ITALY and the ITALIAN EMPIRE 1939

MUSSOLINI

A Study in Power

MUSSOLINI

A STUDY IN POWER

By Ivone Kirkpatrick

HAWTHORN BOOKS, INC.
Publishers • NEW YORK

 All inquiries should be addressed to Hawthorn Books, Inc., 70 Fifth Avenue, New York City 10011. This book was manufactured in the United States of America and published simultaneously in Canada by Prentice-Hall of Canada, Ltd., 520 Ellesmere Road, Scarborough, Ontario. Library of Congress Catalogue Card Number: 64-13278. Suggested decimal classification: 923.145.

First Edition, April, 1964

H-6011

CONTENTS

BOOK III

DECLINE

BOOK IV

FALL

LIST OF ILLUSTRATIONS

The following group of illustrations appears between pages 288 and 289.

The following group of illustrations appears between pages 544 and 545.

CHART AND MAPS

Introduction

EARLY in 1930 I was informed that I was to be appointed Head of the Chancery at the embassy in Rome. I had never been in Italy before. I arrived in Rome for the first time on a glorious April morning, and, as I left the station, I saw the fountains in the Piazza dell' Esedra sparkling in the sunshine. From that moment I became a captive of Rome. It is the only foreign city to which I return with a feeling of breathless joy.

During my term of service I met Mussolini from time to time, but I was, of course, too junior to have official dealings with him. Moreover, until 1932, Grandi was in charge of the Ministry of Foreign Affairs, and my role was to keep in touch with him through his exceedingly competent *chef de cabinet,* Pellegrino Ghigi, a man whom Grandi subsequently described to me as being "as close to me as a brother."

My ambassador, Sir Ronald Graham, probably knew Mussolini better than any foreigner. He had witnessed the March on Rom
and accompanied Mussolini at every stage in his subsequent
velopment. He was a shrewd Scot, who entertained no ill
and who from his long experience in Rome was an excelle
of Italian affairs. From him and from the records of his
versations with Mussolini I was able to form a vivid
Duce. I have incorporated much of this informati

In the autumn of 1933 I was transferred to Be
tinued to follow with a professional interest M
and particularly his relations with Germany.
accompanied Hitler on his first visit to Italy,
of that unfortunate expedition, and I was

the Italian ambassador, Bernardo Attolico, who was a reliable and useful source of information. In 1937 I witnessed Mussolini's triumphal entry into Berlin, and I met him again at the Munich Conference in October, 1938. Six years had elapsed since I had seen him in Rome, and he seemed to me to have deteriorated physically and morally.

In 1939 I became head of the Central Department of the Foreign Office. From this point of vantage I was concerned with the Prime Minister's visit to Rome and with the many diplomatic transactions which led to the war. In June, 1940, I heard on the radio the familiar, raucous voice proclaiming from the balcony of the Palazzo Venezia Italy's declaration of war.

In 1941 I became Controller of the European Services of the B.B.C., and one of my tasks was to follow developments in Italy. It was consequently no surprise when we heard the Italian radio announce the fall of Mussolini. From 1943 to 1945 our task was to seize upon every possible item of Italian news to discredit the Salò Republic.

Thus for fifteen years I was, if from a distance, in touch with Mussolini and his affairs. Accordingly, when my publishers invited me to write a life of Mussolini, which might serve as a companion volume to Alan Bullock's biography of Hitler, I accepted with alacrity. The difficulty, and indeed the impertinence, of an attempt to match Bullock's outstanding work should have deterred me. But I was beguiled by the prospect of travels in Italy. I was also attracted by the challenge. I knew Hitler fairly well, but there is no
doubt that of the two dictators Mussolini was by far the more com-
x and interesting person. Both friend and foe have spoken of his
r to attract men.

s, however, only after I had started work that I began fully
how difficult it is to describe the contradictions of Musso-
er. Nothing can be said of him which is completely
annot be immediately disproved from some reliable
om his own mouth. Nevertheless I have attempted
offer an assessment of the man which, I fear,
who see in him a simple incarnation of evil, or
d me to illuminate the services which he

Some of the material in this chapter relates to events which occurred after the point in his life at which the chapter appears; and it has been represented to me that such an arrangement may rob the subsequent chapters of their interest. It seems to me, however, that Mussolini's conduct, through the tortuous vicissitudes of his career after he became Prime Minister, can only be understood if there is a prior apprehension of his outlook and character. It would have been wearisome to attempt to point the moral at each stage.

There have been few public lives more dramatic and more exciting than that of Mussolini; his appearance like a comet in the European firmament; his rise to a position in which he was almost universally acclaimed as a historical figure of the first rank; his fall and squalid end. All this took place against the background of the most gigantic conflict the world has known. It is unprofitable to speculate on what might have occurred if he had been possessed of more wisdom and stability.

The various judgments passed on Mussolini have, for the most part, been colored by fierce partiality. Benedetto Croce, the philosopher and the foremost intellect of his age in Italy, wrote of him that historians would surely set themselves to discover in the man signs of generosity and genius. They would attempt to rehabilitate him, but, added Croce, they would do so in vain, because he was in reality of limited intelligence, deficient in moral sensibility, ignorant with that fundamental ignorance which did not know and understand the elementary essence of human relationships, incapable of self-criticism or of scruple, excessively vain, lacking taste in every word and gesture, always oscillating between arrogance and servility.

It is a question how far this cruel verdict is justified by the facts. If that were the whole story, would Mussolini have been able to win a world-wide reputation and to retain for twenty-three years his hold on a people as realistic and intelligent as the Italians? It is the strange contradictions in Mussolini's tortured soul that make his life so interesting. That some of his victims should be vindictive is human and understandable; and it would be legitimate to dwell on his many manifest defects. I hope that I have not overlooked them or the damage he did. But many liberal Italians, such as Professor Mario Vinceguerra who was condemned to a long term of imprisonment by a Fascist court, take a more tolerant view of this episode in Italian history. I, personally, am inclined to agree with Grandi, condemned to death at Verona, who in a long conversation with me ended his disquisition on Mussolini's career with a sigh and the two words: "poor Mussolini."

It will be for each reader to judge for himself.

BOOK I

The Road to Power

CHAPTER ONE

Childhood

1883–1901

I

BETWEEN two and three o'clock in the afternoon of July 29, 1883, according to the contemporary press, a thunderbolt fell on the two-headed eagle in the imperial park of Schönbrunn in Vienna and broke off its head, which fell into the lake. At two o'clock on the same afternoon Benito Mussolini was born at Varano di Costa, a small hamlet on the hillside, overlooking the village of Dovia in the Commune of Predappio in Romagna.

The people of Romagna, a region with no defined boundaries which lies west of Ravenna and includes the Republic of San Marino, are jolly, rugged individualists, untouched by industrialism, attached to their sunny, fertile soil, and with a long and turbulent history behind them. They are known for their vengeful character, their sturdy independence, and their love of liberty. A French traveler at the beginning of the last century noted that "the inhabitants of Forlì are warriors, that is to say they are jealous of their rights and always seek to defend them against every foreign oppressor." [1] In the Middle Ages authority was exercised by a succession of local despots, until Alexander VI, who was elected Pope in 1492, extirpated the dynasties of Romagna and brought it under papal sway. Three hundred years later Napoleon annexed Romagna to his Kingdom of Italy, but the Congress of Vienna, over the protests of the inhabitants, returned it to the Pope. In 1821, 1830, and

1848 there were insurrections, but on each occasion they were forcibly suppressed. In 1849 the people of Romagna sheltered Garibaldi when, with a price upon his head, he fled from Rome with his dying wife.

The end of papal rule and the unification of Italy did not bring peace and quiet. In a unified Italy revolt against the foreign oppressor became irrelevant, and, as social and economic issues became more pressing, there was a tendency towards the teaching of the anarchist Mikhail Bakunin, who agitated in favor of the anarchist wing of the First International. Rural Romagna became a center for extreme republicanism, a phenomenon for which there is no rational explanation. In a word, the people of Romagna have never ceased to be in the van of the struggle against the established order. Nor have they changed their character to this day. A modern Italian writer says of them: "When they start a new town in Romagna, they first throw up a monument to Garibaldi and then build a church, because there's no fun in a civil funeral unless it spites the parish priest. The whole history of the province is concerned with spite of this kind."[2] It was this air of nonconformity, anticlericalism, and lusty rebellion which the infant breathed when he first saw the light on that hot summer afternoon in 1883.

II

Benito Amilcare Andrea, the firstborn, was named after Benito Juarez, the Mexican revolutionary, and two Italian revolutionary socialists, Amilcare Cipriani and Andrea Costa, and the second son Arnaldo, who succeeded his elder brother in 1922 as editor of the *Popolo d'Italia,* was christened after Arnaldo da Brescia, a local revolutionary hero in the struggle with the Pope. The last child, born five years after Arnaldo, was a daughter, Edvige, who later made a respectable marriage and settled down to a quiet provincial life in Premilcuore in Romagna. It was not a large family by Italian standards.

In the Middle Ages the name of Mussolini was prominent in Bologna, where there is a Via di Mussolini, and in 1270 Giovanni Mussolini was coruler in the city. Other Mussolini were *Capitani del Popolo,* but in the course of the political convulsions which

MUSSOLINI'S ANCESTRY

Francesco Mussolini (1667-1728) = Benedetta Tartagni

Paulo Mussolini (1702-1779) = Maria Francesca Ghetti

Giacomo Antonio Mussolini (1737-1810) = 1. Maria Francesca Montaguti
2. Maria Paganelli

Giusseppe Domenico Gaspare Mussolini = Maria Angela Frassinetti
b. Calboli 1769 d. Montemaggiore 1822

Luigi detto Giacomo Mussolini = Maria Domenica Frignani
b. Montemaggiore 1805 d. 1829

Luigi Agostino Gaspare Mussolini = Caterina Vasumi
b. Montemaggiore 1834 d. Dovia 1908

Alessandro Gaspare Mussolini = Rosa Maltoni	Francesca = Domenico Gorini	Albina = Domenico Raggi	Alcide = Rosa Caprincoli
b. Collina 1854, d. Forlì 1910 = b. 1858, d. 1905	b. 1856	b. 1862	b. 1865

BENITO MUSSOLINI = Rachele Guidi	Edvige = Michele Mancini	Arnaldo = Augusta Bondanini
b. Dovia 1883, d. 1945 = b. 1893	b. 1888, d. 1957	b. 1885, d. 1931

Edda = Galeazzo Ciano	Vittorio	Bruno	Romano	Anna Maria
b. 1910 = b. 1903, d. 1945	b. 1915	b. 1903, d. 1941	b. 1927	b. 1929

later shook the city, the family was dispersed and no record of their fortunes remains.[3] Little is known of Benito's immediate forebears except their names or the fact that they were small farmers. His grandfather, Luigi, was a lieutenant in the National Guard,[4] who had also been interested in politics and had in his young days been jailed in a papal prison.[5] His father, Alessandro, was a blacksmith and later an innkeeper. But, although he had never been to school, he was by no means an ignorant yokel. A photograph taken not long after his marriage depicts a short thickset man, who with his good features and bright, intelligent eyes might have passed for a successful provincial politician. His Romagnole romanticism was reflected in his definition of socialism, which he published in 1891: "Science illuminating the world: reason mastering faith: free thought overthrowing prejudice: free agreement between men to live a truly civilized life: true justice enthroned on earth: a sublime harmony of concept, thought and action."[6] At an early age he had become a disciple of Bakunin, who first visited Italy in 1864. He established a local branch of the International, drafted Socialist manifestoes, wrote articles in Socialist journals, addressed meetings, attacked the bourgeoisie and the Church, played an active role in local government, and never ceased so long as breath remained in him to profess the doctrine of international socialism. When he died in 1910 Benito, with filial piety, published in the Socialist weekly *La Lotta di Classe* a long obituary describing his father's life-long struggle with the authorities, and he ended with these words: "In many respects he had a tormented existence. His end was premature. Of worldly goods he has left us nothing; of spiritual goods he has left us a treasure: the Idea."

For all his fierce anticlericalism and militant socialism Alessandro was a man not without compassion. The afflictions of the masses, their poverty, their inadequate nourishment, unemployment, and the social conditions which forced them to emigrate, all moved him to constant protest. He gave what he could to the indigent and later, at Forlì, kept open house for the comrades at his inn, where political theory was endlessly discussed. It would have been surprising if in this atmosphere the young Benito had not been drawn to follow in his father's political and journalistic footsteps.

Benito's mother, Rosa Maltoni, was born on April 22, 1858, at

Villafranca, a suburb of Forlì. Her father was a veterinary surgeon. After completing her studies at Forlì in 1876 she received a diploma qualifying her to teach the first three grades in an elementary school. After teaching for two years at Bocconi, a village between Florence and Forlì, she was transferred to Dovia. Here she met Alessandro, whom she married in 1882, to the dismay of her parents, who regarded the union as unsuitable and did all they could to dissuade her. Unlike her husband she was a conformist and took no interest in politics, but she was ambitious for her children and anxious that they should lift themselves out of the artisan class. Deeply religious, gentle, patient, and sensitive, she was able to win the love of her little boy. Writing of his early years he describes his feelings for her:

> My greatest love was for my mother. She was so quiet, so tender, and so strong. Her name was Rosa. My mother not only reared us, but she taught us in the primary school. I often thought, even in my earliest appreciations of human beings, of how faithful and patient her work was. To displease her was my one fear.[7]

She died in 1905 of bronchial pneumonia at the age of forty-six, prematurely aged and worn out by the struggle for existence, for the family led a life of poverty. They possessed almost no furniture and in the winter could afford virtually no heating. There was also very little to eat and on weekdays there was only vegetable soup for lunch and chicory for supper. On Sundays they had a pound of mutton for broth. Benito sincerely mourned his mother's loss, but, although he shared her dissatisfaction with the status of an artisan, she had exercised little influence upon him and he inherited none of her amiable qualities. His character was molded by his early environment and by the uncompromising socialism of his father, who taught him the primitive laws of vengeance and to hate the monarchy, the Church, and society. It was also molded by events.

At the end of the nineteenth century Europe had reached the zenith of its power and prosperity, and there seemed no reason to question the theory of inevitable progress. But on the southern fringe of Europe the Italy in which Alessandro agitated and Benito grew up was not a sleek and contented country. Unification in 1861 and the acquisition of Rome in 1870 had not brought about the millennium. On the contrary: the young parliamentary regime had inherited a poverty-stricken land; there were no railways, virtually no industries, and no primary schools in the South. After forty years of unity 78.70 per cent of the population in Calabria and 48.49 per cent in the Kingdom were still illiterate. The successive Liberal governments, in which the same familiar names appeared and reappeared in different, constantly changing administrations, were unable to grapple with domestic problems, partly because of the mediocrity of their otherwise estimable members, partly because the class from which they were drawn was out of touch with the masses, and partly because the trouble spot, the indigent South, was virtually unrepresented. There was no solid middle class to sustain the country's economic structure, the system of government was overcentralized, and, although Italy was politically unified, there was as yet no sense of national unity. In the face of all these difficulties public dissatisfaction found expression in constant revolt. In 1877 and in 1879 serious disorders requiring the intervention of troops broke out in the South and in Sicily. In 1893 a similar rising, but on a larger scale, took place again in Sicily. With the growth of industry trouble spread later to the North. There was a widespread feeling that parliament and the government were not fitted to cope with the situation. From the Socialist party, which was founded in 1892, the people could have no expectation of a radical change. Its leaders were sober, moderate men, wedded to the parliamentary system, opposed to violence, and unwilling even to pander to the nationalist sentiments of the masses. Enmeshed in their doctrines, which incidentally were repugnant to Catholic thought, they became more and more detached from reality. It was an era of political stagnation rather than one of active political mismanagement.

The difficulty of arousing national consciousness in a country which had for so long been divided was aggravated by the bitter conflict between the state and the Holy See. The problem had a general and a special character. In Italy, as in many other European countries, Liberal theories were in contradiction with the claims of the Church, for liberalism affirmed the primacy of the state and claimed jurisdiction in a wide field including education, ecclesiastical appointments, and even the supervision of religious communities. Elsewhere these contentious issues were to some extent resolved by the conclusion of a concordat and diplomatic representation at the Vatican. But this could not be done in Italy, since the creation of a unified Italy brought with it the dispute over temporal power. In 1871 the new Italian government passed the Law of Guarantees which defined the legal status of the Pope, but the Vatican declined to recognize this law or to enter into relationship with the Quirinal. In 1867 the Pope had declared that it was not expedient that Catholics should take part in politics, and in 1895 an explanatory statement emphasized that the term "inexpediency" meant prohibition. While the ban was not by any means universally observed, it did have the effect of keeping many useful men out of public life, it intensified the hostility of the Liberals, who were impelled to further measures of secularization, and it thus created a painful division in a nation which required unity of purpose to master its problems. In Rome, the capital, the consequences of the conflict were most sharply manifested. Society was split into Blacks and Whites, who were not on speaking terms, while the prisoner of the Vatican sat within his four walls in by no means silent protest against the new regime and all its works.

Finally, in the field of foreign policy there was little to satisfy the aspirations of the people. Since 1882 Italy had been, with Germany and Austria, a member of the Triple Alliance, an arrangement which offered a useful degree of military security to an otherwise defenseless country. The treaty, which contained provisions for consultation and mutual aid in limited contingencies, only obliged Italy to come to the assistance of her allies in two specific cases: if France attacked Germany, or if France and Russia attacked Germany and the Austro-Hungarian Empire. Thus it was not an unsatisfactory instrument, since the price paid for security was not excessive. But it was an unpopular alliance, for Austria was the enemy and alliance with her was repugnant to the irredentists and to those active elements who yearned to see the new Italy extend her domains and grow to the stature of a Great Power. It was bitter that in the scramble for Africa Italy should have been left behind, and she received and expected no sympathy from her allies. So long as poverty reigned at home, so long as government lay in feeble hands, and so long as Italy remained perforce in the straitjacket of the Triple Alliance it seemed as if the patriots' dreams could never be realized. It was fruitful soil for the cultivation of young rebels.

III

Already in his childhood Mussolini was a rebel, a restless, self-assertive, pugnacious rebel. While he was still a baby he fiercely resisted the efforts of his mother and grandmother to teach him to speak. He was taken to a doctor who told the grandmother not to worry: "He will speak. I have an idea that he will speak too much."[8] In his early years Mussolini himself said that he was a violent boy and that many of his companions still bore on their heads the scars he inflicted.[9] After a short time in his mother's school he was sent to the primary school in Predappio, where he was constantly involved in fights with his schoolmates. "I was not displeased," he writes, "that the boys of Predappio resented at first the coming of a strange boy from another village. They flung stones at me and I returned their fire. I was all alone and against many."[10] In his spare time he roamed the countryside with his brother, snaring birds, raiding apple trees, and behaving generally as the mischievous boy he was. He made friends with an old witch in Dovia, *"la vecchia Giovanna,"* who dispensed love philters and quack medicines; and she taught him magic. She must have had some influence over him, since for the rest of his life he was superstitious and always had a strange confidence in his own premonitions.[11]

At home he worked under strong paternal discipline with his father in the smithy and was beaten if he was careless or allowed his attention to wander. In the evenings he listened quietly to political talk. "We lived in a two-roomed tenement. Rarely was there any meat on the table from one week's end to another. There were passionate arguments and quarrels; or just hopes."[12] The effect upon him of these discussions is described in his autobiography.

> Manual labor in my father's blacksmith's shop was not the only common interest we shared. It was inevitable that I should find a clearer understanding of those political and social questions which in the midst of discussions with the neighbors had appeared to me as unfathomable and hence a stupid world of words. I could not follow as a child the

arguments of lengthy debates around the table nor did I grasp the reasons for the watchfulness and measures taken by the police. But now in an obscure way it all appeared as connected with the lives of strong men, who not only dominate their own lives, but also the lives of their fellow creatures. Slowly but fatally I was turning my spirit and my mind to new political ideals destined to flower for a time. . . . These were sad, dark years, not only in my own province but for other parts of Italy. I must have the marks upon my memory of the resentful and furtive protests of those who came to talk with my father.[13]

When the boy was nine years old his parents decided that he should be sent to a boarding school. At first Alessandro objected on anticlerical grounds. At that time all suitable schools were conducted by religious congregations and, although Rosa had been allowed to take Benito to church and make him practice his religion, it was a different matter to hand him over body and soul to the Blacks. Nevertheless both parents agreed that the child was promising, that he required wider horizons for his development, a sense of discipline, and the opportunity to rise above the status of a manual worker. So Rosa triumphed and the boy was taken by his father to the college of the Salesian fathers at Faenza. For all his ambition, Benito went unwillingly to school, which he regarded as imprisonment. He was attached to his birthplace with an affection which never left him. He had no relish for discipline and knew that he would miss his freedom. So when his father had handed him over and said good-by and when the great door of the monastery closed behind him, he broke down and wept.[14]

His record at Faenza was uniformly deplorable. He disliked the loss of liberty, the church ceremonies, and subjection to constant surveillance by the masters. There was also an internal arrangement to which he reasonably took strong exception. In the dining room the boys were divided into three tables, the first for nobles at 60 lire a month, the second for the middle class at 45 lire and the third for the lower class at 30 lire. "I always had to sit in the lowest grade, among the poorest. It no longer troubles me to recall that there were ants in the bread given to the children of the third grade, but the mere fact that we were thus graded still rankles." [15] He was also bored in the classroom. Although he was quick-witted and inquisitive and already showing some of the qualities of the

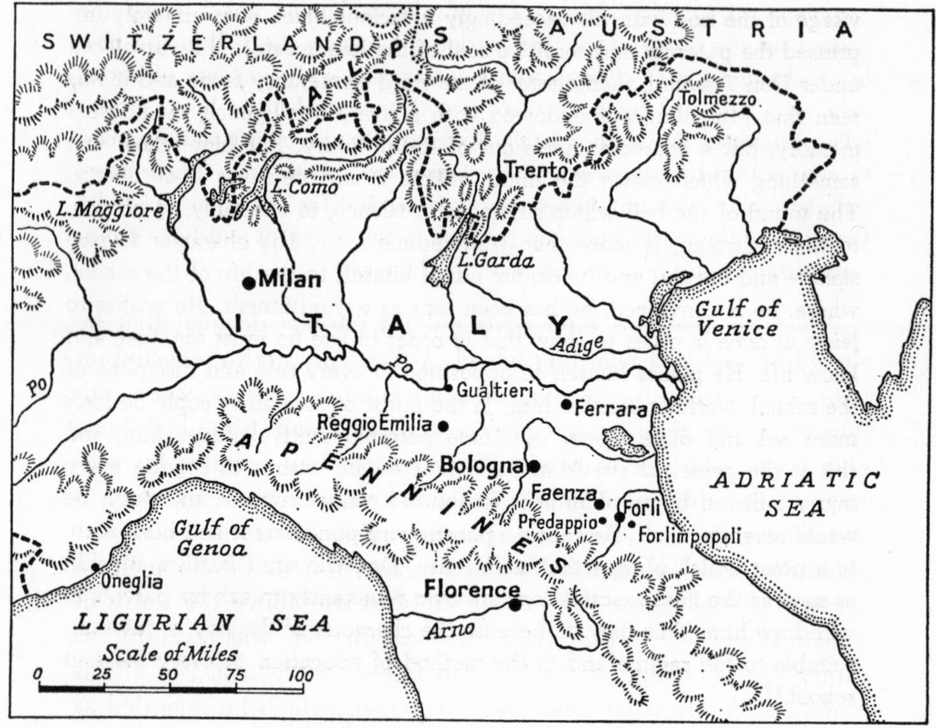

Northern Italy, the setting of Mussolini's early life.

journalist, he lacked application and preferred to read books of his choice rather than those prescribed. In short, he was a dissident in an otherwise ordered society, always in trouble with authority, and constantly kept in or beaten. His troubles culminated at the end of his second year when after an altercation he stabbed an elder boy with a knife. For this offense the headmaster wished to expel him, but, in deference to the representations of the parents and of the Bishop of Forlì, he eventually consented to relent on the understanding that he would leave at the end of the term.[16]

An extract from the record of the Salesian school at Faenza describes, not uncharitably, Mussolini's sojourn in their midst, with only an oblique reference to the incident of the knife.

In September, 1892, Benito Mussolini was entrusted to Don Giovanni Battista Rinaldi, the headmaster of the Salesian school. . . . The square visage of the boy with his exceedingly vivacious black eyes certainly impressed the paternal and sensitive soul of the headmaster. He was placed under Don Traviani, then master of the third elementary form, and it was seen that Mussolini was endowed with a lively intelligence, an unusual memory, but a character quite out of the ordinary. For him school was something which closes the mind, afflicts it and deprives it of liberty. The sound of the bell which summons to silence, to assembly, to church, to the classroom, is more than troublesome. . . . His character is passionate and unruly; and he cannot adapt himself to the life of the school, where, he is convinced, he has been sent as a punishment. He wishes to leave at once in order to show that in order to live he must see, feel, and know life. He places himself in opposition to every rule and discipline of the school. Nothing satisfies him; in the midst of so many people he feels more sad and more alone. . . . One personal motive guides him, and this is the principal streak in his character; he wishes to requite every injury inflicted by an older schoolmate. He cannot support an injury; he wants revenge. . . . He rebels against every punishment and correction, to a point which obliges the headmaster, Don Giovanni Battista Rinaldi, as soon as the final examinations are over reluctantly to ask his parents to withdraw him. This they do because the character of the boy is quite unsuitable to the regime and to the method of education in every Salesian school.[17]

IV

Mussolini's parents were disappointed but not deflected from their purpose by Benito's failure at Faenza. In October, 1895, they managed to send him to the Royal Normal School at Forlimpopolo. This establishment, which had formerly been a Franciscan monastery and had been adapted to its new purpose, looked more like an old provincial hospital than a school. The pupils were principally sons of elementary school teachers in Romagna and the fees for board and lodging were exceedingly modest, 30 lire a month. The headmaster, Valfredo Carducci, brother of the well-known poet Giosuè Carducci, was a gentle, cultivated man who won the respect of all, including Benito.

Despite the institutional character of the place, Benito was less unhappy there than he had been at Faenza. For one thing during his first three years there was no room for him in the school and he boarded with a family in the town, an arrangement which gave him a certain liberty and enabled him to go home on Sundays. Moreover his headmaster seems to have shown more understanding for his wayward pupil than the somewhat rigid pedagogues in the Salesian College. In any event, spurred by ambition to excel and by the desire not to waste the money laid out by his parents on his education he worked quite well; and in 1898 he was moved from the so-called technical school to the senior normal school with a small scholarship. Here he became a boarder.

He was now sixteen years of age. One of his contemporaries, Rino Alessi, describes him as having the aspect of a laborer, with a large pale forehead framed in a crop of black, thick, unruly hair.[18] He was always dressed in black, but his clothes were green with age and showed signs of repairs at knees and elbows. He wore a flowing black tie, which was regarded as a symbol of his individualism. In school society he was not an easy companion and his fellows treated him with vigilant respect, if not with awe. Although he was willing when in the mood to take part in games and discussions, he was more generally a solitary, whose quick temper and biting tongue made it advisable to leave him alone. "He had an indomitable tenacity and pride. . . . To clash with him or to provoke him meant attracting to oneself an instantaneous reaction, which might be one of violence. And who was there who did not beware of doing this?"[19] Altogether the first impression which he made on another classmate, Sante Bedeschi, was "frankly disagreeable."[20]

His relations with the masters were tolerably good, although at times his rebellious nature led him into conflict with authority. On one occasion he organized a successful demonstration against the quality of the bread served to the boys. On another he was guilty of an act of impertinence, which caused the headmaster to address the following letter to his father:

> On Thursday morning your son was due to take lessons in history, Italian, calligraphy, and science. Since the history master was absent on good grounds the Italian master instructed the pupils in the third technical form to write an essay on "Time is Money." Shortly afterwards your son handed up to the master in charge a scrap of paper on which was written: "Time is money, because I am going home to study geometry in view of the imminence of the examinations. Does this not seem more logical? Benito Mussolini." The Council of Masters, having held an emergency

meeting to maintain the prestige of the school and respect for those who frequent it, has suspended your son for ten days. I inform you of this because you will wish to take steps to ensure that your son does not remain idle for so long a period.[21]

During his last years at school Mussolini took an interest in politics and could often be found haranguing the boys in the playground. He also contributed occasional articles to journals published in Forlì and Ravenna. He had an exceptionally good voice and his prowess as an orator caused the headmaster to select him to speak at a public commemoration of Verdi in the local theatre. The speech was less a tribute to Verdi's musical genius than a protest against the social conditions of the age, and the Socialist newspaper *Avanti* of Milan thought it worthy of a short notice. "Yesterday in the Communal Theatre the comrade student, Mussolini, commemorated the Swan of Busseto in a speech which was warmly applauded." It was the first mention of his name in the columns of a newspaper.

Mussolini's last year at Forlimpopolo was a difficult one. He had developed physically and mentally and found it more and more difficult to endure school discipline and the restrictions of an enclosed society. Like a captive wild animal he felt the urge to escape into the outside world. But he was able to master his impulses and in July, 1901, shortly after his eighteenth birthday, he left the normal school with the diploma of an elementary teacher. In his final examinations he received the highest marks of any candidate in history, Italian language and literature, and singing. Armed with his diploma, he gratefully cast off the shackles of childhood and girded himself to face the world.

CHAPTER TWO

The Vagabond

1901–1912

I

FROM Forlimpopolo Mussolini returned home and at once applied for a clerkship in the municipality of Predappio. To the annoyance of his father the application was rejected, ostensibly because of his youth, but more probably because he was known to be troublesome and subversive. His mother was already in bad health and he would have liked to remain at home, but he was obliged to earn his bread, and he applied to the mayor of Legnano for an appointment in the local school. His application failed because he did not submit the necessary supporting documents in time.* He was subsequently able to secure the post of teacher at the elementary school in Gualteri, a "red" commune in Reggio Emilia, at a salary of 56 lire a month. The cost of his board and lodging was 40 lire a month, which left him very little for recreation or even for clothes or other bare necessities of life. He knew the humiliating poverty of the underpaid white-collar worker. In March, 1902, he was elected by the local teachers' association to represent them at an educational congress in Bologna, and he was obliged to apply for a loan of 15 or, if possible, 20 lire from his former schoolmate Sante Bedeschi.[1] A month later he wrote again to ask for 12 lire to settle an urgent debt.[2] Despite his straitened circumstances he made a number of

* His letter was found in the communal archives in October, 1962. *La Notte*, Milan, October 17–18, 1962.

friends, and he danced and played cards in the local inns, where he also talked politics; but he found the Socialists of Reggio Emilia too moderate, too comfortable and pleasure-loving for his liking. He was always apt to expect in others a higher standard of discipline and austerity than he was prepared to apply to himself. Moreover, the life of a school teacher did not appeal to him and he was not unnaturally dissatisfied with his exiguous salary, which was not a living wage. In June, 1902, when he had been less than a year at Gualteri, he wrote to his friend Bedeschi that he had decided to emigrate to Switzerland, where he expected to earn some 90 lire a month.[3] Even if he had not made this decision he would have been obliged to leave his school, for very shortly afterwards he became involved in a violent altercation with the local mayor. He packed his bag at once, leaving behind him his academic gown in part payment for his board and lodging.

It was in July, 1902, that Mussolini at the age of eighteen put into effect his resolve to emigrate. He has been accused of having left Italy merely in order to evade military service, and indeed it may not be a coincidence that his decision was taken shortly before he became liable to conscription. On the other hand he explains in his autobiography that he did not wish to return to the narrow circle of family life and felt the urge to seek wider horizons. The truth probably lies between the two. There could have been no call of conscience to perform military service in a society of which he disapproved, and it was natural that his insatiable restlessness and ambition should drive him to seek adventure abroad. He was determined to abandon the calling of a school teacher and there seemed no other avenue of employment open to him in Italy. He telegraphed to his mother for money for the journey and from her meager resources she sent him 45 lire. On July 9, 1902, he reached Chiasso and, while waiting for his train to Switzerland, he bought a newspaper in which he read that his father had been arrested. At Predappio and at Orte Socialists had smashed ballot boxes in order to prevent the electoral victory of the Clericals; and among the arrested men was Alesandro. He wondered whether he should return home, but he decided to go on. The following day he arrived in Switzerland with 2 lire, 10 centesimi in his pocket.[4]

His first job was at Orbe, where he worked as a hodman to a

builder. In a letter to Sante Bedeschi dated September 2, 1902, he gave a graphic description of his early days in Switzerland:

I reached Yverdon at 11 on Thursday the 10th after 36 hours of train journey. Feeling stupid and weary I made my way into a cheap-looking inn where I had occasion for the first time to talk French. I had something to eat. . . . On Friday I remained for an hour in front of the statue of Pestalozzi, who was born at Yverdon; and for twenty-three hours in bed. On Saturday, together with a painter out of employment I went to Orbe, a neighboring town, to get taken on as a manual laborer. I found work and on Monday the 14th I began; eleven hours work in the day at 32 centesimi an hour. I made 121 journeys with a handbarrow full of stones up to the second floor of a building in process of construction. In the evening the muscles of my arms were swollen. I ate some potatoes roasted upon cinders and threw myself in all my clothes onto my bed, a pile of straw. At five on Tuesday I woke and returned to work. I chafed with the terrible rage of the powerless. The *padrone* made me mad. The third day he said to me: "You are too well dressed." That phrase was meant to convey an insinuation. I should have liked to rebel and to crack the skull of this upstart who was accusing me of laziness while my limbs were giving beneath the weight of the stones. I wanted to shout out in his face: "You coward, you coward!" And then? The man who pays you is always in the right. Saturday evening came. I said to the *padrone* I intended to leave and therefore wished to be paid. He went into his office; I remained in the lobby. Presently he came out. With ill-disguised rage he threw into my hands 20 lire and some centesimi saying: "Here is your money and it is stolen." I remained as though made of stone. What was I to do to him? Kill him? What did I do to him? Nothing. Why? Because I was hungry and had no shoes. I had worn a pair of light boots to pieces on the building stones, which had lacerated both my hands and the soles of my feet. Almost barefooted I went to an Italian's shop and bought myself a pair of shoes, hobnailed in mountaineer's style. I packed off and on the next morning, Sunday, July 20, I took the train at Charornay for Lausanne.

This is not a beautiful city, but it is an attractive one. From the summit of the hill it extends down to the shore of Lake Geneva with its enchanting suburb of Ouchy. It is full of Italians (6,000), who are not looked on with much favor, and the executive committee of the Socialist party has its headquarters here, and the weekly journal *The Future of the Worker,* which I edit in collaboration with the lawyer Barboni, is issued here.

But let us proceed in good order. In Lausanne I lived carefully the first week on the money I had earned at Orbe. Then I was again hard up. On Monday the only piece of metal I had in my pocket was a nickel medallion of Karl Marx. I had eaten a bit of bread in the morning and I did not know where to go to sleep that evening. I wandered about in desperation and presently, a cramp in the stomach preventing me from walking any longer, I sat down on the pedestal of the statue of William Tell which stands in the Montbenon Park. My appearance must have been terrible, for the people who came to inspect the monument scrutinized me with suspicion, almost with alarm.

At five o'clock I leave Montbenon and direct my steps towards Ouchy. I go along the Quay, the very beautiful road by the shore of the lake and evening comes on. In the dark the last rays of the sun and the last sounds of the old bells take me out of myself. . . . A feeling of infinite sadness assails me and I ask myself on the lake's shore whether it is worth while to live another day. While I muse thus, a sweet melody, like a mother's lullaby over the cradle of her little boy, directs the course of my thoughts and I turn back. In front of the splendid Hotel Beau Rivage an orchestra of forty is playing. I lean up against the railings of the garden, amid the dark green firs, and listen intently. The music comforts both my brain and my stomach. But the intervals are terrible, the cramp stabbing into my entrails like red-hot pins. Meanwhile the crowds of holidaymakers are moving about on the pathways of the park, the rustle of silks may be heard and the murmurs of languages which I do not understand. An elderly couple pass close to me. They look English. I would like to ask them to give me money to get myself a bed tonight. But the words die on my lips. The lady glitters with gold and precious stones. I have not a *soldo*, I have no bed, I have no bread. I make off cursing. Ah! that blessed idea of anarchy of thought and action. Is it not the right of the man lying on the ground to murder him who crushes him?

From then until eleven I stay in the public lavatory, from eleven to twelve under an old barge. The wind blows from Savoy and is cold. I return into the town and spend the rest of the night under the Grand Pont. In the morning I look at myself out of curiosity in the windows of a shop. I am unrecognizable. I meet a man from Romagna. I tell him briefly of my affairs. He laughs at me. I curse him. He puts his hand in his pocket and gives me 50 centesimi. I thank him. I hasten to the shop of a baker and buy a piece of bread. I continue walking towards the wood. I feel as though I had a fortune. Having got a long way from the center of the city I bite into my bread with the ferocity of a Cerberus. For twenty-six hours I had not eaten.

I feel a little life flowing through my veins. My courage is returning with the flight of my hunger. I decide to make a struggle. I direct my steps towards the Villa Amina, Avenue du Leman. An Italian professor named Zini lives there. Before making my way into the entrance of the dainty dwelling, I polish my shoes and arrange my tie and cap. I enter. Zini has a head of untidy gray hair; his nose is phenomenal. I have no sooner addressed him in Italian than he discharges at me a volley of: "Oh these nuisances, these eternal nuisances! Holy Christ! What do you want? Eh? I don't know, I don't know! I'll see. Let me see now. Better go to Borgatta, Rue Solitude. I wish I could. . . . Possibly?"

"Oh go to Hell with him who made you, you old slut!" And with this salutation I left him. In my next letter I shall tell you all the rest. I promised you a romance and it has been and is a reality.[5]

This letter gives an impression of the vagabondage of Mussolini's life in Switzerland. It also casts some light on his character at the time, with its mixture of romanticism, resentment against society, disorderly restlessness, dislike of manual labor, and egotistical aggressiveness. He was an unattractive tramp. Gradually he became accustomed to his precarious, feckless existence and came to feel the fascination of it.[6] But he was apt to get into trouble with the police and on one occasion was arrested for vagrancy.

Much of his time during this period was spent in the company of revolutionaries, principally Italians working in Switzerland and political exiles, including many Russian men and women, in whose houses he ate, drank, and talked endlessly. His interest in the women was not wholly Platonic and during his sojourn in Switzerland he formed more than one sentimental attachment. There was, however, one woman with whom his ties were more intellectual than romantic. She was Angelica Balabanoff, a Marxist Socialist, earnest and without a trace of humor, who came from a well-to-do Russian bourgeois family in the Ukraine. As a girl she left home to become a student in western Europe. In Rome she joined the Italian Socialist party and eventually arrived in Switzerland to work among Italian emigrants. She met Mussolini for the first time at a meeting organized in the Italian Socialist branch at Lausanne, at which she was the principal speaker. Her attention was drawn to one member of her audience:

He was a young man I had never seen before and his agitated manner and unkempt clothes set him apart from the other workers in the hall. The emigré audiences were always poorly dressed, but this man was also extremely dirty. I had never seen a more wretched human being. In spite of his large jaw, the bitterness and restlessness in his black eyes, he gave the impression of extreme timidity. Even as he listened, his nervous hands clutching at his big black hat, he seemed more concerned with his inner turmoil than with what I was saying.

After the meeting she made inquiries and was told that he was the son of a Socialist in Romagna, that he was a vagrant, and that he was more of an Anarchist than a Socialist. She approached him and offered to help him with the translation of a German pamphlet for which he had been offered fifty francs. This was the beginning of an association which lasted for twelve years until his expulsion from the Socialist party. Her interest in him sprang partly from pity and partly from the belief that he possessed qualities which would make him useful to Italian socialism. Yet she was not blind to his egotism and to the instability of his character:

> I soon saw that he knew little of history, of economics, or of Socialist theory and that his mind was completely undisciplined. . . . Mussolini's radicalism and anticlericalism were more the reflection of his early environment and his own rebellious egotism than the product of understanding and conviction. His hatred of oppression was not that impersonal hatred of a system shared by all revolutionaries. It sprang from his own sense of indignity and frustration, his passion to assert his own ego, and from a determination for personal revenge.[7]

In the development of his ideas, Mussolini owed much to Angelica Balabanoff. In order to further his political education he attended some lectures in social and political science by Professor Vilfredo Pareto of the University of Lausanne, and by Professor Pascal Boninsegni, a native of Forlì. Boninsegni lived to see Mussolini Prime Minister of Italy and in 1937 visited him in Rome to present him with the diploma of an honorary degree in social and political science at the University of Lausanne. In the course of his studies Mussolini dipped into Nietzsche, Schopenhauer, Kant, Hegel, and Sorel. He also dabbled in Buddhism. On one occasion he was present at a lecture by the moderate Belgian Socialist leader Vandervelde, who spoke about Jesus Christ and described him as the first

Socialist. Incited by his Nihilist companions he rose to join issue with the lecturer and, after attacking Christianity, vaunted the merits of Buddhism. It was a brash, callow performance and the experienced Vandervelde, who had courteously given way to his young heckler, had no difficulty with equal courtesy in covering him with ridicule, while the audience roared its approval.[8] This incident, which received some publicity, together with Mussolini's conduct and political associations, attracted the unfavorable attention of the authorities, who expelled him from the canton.

He took refuge in Annemasse on the French side of the border, where he worked as a laborer and as a part-time teacher in a private school. He might have settled down there, for he found favor with the wife of the *sous-préfet* to whom, drawing on the lore of *"la vecchia Giovanna,"* he acted as soothsayer. But the itch to travel still possessed him and he moved to Zurich. At Zurich he again frequented revolutionary circles, where Marx and Karl Liebknecht were the prophets. He noted with approval the Germanic virtues of order and discipline. He did not hesitate to declare that discipline was what was most required in Italy, but he does not seem to have thought that this had much relevance to himself. His lack of discipline soon led him into further trouble, this time on account of a brawl in a restaurant,[9] and he was expelled from Zurich.

He worked for a short time as a mason in Germany and then in 1903 took up residence in Berne. He was by this time fairly well known as a contributor to Socialist journals and a speaker at Socialist meetings. At Berne he organized a strike of masons; the nature of his activities is described in a letter he wrote to the editor of the Anarchist newspaper *Le Reveil* of Geneva. The language is typical of Mussolini's flamboyant style at this stage of his career.

> Those who showed the most fear among the Italians . . . were the venerable pontiffs of the committee of action for the workers. I will prove it to you by the following fact; the organized workers wished to have a parade of protest and solidarity. Through scruple and delicacy we went, a comrade and I, to carry the result of our deliberations to these gentlemen of the committee of action. . . .
>
> We were badly received. . . . When I announced our intention of going through with the parade whatever the cost, if the Italian workers responded to our call, these ambitious Red pontiffs warned us that they

would do their utmost to prevent us. They even led us to understand that in an extremity they would have recourse to the authorities. At length, having taken note of their declarations and trembling with rage, we left that den of reactionaries.[10]

At about the same time he fought a pistol duel with a fellow Socialist. Neither was hit, but Mussolini was arrested. It is not surprising that the authorities in Berne regarded him as an unwelcome guest. He says himself of his stay in Switzerland: "I threw myself headlong into the politics of the emigrant, of refugees, of those who sought solutions. . . . I took part in political gatherings. I made speeches. Some intemperance in my words made me undesirable to the Swiss authorities." [11] He was expelled from the canton.

To speak of "some intemperance" was a gross understatement. In fact, when expounding his atheistic and revolutionary views, Mussolini, whether in press articles or speeches, used the most violent language. It was not only that he was a true son of Romagna, but he had another motive. As an exhibitionist he felt that extremism was likely to win attention and the prominence for which his egotistical soul yearned.

In October, 1903, he returned home for a short time to see his mother, who was dangerously ill. On November 7 he wrote to Sante Bedeschi from Predappio: "I am at home on account of my mother's health. If the crisis turns out well, as I hope and pray, or badly, I shall go back to my travels. I should like to see you and speak to you one of these days on account of our old friendship. Possibly at the end of November I shall pack my bags again—once more to depart into the unknown. Movement has become a necessity to me. I shall burst if I stay still." [12] His mother recovered and from Predappio he went to Annemasse to see his mistress, the wife of the *sous-préfet*, and he imprudently attempted subsequently to restore his situation in Switzerland by presenting a falsified passport at the Aliens' Registration Office in Geneva. The forgery was detected and Mussolini was imprisoned and expelled from the canton in April, 1904. The affair caused a local stir and there was an interpellation in the Grand Council of Geneva. Replying to a Socialist deputy, Dr. Adrien Wyss, the head of the Police and Justice Department, said that it was not a question of an unfortunate foreigner who had tried dishonestly to obtain a residence permit. It was a question of a man whose presence was dangerous because of the ideas he professed and above all because of the means he preached and the activity which he tried to arouse among his Italian compatriots.[13] The speaker had no difficulty in making his case, for it was undeniable that the Swiss authorities had for two years shown remarkable forbearance.

As a result, however, of the agitation on his behalf on the part of Swiss Socialists, Mussolini was not deported to Italy, where he would have been arrested for desertion, but was taken to the canton of Ticino, where he was set free. In May he returned to Annemasse and he subsequently moved to Lausanne, but he did not stay there long for towards the end of the year, in order to celebrate the birth of an heir to the throne, an Italian Royal Decree amnestied deserters, provided they presented themselves for military service.

He decided to return home forthwith after more than two years of wandering in Switzerland, France, and Germany. He had learned some French and a smattering of German, he had contributed to a number of Socialist journals, and he had seen something of the world—but he was in a sorry state of indecision and disequilibrium. Stuffed with undigested Marxist ideas, he knew that he was dissatisfied with society and wanted revolution; he had spent much time in sterile political debate, he had found fault with many of his Socialist comrades, he was exasperated with the complacent liberalism of the Swiss, but he had no positive aims. He was already feeling the urge for power without much notion of what he wanted to do when he got it. Patriotic sentiment, ambition for Italy as well as for himself, resentment at the failure of society to recognize his quality were confused in a welter of internationalist and Marxist conceptions. This was to be his condition for a number of years, during which he was the prey of conflicting emotions. In this situation he had no alternative but to be an opportunist, a role which was very well suited to his temperament.

His schoolmate Rino Alessi, who was one of Mussolini's most ardent admirers, recognizes this weakness:

> The future agitator already conceived his own political destiny as lying outside the existing political parties. If he later directed his steps towards the Socialist party, it was because of the intuition of the strategist. He was in fact never a Marxist. Not even during the years in which he was

editor of *Avanti* was he able to cure himself of that individualism which was to lead him to sympathize with the doctrines of Nietzsche, Pareto, and Sorel. He had seen in the Socialist party the human mass which was the most numerous and the best organized, on which to work at the opportune moment in the interest of his own doctrine and policy.[14]

This is the verdict of most of his contemporaries; indeed it can be said that at no point in his life was he guided by well-defined principles or convictions. Unlike Hitler he charted no course, but drifted uncertainly on the current of events, determining as each crisis arose how he would set his sail. Often with fumbling fingers he wavered, and the massive jowl, which was later to protrude over the balcony of the Palazzo Venezia, concealed the same instability of character which marked his early years of exile. It will be seen how with the passage of time he gained experience and poise, and so was able to veil this weakness even from some of those who knew him best. But in 1904, although he must have profited from his travels, he was still a very raw, disoriented young man.

His police record, kept at the Forlì Prefecture, listed his many conflicts with the law, but did not speak unkindly of him. The entry giving biographical details up to the beginning of 1904 describes him as a revolutionary Socialist having a very energetic temperament:

Often violent and impulsive, but he has an education that is exceptional among the working classes; he enjoys a good reputation. He shows a certain intelligence and cultivation, having attended the Normal School at Forlimpopoli and secured a teacher's diploma. He mixes with the working classes and obtains some members for his party, but his influence does not extend beyond his own village. He is in relations with the Socialist leaders in Romagna and also with the militants in Berne, Zurich, and Lausanne, where he has lived from 1901 to October, 1903.[15]

II

When he arrived in Italy he presented himself for military service and in December, 1904, was posted to the 10th Bersaglieri Regiment at Verona. He was able to adjust himself to military life and for the first time in his career was involved in no conflict with authority. From time to time he was given leave to go home in order to help his father. In the evening the two men sat before the kitchen fire while one of them read aloud from *The Prince* by Machiavelli, a book which, he claimed, exercised a considerable influence upon him. In May, 1924, in a thesis written for the University of Bologna, he said:

> Now what is quite manifest from even a superficial reading of *The Prince* is the acute pessimism of Machiavelli in regard to human nature. . . . In Chapter XVIII of *The Prince* Machiavelli thus expresses himself: "This may be said generally of men: that they are ungrateful, voluble, deceitful, shirkers of dangers, greedy of gain." . . . Much time has passed since then, but if I were to be allowed to judge my fellows and my compatriots, I could not attenuate in the least Machiavelli's verdict.[16]

Scorn for the masses, for the fellow members of his party, and for the rights of the individual was to inspire Mussolini at every stage in his career. He found also in Machiavelli's verdict on the nobles nourishment for his social grudge: "*Gentiluomini* are called those who live fatly and lazily from the revenues of their land, without even giving themselves the trouble of improving it. In every republic or province they are harmful; but especially where they have castles and vassals who obey them . . . they are the enemies of civilization."

III

It was while he was doing his military service that his mother died, in February, 1905. He was summoned by telegraph, obtained leave, and arrived just in time to be recognized by the dying woman. He was afflicted by her loss: "From me had been taken the one dear and truly near living being."[17] He returned to his regiment and completed his period of military service, from which he was discharged in September, 1906. After an amorous interlude with the new schoolmistress at Dovia, who had succeeded his mother, he was able very soon to secure the post of elementary school teacher at Caneva in the Commune of Tolmezzo in the Friuli region. He was reluctant to return to teaching, but knew no other method of earning a living. For the next few years, freed from the restraints of military discipline, he reverted to his previous nomadic, disorderly existence. At Caneva he was threatened with arrest for subversive speeches and on one occasion he was charged with blasphemy in the classroom. But his energies were not entirely devoted to teaching and to playing politics. He was attracted by women and was not disposed to live the life of an anchorite. Margherita Sarfatti in her biography refers delicately to this aspect of his prowess:

By dint of hard work and sparing, the women in the course of a good summer season will contrive like the ants to amass stores to last them through the severe winter. But during the winter you must not expect sobriety from the Friulani. The weather is Arctic, the houses are kept closed, the countryside is buried in snow: to keep warm there is nothing for it but to drink and eat and make love. The man who does not drink, eat and make love in wholehearted fashion is not held to be a man worthy of the name! [18]

One way and another Mussolini did not give satisfaction to the local authorities, and at the end of his first year they refused to renew his contract. In his autobiography he described his time at Tolmezzo as a year of moral deterioration. His recollection of the period must have been colored by the circumstance that it was at Tolmezzo that he first caught syphilis and was obliged to undergo treatment at the local hospital.[19]

He returned to Dovia, where he spent a few idle months, and early in 1908 he passed an examination in French at Bologna. The diploma which he obtained enabled him, through the good offices of Lucius Serrati, a Socialist leader, to secure a post at Oneglia, on the Italian Riviera, where he was appointed teacher of French in a private school, the Collegio Ulisse Calvi. Serrati had founded a small Socialist newspaper, *La Lima,* at Oneglia and was anxious to entrust the paper to him. In fact Mussolini wrote the entire newspaper himself. Some of the articles were signed "Mussolini B."; others in order to create an illusion of variety carried pseudonyms such as "*Il Limatore,*" "*Vero Erectico,*" and "*Noi.*" Mussolini's stay at Oneglia was not untroubled, for the police, warned from Forlì of Mussolini's revolutionary record, at once began to make difficulties for him and even requested the rector of the school to dismiss him. The rector refused, but Mussolini, far from being intimidated, used the columns of *La Lima* to make venomous attacks on the Catholic Church and to assail the Catholic weekly *Il Giornale Ligure.* Eventually pressure from clericals and conservatives built up and in June, 1904, the police served on him an order to quit Oneglia. In the issue of June 27 he addressed his opponents furiously in *La Lima:*

> In a few days I shall go and, in order that you may be able to report me, I now inform you of my exact address: the house close to the 15 kilometer stone on the provincial road on the river Rabbi, hamlet of Dovia, commune of Predappio, province of Forlì. Make a note of it and try to see whether it is possible also to drive me out of my father's house.[20]

On July 2, 1908, Mussolini returned to Predappio, where he once more engaged in local politics and once more found himself in conflict with authority. Toward the end of the month he was sentenced to a short term of imprisonment for disturbing the peace and seven weeks later to a fine of 100 lire for a seditious speech. Later he published in the local Republican organ *Il Pensiero Romagnolo* an essay, "*La filosofia senza forza,*" attacking the moderate and pacifist views of the Socialist Deputy Claudio Treves. Mussolini's extremist activities made him something of a public figure in the neighborhood and his fame must have spread over the frontier, for early in 1909 the Socialists of the Chamber of Labor at Trent, 150 miles to the north in Austrian territory, offered him the post of secretary at a salary of 120 kronen a month. In addition to the duties of secretary he was to be responsible for *L'Avvenire del Lavoratore,* a small four-page weekly, which was the official organ of the party. This newspaper had been founded in 1895 by Cesare Battista in Vienna and he had later moved it to Trent, where in 1900 he founded his own daily newspaper, the *Popolo,* handing over control of the *Avvenire,* which he continued to print, to the local Socialist party. The *Avvenire,* announcing the news of Mussolini's appointment, said that he was an excellent choice, because he was a proved fighter and an ardent propagandist, particularly versed in anticlericalism.[21]

IV

Mussolini accepted the Trent offer with joy. He longed to make his mark on the world and his new post gave him an opportunity to escape from the squalor of schoolmastering and to put his foot on the first rung of the political ladder. It also gave him his first valuable experience of journalism, the one profession to which he was entirely devoted. He arrived in Trent in March, 1909, and his comrades soon introduced him to Battista, the Socialist irredentist who was to be captured and executed by the Austrians in 1916. The situation which he found was not at all to his liking. The Trentino had not developed industrially and was not attuned to receive his message of revolutionary Socialism. The local party men were law-abiding, reformist, and patriotic, but, so far as extreme nationalism was concerned, they were somewhat inhibited by directives from the central party leadership in Vienna. As editor of the *Avvenire* Mussolini made it his duty to rouse the citizens of Trent by beating the drum of international revolutionary socialism. At the same time he contributed to Battista's irredentist daily, the *Popolo,* and in August, 1909, he became its managing editor. Mussolini's apologists have claimed his association with Battista as proof of his patriotic chauvinism. His detractors invoke his articles in the *Avvenire* as evidence that he was an international socialist and an antimilitarist, one who was out of sympathy with irredentism and only concerned to promote the cause of revolution. The truth is that his background was revolutionary, and everything that had happened to him during his short life had inflamed his revolutionary ardor. On the other hand he was always susceptible to his environment, and this trait, combined with his romanticism, brought him to some extent under the influence of Battista. Thus he was able without too much difficulty to satisfy the requirements of both the *Avvenire* and the *Popolo.* It was not the last occasion on which he was ambivalent in the face of a big issue.

Despite his lack of sympathy for the passive outlook of the Trentino Socialists, Mussolini brought great enthusiasm to his work. It was his first experience as editor of a daily newspaper. In addition to a spate of articles, he wrote serialized stories for the *Popolo's* weekly supplement, *La Vita Trentina.* One of them was entitled: "Claudia Particella, or the Cardinal's Love" and purported to be the love story of Cardinal Madruzzo, a former bishop of Trent. Margherita Sarfatti described it as "just a hotchpotch without beginning or end." [22] He also lectured before workers' groups, made public speeches, and once debated in public with Alcide de Gasperi, who was after the Second World War to become Christian Democratic

Prime Minister of Italy. This exciting and active existence was, however, not to last long, for, as usual, his proceedings aroused the displeasure of the authorities.

The *Avvenire* had declared that he excelled in anticlerical propaganda, and Mussolini more than fulfilled the hopes placed in him. In the language of the gutter he showered a stream of abuse on the Catholic Church and its local representatives. The Vatican he described as a gang of robbers, and a well-known Austrian priest he called a hydrophobic dog. In May, 1909, he was sentenced to a fine of 30 kronen or three days imprisonment for insulting the editor of a Catholic weekly. In June he was condemned to eight days imprisonment and a fine of 100 kronen for incitement to violence. In August he was again sent to prison for seven days, and four days after his release he was again sentenced to seven days for an offense against the press law.[23]

As an Italian living in Austria Mussolini was in a vulnerable position, and during the summer of 1909 rumors became current that the authorities were considering his expulsion. Indeed it says much for the liberalism of the Austrian regime in the Trentino that they tolerated him for as long as they did. Matters were, however, brought to a head when on August 30, 1909, a robbery took place at the Banca Cooperativa at Trent and the sum of about 300,000 kronen was stolen. The authorities regarded the crime as the precursor of an armed irredentist movement, and a number of citizens were arrested. There was no evidence that Mussolini was implicated, but his police record placed him under suspicion and, after his lodgings had been fruitlessly searched, he also was arrested and transferred to the prison at the nearby town of Rovereto. On September 24 he was tried on two charges: first for incitement to violence in a letter to the editor of *L'Alto Adige* and second for sending with this letter a number of the *Avvenire* which had been confiscated. He was acquitted, but not released; and on September 26 he was deported from Austria to Italy. It has been claimed by his apologists that he was deported because of a provocative article in the *Popolo* in which he stated that the Italian frontier was not at Ala, then a border town between Austria and Italy. But the fact is that in six short months he had by his abuse of Austrian hospitality made himself intolerable to the police, and the expulsion of an undesirable alien presented no problem. The Trent Socialists protested against his expulsion and organized a strike, but Mussolini was pleased to return to Italy wearing the halo of a martyred revolutionary and basking in the sunshine of clamorous publicity. He left behind him two mistresses, by each of whom he had had a child, Fernanda Fachinelli and Ida Dalser.

Mussolini's association with Battista marked his first step from international towards national socialism. It was a first, very tentative step, and he cannot be said to have made up his mind, for indeed both in 1911 and in August, 1914, he sided aggressively with the internationalists against the nationalists. But his experience at Trent deepened his dislike of comfortable, moderate, reformist socialism and suggested to him that nationalism and revolution were not incompatible. After he had returned to Italy he published under the auspices of the Florentine review *La Voce* a long essay entitled: "The Trentino as Seen by a Socialist." In describing the Trentino Socialist movement, he declared that its campaign in favor of political and administrative autonomy constituted the finest page in its history. Thus he drew a distinction between autonomy and irredentism, but he also envisaged the possibility of a war with Austria, in which victory to Italian arms would compel the vanquished to cede some of the lost territories.

V

The renown which Mussolini won at Trent secured him the post of Socialist secretary at Forlì at a salary of 120 lire a month. In addition to the secretaryship he undertook to edit a new weekly journal, which he founded himself and to which he gave a title indicative of its aims: *La Lotta di Classe* ("The Class War"). It consisted of only four pages, produced entirely by himself, and its first number appeared in January, 1910. For the first time in his life Mussolini at the age of twenty-six was in the happy position of being in complete control of a newspaper which belonged to him. Forlì was a traditional Republican stronghold in which the Socialists represented a minority, and the struggle which he was obliged to wage appealed to his combative nature. Moreover, while the party in Reggio Emilia, Gualtieri, Tolmezzo, Oneglia, and Trent had been predominantly reformist, he was now at home in the revolutionary atmosphere of Romagna. As usual, he drew inspiration from his environment and *La Lotta di Classe* became the mouthpiece of the extremist wing of the Socialist party.

One man [Menni subsequently wrote], Mussolini, seemed to have the power of being everywhere at the same time in order to fan the revolutionary enthusiasm of the masses. . . . He was ever ready to sacrifice theory to action. "Provided we fight" was his motto. And when there was no possibility of fighting the state, we were to fight each other, since he was of opinion that to do so was to "strengthen our muscles and prepare our minds." [24]

He was thus in constant conflict not only with the Republicans, but with the reformists in his own party, whom he accused of craven cowardice. He complained that the ideals of the movement had given way to naked materialism. He denounced the parliamentary system and condemned electoral pacts, and he demanded direct revolutionary action without equivocation and without compromise. He did not even hesitate to endorse assassination as a political weapon. Referring to a bomb explosion in the Colon Theatre at Buenos Aires, he wrote in *La Lotta di Classe* of July 9, 1910, that the state of society justified the use of violence. "Socialists are too frequently moved by the misfortunes of the bourgeoisie, while at the same time they remain indifferent to those of the proletariat." [25]

A year later the Russian Minister Stolypin was assassinated and Mussolini had this to say in *La Lotta di Classe* of September 23, 1911:

The nemesis of justice struck him dead. So be it. Stolypin (ignoble, sinister, and sanguinary) has deserved his fate. . . . The tragic end of Nicholas II will be the dawn of a new period of revolutionary action. We hope for it steadfastly. While awaiting it, glory to the man who has accomplished the sacred gesture of the avenger.[26]

When the Russian revolution did come, Mussolini had evolved, and the event aroused no enthusiasm in his breast. But that lay in the future. Meanwhile in turgid language calculated to appeal to the extremists he vented his spleen against Christianity, the monarchy, and the established order. His experience in Switzerland made him particularly sympathetic to Russian revolutionaries, and in a Lugano journal, *Pagine Libre,* on January 1, 1911, he made a revealing comment on the famous siege of Sidney Street in London, which he described as a tragedy. The victims he declared were anarchists, but in the elastic sense of the word.

> They hated work, because physical work (one must have the courage to proclaim it once and for all) brutalizes man instead of ennobling him; they hated property because it made irremediable the antagonism between individual and individual; they hated life, and above all the society which they denied and wished to destroy.[27]

He was equally violent in his attacks on Christianity and the Catholic Church. At a congress of the Forlì Socialists in 1910 he presented and carried a resolution defining the practice of the Catholic or any other faith as inconsistent with socialism and expelling from the party those members who followed religious practices or tolerated them in their children. Socialists were enjoined to avoid religious marriage, baptism, or participation in any other religious ceremony.[28] In the columns of *La Lotta di Classe* the tenets of the Christian faith, and in particular the virtues of patience and humility, were assailed with often blasphemous virulence.

He was later to modify his attitude to the Church, as indeed to many other institutions, and the years he spent at Forlì were not a period of his life on which he looked back with any satisfaction. In his autobiography no mention is made of *La Lotta di Classe,* and Margherita Sarfatti merely describes the journal as a vehicle for Mussolini's ideas. It is clear, however, that all that was heard in *La Lotta di Classe* was in fact the voice of a young, vengeful iconoclast, who believed passionately in revolution at the barricades and wished blindly to destroy the idols of the past without knowing what was to be put in their place. It was a voice which shocked many of the moderate Socialist leaders of the day.

It was about this time that Mussolini married Rachele Guidi, if the term can be applied to a union which was neither sanctified in a church nor legalized in a registry office. She was born on April 11, 1892, at Predappio and was the daughter of a small tenant farmer. When she was eight her father died suddenly and the family knew grinding poverty. As soon as she was old enough to do so Rachele went into domestic service, and it was in 1908 while she was with a Signor Chiedini at Forlì that she met Mussolini outside the church. His suit was threadbare and his pockets were bulging with newspapers. He accosted her and asked if she remembered him from the old Predappio days. Rachele's mother Anna Guidi was now living with Alesandro Mussolini, who after his wife's death had left Predappio and become the proprietor of an inn at Forlì called *Il Bersagliere.* Rachele soon left the Chiedini household and went to help at the inn.[29] In the months that followed she and Benito met constantly; and when Mussolini left for Trent he told her to wait for him since he intended to marry her on his return.

Only eight months elapsed and he was back, looking less down at heel and obviously happy. After some delay due to the opposition of Alesandro, Benito rented two rooms in the Palazzo Merenda in the Via Merenda at Forlì and the couple moved in. They were miserably poor on his salary of 120 lire a month, but they managed. On September 1, 1910, when Rachele was eighteen years old, their first child Edda was born, followed later by Vittorio and Bruno and after some years by Romano and Anna Maria. It may be noted that none of the children bore Christian names having a revolutionary connotation. At the time Rachele was a fair, well-built girl with good features and the attractiveness which springs from health and vitality. She made her first appearance with the comrades during the winter of 1913 when she visited the office of *Avanti* at Milan. She was a humble-looking woman and was accompanied by a poorly dressed little girl, who was shivering with cold. Mussolini introduced them as "my comrade Rachele and our daughter Edda." [30]

She was a good wife to him. She knew that her place was in the background and throughout the vicissitudes of their life together she bore patiently with his infidelities and with his changing moods. A humble camp follower, she was always there to give him comfort when he required it; and when the end came she showed him the same love and compassion as she had done in the early days at Forlì and in the time of his prosperity.

In November, 1910, while Mussolini was busy at Forlì, his father died at the age of fifty-seven. Three thousand mourners followed his coffin to the grave, and his death was regarded as a loss to the revolutionary movement. For Mussolini it meant the dissolution of the family home.

As editor of *La Lotta di Classe* Mussolini was now beginning to attract attention, most of it hostile. But he was not disturbed, for he believed that it was more profitable to be feared than loved; and in any event rebellion was more likely than conformity to bring him the publicity he required. In September, 1911, he was given an opportunity to push himself further to the front when the Giolitti government declared war on Turkey and embarked on the conquest of Libya. The recent Austrian annexation of Bosnia and Herzegovina had drawn attention to Turkey's weakness and had encouraged others to seize the first opportunity of dismembering the Sick Man of Europe. Germany had connived at Austria's territorial aggrandizement and was prepared to do the same for her ally Italy. It is true that Libya was not likely to become a valuable asset, but its conquest would assuage the national pride of those who wished to see Italy take her place with other European powers in Africa.

It was a moment of indecision for the Socialists. The moderates, led by Bissolati, were divided between doctrinaire repugnance for colonial adventure and the desire on parliamentary grounds to support Giolitti. Mussolini was equally uncertain, but on different grounds. On the one hand the disciple of Nietzsche had no objection of principle to the use of force and indeed his burgeoning nationalism tempted him to support a war of conquest; on the other hand violent opposition to war might rock the government and pave the way to revolution. For the moderate Socialists doctrine, and for Mussolini revolutionary ardor triumphed; and soon both wings of the party were able to reach agreement on a policy of active opposition. In the struggle Mussolini took a leading part, although no reference to it is made in his autobiography. On September 24, 1911, in a public speech at Forlì he urged the crowd to declare a general strike, to set up street barricades, to tear up railway lines, to stop public transport, and to organize resistance to the government. "His eloquence that day was reminiscent of Marat," wrote Pietro Nenni.[31] There were riots at Forlì and troops were called upon to restore order. Mussolini was arrested, tried on eight charges, and sentenced to twelve months' imprisonment, subsequently reduced to five months on appeal.

His opposition to the war was only of local significance and was not particularly effective since public opinion was in general against him. Nevertheless his trial at Forlì and the subsequent appeal heard at Bologna gave him a plaform from which to expound his political ideas. He was no malefactor, he declared, but a patriotic Italian.

> I have written and said what I have written and said, because I want and love an Italy which is conscious of her duty and struggles to redeem her people from economic and spiritual misery rather than violate the homeland of others in order to extend to it her own pauperism.

Having cleverly struck the patriotic as against the revolutionary note, Mussolini concluded:

> If you acquit me, you will please me because you will restore me to my work and to society. But if you condemn me, you will do me an honor because you find yourself in the presence not of a malefactor, not of a common delinquent, but of an asserter of ideas, of an agitator of consciences, of a soldier of a faith that commands your respect because it bears within itself the presentiments of the future and the great strength of truth.

His speech evoked applause in court and led the prosecutor to remark that the defendant had the gift of speaking most convincingly, a circumstance which made him dangerous.[32] This trial was an important milestone in Mussolini's life, for the publicity it received made him something of a hero in the Socialist ranks, an advantage which he was soon able to exploit.

In the prison of the Rocca in Forlì the Socialist Mussolini shared imprisonment with the Republican Pietro Nenni, also implicated in opposition to the Libyan war. These two men, divided politically but united by similarity of temperament, formed a curious, if distant, friendship which lasted as long as Mussolini lived. They were godfathers to one another's children and shortly before his death Mussolini confided to Carlo Silvestri that it was the one true friendship of his life.[33] The society of Nenni did much to alleviate the boredom of prison life; and Mussolini spent some of his enforced leisure writing a life of John Huss, a capable exercise in anticlerical pamphleteering.

Nenni's description of him during this phase is borne out by other contemporaries.

At that time the future dictator of Italy was leading a life of the utmost simplicity. . . . He was looked upon as somewhat crazy. A lonely, shy man, he was constantly to be seen wandering aimlessly about the countryside, quite alone. In Socialist circles he stood for antireformism and antiparliamentarianism. He made no attempt to conceal his lack of confidence in trade unions and cooperative societies, in which, he maintained, revolutionary instincts were ousted by personal and class interests. Taken all round, he was a solitary and individualistic figure in the ranks of socialism.[34]

VI

Mussolini's release from prison after he had served his sentence was acclaimed by his comrades, who saw in him the makings of a new dynamic leader. At the banquet which they gave him, Olindo Vernocchi, a veteran Socialist leader, concluded his speech with the words: "From today you, Benito, are not only the representative of the Romagna Socialists but the Duce of all revolutionary Socialists in Italy." It was the first occasion on which the term "Duce" was applied to him. Four months later, fortified by this manifestation of support, he traveled confidently to Reggio Emilia to attend the congress of the Socialist party, which took place from July 7 to July 10, 1912. Cesare Rossi describes his appearance on that occasion:

I found myself in the presence of a man with a thin, emaciated, bony face with a thick beard of several days' growth. He wore a gray, large-brimmed hat of Romagnole design, which was threadbare and greasy. His jacket, which had originally been black, had become green with use. His pockets were full of newspapers. He wore an incredibly worn-out flowing tie, a shirt and a collar, which should have been white, but had not been so for a long time, a pair of old fustian trousers with crumpled knees showing long service and disdain for the ironing board, a pair of shoes which for months had not known polish.[35]

When this strange figure stood at the speaker's tribune, his indigent appearance, together with the fame of his recent imprisonment, provoked tumultuous applause.

The congress which Mussolini addressed was an important one. For some time a growing rift had been splitting the Socialist party into two factions: on the one hand the reformists, who believed that the hour of revolution had not struck and that the interests of the working classes were best served by securing social reform through collaboration with the Liberals, and on the other hand the revolutionaries. Mussolini, to whom the parliamentary system was repugnant and who was not prepared to compromise with anyone, was naturally on the side of the revolutionaries.

The circumstances in which Mussolini faced the congress favored his plans. He had acquired a certain notoriety, and he knew that he could now rely on an attentive audience. Moreover an event had recently occurred which gave him an opportunity of striking a telling blow against the reformists. Shortly before the meeting of the congress a lunatic had fired on the King without hitting him and the Chamber of Deputies had decided to tender a loyal message of congratulation. Bissolati, the gentle, moderate Socialist leader, together with other Socialists, had associated himself with this move and thus precipitated a crisis in the party. The activists were already at loggerheads with the evolutionists over Bissolati's attitude to the use of force in domestic politics, and this incident proved the last straw. At the congress Mussolini used his new-found authority to speak for the left wing and his hatred of the monarchy added venom to his words:

> On March 14 a Roman mason fired his revolver at Victor of Savoy. Precedent indicated the line of conduct to be followed by Socialists. . . . One had a right to hope not to see again . . . the incredible spectacle of labor exchanges raising the flag at half-mast veiled in black; of Socialist municipalities sending telegrams of condolence and congratulation; of all democratic and revolutionary Italy prostrating itself at a given moment before the throne. . . . What is a king anyway except by definition a useless citizen? There are peoples who have sent their King packing; others even have preferred to take the precaution of sending him to the guillotine, and those peoples are in the vanguard of progress.[36]

This was the language Mussolini's audience wanted to hear and it intoxicated them. At his behest, four moderates, Bissolati, Bonomi, Podrecca, and Cabrini were expelled from the party, and Claudio Treves was dismissed from the editorship of *Avanti,* the party organ. From now on Mussolini's star was in the ascendant and, under his stimulus, the party was moving towards extremism. He was himself elected a member of the party executive committee, together with

Angelica Balabanoff and Geacinto Serrati, but he did not at once secure the editorship of *Avanti,* which was entrusted to Giovanni Bacci, a nonentity of the left wing. He could afford to wait a little while he gathered the fruits of his triumph. He had made a notable impact on both friends and enemies who recognized that a new force had arrived in Italian politics. The *Corriere della Sera* said that he had pleased the congress, which found in him an interpreter of its own sentiments.[37] Bonomi described him as "a revolutionary in whom the spirit of the barricades is stronger than Marxist discipline."[38] Signor Sarfatti, who had hitherto supported Bissolati, voted with reluctance for Mussolini and in a letter described him as: "a wonderful young man, spare of figure, hard, fiery, most original, with occasional bursts of eloquence; a man with a great future before him. You will see that he is destined to dominate the party."[39] Anna Kuliscioff, a prominent Socialist of Lithuanian origin, was perhaps more perspicacious in her assessment: "He is nothing of a Marxist, nor is he really a Socialist at all. He has not the mentality of a scientific Socialist. Nor is he really a politician. He is a sentimental poetaster who has read Nietzsche." Of course he was more than a dreamy poetaster. He had a streak of egotistical ruthlessness with which to further his boundless ambitions; and he had the capacity to move men's minds. But it was true that he belonged to no party, although he was obliged by political expediency to continue to make use of the Socialists, for there was no other party to which he could turn.

The party congress at Reggio Emilia marked the end of Mussolini's vagabondage. He had fulfilled his first ambition, which was to arrive, to secure for himself a niche in society and a platform from which he could expound his still nebulous views. To the tasks awaiting him he now addressed himself with the animal vitality and enthusiasm of youth.

CHAPTER THREE

The Editor

1912–1917

I

THE appointment of Bacci to the editor's chair of *Avanti* was only a temporary expedient. In December, 1912, Mussolini was able to oust him and to take over the newspaper, but he made it a condition that he should engage Angelica Balabanoff as his assistant editor. His first issue of *Avanti* contained a personal message from the new editor: "I embark on my journey carrying intact the burden of my ideas, and I hope to reach my goal. That is to say, I hope not to be unworthy of the confidence placed in me by the leadership of the party."

One member of the Socialist executive committee, Arturo Vella, had opposed Mussolini's appointment on the ground that he was too much of an individualist; but nobody at that time thought of questioning his fidelity to the cause. Angelica, although she was aware of his lack of political education, felt that his devotion to the movement, his adaptability, his industry, and his ability would enable him to discharge his duties satisfactorily. She believed him to be a sincere revolutionary, and she later ascribed his apostasy to his weakness of character and to the temptations placed in his way by outside influences.[1]

The editorship of *Avanti* improved Mussolini's financial position. He could have obtained 700 lire a month, the salary paid to his predecessor, but he was never interested in money, and he reduced the figure to 500 so as not to encumber the paper's resources. He and Rachele moved into a flat in 19 Via Castel Morrone, in a good part of Milan not far from the City Hall, for which he paid the relatively large rent of 100 lire a month. He was now in control of a national daily with headquarters in Italy's most important industrial city and was henceforth in a position to make his influence felt in a wider sphere. He worked like a demon both in the office of *Avanti* and in the local Socialist party. Under his leadership the circulation of the newspaper rose gradually from 20,000 to nearly 100,000, a large figure for a provincial party newspaper. His leading articles, devoid of logic and not conspicuous for factual accuracy, were effective for the power of his invective and the range of his imagery. He attended and spoke at party meetings all over the country, attacking the reformist wing of the party and the parliamentary system. He wrote to a friend: "Here I work like a dog. I live a solitary life. They attack me from every quarter: from the priests to the Syndicalists." [2] But he was not entirely alone, for at about this time he met and formed an association with a young Mohammedan Anarchist called Leda Rafanelli. It was more of an intellectual than a sensual association and it lasted almost two years. Although Leda was captivated by his charm and by his virile oratory, she was well aware that he was volatile and unstable: "During our long conversations I had occasion to note that Mussolini too easily changed his opinion. At least with me he was not only deferent but ready to share my view, even though at the beginning of the discussion he seemed to be of the opposite opinion." [3] Nevertheless, to the public he presented the figure of an implacable revolutionary, a man who knew his mind and who might one day lead his party to the overthrow of the Italian monarchy. The fact that he sometimes contradicted himself in his public utterances was lost in the turbulence of his eloquence.

Leda Rafanelli gives a picture of him during this period. He came to see her in her Arabic-style flat, elegantly dressed in black, with a high forehead accentuated by premature baldness and carrying a hard hat between his hands. She observed that his knowledge was confined to the topics discussed in his own political circle and that he was avid to learn what she could teach him. He was shy with her, but he explained that he was at his best with crowds: "I feel that I could become a great orator, a modern Demosthenes, a Jaurès. But I should require an immense, emotional crowd which was at a distance and the members of which were unknown to me. I speak more readily in a stadium than in the parlors of local clubs." He told her of his frustrations and ambitions: "I require to be somebody, do you understand me? I want to be not only the man I am. I want to rise to the top. In my youth I wanted to be a great musician [he played the violin] or a great writer, but I understood that I should have remained mediocre. The environment in which I was born enslaved me. . . . I shall never be content. I tell you, I must rise, I must make a bound forwards, to the top." [4]

The years 1913 and 1914 were tumultuous with civil strife and Mussolini used the columns of *Avanti* to support the cause of proletarian revolution and to flay the reformists for their bourgeois cowardice. In 1913 riots in the South were bloodily suppressed by troops who opened fire on the crowds. In 1914 unrest spread to the North and threatened to become general. "Our lack of political understanding brought at least one riot a week. . . . They had their harvest of killed and wounded and of corroding bitterness of heart. Riots and upheavals among day laborers, among the peasants in the valley of the Po, riots in the South. Even separatist movements in our islands." [5]

This was the background against which the Socialist party, with Mussolini in the van, prepared for the general elections of November, 1913, the first to be held under universal suffrage. Mussolini himself stood for Forlì, a constituency in which he had little chance of success owing to its long Republican tradition. He was not elected, but the Socialists won fifty-three seats, a success which was attributed largely to Mussolini's conduct of the campaign. He declared himself delighted with the result and to an applauding crowd assembled under the windows of *Avanti* he said: "Now we can envisage only two blocks, the one conservative and the other revolutionary." [6]

In March, 1914, he was tried at Milan for having written articles which the prosecution claimed to be seditious. The trial lasted a fortnight and once more gave Mussolini a convenient political platform, which he used to such effect that the jury acquitted him. Fresh from this triumph he traveled the following month to the Socialist party congress at Ancona and here again he played a leading role, scoring two notable successes. He had for some time been opposed to Freemasonry, and he induced the congress to pass a resolution declaring that Socialists could no longer be Masons. It might be, he said, that Masonry was humanitarian. But it was time to react against the infiltration of humanitarianism into socialism, for socialism was purely a class problem. Similarly the anticlericalism of Masonry had nothing to do with Socialist anticlericalism since the latter was inspired by class consciousness. Despite the presence of many Masons at the congress Mussolini's resolution carried the day by a large majority.

His second success lay in his ability to dominate the congress and to keep the revolutionary wing of the party in the ascendant. At his instance the congress decided to organize public demonstrations in favor of an Anarchist soldier and against the establishment of penal companies in the army, to one of which the soldier had been posted; and it was resolved to call a general strike in the event of police repression. Sunday, June 7, 1914, was the day selected and, while in Milan the day passed off quietly, there were riots in Ancona, where the police fired on the crowd, killing three and wounding ten of the demonstrators. The general strike, the so-called Red Week, which soon spread like a revolutionary brush fire, was the reply. It was the most serious insurrection united Italy had known, but it collapsed on the seventh day when the Confederation of Labor called off the strike, because it recognized that the movement could not succeed without the support of any armed forces. Respect for strength and contempt for the flabbiness of the masses and their Socialist leaders were the conclusions which Mussolini drew from the events of Red Week and which guided him in his subsequent conduct of affairs. Nevertheless his prestige did not suffer from the fiasco. On the contrary he was able to pin the blame on the cowardice of the moderates, whom he accused of treason, and to garner credit for his own activist role. Bonomi, who was no friend, wrote of him:

> The young revolutionary is now the heart and the brain of the Socialist party. Among the masses and especially among the new recruits, who represent the largest and most enthusiastic element, he is the orator and writer who is most highly considered, most loved and most followed. At

the Socialist congress at Ancona his will became law and his authority was that of a dictator. In his hands *Avanti* has advanced towards a goal which is clear, precise, and admitted, namely to infuse a revolutionary spirit into the Italian masses.[7]

Under the leadership of the extremist wing the Socialist party improved their position at the local elections held in June, 1914. Mussolini was elected at Milan and the Socialists gained control for the first time in many important towns, including Bologna. Mussolini declared proudly that the Socialists had been the only party to campaign without equivocation and promised that the abortive Red Week would be followed by a successful revolution. But it should be noted that he was still without a constructive policy.

II

Hard on these events came the assassination of the Archduke Ferdinand at Sarajevo and the outbreak of the First World War. Once more Mussolini was torn by conflicting emotions. His temperament counseled action and he had not abandoned the alluring expectation that war might bring about revolution and the fall of the monarchy. On the other hand the main body of the Socialist party, with which his fortunes were bound up, favored neutrality, which was perfectly open to Italy under the terms of the Treaty of 1882. Italian opinion was somewhat confused. After 1870 the opposition of France to Italian expansion had evoked as much ill will as the conduct of the hereditary enemy, Austria. Moreover the decadent Austro-Hungarian Empire was now allied and in a sense subservient to Germany, on whom the Italians looked without the same enmity. Indeed, the Italian army respected the Prussian army, the Italian Socialists were impressed by Prussian socialism, and the intellectuals admired the academic institutions of Prussia. On the other hand France's ally was Britain, the traditional friend, who was the best guarantor of Italy's security in the Mediterranean. Thus predilection for Prussia and Britain canceled out the ingrained antipathy of the Italians to the major allies of these two countries.

It is not surprising that in these circumstances the attitude of Italy on the outbreak of the war in August, 1914, should have been one of unqualified neutrality. Only the Nationalists, of whom Federzoni was the spokesman, favored joining Germany and Austria. A few Socialists, including the now completely isolated Bissolati and of course Cesare Battista, supported the struggle of the Western democracies against Prussian autocracy and Austrian imperialism. There was also some disarray in the Socialist ranks caused by the defection of the German and Austrian Social Democrats from the solidarity of the International. The government, however, and the vast bulk of the nation were against intervention on the side of the Central Powers and in favor of neutrality.

Mussolini made it his first task to oppose war in alliance with Germany and Austria. On July 26, 1914, in an article "Down with the War," he declared that Italy must stand aside, and on the following day he threatened the government with violence if they ventured to flout public opinion: "The members of the proletariat are now on the alert. The moment Italy showed inclination to break neutrality in order to back up the Central Powers, the Italian proletariat would have but one duty, we say it clearly and distinctly,—that of rising in rebellion." [8] On July 29 with a number of others he signed a Socialist party manifesto appealing once more to the masses to resist involvement in war. During August and September he continued to thunder against the war and to brand his opponents as traitors and renegades.

Mussolini was, however, battering at an open door, since the country was resolved not to fight for Germany and Austria; and as the months passed it became clear that the issue lay between a small minority who favored Britain and France and the large majority who stood for absolute neutrality. One event, the battle of the Marne, contributed significantly to Mussolini's conversion from neutralism to interventionism. From that moment he ceased to believe in an ultimate German victory; and since regard for power and fear were the two motives which guided him in life, he decided that it might well be a mistake to maintain indefinitely his policy of absolute neutrality.

III

He was, however, obliged by his situation to move prudently. He had in August published an article in *Avanti* accusing a friend,

Ottavio Dinale, of being a warmonger. When Dinale some time later called on him to protest, he explained that international socialism prescribed opposition to war to the point of using the weapon of the general strike. If he were to favor intervention, he would be setting himself up against the tables of the law and would probably be lynched. In consequence he was obliged to adopt prudent tactics and, while clinging to the policy of neutrality, to move step by step to the conclusion that intervention must be linked with the interests not only of the country, but of the proletariat.[9] In conversation with other friends he from time to time revealed that, while he did not intend to abandon his public condemnation of the war, he had not closed his mind to the possibility of intervention. To Libero Tancredi, an Anarchist interventionist, he observed that the neutralism of *Avanti* could fulfill one useful function, namely to give indirect support to the Italian government in eventual negotiations with the Entente, who would certainly seek to pay as low a price as possible for Italian intervention. To Battista, whom he met at the Association of Lombard Journalists, he said that neutrality was nonsense, that the Socialists could not be accomplices of the Central Powers, and that the moment had come for Italy to become a Great Power and to complete the work of the architects of the Risorgimento.

By the end of September it was becoming generally known that Mussolini was vacillating, and Libero Tancredi in the *Resto di Carlino* of Bologna openly accused him of privately favoring intervention, while continuing to oppose it in *Avanti*. But Mussolini was not the only man in Italy to be privately questioning the wisdom of neutrality. The King feared Germany, a number of politicians sympathized with France, and there was always the temptation to grasp any opportunity of frontier revision at the expense of Austria. The nation was still predominantly neutralist, but the tide was beginning to turn; and French money was spent liberally to accelerate the trend. Mussolini took advantage of the change of climate to become bolder. On October 13, 1914, the newspaper *La Voce* noted that he had changed his anti-interventionist policy; and indeed there was ample ground for the charge since on October 10 he had published in *Avanti* an article advocating a departure from absolute neutrality in favor of armed neutrality and concluding:

To refuse to distinguish between war and war and to presume to offer the same kind of opposition to all wars is to give proof of a stupidity bordering upon the imbecile. . . . Do you want to be as men and as Socialists, inert spectators of this tremendous drama? Or do you not want to be, in some fashion or other its protagonists? Socialists of Italy, listen: it has happened at times that the letter has killed the spirit. Do not let us keep the letter of the party if that means killing the spirit of socialism.[10]

IV

It was a sudden reversal of the newspaper's policy, undertaken without previous consultation with his associates and requiring some explanation. It has been alleged by his detractors that he took money from the French government. His apologists have hotly denied this and invoke the findings of a commission of enquiry which was set up to examine the origins of the funds of the *Popolo d'Italia* and which in a report of February 24, 1915, cleared Mussolini of any suspicion of personal gain. It is therefore worth marshaling the evidence, which, incidentally, was not available in 1915 to the commission.

In his book *Laughing Diplomat* Daniele Varé refers to a story told to M. P. Mantoux by M. Julien Luchaire to the effect that the members of a French propaganda mission, hearing that the *Popolo d'Italia* was in financial difficulties, offered a subvention to Mussolini, who accepted it. The sum might have been 100,000 lire or more, but a year later the money was repaid in full by Mussolini with an expression of gratitude for the temporary loan.[11] M. Luchaire, who was interrogated on the point by Gaetano Salvemini, replied as follows:

It is true that in 1915 during the interventionist campaign Mussolini found himself in financial difficulties and one evening in Milan asked me for a loan. I no longer remember the exact sum. It could not have been more than 30,000 lire, perhaps less. I believe, without being able to swear to it, that a few days later Barrère * took my place and provided larger sums. My loan was never repaid. About ten years later, while I was making a tour of the European capitals in my capacity of Director of the Institute of International Cooperation [a League of Nations body] to conclude agreements and collect funds I saw Mussolini again. He as-

* M. C. Barrère, French Ambassador to the Quirinal.

signed an annual sum of 100,000 lire to the Institute and this sum, like the contributions of other nations, was channeled through the League of Nations. It is possible that on my return to Geneva I may have said jokingly to Mantoux or somebody else: "Mussolini has thus repaid the money I lent him." This is almost certainly the origin of the story.[12]

M. Luchaire, although he cannot swear to the part played by Barrère, was in such close touch with the French embassy that his belief can with reasonable certainty be taken as evidence. Nevertheless there is confirmation from another quarter. Some years later Barrère told M. Wapler, whom he sponsored in the French Foreign Service, that he had personally made substantial payments to Mussolini during the interventionist campaign; and that Mussolini, a shabby figure in an old mackintosh, had come regularly to the Palazzo Farnese to collect the money.*

In March, 1925, during a political trial in Paris of certain anti-Fascists for offenses against public order, counsel for the prosecution exhorted the jury to remember that Italy had entered the war in consequence of Mussolini's disinterested effort. Maître Torrès, counsel for the anti-Fascists, retorted that Mussolini had only bestirred himself about France's fate after pocketing the sums earmarked to buy him. This assertion was not further questioned in court, and outside the court Maître Torrès gave the following supplementary information:

> There was a moment quite at the start when the Italian Socialist party was unanimous against the armed intervention of Italy. The French government was concerned and considered the matter in a Cabinet meeting. They examined the question to see if there were not some means of converting some of the Socialists to the cause of the war—a financial means. The name of Mussolini was mentioned. The first payment was 15,000 francs and after that they allowed him 10,000 francs monthly. It was Guesde's † secretary, Dumas, who brought him the money. It was then that the *Popolo d'Italia* was born, immediately interventionist. That is the exact story, which no one will dare to deny for fear of more crushing documentary evidence.[13]

On November 9, 1926, the French deputy P. Renaudel wrote in the *Quotidien:* "Many of us remember that the first numbers of the

* Related by M. Arnauld Wapler to the author.
† M. Jules Guesde, a French Minister of State.

Popolo d'Italia were published with the aid of French money. Marcel Cachin knows it, but does not like it discussed." Marcel Cachin, then a Communist Deputy, had been a Socialist member of the "*Union Sacrée*" during the war and had traveled in Italy on semi-official missions. He had during the 1914 war in the course of a speech in the Chamber hailed Mussolini's conversion as a triumph of Allied propaganda.

On January 9, 1928, M. Paul Faure, a French deputy, wrote in the *Populaire:*

> One day Jules Guesde, then a Minister of State, confided to me that we possessed down there a man, who was one of ours: Mussolini. They had sent him a first payment of 100,000 francs to launch his newspaper. I cannot say exactly who carried the money, but Cachin, if he wished, could enlighten the readers of *Humanité.* He was then in Italy to see Mussolini on behalf of the French government.

It is significant that Cachin, who cannot have enjoyed being labeled as the intermediary of a bourgeois government who launched Mussolini, made no attempt to deny the story.

There is also some evidence from Italian sources, which must, however, be treated with reserve since it emanates from political opponents and there are some factual discrepancies. In 1938 Roberto Marvasi, an Italian refugee, published a book: *Le Roi, Mussolini, le Pape, D'Annunzio,* in which he alleged that Dino Roberto and Alceste de Ambris, two associates of Mussolini, went in March, 1915, to Paris, where Luigi Campolonghi, who was in close touch with French circles, confided to them that some of the leading Italian interventionists were in the pay of the French government. The three decided to pay a visit to Guesde, who summoned his private secretary, Dumas, and instructed him to bring a wad of bank notes. These were handed to de Ambris for transmission to Mussolini. In 1946 Salvemini asked Campolonghi for confirmation and received a long reply to the effect that the story was substantially true, although inaccurate in part. In particular the three men had visited Guesde not to solicit money, but to impress on the French Socialist comrades the need to send envoys to Italy to wean the Italian Socialists from neutralism. During the interview the Socialist Deputy Mario Montet had entered the room carrying a large envelope containing bank notes; and Guesde had handed them to Campolonghi with the words, "Take this envelope to Comrade Mussolini. It contains the monthly contribution which the French comrades send to his newspaper for the interventionist campaign." In the face of the reluctance of the three visitors to undertake the commission, Guesde explained that the money did not come from the French government but from the Socialists, who, wishing to contribute to the interventionist campaign of the *Popolo d'Italia,* had voluntarily made a levy to give the newspaper a sound financial basis. It was De Ambris who eventually agreed to accept the money and act as intermediary.

Salvemini was unable to obtain confirmation from De Ambris, who died before the publication of Marvasi's book. But in 1930, De Ambris, then a refugee, published a book[14] in France in which he stated that Mussolini had taken French money:

> Most people consider Mussolini abominable because he accepted money from the French government to found *Il Popolo d'Italia.* But that was not in itself abominable. If Mussolini had been an interventionist from the beginning, or if he had become interventionist without personal calculation, we should not regard him as guilty for having subsequently accepted money. When one takes a course, in which one's conscience is the guide, one can also accept help which renders it easier to achieve one's aim. The profound, radical, and unpardonable immorality of Mussolini lies in the fact that he deviated from his path, apostasized to obtain a personal advantage.[15]

Guiseppe Pontremoli, who in 1914 was editor of *Il Secolo* of Milan, and in touch with Franco-Italian affairs, published an article in *Il Mondo* of March 25, 1950, in which he alleged that a meeting had taken place between Mussolini and Marcel Cachin. In the negotiations which followed, Filippo Naldi, editor of *Il Resto del Carlino* of Bologna, a conservative interventionist newspaper, had taken part. The upshot was a first payment of 100,000 lire through a French bank with a branch in Italy. Its manager, Giulio Calabi, had given an account of the transaction to Pontremoli and affirmed that he had paid the sum as an advance in respect of advertising space to be allotted in the newspaper. But this payment had not sufficed and had been followed by further subventions from the same source. Unfortunately Pontremoli's version makes it impossible to fix the date of the alleged meeting with Cachin, and it is thus uncertain whether the first payment was made before or after October 10, 1914, the date on which Mussolini published his deviationist article in *Avanti.*[16]

On May 3, 1919 a Milan weekly, *L'Italia del Popolo,* declared that Mussolini had taken French money and challenged him to bring an action for slander. "We have the proof of what we have said and written." Mussolini ignored the challenge, a circumstance which may point to an uneasy conscience.

So much for evidence from Italian anti-Fascist sources. There are also clues to be found in Fascist publications. Thus in Mussolini's autobiography the origin of the *Popolo d'Italia* is explained in the following manner: [17]

I needed a daily paper. I hungered for one. I gathered together a few of my political friends, who had followed me in the last hard struggle and we held a "War Council." When money is concerned I am anything but a wizard. When it is a question of means or of capital to start a project or how to finance a newspaper, I grasp only the abstract side, the political value and the spiritual essence of the thing. To me money is detestable; what it may do is something beautiful and noble.

This book, read and approved by Mussolini, was the joint work of the American ambassador Richard Washburn Child and of Arnaldo Mussolini, who was certainly aware in 1928, when the book was published, of the allegations that Mussolini had taken French money. The wording of the passage and the fact that no attempt is made to repudiate the allegation may be construed as an implicit admission of the charge.

Margherita Sarfatti's defense of Mussolini on this issue is implausible:

Strange rumors were set afloat during the agitated days that followed. The ex-editor of the *Avanti* was declared to have accepted money from France in order to start a paper of his own. Such reports disturbed his friends and sympathizers. We knew him of course to be incapable of taking a sou for himself; but a man afire with a great project and with the sense of an imperative call to fulfill it—who could say but that in a moment of excitement he might feel justified in availing himself of any means to his hand for the purpose? It was decided to acquaint him with what was being said, for the slanders were calculated to damage seriously both Mussolini himself and the cause dear to us all. What was my surprise when I saw the two tiny rooms furnished with only four tumble-down chairs and a rickety table, in which the excellent Alessandro Giuliani, who for many years had been news-gossip on the *Avanti* and who had resigned with Mussolini, was waiting for the return of his chief. Giuliani was pleased by my coming and honored me at once with his confidence by showing me a typewritten agreement embodying a contract for some advertisements—the only economic preparation that had yet been made for the issuing of the newspaper. The contract for these advertisements and a sum of 4,000 lire obtained on a bill of exchange: such was the "capital" available. Quite enough, Mussolini felt. There were only the two factories to be paid at once and the printer and the paper merchant. As for the literary staff, those who were not animated by the fires of enthusiasm could stay at home! And so the new journal came into existence.[18]

It is unlikely that any substantial advertising contracts would have been placed and paid for in advance, having regard to the precarious prospects of the newspaper and the discouraging appearance of its premises. But, however that may be, it is clear that a loan of 4,000 lire, which would not have covered the cost of producing the first issue, was a wholly inadequate basis on which to start the enterprise.

Finally, early in 1932, Gaetano Salvemini published in Paris a book called *Mussolini Diplomate* and sent a copy to Mussolini with a sarcastic dedication. In August, 1947, Gaetano Baldacci, editor of the *Corriere della Sera,* told Salvemini that Mussolini had read the book and had made marginal notes. This bibliographical curiosity was then in Baldacci's possession and he allowed Salvemini to examine it.

Mussolini had written in red pencil on the first page: "Read February 20–21 1932-X." On fifty-six of the 338 pages there were passages which were underlined or marginally marked with a line or an arrow in red or occasionally blue pencil. In the margin of five statements by Salvemini, Mussolini had written the word "false," but when he came to the passage stating that he had taken French money he had merely underlined the name of Maître Torrès, the dates and names of the newspapers in which Renaudel and Faure had made the allegation, as well as the date and name of the weekly *L'Italia del Popolo*. It is significant but not conclusive that against none of these passages had he made the marginal note: "False." [19]

The sum total of the evidence is only circumstantial but it is cumulatively impressive. It is certain that Mussolini cannot have launched his newspaper without money. It is almost certain that he received something from Italian official sources through Naldi, who was in close touch with the Minister for Foreign Affairs; and it may well be that the first payments came from Naldi. Nevertheless the French evidence and in particular the statement of Barrère, who can have had no reason to tamper with the truth, leads to the inescapable conclusion that he accepted substantial sums of money from France. It does not however follow that Mussolini, who was never avaricious, simply sold himself for a bribe. There were many factors at work. He had originally opposed the war because the issue then was neutrality or intervention on the side of the Central Powers. But his inclinations moved more and more towards war against the Central Powers, which after the battle of the Marne seemed likely to be on the losing side. Secondly, he was always susceptible to his environment and he could not fail to be influenced by the changing tide of public opinion, and in particular by the attitude of the Syndicalists, who favored intervention. Finally he had always chafed at party discipline and he knew that he could not enjoy complete independence while he remained editor of *Avanti*. Accordingly he wanted to possess his own daily newspaper, an ambition which his negotiations with Naldi enabled him to realize. His sudden change of front was a calculated act of policy and, if he took money, it was only because he required it in order to found the newspaper in the columns of which he was to preach the cause of intervention.

There is evidence from another quarter that Mussolini was concerned to raise money for his newspaper. At the beginning of the war a certain Matvei Gedenshtrom, Russian Counsellor of State and former Consul General in Melbourne, was living in Milan, "employed in a department of the Russian Ministry of Foreign Affairs." In February, 1915, Gedenshtrom, who had previously undertaken secret missions for the Russian Admiralty during the Japanese war, reported to the Russian ambassador in Rome and to the military attaché, Colonel Enkel, that he was in touch with a very influential Italian revolutionary leader with a view to bringing Italy into the war within six weeks. It is not known how Gedenshtrom and Mussolini met, but it is possible that the intermediary was the Russian wife of Filippo Naldi.

The plan proposed by Mussolini was to stage a large-scale incident on the Austro-Italian border. Over a thousand volunteers would be employed and success was guaranteed. In addition the press was to be influenced in favor of intervention and public meetings would be organized in the same cause. But of course funds would be required and the sum named was a million francs, to be paid by the Russian government. The ambassador and Colonel Enkel, reporting home, endorsed the plan and recommended that, should it receive approval, the money should be remitted to the embassy by telegraph through several different banks.

At first the Russian Supreme Command seems to have viewed the project with favor. The Chief of Staff, General Yanushkevich, "deemed it expedient to avail ourselves of the plan in its entirety, particularly the part which concerns the disposition of the local press in our favor." Nevertheless there were sceptics, particularly among the members of the Russian General Staff in St. Petersburg, and the matter was temporarily shelved.

Towards the end of March, Gedenshtrom traveled to Petrograd in an effort to force the issue. On the advice of an old acquaintance, Admiral Rusin, he drafted a report for the Ministry of Foreign Affairs and General Belyaer, Chief of the General Staff. Both recipients were unimpressed, but Gedenshtrom was not discouraged and appealed to the Supreme Commander, Grand Duke Nicholas, by means of a long memorandum and a request for an interview. He concluded: "Out of prudence I have indicated the name of the important person in Italy . . . by its initial letter M. only, but it is known to Colonel Enkel, the military attaché in Rome, who would not otherwise have made such a positive and favorable comment, and I have also confided it to General Belyaev, Admiral Rusin, and Baron Schilling [Ministry of Foregin Affairs]."

The Grand Duke favored the acceptance of Gedeshtrom's proposal, "sparing no expense in the process." But Belyaev remained adamant in his scepticism and replied that the plan was so naive as to betray Gedenshtrom's "complete lack of experience in matters of this kind." At best, the money would be wasted and, at worst, regrettable complications would arise. The fact that Mussolini was a revolutionary probably prejudiced Belyaev and the Ministry of Foreign Affairs, which supported him, against any transaction with so dubious a character.

On April 12 the name of Mussolini appeared for the first time in the correspondence, when Belyaev, with evident relish, informed Yanushkevich that "Mussolini, the person proposed by Gedenshtrom, has been arrested." Mussolini had in fact been arrested in Rome on April 11 in the course of an interventionist disturbance. But the indefatigable Gedenshtrom, who was extremely well informed on Italian internal affairs, assured Belyaev that the arrest was of no importance and that Mussolini would soon be set free. As it happened, he was released within a few hours. Nevertheless the Russian government resolved on a number of grounds not to proceed any further in the matter, and it was allowed to drop.

The last word, however, lay with Gedenshtrom, who on June 7, 1915, addressed a revealing memorandum to I. K. Grigorovich, Minister of Marine. In this document he deplored the rejection of his plan, but reverted to Mussolini and urged the advantage of winning over "such an influential political figure." Mussolini's sources of information, he argued, were excellent, and, moreover, it had been possible to induce him to publish in the *Popolo d'Italia* useful articles advocating the extension of Russian influence in the Mediterranean. Of course, Gedenshtrom concluded, it would be necessary to keep all transactions secret, since otherwise "he and his party will immediately lose all prestige and influence in Italy."

Gedenshtrom's memorandum and the related issue of influencing the press in Italy and other countries were placed on the agenda of the cabinet session on June 29, 1915, but no record of the proceedings has survived. Nor has any further trace of Gedenshtrom been found. He disappeared, and with him the only firsthand witness of a curious episode in Mussolini's career.*

* The documents on which this account is based were found by the Leningrad historian Alexei Korneyev in the archives of the Foreign Office, the Central State Historical Archives of the U.S.S.R., the Central State Naval Archives, and the Central State Archives of Military History. They were printed, with

There has been some debate as to whether Mussolini, before breaking with the Socialists had already completed his arrangements with Naldi and the French for the foundation of his new daily the *Popolo d'Italia.* It is a point which will never be cleared up, but it can be said that it would have been out of character for him to take the plunge without making provision for his future. He was essentially an opportunist and there was no particular reason to show his hand prematurely. Moreover it is significant that the first number of the *Popolo d'Italia* appeared less than four weeks after he left *Avanti.* It is therefore reasonable to suppose that it was only when everything had been arranged to his satisfaction that he made his move.

The Socialists were of course exceedingly angry at Mussolini's defection, and an emergency meeting of the executive committee of the party was held on October 19 at Bologna to consider the position. The comrades all pressed Mussolini for an explanation and one of them inquired why he did not resign as soon as he realized that he was no longer in agreement with party policy. But Mussolini made no reply and the meeting resolved to relieve him of his post as editor. Angelica Balabanoff proposed that he should be paid an allowance until he was able to find new employment and provide for his family. He angrily rejected the offer, saying that he could find work as a mason. Whatever action the committee might take, he added, he would remain true to socialism; and he looked at his former colleagues with cold, animal, vengeful eyes. It was his last transaction with Angelica Balabanoff.[20] His condemnation by the executive committee of the party also caused a breach with Leda Rafanelli, who declined to have any further dealings with him. He

---

an introduction by A. Korneyev, in the issue of *Istoricheskiy Arkhiv* of September–October, 1962, published by the Academy of Sciences of the U.S.S.R. I am indebted to Sir Frank Roberts, British ambassador in Moscow, for putting me on the track of Korneyev's work and to M. A. Soldatov, the Soviet Ambassador in London, for very kindly sending me a copy of the publication as soon as it appeared.

Some confirmation of the Gedenshtrom story is to be found in a published conversation between Professor R. Battaglia and Dino Roberto, a former journalist on the *Popolo d'Italia* (*Unità,* July 31, 1959). According to Roberto, Mussolini wished to entrust the leadership of the frontier operation to Filippo Corridoni; and when Corridoni refused he turned to Garibaldi, commanding the volunteers detachment of that name. The idea of a frontier incident is in line with Mussolini's juvenile romanticism.

soon consoled himself, however, by renewing a liaison, begun at Trent in 1909, with Ida Dalser, who had since migrated to Milan. She was a woman of about his age, not particularly good looking, but with a certain intelligence and impulsive charm. She was both jealous of Rachele and intemperate in her demands on Mussolini; and while he treated her as shabbily as he did any other woman, she was not equally pliant. Indeed she was later to give him considerable anxiety and trouble.

V

The first number of the *Popolo d'Italia* appeared on November 15. In order to emphasize that he was still a Socialist, albeit an independent Socialist, it carried the subtitle: "A Socialist Daily." But it also printed in the margin two un-Socialist and Mussolinian maxims which he borrowed from Blanqui and Napoleon, respectively: "He who has steel has bread" and "Revolution is an idea which has found bayonets to support it." The subtitle represented the residue of the convictions on which he had been nurtured, the maxims the fruit of his reflections on the fiasco of Red Week. The leading article in the first issue was entitled "Audacity" and appealed to the young men of the country to take up war.

The appearance of the *Popolo d'Italia* so soon after Mussolini's dismissal from *Avanti* and the tone of his uncompromising leading article still further inflamed Socialist opinion. On November 25, 1914, there was a tumultuous meeting of the Milan party branch in the People's Theatre and hundreds came to hear his defense. He was still anxious to avoid an irrevocable breach with the party, but the angry comrades were not of a like mind. When he rose to speak, pale and unshaven, he was greeted with shouts of "Who is the paymaster" and "traitor, hireling, assassin." As soon as he could make himself heard he declared that he was and remained a Socialist: "Do not think that by tearing up my card you will deprive me of my Socialist faith and that you will keep me from fighting for the cause of socialism and the revolution." [21] But the mood of the meeting was not favorable to any form of compromise and without any further ado he was expelled from the party. His reaction to this event was characteristically violent. In a long article in the *Popolo d'Italia* he denounced the Socialist leaders and warned them that he would fight them implacably with all his strength. "That is why I have forged for myself a weapon with which to enlighten the proletariat and to remove them from the influence of these sad preachers." [22]

Mussolini's breach with the Socialist party was to exercise an influence on him for the rest of his life. It is true that he had never been entirely happy in the party and resented being shackled by Socialist doctrine. There was also a personal grievance against some of the leading comrades. In particular Anna Kuliscioff, Turati's wife and a Socialist of Marxist complexion, presided over a political salon to which Mussolini had sought admittance in vain. His failure aggravated his inferiority complex and filled him with rancor against his political associates. Nevertheless the severance of his ties with the party left him with a sense of guilt. He acquired the mentality of a renegade, and felt constantly impelled to make his peace with the Socialists. It was this sense of guilt which later fortified his resolve to remain loyal to the German alliance and which in the last months of his life inspired the pitiful attempt to revive socialism in his Salò Republic.

For the moment, however, it was convenient to be independent. He says himself: "I felt lighter, fresher. I was free. I was better prepared to fight my battles than when I was bound by the dogmas of any political organization." [23] He was now able to campaign for intervention without equivocation or reserve, supported by Filippo Corridoni's Syndicalists, Libero Tancredi's Anarchists, Battista, and even by Bissolati. With Corridoni's aid he created the *Fasci di Azione Rivoluzionaria,* groups of young men who demonstrated for war. It was here, incidentally, that he first met Dino Grandi, then a nineteen-year-old student at Rome University. Both took part in a prowar demonstration and both were arrested. They were not to meet again until after the war, when Grandi returned with a gallant record of service with the Alpini.

Demonstrations in the streets were supported by vibrant articles in the *Popolo d'Italia* appealing to the patriotism of the nation and extolling the valor of the *Fasci.** Although Mussolini was later to

---

* These articles had a great success. Freya Stark saw a *Popolo d'Italia* by chance and "so much admired the leading article that I stuck to the *Popolo*

identify the *Fasci* with the bundles of rods carried by the Roman victors, the appellation in 1915 carried no special significance. The word *fascio* was then in current use to describe a political group. For example, under Crispi, "*Fasci Siciliani*" had been formed to voice the grievances of the local peasantry, and in later years there had been a Neapolitan *fascio,* created to fight abuses in the town's administration.

Mussolini's advocacy was doubtless useful to the Allies, but it was in no sense decisive, and there was little basis for the subsequent Fascist legend that Mussolini had brought Italy into the war. D'Annunzio, who was also calling for intervention, exercised a greater influence; and more important, the Italian government was moving in the same direction.

If Italy were to remain neutral throughout a war which might last some time, it seemed reasonable that Austria should pay a price for Italian nonbelligerence. A million Italians lived under Austrian rule and Italian sentiment demanded that a victory of the Central Powers should not perpetuate this state of affairs. The liberation of these people could only be achieved in one of two ways: by agreement, as a price to be paid by Austria for continued Italian neutrality, or by conquest.

Under the Treaty of 1882 Italy was entitled to claim from Austria some compensation for her disturbance of the previously existing balance in the Balkans. This the Italian government did, but the negotiations proved abortive. Accordingly the conversations were broken off and on March 3, 1915, the Italian ambassador in London was instructed to open secret negotiations for an agreement with the powers of the Entente. The outcome was the signature in the following week of the Treaty of London, which defined the price to be paid by the Allies for Italy's entry into the war: South Tyrol, Trieste, Gorizia, Gradisca, Istria and the islands of Cherso and Lussiu, Dalmatia to Cape Planka, Valona, Rhodes and the Dodecanese group, a zone of influence in Asia Minor with eventually a share in its partition, and a loan of fifty million pounds. Had Baron Sonnino, the Italian foreign minister, not believed that the war

from then on." She asked about Mussolini, "as I was so much impressed by the writing, and no one could tell me anything about him." [Freya Stark, *Travellers Prelude* (London, 1950), chapter 13.]

would be short, a larger loan would certainly have been demanded.[24] Once the treaty had been signed, events moved fast. The King asked Giolitti to resign and Salandra was appointed in his place. On May 24, 1915, Italy declared war.

The entry of Italy into the war represented a personal success which Mussolini proceeded systematically to exploit. For this purpose he had a ready instrument in the *Popolo d'Italia,* which exerted itself during the war years, not without success, to create a Mussolini myth.

On the new *Popolo d'Italia* Mussolini of course needed trained staff, for he could not hope to produce a daily newspaper single-handed, as he had done with *La Lima* and *La Lotta di Classe* at Oneglia and Forlì. He was lucky to secure the services of Giuseppe De Falco, who came to him from Switzerland, where he had edited the *Avvenire del Lavoratore.* But Mussolini in his newspaper office, as elsewhere, was intolerant of people with a mind of their own. After two or three years De Falco, when he had served his purpose, was ruthlessly discarded. When Mussolini was reproached for his ingratitude towards a companion who had taken a professional and political risk in rallying to him at a critical moment and who had spent himself in the service of the newspaper, he replied with callous indifference: "After all it was I who created this Signor De Falco. Who had ever heard of him before?" [25]

VI

It was not until August 31, 1915, that he was called up with his class and was posted as a private soldier to the 11th Bersaglieri. While his conduct was unexceptionable, his period of service was undistinguished and he never rose above the rank of sergeant. He explains in his autobiography that his political past was enough to discourage his superiors from sending him to an officer training school,[26] and it may well be that this was the case. He arrived at the front on September 16 and settled down to the monotony of trench war in the Alto Isonzo zone. The story of his military experience is told in his *Diario di guerra,* a book of remarkable banality, published in 1923 as part of the propaganda campaign to magnify the Duce. The entries describe the landscape, the weather, the hardships, and the courage of the Italian soldier. He mentions that at Christmas he attended Mass, a thing his father never did, and there was a patriotic sermon which appealed to him. He had altogether three spells of duty, totaling about nine months, in the front-line trenches, interrupted in November, 1915, by an attack of paratyphoid fever. He was on good terms with his comrades and his officers, who were pleased to have a well-known Milanese editor in their ranks.

He was able to use his sick leave to clear up certain domestic entanglements. In September, 1915, Rachele had given birth to a son, their second child. Mussolini sent instructions that he was to be called Vittorio in honor of victory and Alessandro after his father and after a certain unnamed English captain who had recently distinguished himself by his heroism; but the child was not to be baptized. In view of the addition to his family Mussolini decided to regularize Rachele's position and on December 16, 1915, he contracted a civil marriage with her at Treviglio. Meanwhile Ida Dalser had advised him that on November 11, 1915, she also had given birth to a son and had called him Benito Albano. On January 11, 1916, before notaries in Milan, he formally recognized the infant and was subsequently ordered by the courts to pay an allowance of 200 lire a month to the mother. Ida Dalser subsequently became a source of much embarrassment to Mussolini. She claimed to be his wife and invaded Rachele's apartment; she made a scene at the office of the *Popolo d'Italia;* and for self-protection when he became Prime Minister Mussolini placed her under police surveillance. Eventually, in 1926, she was declared to be mentally unhinged and was kept in confinement in mental hospitals until her death in December, 1935. Benito, the son, was left in charge of Ida Dalser's brother-in-law for a time and eventually died in the mental hospital at Mombello near Milan in July, 1942.[27]

Mussolini, having settled these tiresome domestic affairs, returned in February, 1916, to duty at the front. Here on no occasion was he involved in any pitched battle, nor was he given much opportunity of winning renown. He led the life of a static infantry soldier in the Alps and, since the Italian army was not particularly well equipped, he must have suffered privation and discomfort. He was promoted to the rank of sergeant and even his bitterest enemies have been unable to unearth any discreditable episode in his military record. During these months he was careful to ensure that through the *Popolo d'Italia* the public should be kept informed of his exploits; and he also contributed anonymous articles designed to maintain the war fervor of the nation. Eventually on February 22, 1917, he was wounded by the accidental explosion of a mortar bomb in his trench. His condition was not dangerous, but a large number of splinters (he relates that there were forty-four of them) [28] entered his body, and he was not discharged from the hospital until August, 1917.

Of course the *Popolo d'Italia* made much of the event and it was not alone, since Mussolini was now a prominent figure and in war every expedient is used to boost national morale. The King, who had already been to see him when he was ill with paratyphoid, came again to visit him in the hospital. These were the first meetings with his sovereign whom he had publicly reviled at Reggio Emilia in 1912; and Mussolini expressed his gratification at this mark of royal favor. He was still on crutches when he left hospital to return to Milan. There Margherita Sarfatti went to see him:

> He was so exhausted he could scarcely speak. He smiled out at us from his pale face, his eyes sunken in great hollows. His lips scarcely moved; one could see how horribly he had suffered. Someone asked if he would like a book to read. He refused. "I read only this because it is familiar. I cannot read anything new," and he showed a volume of Carducci's poems, a tonic for weary souls.[29]

He never returned to the front, but made a successful application for exemption from further military service on the ground of his journalistic indispensability and he came back with all the prestige of a war hero to the office of the *Popolo d'Italia.* A new chapter in his life was about to begin.

CHAPTER FOUR

The Party Leader

1917–1922

I

IT was a different Mussolini who returned from the war once more to occupy the editorial chair at the office of the *Popolo d'Italia* in Milan. It cannot be said that his character had changed, but his appearance had done so and there was a new outlook. He was no longer indigent, bedraggled, and dirty. He wore a neat dark suit with a stiff white collar. The flowing tie and the large soft hat had disappeared and all that remained of his revolutionary appearance were two protuberant black eyes which lit up his sallow face when something occurred to arouse him. His eyes were the feature which seems to have impressed most observers. His experiences in the army had toughened him, he had learned to adjust himself more readily to circumstances, he had matured, he knew that he had the capacity to move crowds, he had learned many of the tricks of the journalist's trade, and he no longer writhed under the frustration of obscurity. All this gave him a degree of self-confidence which he had previously lacked. Moreover he had discovered that revolutions cannot be made simply by flinging verbal challenges at the authority and the force wielded by the state. He had not abandoned his revolutionary ideas, and his problem, to which as yet he saw no clear solution, was to create or to take advantage of conditions in which he might realize his aim. The circumstance that he had broken with the Socialists and that he was now a man without a party both simplified and complicated his task. On one hand he was no longer obliged to compromise with party associates, but on the other, if he wished to enlist popular support, it would be necessary to appeal to the masses over the heads of the Socialist leaders and to summon new forces to his standard.

All this lay in the future, for it was clear to him that unless the war with which his personal fortunes were so closely involved were won, his prospects would be dim indeed. Already the neutralists, now termed pacifists, were joining issue with the interventionists; and their campaign was assisted by Pope Benedict XV, who in the summer issued an appeal for a compromise peace. A wave of weariness and defeatism flowed over Italy, and the Socialist Claudio Treves coined a slogan which soon gained nationwide currency: "Next winter, no longer in the trenches."

In this predicament Mussolini decided that there was no need to devise a policy until after the war was won. First things must come first and his immediate aim must be to concentrate on stimulating the national war effort. To this task he applied himself with ardor in speeches and press articles, rather in the manner of Horatio Bottomley.

Very soon, in October, 1917, came the stunning news of the Italian disaster at Caporetto, the impact of which was accentuated by a communiqué from Cadorna, the Commander-in-Chief, bitterly criticizing the troops engaged. This reverse seemed to justify the predictions of the neutralists, and all those who shared responsibility for Italy's entry into the war felt themselves to be on trial. Nevertheless the Italian nation rallied strongly. A new government was formed under Orlando, with Nitti as its most powerful member, while Giolitti with other ex-premiers and Turati, speaking for the Socialists, joined in exhorting the nation to steadfastness.

Among the many voices raised in patriotic ardor none was louder than that of Mussolini, who fulminated daily for unity, for resistance, and for discipline. He demanded action against slackers, the organization of a volunteer army, military rule in the North, the suppression of Socialist newspapers, and more humane treatment for soldiers. The gravity of the hour, he declared, required that the nation should show the world that it could rise to the greatest heights. Every sacrifice should be made.

> Political liberty is for time of peace. In time of war it is treason. It is not possible that while on millions of men there is laid the obligation to fight for their country, a few thousands can be allowed freedom to betray their country . . . we must abandon the great phrase "Liberty." There is another which in this third winter of war should be on the lips of the cabinet when they address the Italian people, and it is "Discipline." [1]

The man, who in his youth had hailed with gloating anticipation the liquidation of the Russian Emperor now demanded that Leninism should be repudiated. It was a clever and effective press campaign, which required a certain courage since it was calculated to isolate him completely from the parties of the Left at a time when he could find no political haven with the Right. During this period he was content to be a lone wolf; and when he was asked why he did not join a projected union of the Italian Socialist party and the Syndicalists, he replied that he could not do so because he possessed the individualistic temperament of the Anarchist and because he was an unsociable and not easily organized animal.[2]

The first prominent Englishman to come across Mussolini was Sir Samuel Hoare, who was serving as a staff officer in charge of certain branches of military intelligence in the British forces despatched to the Italian front under Lord Cavan. Hoare was appalled at the sight of the broken, retreating Italian army and at the growing ascendancy of the defeatists and the pro-Germans in Rome; and he was advised by a number of his staff to turn to the editor of the *Popolo d'Italia* who might help to arrest the debacle. "Who is this Benito Mussolini?" was Hoare's question and the answer was that he was a powerful mob leader in Milan, who had helped to bring Italy into the war and was then hesitating on which side of the barricades to fight. Hoare accordingly obtained sanction from the Director of Military Intelligence in London to approach the unknown agitator, and money was made available with which to finance propaganda for the war. "Leave it to me," was Mussolini's reply to the intermediary; and he was as good as his word, for the *Fasci di Combattimento* soon made short work of the Milanese pacifists. Mussolini was not in the least embarrassed when, nearly twenty years later, Sir Samuel Hoare brought to his recollection this incident in his early career.[3]

As the months passed, the crisis at the front was surmounted, not without military aid from the Western Allies, and the Italian army recovered to play its part in bringing about the collapse of the Central Powers in the autumn. In Italy, as well as elsewhere, the common victory was acclaimed and hopes ran high for the future. Mussolini took a prominent part in the peace celebrations at Milan and his sister Edvige records that he seemed transfigured with joy.[4] But the mood of elation did not last long, for peace brings with it more intractable problems than war, and soon Italy was deep in difficulties both at home and abroad.

II

At home revolution was in the air. The European order which for a hundred years had held sway had suddenly collapsed. In Petrograd, Berlin, Vienna, and Budapest, amidst the ruins of the former empires, new forces were in ferment. Millions of Italian soldiers released from the restraints of military discipline and nourished for years on the hopes of a new and better world, were being cast into civilian life where they found neither work nor prospects. The war, far from curing Italy's economic ills, had only aggravated them. Many of Italy's traditional emigration outlets, through which nearly a million workers passed in 1913, were now closed to her and the transition from a war to a peace economy was beset with difficulty. The public debt had risen alarmingly, the merchant navy had suffered grave losses, raw materials were lacking, Italy's best customers, Germany and Austria, lay prostrate, and unemployment increased. On the moral plane the process of adjustment was equally painful. Thousands of students, clerks, and artisans had earned promotion to commissioned rank and were unwilling to resume their former places in Italian society. Many of these bewildered and discontented men, wavering between the parties of the Left and the Nationalists, were to join D'Annunzio's legions at Fiume, and, when he failed, Mussolini's Fascists. It is not surprising that in this situation the bacillus of revolution should have crossed the frontier and infected the Italian mind. Communism and extreme nationalism began to rear their heads. Political tension was aggravated by the circumstance that with the end of the war the parties abandoned any pretense of maintaining national unity and relapsed into naked sectarian strife. There soon appeared a cleft between the former neutralists on the one hand, who claimed that Italy's entry into the war had been a mistake and invoked events to prove their case, and on the other hand the interventionists who pinned the blame for Italy's misfortunes on the Allies and on the home government. Mussolini as an interventionist was thus pushed remorselessly in the direction of nationalism.

The general unrest was stimulated by events abroad. In Paris the peace conference with leisurely steps was plowing through the settlement, first with Germany and then with Austria, Bulgaria, and Turkey. Its proceedings gave little satisfaction to anyone, but the Italians had three particular grounds of complaint. In the first place the wrath of the Western Allies seemed to be concentrated on Germany, while Austria, which had instigated and started the war, Austria, which was Italy's principal enemy, seemed to be regarded merely as a minor delinquent. Secondly it soon became clear that the situation envisaged in the secret Treaty of London no longer existed and that Italy was not going to be given all that had been promised in that agreement. Very few were acquainted with the exact text of the treaty, but it was commonly known that its provisions were not being completely executed. The circumstance that Italy was to obtain South Tyrol, that the new and fashionable doctrine of self-determination, recently proclaimed with so much unction, was to be thrown at once on to the scrap heap in order to accommodate her, was of little account. Italy, who had lost 652,000 dead, wanted her sacrifices to be recognized in full and the failure of the Allies to do so was not only resented on material grounds, but was offensive to Italian pride.

Finally the Italian delegation was not treated with the requisite deference. A contributory factor was the disunity and lack of purpose among the delegates themselves. For example, Sonnino refused to reveal to a member of his delegation, Vittorio Scialoja, the text of the Treaty of London on the grounds that it was a secret document. Scialoja applied to the British delegation, explaining that he had mislaid his copy, and at once received what he required. The fact that the failures at Paris were recognized to be as much the fault of the Italian delegates as of the Allies did not assuage, but only added to the bitterness.

The general mood of dissatisfaction with the issue of the war created an unhappy situation for the man who had acquired notoriety in promoting Italian intervention; but Mussolini was undismayed, and he resolved to exploit the popular mood of angry disillusion. In an article of January 1, 1919, the *Popolo d'Italia* complained of the profound humiliation of Italy and of the miserable spectacle presented by her disunity, while England and France gave an immense impression of solidarity. Mussolini demanded the annexation of Fiume and Dalmatia. He attacked the government for failure to make provision for demobilization or to put forward a policy of social reform or to give the returned soldiers their due. Soon he was in conflict with those Socialists led by Bissolati who opposed irredentism on grounds of principle.

III

In February, 1919, the first Communist demonstration took place in Milan and Mussolini determined to revive his *Fasci,* now called *Fasci di Combattimento.* On March 23, 1919, the Fascist party was born at a meeting held in a hall in the Piazza San Sepolcro at Milan and chaired by an officer of the Arditi. It was an inauspicious beginning. Although the meeting had been well advertised in the *Popolo d'Italia* as having for its object the foundation of a new movement and the establishment of a program which would ensure victory in the fight against the forces dissolving the nation, it attracted little public support. Only 145 men attended,* and few of them were persons of any consequence. Not very far to the North Hitler was also making a beginning, but in still more discouraging circumstances.

The formulation of a Fascist program presented great difficulty, since Mussolini still had no clear idea what he wanted. It was not easy to sort out the confused ideas and aspirations which filled his mind. He disliked the monarchy, the Church, the Socialist party, and the established order; he retained something of the doctrines of socialism, yet he yearned as much as any nationalist to see Italy

---

* The number may well have been smaller. Cesare Rossi said that when it came to electing the executive committee Mussolini picked at random enthusiasts in the front row, some of whom turned out to have police records.

extend her territories and assume the status of a Great Power; he stood for the equalization of wealth, yet he opposed communism; he sympathized with the aspirations of the proletariat, yet he despised the masses; above all he was determined to acquire power and, since he could not exactly foresee where he would obtain the necessary support, he could not afford irrevocably to antagonize either the dissatisfied masses or potential allies in other segments of society. He himself admitted ten years later that in 1919 he had no policy and no program.

> When, in the now distant March of 1919, I summoned a meeting at Milan through the columns of the *Popolo d'Italia* of the surviving members of the Interventionist party who had themselves been in action and who had followed me since the creation of the Fascist Revolutionary Party (which took place in the January of 1915), I had no specific doctrinal attitude in my mind. I had a living experience of one doctrine only —that of socialism from 1903–1904 to the winter of 1914—that is to say about a decade. . . . Even though I had taken part in the movement first as a member of the rank and file and then later as a leader, yet I had no experience of its doctrine in practice. My own doctrine, even in this period, had always been a doctrine of action.[5]

Mussolini not only had no policy, but his exposed position compelled him to be prudent; and his apologists admit that at this stage he was more swayed by considerations of expediency than by conviction. For example, when President Wilson visited Italy in January, 1919, the *Popolo d'Italia* published an article entitled "Viva Wilson." The President and his policy were of course profoundly repugnant to Mussolini, but he defended his attitude by explaining that the whole of Italy was infatuated with Wilson and that he could not afford to run against the current of public opinion, however volatile it might be. He therefore judged it best to put a good face on the arrival of the American Messiah in the hope that it would predispose him to Italian claims at the peace conference.[6] He was invited to the banquet given to Wilson at Milan and borrowed from a friendly tailor, the father-in-law of the publicity manager of the *Popolo d'Italia,* a dress suit which had been made for an industrialist. Unfortunately he absentmindedly put the menu into the pocket of the coat and the suit was subsequently delivered to its angry owner with this incriminating evidence.[7]

In view of the Leader's uncertainty it is perhaps not surprising that the inaugural meeting of the *Fasci di Combattimento* displayed an inglorious reticence somewhat out of harmony with their title. In the morning they passed three anodyne resolutions. The first paid a tribute to the fallen and undertook to support the rights of ex-servicemen. The second opposed imperialism in other peoples which would be prejudicial to Italy and any eventual imperialism in Italy which would infringe the rights of other nations; and accepted the "fundamental principle of the League of Nations, which presupposes the geographical integrity of every nation." "This, as far as Italy is concerned, must be realized on the Alps and the Adriatic with the annexation of Fiume and Dalmatia." The third resolution pledged the party to oppose the candidature of neutralists of any party.[8]

This was a somewhat jejune program for a new party, but in the afternoon Mussolini made a second speech in which he embroidered his ideas and, somewhat tentatively, put forward one new proposal.

We declare war on socialism not because it is Socialist, but because it has acted against the nation. On the essence of socialism, its program and its tactics we can all debate, but the official Italian Socialist party has been definitely reactionary, completely conservative, and if their ideas had triumphed, there would today be for us no possibility of life in the world. . . . We must be an active minority, we wish to separate the official Socialist party from the proletariat, but if the bourgeoisie think that they will find lightning conductors in us, they deceive themselves. We must meet labor. . . . We must meet the demands of the working classes. Do they want the eight-hour day? Will the night workers tomorrow demand the six-hour day; or sickness and old-age pensions; the control of industry? We shall support these demands because we want to accustom the workers to control of the enterprises and also to convince them that it is no easy thing successfully to direct an industry or a commercial enterprise. . . . We demand universal suffrage for men and women, regional electoral lists, proportional representation. From the new elections will emerge a national assembly which we shall require to determine the form of government in the Italian state. . . . The present method of representation cannot suffice; we want a direct representation of the individuals concerned. It may be objected against this program that it is a return to the conception of the Corporation, but that is no matter.

This was the first Fascist reference to the Corporative State.[9]

In the months that followed Mussolini made speeches all over the country and poured forth a stream of articles in the *Popolo d'Italia* in which he sought to appeal as a demagogue to the masses, and at the same time to reassure the bourgeoisie by disclaiming revolutionary intentions and by playing on their nationalist sentiments. Speaking at Milan on July 22, 1919, he said:

In 1913 when the Socialist party was already rotten, it was I who put into circulation the words which made the pulses of the big men of Italian socialism beat: "This proletariat is in need of a bath of blood," I said. It has had it and it lasted for three years. "This proletariat is in need of a day of history." And it has had a thousand. It was necessary then to shake up the masses, because they had fallen into a state of weakness and insensibility. Today this situation exists no longer. Today the only way not to live in fear of a revolution is to think that we are now in the full swing of one. . . . I am not afraid of the word. I am a revolutionary and a reactionary. Really, life is always like this. I am afraid of the revolution which destroys and does not create. I fear going to extremes, the policy of madness, at the bottom of which may lie the destruction of this our fragile mechanical civilization, robbed of its solid moral basis, and the coming of a terrible race of dominators who would reintroduce discipline into the world and re-establish the necessary hierarchies with the cracking of whips and machine guns. At the same time, as regards reaction and revolution, I have a compass in my pocket which guides me. All that which tends towards making the Italian people great finds me favorable and, vice versa, all that which tends towards lowering, brutalizing, and impoverishing them finds me opposed.[10]

Mussolini's ambivalence was not entirely cynical, for he was at heart a timid man and the closer he found himself to power the more he recoiled from the consequences of his own revolutionary preaching. Moreover the bourgeoisie required to be reassured, since the tone of Mussolini's articles in the *Popolo d'Italia* and the program of the party were calculated to alarm them. On June 6, 1919, the *Popolo d'Italia* had published a document which purported to embody the aims of the Fascist movement. It called for:

1. Universal suffrage, regional lists, proportional representation, and votes for women.
2. Reduction of the age of electors to eighteen; and of Deputies to twenty-five.
3. Abolition of the Senate.

4. Convocation of a National Assembly which would in three years determine the future Constitution.

5. Formation of National Councils of experts in labor, industry, transport, social hygiene, communications, etc., elected by the respective professions and trades, with legislative powers and with the right to elect a Commissioner who would have the powers of a Minister.

6. The promulgation of a law laying down an eight-hour day for all workers.

7. A minimum wage.

8. Participation of workers' representatives in the technical direction of industry.

9. The control of industry and public services by such proletarian organizations as are morally and technically worthy.

10. Immediate reorganization of railways and transport.

11. Modification of the draft law on sickness and old-age insurance, reducing the age for the latter from 75 to 55.

12. Creation of a national short-service militia of a purely defensive character.

13. Nationalization of all armaments factories.

14. A foreign policy calculated to enable Italy to take her proper place in the peaceful competition between civilized nations.

15. A heavy progressive tax on capital which would have the character of a partial expropriation of wealth.

16. Confiscation of all property belonging to religious congregations and the abolition of bishops' stipends.

17. The revision of all war contracts and the confiscation of 85 per cent of war profits.

This was at last something of a program, but it will be seen later how much, or rather how little, was ever put into effect when Mussolini had taken the reins of power into his own hands.

In the field of foreign affairs he was able to indulge his natural feelings of resentment, and at the same time to satisfy the aspirations of the young chauvinist elements, whose support was essential to his cause. He had been brought up to hate wealth and power at home; and these sentiments were readily translated in international politics to hatred of the "haves" among the nations. His natural antipathy to the Western plutocracies was of course sharpened by their opposition in Paris to the full extent of Italy's territorial claims. He spoke of the collapse of the traditional friendship between England and Italy and of the need to secure justice for the proletarian Italians in the face of the largest and most bourgeois nation in the world. "In the West there are the 'Haves.' They are our rivals, our competitors, our enemies; and when they sometimes help us it is not an expression of solidarity, but rather something between almsgiving and blackmail." He thought vaguely of a foreign policy aiming at an understanding with the East. "The proletariat must understand that in order to liberate itself from the yoke of the bourgeois and plutocratic 'Haves' of the West it must go East, but not with empty hands. In labor and in production lie not only the sources of internal well-being but also the certain guarantee of our liberty and national independence." [11] At the same time he was careful, while attacking the Western powers, to reply to the Socialist charge that Italy had gained nothing from the war and that intervention had been a mistake. So he laid emphasis on the value to Italy of her territorial acquisitions and pursued his campaign for the annexation of Fiume and Dalmatia. On May 22, 1919, he addressed an enthusiastic nationalist meeting in the Verdi Theatre at Fiume. Here he once more attacked the Western powers with reckless impartiality and called for the expulsion of all foreigners from the Mediterranean, aid to Egypt, the liberation of Malta, and the end of France's Mediterranean Empire beginning with Tunis. A contemporary account refers to him as "an Italian journalist called Mussolini." [12]

IV

Meanwhile at home disorder was threatening the structure of the state. Strikes swept the country and a number of factories were occupied by the workers. The Fascist central committee proclaimed solidarity with the strikers and the *Popolo d'Italia*, following their line, went so far as to say that a few monopolists hanged on the lampposts would serve as an example. Fraternization with the strikers, however, was not held to be inconsistent with continued attacks on the Socialists, who, the Fascists declared, were giving no effective support to the working classes. In order to emphasize the breach between Fascists and Socialists the subtitle of the *Popolo d'Italia* was changed from "The Socialist Daily" to "Journal of the Fighters and Producers." The truculent claim of the Fascist party to be the only friend of the working man naturally created great bitterness in Socialist circles. On April 15, 1919, there was a bloody clash in Milan between a marching Socialist-Marxist column and a body of Fascists. The victorious Fascists then attacked and destroyed the premises of *Avanti,* and in the tumult a soldier was killed. This incident inflamed passions on both sides. The Socialists retaliated in kind, and a Fascist was barbarously murdered in Florence. The conflict brought many new recruits to the Fascist ranks, not all of them estimable, and with the increase in their numbers the area of disturbance grew until there were daily clashes all over the North. It was a situation which repeated itself not long afterwards in Germany, when street battles between Brownshirts and Communists were the order of the day. In both countries fear of communism aided the new movements. In Italy at this stage the government tolerated, if it did not actively support the Fascists, for it regarded Mussolini as a useful bulwark against communism. In the turmoil the Fascists prepared for the general elections to be held in the autumn of 1919.

They were not the only new party on the scene, for at the same time a formidable rival had entered the lists. In January, 1919, posters had appeared all over the country announcing the formation of the *Partito Popolare Italiano,* a Catholic democratic party under the leadership of the forty-eight-year-old Sicilian priest Don Luigi Sturzo. Its program was progressive and called for reforms in the electoral law, in the system of taxation and in the ownership of land, for a solution of the Southern question, and for a campaign against illiteracy. Foreign policy was to be based on the ideals of the League of Nations. The new party was not to be a Catholic party as such, but rather a party composed of Catholics, which would be unconnected with the Vatican and ready to cooperate with other parties. The program was designed to appeal particularly to those progressive elements which were unable to work with Marxist and anticlerical Socialists and which opposed the violent social upheaval demanded by the Left. The foundation of this party represented a notable innovation in Italian public life, since Catholics had hitherto been forbidden to enter politics, and Don Sturzo before embarking on his project took care to obtain the assent of Cardinal Gasparri, the Papal Secretary of State. Moreover, for the first time a party was created to bring under its confessional banner elements from the Right and the Left, which hitherto had either stayed out of politics or had been drawn to the traditional parties. The chief sufferer was the Liberal party, which had formed the backbone of the Italian parliamentary system since the Risorgimento and which was already shaken by the postwar convulsions.

The elections of November, 1919, reflected both this development and the mood of the dissatisfied electorate; and it marked the passing of the old oligarchy. The result was a triumph for the Socialists, who for the first time became the largest party, and to a lesser degree for Don Sturzo. The distribution of seats in the Chamber was as follows:

Official Socialists (Extreme)	156
Reformist Socialists (Moderate)	19
Liberals	129
Partito Popolare (Don Sturzo)	101
Democrats and Radicals	73
Others	50

The Fascists, whose candidates included Arturo Toscanini, failed to obtain a single seat. It was a serious blow, since Mussolini had used every art to appeal to the masses and he had hoped to enroll some Nationalists. Yet his failure was complete. In Milan he only polled 4,064 votes whereas his successful Socialist opponent, Turati, received 180,000. Above all, the success of the *Partito Popolare* represented perhaps the most serious threat to his prospects, and he never forgave Don Sturzo for his success. Charlatans, he declared, who added the hope of Paradise to their promises, would not succeed. Don Sturzo, the little long-nosed Sicilian priest, might well talk of Paradise, but on earth he would accomplish nothing.[13] Don Sturzo for his part reciprocated Mussolini's antipathy and was equally scathing in his assessment of his adversary:

Of mediocre culture and meager political experience, Mussolini has the brilliant qualities of the extemporizer and none of the scruples of those who, convinced of an idea, fear to be false to it. . . . He was an anti-militarist, opposed to colonial enterprise, denying the duty of defending his country—and he became an interventionist with imperialist tendencies. . . . His mind, given to excessive simplification, is bound by no formula; he can pass from theory to theory, from position to position, rapidly, even inconsistently, with neither remorse nor regret. In this game he has one constant aim—to lay hold of the elements of imagination and sentiment that make for success. Hence his speeches are always attuned to the state of mind of the public to which he is speaking; if the public were other, he would use other language. . . . His friends and companions he holds in esteem so long as they are useful to him; he fears them when he cannot do without them; he abandons them to their fate when they are in his way.[14]

Both judgments have substance. Mussolini's strength lay in his plausible inconsistencies, his lack of scruple and the agility which knew how to turn events to his advantage, while Don Sturzo's weakness lay in his serene detachment, which rendered him unfit to play the part of a successful politician in the Italy of his day.

The Socialists were intoxicated no less by their own success than by the humiliation of the Fascists. *Avanti* reported that a corpse, identified as that of Benito Mussolini, had been dragged out of the river. A mock funeral procession, with mourners singing ribald psalms, paraded through the streets of Milan and the crowd halted outside Mussolini's house to invite him to attend his own funeral. Posters were printed with the words: "Turati [the Socialist candidate] 180,000; Mussolini 4,000." It was understandable that the Socialists should have gloated over the renegade's discomfiture, but they were to pay later for their temerity, for he was not a man to forget a wrong or to forgive an insult.

Mussolini was now assailed on two flanks, from one side by the triumphant Socialists and from the other by Don Sturzo's new party, which was the more dangerous since its success threatened to attract further masses of Catholic voters, particularly in the South. In this difficult situation the Fascists had little to offer except anti-Socialist slogans, turgid expressions of patriotic devotion, and an almost meaningless and completely equivocal program. The outcome of the November elections had been as encouraging to the Socialists and the *Partito Popolare* as it had been depressing to the

Fascists. The Fascist central committee had been dispersed; some had been arrested, others had disappeared. The *Popolo d'Italia,* which was losing circulation, was sometimes sequestrated and often censored. Two members of the staff resigned in protest against Mussolini's policy. The movement was at low water and Mussolini himself went through a phase of discouragement. "Fascism," he said bitterly, "has come to a dead end," and he spoke of leaving journalism and politics for the theater and fiction.[15] But an event occurred just before the elections which, as it turned out, was to have a profound effect on the future evolution of the movement. On September 12, 1919, D'Annunzio, with Mussolini's prior knowledge, suddenly occupied Fiume.

V

Under the terms of the Italo-Austrian armistice Fiume did not fall within the area to be occupied by Italy, but it did lie within the area covered by the armistice between the Commander of the Army of the Orient, General Franchet d'Esperey, and the Hungarians. Moreover Fiume was not promised to Italy under the Treaty of London. Nevertheless, immediately after the armistice Italian naval forces appeared off Fiume, and on November 15, 1918, a Serbian battalion arrived to make a counterdemonstration. They were persuaded to withdraw and on November 18 an American battalion disembarked, followed by British and French contingents. Meanwhile Italian troops, which were eventually raised to the strength of a division, gradually infiltrated into the city. General Grazioli, the Italian commander, who was the senior officer at Fiume, used his rank to buttress Italian influence. The Italian flag was the official flag, the Italian penal code was imposed on the courts, an Italian legislative assembly was created, and a small Italian militia was recruited. These measures evoked protest from the three other military commanders, but in vain. Inevitably friction developed, particularly between the French and the Italians, and in June and July, 1919, there were riots, in the course of which four French soldiers lost their lives. In consequence of these events, which greatly excited public opinion in France and Italy, an inter-allied military commission, composed of senior British, French,

Italian, and American generals, was dispatched to Fiume with instructions to hold an inquiry. On August 8, 1919, it made a number of recommendations designed to remove Italian control and to entrust the administration of the city to an international and impartial body. But before these recommendations could be put into effect D'Annunzio struck.

The occupation of Fiume by the romantic and degenerate poet struck a grievous blow at authority in Italy, but it was superficially a comedy. Attired in a variety of flamboyant uniforms D'Annunzio made daily speeches and held parades of his Arditi. At the conclusion of the proceedings came the stock ceremony. "For Gabriele D'Annunzio," and the parade replied "*Ayah, ayah, alala.*" "For the people of Fiume!" "*Ayah, ayah, alala.*" "For whom the future? For whom Italy? For whom the power and the glory?" "For us." The troops raised their daggers aloft and cheered the Regent. There were constant fanfares, processions, and distributions of new medals. Raids were organized, prize ships were brought into port, and islands annexed. The so-called legislative body was composed of ten corporations, of which the last was described in the Statute of the Province of Fiume as being "for the mysterious forces of nature and adventure"; but in fact D'Annunzio was the dictator.

All this would have been harmless enough, but for the fact that D'Annunzio's defiance of the government undermined the discipline of the army and navy and brought about a widespread contempt for authority which was later to have serious consequences. Fiume was also the proving ground for fascism, just as the Spanish Civil War was to be for the Second World War. D'Annunzio had conceived the idea of the uniforms with their black fezzes, the assemblies, the slogans, the administration of castor oil to political opponents, and the claptrap of a Fascist regime. He had appealed to chauvinism, to the adventurous spirit of youth, to the desire of the masses for colorful pomp, and to the ideal of force. Mussolini, who had hitherto relied on inflammatory rhetoric and journalism, was clever enough to see that these meretricious devices of political pageantry could be developed and usefully applied to his own wider purpose. D'Annunzio's success in capturing the city with small forces encouraged Mussolini to believe that his own will to power would bring him a similar, if larger, reward.

At first the occupation of Fiume was received with enthusiasm in Italy, and Mussolini, after waiting prudently to assure himself of the expedition's success and of the acquiescence of the Nitti government, added his voice to the general acclamation. On September 13 he declared to a crowd assembled outside the *Popolo d'Italia* that he saluted the hero and would obey his every command. He campaigned against the Nitti government and raised substantial funds for Fiume. In October he flew to the city and held a long conversation with D'Annunzio, in the course of which the possibility of a march on Rome was discussed; but Mussolini privately begged the poet not to undertake anything before the elections.* In short, so far as the public were concerned, D'Annunzio had no more ardent supporter than Mussolini. Nevertheless on this issue he was as unstable as he had been on any other. His hatred of the Rome government, his desire to flout the Western Allies, his romanticism, and his genuine desire to extend Italy's dominions all combined to predispose him in favor of the adventure. But there were other considerations to be weighed. He was not prepared to play second fiddle to D'Annunzio for very long. Nor could he afford to be associated too closely with a failure; and it became clear very soon that the antics of the eccentric Regent were more likely to end in tears than in glory. D'Annunzio must have sensed this, since as early as September 16, 1919, he sent Mussolini a letter in which he upbraided him bitterly for the tepidity of his support. So in the face of public opinion and of D'Annunzio's reproaches Mussolini found himself once more in the situation of August, 1914. He was publicly committed to the support of a cause while privately entertaining every reservation. Accordingly he continued vociferously to acclaim D'Annunzio and to demand the annexation of Fiume, while at the same time he sought to impede any new adventure such as a march on Rome and awaited the first opportunity to disengage. Meanwhile

* Mussolini had sent a memorandum to D'Annunzio sketching the character of the coming revolution: not reactionary, but Republican, D'Annunzio to be head of the state, religion and the Vatican to be respected. Tactics were discussed, the need to avoid a general strike was emphasized and the view was expressed that conditions for a revolt would not exist until the spring of 1921. (Pini and Susmel, *op. cit.*, II, 80–81). It is, however, clear that Mussolini never took this project seriously. In the course of his conversation he postponed the date until the end of 1921; and he never gave the matter another thought.

he made such use as he could of Fiume's resources to advance the fortunes of his own party.

As the months passed the situation at Fiume continued to engage the attention of the Italian government and people. But it did not arouse much interest abroad. The London *Times* for example, while faithfully reporting events in Fiume and the long and fruitless negotiations between the Italian government and the poet, gave them little space or prominence. A railway strike had broken out in England and there were many other events to report of greater cosmic interest and significance. Fortunately for the Italian government time was on their side, for there was a gradual deterioration in the economic position of the city, and the people gradually realized that they could not live on parades, pomp, and poetry. Diminishing local support fortified the Italian government, and eventually in November, 1920, Count Sforza, Minister for Foreign Affairs in Giolitti's administration, concluded an agreement at Rapallo with Yugoslavia under which Fiume became an independent city and Italy acquired Istria, the islands of Lussiri and Cherso, and Zara.

The signature of the agreement was advantageous to both Mussolini and the Italian government. It offered Mussolini the opportunity, for which he had been waiting, to discard D'Annunzio, and it created conditions in which the Italian government could safely bring the occupation of Fiume to an end. Mussolini was cautious, but he made his position plain. He spoke of the conflict between his emotions and the dictates of realism. The treaty with Yugoslavia, he said, while not in every way satisfactory, was not a disaster; and moreover it was not eternal. The Italian people were exhausted and not in a mood to struggle further. In these circumstances it would, he claimed, have been quite impossible to organize a Fascist revolt, and he had no alternative but to respect the treaty. So far as his own relations with D'Annunzio were concerned, he discharged his obligations by emphasizing that if Fiume had not become Yugoslav, it was due to the valor of the poet and his legionaries.

Encouraged by Mussolini's attitude and the apathy of the nation, the Italian government took steps to evict D'Annunzio. On Christmas Eve, 1920—the time was cleverly chosen since no newspapers appeared for two days—an Italian squadron bombarded Fiume and after four days D'Annunzio left the city saying that its inhabitants had not proved worthy of him. Indeed most of them were heartily sick of the sterile adventure and looked forward to the opportunity of restoring their shattered fortunes within the framework of a free city. Mussolini, while paying perfunctory tribute to D'Annunzio, gratefully accepted the forcible solution of a problem which had become an embarrassment.

Of course the legionaries and many Fascists were indignant at his treachery and accused him of having abandoned Fiume at the decisive hour. But Mussolini retorted blandly that the legionaries in the mystical and heroic atmosphere of Fiume were out of touch with Italian opinion and with realities, that a Fascist insurrection would have been doomed to failure, and that it would have been wrong to prejudice the future of the party by playing into the hands of the antinational forces.[16]

In a speech at the end of January, 1921, he explained that he had never undertaken to make a revolution in the event of Fiume being attacked:

> Revolution is not a surprise package which can be opened at will. I do not carry it in my pocket. . . . Revolution will be accomplished with the army, not against the army; with arms, not without them; with trained forces, not with undisciplined mobs called together in the streets. It will succeed when it is surrounded by a halo of sympathy by the majority, and if it has not that, it will fail.[17]

It was not heroic language, but the Italians are realists and his audience must have heard with some gratification that they were not being called upon to take part in a forlorn hope.

In the course of the recriminations arising from the collapse of the Fiume expedition two specific allegations were leveled at Mussolini; first that he had misappropriated for his electoral purposes funds which he had collected for Fiume; and second that he had made a secret deal with Giolitti under which the Italian government would give the Fascists a free hand to attack the Socialists and the labor organizations in return for Mussolini's acquiescence in the bombardment of Fiume. There is some foundation for the first allegation. The issue was taken to a tribunal of the journalists' association and Mussolini was acquitted, largely because he was able to produce a letter from D'Annunzio absolving him from the charge. But Mussolini did admit that some hundreds of armed men had come from Fiume during the last week of the electoral campaign and that he had paid them a daily wage of from 20 to 25 lire.[18] It is unlikely that he could have met this expenditure from any source other than the Fiume fund, and he probably had no difficulty in persuading himself that he was entitled to use this money to pay Fiume legionaries who had come to support the electoral campaign of a party devoted to their cause. The impropriety of using armed bands in an election does not appear to have occurred to him.

The second allegation is more serious. No record exists of any transaction with Giolitti and any verdict must be speculative. Alceste de Ambris, D'Annunzio's so-called Prime Minister, categorically accused Mussolini of the pact, and it may not have been a coincidence that in 1921 the Italian government began to show a remarkable degree of tolerance towards the violence of the Fascists. Giolitti was contemptuous of Mussolini and regarded him as a transient phenomenon in Italian politics. He made the same mistake as did the German industrialists ten years later when they began to compound with Hitler. Giolitti believed that he could use Mussolini against the Socialists and discard him or at least control him when he had served his purpose. Mussolini for his part must have felt that history was repeating itself. In 1914 he had come to be embarrassed by his own advocacy of neutrality and he had gratefully grasped the opportunity of changing his course, even though it meant betraying his former associates. Now he was being offered favorable terms to liquidate his participation in an enterprise which could no longer be expected to pay a dividend and might even compromise his future. It would have been out of character for him to have rejected so advantageous a deal simply because of a personal commitment to D'Annunzio. There is no proof, but it is not unfair to infer that this is precisely what he did.

It might have been thought that the eviction of D'Annunzio, coming so soon after the electoral disaster, would have still further demoralized the Fascists and diminished Mussolini's position. It is true that for a time a number of Fascists were disaffected, but there were many other compensating factors. D'Annunzio was now in obscurity and with his disappearance Mussolini became the undisputed leader of the revolutionary paramilitary forces. Many of the Arditi and legionaries from Fiume flocked to his standards and this infusion of new blood not only strengthened his Fasci, but attracted new men to the movement. Secondly Mussolini had correctly assessed public opinion which, far from resenting his betrayal of Fiume, was grateful to him for having helped to bring the affair to an end. Finally D'Annunzio at Fiume had set the pattern for the future of fascism: a corporative dictatorship with all its trappings, the uniforms, the marches, the assemblies, the slogans, and the pomp. Now at last Mussolini began to perceive the outward form which his regime would assume. Within this framework he would create the image of himself as the Leader, the man of destiny, the man of iron will, the man with a policy which would promote Italy to a foremost place among the nations. The form of fascism was henceforth settled, but he remained as vague as before about the substance. He had, however, reached one practical and prudent conclusion. After his own experience of Red Week and D'Annunzio's experience at Fiume he resolved not to involve himself in conflict with the army.

VI

While D'Annunzio had been busy at Fiume, the situation of Italy had been slowly deteriorating at home and abroad. There was a steady fall in the value of the lira; credits were exhausted and the Italian government appealed in vain to Britain for a loan; a shortage of coal hampered industry and inflicted hardship on the individual; and the price of bread rose. Sir George Buchanan, the British ambassador in Rome, reporting on April 17, 1920, said that Italy presented a somber picture, which did not necessarily presage revolution, although it was likely that outbreaks, especially in the North, would have the effect of isolating large areas for a considerable time. Sir George, who had witnessed the Russian revolution in St. Petersburg, was inclined to see a Bolshevik in every unruly Italian, but his forecast was not far wide of the mark.

Popular dissatisfaction manifested itself in a wave of violent strikes which paralyzed the country—there were altogether 1,881 strikes in 1920—and in September disorder reached its peak when the workmen of Piedmont and Lombardy forcibly occupied the factories and set up workers' councils according to the Russian revolutionary formula. Mussolini, following his practice of outbidding the Socialists, gave overt support to the strikers. In a speech at Trieste on September 20, 1920, he said: "I not only accept the unprecedented control of the factories but their social and cooperative management as well. . . . I demand that the factories increase their production. If this is guaranteed to me by the workers in place of the industrialists, I shall declare without hesitation that the former have the right to substitute themselves for the latter." In private, however, he reserved his position, for he was always sceptical of the ability of the proletariat to impose their will by force and he did not believe that this particular movement would in fact succeed. Nevertheless it was useful for his ulterior ends to dangle before the terrified bourgeoisie the specter of revolution. Giolitti, the Prime Minister of the day, refused to be stampeded into action, for he regarded the Socialists as being in decline and feared that the use of force against the workers might revitalize the party. His policy, which was much criticized by the industrialists, was to wait on events and to buy the workers off by improvements in pay and conditions. Events proved his judgment right. The workmen, unable to persuade technicians and administrators to collaborate, found themselves unable to maintain production. The movement petered out and by the end of the month the factories were quietly evacuated. But the episode was a shock to the country.

Simultaneously mutinies broke out in several military garrisons, and officers were arrested by their men. Some units declined to embark for Albania,* and in Ancona there was serious trouble which resulted in a number of casualties. Under the pressure of these events the government decided to abandon Albania and ordered the evacuation of Valona. Mussolini, who continued to combine support of the working classes against society with ag-

* In December, 1914, Italian troops had occupied Valona and in 1916 the whole of southern Albania. After the armistice the Italians extended their hold and occupied most of the country.

gressive nationalism, protested violently at the humiliation of Italy and predicted gloomily that withdrawals from Dalmatia and from Africa would shortly follow. The French, he declared, would in contrast fight to maintain themselves in the Levant; and the British would not abandon Mesopotamia and Malta, nor surrender Gibraltar to Spain, Egypt to the Egyptians, Ireland to the Irish. Disorder at home and reverses abroad shook public confidence and attracted new adherents to the Fascist movement, particularly from the younger generation who were tired of the old political parties and ready for something new. In the autumn communal elections the Fascists succeeded in winning four seats in the Socialist stronghold of Bologna and in Milan the Socialists only retained their hold by a greatly reduced majority. At the inaugural session of the municipal council in Bologna on November 21, 1920, there was a disturbance and one of the Fascist members, Giulio Giordani, was killed by a revolver shot. This incident was important, for it provoked the first organized reprisals, and Mussolini publicly warned his opponents that while he deprecated all wars, and in particular civil war, he intended to react with force against the violence of the extremists. From this moment the conflict between the Fascists and the Left became more widespread and more bitter. It also hampered the efforts of the government to stimulate the recovery of the economy.

In the country the Fascists were dependent on the financial and moral support of the owners of land, in most cases smallholders. The old landed proprietors, terrified by peasant agitation and by the climate of opinion created by events in Russia, had found it prudent to surrender much of their land to tenants. The new owners were much fiercer than their predecessors in the defense of their newly acquired property, and regarded the Fascists as a bulwark against claims of the farm workers and the subversive elements of the Left. It might have been thought that Mussolini, who purported to be the champion of the masses, would have been reluctant to accept aid from such a quarter, but he welcomed support where he could find it. Bands of Fascists roamed the countryside beating up Socialists, dispersing their meetings or destroying their premises without much interference from the police. Soon almost every northern country town had its *Fascio* and its detachment, termed a *Squadra.*

In Ferrara, the most active and efficient center, the leader was Italo Balbo, who had served without particular distinction in the Alpini during the war and had taken a degree in political science at Florence University. He was not one of the early Fascists and only joined the movement in 1920 when the landowners association decided to finance it and offered him the local secretaryship with an appropriate salary. He was then a thin young man of revolutionary and anticlerical sentiments, with long disheveled hair and a black musketeer beard. At about the same time Dino Grandi joined the Fascists and became a leader in Bologna, where he soon acquired a considerable reputation both for his ability and for the violence of his conduct. There were a few other leaders of this stamp, but the *Squadre* were for the most part composed of hooligans or of young men inspired by the spirit of adventure and the desire to have a new deal in Italy. In the excitement of continual battle they were not too much concerned with the details of the movement's program nor with the political consistency of their Leader.

In the midst of these stirring events Mussolini began in 1920 to take flying lessons from a well-known aviator, Cesare Redaelli, who found him an interesting but not an altogether satisfactory pupil. It was difficult to fit flying in with his many engagements, and in the ten months from July 20, 1920, to May 12, 1921, he was only able to take fourteen lessons and to complete six and half hours of flying time. He had one crash from which he escaped not without injury and eventually pleaded overwork in order to break off his course of instruction before getting his pilot's license. Nevertheless he had achieved what he had set out to do, namely to mark publicly the importance he attached to the future of Italian aviation. The flying lessons were part of his policy, which was to build up the image of a new man with modern ideas, anxious to break with the past, a man who was a veritable Duce, who had the imagination and the drive necessary to bring about a revolution in the national life. Hence the short, staccato sentences in his speeches and press articles, the uncompromising and omniscient tone, the imperious gestures, and the other tricks designed to create the impression of sincerity, conviction, and resolution. In addition to being a journalist he became a practiced and accomplished actor—he had always possessed great histrionic talent—and while in private he was often timid and always uncertain, the face he presented on the boards was that of an indomitable leader.

VII

The year 1921 saw the Fascists begin the advance which was to sweep them into power. Several factors were operating in Mussolini's favor. The public was becoming tired of the inconvenience caused by strikes and disorder, the bourgeoisie was afraid of communism and not only the landowners but the industrialists were supporting fascism, while internal dissensions between the Communists and the others were beginning to destroy the coherence of the Socialist party. Finally the government made a notable change of policy. During 1920 Giolitti had covertly tolerated the Fascists, but he did not go further since he still hoped to maneuver the Socialists into parliamentary collaboration. But in 1921 he abandoned this hope and began to give overt support to the anti-Socialist campaign of the Fascists. Not only did the authorities give protection to the *Squadre* guilty of murder, arson, and pillage, but they gave them money and arms. Under the pressure of legalized violence the Socialists, already weakened by schism, began to dissolve and scarcely dared defend themselves. The Communists had split from the Socialists, and there was still dissension in the Socialist ranks between the reformist parliamentarians and the left-wing revolutionaries. Far from being assuaged by the visible collapse of the enemy, the Fascists with ever greater ardor increased the number and violence of their assaults. Between January and May of 1921 they destroyed 120 labor union headquarters and invaded over two hundred Socialist centers, killing 243 and wounding 1,144. Their own casualties, while they were fewer, were not inconsiderable. The struggle between Red- and Blackshirts was to continue all through 1921 and most of 1922, but already on July 2, 1921, Mussolini was able to write in the *Popolo d'Italia:* "To say that a Bolshevist peril still exists in Italy is to want to charge with reality certain fears that are not to be acknowledged. Bolshevism is vanquished." *

The attitude of Giolitti, the wily old Liberal politician, appears inexplicable in the light of subsequent events, particularly since he never at any time regarded communism as a serious danger in Italy. But he was overconfident in his own skill as a politician and, having failed to make the Socialists toe his line, he determined to destroy them, using the first instrument that came to hand. He despised Mussolini for his inexperience and brashness and believed that, having liquidated fascism when it had served his purpose, he could safely return to the old parliamentary game which he had so successfully played for forty years. It was grievous miscalculation, for the old man had not perceived that increasing numbers from the most virile section of the population, tired of parliamentary maneuvers, were turning against the whole system.

Mussolini was now to some extent the prisoner of the industrialists and landowners whose financial and moral support was essential. There was also the danger that the hotheads leading the Blackshirt *Squadre* would assume control. During the months to come Mussolini made spasmodic efforts both to disengage from the Right and to restrain the excesses of his Blackshirts, but in neither enterprise was he entirely successful since he could not afford to break with his financial backers nor with his armed bands. Speaking at Bologna on April 3, 1921, to a Fascist rally, he said that the movement did not worship violence for the sake of violence. What they were doing was to make a revolution designed to break the Bolshevist state pending a settlement of accounts with the Liberal state which remained, for they had no intention of being the agents of the reactionaries and conservatives.

These brave words were no sooner uttured than they were eaten. Giolitti had felt for some time that he should call an election in order to obtain a working majority. There seemed no doubt that the Socialists, weakened both by divisions in their ranks and by Fascist attacks, had lost ground since the elections of 1919 and that the

---

* Nevertheless fear of bolshevism persisted. As Professor Chabod points out (p. 43), it was retrospective.

Partito Popolare had also forfeited support through the ineptitude of their party administration. In these circumstances he hoped that a Liberal-Democratic bloc led by himself would win some three hundred seats and so render his government independent of Socialist or *Partito Popolare* support. Accordingly he decided to dissolve parliament and to hold new elections on May 15, 1921, and he proposed to the Fascists that they should form part of his so-called constitutional electoral bloc. He hoped in this way to profit electorally from the accession of fresh, young, virile elements,[19] who could be relied upon to intimidate the Socialist and *Partito Popolare* voters and at the same time bring the Fascists under his parliamentary control. "They are our Black-and-Tans," he told a high British official.[20] Mussolini, who had always inveighed against electoral pacts, now accepted the offer and defended his decision on tactical grounds. The Fascists, he said, did not fear contamination for they were strong enough to preserve their autonomy from the dangers of hybrid contacts. It would be his task to be on the watch; and if any industrialists, landowners, or bankers entertained any illusions in this respect, they would do well to discard them immediately.

Although there was some disorder provoked by the Fascists, the elections were held in a relatively calm atmosphere and returned a new parliament constituted as follows:

Liberal Democrats	159
Socialists	146
Partito Popolare	104
Fascists	35
Agrarians	26
Communists	11
Nationalists	10
Republicans	7
Slavs, Germans, etc.	12

The result was a bitter disappointment for Giolitti since it gave him no majority for his constitutional bloc. Some politicians thought that if the elections had been held three weeks earlier, the socialists might have lost more seats, but the violence of the Fascists and their wanton destruction of property was gradually alienating public opinion, which reacted in favor of the Socialists and of the *Partito Popolare*. The Fascists, favored by the electoral pact, won thirty-five seats, a more favorable outcome than Giolitti had foreseen. They were still a small party, but it was a beginning, and after the fiasco of 1919 the result was received with grateful satisfaction. Among the successful candidates were Mussolini, who was elected in Bologna-Ferrara-Ravenna-Forlì as well as in Milan-Pavia, and Dino Grandi, who was elected in Bologna. In Milan Mussolini received 124,918 votes as against the 4,064 cast for him in 1919. The entry of the small Fascist group into the Chamber attracted surprisingly little public attention. They distinguished themselves principally by their disorderly behavior, and it does not seem to have occurred to anyone in Rome that within eighteen months their leader would be in power. Indeed events after the elections were so inauspicious for Mussolini as to excuse this lack of foresight.

CHAPTER FIVE

The Parliamentarian

1921–1922

I

THE new parliament met on June 11, 1921, to hear the speech of the Crown. There was some discussion among the Fascists as to whether in view of their attitude to the monarchy they should attend on the opening day when the King would be present. Mussolini strongly argued for abstention, but when the issue was put to the vote eighteen, including De Vecchi and Count Costanzo Ciano (father of Galeazzo Ciano), favored attendance and only fifteen voted with Mussolini. Mussolini made no attempt to hide his displeasure at the outcome of the vote, but the difference was symptomatic of the internal dissensions, which during the year were to threaten Mussolini's authority and the future of the movement. He was hard put to it to retain control and in order to do so he was obliged to oscillate with extraordinary agility between monarchism and republicanism, parliamentarianism and revolution, legality and violence. Sometimes he was the leader, other times he had quickly to reverse his steps in order to regain contact with his flock. Only a resolute man of infinite resource could have steered his devious course through the pitfalls that awaited him.

In the course of the debate on the address, Mussolini made his maiden speech. It was for the most part a conventional, nationalist attack on the Socialists, on the foreign policy of Count Sforza, and on the domestic policy of the government, and as such it received loud applause from the Right. But it contained one significant and interesting passage. Fascism, he declared, neither preached nor practised anticlericalism. There were domestic problems to be solved such as the attitude of the state to divorce and education, but there was one historical problem of transcendent importance, namely that of the relations between Italy and the Vatican.

All of us [he said], who have been nourished on the writings of Carducci have hated the "old bloody Vatican wolf" of which I think Carducci spoke in his ode to Ferrera. . . . All this, regarded purely as literature, may be very brilliant, but today to us Fascists with our unbiased outlook it seems something of an anachronism. I here affirm that the Latin and imperial tradition of Rome is today represented by Catholicism. If, as Mommsen said, twenty-five or thirty years ago, one cannot be in Rome without the sense of a universal idea, then I believe and assert that the only universal idea which today exists in Rome is that which radiates from the Vatican. I am much exercised when I witness the formation of national churches, because I reflect that there are millions and millions of men who no longer look to Italy and to Rome. This is the ground on which I believe that if the Vatican will renounce its temporal dreams—and I think that it is already on the way to doing so—Italy, the lay government of Italy, must give the Vatican the material help, the material facilities for schools, churches, hospitals, and other establishments which a lay power has at its disposal. I say this because the development of Catholicism in the world, an increase in the numbers of the 400 millions who in every part of the world look to Rome, is a matter of interest and of pride also to us who are Italians.[1]

In this speech Mussolini voiced, not for the first time, his pride in and attachment to the glory of Rome. It was also an expression of his wish to settle the Roman question and as such it can be described as one of the few statements of policy to which he adhered when later he was in control of Italy's affairs. It will be seen later with what persistence he addressed himself to the task.

The debate on the Address lasted several days and ended with a vote of confidence in the Giolitti government by a majority of thirty-four. The Fascists without regard to the electoral pact voted against the government. Very soon, however, Giolitti decided to resign because he knew that some days later the *Partito Popolare* would vote against his bill for full powers to reform the bureaucracy; and without the *Partito Popolare* there could be no majority. Giolitti suggested to the King that his successor should be either De Nicola, the President of the Chamber, or Bonomi, who had been in the Giolitti cabinet. The King consulted the other leaders of parliamentary groups, among them Mussolini, who recommended De Nicola. It was Mussolini's first conversation with the Sovereign since they had met at the military hospital in 1917 and the interview passed off amicably. As it happened, the King chose Bonomi, the reformist Socialist, for whom he had always had a certain predilection on account of his modesty and simplicity.

With the advent to power of the new government an effort was made to restore order, but the army, police, and the provincial administration, many of whom sympathized with the Fascists, had been demoralized by months of connivance at Blackshirt outrages and the infiltration of sympathizers into key positions. Mussolini, for his part, took the earliest opportunity to announce that he regarded himself as under no obligation to support the governmental bloc and that in fact his group would sit in the Chamber with the opposition. Hitherto fascism had been a revolutionary, republican, antiparliamentarian movement, but in an interview with the *Giornale d'Italia* on May 21, 1921, he did not exclude the possibility that the movement would become an autonomous parliamentary political party.

II

Meanwhile violence in the provinces continued unabated. Outrages on both sides were followed by reprisals and counterreprisals; and the Blackshirts, who gradually developed the technique of concentrating their detachments on their objective, were generally victorious. At Sarzana, however, they lost sixteen killed and thirty wounded, and their column narrowly escaped annihilation. Despite this and other occasional reverses the young adventurers who joined the ranks of the Blackshirt detachments enjoyed their guerrilla war. The sufferers were the people of Italy, who never knew from day to day whether trains would run or food be obtainable, or whether they would find themselves involved in a street battle. Gradually resentment against the Fascists mounted. Orderly citizens, who had previously regarded fascism as a useful or indeed laudable antidote to bolshevism now began to view the excesses of the *Squadre* with repugnance. Mussolini, who was highly sensitive to any change in the climate of public opinion and was resolved to avoid a conflict with the army, began to call for moderation and even ventilated the possibility of cooperation with the Socialists and the *Partito Popolare*, who both represented the interests of the working classes. On June 21 Mussolini, speaking in the Chamber on foreign affairs, let fall the observation that the Fascists were prepared to disarm, provided their opponents would do likewise; and on June 30 Filippo Turati, the moderate Socialist, made a speech also in the Chamber urging both sides to abandon methods of violence.

Encouraged by this development Bonomi in July suggested a meeting of Socialists and Fascists with a view to a truce. Mussolini seized the opportunity thus offered and did all he could to further Bonomi's plan despite much bitter opposition on the part of his own followers, who at a meeting of the National Fascist Council on July 12 adopted a resolution that the moment was not opportune for any form of agreement with their opponents. Undeterred by this step, Mussolini went ahead with the project as rapidly as he could, and on August 2, 1921, an agreement was concluded in Rome under which the signatories undertook to renounce violence and to submit differences to arbitration. Mussolini, Cesare de Vecchi, and Giovanni Giuriati signed for the parliamentary Fascist group; Cesare Rossi and four others for the *Fasci di Combattimento;* while the Socialist signatories included Bacci, Mussolini's predecessor at *Avanti.*

The news of this agreement created grave dissension in the Fascist ranks. Mussolini courageously defied his critics when he wrote:

> I will defend with all my forces this treaty of peace, which in my view attains the importance of a historic event on account of its singularity without precedent. For this purpose I will apply the old and very wise proverb: "Whoever does not employ the rod, hates his own son." Well if Fascism is my son—which everyone has always known it to be—I swear with the rods of my oath, of my courage, of my passion, I will either correct him or I will make his life impossible.[2]

The man, he said, who had founded and led the movement was entitled to take a broad and not a local, parochial view of events. In any event, if fascism would not follow him, no one could oblige him to follow fascism. Again these were brave words, but he was compelled to eat them before many weeks had passed.

There were now two distinct trends which threatened to divide the Fascist movement. The first was represented by many provincial *Fasci,* principally in Tuscany, Emilia, and Romagna. For them and their financial patrons the primary task of fascism in the so-called fight against communism was to destroy the tyranny of socialism over the working classes exercised through the Socialists' trade unions and employment agencies. These they planned to eliminate, creating in their place Fascist trade unions and employment agencies. They attached no importance to parliament or the establishment of a Fascist political party, and they regarded the truce as a hindrance to the accomplishment of their mission. The minority, led by Mussolini, regarded the aims of the movement as wider and more important than mere anti-Socialist reaction. They wished to make it a great national political party with an aggressive foreign policy and a new deal at home. For this purpose they were prepared to sacrifice the Fascist trade unions; and it was this appeasement of the Socialists rather than the truce itself which constituted the basis of the dispute. Mussolini, however, saw that to be content with the limited aims of the provincial *Fasci* would lead him nowhere. Once the power of socialism had been destroyed, the purpose of the movement would be fulfilled and there would be no reason for its continued existence.

The rank and file were not to be won over and Mussolini was faced by open rebellion on the part of most of the provincial *Fasci.* The local "*ras,*" as the provincial leaders were termed, came out openly on the side of the rebels. Prominent among them were Farinacci, Balbo, and Grandi, the last of whom repudiated Mussolini's leadership and sought to bring about his fall. It was Grandi's first attempt to unseat his chief, and he did not repeat it until 1943. In Bologna, Grandi's stronghold, men began to circulate the slogan: "He who has once betrayed, will betray again." Mussolini was accused of going over to parliamentarians and of abandoning his followers in the midst of the struggle.[3] Under the influence of their agrarian and industrialist paymasters the *ras* claimed that the task of liquidating the subversive and antinational elements was not completed and that a truce would enable the enemy to rally his forces. It seemed to the young romantics in the *Squadre* that a halt had been called to a revolution against the old order. Feeling against Mussolini gradually mounted.

On August 16, 1921, at Bologna a congress was held of *Fasci* from Emilia-Romagna, Mantua, Cremona, and Venice. With the support of Balbo, Farinacci, and several other prominent Fascists it approved a resolution condemning the truce. The attitude of the delegates was hostile to Mussolini, who was thought to have left his comrades in the lurch for the prospect of an illusory parliamentary collaboration with implacable adversaries; and he must have felt that he might once more find himself a man without a party. He did not himself attend the congress, but on receiving the news of the vote he at once resigned from the executive committee of the Fascists. But just as in 1914 he had claimed that he was still a Socialist, so he now affirmed that he remained a Fascist. "The matter is settled. The man who is defeated must go. And I leave the top rank. I remain, and I hope I may remain, an ordinary private soldier in the Milan *Fascio*." [4]

In one respect, however, Mussolini was in a much better position than he had been in 1914, for he now possessed an established, influential newspaper, in the columns of which he could fight his battle. Moreover, whereas in 1914 he had left the Socialist party as a lone, execrated figure, in 1921 a number of the *Fasci* were on his side and he had some supporters in the upper ranks of the movement, among them Cesare Rossi, who resigned his post of vice-secretary as a gesture of sympathy with Mussolini.

While the storm blew, Mussolini waited, well poised for movement in any direction, to see how events would shape. Ever since his experience of Red Week he had doubted whether he could attain power by revolutionary action and he remained convinced that he could not do so unless the army were on his side or at least neutral. The majority of his followers, intoxicated by excitement and by the success of their guerrilla operations, had no such misgivings; and he wavered between yielding to their solicitations and attempting to attain power by some parliamentary combination.

The only thing that mattered was power, and he was not particular as to the means by which he was to realize his ambition. He must therefore try to avoid an irrevocable breach with the *Fasci*, who were now completely out of control, and at the same time keep the door open for negotiations with the political parties. It might even be expedient to find a synthesis between fascism and parliamentarianism. Hence the idea, which began to assume increasing importance in his mind, of converting the movement into a political party. He was also influenced by the consideration that once the so-called Bolshevik danger had been conjured, there was, unless the movement became a political party, no reason for its continued existence.

On August 26, 1921, the national Fascist council met at Florence to consider the position. Feeling against Mussolini, who was not present, was still running high, but the members were aware that the loss of their leader would be a grievous blow to the movement and many of them, knowing his volatile character, hoped not unreasonably that he could be brought to change his mind. They therefore decided prudently to postpone a solution of the crisis until it could be considered at the full congress, which was to take place in Rome in November. Meanwhile the situation in the country deteriorated rapidly and under the leadership of Balbo and Grandi the *Squadre* resumed their far-flung operations, although not with the same intensity as before the truce. At Modena eight Fascists were killed by the government forces, and Mussolini attended the funeral to make a speech in which he indicated clearly that while he remained opposed to undisciplined violence, his heart was still with the Fascists. The country, he said, yearned for peace, but there could be no real peace so long as Fascists were called assassins, mercenaries, and adventurers. If any Fascists deserved these appellations he would be the first to condemn them, for fascism was an ideal and the youths who had fallen had died not for a bourgeois or proletarian Italy, not for an Italy represented by those who governed or rather misgoverned the nation, but for an Italy whose greatness lay not only in its glorious future.[5]

Mussolini's presence at Modena and his speech marked the beginning of a process of reconciliation which culminated at the Rome congress six weeks later. Meanwhile preparatory conversations in which Mussolini took part showed that there was still very strong opposition in the movement to his proposal to create a Fascist party, but he used his personal influence and the *Popolo d'Italia* to propagate the idea and to call for discipline in the Fascist ranks. In the midst of these activities he received a challenge to a duel from a former Socialist friend and colleague, Francesco Ciccotti, the editor of Nitti's newspaper the *Paese,* on account of an attack on him in the *Popolo d'Italia.* Mussolini was under constant police surveillance and it was difficult to organize the duel, but it eventually took place in a villa at Leghorn and ended inconclusively after the fourteenth assault because the doctors declared that Ciccotti's weak heart was in no fit state to endure a further prolongation of the conflict. The *Fascio* at Leghorn gave Mussolini a warm and encouraging welcome. He was beginning slowly to recover the ground he had lost.

The outcome of the Socialist congress at Milan in October, 1921, was not without influence on the evolution of the dispute within the Fascist movement. At the instance of the party's left wing a resolution was passed declaring the Socialist party to be a revolutionary party and the presence of collaborationists and Social Democrats in its ranks to be incompatible with its aims. Despite the fact that the Communists had broken with the Socialists, the congress stated that, as far as circumstances permitted, the party would conform its action to that of Moscow. The victory of the extremists at Milan and the eclipse of the reformists not only split the party and weakened its capacity to resist the Fascists, but it was also a signal that there could be no prospect of a parliamentary deal between the Fascists and the Socialists; and Mussolini began to edge towards the Right. He also prepared the way for his own surrender over the truce, by declaring that the Socialists had first broken it and that the current disorders were brought about by their provocation. In fact the offense of the Socialists was to take steps to defend themselves. In August a young ex-soldier named Argo Secondari had founded the *Arditi del Popolo* to fight the Fascists. It was nominally nonpolitical, but it naturally attracted recruits from the Socialists and from those members of the *Partito Popolare* who felt themselves threatened by the *Squadre.*

On November 7, 1921, four thousand Fascist delegates, drawn

from every part of Italy, met in the Augusteo in Rome in an atmosphere of considerable tension. But, as so often happens on such occasions, the ground had already been cleared behind closed doors before the congress met. At a private meeting some days previously between leading protagonists and opponents of the truce, Mussolini had indicated that although the truce could not be formally repudiated and must remain nominally in force, he would do nothing to impede the operations of the *Squadre*. On this basis unity was re-established and it was unanimously decided not to debate the issue at the congress. This face-saving formula cloaked Mussolini's surrender, but the affair taught him a valuable lesson and he resolved, if ever he attained power, to render himself independent of the power of the *Fasci*.

When Mussolini spoke on the second day of the congress he said that at a meeting at the Hotel des Princes between representatives of both schools of thought it had been decided not to provoke a debate on the truce and not to put the issue to the vote. But, if, as seemed to be the case, the congress wished to open a discussion, he was ready to make a full defense of his policy. At this point Grandi rose and said that everything had been satisfactorily cleared up and the treaty could be buried; and as Mussolini retorted "bury the debate, not the treaty," Grandi rushed forward to embrace him. The delegates, who were really more concerned to end the schism than to explore the finer points of the compromise, cheered loudly.[6] From that moment Mussolini was once more in command and, sensing the mood of his audience, was able to bend it to his will. But he had been obliged to give ground, the basic difference between himself and the rebels had not been resolved, and the next eleven months were to see a constant tug of war between the *Fasci*, shouting for action, and Mussolini counseling restraint.

III

In the meantime Mussolini, now restored to the executive committee, was glad to make use of his ascendancy to push forward his plans for the constitution of a political party with a political program. A resolution proposed by Michele Bianchi, secretary of the Milan *Fascio*, that a Fascist party should be constituted was carried by a large majority against the votes of Grandi and the Emilian delegates. Mussolini was elected head of the executive committee and his henchman, Bianchi, secretary-general of the party. The new program can conveniently be summarized as follows:

1. Functions of the state to be limited to those of a purely political and juridical nature; other functions to be delegated to technical national councils elected by professional and economic corporations.
2. "Agnosticism" as regards the question of the monarchy versus republicanism.
3. Extension of public ownership of land in such areas as were suitable. No socialization of the land.
4. Economy: administrative decentralization * and bureaucratic reform.
5. Withdrawal of the right to strike in the public utility services.
6. No monopolies and no subsidies. Private industry to be encouraged and unprofitable state industries given up.
7. Revision of the peace treaties, to be based on economic considerations.
8. Maintenance of an efficient army and navy.

As usual, the definition of Mussolini's aims was expressed in deliberately vague terms and there were obvious lacunae, but the substance of the program illustrated clearly how far he had traveled in two years from the Left to the Right. Fascism was no longer a movement of dissatisfied ex-servicemen directed against foreign and domestic plutocracy, no longer a movement of the Left, but a party vowed primarily to the destruction of socialism. Its character was underlined towards the end of the year when the Fascist group in the Chamber agreed to collaborate with the Nationalists and with Salandra's group of Liberal Democrats, thus constituting a bloc of sixty-two deputies of the Right.

Immediately after the conclusion of the congress Mussolini duly fulfilled his part of the bargain and announced that the truce had lapsed because it had been broken by the Socialists. At the same time he took advantage of the personal ascendancy he had regained

* Overcentralization, imposed on a recently unified country, was one of the evils of the existing system. But in fact Mussolini did nothing when he had power.

to float the idea of a new regime for Italy. In an article published in the *Popolo d'Italia* of November 22, 1921, he said that recent political events could lead to the beginning of a great restoration in Italy. It was by no means certain that the country stood on the threshold of a new age, which would bring with it greater liberty and a wider democratic system. On the contrary it was possible that the next ten years would see an inglorious end to all these so-called democratic advances. It was probable that the people would turn from government by the masses to government by a few men or by a single man. Already in the economic field government by the masses had failed and Russia was reverting to dictators in the factories. Soon universal suffrage would be out of date and men would perhaps yearn for a dictator. Anna Kuliscioff wrote to Turati: "I enclose a *Popolo d'Italia* with an article by Mussolini, who proclaims the need for a dictatorship or rather for a dictator—who is to be himself—to save Italy." It was the first occasion on which Mussolini publicly stated his claim to be the sole ruler of his country, but he was thinking in terms of a decade and did not foresee that the next eleven months would see the collapse of the regime and the early realization of his dreams.[7]

In December, 1921, the economic situation in Italy deteriorated further and was aggravated by the failure of the Banca di Sconto, which ruined thousands of small depositors and shook the position of the government. Any prospect of recovery was destroyed by constant strikes and by the revival of the guerrilla war between Fascists and Socialists on an ever ascending scale. Mussolini made an occasional call for discipline and for the avoidance of unprovoked violence, but it was known throughout the party that he had in fact given the *Squadre* a free hand to liquidate their enemies.

IV

The year 1922 saw the Fascist operations in the North assume a paramilitary character under the energetic leadership of Italo Balbo. He was a typical product of the war, a young man, then tweny-five years of age, who was unable to settle down to a humdrum peacetime existence.

When I came back from the war [he relates in his diary], I, like so many others, hated politics and politicians, who, it seemed to me had betrayed the hopes of the fighting men and had inflicted on Italy a shameful peace and on those who worshiped heroism a series of humiliations. Struggle, fight to return the country to Giolitti who had bartered every ideal? No. Better deny everything, destroy everything in order to build everything up again from the bottom. Many at that time, even the most generous souls, turned towards nihilist communism, which offered a ready and more radical revolutionary program and was engaged on two fronts in a struggle against the bourgeoisie and against socialism. It is certain, I believe, that without Mussolini three-quarters of the Italian youth coming home from the trenches would have become Bolsheviks. They wanted a revolution at any cost.[8]

Now that Mussolini and the Rome congress had given the *Squadre* a free hand, Balbo's aim was to organize them on military lines and intensify their operations. Early in 1922 he attended a meeting at Oneglia in the house of General Gandolfo and it was decided to group the *Squadre* in regional commands. To Balbo were assigned the detachments from Emilia, Romagna, Mantua, the Marches, Venice, the Trentino, Istria, and Zara. Thus the most important and the largest units in the Fascist forces came under Balbo's direct control, and he returned from Oneglia resolved to make active use of them.

The first weeks of the year were spent in preparation and planning, and operations were confined to small-scale raids on the pattern of 1921, but by April Balbo was beginning to make his presence felt, to a point which threatened the authority of the state. For example, when the Minister of Agriculture visited the province of Ferrara, accompanied by the prefect of Bologna, Balbo with a party of Fascists called on him to present a memorandum on problems of local agriculture. During the course of the interview Balbo took the prefect aside to inform him coolly that he proposed to kidnap the Minister unless some Fascists who had recently been arrested in Bologna were immediately released. The prefect assured him that the men had been arrested purely as a precautionary measure and undertook to set them free within two days. He was as good as his word.

In May Balbo organized his first major operation. At the end of April the Fascist trade unions in the province were alerted and told that if the government did not initiate local public works in order to diminish unemployment, there would be a demonstration of force at Ferrara and the invading detachments would not leave the town until the government had given way. On the appointed day, May 12, 1922, 63,000 armed Fascists appeared at the gates of Ferrara. From seven o'clock in the morning the whole life of the city was paralyzed. Hotels, restaurants, and shops were compelled to close, public transport was halted, and all access from outside was barred. The schools were requisitioned as quarters for the invading army, many of whom camped in the streets, and foodstuffs were seized in order to provide rations. The *carabinieri,* the gendarmerie, and the police were ordered to withdraw to their barracks. In a very short time control of the city passed into the hands of the Fascists. In this predicament the prefect asked to see Balbo, who told him that the Fascist army would not leave Ferrara until the government had capitulated. If no satisfactory reply were received within forty-eight hours, he would pass to the offensive and his first objective would be the prefecture. After some frenzied telephoning to Rome news was received that the government had given way, and on the following day Balbo withdrew his victorious and elated cohorts from Ferrara.

Encouraged by this success, Balbo looked around for another suitable target. He found one in Bologna where the Socialists had recently killed a Blackshirt and where the prefect was thought to be unfavorably disposed to the Fascists. On May 29, 1922, the city was occupied by some 20,000 Fascist militia and on the two following days they were reinforced by the arrival of further detachments. Unfortunately for Balbo the prefect of Bologna was made of sterner stuff than his colleague at Ferrara and refused to give way. After five days it seemed as if the deadlock could only be broken by conflict between the Blackshirts and the governmental forces, which were much stronger at Bologna than at Ferrara. In this situation Mussolini, who had always been resolved to avoid a breach with the army, wrote to Balbo from Rome instructing him tactfully to suspend the occupation:

> Dear friend, it is necessary to terminate, for a period which will be very short, your magnificent action. The state has resolved to display for the first time and after many abdications its capacity to live and to resist. . . .

A pause is necessary. We must not exhaust our superb militia. I am sure that you will obey my order with the same discipline as you showed in your mobilization.

Such was Mussolini's personal ascendancy that this somewhat disingenuous letter achieved its aim and Balbo immediately ordered the withdrawal of the invading detachments and the return of the city to normal. In order to gild the pill Mussolini on the following day sent a telegram of congratulation to Balbo; and Bianchi, secretary of the party, published a statement commending the behavior of Balbo and his lieutenants. Nevertheless the episode represented a notable success for the government. It was also a success for Mussolini's more cautious policy. The self-evident fact that at the critical moment it was his, and not the government's, nerve which had failed, did not diminish his stature in the eyes of the rank and file although it exasperated their frustrated leaders.

On July 26, 1922, Balbo with detachments from Ferrara and Bologna occupied Ravenna as a reprisal for attacks on Fascists by the Socialists. Again the schools were requisitioned, and on July 27 the Fascists seized the Republican headquarters and threatened to set fire to it if the party did not dissociate themselves from the Socialists. On July 28 the premises and contents of the Confederation of Socialist Cooperatives were completely destroyed by fire. At this juncture Mussolini again intervened, on this occasion because he did not wish to alienate the Republicans, some of whom at the recent elections had cast preference votes for Grandi. Balbo to his great displeasure received a telegram from Bianchi, ordering him to await the arrival of Grandi before taking any further action against the Republicans. Later in the day Grandi arrived and after a meeting with the Republicans issued a joint statement to the effect that a *modus vivendi* had been agreed and that hostilities would cease. On July 30, the Republican headquarters were formally handed over and the Fascists began to evacuate Ravenna.

This reverse, for which Balbo blamed Mussolini, did not, however, cool his adventurous ardor. A few days later, on August 3, 1922, he received news that the situation at Parma was unsatisfactory and that the local party leaders wished him to come and take the city over. That same night he left by road for Parma, but found the bridge at Reggio Emilia blocked by the gendarmerie. He bluffed the not unfriendly police superintendent of Reggio Emilia into giving him an official pass with which he made his way into Parma, where he set up a military headquarters in the principal hotel. A situation report showed that he was confronted for the first time by an armed and organized enemy force which was able and resolved to offer determined resistance. Accordingly on August 4 he mobilized the *Squadre* of Piacenza, Cremona, Mantua, Reggio Emilia, Modena, Bologna, and Ferrara, which soon began to enter the city. The station was occupied, the schools were requisitioned, and the trunk roads leading into Parma brought under control. While this was going on the Socialist *Arditi* were not idle. Barricades were put up in the streets and from these and from the housetops an intermittent fire was directed on the invading Fascists.

In the morning of August 4 Balbo, escorted by a hundred armed Blackshirts, called on the prefect, who received him in the presence of the local general officer in command, General Lodomez, the chief of police, and other authorities. Balbo in the manner of the commander of a victorious occupying army addressed the prefect in peremptory terms. He complained of the acquiescence of the government in the military measures of the Reds and declared that if within twelve hours normality was not restored, barricades removed, and the Reds disarmed, the Fascists under orders from the party leadership would take over authority from the state. The prefect asked for two hours' grace, which was accorded to him, and at 2 P.M. General Lodomez' troops entered the areas occupied by the Reds and removed the barricades, but without taking any steps to disarm the *Arditi*. In the evening Balbo, again escorted by his Blackshirt force, called on the prefect to inform him that in the circumstances the Fascists had no alternative but to use force. That evening further Blackshirt detachments arrived and battle was joined with the Reds. In the midst of the turmoil a telephone message was received from Bianchi in Rome to the effect that a conflict with the troops must be avoided at all costs. Balbo remarked acidly that while a battle was raging it could not be effectively limited and he decided to ignore the directive. Nevertheless, on the only occasion on which his forces were confronted by resolute troops he in fact gave the order to withdraw. Disappointed at events in the precincts of the city, Balbo used the detachments camped in Parma to make forays against the Socialists throughout the province, where they left a trail of destruction behind them.

On the morning of August 5 he had a third meeting with the prefect, to whom he declared that he would not suspend his operations until power had been handed over to the army. In the evening he received the Bishop of Parma, who offered himself as an honest broker with a view to the restoration of peace. The Bishop, while he was treated with the utmost deference and accorded a guard of honor, was courteously told that his offer could not be accepted and that the Fascists would not evacuate Parma until their conditions had been met.

At midnight Balbo reaped the reward of his persistent determination. General Lodomez called at his headquarters and informed him that the government had yielded. A state of siege had been declared and all power transferred from the prefect to the military. On August 6 Balbo held a victory parade in the Piazza di Parma and during the course of the day his detachments left the city. After two failures he had won a resounding victory, which was not without influence on the course of events. Indeed it could already be said that there were two governments, at all events in the North: one *de jure* government in Rome which was nominally anti-Fascist and one *de facto* Fascist government, with which the local authorities were obliged to treat. It was a situation which might have spurred Mussolini to attempt to force the issue. But he continued to prefer more cautious tactics and, like the Duke of Plazatoro, to lead his army from behind.

Although Mussolini's position remained unassailable and the unity of the party was no longer in question, he was aware that Balbo bitterly resented his constant interference, and Bianchi was accordingly instructed to despatch a letter in Mussolini's name designed to smooth Balbo's ruffled feathers. After explaining why it had been necessary to suspend operations against the Republicans at Ravenna, he sought to attenuate the impact of the telephone message which had so annoyed Balbo at Parma. He concluded with a placatory message: "It is ridiculous that you should doubt my complete, unconditional, unlimited, fraternal confidence in you.

My confidence in you has no limits, just as there are no limits to my wishes for your welfare.[9]

While Balbo had been leading his Blackshirt cohorts from one city to another in Northeast Italy, similar incidents, though on a smaller scale, took place in many other towns in Piedmont, Lombardy, Tuscany, and the Marches. By the end of August Socialist resistance was broken, the Fascists were everywhere in the ascendant and, more important, it became evident that many elements in the army were well disposed to the movement thanks to Mussolini's resolve that there should be no clash with the troops. Thus it could be said that the conditions for a successful revolt already existed; and the more forward elements in the Party were eager for action, but Mussolini had not yet made up his mind. During the first eight months of 1922 he had played two roles. He was the leader of the revolutionary Blackshirts, over whom he maintained an unquestioned although possibly precarious authority, but he was also the journalist parliamentarian, who did not exclude the possibility of a constitutional solution. On the whole his instinct was to prefer the latter, less hazardous course and his conduct was designed to give himself for as long as possible the greatest possible liberty of maneuver.

V

In January, 1922, he had traveled to Cannes in order to cover the international conference for the *Popolo d'Italia*. There he was received by M. Briand and the interview was the occasion for an odd sartorial fashion, which he affected for some considerable time. Noticing that his shoes were so shabby as to create a bad impression on M. Briand, he covered them with a pair of white spats, which so delighted him that he continued to wear them in and out of season, even when reviewing Blackshirt parades. While he was at Cannes he had a curious conversation with Pietro Nenni, with whom he was united by temperamental affinity and by the ties of old friendship and common trials, although their respective paths had widely diverged. It was a sad, nostalgic conversation which led nowhere and only served to show that the views of the two men were now irreconcilable. Mussolini said that the civil war had been a tragic necessity, but that at a given moment he had had no hesitation in proclaiming that the time had come to break the sanguinary circle of violence. Nenni retorted that this move had isolated him in his own party. Mussolini replied that a great coalition between Fascists, Socialists, and Catholics was the only solution, but since no one wanted peace, it must be war. Nenni told him that his individualism had led him astray, that he had forgotten that he was once the leader of the Socialist party, and that it was now his voice which made Socialists the victims of the Fascist daggers. As dawn broke, the conversation ended on a hopeless note. "Your friends," said Mussolini, "must learn to understand me; I am ready for either peace or war." "The choice no longer rests with you," was Nenni's reply. "In that case it will be war," and on this somber note the two men parted.[10]

George Slocombe, correspondent of *The Daily Herald,* also met Mussolini at Cannes and gives an interesting account of the impression he then made. Mussolini was lodged in an old-fashioned hotel and was already protected by Fascist guards, who stood vigilantly at the door. Slocombe suspected in him a strong inferiority complex only mastered by a powerful will. In the course of a desultory conversation they talked of contemporary politics and of the theories of Sorel on violence. Lenin was the only contemporary for whom he would express respect, while for living Socialist leaders in France or elsewhere he showed indifference or contempt. Slocombe fell a victim to Mussolini's charm and seems to have preferred his rugged nationalism to the flabby intellectualism of the Italian Socialist leaders. After leaving Mussolini he told a prominent Italian colleague of his own conviction that the Fascist leader was destined to play an important role. "Mussolini?" the Italian journalist replied, "Nonsense, my dear fellow. A humbug. A poseur. A ridiculous charlatan." [11]

In March, 1922, Mussolini paid a visit to Berlin where he met, among others, Chancellor Wirth, Gustave Stresemann, and Walther Rathenau, who made a considerable impression on him. He was now beginning to move in international society, he was being treated as a person of some importance, and the result was to attenuate the revolutionary ardor of his youth. Like a man who has moved into a higher stratum of society, he was beginning to wonder whether loyalty to his old associations would be as profitable as conformity with the outlook of his new and more important acquaintances.

On his return to Milan he published an article in which he maintained, wrongly, that monarchist sentiment was still strong in Germany, and rightly that democracy and pacifism were but a mask. As a result of his visit he came to the conclusion that in the matter of reparations Italy should support Britain rather than France. On all other issues, however, he was bitterly hostile to Britain and British policy. In many speeches and articles over a considerable period he attacked British policy in Palestine and in Egypt; he complained of British egotism and the violation of Italian rights; he spoke of British decadence and voiced his innermost thoughts when he said: "The English are a bourgeois nation; we are a proletarian one." [12] He was of course appealing to a sense of Italian nationalism, but he came to be regarded in the British Embassy and elsewhere as something of an Anglophobe.

Meanwhile two events of domestic importance occurred. On January 22, 1922, Pope Benedict XV died. Mussolini took the opportunity to write that the Papacy represented the largest and the oldest empire in the world. At that moment men of every race in every continent were turning their eyes to Rome, a fact which could not be brushed aside by the lay world and which reflected the enormous spiritual power of Catholicism. Charlatan anticlericalism, he continued, was on the way out, for men still nourished the hope of another world and were inspired to take refuge from the miseries of life in an absolute faith.[13] He went down to St. Peter's in the hope of seeing the white smoke indicating that the conclave had made its choice, and when Pius XI was elected he expressed the belief that with this new Pope on the throne relations between Italy and the Vatican would improve.[14] All this was a far cry from the violence of his youthful anticlericalism, but two forces had been at work to bring about the change. His romanticism exulted in the glory of Rome of which the papacy was the principal symbol, and he realized that just as he could not risk a conflict with the army, so he could not afford to antagonize the Catholic Church.

VI

In February, 1922, the Bonomi government, weakened by the failure of the Banca di Sconto and the mounting economic crises, resigned. At the last moment a desperate effort was made by Signor Celli, a Reformist Socialist, and Signor Modigliani, one of the ablest tacticians in Parliament and a leader of the collaborationist fraction of the Socialist party, to commit the Chamber to a declaration in favor of a government which would concentrate towards the Left and would exclude the Right. Such a government would have been free without inhibitions to take energetic measures against the Fascists. But Mussolini, sensing the danger, skillfully defeated the maneuver by giving his own interpretation to Celli's motion and declaring that it contained nothing which could not be accepted by the whole Chamber. The motion was thus accepted virtually without opposition, but a subsequent Social Democratic motion expressing lack of confidence in the government was carried by a large majority. The only supporters of the government were the *Partito Popolare* and the reformist Socialists. There was thus no alternative for Bonomi but to tender the resignation of his cabinet to the King.

The fall of the government just before the Reparations Conference at Genoa, where Italy hoped to play an influential part, was ill received in the country. In Bologna and other cities crowds paraded, shouting: "Down with Parliament. Long live military dictatorship." The crisis lasted some time and the Fascist parliamentary group resolved not to participate in any government, even in a combination with right-wing tendencies, which had been proposed by Orlando in a private conversation with Mussolini. Eventually on February 25 Luigi Facta, one of Giolitti's followers and a man of weak character and mediocre talent, was entrusted with the formation of a new administration. The demonstrations against parliament, the length of the governmental crisis, and the character of Facta encouraged the Fascists to believe that their hour had struck. In an article in *Gerarchia,* a review which he founded in January, 1922, Mussolini repeated that the age of democracy had died during the war and that the world was now moving to the Right. New aristocracies were arising. Sensitive as ever to his environment Mussolini was reflecting the mounting tide of public dissatisfaction with the parliamentary regime.

In March, 1922, he returned from Berlin to deal with some party deviationists led by Piero Marsich and including a Major Cristoforo Baseggio. The ensuing altercation caused Bassegio to challenge Mussolini to a duel, which took place without any police intervention and resulted in a reconciliation after Mussolini had had the best of the encounter. Two months later in May he fought the last duel of his life with Mario Missivoli who, in a letter to D'Annunzio, had accused him of being in league with the landowners. The duel ended inconclusively without a reconciliation.

VII

On July 21, 1922, the Facta government fell. The immediate cause was his failure to deal with a Fascist demonstration at Cremona on July 13, when invading forces under Farinacci sacked the Socialist headquarters, occupied the municipal buildings, and burned the apartment of the *Popolare* Deputy Guido Miglioli. This outrage brought together in opposition to the government the Socialists and the *Popolare* who constituted a majority in the Chamber. The Fascists also voted against Facta, who was defeated by 392 to 103 votes. In the debate, in which Mussolini spoke for the last time as a backbencher, he declared that fascism which was fighting the government in the country could not support it in the Chamber. Fascism, he continued, might shortly have to state publicly whether it wished to be a constitutional party or a revolutionary party, in which latter case it could not form part of any governmental group or even feel obliged to sit in parliament. In consequence the problem of finding a new government only interested the Fascists up to a certain point. He concluded by saying that the Party had at its disposal large, well-disciplined, and well-organized forces.

If from this crisis a government emerges which resolves the urgent, anxious problem of the hour, that is to say the problem of pacification and of the normalization of relations between the various parties, we will happily accept it and we shall seek to bring our rank and file to recognize the need, deeply felt by the whole nation, for order, work, and discipline. But if perchance there emerges a reactionary government of violent anti-Fascist complexion, take note, gentlemen, that we shall react with the utmost energy and resolution. To reaction we shall reply by insurrection: I must in all frankness say that of the two eventualities I prefer the first on patriotic and humane grounds. I prefer that Fascism, which is a force which you Socialists can no longer ignore and still less think to destroy, should come to participate in the life of the State by legal means after preparing for a legal conquest of power. But there is also the other contingency to which in conscience I must refer. Each of you in the impending crisis, and in the discussions between your groups with a view to finding a solution, must take account of my declaration which I entrust to your meditation and to your conscience. I have finished.[15]

Fruitless negotiations took place between the King and the party leaders. Orlando was tried, then Bonomi, Meda of the *Popolare,* De Nava of the Liberal Democratic group, and finally Orlando for the second time. Mussolini would have been ready to join a cabinet of national union under Nitti or a less comprehensive coalition under Orlando, but every possible combination foundered on the stubborn refusal of the parties to abandon the positions in which each had entrenched itself. The mood of exasperation in the country was reflected by Pietro Nenni when he subsequently wrote of the moral collapse of parliament:

With but few exceptions the ruling class in Italy was morally decadent. It entirely failed to realise the perils threatening the country. Its mediocrity was such that it was incapable of rising above its petty quarrels and personal jealousies to a general view of the crisis. . . . The country demanded a man at the head of the government, and all it could offer was a grotesque and ridiculous puppet in the person of Signor Facta, a moral and physical caricature of authority. A fortnight of crisis and of coming and going from the Chamber to the Quirinal, from the Quirinal to the Chamber, of bombastic utterances and speeches, of orders of the day and polemics; a fortnight of palaver and ingenious attempts to combine ingredients so as to form a cabinet representing all party groups and sugbroups in equitable proportions, without any program whatsoever. . . . Such was the senseless idea of the parliamentarians, who were under the delusion that they were cleverness itself; they fed the flame they should have quenched. Wait and see. Such was the program of a majority which had no sense of its obligations, had no ideals and was staggering along the road to its last and definite defeat.[16]

After twelve days of classic parliamentary maneuver no solution could be found except to entrust Facta with the formation of yet another administration, the seventh that Italy had known in the short space of three years. The reappointment of this insignificant man proved to be the deathblow to the parliamentary system in Italy. Public opinion, already disturbed by the governmental crisis of February, felt frustrated by its renewal little more than four months later, and there was a growing conviction, which the Fascists did nothing to dispel, that a second weaker Facta government could not last long and that only a radical change would save the country.

The situation further was aggravated after Facta had been in office for only twenty-four hours. On August 1 the Socialist Labor Alliance proclaimed a general strike as a protest against Balbo's proceedings in Romagna and on the same day Mussolini, after mobilizing his *Fasci* from Rome, gave the government forty-eight hours in which to take action against public servants on strike, failing which he reserved liberty to adopt repressive measures. The government did nothing, but the Fascists with some public support were able to keep essential services running and in consequence the strike collapsed ignominiously on August 2. It was a notable success for the Fascists and a blow to the prestige of Facta and of constitutional authority. The reformist Socialists in their newspaper, *Giustizia,* on August 12 admitted the magnitude of the victory:

> We must have the courage to admit that the general strike proclaimed by the Alliance of Labor has been our Caporetto. We emerge from this test well beaten. We have played our last card and lost Milan and Genoa, which seemed the strongest card in our defence. In the Lombard capital the party newspaper has once more gone up in flames, the administration of the town has been snatched from its lawful representatives. . . . It is the same elsewhere. Every important center bears the marks of the Fascist hurricane. We must face facts: the Fascists are masters of the field. Nothing is to prevent them dealing more heavy blows in the certainty of winning fresh victories.[17]

The demoralization in the ranks of the Socialists was matched by the increasing self-confidence of the Fascists, who followed up their success by launching new attacks on the Socialists in Genoa, Leghorn, Parma, and Ancona. In Milan they once more destroyed the premises of *Avanti,* seized the town hall, and expelled the Socialist administration. Mussolini was still in Rome and in his absence the Fascist leaders invited D'Annunzio to appear on the balcony of the captured town hall to address the crowd. An effort was made by Mussolini's friends, who deprecated the reappearance of D'Annunzio on the public scene, to communicate with Mussolini in Rome, but he was nowhere to be found since he had disappeared on a sentimental adventure with a woman. Mortified by his failure to keep abreast of events, Mussolini as soon as he became available had no alternative but to draft a message to Milan expressing his pleasure at D'Annunzio's intervention and approving the operations of the Milan *Fascio.*

On August 6 *Avanti,* which had provisionally transferred publication to Turin after the destruction of its Milan office, published an article stating that the Fascists were planning an attack on Rome and accusing the government of inaction in the face of the danger. The *Corriere della Sera* ventilated the possibility that the Fascists would take advantage of the crisis of the parliamentary system and the strike organized by the Socialists to establish a dictatorship with the support of D'Annunzio. Rumors were in the air. But Mussolini did nothing to whip his followers up or to inspire terror in his opponents. On the contrary, he continued to temporize and hoped that with time he could create conditions still more favorable to himself. In an interview published in the *Mattino* of Naples on August 11 he said that the March on Rome was in a sense already in progress. He did not mean a march by some hundreds of thousands of armed Fascists. Such a march was strategically possible, but it was not yet politically inevitable. Fascism naturally wished to become the power in the state, but it was by no means certain that a *coup d'état* would be necessary to attain this objective. He had no confidence in the Facta government and favored new elections, which would return a parliament more representative of the will of the nation.[18]

In the six weeks which followed until he became Prime Minister Mussolini was torn between fear of launching a premature enterprise which might fail and the need to maintain his hold on the belligerent *Fasci,* who were stridently demanding immediate action. He knew that failure might irrevocably compromise his future and he had little confidence in the efficacy of revolutionary action.

On the other hand he could not afford to lose the support of the *Fasci,* whose leaders, drunk with victory, were now convinced that the parliamentary system would collapse at the first blast of their trumpets. The government nervelessly waited on events, while Mussolini also waited.

Mussolini's judgment was not at fault. As the week passed public opinion was becoming more and more exasperated at the state of the nation, and many who were not Fascists began to turn to Mussolini as the man of destiny. Even the army was disaffected, and on August 13 the prefect of Milan reported gloomily to the Minister of the Interior that the attitude of the military was not clear and that they could not be relied on in an emergency. By that date the Fascist movement had grown enormously. It was calculated that there were then a million Fascists in Italy, of whom about two hundred thousand were organized in the militia formations. This increase was due partly to the revulsion of feeling against parliament, partly to the success of the guerilla operations and partly to the skill with which the Fascists had lured hundreds of thousands of working men from the Socialist trade unions into the ranks of their labor organization, the so-called National Syndicates. The increasing political stature of Mussolini led to abortive conversations with Salandra, who wanted a government of the Right, led by himself, Mussolini, and Federzoni, the Nationalist leader; and with Facta, who never abandoned hope of yoking the Fascists to his chariot. But no means could be found of breaking the deadlock and Italy continued to live in an uneasy lull. Nothing could have suited Mussolini better.

CHAPTER SIX

The March on Rome

1922

I

THE weeks that preceded the March on Rome were for Mussolini a period of intense activity. He may be said to have opened his campaign on September 20 at Udine, where at a Fascist rally he made an important speech designed to impress the nation with his statesmanlike moderation and patriotism. He dealt at some length with the problems of violence and the monarchy, both of which were exercising public opinion. Violence, he declared, was not intrinsically immoral; it could be moral and necessary when it was used to resolve a cancerous situation. But violence without discipline and without reason must be repudiated; it should be adapted to the needs of the moment and not made a doctrine or a sport. He was not enamored with the masses and he did not believe in the democratic theory that the majority was always right. But the masses formed an integral part of the nation and the task of fascism must be to weld the nation into an organic whole which would work for the greatness of Italy. When they were asked what was their program, the answer was simple: they wished to govern Italy and it was not programs which were lacking but men and resolution. He then passed to the delicate topic of the monarchy and made it clear why he had abandoned republicanism. It was a question of political expediency. A great section of the country would view with suspicion a change in the governmental system which went so far as to threaten the monarchy. In fact it was possible to introduce radical reforms without bringing the throne into question and there was no reason to believe that the monarchy had any interest in obstructing the Fascist revolution. To a heckler who shouted "*Viva Mazzini*," he replied that Mazzini had not thought it inconsistent with his republican convictions to accept a unified Italy under a monarch. It was not his ideal, but one could not always achieve the ideal. Mussolini concluded on a high patriotic note. The Fascists did not intend to destroy everything, but merely to demolish the social-democratic superstructure of the past. The state they would create would not represent a party but the nation; it would embrace all, protect all, and oppose all who threatened its sovereignty. This was the state which would issue from the Italian victory of 1918 and would be the guarantor of Italy's greatness.[1]

In order to support Mussolini's effort to create an image of Fascist moderation, Bianchi in an interview published in the *Giornale d'Italia* on October 7 denied the imminence of a revolutionary stroke and said that in order to regularize the position the Fascists demanded new elections before the end of the year. Nevertheless, despite the caution of Mussolini and his spokesman, there was a general sense that the Fascists were surging forward on an irresistible tide, and at Cremona four days later Mussolini was received by shouts of "To Rome, to Rome." It was becoming more and more difficult to remain immobile. The country expected action and the Blackshirt leaders were resolved that there should be no further delay in mobilizing the *Fasci* for the revolutionary action which would bring the Party into power. Mussolini was infected by their optimistic enthusiasm and indeed he had no option but to go forward if he was to retain their loyalty.

In the month of October two events occurred which immediately paved the way for the so-called March on Rome. On October 16, 1922, Mussolini held a meeting in Milan at which the plans for military action were laid, and on October 24 the congress of the Fascist party was held at Naples. Of these events the Italian government was a helpless spectator; the only move it made was a tentative approach designed to lure Mussolini and some of his lieutenants into a coalition national government. Never did a nation and its government await the onslaught of a revolution with such complacent indifference.

Towards the end of September the Fascists, with the support of Nationalist elements, had occupied Bolzano and Trent, and on October 6 Mussolini had a conversation with Balbo at which the prospects of a march on Rome were ventilated and it was agreed to stage a second attack on Parma. But between October 6 and October 10, Mussolini began to take the view that the moment was ripe for action. In a conversation with Cesare Rossi he summed up his position as follows. Fascism was spreading everywhere and its opponents were not in a position to organize effective resistance. The *carabinieri* and gendarmerie, especially in the provinces, were well disposed and the army at the worst would be benevolently neutral. The Facta government would not fire on the Fascists and the monarchists were reassured by the Udine speech, which he would repeat more explicitly at Naples. Finally the parliamentarians had only one idea, namely to stand well with the Fascists. The black spots were Parma, D'Annunzio, the King, and the lack of discipline of the Fascists. Nevertheless D'Annunzio could be managed and there were elements around the King who could make him function.[2]

In the new circumstances Mussolini on October 11 instructed Balbo to suspend the Parma operation and instead to meet him at Milan on October 16. At the same time other Fascist commanders and two generals on the active list, Generals Fara and Ceccherini, were also summoned to the meeting, which was held in circumstances of great secrecy.

II

On October 16, 1922, those leaders of the Fascist party who had been summoned by Mussolini gathered at Milan in the premises of the local *Fascio* in the Via San Marco in order to review the situation. Bianchi said that after the recent Fascist victories the time had come to face the alternative of seizing power by legal means or by force. But Mussolini, who was in the chair, declared that while they were all agreed that fascism should become the government not in the interests of a party but of the nation, it was necessary to reflect deeply and to weigh imponderables before choosing between new elections and insurrection. Balbo, with the support of Bianchi, proposed that the Fascist militia should be reorganized under a unified command. This was approved and after some discussion it was decided to vest the command in a triumvirate composed of Balbo, De Vecchi, and General De Bono, a regular soldier who had recently retired from the command of the Army Corps at Verona.

As soon as Mussolini had opened the proceedings, De Bono at once objected to the presence of the two generals on the ground that they were not members of the Fascist militia and that its high command could not without danger be enlarged. Mussolini, however, replied that in the course of revolutionary action it would be useful to have generals in uniform at the head of insurgent groups; and he carried his point on the understanding that there would be no interference with the functions of the Fascist high command.

Having thus cleared the ground, Mussolini proceeded to make an appreciation of the position. Events, he declared, were threatening to run away with them, and fascism could be faced at any moment with the need to launch an insurrectionary movement. He thought that such a movement should converge on Rome, occupy the city, compel the government to surrender its powers, and induce the Crown to entrust them to a Fascist administration. He did not think a constitutional solution possible, but the current parliamentary maneuvers would serve to distract the attention of public opinion and of the government. He asked those present to say quite frankly whether they considered the Fascist military forces to be materially and morally ready for a revolutionary enterprise.

De Bono and De Vecchi expressed the view that the Fascists were not yet ready and that it would be advisable to wait for some time. Balbo on the other hand was disturbed at the recent turn of events and thought that any delay would be most dangerous. If the stroke were not attempted immediately, it would be too late in the spring, for in the warmth of Rome the Liberals and the Left would reach agreement and it would not be difficult for a new administration to take more energetic steps to deploy the police and the army against fascism. At the moment the Fascists enjoyed the advantage of the element of surprise; and it was better to act at once, even if preparations were not complete, rather than later when the enemy would also be more ready.

Mussolini said that he agreed with Balbo. Nevertheless he refused to commit himself to an immediate decision and ruled merely that the insurrectionary movement should be launched as soon as a favorable opportunity arose. He proposed that consideration of the date should be deferred until after the Fascist congress at Naples on October 24.

The meeting then passed to an examination of ways and means. Mussolini thought that there should be three large concentrations of Fascist formations in Emilia, Tuscany, and the Marches which would march to Rome on converging roads. De Bono and De Vecchi, with the support of Generals Fara and Ceccherini, pleaded that so long a march down half the length of Italy would compromise the success of the enterprise. Balbo on the other hand said that experience had shown that it was possible to concentrate Fascist forces by despatching them in small detachments to the selected point. He proposed that places close to Rome should be chosen and that the Fascist forces should be instructed to proceed there by normal or special methods of transport, according to the circumstances. It was accordingly decided that three columns should be concentrated: one close to Civitavecchia, composed of forces from Tuscany, Liguria, and northern Italy; one close to Monterotondo, for the forces from Emilia, Venice and Lombardy; and one at Tivoli, for the forces from the Marches, the Abruzzi, Lazio, and the South.

As regards the location of the headquarters and the reserves it was agreed that subject to investigation and report by Balbo the former should be at Perugia and the latter at Foligno. Finally Mussolini declared that as soon as the military action began the party leadership would surrender full power to a quadrumvirate composed of the three Blackshirt commanders, De Bono, De Vecchi and Balbo, to whom would be added Michele Bianchi, the secretary of the Party. He then produced the following draft proclamation to be signed by the quadrumvirate and not by himself:

Fascists, Italians!

The hour of the decisive battle has struck. Four years ago the national army at about this time launched the supreme offensive which led it to victory. Today the army of the Blackshirts grasps that mutilated victory and, moving resolutely on Rome leads her back to the glory of the Capitol. Today leaders and legionaries have been mobilized. The martial law of fascism has been put into force. By order of the Duce the military, political, and administrative functions of the party leadership have been vested in a secret quadrumvirate with dictatorial powers.

The army, the last reserve and safeguard of the nation, must not take part in the struggle. Fascism renews an expression of its deep admiration for the army of Vittoria Veneto. Nor does fascism march against the members of the public administration, but against a class of imbecile and weak-minded politicians, who for four long years have not known how to give a government to the nation. The classes which constitute the productive bourgeoisie know that fascism wishes to impose discipline only on the nation as a whole and to give aid to all those forces which advance its economic expansion and well-being.

The working classes, those in the fields and in the factories, the transport workers and the clerks have nothing to fear from Fascist rule. Their just rights will be loyally preserved. We shall be generous to our unarmed adversaries; to the others we shall be ruthless.

Fascism draws its sword to cut the many Gordian knots which enmesh and strangle Italian life. We call upon Almighty God and on the spirits of our five hundred thousand dead to witness that only one impulse moves us, only one desire unites us, only one passion inflames us: to contribute to the salvation and to the greatness of our country.

Fascists of all Italy!

Summon your spirit and your strength. We must conquer. We shall conquer.

Long live Italy. Long live fascism.

The Quadrumvirate.

After undertaking to observe complete secrecy as to the plans that had been laid, the meeting broke up in a mood of high exaltation. It seemed as if power lay at last within their grasp. Mussolini himself was now more than ever impressed with the need for speed. The feeble Facta government might be replaced by a stronger administration and the forcible eviction of D'Annunzio from Fiume was fresh in his mind. Public opinion which was moving his way might at any moment veer, and he could not be certain that his relations with well-disposed elements in the army would not be compromised by his ebullient Blackshirts. In a word the omens were favorable and while his position could not be expected to improve significantly in the near future, it might very quickly deteriorate. "If Giolitti returns to power," he said, "we are done for." [3] Nevertheless he adhered to his decision to take no irrevocable step before the party congress at Naples on October 24.

He was, however, more solidly committed to the enterprise than prudence counseled and he resolved to reduce its risks to a minimum. Skill was required to allay suspicion and to forestall preventive measures by his adversaries, to gain allies, and to ensure the neutrality of the armed forces. During the three weeks to come he neglected no step to protect his position. His first move was to conciliate D'Annunzio, whose equivocal attitude had been causing him anxiety. In order to effect this he made an apparently massive, but in reality illusory, concession in the matter of the Federation of Maritime Workers. This union had placed itself under D'Annunzio's protection and had made him valuable gifts of cash. After the Fascist conquest of Genoa, however, the local leaders demanded its liquidation and its replacement by the Fascist union, the National Maritime Corporation. Mussolini resolved the threatening conflict by an agreement with D'Annunzio in which he undertook within thirty days to dissolve the Fascist union. The agreement, unpopular as it was in Fascist circles, brought Mussolini substantial advantages. It flattered D'Annunzio, it assured him of the support of the Federation of Maritime Workers, and involved no onerous commitments. It did not come into force for thirty days and before they were past the March on Rome or the constitutional seizure of power would have taken place. By then he would have no further need of D'Annunzio and he could destroy the pact if it proved inconvenient.

Meanwhile Mussolini had also been conducting negotiations with Giolitti through Alfredo Lusignoli, the prefect of Milan. Giolitti was only prepared to offer the Fascists a modest participation in an administration led by himself, but Mussolini for tactical reasons deliberately prolonged the negotiation by pitching his demands higher and higher at each stage. In an interview given to *The Manchester Guardian* he sought to prepare and to placate foreign opinion. Fascism, he declared, which only desired peace and reconstruction, was now for the third time rendering a service to Europe after

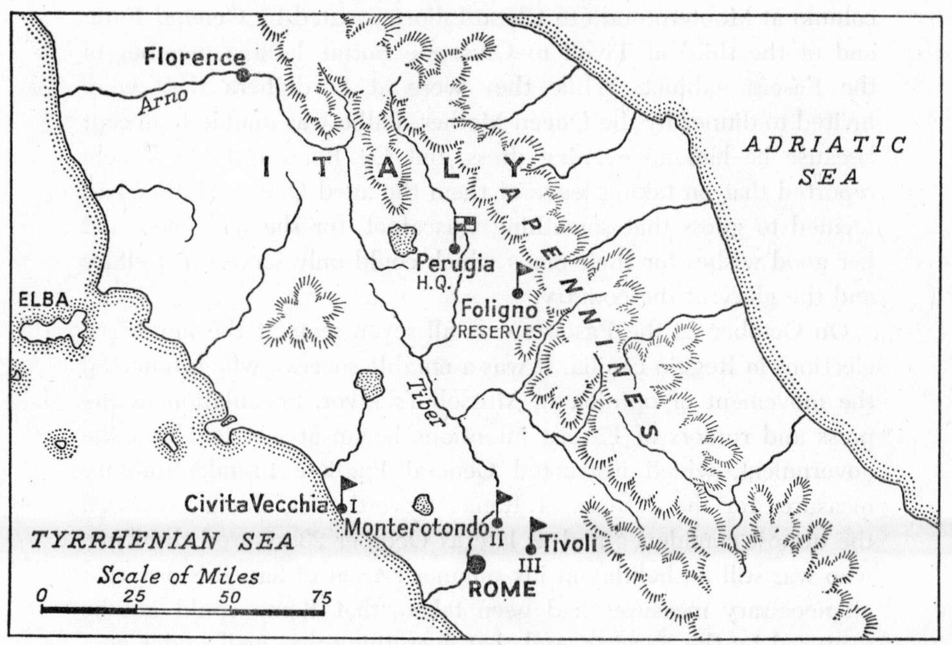

The Fascist deployment for the March on Rome.

supporting intervention and suppressing bolshevism. They were proposing to impose new elections on a feeble, inefficient government and only if they failed would they proceed to more energetic action. When fascism was in power, the Blackshirts would remain at the disposal of the new government to protect the nation. The party stood for collaboration between all classes; the rights of the workers; friendship with all countries, subject to the maintenance of Italy's rights; liberty for all, subject to the nation's interests; reduction in public expenditure; greater production; and the balancing of the budget. Finally in the new government the Fascists would demand the portfolios of the Interior, Foreign Affairs, War, Navy, and Labor.

While Mussolini was engaged on these political maneuvers, Balbo, De Bono, and De Vecchi met at Bordighera to elaborate their plans for the March on Rome. They decided to entrust the command of the first column near Civitavecchia (Santa Marinella) to Perrone Compagni, assisted by General Ceccherini; of the second column at Monterotondo to Ulisse Igliori, assisted by General Fara; and of the third at Tivoli to Giuseppe Bottai, later a member of the Fascist cabinet. While they were at Bordighera they were invited to dinner by the Queen Mother. Balbo was unable to accept because he had no evening dress, but De Bono and De Vecchi reported that on taking leave of them the aged Queen Mother had seemed to guess that something was afoot, for she had expressed her good wishes for their plans which could only serve the welfare and the glory of the country.

On October 22 the Fascists won all seven seats at the municipal elections in Reggio Emilia. It was a notable success, which reflected the movement of opinion in Mussolini's favor. Speculation in the press and rumors of Fascist intentions began at last to alarm the government, which instructed General Pugliese to take military measures for the defense of Rome. Nevertheless, Facta professed the utmost confidence and as late as October 23 assured the King, who was still on holiday at his summer retreat of San Rossore, that all necessary measures had been taken, that Rome could not be captured by the Fascists, and that everything was well under control.

III

This was the situation when on the morning of October 23 Mussolini himself arrived at Rome from Milan on his way to Naples. During his few hours in the capital he had a brief, inconclusive conversation with Salandra, in the course of which he demanded the immediate resignation of the Facta government and the award of five portfolios to the Fascists in the new government. He was still behaving as if he had not abandoned hope of collaborating with other parties in the existing parliamentary system, but the improvement in his own position and the fumbling incompetence of the government encouraged him to stiffen his terms and to state them with increasing self-assurance.

That afternoon he left Rome for Naples, which he reached in the evening. On the following day he made his speech to the party congress. It was an aggressive speech, which reflected the influences which were being brought to bear upon him. The enthusiastic welcome of thousands of young men ardent for action, the impression of power created by their assembly at Naples, the irresolution of the government which he had scented during his brief sojourn in Rome, the atmosphere of expectancy in the nation at large, and the nagging fear that he might miss his best opportunity spurred him forward to the brink. But there he stopped, for he intended to give the government one last chance to meet his demands. He was more confident than he had ever been before and it was common sense rather than cowardice which counseled him to prefer the certainty of a negotiated compromise to the hazards of an insurrection.

In his speech Mussolini recalled that the problem facing them was to choose between legality and a parliamentary success on the one hand, and insurrection on the other, since by one or other of these methods fascism was determined to obtain power. He had demanded new elections and five portfolios as well as the Commissariat of Aviation, but all he had received was the derisory offer of a few places in the government without portfolio. The Fascists, however, were not prepared to enter the portals of power by the tradesmen's entrance and to sell their birthright for a miserable bowl of ministerial pottage. Consequently the problem was now one of force, and strength resided in the disciplined formations of the Fascist legions.

As regards the issue of the monarchy, there was no doubt that Italian unity rested on the royal House of Savoy; and it was certain that the Italian monarchy, having regard to its history and traditions, would not seek to arrest the strongly flowing current of national opinion. The Fascists did not even intend to liquidate parliament, even though the public might eventually tire of this plaything. The army also should remember that it was the Fascists who came to its defense when it was betrayed by the ministers. Finally he promised that the Fascists would be a national party which would bring an end to the civil war which was tormenting the nation.[4]

In the afternoon Mussolini reviewed 40,000 Fascists, who marched past in the Piazza del Plebiscito. Addressing them he said:

Today without striking a blow we have conquered the soul of Naples and of the whole of Southern Italy. The demonstration is an end in itself and cannot become a battle. But I assure you in all solemnity that the hour has struck. Either they give us the government or we shall take it, by falling on Rome. Now it is a matter of days or hours. It is necessary that you should return promptly to your homes in order that our action may be simultaneous and that in every part of Italy we should be in a position to take by the throat the miserable political dominating class. I guarantee and swear to you that the orders, if they are necessary, will reach you.

These were menacing words, but Facta simply because there had been no disturbance of public order at Naples felt that the danger had passed and telegraphed to the King: "I believe that the prospect of a March on Rome has faded away. Nevertheless the greatest vigilance should be maintained."[5] In reality that night Mussolini met the *Quadrumviri* and other leaders in the Hotel Vesuvio at Naples to make the final arrangements for the March on Rome. It was agreed that the political leaders of the party should hand over their powers to the Quadrumvirate at midnight on October 26. The aim of the movement must be the seizure of power with a cabinet including at least six Fascist ministers in the most important posts. Secret mobilization was fixed for October 27, and on October 28 action was to be taken against local objectives such as prefectures, police stations, post offices, radio stations, anti-Fascist newspapers and clubs, and trade union premises. Once the towns were conquered there was to be a concentration of the Fascist formations on the three selected points. Where the conquest of a town was impossible or doubtful, no assault should be attempted and every single available Fascist should be despatched to the concentration points. On the morning of October 28 the three columns would together advance on the capital. In the event of resistance by the armed forces every effort should be made to avoid a conflict with the army, which should be treated with marks of sympathy and respect; no offer of help by the troops should be accepted. Work would be suspended throughout Italy and all towns would display the national flag.[6]

Having laid down these plans, Mussolini brought the meeting to a close. Outside the hotel the town was festively illuminated and in the early hours of the autumn morning parties of Blackshirts still roamed the streets, triumphantly singing their Fascist songs and shouting: "*A Roma, a Roma.*" In his hotel room Mussolini was receiving General Federico Baistrocchi, commanding the Naples district, who called with the welcome tidings that the army formations in the South looked with great sympathy on fascism and its Duce.

IV

On October 25 Mussolini in secrecy left Naples for Milan. Many of the militia commanders also went home to prepare the mobilization of their local units, but the congress continued to sit largely for the purpose of deception. Nothing occurred of any note except an intervention by Grandi, the former activist, who now declared himself opposed to insurrection. Despite his views, he was nominated Chief of Staff to the Fascist high command at Perugia, a circumstance which did not deter him from continuing to explore the possibility of a parliamentary arrangement.

After an all-night sitting, the congress dispersed on October 26. Mussolini was at Milan, the Fascist commanders with a few exceptions were at their posts, the final plans were laid. Everything seemed in order, but in fact the next five days were a period of extreme confusion both in Rome and in the Fascist camp. On both sides efforts, some of them uncoordinated and unauthorized, were still being made to find a compromise which would exorcise the peril of a Fascist stroke. The government, which had feared that the Fascists would march on Rome from Naples, now believed that the danger had passed, a comforting illusion which gave their dilatory negotiations no sense of urgency. Salandra, who proposed to lead a new administration with Fascist participation, hoped to forestall a similar move by Giolitti and called on Facta on October 26 to advise him to resign. Facta, who was contemplating the prolongation of his own government's life with the inclusion of some Fascists, telephoned to the prefect of Milan to inquire how Mussolini's negotiations with Giolitti were progressing. While these traditional transactions were pursuing their languid course, the Fascists were playing their part in the political game. De Vecchi, after urging that the King should return, called on Salandra to inform him that unless Facta were dismissed the Fascist assault would be launched. The Facta cabinet met in the afternoon and decided not to resign, but to place their portfolios in the Prime Minister's hands in order that he should be free to reconstruct the government if need be. It was also agreed that the King should be invited to return to the capital from San Rossore. Thus the whole day was frittered away.

On October 27 the prefect of Milan telephoned to Facta that Giolitti intended to reach agreement with Mussolini and that the latter was expected shortly at the prefecture for discussions. At almost the same time Mussolini telephoned to Salandra to inquire whether, if Facta resigned, he would consent to form the new government. Salandra, anxious for a combination with the Fascists, invited Mussolini to come to Rome, but Mussolini, who was in a strong position and preferred to be courted from a distance, replied that he must remain in Milan. Meanwhile De Vecchi and Grandi, who should have been at Perugia, remained in Rome and continued to press Salandra to find a solution which would put a stop to the imminent Fascist move. But Salandra could only reply that he was powerless so long as Facta remained in office; and Facta was doing all he could to keep Salandra and Giolitti out while he negotiated some arrangement whereby he could remain Prime Minister in a new administration composed of Mussolini and other Fascists. Despite the gravity of the hour, he was still intent on playing the old conventional game of parliamentary combinations.[7]

In Rome Michele Bianchi was becoming anxious lest Mussolini might be lured into some coalition arrangement. Ot 2:40 P.M. he telephoned to Rossi at Milan to seek reassurance. Both Rossi and Aldo Finzi, who was also at Milan, replied that no concessions would be made and that the plan laid down at Naples would be executed. But Rossi said there might be a delay of a day or two for purely tactical reasons. At 3 A.M. Bianchi, disturbed at Rossi's reservation put through a call to Mussolini and the following conversation took place:

Bianchi: Benito . . .

Mussolini: What is it, Michelino?

Bianchi: I and my friends want to know what instructions you have for us.

Mussolini: Instructions from me?

Bianchi: Yes. What is the latest news?

Mussolini: The latest is this: Lusignoli has been to Cavour [to see Giolitti] and says that it is possible to extract from Giolitti four important portfolios and four undersecretaryships.

Bianchi: What would these portfolios be?

Mussolini: Marine, Treasury, Agriculture, Colonies. There would be War, which would be given to one of our friends, and finally the four undersecretaries.

Bianchi: And then?

Mussolini: Then he sent me a telephone message from Cavour that he would be back at 9 o'clock this morning.

Bianchi: Benito . . .

Mussolini: Yes?

Bianchi: Benito, do you want my opinion? Will you hear my firm, irrevocable advice?

Mussolini: Yes, yes.

Bianchi: Reply, no.

Mussolini: Of course. The machine has now been put in motion and nothing can stop it.

Bianchi: The die has been cast. There is now no longer any case for discussing the portfolios.

Mussolini: Of course.

Bianchi: Then we are in agreement. May I also communicate this in your name?

Mussolini: Wait. Let us first hear what Lusignoli has to say. Tomorrow we can discuss it again.

Bianchi: Very well.

Mussolini: Yes, because thus you will be brought up to date. I will tell you the report Lusignoli makes to me.

Bianchi: Good.[8]

Meanwhile during the course of October 27 the Fascist mobilization was in full swing and, despite all efforts to keep movements secret, alarming reports poured into Rome of concentrations in a number of provincial cities. The cabinet met and after a long debate decided to resign. In the evening Facta called on the King, who had returned to Rome, and formally tendered the resignation of the government. He spoke of the need to defend Rome and suggested the proclamation of a state of siege, but the King thought that it would be wise to postpone so extreme a measure.

At Perugia, Balbo, Bianchi, and De Bono were installed in the

Hotel Brufani close to the prefecture, which had been seized without bloodshed. The troops were confined to barracks and the town was completely under the control of the Fascist militia, which had poured in from many provincial centers. In view of the fact that Facta's resignation fulfilled one of the demands put forward by the Fascists, the Quadrumvirate thought it prudent to await developments and to suspend all action for twenty-four hours. Instructions to this effect were sent to Farinacci at Cremona, but he at once telephoned to Mussolini at Milan protesting that military action had been started and could not now be halted without risk of disaster. Mussolini purported to agree, but in fact the original plan to make a concerted move at midnight on October 27/28 was not completely executed and there were only sporadic outbreaks of Fascist violence, principally in areas not under the direct control of the Quadrumvirate, who were somewhat isolated in Perugia. Moreover they were still deprived of the presence of De Vecchi, busy huckstering in Rome. It was a situation of the utmost confusion.

Mussolini, who was concerned to ensure that the party leaders should not coalesce against him, had despatched Count Costanzo Ciano to Rome with instructions for further negotiations. It was a purely tactical move. Ciano was to demand as a minimum the portfolios of the Interior, Justice, War, Labor, and Education or Public Works and the dissolution of the Chamber. At the same time in order to keep up the pressure he made arrangements to publish the proclamation of the *Quadrumviri* in the *Popolo d'Italia* on the following day. But before Ciano could reach Rome to carry out his instructions events occurred which hopelessly compromised Facta's position.

V

During the night of October 27/28 Facta's principal private secretary remained on duty to deal with the information flowing into the Prime Minister's office, for although Facta had resigned, his cabinet remained in charge of affairs pending the appointment of a successor. As the night wore on, reports were received of the seizure of post offices, of fraternization between Fascists and army units who were handing over arms, of requisitioned trains which were carrying armed formations in the direction of the capital. At about 3:30 A.M. Bianchi telephoned from Perugia to say that nothing could now stop the Fascist machine and that he hoped that Facta would not cause Italian blood to be shed. In view of the mounting gravity of this intelligence Facta had been alerted at about 3 A.M., and at 5 A.M. on October 28 he held an emergency meeting of his cabinet. It was decided, thanks to the insistence of the Minister of the Interior and against Facta's inclination, to proclaim a state of siege at noon. The proclamation was drafted on the spot, printed, and affixed to the walls of Rome by 8:30 A.M. The army commander was instructed to use every means to prevent the access of Fascists to the city and the prefects were ordered to maintain order and to arrest immediately all disturbers of the peace.

The Prime Minister repaired at once to the Villa Savoia in order to obtain the Sovereign's signature to the proclamation. The King, however, refused to sign. Several factors contributed to his decision. He had during the preceding night received Generals Diaz and Pecori Giraldi, who had expressed the view that the military would do their duty, but that it would be well not to put them to the test.[9] The King had also received unconfirmed but circumstantial reports that the Duke of Aosta and certain army leaders were in league with the Fascists; and he had no intention of imperiling his throne in order to make way for the Duke whom he disliked. In any event he was tired of the antics of the politicians and had no reason to plunge the country into civil war to suit their convenience; and if these considerations were not enough to sway his judgment, he had seen enough of Facta to have no confidence whatever in his ability to make effective use of any extraordinary powers he might be given. The King reached the conclusion that a conflict must be avoided at all costs and bluntly told Facta that he was not prepared to accede to his request.

Facta returned to announce to his dismayed colleagues the failure of his mission. There was a general, well-founded impression that he had not presented his case with much vigor or conviction. He had admitted to the King that after his own resignation his government could have little authority; he deprecated bloodshed and he expressed the hope that Mussolini would prove reasonable.* In any event the cabinet later in the day despatched their reluctant Prime Minister to see the King for the second time in order to extract his signature. Once more the Prime Minister came back disconsolately with the news that the King had categorically refused. This decision, which involved the withdrawal of the proclamation and of the instructions to the military and the prefects, was a fatal blow to the government. It meant in effect that the forces at the government's disposal would not be used against the Fascist columns concentrating around Rome, and it thus opened the portals of power to Mussolini and the Fascists. It only remained to negotiate the terms of surrender, a matter on which many people had many different views. But Mussolini, who had throughout used every expedient to avoid or postpone an armed clash, now felt secure from that peril and was emboldened to be intransigent.

The day of October 28 was spent in consultations. Like ants scurrying hither and thither on a disturbed antheap, men ran around Rome in the search for a formula. Federzoni after seeing the King telephoned to Mussolini at Milan to say that he was in touch with Salandra and begged Mussolini to come to Rome, where he was required for conversations at the Palace. Mussolini replied that he was unable to leave Milan. Costanzo Ciano arrived in Rome and, although his instructions had clearly been overtaken by events, called on Salandra to present Mussolini's demand for five portfolios. Meanwhile the King was interviewing all the members of the old gang except Giolitti, who on Facta's disingenuous advice had stayed in the country. He also received De Vecchi, the self-appointed Fascist spokesman in Rome. The upshot of these interminable consultations was a decision reached by the King in the evening to entrust Salandra with the formation of a government. Salandra at once received Ciano, De Vecchi, Grandi, and Federzoni to inform them of his plan, namely the formation of a government of the Right with the participation of Mussolini. The Fascist representatives decided to recommend their solution by telephone to Mussolini, who dryly replied: "It was not worthwhile mobilizing

* Sforza, *op. cit.*, p. 257. According to Marcello Soleri, Facta even advised the King not to sign (see Chabod, *op. cit.*, p. 59), on the ground that it would have led to a conflict between the army and the Fascists.

the Fascist army, causing a revolution, killing people, for the sake of a Salandra–Mussolini solution. I will not accept"; and they heard the click of the replaced receiver.[10]

All these maneuvers were as unreal as the proceedings of the Doenitz government at Flensburg during the closing days of the Second World War. Mussolini, fortified by the obvious disarray in Rome and by the knowledge that he would not be opposed by the army, was now determined not to serve under Salandra or any other politician. He had already neutralized the prefect of Milan by slyly showing him a bogus list of prospective Fascist ministers on which he figured as Minister of the Interior. Assured of the prefect's protection he could afford to bide his time. Accordingly, when General Cittadini, the King's aide-de-camp, telephoned at De Vecchi's behest to invite him to Rome, Mussolini replied that the time was past for consultations or ministerial combinations. He did not intend to leave Milan unless he were formally entrusted with the formation of a government. To a similar message from Salandra he sent the same reply. Thus the day of October 28 ended seemingly in a deadlock, but Mussolini had in fact already won the battle, a victory which he gleefully reported in a message to D'Annunzio: "The latest news crowns our triumph. Tomorrow Italy will have a government. We shall be discreet and intelligent enough not to abuse our victory. I am sure that you will greet it as the happy culmination of the renewal of our Italian youth." [11]

On October 29 Mussolini published in the *Popolo d'Italia* his last article written in the capacity of a journalist:

> This is the situation. The greater part of northern Italy is in the hands of the Fascists. Central Italy—Tuscany, Umbria, the Marches, Alto Lazio—is occupied by the Blackshirts. Where the police headquarters and the prefectures have not been taken by assault, the Fascists have occupied stations and post offices, which are the nerve centers of the nation. The political authority—a little surprised and much dismayed—has not been able to cope with the movement, because a movement of this character cannot be contained and still less broken. A tremendous victory is in sight, with the almost unanimous approval of the nation. But victory is not to be mutilated by eleventh hour combinations. It was really not worth the trouble of mobilizing merely in order to reach a deal with Salandra. The government must have a clear Fascist character.

Fascism will not abuse its victory, but is determined that it shall not be diminished. Let that be clear to all. Nothing shall disturb the beauty and the ardor of our offensive. The Fascists have been and are admirable. Their self-sacrifice is great and must be crowned by complete victory. Any other solution is to be rejected. Let the men of Rome understand that the hour has come to finish with the old conventional procedures, which have on countless occasions in less grave circumstances been discarded. Let them understand that up to the present moment a solution of the crisis can be still obtained within the framework of the most orthodox constitutionalism, but that tomorrow it may perhaps be too late. Some politicians in Rome show a lack of perception which oscillates between the grotesque and palsied helplessness. Let them decide. Fascism wants power and will have it.[12]

VI

Mussolini's assessment was proved correct and his self-confidence was justified by the events of October 29. In the early hours of the morning a second effort was made by telephone to induce Mussolini to enter a Salandra administration, a course still favored by Ciano, Grandi, and De Vecchi, but he curtly refused. A few hours later the three Fascist leaders informed Salandra of their failure; and shortly afterwards Senator Albertini telephoned from Milan that an ugly situation was developing in the streets and he advised that no further time should be lost in entrusting Mussolini with the formation of a government.

Salandra was now convinced that his own plan to form a government had broken down and later in the morning he formally apprised the King that his efforts had failed. In these circumstances and under advice from prominent politicians and industrialists in Milan, he advised the King to call upon Mussolini. De Vecchi was immediately summoned to the Palace and the King instructed him to invite Mussolini to come to Rome to receive the appointment of Prime Minister. The confusion, which had attended each successive move during the preceding three days, persisted to the end. It was now impossible to communicate with Mussolini for the simple reason that he could not be traced either at his office or at home. Rachele Mussolini describes how when the telephone rang in the flat, she ran to answer it because Benito was out. "I heard the voice of the operator and then a masculine voice who asked for my husband. I answered: 'He is not here. You will find him at the *Popolo d'Italia.*' I am about to give the number when the voice interrupts: 'He is not there either; we want to know where to find him. It is a most urgent matter; it is the Palace speaking.' 'But I don't know where he has gone,' I reply. Later they telephone again. This time it is the King's aide-de-camp himself, who insists on finding Mussolini. I told him that I did not know. Where could Benito be? Later he telephoned himself and concluded: 'Yes, I have made contact with the Palace. Pack my bag with some things and a suit. I have to travel to Rome!"

Mussolini, however, was not prepared to rely on a telephone message. He wished to be certain that a definite decision had been taken and that he would not be trapped into further negotiations or, still worse, handed over to his enemies. He had therefore stipulated that before actually leaving Milan he must receive a telegram from General Cittadini confirming that the King intended to appoint him Prime Minister. He knew that oral messages were not reliable and he was determined that there should be no last-minute hitch after his arrival in Rome. The telegram duly arrived at about noon and Mussolini, turning to his brother Arnaldo, exclaimed: "If only our father were alive."

There was no immediately available train to Rome and Mussolini spent the afternoon clearing up his affairs. He prepared a special edition of the *Popolo d'Italia* and transferred control of the newspaper to his brother Arnaldo. He saw Cesare Rossi and gave him instructions for the scientific destruction of the premises of *Avanti* and *Giustizia.* The good news was communicated to the Fascist headquarters at Perugia and to the local militia units. He said farewell to Rachele and the children and in the evening left for Rome by train. At the station large numbers of Fascists were on the platform to give him an enthusiastic welcome. To the stationmaster, who was in attendance, he said: "I want to leave exactly on time. From now on everything has got to function perfectly." Lady Sybil Graham, wife of the British ambassador in Rome, who happened to be traveling by the same train, witnessed both the Duce's triumphant departure and the birth of the myth of Fascist punctuality on the Italian railway system. At 9:30 in the morning the train stopped at Civitavecchia, where Mussolini alighted to review some of the Fascist militia who were concentrated there. An hour later he reached Rome and, still wearing his black shirt, drove to the Quirinal where the King formally entrusted him with the formation of a government. It was a cordial meeting and the friendly reception given to the new Prime Minister only reflected the general sense of relief throughout the country at the peaceful end of the crisis. To Vittorio Solaro del Borgo, one of his gentlemen-in-waiting, the King expressed his satisfaction: "I seem, Solaro, to have come out of a long nightmare. I know that Orlando, Salandra, Giolitti, all the leaders and the best men in the country are pleased. Look, I have here thousands of telegrams from all over Italy and elsewhere which have arrived at the Quirinal to tell me that I have done well." He went on to say that he had rightly refused to sign Facta's proclamation in order to save a government of poltroons; and when Solaro asked him what impression he had of his new Prime Minister, he replied: "He is really a man of purpose and I can tell you that he will last some time. There is in him, if I am not mistaken, the will to act and to act well. When I told him to put together an administration on a broad basis and with capable men, I felt that he agreed and was close to my views. I had previously formed quite a different impression of him." [13]

Having accepted the task of forming a new administration, Mussolini undertook in the course of the day to submit his list of ministers. Then with the King he appeared on the balcony of the Palace to be cheered by an enthusiastic crowd. Rome was in a holiday mood and few critical voices were raised from any quarter. At about 7 P.M. Mussolini returned to the Palace in a borrowed frock coat to present the following list of ministers:

Benito Mussolini *	President of the Council (Fascist) Interior Foreign Affairs (*ad interim*)
Senator General Armando Diaz	War (Nonparty)
Senator Admiral Paolo Thaon di Revel	Marine (Nonparty)

* These men were already deputies in the Chamber.

Luigi Federzoni *	Colonies (Nationalist)
Aldo Oviglio *	Justice (Fascist)
Alberto de Stefani *	Finance (Fascist)
Vincenzo Tangorra *	Treasury (*Popolare*)
Professor Giovanni Gentile	Education (Nationalist)
Gabriello Carnazza *	Public Works (Social Democrat)
Giuseppe de Capitani d'Arzaso *	Agriculture (Liberal)
Senator Teofilo Rossi	Industry and Commerce (Democrat)
Stephano Cavazzoni *	Labor and Social Welfare (*Popolare*)
Giovanni Colonna di Cesaro *	Posts and Telegraphs (Social Democrat)
Giovanni Giuriati *	Liberated Provinces (Fascist)

Undersecretaries

Giacomo Acerbo *	Presidency (Fascist)
Aldo Finzi *	Interior (Fascist)
Ernesto Vassallo *	Foreign Affairs (*Popolare*)
Carlo Bonardi *	War (Social Democrat)
Costanzo Ciano *	Marine (Fascist)
Alfredo Rocco *	Treasury (Nationalist)
Cesare Maria de Vecchi *	Military Pensions (Fascist)
Pietro Lissia *	Finance (Social Democrat)
Giovanni Marchi *	Colonies (Liberal)
Umberto Merlin *	Liberated Territories (*Popolare*)
Fulvio Milani *	Justice (*Popolare*)
Dario Lupi *	Education (Fascist)
Luigi Siciliani *	Fine Arts (Nationalist)
Ottavio Corgini *	Agriculture (Fascist)
Alessandro Sardi *	Public Works (Fascist)
Michele Terzaghi *	Posts and Telegraphs (Fascist)
Giovanni Gronchi *	Industry and Commerce (*Popolare*)
Silvio Gai *	Labor and Social Welfare (Fascist)

It was a moderate cabinet of national concentration. Of the fourteen ministers there were only four Fascists and only nine among

* These men were already deputies in the Chamber.

the eighteen undersecretaries. Mussolini explains that he discarded the idea of a purely Fascist administration because he wished to give the country the impression of a normal life far from the selfish exclusiveness of a single party.[14] This was true up to a point, but he had other grounds for acting as he did. He intended to govern through parliament and there were few Fascists who possessed either parliamentary or administrative experience. Of the four *Quadrumviri* only De Vecchi received office; while Grandi, who had long been a prominent leader in Bologna and possessed the necessary intellectual qualities, was excluded because of Mussolini's annoyance at his behavior in Rome at the time when he was seeking to promote a coalition with Salandra. He was not the only disappointed Fascist and the fact that Mussolini was able to construct a government on so broad a basis was a measure of the personal ascendancy which he had been able to re-establish in the party.

VII

He deserved his position, for it was he who had been in control throughout, whereas the Quadrumvirate had in reality exercised none of the powers which had nominally passed into its hands. The mobilization had been arranged at Naples, but the headquarters at Perugia was out of touch and unable to control its fortunes. Indeed one member of the Quadrumvirate, De Vecchi, and its chief of staff, Grandi, had detached themselves in order to conduct independent negotiations in Rome with a view to promoting the formation of a Salandra government, while De Bono, Bianchi, and Balbo at Perugia were issuing a statement to the effect that the only acceptable solution was a Mussolini cabinet. At the critical moment it was Mussolini who rejected the proposal for a Salandra government without any reference to the Quadrumvirate; nor did he at any time consult them about the composition of his government. Thus the supreme command at Perugia came to an end without having commanded anything.

The mobilization and concentration of the Fascist formations were equally ineffective. By the morning of October 28 there were only some 4,000 men under Perrone Compagni in the Civitavecchia area without quarters, little food, or any rail transport; 2,000 at Monterotondo under Igliori and 8,000 at Tivoli under Bottai; altogether about 14,000 men, shoddily armed, to whom must be added 3,000 men comprising the reserves at Foligno about seventy miles away. The three columns were not in communication with one another nor with Perugia, and it would have been easy for troops equipped with guns and tanks to attack them singly and put them to flight. Fortunately for the Fascists their strength was never put to the test, and it was the disintegration of the parliamentary system rather than a purely military threat which brought about Mussolini's success.

The Fascist columns did not in fact move from their concentration points until Mussolini had become Prime Minister and had given them the order to march. At that stage their presence in Rome had become unnecessary, but Mussolini was anxious to reward his men with the panoply of victory and to demonstrate that he had behind him both the resources of the state and the formations of the Fascist party. Although he probably did not foresee it at the time, the appearance in Rome of his legions was later to serve a useful purpose in clothing the whole transaction with an aura of heroism and glory.

Having settled the composition of his government, Mussolini's most urgent task was to deal with the thousands of enflamed Fascists whom he had brought into the capital and who now constituted a threat to public order. A review attended by the King was organized, after which Mussolini gave orders that the various formations should return home forthwith. It was not easy to provide transport at short notice for so many men, but thanks to Mussolini's energetic intervention the last trains bearing the victors of the March on Rome steamed out of the terminus during the night of October 31.

Meanwhile Mussolini had spent the day of October 31 taking over his two ministries. At the Ministry of Foreign Affairs he made the acquaintance of the senior officials and despatched the routine telegrams informing foreign governments of his assumption of office. In confronting the task before him he was sustained by the almost universal goodwill of the nation. Even Giolitti and Salandra declared that the new government made a good impression, while General Cadorna approved it without reserve.[15] As night fell on October 31 a new chapter opened in Italian history. The celebrating in the streets had ceased, the formal steps for the transfer of power had been taken, the glorious March on Rome was over. It was now time to settle down to the stern task of government.

Mussolini has been much criticized by his enemies for the part he played during these fateful days. The hero, they say, skulked at Milan close to the Swiss border while his lieutenants were exposed in forward positions; and he timidly declined to make the journey to Rome until he was assured that he would be subjected to no personal risk. It is not surprising that the ludicrous legend of the March on Rome, subsequently manufactured by Fascist propaganda, should have produced a reaction and involved Mussolini in charges of personal cowardice. Indeed it cannot be said that he played a particularly glorious role. On the other hand he was concerned to seize power rather than to achieve personal glory. Unable to make up his mind almost until the last moment whether to use force or to accept a parliamentary combination, and resolved not to fight the army or make a premature move which might fail, he decided to withdraw to Milan and await developments. In doing so he adopted a well-tried practice, to which it might be useful to revert in the conduct of international affairs, namely to keep the principal at a distance while subordinates are entrusted with the negotiation. From Milan he watched the gradual disintegration of the Facta government, and he moved only when he saw clearly that there was no need to compromise. On this occasion his patience, his judgment, and his timing could not have been bettered. Events, it is true, conspired to help him, but he seized his chance to effect a bloodless revolution and to be lifted by a grateful nation from the leadership of a small parliamentary fraction to the highest post in the state. His tactics were not to the taste of all his followers, but this circumstance did not rob him of his authority and prestige. If success be the touchstone by which politicians are judged, he had no reason to fear the verdict of history. He could now face the future in the knowledge that, for the moment at all events, he enjoyed the support of the King, the army, an obedient parliament, his Fascist followers, and the majority of the nation. After the sanguinary civil strife which for three years had torn the Italian nation apart, it was a happy situation in which to embark on the tremendous task before him.

BOOK II

Power

CHAPTER SEVEN

The Duce

I

MUSSOLINI became Prime Minister at the early age of thirty-nine and was the youngest in the line of twenty-four who filled the office, many of them more than once, during the sixty years following the unification of Italy. Of his better known predecessors Giolitti was fifty when he was Prime Minister for the first time, Nitti fifty-one, Sonnino fifty-seven, Orlando fifty-seven, Salandra sixty-one, and Crispi sixty-eight. He enjoyed two unusual advantages, first his youth and secondly the circumstance that outside Lombardy and Romagna he was comparatively little known. He had been the leader of his new movement for less than four years, in the Chamber of Deputies for only eighteen months and, except for his period abroad and occasional excursions to Rome and the South, had virtually spent his whole working life in Forlì and Milan. In the rarefied atmosphere of the Italian capital few people in the governing classes had even met him, and he appeared as a mythical figure from the distant provinces. An Italian diplomat returning from abroad shortly after Mussolini's seizure of power asked a friend what manner of man he was and received the vague reply: "I have very little idea, but I am told that he is a wild man from the north."[1] It was remarkable that the advent of this unknown man should have been so widely welcomed, but the people were tired of the old politicians and the accent on the new administration was novelty and youth. With Mussolini youth was a fetish. He resented the inroad of advancing years and after he had reached the age of fifty forbade any celebration of his birthday or even mention of his age.[2]

His physical appearance was not unimpressive. Although small in stature, he was as solidly built as a blacksmith's son should be, and he held himself well, so as to give the impression of greater height than he possessed. The impression of power and animal vitality which he exuded was reinforced by an authoritative manner of speech and the quick nervous gestures which accompanied it. His face was sallow, his black hair was fast receding from a lofty brow, the mouth was large, his features mobile, the jaw massive, and in the center of the head two large, very black piercing eyes which seemed almost to protrude from his face. His eyes were perhaps his most striking feature. When interested or anxious to emphasize a point, he had a trick of "rolling his eyes," as many of his visitors described it. In reality he was able to raise the upper eyelid and depress the lower, so as to display two vast white orbs.

In the early days of power he almost always wore a neat, dark suit with a hard butterfly collar and an unobtrusive but expensive tie. He possessed a musical voice which he used to good advantage and his demeanor in private was reserved and unassuming. In conversation he was courteous and natural without pose or affection, with a certain mordant peasant wit, but also without much vestige of humor. When he wished to do so, he could employ great charm; and the picture he presented to those who met him for the first time was that of a young, ardent, but modest politician, conscious of the difficulties before him, but resolved to face them with courage and a sense of responsibility.

In public he was a very difficult man. Here he relied on his considerable ability as an actor to create the image of an iron, indomitable Duce, who knew exactly what he wanted and where he was going. The imperious gestures, the head tilted back, the chin pushed forward, hands on his hips, and the torso stiff as a ramrod were the hallmarks of the Leader. These calculated artifices on one occasion saved his life. In 1926 an unbalanced Irishwoman, Miss Violet Gibson, shot him with a revolver as he was leaving the capitol after opening a medical congress. As he emerged into the public gaze the band struck up the Fascist anthem and Mussolini, in accordance with his usual practice, threw his head back with the result that the bullet, fired at point-blank range, instead of inflicting a mortal wound, merely passed through his nose.

In order to retain his hold on the masses he relied to a great extent on the influence of a servile press. But he did not overlook the power of speech. As an orator he was a master of every trick with which the demagogue binds his audience. His style, and he prided himself on the fact, was peculiar to himself and essentially un-Italian. The official designation of it was "lapidary," an appropriate description, for his speeches were declamatory rather than persuasive and consisted mainly of short staccato sentences breathing self-assurance and conviction. But he could, when required, dramatize himself, using a raucous voice and ample gestures to pour scorn on his adversaries and to whip up the enthusiasm of the crowd. In 1921 Ugo Ojetti, writing in the *Corriere della Sera,* gave the following description of him speaking at the Fascist congress in Rome:

> He is a most expert orator, master of himself, who before his public always assumes the mien which best suits his subject and the moment. His gestures are sparse. He only gesticulates with the right hand. At times he puts both his hands in his pockets. This is his statuesque moment in which, having drawn his threads together, he comes to an end. On the rare occasions on which this reserved figure of an orator opens out and gives himself freedom the two arms rotate above his head, the ten fingers wave as if they were seeking to pluck strings in the air, and the words pour forth from his lips in a torrent. In an instant Mussolini returns with a frown to graven immobility and with two fingers gropes for the knot of his tie to assure himself that it has not moved from the perpendicular. These moments of tumultuous gesticulation are not the moving moments. They represent for him rather the end of his logical demonstrations, a method of summarizing to the public the multitude of the other arguments which he has enumerated, emphasized, or passed over for the sake of brevity, in a word a means of saying "et cetera" most effectively mimed.[3]

Sixteen years later he still possessed some magic in his oratory. In the spring of 1937 an English visitor, A. L. Rowse, went to hear him speak from the balcony of the Palazzo Venezia: "By and by he came out: a short stocky butcher, with a heavy ill-shaven jowl. He spoke with the hoarse voice of a Lansbury, the vocal chords worn out with much outdoor speaking; but what struck me was the beauty of this ugly customer's gestures—there *was* something of the artist in him, of the artistry of his people." [4]

The importance Mussolini attached to speech as a weapon in his armory reflected his view that a modern ruler must carry the masses with him. For this purpose no means should be neglected. "Every revolution," he declared to Emil Ludwig, "creates new forms, new myths, and new rites; and the would-be revolutionary, while using old traditions, must refashion them. He must create new festivals, new gestures, new forms, which will themselves become traditional." [5] And again: "Music and women allure the crowd and make it more pliable. The Roman greeting, songs and formulas, anniversary commemorations, and the like—all are essential to fan the flames of enthusiasm that keep a movement in being. It was just the same in ancient Rome." [6] In public relations he was a master and excelled as no politician has ever done in the art of self-advertisement. Arturo Jemolo says of him that he had an extraordinary understanding of the masses. "He always knew what he could require of them and to what point he could go. He knew how to bemuse them, to appeal to their baser instincts, and to lead them where he willed." [7]

Nevertheless, while he recognized the need to appeal to the masses, he never disguised his contempt for them, which sprang originally from his belief that only an elite and never the proletariat could make a revolution. As the years passed his experiences in the Socialist party and his increasing repugnance for all democratic processes reinforced his dislike of the masses. "In the workers he addressed he saw not his brethren, but merely a force and an instrument which he intended to bend to his own ends." [8] He openly declared that nothing was more absurd than rule by the will of the majority and he was not afraid to allow Ludwig to publish the following revealing passage: "For me the masses are nothing but a herd of sheep as long as they are unorganized. I am nowise antagonistic to them. All I deny is that they are capable of ruling themselves. But if you would lead them, you must guide them by two reins, enthusiasm and interest." [9] He was convinced that the people were not attached to liberty, were interested only in their own material welfare and had no desire to shape their destiny. The era of democracy was passing in favor of a fashion for autocratic rule: "When political matters are discussed on the wireless, they listen to a sentence or two and then switch off. Nobody studies politics. The people do not want to rule, but to be ruled and to be left in peace." [10] Ludwig asked him whether a dictator could be loved. "Yes," answered Mussolini, "provided that the masses fear him at the same time. The crowd loves strong men. The crowd is like a woman." [11] He summed up his attitude to the masses in a word:

> It is faith that moves mountains, not reason. Reason is a tool, but it can never be the motive force of the crowd. Today less than ever. Today people have not so much time to think as they used to have. The capacity of the modern man for faith is illimitable. When the masses are like wax in my hands, when I stir their faith or when I mingle with them and am almost crushed by them, I feel myself to be a part of them. All the same there persists in me a certain aversion, like that which the modeler feels for the clay he is molding. Does not the sculptor sometimes smash his block of marble into fragments because he cannot shape it to represent the vision he has conceived? Now and then this crude matter rebels against the creator. Everything turns upon one's ability to control the masses like an artist.[12]

In later years Mussolini used to say that experience had shown him that it would take a generation to fashion the Italian people to his liking.

Behind the façade of arrogance and self-assurance Mussolini was a curiously indecisive character. At times he believed that he was a modern Messiah, who would create a new order in Italy and set a new pattern of government for the world. In this belief he was sustained by the adulation of many of his contemporaries. As early as 1913, for example, Georges Sorel had said: "Mussolini is no ordinary Socialist. One day you will see him at the head of a consecrated battalion, greeting the Italian banner with his dagger. He is an Italian of the fifteenth century, a *condottiere*. You do not know it yet. But he is the one energetic man who has the capacity to correct the weaknesses of the government." [13]

At other times Mussolini suffered from doubts, hesitations, and an inferiority complex so marked as to attract the attention of his doctor.[14] This hesitance and sense of inferiority sprang partly from his natural timidity, on which Angelica Balabanoff, among others, commented in his youth, partly from the conflict between the influence of his early upbringing and his romantic, nationalist temperament, partly from his inordinate susceptibility to his ever changing environment, and partly from envy of men of good birth and education, and an inner awareness that he was not equipped either by knowledge or experience to be at the helm of a large country at a critical moment in its history. He was in the situation of an adventurous boy who steals a boat and puts out to sea without knowing exactly what he will do when the winds begin to blow. He said himself: "I am always on the watch, particularly when a changing wind fills the sails of my ship of fortune." [15]

Consistency in Mussolini's eyes had no intrinsic virtue. Far more valuable was the capacity to change course rapidly as soon as expediency required it. Thus he had originally been a Socialist pacifist, but campaigned for intervention when the moment had seemed opportune. He had been a rampageous republican, but became an ardent supporter of the monarchy. He had undertaken to sustain the League of Nations, only later to deride it. As late as 1919 in a speech at Milan he had condemned the system of dictatorship which he was later to espouse. He had attacked and indeed persecuted the Church with the zeal of St. Paul, but he made his peace with the Vatican, restored religious education in the schools, and brought a happy end to the long conflict between the Quirinal and the Holy See. There was scarcely an issue on which he did not change his opinion or on which his restless, sceptical mind could be relied upon to remain constant. Moreover he was able to communicate wholly inconsistent impressions to different people at the same time.

As Mussolini himself admitted, he was a man without a program, who relied on faith, will power, and intuition rather than on intellect. He was much too volatile to wish to be tied down by any carefully elaborated philosophy of life; and if he enunciated a principle, it was only to justify a particular policy to which he was momentarily attached. If subsequently he wished to alter his policy, it was not difficult to find another principle to justify the change. "Every attempt he made to place his actions on a theoretical basis was shipwrecked on the rock of his own pragmatism. His system consisted in having none. Action, action, action—this summed up his whole creed."[16]

His instability and superficiality, although useful in so far as they gave him room for elastic maneuver, rendered him unfit to be the sole ruler of a nation. He was really miscast as a politician, for he was by profession and temperament a journalist. Each day had brought the task of producing a new edition of his newspaper, and everything had to be subordinated to that end. No need to peer far into the future, no need to dig up detailed programs; all that was required was to take a line on the events of the day without too much regard to the past or what the coming months might bring. If from time to time the newspaper changed its tune, it was unlikely that many would notice it and it could in any event be claimed that it was the circumstances which had altered. In 1919 he was at first not disposed to stand as a candidate in the general elections. When, one day, Mussolini told Margherita Sarfatti that he had suddenly changed his mind and she reproached him, he replied blandly: "Yesterday was yesterday; today is another day."[17]

His reading reflected this innate superficiality. He was a very fast reader and used to peruse an official file at the rate of several pages a minute, a process which enabled him to grasp the gist without apprehending any of the detail. His detractors have claimed that he was wholly uneducated and Count Sforza in particular has alleged that it was untrue that he had ever read Nietzsche, Pareto, or Sorel, for throughout his life he had never read anything but newspaper articles. This is an exaggeration. In fact Mussolini read widely, or rather he skimmed books in the hope of picking up ideas which he could appropriate and repeat in the form of vivid aphorisms to meet any future requirement. Speech was only of value in his eyes in so far as it fulfilled his purpose, and he was not concerned with the truth of his words. If they produced the result he desired at the time, they were justified. Consequently it would have been wrong to deduce that statements of policy, promises, or threats would necessarily lead to action, for in his eyes there was no connection between words and deeds. Similarly principles had no reality, since only action counted and, on the plane of action, success or failure was the only material consideration.

Cesare Rossi gives an example of Mussolini's capacity to make use of something he had read in a book. Before a session of the Senate in 1923 Rossi had accompanied to the Palazzo Chigi Professor Saverio Cilibrizzi, who was to present to the Duce a copy of his book: *Story of the Italian Parliament from Novara to Vittorio Veneto.* Mussolini thanked him perfunctorily and began idly to turn the pages of the book. All at once he stopped and looked at a certain passage with a gesture which betokened interest and surprise. In the afternoon in his speech to the Senate he attacked the liberal conception and cited the case of Cavour who during the second parliament had been beaten at a by-election in Turin by a certain lawyer Pansoia. On this unknown local politician Mussolini heaped irony, deriding the system of democratic egalitarianism which had almost deprived Italy of her greatest statesman. The senators were most impressed. "How well he knows the history of the sub-Alpine parliament," was the comment in the lobby after the speech. But Mussolini was only repeating a story which had caught his eye that morning in Professor Cilibrizzi's book.[18]

Unfortunately Mussolini's superficiality was translated from the headquarters of the *Popolo d'Italia* in Milan to the office of the Prime Minister in Rome. There, although he kept long hours, he did little genuine hard administrative work. He scrutinized the newspapers of the world with a professional eye; and articles which were critical of Italy or of himself excited his wrath to a degree quite out of proportion to their importance. He saw the chiefs of the carabinieri and the police and studied their reports. He also read with particular care all secret service reports, for to the dismay of his advisers he was, like most amateur politicians, apt to attach much greater importance to these often dubious documents than to reports from the regular public service. There was on his desk every day a file of secret reports; memoranda from the secret police, telephone intercepts, censored letters, the results of secret inquiries into the proceedings of his ministers and accounts of dinner-table conversations concocted by servants in the pay of the police; * and

* An account of Mussolini's personal and secret files on his ministers, party leaders, service chiefs, members of the bureaucracy, members of the royal family, and a vast number of lesser folk will be found in Emilio Re, *Storia di un archivio: le carte di Mussolini* (Milan, 1946). The loss of these archives was a source of particular affliction to him when he fled to Como in April, 1945.

any report of an ill-considered critical comment by an individual would cause the author to be entered into his bad books, for he took a personal view of policies. If their protagonists were considered friendly, he tended to support them and in the contrary case to oppose them. Thus, the circumstance that he regarded Sir Ronald Graham, who was British ambassador in Rome from 1922 to 1934, as friendly caused him to look on British proposals with a more favorable eye than he otherwise would have done. This was generally known in Rome and if, during Sir Ronald's term, there was any difficulty with any Italian ministry, it was only necessary in order to obtain satisfaction to mention that the ambassador might take the matter up personally with the Duce. This state of affairs ended when at about the same time Sir Ronald, despite Mussolini's protest, was recalled from Rome and the Duce embarked on a series of adventures which strained Anglo-Italian relations and drove him inexorably into the power of Hitler.

Mussolini knew very little about the machinery of government or economics or foreign countries. His ignorance was sometimes staggering, as is shown, for example, by his reference, in his Senate speech of February 4, 1923, to the well-known American Senator Borah as "the head of one of the many parties in the star-spangled republic." In the course of his conversations in 1932 with Emil Ludwig he showed that he entertained the oddest ideas about the position of the President of the United States:

Ludwig: Curiously enough, in the course of my travels I have found you more popular in America than anywhere else. In a hundred interviews I was asked: "How do you like Mussolini?" Yet the Americans are opposed to dictatorship in any form.

Mussolini: You are wrong; the Americans have a dictator. The President is almost omnipotent, his power being guaranteed by the constitution.

Ludwig: True, he might be omnipotent.

Mussolini: No, he actually is all-powerful.[19]

His ignorance of America was not confined to misapprehensions about the system of government and conditions in that country. He was also unaware of the growing importance of the United States in world affairs. In 1932, when Grandi left the Ministry of Foreign Affairs and Mussolini took over the portfolio he decided to make a clean sweep. He accordingly sent for Rosso, the permanent head of the department, and told him that he would be promoted to be an ambassador. "Unfortunately," he added, "there is no post vacant for you in Europe. So you will have to be satisfied with the Embassy in Washington." [20]

One consequence of Mussolini's superficiality was that he almost never spent time or energy delving deeply into the details of governmental administration. Figures meant little or nothing to him. One million was a large figure. So was ten million or a hundred million; and he found it difficult to distinguish between them. Thus he was vastly impressed when shortly before the war Goering told him that Germany had effectively provided against a blockade by building up a stock of eighty million tins of canned meat.[21] The fact that this hoard would provide each inhabitant with little more than one tin of meat simply did not occur to him. All he knew was that eighty million sounded like a large figure and must represent a notable German achievement. He was later to be equally impressed by some of Hitler's claims.

Having no stomach for the grind of administrative work, it was Mussolini's practice in the early days to leave to his ministers the management of their departments, only reserving to himself major decisions of policy and the right to intervene capriciously in details such as the determination of the date on which the Rome police changed into their white summer uniforms. In his ignorance he was nervous about differing from the more knowledgeable members of his cabinet and he would sometimes write the word "Approved" on two conflicting memoranda emanating from two different ministries. It was a habit which caused some confusion, only cleared up by a subsequent snap decision or by a laborious and unsatisfactory compromise. If he had been less remote from the day-to-day conduct of affairs, he would not have been surprised to discover exactly how ill-found and ill-prepared his Italian army was to face the hazards of modern war. During the years of peace he had been proudly calling the attention of the nation and the world to the millions of bayonets which he could muster. He would have been better advised before indulging in the luxury of these bellicose gestures to examine more closely what stood behind the bayonets and the men who carried them.

In fact his superficiality and the defects in his machinery of government combined to make him extraordinarily ignorant of the situation of Italy's armed forces. So out of touch was he that in September, 1939, he was unaware of Italy's air force strength, and Ciano actually suggested to him that he should obtain the figures by instructing each prefect to count the aircraft lying on the airfields in his district.[22]

In September, 1940, he invited the German and Hungarian military attachés to be present at his review of three cavalry divisions near Udine. The ride past of the twelve cavalry regiments presented a splendid spectacle, but it did not seem to occur to Mussolini that the horse in war was outmoded or that the parade was no advertisement of Italy's preparedness for war. On the following day he visited infantry divisions on the Yugoslav border and for a few minutes viewed a military exercise from an observation post. The German military attaché noted that he showed little interest in the exercise and had no eye for the weapons and equipment of the troops, which were hopelessly out of date. Mussolini believed that the only thing that mattered in war was morale; and, if the men sang lustily as they marched past, he was satisfied. Despite the warnings of his military advisers, he declined to recognize that troops cannot maintain morale if their equipment is conspicuously inferior to that of their adversaries or the allies at their side.[23]

If Mussolini was ill-informed, uncertain, and vacillating at home, he was equally so in his conduct of foreign affairs. Here he was torn in every direction by ingrained prejudice, ignorance, passing predilections, ambition, and above all by fear. His first aim was to make Italy respected abroad and to ensure her participation on an honorable footing in all major international negotiations. In this enterprise he was at first almost wholly successful, though it is fair to say that in 1919 Italy had secured a permanent seat on the Council of the League of Nations and was thus already entitled to be heard on all matters of great importance. Mussolini did, however, in a very short time improve the international standing of his country, an achievement which won him the grateful respect of Italians all over the world. The situation of Italy before the Fascist era had been a source of national humiliation. "One has to be in the diplomatic service to realize how little Italy counts in the world," said the Italian minister in Berne; and the Marchese di Saluzzo observed: "When Italy was divided up into little states, the Kingdom of Piedmont had more dignity and prestige than Italy since the war."[24]

For the rest, Mussolini allowed himself to drift in any and every direction; and his changes of course were often as unpredictable as the weather. The British Ambassador wrote of him in September, 1935: "My own constant impression is of a man who is the victim, not the master, of his destiny."* At times he was surprisingly conciliatory, as, for example, in certain negotiations with Yugoslavia. At others he was rigid and unbending, as during the months immediately before the Abyssinian campaign. Basically he was a xenophobe and objected to the intrusion of any foreign influence: "It is the upper classes in society, who are the first to ape French manners, to Anglicize and to Americanize themselves, to adopt the dress of other countries, often their psychology, more often their defects."[25]

In consequence he was apt to dislike any organization concerned with international cooperation, from the League of Nations to the Rotarians, and for him a choice of foreign friends was a choice of evils. In 1914 he had professed to see the danger to Italy of a German victory and he hotly supported the cause of the Western democracies. After the war he was disillusioned by the treatment meted out to Italy, but he had other grounds for disliking Britain and France. He was opposed to democracies, both because he objected to their system of government and because he felt instinctively that they must be hostile to him: "It is wholly in the logic of things that the international Socialist, Democratic, Liberal, Masonic, and Bolshevist world should be furiously anti-Fascist." Moreover he had been brought up as a revolutionary to hate the wealthy and he translated this aversion into the sphere of international politics. "The English are a bourgeois nation, we a proletarian one," he wrote in the *Popolo d'Italia* of July 8, 1922. Moreover the Western Allies represented in his mind the old drowsy order, liberal, humani-

* Mussolini was later to confirm this verdict. In March, 1945, he said to an Italian journalist: "I shall go wherever destiny sends me, for I have done what destiny has told me to do." (Pini and Susmel, *op. cit.*, IV, 486). Mr. De Valera, who saw him not long before the war, gained the impression that he had abandoned any attempt to control his fate.

tarian, pacifist, played out and ready to be swept away like the old Italian political parties. Hence he tended to sympathize with treaty revisionists and with any revolutionary—such as the Grand Mufti—who was tilting against the established order. His prejudice against England was compounded with ignorance. He did not know, for example, that Kipling was becoming somewhat out of date and he believed moreover that British colonial rule was harsh and brutal; and he had no idea of the meaning of freedom of speech or of the press, so that he was apt to conclude that any letter printed by the (London) *Times* represented the view of the editor, the government, and the country. More serious, he was convinced that Britain was in decline, and to a man who respected only force and whose policy was dictated principally by fear, this was the most damning indictment which could be made of a nation.

A minor grievance against England flowed from the attitude of English tourists who, he alleged, regarded Italy with patronizing affection as a country merely possessing ancient monuments and living on an equally ancient glory. He boasted that he had not set foot in a museum three times in his life; and he fiercely repudiated any suggestion that Italy was not a modern, forward-looking country, which must be taken seriously as a new force in world affairs: "An end to the representation of Italy as a nation of innkeepers, the goal of every loafer armed with his odious Baedeker. . . . We are and are resolved to be a nation of producers." [26]

Towards France Mussolini's feeling was somewhat reminiscent of Hitler's attitude towards England. From time to time he seemed to desire an accommodation, but always on his own terms. When Hitler spoke to Lord Halifax at Berchtesgaden in 1937 he said that Anglo-German relations could only be placed on a friendly footing if there were no criticism of Germany in Parliament or in the British press. Similarly Mussolini believed that any agreement with France in the international field must be extended to French domestic politics and thus bring about an end to any expression of antifascism in France. His resentment against the French parties of the Left was fanned by their traffic with the many Italian political exiles on French soil, a situation which caused continual friction between the two countries.

His outlook towards France was further poisoned by a deep

sense of inferiority, which made him long to humiliate her. The contempt for Italy, which certain French politicians made little effort to conceal, increased his sense of exacerbation. In 1923 he said to Rossi: "In France we have no friends. All of them are against us. In the eyes of every Frenchman we are only *'sales macaronis.'* "[27] Finally he came to the conclusion that France also was in decline and that it was not worthwhile making any effort to win her friendship. All in all his feelings for Britain and France were informed by an irritated frustration, envy of their wealth and possessions, dislike of their democratic traditions, and contempt for their pacifism rather than by any deep rational hatred.

At the same time he was apt to disclaim any animus against Britain, whom he might need one day, and for certain of whose statesmen—Macdonald, Austen Chamberlain, Curzon—he had a certain sympathy. Thus when Ludwig asked him why the British were not popular in Italy and suggested that it might be because they were the strongest pillars of that democracy which he repudiated, he replied:

It is not the English in particular who are unpopular. Foreigners in general are disliked. All our sympathies with the world outside Italy have waned. A new movement such as ours makes short work of traditional phrases. For half a century, at least, the friendship between Italy and England has been a catchword. We scrutinize the problem and inquire: "Is there any substance in this alleged friendship?" Then the talk is about "the brotherhood of the Latin nations." Are the French "Latins" and have they shown any sense of fraternity with us? Such revisions as these are altogether in the spirit of fascism.[28]

Mussolini's attitude towards Germany was of a very different order. In 1914 he had inveighed against the Empire and during his visit to Berlin after the war he had shrewdly noted that militarism was once more rearing its head. He objected to Pan-Germanism because it was dangerous to Italy, and to the racial theories of Houston Stewart Chamberlain and others, which were subsequently adopted by Hitler, because they seemed to him ridiculous. He was also opposed to anti-Semitism on the ground that the Jews were a useful element in Italian society. It is true that immediately after the First World War he seemed to favor Germany when he advocated a reduction of the reparations burden, but he did so on practical grounds, and in the framework of a general debt settlement, rather than from any sympathy with the Germans, whom he found aggressive, domineering, and unpleasant. He once remarked to Sir Ronald Graham that the Germans were their own worst enemies and that they were an exceedingly difficult people to help.

After Hitler's accession to power he became more urgently aware of the German threat to Europe's well-being, but unfortunately, much as he disliked the Germans, it was their discipline and strength which he admired. He had little confidence in the resolution of the Western powers, and the principal motive which guided his relations with Germany was once again fear. As the years passed, and the Germans became more powerful, he gravitated reluctantly and fatefully towards them. He did not do so willingly, for Hitler's rise threatened his own position, and at times he made feeble, spasmodic efforts to break loose. At others he strove to salve his wounded pride by seeking to emulate the German conqueror. Thus after the German seizure of Prague in March, 1939, Ciano, echoing his master, noted: "It is useless to deny that all this worries and humiliates the Italian people. It is necessary to give them satisfaction and compensation. Albania." [29]

Mussolini's attitude to Germany was reflected in his relations with Hitler. He disliked Hitler as a man. His outspoken brutality, overbearing loquacity, and indifference to the interests of Italy were utterly repugnant. Mussolini at the first meeting in Venice at once recognized in him a man of wrath, who would bring crashing to the ground the pillars of European civilization.[30] Yet at the same time the Fuehrer's strength of purpose and the power which he wielded exercised an extraordinary fascination on the Duce. From every meeting, however awkward or even humiliating, Mussolini returned fortified and refreshed. In the intervals there were passionate outbursts of anger against the Germans, but when the two men were together Mussolini could not bring himself to debate with his formidable antagonist or even to doubt his word, that word which he had so often and so flagrantly broken. His failure to stand up to Hitler or to trade on the esteem in which the German dictator held him was the despair of his advisers. Thus, Dino Alfieri, the Italian ambassador in Berlin, writes that his mounting sense of inferiority caused him to adopt in his relations with Hitler that humble, passive, secretly hostile attitude, which not only had repercussions on every phase, every incident of the war, but did incalculable injury to his country's cause. Now and then the Italian Condottiere would pull himself together and show signs of fight. Sometimes he would formulate a proud and inflexible resolve. But these were mere expressions of his pent-up feelings—ineffectual babblings, destined to reach the ears of none outside the circle of his immediate colleagues.[31]

Such was the character of Mussolini's relations with the principal powers in Europe. But his foreign policy was also conditioned by his juvenile romanticism. The resurgence of Imperial Rome under his leadership became his dream. As he looked back with envy on the history of the popes and on their world-wide sway, he felt the urge to emulate and to surpass them. Just as a small band of indigent Apostles had realized the parable of the mustard seed, so he, with his Fascist elect, would regenerate the world. Not only would he extend the bounds of Empire across *"mare nostrum"* to Africa and beyond, but Rome would become once more the inspiration of every civilized man. These wild and passionate ambitions, often the subject of hysterical language, found their expression in the trappings with which he clothed the Fascist state: the *Fasci*, the bundles of rods carried by the Roman lictors; the organization of the militia, with its ranks and formations on the Roman model; the Roman salute; the so-called Roman parade step; the Roman wolf kept encaged on the Capitol, which incidentally evoked protest from animal-loving Britons; and the constant evocation of Rome as the mainspring of Italian life. Of course realism was often in conflict with romanticism, and there were times when prudent counselors were able to induce him to renounce some flamboyant gesture. But there was always the danger that he would refuse to do so, and his Ministry of Foreign Affairs lived in constant dread of having to rescue him from the consequences of some romantic impulse.

II

It will be seen later how, in this welter of resentments and emotions, his foreign policy oscillated, and how uncertain was his guiding hand. If he had had greater experience and a less volatile character, or if he had relied on good advice, he might have steered a straighter, safer course. But he was a gambler, ready to stake his own fortunes and those of his country. After the March on Rome he said to Grandi: "I was right to trust my star"; and with the passage of time he was more and more inclined to rely on intuition. Unfortunately his judgment of men and events was more often than not astray. For example, in 1922 he declared in the Chamber that Italy had nothing to fear from Russia and he prophesied that the Soviet Union would evolve into a bourgeois country of small proprietors. And again, although he disliked Hitler, he believed almost until the end and in the face of all the evidence that he was a man on whose word reliance could be placed. His often ingenuous credulity was a failing on which his German doctor was later to comment sadly.[32] As is usually the fate of dictators, Mussolini became more and more isolated, more remote from events, more incapable of piercing the smoke screen thrown by his less competent subordinates around their proceedings, and more inclined to accept the views of the last plausible man he had seen. These were subsequently imparted as his own to respectful listeners and thus gained a currency which they did not deserve.

By the exercise of his charm, and by judicious flattery, he could draw most of his Italian and almost all his foreign visitors into his net. Bemused by the atmosphere of the big room in the Palazzo Venezia, by his reputation as a European statesman and by the calm assurance with which he spoke, they came away with the impression that they had heard the voice of the oracle. In the memoirs of the many European politicians who visited Rome between the wars, the same descriptions of Mussolini may be found. All speak of his economy of words, the clarity with which he expressed his thoughts, and his mastery of his subject.

It probably sounded fine at the time, but when the records of his conversations are read in cold print and with the advantage of hindsight, it is clear that, while from time to time a shaft of intuition illuminated a problem, there can have been few public men in Europe who uttered more nonsense, or whose predictions were more often falsified by events. Two typical examples are observations which in 1937 he made about England: "The next great surprise for England will be provided by the growth of English communism.

That would be a good lesson, particularly for Mr. Eden himself"; [33] and "English land forces cannot survive long in Egypt and in particular could not operate there. Those which were moved towards our frontiers on the occasion of the Abyssinian conflict were very soon smitten by dysentery and had very heavy losses." [34]

His situation would have been improved if he had enjoyed the advantage of intercourse with men of quality. But from the days of his childhood he had always been a singularly friendless creature, and after he became Prime Minister he lived entirely alone. After a short spell in a hotel he moved to a small rented apartment in the Palazzo Tittoni in the Via Rasella, a narrow, mean street close to the Piazza Barberini. It was a dilapidated building with the appearance of a tenement, and here he led a simple existence with one devoted general servant, Cesira Carocci, whom he acquired from D'Annunzio. There was no kitchen in the flat and when he was at home any meals required were sent up by the landlord, Baron Fasani, who lived below. Later he occupied the more ample Villa Torlonia in the Via Nomentana where, except during Rachele's visits, his only companion was the fencing master, a former cavalry noncommissioned officer named Camillo Ridolfi, who for many years had helped him with his duels.

The Villa Torlonia was a substantial house of vulgar neoclassical design surrounded by a large garden, almost a little park, of some twenty acres with a tennis court and a riding track. The already tasteless interior was not improved by the display of numberless objects which he had from time to time received as gifts. His translation to these comparatively comfortable surroundings did not bring with it any change in his Spartan way of life, except in so far as he was now afforded a better opportunity of taking physical exercise. He rose at six o'clock and after a brief bout of gymnastics went out for a ride in the garden. There were a few small hurdles to jump, which by a judicious tilt of the camera could be given for publicity purposes the appearance of quite formidable obstacles. He also fenced and occasionally bicycled or played lawn tennis. Breakfast consisted of fruit, whole-meal bread, and milk with a little coffee. A rapid, heavily protected motor drive brought him to his office in the Palazzo Venezia shortly after eight o'clock. For lunch he ate spaghetti, vegetables, and fruit with no coffee. He never smoked or drank spirits and his only indulgence was a very occasional glass of wine. He came home from the office at about nine o'clock in the evening and supped on clear soup, vegetables, and fruit. He was a small eater, always in a hurry over his meals, which never lasted more than a few minutes. After supper he drank an orangeade or camomile tea and went to bed at about half-past ten. He was usually a good sleeper.

To some extent the simplicity of his regime was imposed on him by his state of health, for although he was endowed with a robust constitution, he had contracted syphilis in his youth and in 1925 he fell seriously ill with gastric ulcers. He was treated for the ulcers by a number of doctors, but his condition eventually became so alarming that a well-known Italian doctor, Professor Aldo Castellani, was hastily summoned from London to see him. He found Mussolini barely able to sit at a table piled high with papers and by his side was a basin into which he had been vomiting blood. He looked wretchedly ill and the doctor diagnosed duodenal ulcer and enlarged liver. The patient was ordered to bed at once and placed on a strict diet with alkaline treatment. After a few days he was so much better that Castellani sought and obtained permission to return to his practice in London. But the patient was obliged to continue to be careful of his food.

Mussolini was aware of the rumor that his illness was due to the aftereffects of syphilis and much resented it. He accordingly asked Castellani whether it would be possible to have a blood test made in England. It was arranged that this should be done, but he was impatient to hear the result and wrote to Castellani: "I should like to know the result of the Wassermann test. I am better and no longer have severe pain in the region of the liver." Castellani in reply was able to assure him by telegram that the blood test was absolutely negative. This finding was subsequently confirmed, and there is no ground for the reports that his health was permanently impaired by the aftereffects of syphilis.

A year later Castellani saw him again and found him much improved in health. Mussolini, who was much annoyed at the alarmist rumors flying around Rome about his health, was delighted at the doctor's verdict and at once drafted the following statement for publication:

Professor Castellani, who is a great doctor and whom I greatly esteem, in passing through Rome came to visit me as he has already done on previous occasions. He came at 9:15 in the evening. I had just returned from my work. I was in excellent humor. He examined me before dinner and found me in very good health. My dinner lasted exactly three minutes, timed by the Professor with a watch in his hand. Professor Castellani examined me again afterward and came to the same satisfactory conclusion as before. I feel well. The Professor found me *rejuvenated*. And it is so. This may be told to all those who are interested in my health.[35]

Not only did Mussolini lead a very simple life, but he never went out into society and only very seldom made an appearance at a foreign embassy on some special occasion, such as the visit of some foreign statesman or other notable. When he did so the secret police would occupy the embassy and from behind the garden bushes or other suitable vantage points assure themselves against the admission of intruders. At the party Mussolini would move among the guests, conversing easily with all and sundry. His social graces were, however, not natural and were only acquired with some difficulty. As soon as he became Prime Minister he realized that he would have social responsibilities and that he was not equipped to discharge them. He accordingly engaged a young man from the Foreign Office, Mario Pansa, to teach him English and to act as social mentor. It was Pansa who induced him reluctantly to discard the white spats to which he had been addicted for so long. Shortly afterwards Mussolini had an engagement to dine at the British embassy and Pansa advised him for safety's sake to follow carefully what was being done at table by another Italian guest, Alberto Theodoli. All went well until the fish when Theodoli noticed to his horror that Mussolini was shoveling the food into his mouth with a knife. He caught the Duce's eye, ostentatiously raised his knife on high, and then laid it firmly on the table. Unfortunately Mussolini followed Pansa's advice too literally and proceeded to lay his own knife covered with yellow fish sauce on the damask tablecloth.[36]

Mussolini was, however, so quick and adaptable that it was not necessary to prolong for more than a short time the period of his initiation. His character was full of contradictions and it may seem strange that a man with his revolutionary and nonconformist background should have taken so much trouble to bring his behavior into conformity with the requirements of his new position and with the usages of polite society. But he had a high regard for his status as Prime Minister of a Great Power; and in his view it would have been not only wrong to flout convention but characteristic of the Socialists and the Democrats, whom he despised. Thus, although he wore his black shirt when he saw the King after the March on Rome in order to mark the revolutionary character of his movement, he returned the same day in a silk hat and borrowed frock coat to present his list of ministers. He was always meticulous about his dress and deportment whenever he had to see the Sovereign. To Cesare Rossi he once said: "I do not understand Bissolati, who after all was not a common vulgarian, going to see the King in a suit. When one goes to confer with the head of the state a certain outward dignity must be observed." Rossi in reply explained that Bissolati possessed no formal clothes and had made known his embarrassment to the Minister of the Court. The King, to whom the matter was referred, had indulgently replied that Bissolati could come dressed as he liked. But Mussolini was by no means satisfied with the explanation and remarked: "When one is Sovereign of a kingdom of thirty-eight million inhabitants, one does not compromise in matters of etiquette and protocol." [37]

Mussolini's sense of propriety governed his relations with the King. There were times when he was irritated with the monarch, for example when he demurred at the new electoral law or when he objected to the risk attached to Mussolini's journeys by airplane; and he would mutter that he would become a republican again, or that the King was too small a man for an Italy which was on the road to greatness. But during his long intercourse with the King, he always came to recognize that the monarchy by its tradition represented a valuable focus of national unity; and his realism and tactical sense counseled him to use it rather than to fight it. He remained deaf to Hitler's warnings, and if there was one man to whom he was consistently loyal during his life, it was the King. It was therefore a surprise and a bitter blow that the King should have been the instrument of his downfall.

Although Mussolini was resolved to fulfill his official obligations, he did not regard himself as in any way bound to attend purely social functions. There were of course a number of public appearances which he was obliged to make: visits to provincial cities, industrial fairs, agricultural enterprises, and military establishments; and from time to time he went to the Opera in Rome or Milan, for he was fond of music and had learned to play the violin when he was a boy. But these were only occasional departures from the routine of his daily life spent between his office and the lonely Villa Torlonia.

III

His dislike of society was accentuated by his uneasiness in the presence of educated and intelligent men. This weakness was manifested when he made his first appearance at a conference at Lausanne in December, 1922. There, despite his somewhat puerile expedients to buttress his own position, he was plainly uncomfortable and awed by Curzon and Poincaré, an experience which he never forgot and which colored his outlook towards participation at international gatherings. This diffidence, which constituted one side of his complex character, was reflected in remarks which he let fall from time to time. Thus he said shortly after he became Prime Minister: "What have I achieved after all up to now? Nothing. I am a small journalist and a minister for the moment, like so many others"; and he added: "But I have a frenzied ambition which burns, gnaws, and consumes me like a physical malady. It is, with my will, to engrave my mark on this age, like a lion with his claw." [38] Some years later a member of the British embassy had occasion to thank him for receiving a British journalist and he replied with a deprecatory smile: "I am a journalist by trade and it is to journalism that I must look for my bread and butter if, as is possible, I one day lose my present job."

There was diffidence also as well as jealousy and suspicion in his relations with his ministers and the party leaders, which were strange and unsatisfactory. He was sensitive to the emergence of any possible rival and he viewed all men with a peasant's suspicion. During the Matteotti crisis he was heard to say: "If my sainted mother were to return to life, I should no longer trust even her." [39] His cabinet colleagues rarely saw him and most transactions were done on paper, but they were terrified of him for they knew that he was unpredictable and that at any moment he could dismiss them; and since most of them had joined the movement as young men before they could establish themselves in a profession, they had no other means of earning a living. At meetings of the Grand Council he was a brisk, authoritative chairman, ready to listen to the views of those around the table and clear in his summing up of the Council's decisions, which in the last resort were his own. But he was far less impressive in his day-to-day dealings with his ministers. Here he was shy of forcing the issue with any individual, for he disliked a row and was afraid of being bested in an argument. So he preferred to agree, when he could do so, to paper over the cracks when his ministers were in disagreement, and when neither course was possible to organize a reconstruction of his government, a process which he euphemistically termed "the changing of the guard." In Fascist Italy no one in authority ever failed, and if men disappeared from public life, it was only because in the natural order of things one guard was replaced by another. This device ensured that he was never involved in any unpleasantness. Even when he discovered during the war that Ciano was no longer to be relied on, there was no angry confrontation and no dismissal of the recalcitrant minister. Instead Ciano was removed from the Ministry of Foreign Affairs in the course of a ministerial reconstruction, and he was asked in the most friendly manner possible where he would like to go. When he selected the embassy to the Holy See, his wish was immediately granted.

If Mussolini treated his ministers with a mixture of tyranny and moral cowardice, their attitude to him, which was compounded of fear, dislike, and veiled disloyalty, was equally discreditable. They cannot altogether be blamed, for Mussolini's lack of generosity and ruthlessness were so notorious that no associate could trust him. Time and again a man who had served his purpose was dropped in the gutter like a squeezed lemon. Mussolini himself did not regard this fault as a weakness, for he preferred to be feared rather than loved and he boasted of his capacity to act without regard to any sentimental consideration. With a profound contempt for mankind and wide experience of human frailty, he enjoyed exercising his talent to degrade men and bring out their worst qualities. He was a great corruptor. In his view men were only the material with which to build the structure of his own personal domination. To Cesare Rossi he put it more elegantly: "The individual only exists in so far as he is a member of the state and is subordinated to the interests of the State." [40]

His individualism was another characteristic which governed his human relationships. Before he came to power he proclaimed it in a public speech:

> I am for the individual and I strike at the state. Down with the state in all its forms and incarnations. The state of yesterday, of today and of tomorrow. The bourgeois state and the Socialist state. In the gloom of today and in the uncertainty of the morrow the only faith which remains to us individualists, who are destined to perish, is the religion which is today absurd, but eternally consoling, of anarchy.

He could never act as a member of a team, disliked being crossed, and was only happy when he was in a position to impose his will, even when he was not quite sure that he was on the right tack. His failure to establish any basis of trust between himself on the one hand and his ministers and the bureaucracy on the other was exceedingly damaging to the orderly conduct of affairs. He said to Ludwig: "I cannot have any friends. I have no friends. First of all because of my temperament; secondly because of my view of human beings. That is why I avoid both intimacy and discussion." [41] His conception of government was personal rule; and he arrogated to himself the right to take the reins in his hands, when intuition or inclination bade him do so, and to drop them equally suddenly. This was particularly the case in his treatment of international affairs. At times he summarily rejected advice designed to keep him within the bounds of prudence. At others he overruled his experts and, on the grounds of so-called higher policy, insisted on making unnecessary and ill-timed concessions for which he received no counterpart. Sometimes he happened to be right, but these apparently capricious decisions were often taken suddenly without knowledge of the facts or time to give them the necessary consideration. With the possible exception of his brother Arnaldo, who died prematurely, there was no single man with whom he was on intimate terms or who at any time during his period of office exercised the slightest influence upon him. But even Arnaldo's beneficent influence was limited, since Mussolini regarded him as excessively moderate. He complained of him to Ludwig: "He lacked the passionate impetus of that Arnaldo after whom he was called. A revolutionary is born, not made."[42]

The solitary life he elected to lead, which surrounded him with a useful aura of mystery, was in fact congenial. So was its simplicity. He had no taste for luxury. Nor was he in the least interested in money, except in so far as it was required to meet his elementary requirements. He never carried any in his pocket and never spent more than was required for his horses, his sports car, and his relatively modest establishments in Rome and his country residence at Rocca delle Caminate, close to his birthplace in Romagna, which he loved. He was equally uninterested in titles or other empty honors. So the example of austerity which he gave to the Italian nation involved no personal sacrifice.

IV

In one respect, however, he was self-indulgent to a degree which impaired his health and eventually coarsened the fabric of his character. It was not a matter which he ever discussed with any but his closest associates and in his maturer years he was as discreet about it as he could be, but from his youth he had never been able to resist the attraction of women. As he moved from place to place he left behind him a chain of more or less disconsolate mistresses; and his cohabitation with Rachele did nothing to diminish his promiscuous ardor.

At the end of March, 1924, just before the elections, Mussolini traveled to Milan to attend the funeral of a Fascist murdered in Paris. There he stayed for ten days until the elections were over, but he did not spend his nights at home with Rachele in their Milan flat. He was ostensibly sleeping at his office, but in fact was with the widowed Margherita Sarfatti, with whom he had for some time maintained a liaison. Rachele, who was aware of this and other irregularities, for once reacted vigorously and left Milan in dudgeon for Forlì, taking with her the infant Bruno. The family doctor, Ambrosio Binda, asked Cesare Rossi to intervene, but Mussolini airily claimed that the whole thing was a storm in a teacup and that Rachele was taking umbrage for no reason: "I sleep in the prefecture simply because the babies make so much row at home. That is all." [43]

Mussolini was no more faithful to Margherita Sarfatti, with whom his relations were perhaps more intellectual than romantic, than to Rachele or his many other mistresses. She was a Jewess, who married Cesare Sarfatti, a coreligionist and a lawyer. Both left the Socialist party when Mussolini founded the *Popolo d'Italia* and Margherita was employed on the artistic side of the newspaper. In 1921 she became editor of the Fascist monthly *Gerarchia,* wrote a biography of the Duce, and during the early years of Mussolini's premiership continued, to Rachele's annoyance, to exercise a certain influence on him. Eventually, when his liaison became the subject of gossip, he dismissed her from the *Popolo d'Italia,* and in 1934 he broke with her completely. In 1937 it was becoming apparent that the situation of the Jews in Italy was deteriorating and she emigrated. Alma Mahler-Werfel saw her two years later in Paris, embittered by poverty and by rancor against her former lover.[44] She returned to Italy after the war and died in 1961 at the age of seventy-eight. According to press reports she had previously sold to a foreign purchaser for a sum said to exceed sixty million lire an enormous bundle of letters from Mussolini on the understanding that they were not to be published until after her death.

Another episode was a scandal caused by a French actress, Mlle. Fontanges, whose real name was Magda Coraboeuf. She came to Rome in 1937 and on her return to Paris revealed to the press that she had been Mussolini's mistress. In order to protect himself Mussolini informed the French ambassador that he had given instructions that Mlle. Fontanges would not be allowed to come to Rome again. She was an unbalanced woman and seems to have held the French ambassador, the Comte de Chambrun, responsible for her misfortune, for she shot and wounded him, an offense for which she was sentenced to a year's imprisonment. The fact that she was French only added to Mussolini's angry embarrassment.

Mussolini's treatment of his women was Eastern in its callousness. He had no great opinion of the opposite sex and observed to Schuschnigg that history proved that the intervention of women in politics was usually disastrous.[45] Nor did he believe in chivalry towards women, who "prefer brutality in a man to courtesy." [46] Like a pasha he was apt to summon them suddenly when they were required and to dismiss them equally abruptly. Even Clara Petacci was expected to wait in the apartment above her lord's office in the Palazzo Venezia in the hope, not always fulfilled, that he might require her. He must have been attractive to women who enjoy submitting to the caprice and violence of a ruthless master. One foreign artist, to whom he gave a few sittings, quickly fell a victim to his sorcery and relates that she came away not only with a work of art, but with a child.

Mussolini knew that his conduct was a source of grief to his wife, but he was neither willing nor able to control his passions; and in the conflict between sensuality and his feeble sense of duty towards her, it was always sensuality that won. Rachele, who understood and forgave his infidelities, lived in seclusion, devoting herself to her five children and obediently fulfilling her husband's slightest wish. He did little to requite her love, though he was fond of her as one might be of any familiar piece of furniture.

It has been said by some that Mussolini's promiscuity has been much exaggerated. It is true that he was an exhibitionist, who enjoyed dramatizing himself and that he took pride in his own youth and virility. But the stories of his adventures do not stem from him and they are so well documented and confirmed by so many reliable sources that they cannot be discarded.

Like all Italians he was devoted to children and, though he was in no sense a family man, he was on the whole indulgent to his own children. Edda was his favorite, but he showed a certain affection towards them all, and he was sincerely afflicted when his second son Bruno was killed in the war. When his youngest daughter contracted poliomyelitis, he was distraught and on one occasion actually broke down in public. At the official opening of a new press center the president of the Foreign Press Association presented him with a doll for the sick child. The Duce's eyes filled with tears and he walked to the window, muttering to Alfieri: "I can't reply. You must say something." [47]

As the mother of his children, Rachele received some of the consideration to which she was entitled. When they were separated, he took the trouble to keep her abreast of important events by telephone; and he satisfied all her modest material requirements. But he was not prepared to put himself to any real inconvenience on her account and, where other women were concerned, he treated her with egotistical indifference.

V

He might have behaved more generously to Rachele if he had possessed any moral principles or a greater degree of natural virtue. There are a number of faults of character which men tolerate, but his were those which are less easy to forgive. The driving force of his life was ambition and lust for power for power's sake. To this end he was prepared to betray his associates, to compromise with truth and justice, and to condone the use of force against his adversaries, whom he persecuted with all the zest of his revengeful nature. When Ludwig asked him whether the memory of his own prison experiences did not sometimes give him pause, he replied: "By no means. It seems to me that I am perfectly consistent. They began by locking me up. Now I pay them back in their own coin." [48]

Ambition was sustained by vanity and egotism. He had always believed that he was in a special category and his early sense of grievance against society arose from its refusal to recognize this self-evident fact. Consequently he was above the law and did not feel obliged to apply to himself the standards which he was ready to exact from others. For example, while he demanded discipline from the Italians, he saw no reason to practice that virtue himself.[49] As far as his own conduct was concerned, he was moved by one consideration only, the promotion of his own interests. Thus, if the use of force was necessary to advance him on the road to power to keep him in office, it was legitimate; if it prejudiced his prospects, it was wrong.

His attitude to the morality of violence was dishonest and colored by the misgivings of an uneasy conscience. Basically he did not like violence for its own sake. He was fastidiously squeamish and on one occasion refused to visit a morgue to identify a corpse. He was affronted by the brutality and blood lust of Hitler. Yet he never recoiled from violence when it served his end and was eager to use it in order to intimidate his opponents. His sister Edvige, writing of his outlook, said: "My brother did not like violence. He accepted it, he even foresaw it, just as one foresees fever in a sick organism. It was the inevitable road into the national political struggle which must be taken by the outsiders, the irregulars, those whom the large political parties had so wrongly ignored."[50]

After he became Prime Minister he was at pains to find a moral justification for his use of violence: "Violence is perfectly moral, more moral than a compromise or a deal. But because it possesses the justification of its lofty morality, it must always be guided by an ideal and never by base calculation or shabby self-interest."[51] At the same time self-interest demanded that he should be the censor of morals and that the use of violence should be subject to his personal control: "When the party of the revolution holds the reins of power, violence must become exclusively an instrument of the state."[52]

The vice of jealousy must be added to the catalogue of his unpleasing failings. Jealousy of men and of countries more favored than himself or his own country warped his judgment and led him into enterprises he would otherwise never have undertaken. Thus it was jealousy of Germany that impelled him to launch the disastrous invasion of Greece and to suffer the humiliation of rescue at the hands of Hitler.

Mussolini's vanity and egotism rested on a mystical and irrational belief that he had been called to regenerate his country. Equally irrational was the deeply rooted superstition implanted in him during his childhood by *"la vecchia Giovanna."* He not only thought that he was endowed with a second sense, which was more reliable than the process of reason, but he was a prey to vulgar superstitions. Thus he was openly afraid of *jettatori,* men with the evil eye. On one occasion he insisted on flying to Pisa in bad weather, but abandoned the project at short notice when he was told that two deputies known to be *jettatori* were in his anteroom asking to be received.[53]

King Alfonso of Spain was also reputed to have the evil eye and Mussolini, after calling on him in Rome, a duty which he could not evade, instructed his chauffeur to drive very slowly. He was also very sensitive about anything which might bring him bad luck.

When he heard of Lord Carnarvon's sudden death in Egypt he immediately lifted the telephone to give instructions that a mummy which had recently been presented to him should be disposed of without delay. He was rather ashamed of this episode, and when Ludwig taxed him with it, admitted to being superstitious, but claimed rather feebly that in this particular case he had not been moved by superstition, but by the conviction that it was a profanation to traffic in dead bodies.

His superstition colored his attitude to religion, which was characteristically contradictory and confused. As a boy he had been made to go to church and disliked it. "I followed the practice of religion with my mother, who was a believer, and my grandmother, but I could not remain for so long in church, especially during the grand ceremonies. The rosy light of the candles, the penetrating smell of incense, the color of the sacred vestments, the slow, monotonous singing of the faithful, and the sound of the organ all disturbed me profoundly."[54] His sister relates that as children they were compelled to say long prayers and that Benito once remarked: "With so many rosaries we shall certainly gain paradise, even if for the rest of our lives we forget to pray."[55]

The religious discipline of the Salesians at Faenza and his father's aggressive atheism, reinforced by the anticlericalism of his Socialist comrades, deepened his dislike of the Church. The Christian doctrines of charity and humility affronted him. He published anticlerical works and constantly attacked the Vatican in speeches and press articles. In 1918 he refused to solicit information from the Vatican about the safety of Edvige's husband, who was believed to be a prisoner of war. Addressing his followers on January 1, 1920, he spoke of the rival papacies of Moscow and Rome, with their respective encyclicals: "We are the heretics of both religions. We have torn to pieces all the revealed truths, we have spat upon all the dogmas, rejected all the paradises, scoffed at all the charlatans, red, white, and black, who market miraculous drugs to give happiness to mankind. We do not believe in programs, in schemes, in saints, in apostles; we do not, above all, believe in happiness, in salvation."[56]

A few months later he was quite suddenly enlightened and came to recognize that the grandeur of Rome was bound up with the prestige of the Holy See. He understood that he could no longer afford to violate the feelings of millions of his countrymen, and he began to prepare his followers for a radical change in his policy. Later when he became Prime Minister he paid a visit to the Pope and began to attend official religious functions. "Beyond question power and harmony are promoted for a statesman if he adheres to the religion of his countrymen," was his explanation to Ludwig.[57] This consideration probably led him to arrange in April, 1923, that his children, Edda, Vittorio, and Bruno should be baptized and subsequently confirmed; and towards the end of 1925, in deference to the wishes of Pope Pius XI, he went through a religious marriage ceremony with Rachele.

In the public sphere he restored religious education and brought the crucifix back into the schools. The Fascist state was officially declared to be a pillar of religion:

The Fascist state is not indifferent to religious phenomena in general, nor does it maintain an attitude of indifference to Roman Catholicism, the special positive religion of the Italians. The state has no theology, but it has a moral code. The Fascist state sees in religion one of the deepest of spiritual manifestations, and for this reason it not only respects religion, but defends and protects it. The Fascist state does not attempt, as did Robespierre at the height of the revolutionary delirium of the Convention, to set up a "god" of its own; nor does it vainly seek, as did bolshevism, to efface God from the soul of man. Fascism respects the God of ascetics, saints, and heroes, and it also respects God as conceived by the ingenuous and primitive heart of the people, the God to whom their prayers are raised.[58]

Mussolini's conversion was not permanent and there were times when he relapsed into the fiercest anticlericalism. There is no doubt that his transient change of heart was imposed on him by his sense of opportunism. Yet expediency may not have been the only consideration which dictated this difficult and delicate move, for underlying everything there was a superstitious and niggling uncertainty about the supernatural. Thus as a soldier he went to Mass on Christmas Day, and after his son Bruno had been killed he asked that a Mass should be said for his soul. It was a form of reinsurance. He may have heard the story of Voltaire who told a pious lady that she would be painfully surprised when she discovered that there was no Heaven and received the retort that he would be more painfully surprised to find that there was a Hell.

The most serious charge leveled at Mussolini was that he was a coward. It was a charge which had some substance, for he was a curious mixture of combative aggressiveness and prudence. It is surprising how many of his former associates use the word "timid" to describe this aspect of his character. In his youth Angelica Balabanoff noted that whenever he was called on to face an unpleasant situation, to refuse an article for *Avanti,* to dismiss a member of the staff, or conduct an awkward interview, he would ask her to act for him.[59] When Italy in 1915 entered the war—which he had demanded—he did not rush, as others did, to be enrolled as a volunteer; nor did he return to the front after he had been wounded. Similarly when the Fascist squads were rampaging over northern Italy or concentrating for the March on Rome, he was never in the front line, but elected to squat far from the scene of action in his headquarters at Milan. After he had become Prime Minister he was notoriously frightened of assassination, although he was calm and brave in the hour of peril. "Fancy, a woman," was his only comment when Miss Gibson shot him in the nose; and his instinct of an actor drove him with admirable presence of mind to take full advantage of the situation: "If I go forward," he told the bystanders after he had been bandaged, "follow me. If I go back, kill me. If I die, avenge me." [60] In his dealings with individuals or with his problems of domestic policy he rarely showed moral courage. He was something of a bully, who trampled on the weak and showed respect for men of independent outlook.

His enemies allege that he was a man altogether devoid of courage. Yet it would be an oversimplification to brand him as a coward, since he was brave on occasion and did not recoil from taking a calculated risk. A. Rossi, who was no friend, shows insight in dealing with this aspect of his character:

To talk in terms of current psychology of his cowardice or courage is to miss his real personality. Mussolini was too shrewd to be really brave, but he was shrewd enough not to be the slave of his nerves. He had a fine instinct for the road to success and eventually always managed to take it. With no love of danger for its own sake he would do all he could to avoid or reduce it, but when it was a question of asserting himself or of self-preservation he was ready to accept whatever the situation dictated.[61]

As Rossi says, his quality lay in the cynical agility with which he seized every fleeting opportunity to turn events to his own advantage. He skillfully deployed his talents as an orator, an actor, and an impresario to enthrall the masses, and his gift of imagination was used to forge many of the weapons in his armory: the pomp, the uniforms, the rallies, the slogans, and the ceremonies, all of which were later gratefully imported into Germany by the Nazis. His will power and vitality were other qualities which enabled him for a time to impose himself on the nation. As is usually the case with dictators, it was the ruling classes which first began to criticize and turn against him. The loyalty of the masses he was able to retain until, in the period of his decline, he led them into a war which they did not want, submitted them to the voracious exigencies of the German invader, and brought them face to face with ignominious defeat. Even so, he was enthusiastically received in Milan a short time before his death and today he is regarded with more indulgence in modern Italy than is Hitler in the German Federal Republic.

VI

It is easy to see how in the course of his life his qualities and defects shaped his conduct at each stage. In the first phase he was a revolutionary, a restless, disheveled vagabond who carried no ballast, but was moved by only one idea, to cut a figure in the world. During this period he learned the rudiments of journalism, acquired facility in public speaking, and served his apprenticeship in a political party. His attitude and the views he then expressed were the reflection of his circumstances. He was never happy in the Socialist party, but used it purposefully to advance his own career. By his behavior during the Tripoli campaign and his deft handling of the Socialist congress at Reggio Emilia he acquired a leading position in the movement. With the outbreak of war in 1914 his instinct stood him in good stead and, without any consideration for his former associates, he seized the first opportunity to pass into the interventionist camp. It was a hazardous move, perfectly timed and justified by events. It gave him the ownership of a national newspaper and, thanks to the publicity given to his agitation for the war, he was now for the first time a completely independent figure in politics. He owed his success to persistence, shrewdness, and a bland refusal to be inhibited by accusations of inconsistency and disloyalty to his former party.

In his second phase his circumstances and outlook had altered. He had realized his first ambition. He was a somebody and he was assuaged by the knowledge that he had arrived. He was earning a modest but sufficient income and had discarded the rags of his youth in favor of the uniform of the bourgeois. His task was now to hoist himself into the seat of government. For this purpose he cheerfully cast aside one by one the articles of his previous faith. He sought allies where he could find them, among the landed proprietors, the industrialists, and the army, for he knew that otherwise his unfledged Fascist movement must perish. It was during these three years that Mussolini's tactical skill, which was almost political genius, was seen at its best. Beset on one side by the indiscipline of his party bosses in the North, and on the other by the threat of a parliamentary combination which might summon resolution to squash him, he steered his way past successive rocks and whirlpools.

At first he set his sights no higher than participation, with a few portfolios in some coalition government; and the man who had previously fulminated against the system of parliamentary combinations and indeed against parliament itself, negotiated in turn with Giolitti, Orlando, and Salandra as if to the manner born. At each stage he allowed himself the maximum liberty of maneuver, he conciliated churchmen and monarchists, and, when the Facta government began to disintegrate, he was the first to take note of the portents. It was then that against the pressure of his less adventurous followers he resolved to have no further truck with political combinations and to demand power for himself. So skillful was his handling of the situation that his appointment as Prime Minister was made to appear the logical and inevitable solution; and he arrived in Rome without any constitutional disturbance, to be greeted as the savior of the nation. While other men might have been thrown off balance by the heady wine of sudden and unexpected success, he lent an ear to the counsels of prudence and formed his government on the broadest possible base. It was an achievement on which any politician could look back with pride.

The third phase, which lasted until 1934, brought Mussolini to the summit of power and success. After surmounting the Matteotti crisis he was able to abolish parliament, to extinguish civil liberties, to bring the Fascist formations under control, and to remove all recalcitrant politicians from his path by imprisonment or exile. It was a period of personal rule, untidy but not ineffective, in which he was unhampered by any outside influence. The trains were punctual and this, together with other administrative reforms, well advertised by Fascist propaganda, led the world to accept the dictum that Mussolini had done great things for Italy. There was no man in Europe whose prestige stood higher. In 1933 Ramsay Macdonald, who had virulently attacked Mussolini some years previously, paid a visit to Rome accompanied by Sir John Simon. There were conversations and reciprocal entertainments, and the British party returned to London much impressed by their host. Ramsay Macdonald in particular was bewitched by Mussolini's imaginative ingenuity and in the cabinet rather bored his colleagues with a fulsome account of the Duce's quality. Mussolini, for his part, took to Macdonald and told Rachele that: "He realizes that Italy is no longer the country she was in the immediate postwar period. I am grateful to him for this and for his welcome cordiality." [62]

Ramsay Macdonald was not singular in his assessment, for by that time Mussolini had acquired sufficient experience and poise to be able to persuade all his foreign visitors that he was a European statesman of the first rank. Gandhi, who visited him in 1931, described him as the savior of the new Italy. The Mahatma called on Mussolini at the Villa Torlonia accompanied by his goat; and when after the interview Mussolini found his sons laughing at the goat he looked at them severely and said: "That man and his goat are shaking the British Empire." [63] Franz von Papen, who came in 1933, wrote of Mussolini:

> I found the Italian dictator a man of very different caliber to Hitler. Short in stature, but with an air of great authority, his massive head conveyed an impression of great strength of character. He handled people like a man who was accustomed to having his orders obeyed, but displayed im-

mense charm and did not give the impression of a revolutionary. Hitler always had a slight air of uncertainty, whereas Mussolini was calm, dignified, and appeared the complete master of whatever subject was being discussed. I felt he would be a good influence on Hitler; he was much more of a statesman and reminded one of a diplomat of the old school rather than a dictator.[64]

Papen's master, Hitler, also fell under the spell of Mussolini, for whom he had unbounded admiration, which bordered on veneration. He had no opinion of the Italian people and regarded it as Mussolini's misfortune that he should be at the head of a nation so effete, so racially impure, and so infected by Christian sentiment. But Mussolini's success in storming the bastions of the old order had been Hitler's guiding star during the weary years of his struggle for power; and he never ceased to regard him as a genius, a singular prophet who had pointed and prepared his own way: "The brown shirt would probably not have existed without the black shirt. The March on Rome in 1922 was one of the turning points of history. The mere fact that anything of the sort could be attempted, and could succeed, gave us an impetus." [65] Speaking to a vast crowd on the Maifeld in Berlin, on September 28, 1937, Hitler described Mussolini as "one of those lonely men of the ages on whom history is not tested, but who are themselves the makers of history." As late as February, 1945, speaking in the Berlin bunker, he said: "The Duce himself is my equal. He may perhaps even be my superior from the point of view of his ambitions for his people." [66] Another very different German, Emil Ludwig, wrote of him in 1932: "I have no hesitation in describing him as a great statesman." [67]

A number of English visitors, including Duff Cooper,[68] were equally enthusiastic. Sir Winston Churchill made no effort to conceal his sympathy with and respect for the Italian dictator: "On the two occasions in 1927 when I met Mussolini, our personal relations had been intimate and easy." [69] Years later in his broadcast to the Italian people on December 23, 1940, he said of him: "That he is a great man I do not deny." [70] Lord Avon (Sir Anthony Eden) wrote of him that he was a man whose personality would be felt in any company.[71] It was part of the contradiction in Mussolini's nature that clarity of expression, on which his visitors commented, should have flowed from confusion of mind.

This third phase of Mussolini's life was the heyday of his career. He was still prepared to listen to, if not always to follow, professional advice, and his qualities were sufficient to keep him out of trouble. A member of his personal secretariat during this period describes him as a pleasant master to serve, though he could be rude and impatient.[72] He had in particular a disconcerting habit of ringing the bell to put incoherent questions which were quite impossible for a secretary not sharing his thoughts to answer. He might, for example, look up from his desk to inquire: "What on earth are we to do with this man?"; and he would display annoyance when no answer was forthcoming. On occasions he would indulge in a somewhat primitive peasant humor. Once, after he had become president of the Antiblasphemy League, he complained that rain was badly needed and walking to the window to survey the cloudless sky turned to his secretary and said: "I am now the president of the Antiblasphemy League, but if it doesn't rain within two days, I shall have to order the nation to blaspheme."

His personal staff and political associates were not always so impressed with him as were his visitors, on whom he turned the full flow of his magnetism, but they respected him for what he had done for Italy, in particular for the establishment of order, the inculcation of patriotism, the higher standing of the army, and the growing prestige of Italy abroad. And when the time came for a transfer to another post and Mussolini sped them on their way with a signed photograph and a graceful expression of his thanks, they left him with sentiments of affection and regret.

During those golden years neither Mussolini's defects nor the weakness of his personal system of government had become apparent or led to visible failure. But the seeds of his eventual destruction were being sown. Surrounded by adulation at home and abroad, he allowed his natural arrogance, untempered by any reverse, to grow to dangerous proportions.

It was in 1935 that in his fourth phase he began almost imperceptibly to go downhill. Corruption by power, which prevents every dictator from keeping abreast of events, freedom from domestic criticism, the tendency to fall a victim to one's own propaganda, and his own lack of thoroughness and administrative capacity were all contributory factors. But the principal cause of his ruin was the rise of Nazi Germany, which excited his jealousy and his apprehensions. Jealousy, aggravated by his natural egotism, drove him to attempt to match the German dictator and so to embark on a series of adventures. In this later process the earlier conquest of Abyssinia proved more damaging than any other enterprise. He embarked on this war with many misgivings and against the advice of his experts; but, when he emerged from it with more than a modicum of glory and without a scratch, he became convinced of his own infallibility and was no longer prepared to listen to the voice of reason.

As Hitler became more powerful, jealousy was overlaid by fear, since Mussolini appraised Hitler's character sufficiently well to realize the mortal danger of thwarting the German dictator. He might have been more robust had Britain and France shown more resolution in resisting Hitler's growing pretensions, but Mussolini was convinced that the democracies were pacifist at heart; and in their conversations with him the British and French leaders emphasized their desire for peace rather than their military strength. This was a mistake which Hitler did not make. Mussolini was interested only in power, and with anguish he drew the inevitable conclusion from the terrifying and rapid rise of Germany's military might. As the years passed, he fell more and more under the personal domination of Hitler, who filled him with an admixture of hatred and admiration. Mussolini knew very little about the art of war, and Hitler was able with a flow of statistics and military jargon to persuade him that Germany was invincible. From his encounters with the German Fuehrer the doubting Italian Duce returned confident in the victory of the common cause. Nevertheless there were moments when, like a cornered animal, he sought desperately a means of escape. For example, when Hitler invaded Norway, Mussolini joyfully looked forward to a resounding German defeat which would restore to him some liberty of movement. But the failure of the Western Allies soon convinced him that he must continue to maneuver as best he could within very narrow limits under ever more ruthless German pressure. With impotent rage gnawing at his heart Mussolini was dragged, a reluctant and despised vassal, in Hitler's wake along the road chosen by his master.

His decline was accompanied and accelerated by physical degeneration. His ulcers troubled him, depression overcame him, and his whole fabric coarsened. The spry, youthful dictator was now a fat, bald, prematurely aged figure. His grip on affairs had loosened and he consoled himself for his political impotence by the demonstration of his prowess in the boudoir. Indeed there was no other field in which he could claim to be his own master. The conduct of the war was entirely in German hands and at home he was obliged to submit to German wishes, even to the extent of tolerating the maltreatment of Italian laborers in Germany. His only hope lay in the success of German arms and in the fruits of an ultimate victory in which he might be allowed some share.

When this hope evaporated at the end of 1942 Mussolini suffered a moral and physical collapse. In the last phase he stumbled from one disaster to another. Without faith in himself or in his star, without dignity, and without any effort to escape his impending doom he allowed himself to be carried helplessly on the tide of events. He was a broken, disillusioned man.

VII

His end obscured his achievements, which were considerable. His place in history is assured if only because he was the first man to launch a new form of socialism, the socialism of nationalism, a system which was later adopted by many other countries and which altered the face of Europe in his generation. Despite the material benefits he conferred on Italy, it was not a beneficent innovation and the fashion which he set had calamitous consequences. Nevertheless his revolution was a significant event.

It is difficult to say when exactly he came to the conclusion that nineteenth-century socialism was out of tune with the requirements of the day, that it would never gain power, and that it should be replaced by a form of state control not far removed from Marxism, but cut to an aggressively nationalist pattern. His ideas were of course to some extent derived from Sorel, Nietzsche, Blanqui, and other apostles of force, but the process of his evolution was gradual and was to some extent conditioned by events. There was always in his outlook an element of dissatisfaction with the Italian Socialist party; and the First World War and the need after the war to justify intervention precipitated his move from revolutionary republicanism within the Socialist ranks to nationalism. He did not, however, abandon the idea of revolution. Instead of effecting it on the barricades, in his view a hopeless prospect, he planned to enroll followers under the standard of nationalism and eventually to obtain peaceful possession of the machinery of government. In the exposed situation in which he thus found himself he was obliged to seek support on a broad basis; and he discarded republicanism, anticlericalism, and the nationalization of industry. He even tried to govern through parliament despite his dislike of the system. Once again events intervened and he was able sooner than he had thought possible to dispense with parliament and to create a monolithic, nationalist state under the leadership of one man. With this act his revolution was accomplished.

To have achieved so much in so short a time required a high degree of talent and imagination. Without any advantages of birth, education, or political experience he launched a new movement in 1919, and within a period of thirty months had scattered the traditional parties to wrest power for himself. Under the burden of office the youthful leader did not falter. Indeed during the first ten years of his rule he had won a prestige which raised the international status of Italy and earned for his person the deference of the world.

It is remarkable that a man with so many obvious defects should have done all this. The explanation is that his very considerable talents matched the situation. He came into politics at a moment when the war, for which he had campaigned, had shaken the basis of society. Revolution was in the air, but Catholic Italy, while demanding a change, was not ripe for communism on the Russian model. Mussolini's brand of national socialism met the mood of the nation. His appeal for a new deal, backed by the most intense and skillful propaganda, fell on ready ears, but he still would not have triumphed but for the self-seeking blindness and incapacity of the old political parties.

In his *Letter to a Comrade* of October, 1917, Lenin laid down the conditions of a successful revolution: incapacity of the governing class, general hostility to the established order, and middle-class sympathy. All these conditions were present in the Italy of 1922. After Mussolini's advent to power his qualities—mental agility, shrewdness, ruthless opportunism, and histrionic and rhetorical talent—kept him afloat in a flabby world, in which for a time he was not subjected to much competition, and people were prepared to accept him at his own valuation. But during this halcyon period his defects were rotting the fabric he had created and, when he came to be severely tested, his jealousy, lack of courage, vanity, egotism, ignorance, and superficiality led him into policies which were the logical consequence of his own errors and inexorably plunged his country into servitude and disaster.

It is difficult to fix Mussolini's fluid, kaleidoscopic character. To say that he was stupid belies the skill and tactical ability he showed in several critical situations, while on as many occasions he was guilty of crass errors of judgment. He could be generous more from motives of pride than of charity, but he was as often vindictive and amoral. He combined cowardice with a certain degree of courage. Unpredictable, romantic, and unstable he could play any role. So it is that the differing judgments passed on him by supporters and enemies and the evidence on which they are based cannot be wholly accepted or rejected. Some may accept the verdict of Hegel that "the great man of the age is the one who can put into words the will of his age, tell his age what its will is and accomplish it." In this sense it might be argued that Mussolini was a great man. But the truth in relation to this complex character is surely that he is likely to enjoy fame, but that he can lay no claim to real greatness. He was an agile, imaginative pragmatist; and in the sense that he was never at any time able to fill the role for which he had cast himself, he was a pathetic figure. Count Sforza speaks of him in the words of one of Alfred de Vigny's characters: "His attitude, his voice are only an actor's pantomime, a miserable parade of sovereignty whose vanity he must know. It is impossible that he believes in himself so sincerely. He prevents all of us from raising the veil, but he sees himself naked beneath it. And what does he see? A poor ignorant wretch, like all of us, and under that disguise the weak human creature." [73]

For all his misdeeds and the damage he did to Italy and the world, it is difficult not to feel compassion for the young man of thirty-nine as with the mingled optimism and secret misgivings born of his inexperience he set out on his journey.

CHAPTER EIGHT

The Prime Minister

1922–1924

I

THE world into which Mussolini found himself so suddenly projected was a strange one. He had a short experience of the Chamber of Deputies, but he had never set foot in a government department and he required a little time to familiarize himself with the workings of the two key offices over which he was to preside—Foreign Affairs and the Interior. During the early days he was concerned to create two different and somewhat contradictory impressions; first that a new broom was at work with feverish energy, and, secondly, that moderation would be his watchword at home and abroad. He was of course insistent that Italian rights and dignity would have to be respected. He could hardly be expected to do less, but he assured all and sundry of his devotion to peace and of his desire to establish good relations with foreign countries. At home, the composition of his government and the expression of his intention to govern through Parliament offered an assurance that there would be no violent upheaval. He was cautiously feeling his way and it was important to do all he could to allay misgivings. It can be said that in both enterprises he was successful.

One of his first engagements was to receive the British ambassador on November 1, 1922. It was a very friendly interview and Sir Ronald Graham reported that the Duce had been quiet in his demeanor and had spoken with studied moderation. On domestic affairs he had said that faction was at an end, that he would impose discipline on the nation, and that all would henceforth work together for the greatness of Italy. The only substantial change he had in mind was a reform of the electoral law. The army would be nonpolitical, and he had just forbidden (this was true) a proposed military demonstration in his honor. After some conversation on current diplomatic affairs, on which Mussolini disarmingly admitted his ignorance, he assured the ambassador of his desire to have good relations and cooperation with England. On this point Sir Ronald Graham reported that a mutual friend had asked Mussolini whether his recent public criticisms of England might not prove embarrassing and had received the reply: "Not at all; those are things which one says when one has no responsibility, but forgets as soon as possible the moment one has." Altogether it was a very satisfactory interview and Sir Ronald, who had expected to meet a hothead, came away with the feeling that Mussolini was a man with whom one could do business.

On the following day Mussolini gave an interview to a representative of *The Sunday Express* in which he said that Italy wished to be treated by the Great Powers as a sister and not as a servant girl. Nevertheless he denied that he wished to beat the Italian drum in order to obtain a solution of the whole Adriatic problem or indeed to embark on any risky adventure. He denied that fascism was militaristic and reactionary, but he said that a Conservative Italy expected the support of a Conservative England. A week later, addressing the French newspaper correspondents in Rome, he spoke of his hope of a cordial understanding with France and announced the imminent signature of a Franco-Italian commercial agreement.

II

Having thus prepared the way for his first appearance on the international stage, Mussolini left Rome on November 18 to attend the Lausanne Conference on Turkey. It was an important conference, held under the shadow of the Chanak incident which had so nearly precipitated a war. Lord Curzon had wisely declined to enter the conference unless an explicit understanding were reached in advance that a united front as between Britain, France, and Italy should be constituted and subsequently maintained. Poincaré reluctantly agreed and a joint telegram was sent to Mussolini inviting him to meet the British and French ministers at Lausanne on the evening of November 19 before the conference opened.

Mussolini enjoyed a triumphant progress as his train moved up through Italy. At each station on the way he was received with manifestations of popular enthusiasm. It was a spontaneous acclamation for the new man who was going abroad to defend the national interest and to ensure that Italy should receive the fruits of victory of which she had unjustly been deprived. Salvatore Contarini, the Secretary General of the Ministry of Foreign Affairs, and Raffaele Guariglia, who accompanied Mussolini, wondered how the Duce would bring anything back from Lausanne to satisfy the aspirations of the pathetically trustful masses. But Mussolini, without consulting them, had already conceived his first theatrical diplomatic stroke. He suddenly gave orders that a telegram should be sent to Curzon and Poincaré asking them to meet him at Territet before going to Lausanne.

On the morning of November 19 Curzon and Poincaré traveled from Paris to Lausanne in the same train and, on reaching Pontarlier, received Mussolini's message. This communication caused some consternation and it was suggested by someone that Mussolini was unwilling or unable to come to Lausanne because the expulsion order served on him during his youth was still in force. In fact it had been courteously rescinded by the Swiss government as soon as he became Prime Minister. Poincaré of course recognized at once that the move was designed to bolster Mussolini's prestige, and Curzon agreed. But while the Frenchman resented the implication, the Englishman was indulgently ready to pander to the Duce's pride, particularly since Poincaré seemed to be so angry about it all. After some parley it was agreed to travel on to Territet without the members of the delegations, who were dropped at Lausanne station to the discomfiture of the Swiss reception committee, drawn up to receive the distinguished visitors.

At Territet Mussolini received Curzon and Poincaré in the Grand Hotel and without a word to his experts asked that the conversation should be restricted to the three men. After a short time they emerged and, to the consternation of the Italian experts, produced an agreed communiqué stating that Italy would be treated at the Lausanne conference by her allies on a footing of equality. The professionals felt, not without reason, that an undertaking to treat Italy as an equal implied a degree of inferiority. Nevertheless this fine point was not taken by the Italian masses, who regarded Mussolini as having captured the first trick. Lord Curzon, who in return had received an assurance of Italian solidarity in the face of the Turks, was equally satisfied. Only Poincaré was displeased, for he had nothing to show from the expedition to Territet; and his annoyance was increased when he perceived that Mussolini had made arrangements to precede him to Lausanne in his private train.

Encouraged by this success, Mussolini adopted similar tactics when the conversation was resumed the following morning in Lord Curzon's sitting room at the Hotel Beau Rivage in Ouchy. At the appointed hour Poincaré with his delegation appeared together with the members of the Italian delegation, but there was no Mussolini. As the time passed Poincaré's irritation grew visibly and Victor Cavendish-Bentinck of the British delegation was dispatched to Mussolini's apartment in order to accelerate his arrival. There he met Mario Pansa, who inquired whether Curzon and Poincaré were already at hand. On receiving an acid affirmative reply he undertook to produce the Duce, who slowly entered the conference room and got down to work. Having made his gesture, Mussolini was not uncooperative and Lord Curzon attained his first objective, the affirmative of an Allied united front.

It cannot be said that Mussolini made an overwhelming impression at this, his first, conference. Sir Harold Nicolson, who was present, was struck by his lack of ease, evinced by a constant wriggling in clothes which appeared too tight or too stiff. "Mussolini—a shade embarrassed by being thus confronted at his first diplomatic conference by such giants of the profession—chafed uneasily against his stiff white cuffs, rolling important eyes. He said little. '*Je suis d'accord*' was the most important thing he said." [1]

It has been alleged that Curzon privately described Mussolini as a boor and a charlatan, but this is quite untrue. On the contrary, he recognized in the somewhat awkward figure a politician who was likely to play a prominent role in Europe, and he deployed all his charm not without success to captivate the dictator.[2] Mussolini for his part enjoyed the attention and on taking leave of Lord and Lady Curzon after his three days at Lausanne undertook to learn sufficient English within a month to write them a letter in English. Lord and Lady Curzon were hereafter classified in Mussolini's mind as friendly.

III

A month later Mussolini attended his second conference, this time the German reparations conference in London, where he met Bonar Law and Poincaré. It was an inconclusive meeting because of Franco-German differences and after four days he went home. He did not like London. He found the weather depressing—he was always very susceptible to weather—and he complained that the grime obliged him to change his collar three times a day. To his wife he said that he hoped that he would never have to go back to England. "Good manners, all right, but nothing tangible, Rachele. They don't or don't want to understand our needs. To them Italy is small beer, but we'll change all that. If they want me, they'll have to come to Italy for me." [3] He never saw England again, and, except for a scurry to Locarno, sixteen years were to elapse before he again ventured abroad to an international conference, which was to be his last.

IV

Meanwhile domestic affairs were also claiming his attention. His first important engagement was on November 16, 1922, when he presented his government to the Chamber of Deputies. His speech was a characteristic admixture of the carrot and the stick. On foreign policy, he pledged himself to fulfill all existing treaty commitments whether they were favorable or not. For the rest he would be tough and realistic:

> Italy today has a new importance which must be reckoned with adequately, and this fact is beginning to be recognized beyond her boundaries. We have not the bad taste to exaggerate our powers, but neither do we wish to belittle them with excessive and useless modesty. My formula is simple: "Nothing for nothing." Those who wish to have concrete proofs of friendship from us must give us the same. Fascist Italy,

just as she does not intend to repudiate treaties for many reasons, political, moral, and economic, does not intend either to abandon the Allies. Rome is in line with London and Paris; but Italy must assert herself and impose upon the Allies that strict and courageous examination of conscience which has not been faced by them from the time of the armistice up to the present day.

On domestic affairs he was first conciliatory. He undertook to restore internal order, violence would cease, religious liberty and civil rights would be respected, and he would govern in the interests of the nation rather than of any faction. His policy could be summed up in the three words: economy, work, and discipline. Having promised to work within the framework of the constitution, Mussolini reminded the Deputies that they were in his hands:

Revolution has its rights and I am here to defend and develop the revolution of the Blackshirts. I refused to make an outright conquest as I could have done. I put a limit to my actions. With my three hundred thousand armed men, prepared to dare everything and ready, almost mystically, to obey my orders, I could have punished those who have defamed and bespattered fascism. I might have made this bleak hall a bivouac for my platoons. I might have closed parliament altogether and created a government of Fascists alone. I could have done that, but such, at least for the present, has not been my wish.[4]

He concluded by demanding full powers for financial and bureaucratic reform and offered his bemused listeners the prospect of cooperation under the threat of force if they declined to collaborate.

I do not wish, as long as it is possible to avoid it, to govern against the wishes of the Chamber; but the Chamber must understand the peculiar position it holds, which makes it liable to dismissal in two days or two years. We ask for full powers because we wish to take full responsibility. Without full powers you know that not a penny—a penny I say—would be saved. By this we do not intend to exclude the possibility of voluntary cooperation, whether it be from deputies, senators, or single, competent citizens.[5]

Speaking eleven days later in the Senate, Mussolini once more reminded his audience that nothing could have prevented him from closing parliament and proclaiming a dictatorship. But after claiming credit for his moderation, he again issued a warning: "I do not intend that liberty shall degenerate into licence."[6] Despite his authoritative tone, or perhaps because of it, his speeches were well received and both houses of parliament voted him his full powers by substantial majorities. It was a notable parliamentary success. Mussolini told the British Ambassador after the debate that he was well aware that many members of the Chamber hated him. He had purposely addressed them in severe terms and had thought at one moment that a portion at least of them would have protested or resigned in a body. If they had followed this latter course no one would have been better pleased than himself, but they had evidently preferred life, even a short life, to an immediate death.

Having fixed parliament, Mussolini set about consolidating his position in the country. With his flair for propaganda and skill at promoting the cult of the individual he decided to leave his desk in Rome and to show himself all over Italy, including Sardinia, which he was the first Prime Minister to visit. It was a wise move, for it enabled him to bring multitudes who had never seen him under the spell of their new dynamic leader.

His political prospects were quite fortuitously improved by a severe and unexpected blow to the *Partito Popolare*. The party held its annual congress at Turin in April, 1923, and the principal subject of debate was its policy towards the Fascist government. The delegates were split into three sections, the Right, which supported the government; the Left, which demanded opposition; and the Center, led by Sturzo, which favored collaboration under conditions. This lack of unity was inevitable in a party which had drawn its adherents from every element in the political spectrum.

Don Sturzo was, however, able to carry the congress with him. In a remarkable speech he advocated the maintenance of Christian liberty against the encroachments of the pantheist state. If the government accepted this premise, the party would collaborate, but, he added, "one collaborates standing, not kneeling." The congress endorsed his policy by a large majority and Mussolini, in dudgeon, called on his *Popolare* ministers to resign.

Immediately afterwards the Fascist press launched a scurrilous campaign against Don Sturzo, which received support from the right wing of the party. An article in the Catholic *Corriere d'Italia* even accused Don Sturzo of causing embarrassment to the ecclesiastical authorities. To what extent the Vatican was implicated is not likely ever to be known, but in this new situation Don Sturzo resigned; and the party, already weakened by dissension, ceased to be a political force which might have offered a dangerous challenge to fascism. It was a fortunate change of wind for Mussolini.

On his return from the provinces he solved the problem of his paramilitary formations by abolishing the gendarmerie and creating a voluntary Militia of National Security, to be recruited exclusively from the old Fascist militia, the cost to be borne on the vote of the Ministry of the Interior. He also removed any threat of competition from the hated Masons by moving the Grand Council to declare that Freemasonry was incompatible with fascism. The Mason members of the Council who were obliged to resign immediately from their Lodges included Balbo, Acerbo, and Rossi.

V

In July he brought in his electoral reform bill, which abolished the system of proportional representation, introduced after the war, in favor of one designed to ensure that the government should enjoy a safe parliamentary majority. Under the terms of the bill the whole kingdom was to be regarded as one constituency, divided into fifteen electoral districts. The aggregate votes would be counted and two-thirds of the seats in the Chamber of Deputies (357 out of 535) would be automatically allotted to the party obtaining the greatest number of votes, always provided it received more than 25 per cent of the total votes cast. The remaining seats were to be divided among the other parties in proportion to the number of votes they received.

Of the outcome of an election held under this law there could be no doubt since Mussolini enjoyed the backing of the majority of the nation. The London *Times,* reviewing his first year of office, had this to say on October 31, 1923:

> It is incontestable that Italy has never been so united as she is today. . . . People have become impressed by the fact that *Fascismo* is not merely the usual successful political revolution, but also a spiritual revolution. *Fascismo* has abolished the game of Parliamentary chess; it has simplified the taxation system and reduced the deficit to measurable pro-

portions; it has vastly improved the public services, particularly the railways; it has reduced a superfluously large bureaucracy without any very bad results in the way of hardships or unemployment; it has pursued a vigorous and fairly successful colonial policy. All this represents hard and useful work, but the chief boons it has conferred upon Italy are internal security and national self-respect.

The electoral law was an ingenious expedient designed to put an end to the old game of political combinations and, as such, since the Chamber would not reflect the mood of the country, it was bound to arouse the opposition of the parties. In consequence Mussolini had originally intended to impose the change by decree, but the King, who disliked the law, insisted that it should receive parliamentary sanction and Mussolini reluctantly complied. It was his first brush with the monarch and on his return from the audience he muttered that if the monarchy continued to put spokes in the wheel, he would open the door to republicanism, which he had never definitely closed. The outcome of the debate was awaited with interest and on the part of the Fascists with some trepidation, since they held only thirty-five seats in the Chamber and defeat might create a difficult situation. Mussolini, fearing a hostile combination of all the parties in the Chamber, cunningly appointed three former Prime Ministers, Giolitti, Orlando, and Salandra to be members of a Committee to study and report on the bill. He knew all three to be hostile to proportional representation and therefore likely to welcome the new system. The event proved him right, for all three reported in favor of the bill.

Nevertheless Mussolini, aware of the deep current of opposition and sensing the mood of the House made a speech which was firm in substance but exceedingly conciliatory in tone. He promised a return to order, to parliamentary methods, to concord between citizens, and to respect of parties: "I beg you to consider that fascism is in favor of elections. That is to say, it calls for the elections in order to conquer the communes and the provinces. It has called for them in order to send deputies to parliament; it does not therefore seek to abolish parliament. On the contrary, as I said before and I repeat it, the government wants to make of parliament a more serious, if not more solemn institution: it wants, if possible, to bridge over that hiatus which undeniably exists between fascism and the country." [7] It was one of his finest speeches, which brought him a signal victory by 163 votes, including those of a number of members of the *Partito Popolare*. At its conclusion Giolitti, Salandra, and Orlando came down from their seats to congratulate the Prime Minister. The Senate subsequently approved the law by 165 to 41 votes.

Mussolini was, however, wise enough to know that a hardly won parliamentary triumph offered no guarantee of success at the polls. He determined therefore not to hold fresh elections until he was more assured of sufficient electoral support. There was no particular hurry, since he had armed himself with full powers and had no immediate need of a parliamentary majority. To the British ambassador he gave the disingenuous explanation that the country needed a period of quiet and should not be subjected to the turbulence of an electoral campaign.

VI

Hard on these events came the first crisis of Mussolini's premiership. A Boundary Commission in Albania had been appointed by the Conference of Ambassadors in Paris; and on August 27, 1923, the Italian General Tellini and all the Italian members of the Commission accompanying him were assassinated on Greek territory a few miles from the frontier. On receipt of this intelligence Mussolini was not only exceedingly angry, but seriously embarrassed. The man who had always derided previous governments for their feebleness in defending Italian interests now faced a situation in which he could not afford to subject himself to the same criticism. All that he had achieved during the previous ten months could be lost in a moment.

He was with difficulty dissuaded from taking immediate forcible action against Greece. Instead he addressed a seven-point ultimatum to the Greek government in which he demanded:

1. An unreserved public apology.
2. A memorial service for the victims in the Catholic Cathedral at Athens in the presence of the Greek government.

3. Honors to be paid by the Greek fleet in the Piraeus to the Italian flag, to be represented by a naval squadron despatched for the purpose.
4. Inquiry on the spot to be carried out in the presence of the Italian military attaché and to be completed in five days.
5. Capital punishment for all authors of the crime.
6. Military honors to be rendered to the bodies of the victims at the port of embarkation.
7. Payment of an indemnity of 50 million lire within five days.

These were stiff terms and the Greek government, who not unreasonably claimed that there was no evidence that they or indeed any Greek had been responsible for the outrage, offered only partial satisfaction. Whereupon, on August 31, the Italian navy bombarded Corfu, killing a number of civilians, and landed a substantial force of marines to occupy the island. Foreign opinion, led by the British press, was exceedingly hostile, but in Italy the public gave unqualified support to the enterprise.

The matter came up before the Council of the League of Nations on September 1 and the debate, in which Lord Robert Cecil played a leading part, reflected the almost universal disapproval with which Italy's action had been greeted. The Italians claimed that the Conference of Ambassadors was the body to whom the dispute should be referred, and on September 4 Mussolini threatened that he would leave the League of Nations if it declared itself competent. On September 6 the Council drew up proposed terms of settlement and, since no agreement could be reached at Geneva, transmitted the minutes of their proceedings to the Conference of Ambassadors in Paris.

Here the Italians found a more favorable atmosphere because the French, who were at grips with the Germans in the Ruhr, were anxious not to alienate Italy, and only the British representative could be expected to cause trouble. On September 7, the Conference of Ambassadors, acting with commendable speed, presented the following demands to the Greek government.

1. Apology by the highest Greek military authority to the representatives of the three Allied Powers.
2. Funeral service at Athens.

3. Salute by the Greek fleet to the Italian, British, and French flags.
4. Military honors to the bodies of the victims on embarkation.
5. Investigation of the outrage and punishment of the victims.
6. Supervision of the inquiry by a commission of Italian, British, and French delegates under a Japanese chairman.
7. Indemnity to be determined by the Permanent Court of International Justice at The Hague, to be based on the report of the Commission. Meanwhile the Greek government was to deposit 50 million lire with the Swiss National Bank.

These terms represented a considerable attenuation of Italy's original demands, but they were stiff enough in all conscience. The Greek government gave way. The first report of the Commission of inquiry was submitted on September 22, and on September 27 the Conference of Ambassadors decided to hand over to Italy the whole sum of 50 million lire deposited by the Greek government. The Italians for their part, after the demands presented in Paris had been met, evacuated Corfu.

The Italian press greeted the outcome as a triumph for Mussolini; and indeed, thanks to the connivance of the Conference of Ambassadors, he was able to extricate himself without damage and with a semblance of glory from a situation which might have proved untenable. Nevertheless Mussolini was not too pleased and, when Sir Ronald Graham saw him on September 16, he found him in a state of great nervous excitement and angry agitation. He said that he regarded the proceedings in the Council of the League and the terms of settlement, which the Italian ambassador had no business to accept, as grotesque. He inveighed against the League of Nations in general and in particular against the attitude of England as manifested by the press, by Lord Robert Cecil in Geneva, and the British ambassador in Paris. It was an unpleasant interview and Sir Ronald found that no defense or explanation of the British case made the slightest impression on the Duce.

Many responsible Italians, however, thought that Mussolini had gone too far and were much relieved that means had been found to bring the dispute to an end. This sentiment gradually percolated up to Mussolini. He began to realize that he was perhaps lucky to have escaped unscathed and to have misgivings about the wisdom of his own impetuosity. Moreover he was anxious to repair the damage caused to relations with England on whom he was dependent for concessions in Africa and elsewhere. Accordingly, when Sir Ronald Graham called on him a month later, the atmosphere was very different. Mussolini was calm and friendly. He admitted that he had misjudged Britain, which he recognized had not been actuated by hostility to Italy, but by motives which, though they might be difficult for the Italian mentality to appreciate, were worthy of respect. Of course he did not regard the League of Nations with much friendliness. Nevertheless it would be a mistake for Italy to leave the League or to antagonize it, and he had no intention of allowing anything of the kind. He concluded by expressing his sincere desire for friendly collaboration between Italy and Britain. The sudden change in his demeanor, brought about by susceptibility to the opinions of others, lack of reflection, and self-interest, was characteristic of Mussolini, in whom fluidity was at once a source of weakness and of strength.

The Corfu affair was an important episode in Mussolini's career. It strengthened his position at home at a time when he was still feeling his way, but it also brought him for the first time into conflict with world opinion. Sir William Tyrell * observed that it would soon be possible to assess his character, for the experience might impel him to further similar exploits or it might teach him prudence. As it happened it taught him prudence, and a very long time was to elapse before he embarked on another foreign adventure. In his new mood of caution he set himself to repair the damage and to initiate a period of close Anglo-Italian collaboration.

VII

Meanwhile Mussolini, under the impulse of his professional advisers, took a personal hand in expediting negotiations with Yugoslavia for a Fiume settlement. After the eviction of D'Annunzio in December, 1920, elections in Fiume had resulted in the defeat of the Italian Nationalist party and the victory of the Autonomists

* Deputy Undersecretary in the Foreign Office, later Permanent Undersecretary.

led by Riccardo Zanella, a former supporter of D'Annunzio, who now considered that only by fulfilling the Rapallo treaty could Fiume recover her former prosperity. However, before the election results could be made public, the ballot boxes were burned by the Nationalists and the local Fascist leader Francesco Giunta occupied the city hall. The provisional government resigned and the Italian government appointed a local Nationalist leader as Commissioner Extraordinary. An attempt to form a coalition government failed because Zanella had taken refuge in Yugoslavia, but in October, 1921, the Constituent Assembly was convoked and a government was set up by Zanella who attempted to set up an independent state with Italian financial aid. In March, 1922, the Fascists, led by Giunta and Guiriati, seized the city and once more Zanella fled to Yugoslavia.

The Genoa conference of April, 1922, had given the Italian and Yugoslav governments an opportunity to review the problem. A conference was subsequently held in May at Santa Margherita and a new Italo-Yugoslav agreement and three conventions were signed at Rome in October, 1922. This agreement aimed at the execution of the Rapallo treaty and provided that within twelve days from ratification Italy should evacuate the third Dalmatian zone around Zara. In regard to Fiume, it was stipulated that the Italians should evacuate Susak within five days from ratification, and that thereafter a mixed Italo-Yugoslav commission should delimit the frontier of the Free State of Fiume, open traffic with the city and organize the local administrative services in accordance with the terms of the Rapallo treaty. The commission was to complete its work within a month and differences would be submitted to the arbitration of the President of the Swiss Republic. Ratifications of the agreement were exchanged on February 26, 1923, the mixed commission met on March 1 at Abbazia, and Italian troops evacuated Zara and began to move out of the third Dalmatian zone. But at this point the commission got into difficulties. The Italians refused to hand over the Delta and Port Barros until a consortium for the common administration of the whole port had been constituted, while the Yugoslavs refused to reopen railway communications with Fiume until they took possession of the Delta and Port Barros. The deadlock was complete.

Apart from the damage to relations with Yugoslavia, Mussolini, who was already faced with an enormous budgetary deficit, had reason on financial grounds to seek an early solution. While the dispute was dragging on, Fiume was gradually being ruined. Its factories were closed, trade was at a standstill, the railway, which had been cut when D'Annunzio entered the town, had not been reopened and only substantial subsidies from Italy saved the inhabitants from starvation. Accordingly, in July, 1923, Mussolini made a compromise proposal: the abolition of the Free State and the incorporation of Fiume in Italy in exchange for the cession to Yugoslavia of the Delta and Port Barros. As negotiations dragged on Mussolini peremptorily demanded that the work of the mixed commission should be completed by September 15, 1923. On that date the Italian president of the local government resigned and Mussolini despatched General Giardino to Fiume to take charge of the local administration as Governor in the name of the Italian government. Faced by this situation, the Yugoslavs, who had vainly sought to obtain support in Paris, saw that the Italian annexation of Fiume had become inevitable and resolved to accept Mussolini's proposal.

On January 27, 1924, the Pact of Rome was signed by Mussolini and a Yugoslav delegation. Under this treaty Yugoslavia recognized Italy's full sovereignty over the city and port of Fiume and received the Delta and Port Barros. The new frontier was traced and Italy leased to Yugoslavia for fifty years, at a rent of one gold lira a year, the Thaon di Revel basin in the center of the port of Fiume. There was also a protocol providing for the amicable settlement of general Italo-Yugoslav questions. The treaty was welcomed in both countries, although in Croatia and Slovenia it represented a painful sacrifice in the interests of peace. For Mussolini the outcome was particularly gratifying since it expunged his betrayal of the cause of Fiume at the time of D'Annunzio's surrender. In recognition of the part which he had played in securing Fiume for Italy Mussolini was awarded the Collar of the Annunziata, the highest distinction which the King could bestow and which gives the recipient the title of Cousin to the Sovereign. D'Annunzio was not forgotten and was created Prince of Monte Nervoso. On February 22, 1924, a Royal Decree formally annexed Fiume to Italy and on

March 16 the King took possession of the city. It was another success to reinforce Mussolini's claim to be the only effective custodian of Italian interests.

VIII

It now seemed a suitable moment to hold general elections under the new electoral law. On January 25, 1924, parliament was dissolved and April 6 was declared to be polling day. With all the resources and the government behind him to make the elections in the time-honored manner, Mussolini could be assured of the outcome. Nevertheless he took every precaution to avoid an unpleasant surprise. In the South, in Sicily, and in Sardinia, where his movement was weak and tradition died hard, he decided in principle to include in his list national figures and local notables from other parties who could be regarded as fellow travelers.

At the same time Mussolini was unable and unwilling to conceal his displeasure at the whole electoral procedure. On January 28 he held a meeting in the Palazzo Venezia of all the leaders in the Fascist party. He told them that it was mortifying to have to embark on an electoral campaign, but that nevertheless it must be competently conducted. After derogatory remarks about the other parties, particularly the Socialists and the *Partito Popolare,* he assured his listeners that he would repel proposals for an alliance, although he would take, where he could, men who were ready to afford active and disinterested collaboration. But if by so-called normalization was meant the dissolution of the militia, he would reply: "He who touches the militia will receive a charge of lead." He concluded by pouring scorn on the system of elections. Nothing, he said, could be more ridiculous than to think of a Mussolini wasting his time compiling electoral lists.

In order to mark his detachment from the whole business he confided the task of drawing up his electoral lists to a committee of five: Giunta, Bianchi, Finza, Rossi, and Acerbo. Of the old gang of politicians they were able to secure Salandra and Orlando. Giolitti preferred to make a list of his own, while declaring that this did not signify hostility to the government and De Nicola, President of the Chamber, who had agreed to appear on the list, decided at the last moment to withdraw into private life. There were in addition a large number of Liberals and some deviationists from the *Partito Popolare* and parties of the Left. In order to guard against betrayal by these new allies, who were electorally useful, the committee were careful to pack a sufficient number of faithful Fascists in the list to assure an over-all majority in the new Chamber.

The accession of men from other parties was also important to Mussolini because it served to create public confidence in his administration. The Italian industrialists were contributing a large sum to his election expenses and they believed that the new recruits would use their influence to safeguard civil liberties and constitutional forms. The German industrialists and nationalists made the same mistake when they supported Hitler in 1933 and decided to enter his government.

When the committee presented the results of their arduous labors Mussolini received them with demonstrative ill humor, for like a sulky boy he was still at pains to show how much he disliked the system. After the meeting he said to Rossi: "This is the last time elections on this model will be held. Next time I will nominate them all." [8]

Although Mussolini personally had undertaken that the electoral campaign should be conducted in order and liberty, it was in fact marred by disgraceful acts of Fascist violence. In Genoa, Milan, Turin, Udine, Savona, Urbino, and Rome opposition members of parliament and party leaders were assaulted. One Socialist candidate, Antonio Piccinini, was kidnaped from his home and brutally slain. Inflamed by their battle with the *Partito Popolare,* the Fascists attacked individual priests, Catholic laymen, and Catholic establishments. In a few cases voters were intimidated and returns falsified. Deplorable though this conduct was, it cannot be said that it exercised a decisive influence on the outcome. Indeed in those areas in which Fascist violence was most prevalent the government list did least well.

Polling took place on April 6, 1924. The total result gave over four and a half million votes to Mussolini's list and nearly three million to the opposition. Under the electoral law Mussolini's list automatically obtained 355 seats in the chamber and the remainder were distributed as follows:—

Popolari	40
Unitary Socialists	29
Democrats	25
Giolittians	25
Communists	19
Maximalist Socialists	14
Republicans	8

The number of votes cast for the opposition, particularly in the North, was disappointingly large. In Piedmont, Lombardy, Liguria, and Venice the opposition secured 1,317,117 votes as against only 1,194,829 for the government list. The outcome in Milan was regarded as a personal affront by the Duce. Nevertheless, the elections gave him both the manifestation of popular support and the large parliamentary majority he required, and his political barometer was set fair when out of a clear sky an unpredictable storm burst over his head. Matteotti, the Socialist leader, was murdered. This event, which shook the Fascist movement to its foundations, was to have a profound effect on the evolution of Italian political life and on the outlook of Mussolini himself.

CHAPTER NINE

The Murder of Matteotti

1924

I

GIACOMO Matteotti was born in 1885 of a well-to-do family of Trentino origin. He soon joined the Socialist party and was present at the congress of Reggio Emilia in 1912, at which Mussolini first came into prominence. In 1919, at the age of thirty-four, he was elected Socialist deputy for Ferrara-Rovigo; and he was re-elected in 1921 and again in 1924. During these years he distinguished himself by his forceful and effective opposition to the Fascist movement. In the Chamber he attracted the unfavorable attention of the Fascists by his savage attacks on the proceedings of the Blackshirt militia in the North. On one occasion the violence of his invective provoked such a scene that the president of the Chamber was obliged to suspend the session. Tall, dark, ascetic, and fanatical, he was a figure to be feared. One of his friends likened him to a matador in the ring; and it is not surprising that his skill in debate, his vitality, his use of cold irony, and his thin sharp voice without inflection should have exasperated his opponents.

Matteotti was thus a marked man when, on May 24, 1924, he attended the opening of the new parliament. The atmosphere was charged with excitement, for in the Chamber the majority were now young men who had served in the war and taken part either in D'Annunzio's expedition to Fiume or in the guerrilla operations of the Fascist militia or in the March on Rome. They were ignorant of parliamentary procedure, excited by victory, and not in a mood to brook any manifestation of opposition.

The debate on the address passed off in relative calm, although Matteotti made an intervention which aroused some Fascist protest. On May 30, however, the President of the Chamber unexpectedly called a motion confirming the result of the elections. There was a moment of silence and the President was about to declare the motion carried when Matteotti rose to speak *extempore*. He declared that in various constituencies, which he named, violence had been used against the opposition parties. He demanded a return to the rule of law and proposed that no decision should be taken in regard to the validity of the election pending further examination of the electoral returns. The Fascists were so exasperated, their interruptions and brawls on the floor of the Chamber so violent and prolonged that the speech, which should have taken twenty minutes to deliver, lasted for an hour and a half. On the following day the *Popolo d'Italia* described it as a monstrous provocation. Meanwhile it was rumored that Matteotti was preparing another, more damaging speech, in which he intended to expose financial scandals implicating prominent men in the government.

On June 4 Matteotti had a lively passage of arms with Mussolini in the Chamber; and two days later Mussolini, smarting under the constant attacks of the opposition, could contain himself no longer and turning to the parties of the Left shouted: "You should receive a charge of lead in the back." The Fascist newspaper *Impero* wrote that the Fascist giant was about to deal its opponents a terrible blow and that there was nothing to prevent the movement setting up in every *piazza* in Italy the execution squads which should have been put to work in October, 1922. In Milan, Marinelli, the treasurer of the party, declared that he would carry out with lightning speed any order for action which he might receive from the Duce or the party leadership. Thus the stage was set for the tragedy which followed.

II

On June 11 it was noticed that Matteotti had disappeared, and as the hours passed the conviction grew that he had been abducted by the Fascists. On the following day Mussolini gave an assurance to an excited Chamber that all the resources of the government would be used to discover and punish the miscreants. On June 13 there was another agitated debate in the Chamber. After Grandi and Carlo Delcroix, speaking for the Fascists, had deplored the crime and promised retribution, Mussolini rose. He announced that three arrests had already been made and that the police hoped very shortly to lay their hands on all those who had taken part in the crime. If there was anyone in the House who was entitled to feel grieved and exasperated at what had occurred, it was himself. He had hoped that the country and indeed the Chamber were entering a period of pacification when suddenly this bestial crime had disturbed, not irreparably he believed, the process of moral reconstruction. He appealed for national unity and concluded by giving an assurance that the police would do their duty and that the law would take its course.

The opposition were, however, not in the Chamber to hear either the appeal or the undertaking, for in the morning they had resolved to take no further part in parliamentary proceedings so long as the mystery of Matteotti's disappearance was not cleared up. Twenty-three years elapsed and a global war was fought before this requirement could be fully met. Thanks to the action of the postwar Italian government, this sordid episode in Italian history was fully investigated and the facts made known to the world. Meanwhile the opposition, invoking the by no means analogous circumstances in which the Roman plebs proceeded to the Aventine Hill, declared that they had withdrawn to the Aventine. There they remained and with the exception of the Communists, never returned to the Chamber.

In the perpetration of the crime the principal actor was Amerigo Dumini, a young adventurer with a good war record, who at the time was acting as personal assistant to Cesare Rossi, head of the Prime Minister's press department. He had previously been sent to Paris by Marinelli to investigate the murder of Fascists by opposition exiles and had been wounded in a fray. He was thus by character and experience suited to undertake the liquidation of Matteotti. Dumini himself alleges that Marinelli became convinced that Matteotti was concerned with anti-Fascist operations in France and that the object of his abduction was to extract from him the information on this subject which the Fascist authorities required.[1] Dumini is, however, not a reliable witness and there is no doubt that the motive of the crime was to intimidate, if not to remove, an inconvenient opponent.

The second principal was Cesare Rossi, a Tuscan by origin. He began life as a worker in a printing office and subsequently joined the staff of various Syndicalist newspapers between 1905 and 1910. He was originally a pacifist, but like many Syndicalists favored intervention in 1914. He subsequently joined the *Popolo d'Italia* and after the March on Rome was called by Mussolini to manage the press, with an office in the Ministry of the Interior. There he became involved in a number of discreditable enterprises against enemies of the regime.

The third principal was Giovanni Marinelli. Born in 1880, he was a member of the Socialist party and was president of the Committee directing the abortive Red Week. He left the party with Mussolini and became treasurer of the Fascist party. He was a man of mediocre intelligence, but since all payments had to pass through his hands, he was intimately concerned with the secret measures taken against anti-Fascists at home or abroad.

The plot against Matteotti was carefully prepared. A large seven-seater automobile was procured and for some days Dumini and his associates kept Matteotti under observation so as to become acquainted with his movements. Matteotti lived in the Via Mancini, a small street which joins the Via Flaminia and the Lungo Tevere Arnaldo di Brescia. At about 4 P.M. the car drew up in the Lungo Tevere at the bottom of the Via Mancini. A man called Augusto Malacria was at the wheel and beside him sat Dumini, while the remainder of the party loitered on the pavement. Dumini avers that the car was only halted when they accidentally saw Matteotti in the street,[2] but there is no evidence to support this unlikely story; and it seems certain that the kidnapers were aware that he was due to leave his house to proceed to the parliament building and had laid their plans accordingly.

Punctually at the expected time Matteotti emerged from his dwelling on to the Lungo Tevere carrying his papers under his arm. The toughs on the pavement seized him; there was a short struggle in the course of which he was dealt violent blows, and he was bundled into the car which drove off at a furious speed in the direction of the Ponte Milvio. Matteotti managed surreptitiously to throw out of the window the railway pass issued to all deputies, which bore his name. But, more unfortunately for the perpetrators, a lawyer and a street cleaner witnessed the incident and the former was able to take the number of the car and to communicate it to the police.

With this valuable clue the police were soon on the track of the criminals and in the course of the next few days they arrested Dumini, Aldo Putato, Albino Volpi, Giuseppe Viola, and Amleto Poveromo, who were charged with the abduction of Matteotti. Malacria had fled to France, but was subsequently extradited. The police also arrested Filippo Filippelli, editor of the *Corriere Italiano*, who was charged with complicity in the crime inasmuch as he had lent the automobile in which Matteotti had been abducted.

III

Events moved so fast that by June 19 the judge entrusted with the investigation of the case was able to begin his work.[3] This task devolved on Mauro del Giudice, president of the criminal section of the Court of Appeal, who was assisted by Umberto Tancredi of the Procurator-General's department. Both of them were upright men who remained impervious to the pressure brought to bear on them from various quarters to conduct the case in such a manner as not to embarrass Mussolini. The wildest rumors were afoot and no one knew what an impartial investigation would reveal nor how high responsibility lay. The Procurator-General, Vincenzo Crisafulli, sent an emissary to Del Guidice to suggest that in view of his advanced years (he was sixty-eight) it might be wiser to step down and allow a younger man to undertake the work; and he named as the proposed substitute a judge well known for his Fascist tendencies. Del Guidice repulsed these and other advances and lost no time in beginning the "instruction," that is to say the private interrogation of the suspects.

As was to be expected, Dumini and his associates were uncommunicative and baldly denied all complicity in the crime. Filippelli, however, was ready to reveal all that he knew. He declared that at the beginning of June Dumini and Putato had asked him to lend a car for a few days because they were anxious to show Rome and its surroundings to some Fascist friends who had arrived from Milan. On the evening of June 10 Dumini and Putato had come to the office of the *Corriere Italiano* in a state of some agitation and Dumini had said: "Filippelli, there has been a sad bungle today, which we must promptly put right. Matteotti died today."

Dumini had then gone on to explain that after Matteotti's violent speech in the Chamber against fascism in general and Mussolini in particular, Mussolini had let it be understood that Matteotti must be taught a lesson. In consequence of instructions from Mussolini through Marinelli, Dumini and his associates had that day waited for Matteotti and abducted him as he was leaving his house for the Chamber. In the car Matteotti had struggled with Dumini's associates, who had then slain him. Unfortunately the car had been badly stained with blood, and it had become necessary to dispose of it quickly. Accordingly Dumini had asked Filippelli to arrange for the car to be garaged for the night until it could be made to disappear on the morrow.

In view of the gravity of this statement the judge issued a warrant for the arrest of Marinelli and Cesare Rossi. Marinelli was delivered to the prison without delay but declined to make any statement. Rossi had fled, but after a week in hiding during which he abandoned hope that Mussolini would help him to cross the frontier with a false passport, surrendered to the authorities on June 22.

Like Filippelli, Rossi was cooperative from the start. Del Giudice describes him as a tall, handsome man of cultivated appearance, with features which revealed that he was not at all the same type as the gangsters who had actually committed the murder. Rossi, under examination, stated that in order to understand what had happened it was necessary to advert to previous Fascist assaults on the persons of the opposition Deputies Amendola, Cesare Forni, and Alfredo Misuri. Mussolini, he declared, was anxious to impose an absolute dictatorship on Italy and had proposed to Rossi, Marinelli, and De Bono the constitution of a secret organization, whose task would be to intimidate the opposition, and Matteotti in particular, by means of acts of violence—woundings, beatings, administration of castor oil, and, if necessary, the killing of the most dangerous adversaries, thus reducing them all to silence.

According to Rossi, Mussolini had asked him to suggest the name of a courageous Fascist without scruples who could be relied on to carry out any task assigned to him. Such a man would have to select other Fascists of the same stamp and form a gang which would be ready to act whenever required in any part of Italy. In reply Rossi named Amerigo Dumini and Mussolini had said: "I also know him. He is just the man for the business." The gang of assassins was duly recruited and carried out asssaults on the persons of the three deputies as well as the destruction of Nitti's villa.

Rossi went on to give his interrogators details of the gang's exploits. He said that after Amendola had been assaulted and very severely injured, De Bono had telephoned the news to Mussolini, who had replied: "I shall now go to lunch with a better appetite." Later Mussolini had given De Bono orders to organize an assault on Misuri, who had been making hostile speeches in the Chamber. The attack was duly carried out and in the evening of the same day De Bono duly reported. Mussolini had been delighted and had exclaimed: "Splendid. For the moment this first lesson will suffice. If afterwards he makes another hostile speech, we shall have to liquidate him"; and De Bono had retorted: "But in that event let us kill him now and thus avoid the risk of a second hostile speech."

At this point the judge asked Rossi about his part in the abduction of Matteotti, and he replied that he knew nothing about it. Pressed to explain why he was familiar with the details of the assaults on the three deputies and yet knew nothing of the case of Matteotti, which must have been of particular interest to Mussolini, Rossi said: "The good general reserves his best blows for the decisive moment of the battle. When we appear at the Assizes I shall reveal from the dock all the crimes which Benito Mussolini has committed and those which he intended to commit in the future."

With Rossi's important statement on the file, Del Giudice felt that he was well on the way to elucidating the crime. Aldo Putato, one of Dumini's gang, confronted with Rossi's evidence, decided to speak and declared that after Matteotti's violent speech in the Chamber he had been informed by Dumini that the Duce had issued instructions that the gang was to hold itself in readiness to give the Socialist deputy a lesson. At first Putato had believed that it was a question of a physical assault or possibly a dose of castor oil, but Dumini had explained that Mussolini in his rage against Matteotti was insistent that he should be killed and the body made to disappear. At first Putato had refused to take part in a murder, but under Dumini's threats and pressure had reluctantly consented to comply.

Putato's statement was subsequently confirmed by a certain Thierskwall, a Yugoslav employed by Marinelli as a secret agent. This man, posing as a Socialist, had insinuated himself into Matteotti's household and had thus been able to give the gang important information as to his way of life and movements. He was arrested by the police and under examination stated that when on the morning of the crime Dumini had told him that Matteotti was to be killed, he had declined to have anything to do with the affair. Since then he had not seen Dumini or any other member of the gang.

The abduction had been facilitated by the circumstances that two or three days before June 10 the plainclothes police guard had been withdrawn from Matteotti's house. A policeman, Salvatore Siciliano, informed Del Guidice in confidence that at police headquarters the rumor was current that the order to remove the guard had come from the Ministry of the Interior and had been executed by the head of the police, Giovanni Bertini. There were also allegations in the anti-Fascist press that Bertini had been an accomplice in the crime, and Mussolini in order to satisfy public opinion dismissed him. Some months later he was promoted to the rank of prefect.

In view of the possibility that the Ministry of the Interior was implicated, Del Giudice, with rare courage, and despite hints from Fascist quarters that he would do well to show less zeal, decided to examine Aldo Finzi, the Fascist Undersecretary of State at the Ministry of the Interior. Finzi denied categorically that he had taken any part, direct or indirect, in the Matteotti affair. He added that he had repeatedly called the attention of the competent authorities to the damage and discredit brought upon the Fascist party by the epidemic of violence afflicting all Italy, but his advice had not been heeded. He had been obliged to allow Dumini and Putato, who enjoyed the protection of the Duce and Rossi, to have a room in the Ministry of the Interior, but he denied that money for Fascist crimes in Italy had come from the secret funds of the Ministry of the Interior. He let it be understood that payments had been made from the secret funds of the party, administered by Marinelli, and from the secret fund allotted to Rossi for the corruption of the press. Nevertheless he admitted that on Mussolini's orders he had some time before Matteotti's murder made a significant payment from secret funds to Dumini, who was proceeding to France with Albino Volpi on a mission entrusted to him by the Prime Minister.

Shortly after giving evidence, Finzi was dismissed by Mussolini, and De Bono, the Director of Public Security, whose name had been linked in the press with that of Finzi, came forward spontaneously and insisted on being heard as a witness. He declared that on June 12, after the arrest of Dumini and Putato, Mussolini had instructed him to hold a midnight meeting to consider the position with Finzi, Marinelli, and Rossi. He was to report the result of their deliberations by telephone to Mussolini.

The meeting took place and Rossi, who was the first to speak, asked De Bono and Finzi if they were determined to keep Dumini and Putato under arrest. On receiving an affirmative reply from De Bono, Rossi begged them to beware of the consequences, for the fate of the Fascist party was at stake. These men were courageous adventurers, but could not be relied on to tolerate a long imprisonment and to keep their mouths shut. When De Bono asked what they could reveal, Rossi replied that they would say it was the Prime Minister who had ordered the abduction of Matteotti. "Be careful what you say," had been De Bono's retort, but Marinelli, who until that moment had been silent, had intervened to say that Rossi was right. After this inconclusive meeting De Bono reported to Mussolini, who remarked: "I understand, they wish to blackmail me. Very well, we shall see. Tomorrow you will tell me everything."

On the following day Del Giudice summoned Finzi again and confronted him with De Bono's statement. Finzi made a gesture of surprise and said: "So he has spoken. Very well, I also will reveal everything and thus we shall all appear before the High Court." Whereupon he made a statement substantially confirming all that De Bono had said. The only material difference in his deposition was that, according to his account, De Bono in reply to Rossi's statement that the prisoners would reveal Mussolini's guilt had shaken his head and said: "That blessed man has never been ready to listen to counsels of moderation."

At this point in the investigation in the middle of August, Matteotti's body was found buried in a ditch in a wood on the Via Flaminia some twelve miles from Rome. There was now no doubt whatsoever that he had been murdered by his assailants.

Shortly afterwards it came to the knowledge of Del Giudice that on the afternoon of June 10 Rossi and one of his boon companions, Carlo Bazzi, editor of the Fascist newspaper *Il Nuovo Paese,* had been seen in a fashionable restaurant at Frascati in the company of two ladies of the town. The young women were summoned and deposed that on the morning of June 10 Rossi and Bazzi had invited them to make a trip into the country and to dine at Frascati. They had accepted and their two hosts had returned at 3 P.M. to pick them up in a smart car. At the dinner table Rossi and Bazzi had discussed politics together and at a certain moment had hinted that a significant event was then taking place in Rome. The following day Del Giudice visited Rossi in prison and told him that the evidence of the young women showed that he had foreknowledge of Matteotti's abduction and thus constituted further proof of his complicity in the crime. Rossi made no reply.

The investigation was completed in November, by which time the depositions and the written material accumulated by Del Giudice had filled forty-four large volumes. The Attorney General, at the instance of the Minister of Justice, for fear of incriminating the Fascist party, refused to allow the assaults on the three deputies to be linked with the Matteotti affair. Accordingly Del Giudice and Tancredi decided to commit all the accused for trial on a charge of abduction and murder, namely Rossi, Marinelli, Dumini, Putato, Poveromo, Viola, Malacria, Filippelli, and Thierskwall. On December 27 the *Mondo* published the famous memorial in which Rossi accused Mussolini of the murder. The document had been smuggled out of the Regina Coeli prison by Signora Rossi, who arranged for its publication with Amendola and Albertini.[4] It added nothing to Rossi's deposition before Del Giudice, and the King told Mussolini that he was glad that he had allowed the nonsense to be published. The actual trial which Del Giudice had so carefully prepared was, however, delayed by an unexpected event. Giuseppe Donati, editor of the Catholic newspaper *Il Popolo,* suspecting without reason that Fascists in high places were being protected by Del Giudice, lodged a formal accusation against Senator De Bono for complicity in the Matteotti affair and demanded that he should be tried by the Senate. Del Giudice was required to transmit all the papers to the Senate so as to enable the trial to take place. In view of the fact that the Senate ten days after the disappearance of Matteotti had passed a vote of confidence in Mussolini and that the president of the Senate, Tittoni, was indebted to Mussolini for having secured him the award of the Collar of the Annunziata, it seemed unlikely that trial before the Senate would serve any purpose except to delay and defeat justice. So it proved. The trial of De Bono lasted six months and resulted in his acquittal.

Meanwhile Tancredi had been promoted and replaced by another more pliant member of the Procurator-General's department and Del Giudice himself was conveniently promoted to be Procurator-General in the Court of Appeal at Catania in Sicily. In order further to safeguard the position, the government on July 31, 1925, issued a decree granting an amnesty to all those convicted of, or about to be tried for, any crime—except the perpetration of murder—which was committed in the national interest. The stage was thus set for the trial of Matteotti's assailants in conditions which assuaged any anxiety that Mussolini may have entertained.[5]

The refurbished prosecution took the line that the abduction of Matteotti was premeditated, but that his killing arose from unforeseen circumstances and was not premeditated. They also found that Rossi and Marinelli had been responsible for organizing a crime of violence, but not of murder, and that they thus came within the terms of the amnesty. They were accordingly released on December 2, 1925, as was also Filippelli for the same reason. Marinelli was shortly afterwards appointed Inspector-General of the Fascist party. Rossi was less fortunate. He remained under police supervision until February, 1926, when he escaped to France. In August, 1928, he was lured to the frontier zone, kidnapped, tried, and sentenced to thirty years imprisonment by the Special Tribunal.

The trial of the remaining defendants, Dumini, Volpi, Viola, Poveromo, and Malacria, took place on March 16, 1926, at Chieti, which was chosen for its remoteness. Roberto Farinacci for the defense admitted that Matteotti had been stabbed in the car. But after a violent attack on the character of Matteotti he claimed that the crime, admitted by the prosecution to have been unpremeditated, had been committed under grave provocation, a circumstance which attenuated guilt and which should reduce the penalty. The court found that the murder was unpremeditated and that Matteotti was suffering from a disease which contributed to his death. Viola and Malacria were acquitted and Dumini, Volpi, and Poveromo were sentenced to imprisonment for five years, eleven months, and twenty days. This sentence was reduced by four years under the amnesty of July 21, 1925, and, since account was taken of the period they had spent in jail, they were almost immediately released.

IV

The real trial of the assassins took place more than twenty years later at the instance of Matteotti's widow. On January 22, 1947, before the criminal court at Rome the case was reopened. Dumini, Rossi, Poveromo, and Francesco Giunta, who did not appear at the first trial, were in the dock. Malacria, who had died, Viola, and Filippelli, who had vanished, were tried in their absence, as well as Filippo Panzeri, who did not appear at the first trial.

An important witness was Carlo Silvestri, a Socialist journalist who had been employed for sixteen years on the *Corriere della Sera* and had suffered imprisonment at the hands of the Fascists. He had on occasion acted as intermediary between the Duce and the Socialists; and he had been in close touch with Mussolini during the period of the Salò Republic. He cannot be regarded as completely reliable. On the other hand, as a Socialist and former victim of the Fascist regime, he had no reason to whitewash Mussolini, except in so far as he professed himself anxious after the war to heal the divisions between the Italian parties and the present a common front against communism.

In court Silvestri threw a new light on Mussolini's part in the affair. According to him, the murder of Matteotti was committed in order to create an irrevocable breach between Mussolini and the

Socialists. As early as August, 1922, Mussolini had spoken to him of the need to have an understanding with the Socialists and the *Popolari*. On October 29, 1922, while the Fascist congress was meeting at Naples, Mussolini had said to him: "Silvestri, we are in agreement. If you receive a conventional telegram from me, make in my name an offer to the Unitary Socialist party to participate in the government and tell them that I will give sufficient guarantees to enable an agreement to be reached." The Socialists, however, declined participation and Mussolini was forced to abandon the idea in consequence both of a threat by the Nationalists to secede and the opposition of the Tuscan Fascists. When Mussolini returned from the Quirinal he said to Silvestri: "I regret profoundly that I have been obliged to renounce my plan for the moment. But what is not possible today will be possible in six months, a year or two years. This is my program because collaboration with the Socialists and the *Popolari* is the only possible solution for the salvation of Italy."

Silvestri went on to recall a conversation in 1934 with Emilio Caldara, former Socialist mayor of Milan, at a time when Mussolini was using him in a last desperate attempt to reach an understanding with the Socialists. Knowing the high moral character of Caldara, Silvestri was sure that he would never have lent himself to this maneuver if he had believed Mussolini to be guilty of Matteotti's murder.

Finally Silvestri referred to a conversation early in 1945 in the course of which Mussolini had said to him:

> The greatest tragedy of my life was when I no longer had the strength to repel the embrace of the false Corporatives, who were in reality acting as agents of capitalism and who wished to embrace the Corporative System in order better to suffocate it. All that happened afterwards was the consequence of the corpse which on June 10, 1924, was thrown between me and the Socialists, in order to prevent an agreement which would have given an entirely different orientation to the national policy, and possibly not only to the national policy.

Silvestri concluded his evidence by saying that his examination of the facts had convinced him that Mussolini could never have given the order to kill Matteotti, if only because Matteotti was the secretary of that Socialist party to which Bruno Buozzi, Gino Baldesi, and Emilio Colombino belonged, all of them men whom he intended to invite to become members of his government. "In undertaking," he added, "to tell the whole truth, I wished in the first place to reveal to the Italians the dark origins of the crime imputed to Mussolini, which in effect had the result of preventing a policy of collaboration with the Socialists, a policy which alone could have prevented the march towards totalitarianism, the dictatorship, and the war. With my evidence I did not wish to defend Mussolini who has so many other sins to expiate before history, but to accuse those who succeeded in evading responsibility for a crime which was antiproletarian and anti-Socialist in its intentions." [6]

Silvestri's evidence made some impression on the court. Under cross-examination he maintained his opinion and expressed the conviction that it was Marinelli who had given Dumini the order to slay Matteotti. Giunta in the witness box confirmed what Silvestri had said: "Mussolini did not have the courage in 1922 to include the Socialists in his government, but he would have done so at the end of June, 1924, because his great passion, his nostalgia, and his ambition was to return to his Socialist comrades and so to be united once more with the working classes."

The prosecution kept an open mind as to the degree of Mussolini's guilt. The Attorney General said that the facts surrounding the murder were quite clear. He repeated that the car had arrived at its post at about 4 P.M. on June 10 and had remained there until about 4:30 P.M., when Matteotti appeared. Malacria was at the wheel and the others on Dumini's orders advanced to capture Matteotti, who defended himself stoutly. He was, however, struck to the ground and carried towards the car, which meanwhile had moved towards the group. But before he could be pushed into the car Matteotti made one more effort to resist and continued to do so after he was in the car, where he broke the glass partition between the driver's seat and the passenger's compartment. He continued to struggle and to shout during the passage of the car towards the Ponte Milvio in the hope of attracting the attention of a passer-by, but according to a witness his shouts were drowned by the horn.

The Attorney General rejected the finding of the Chieti court that Matteotti's death could be in part attributed to his state of health. He was undoubtedly stabbed by a knife or a dagger. He also rejected the finding that the crime was not premeditated, since all the evidence pointed the other way. The assassins were all armed with daggers or revolvers for the enterprise, the body had been stripped before burial so as to render identification difficult, and the abduction had been so carefully prepared and efficiently carried out as to lead to the conclusion that the victim's death was no accident.

As to Mussolini's complicity, the Attorney General said that Rossi had spoken of Mussolini's impulsive and vindictive character and had said that immediately after Matteotti's speech in the Chamber the Duce had remarked in a menacing tone: "After that speech the man should no longer be in circulation." Moreover the minds of the Fascist leaders were further inflamed by the knowledge that Matteotti intended to make another damaging speech on the estimates. The question therefore arose: did Marinelli issue his instructions to Dumini in conformity with the Prime Minister's wishes? Marinelli, Rossi, Filippelli, Finzi, and Dumini had all at one time or another given an affirmative reply to these questions and their statements seemed to be confirmed by the close interest evinced by Mussolini in the trial and in the fate of the accused and by the amnesty of July 31, 1925.

On the other hand account must be taken of the evidence of eminent parliamentarians of the day and of those closest to Mussolini. Every word of his was an order and his henchmen competed to interpret his most hidden thoughts and to translate into acts his wishes, whatever the form of their expression. It was thus quite possible that Marinelli, believing that he was executing an order from the Prime Minister, instructed Dumini to liquidate Matteotti without taking into account the very grave consequences of the act.

After thirty-two sessions the sentence of the court was pronounced on April 4, 1947. Dumini, Poveromo, and Viola, who were found guilty of abduction and premeditated murder, were sentenced to life imprisonment, commuted to thirty years. Filippelli was convicted of complicity but freed under an amnesty; and Panzeri, Rossi, and Giunta were also freed, though Giunta was held for trial on another charge. In view of Malacria's previous death no sentence was passed.

V

With this third trial the Matteotti case was finally closed. In order to determine how far Mussolini was personally responsible, it is necessary to examine his conduct from the time of Matteotti's speech of May 30 until June 10 as well as during the long period of the preliminary judicial investigation. There is no doubt that Mussolini was excited and exasperated by Matteotti's speech; and that he uttered words which could reasonably have been interpreted as an expression of his wish to see Matteotti disappear. What the court at the postwar trial was unable to resolve was whether Mussolini gave an explicit order and whether he had foreknowledge of the crime.

Mussolini was by nature intolerant of criticism and resentful of opposition. Moreover he believed that he had been called to govern Italy, and his enormous egotism led him to regard political opponents as factious and irresponsible. In his later years any opposition was described as criminal. Of all his opponents Matteotti, with his dynamic personality and cutting tongue, was the man he hated most; and his hatred was inflamed by the indignation which Matteotti's proceedings aroused in the breast of every loyal Fascist.

Nevertheless Mussolini's reaction to Matteotti's speech was surprisingly mild. He was in a conciliatory mood. A short time previously he had said to an opposition journalist, Giuseppe Borgese: "My opponents do not take into account the fact that a revolutionary movement like this drags with it a wake of criminality. Instead of making my life work difficult they should help me to master these forces of darkness." [7] Accordingly, when on June 7 he wound up the debate on the Address, he told the Chamber that the country had followed with distaste their acrimonious debate, which had raised the problem of coexistence between the government and the opposition. The question which had been posed was whether their reciprocal susceptibilities would allow parliament to function. He hoped that it would, if they all paid regard to their own personal and political responsibility.

He then went on in pained rather than angry terms to rebut the charges that Italy was living under a tyranny and that the elections had been fraudulent or violent. On the first point he effectively quoted opposition newspapers which called for the forcible overthrow of the government. On the second point he recalled that in Italian history the defeated parties had always complained of fraud. As regards violence, the opposition complained of one death, but the Fascists had lost 18 killed and 147 wounded.

He concluded by saying that in no circumstances would he return to the old system, under which the executive was deprived of its authority by the Chamber, but he held out an olive branch to his opponents. He promised that illegal violence would cease and that he would not oust politicians belonging to the old parties, for there were among them men of courage and integrity who possessed valuable administrative experience. He recognized the usefulness of an effective opposition: "There must be an opposition. If it did not sit on the Left, it would sit among us; and I prefer that it should be there rather than that it should divide our own ranks. The opposition is necessary. I go further and say that it can play an educative and formative role." [8] He went on to speak of the inmmense problems confronting the country and he proposed collaboration between the parties. He made no claim to infallibility, for he was only a man with all the defects and qualities which were proper to human nature. He would repel no offer of help. The work of reconstruction was arduous and would require the support of all men of ability and good will. He put the question to them as one of conscience. Let them cease to take up a sterile negative attitude and address their minds to fruitful cooperation: "We have the right and the duty to scatter the ashes of your and also of our past rancors." [9]

The speech made a good impression and Mussolini received a vote of confidence by 361 to 107 votes. Orlando declared that it had put things to rights and Mussolini was optimistic enough to think that it might lead to an accommodation between the three major parties. In conversation with Giunta and Acerbo he spoke of the possibility of forming a government of national concentration with the inclusion of well-known Liberals, Socialists, and Popularists. He even envisaged the dissolution of the militia and the Grand Council. There was a feeling of relaxation in the air and Mussolini went to the seaside for a few hours' rest.

Four days later the news of Matteotti's disappearance was public property. Not only political and journalistic circles, but the public at large was shocked at a crime which seemed to represent the culmination of four years of Fascist violence. There was talk of a secret Fascist criminal organization, the so-called Cheka, for the liquidation of opponents, of the scandalous protection given by the police to Fascist thugs, of the arbitrary character of the government's proceedings, and of Mussolini's extreme resentment at Matteotti's speech. It was said that, in view of all this and of Mussolini's character of an unscrupulous demagogue, it was reasonable to believe that he must have had some responsibility, direct or indirect, for Matteotti's assassination.

There was a sudden swing of popular opinion against the Duce. Instead of admiration for his success and confidence in the future, the prevailing sentiment was now one of disillusion, hostility to his policy, and fear of coming disaster.

The mounting tide of indignation in the Chamber, in the country, and abroad,* spread panic in the Fascist ranks. The Grand Council held an excited and inconclusive debate in the course of which Giunta accused Rossi of the crime, while three of Mussolini's more reputable ministers, Federzoni, Oviglio, and De Stefani called on him to eliminate suspect members of the government and the party. Very soon Mussolini was virtually isolated, and his waiting room, which had hitherto been full of sycophants and eager suppliants, now stood empty. He was alone and only Navarra, his faithful attendant, remained at his side.

For a time Mussolini himself was as demoralized as his party. Indeed it is no exaggeration to say that he was close to a nervous collapse. When on June 13 he assured the Chamber that the resources of the state would be deployed to track and punish the criminals he gave the appearance of a distraught and broken man. In his diary Marshal Caviglia expressed the view that Mussolini had behaved like a chicken and that he should have taken one of two courses: either, as a Fascist revolutionary, to take responsibility for the punishment of Matteotti for taking foreign money and engaging

* The foreign criticism was very severe and much alarmed Mussolini. His reactions are reflected in his correspondence with Italian missions. (*Documenti diplomatici italiani settima serie,* III, 154–393.)

in anti-Fascist crimes abroad, or to punish the perpetrators and then make a personal appearance at Matteotti's funeral rites.[10] In fact for a long time Mussolini characteristically steered a middle course, making such concessions to public opinion as seemed necessary, reacting when it was safe to do so, and hoping that the exercise of patience would eventually cause the storm to pass.

On June 13 Rossi and Finzi were dismissed, and two days later De Bono was discarded, while Mussolini himself surrendered the Ministry of the Interior to Federzoni. But these half measures did nothing to appease the nation and, as the days passed and no trace of Matteotti's body was found, groups of angry citizens began to gather menacingly in the streets. Sforza suggested to Turati and other opposition leaders that the moment was ripe for forcible action against Mussolini, but the opposition was as paralyzed as the Duce. If Mussolini had known how feeble was the attitude of his enemies, his courage might have revived, but he was too isolated to be aware of what was going on around him.

Speaking to Carlo Silvestri in 1945 of the crisis he said:

> I was so terrifyingly alone in the week after Matteotti's murder that I one day invited Luigi Veratti behind the balcony of the Palazzo Chigi looking out on to the Piazzo Colonna and I said to him: "Twenty men resolved to reach me would find no resistance and no defender. Here I have good revolvers. But I have not yet made up my mind whether I should fire when they burst in or whether I should passively accept my fate." [11]

Another version is that of Marshal Caviglia, who relates that a war veteran, Ponzio di San Sebastiani, was with Mussolini in a room on the first floor of the Palazzo Chigi while a hostile crowd was gathering outside. The Duce, who looked troubled and agitated, suddenly seized a rifle and said: "If that crowd advances, I shall open fire." [12] So precarious was his situation that for a moment Mussolini toyed with the idea of advising the King to turn to the Socialists and to invite Turati or Buozzi to form a government.[13]

This was the lowest point to which Mussolini's fortunes sank. Two factors were to improve his position. The opposition, which had withdrawn from the Chamber to the so-called Aventine, remained irresolute and ineffective. They could have organized the liquidation of the Duce or they could have mobilized public opinion and so have swept the tottering Fascist government from power. But they did neither; and as the days and weeks passed without any action on their part their influence and power waned. Secondly there was a reaction in Mussolini's favor in the provinces. In particular Grandi was extremely active at Bologna, where fifty thousand Fascists gathered to demonstrate in support of the government. For his services he was appointed Undersecretary at the Ministry of the Interior.

On June 24 Mussolini presented himself to the Senate. He was in better heart, but he was still in an uncertain defensive and placatory mood, for he knew how precarious was his hold on power. He admitted that fascism had been shaken, but claimed that it had not been struck down. He expressed his horror at the murder of Matteotti, which like the execution of the Duke of Enghien, had been not only a crime but an error. He could assure the House that the courts would deal with it. Nevertheless the incident should not be allowed to disturb the work of pacification which he had begun. He promised that the Fascist militia would be placed on a constitutional basis, that the party would be disciplined, and that he would govern with parliament. He concluded by saying that the objectives of the government remained the same, namely to secure at any cost by respect of the law a return to normality and a restoration of peace to the country. Only 21 out of 252 senators voted against the motion of confidence in the government. But Mussolini was not yet safe. The discovery of Matteotti's body on August 16 set in motion a new and perilous wave of agitation against the government. The circulation of the opposition newspapers rose to unprecedented heights, protests became more vocal, and the extreme wing of the Fascist party led by Farinacci began to inveigh against Mussolini for his passivity. In particular they took exception to the instruction issued to the prefects and to the police by the new Minister of the Interior that public order should be maintained, thus inhibiting violence against the enemies of fascism.

In this predicament Mussolini continued to oscillate between defiance and conciliation. In July a decree law gave the prefects power to sequestrate a newspaper and eventually to suppress it for publishing false news, or matter calculated to disturb order, to incite to crime, to evoke class hatred, or attacking the King, the royal family, the Pope, religion, or the institutions and powers of the state. It was Mussolini's first move against the liberty of the press and at the outset he used his new power with caution. On August 31 in a speech addressed to miners at Monte Amiata he declared that if the opposition were to move from vituperation to deeds, he would make of them litter for a Fascist encampment.[14] On the other hand in an interview with the director of the *Giornale d'Italia* he spoke of his desire to work with the Liberals. Fascists, he said, who violated the law would be committed to prison. The constitution would be observed and, if the nation one day became tired of him, he would go quietly.

During the months following, the opposition continued to growl ineffectively from the Aventine and the Fascists murmured against their leader. Mussolini maneuvered uneasily between the two. Although during this period his position slowly improved, thanks to the incompetence and incoherence of the opposition parties, he suffered a reverse in November when Balbo inadvisedly brought an action against the *Voce Republicana* for accusing him of the murder of a priest. The defense was able to take the opportunity of proving that Balbo had been responsible for a number of acts of violence in Ferrara in 1923; and before the case was actually lost Balbo tendered his resignation as commander of the militia.

It seemed to Mussolini that he would never extricate himself from his difficulties. Only his will to remain in power sustained him. In an interview with the British ambassador on November 8, 1924, he confessed that he was much concerned at the internal situation and at the mounting violence on both sides. At the moment a thousand Fascists were in jail and five thousand more were awaiting prosecution. He professed the resolve to restore order at any cost.

If Mussolini had been concerned only to restore order and to placate his parliamentary critics, the prosecution of Fascists would obviously have improved his position. But he was under pressure from the extremist wing of his party to give them a free hand to deal with their enemies; and in his precarious position he could not afford to antagonize his extremists. For the moment, however, he decided on a placatory policy.

Accordingly on December 5, 1924, Mussolini delivered in the

Senate a long, apologetic speech which was almost groveling in tone. He said that on the morrow of the revolution two courses had been open to him, to govern within or outside the constitution. He had chosen the first course and he had kept all his promises. He had undertaken to repress illegal violence and the number of prosecutions was evidence that he had not broken his word. He had undertaken to discipline the party. This had been done. He had undertaken to reopen parliament and to make it function. Parliament had been reopened and was functioning. He had been told that he was determined to stay in power at any price. This was not the case. Before a vast crowd at Cremona he had recognized the rights of the nation and of the King. If His Majesty after the present session of the Senate were to send for him and tell him to go, he would stand to attention and obey. He spoke advisedly of His Majesty King Victor Emanuel; but if it were a question of His Majesty the *Corriere della Sera,* then no. The militia, he went on to say, would in accordance with his undertaking be brought within the framework of the constitution and the necessary bill, which had already been approved by the cabinet, would be laid before them.

He then repudiated the charge that liberty had been suppressed in Italy. Only the previous Sunday an opposition meeting had been held in Milan, violent speeches against the government had been made, and news of these proceedings had been disseminated throughout the country by a number of newspapers. If this were not liberty, they would have to alter their political vocabulary.

As regards the internal political situation, he was the first to recognize that the country was traversing a period of crisis and of uncertainty in regard to its attitude towards Fascism. The causes were complex: errors, acts of violence, offenses. There were also mistakes on the part of the government, but what government had never made a mistake. He had told the National Council of the party that they had sinned through vanity and careerism. But there had been scandals in Italian politics long before fascism appeared on the scene, and the party, which had captured the hearts of Italian youth, would not dissolve like mist under a summer sun.

During the past months, he added, he had acquired vast experience of human nature. There were some men who were excessively sensitive to the movement of public opinion. It was better to lose them than to recruit them. There were those who under the shadow of the processes of the law had thought it safer to pass to the ranks of the opposition. There were those who, after burning before him an amount of incense which would have stunned an ox, had left him because they thought they could make a fortune more quickly elsewhere. Nevertheless he was still resolved to bring about an era of pacification. All who knew him were aware of his suffering when news was brought to him of incidents, disorder, and violence. They all knew that he deprecated violence and that he would regard himself as having failed in his task if he did not give peace to the Italian people. But peace did not rest with him alone; and he appealed to the opposition on the Aventine and to their love of country to come some way to meet the Fascists.

VI

This conciliatory speech won Mussolini a vote of confidence by 205 to 54 votes, a smaller majority than he had enjoyed on June 24. But, although he did not yet know it, he was not to show moderation for very long. Two years later he was to tell that same Chamber: "An opposition is not necessary to the functioning of a healthy political system. An opposition is silly and superfluous in a totalitarian regime such as the Fascist regime," [15] and within days he was to swing the tiller towards reaction under the influence of the extremists in his party, who were now on the verge of revolt against his weakness.

At the beginning of December a number of leaders, convoked by Balbo, met to consider the situation and decided to appoint a committee of five, which would assume command of the militia and of the old *Squadristi* in the event of an emergency. At the end of the month a delegation of some thirty senior militia officers called on Mussolini, ostensibly to present New Year wishes, but in reality to protest against a policy of appeasement. It was a painful meeting, held in the presence of De Stefani and General Gandolfo, the new commander of the militia. Aldo Tarabella, the spokesman for the party, declared that they were tired of clinging to the past. Either every Fascist should be in prison including the Duce or all should be at liberty. But the prisons were now full of Fascists and men were putting fascism in the dock, while he, the Duce, refused to take responsibility for the revolution. This responsibility the delegation would assume, and that very day they would present themselves to the judicial authorities, who would doubtless be delighted to incarcerate them in the Regina Coeli prison.

Mussolini spoke of discipline and called the party to order, but Tarabella replied: "What! You who have inflamed so many young hearts, you who have exalted these blessed mobs, you who have led so many young men to acts of sublime heroism, do you suppose that these very mobs are going to stay quiet at a wave of your magic wand?" Mussolini sought to defend himself and spoke of his isolation caused by the corpse which had been thrown between his feet, and Tarabella angrily retorted that a corpse could not stop a revolution. He went on to protest that the militia had been entrusted to the command of generals who were not Fascists and heaped sarcasm on Mussolini's head. To these charges Mussolini could only reply that the militia leaders who had left their posts without leave had rendered themselves liable to disciplinary penalties; and some of the less resolute members of the delegation declared that they were not in agreement with Tarabella. After an unseemly exchange of recriminations among the visitors the whole party left except Tarabella, who remained behind to pursue the argument.[16]

Another important event occurred at the end of December. On the twenty-seventh of the month the *Mondo* published Cesare Rossi's memorial accusing Mussolini of responsibility for Matteotti's murder. The publication of this document and the stormy meeting with the officers made it clear to Mussolini that he could no longer sit on the fence and at the same time retain the loyalty of the Fascist militia. Not for the first time in his political life he decided to yield to the pressure of his supporters. In the evening some of the militia leaders were summoned to the militia headquarters, where General Gandolfo told them that he had been charged by the Duce to thank them. Mussolini was glad to know that there were still men disposed to sacrifice themselves and he wished to inform them that the counterattack would immediately be launched. That evening anti-Fascist newspapers were sequestrated and the premises of anti-Fascists were searched; and Mussolini began to prepare for the change of course which three days later he was to announce to the Chamber on January 3, 1925.

He had narrowly escaped shipwreck. There is evidence in his speech of June 7, and from the statements in the witness box of Silvestri and Giunta, that he was contemplating a parliamentary accommodation with the other parties, particularly the Socialists, whom he wished to include in his administration. There is confirmation of this story from De Bono, who told Marshal Caviglia in 1941 that Mussolini had been edging to the Left, when the murder of Matteotti and its sequel drove him irrevocably on to the course he ultimately took.[17] Cesare Rossi, who was close to him at the time, relates that the idea of returning to socialism was deeply rooted in Mussolini and that he was dominated by the hope of reconciliation.*

Moreover, Mussolini was by nature disinclined to burn his boats and he could not have failed to foresee that the murder of Matteotti, quite apart from wrecking any hopes of political conciliation, would compromise his own position which he had not yet consolidated. Finally, his conduct throughout the months which followed the murder was that of a man perplexed and distraught at an unexpected blow. This was the impression of Camille Barrère, who held the post of French Ambassador in Rome for over twenty years. He subsequently related that while he was shaving in the morning he was advised of Matteotti's murder by his valet. He at once telephoned to Mussolini at his private number and obtained an immediate appointment at the Palazzo Chigi. Barrère, pushing the ushers aside, bounded into Mussolini's office, where he found him alone. Mussolini rose and before the Ambassador could open his mouth exclaimed: "The imbeciles. They have assassinated him." In the conversation which followed Mussolini indicated that the Fascists had intended to "humiliate" Matteotti, but that in the struggle he had been killed. Barrère, who knew his man well, left the Palazzo Chigi convinced that Mussolini had not been acting a part and that he had no foreknowledge of the murder.[18]

* Cesare Rossi, *Trentatre vicendi mussoliniane, op. cit.*, p. 443. Count Grandi, in conversation with the author, went further, and stated categorically that Mussolini had actually arranged to take in Baldesi and other Socialists.

Thus the balance of probability leans heavily on the side of Mussolini's innocence in the matter of direct complicity. But he cannot be acquitted of guilt. He had for many years condoned and indeed encouraged the perpetration of assaults on opponents of the regime. It was a system for which he was personally responsible, and his lieutenants had every reason to believe, both from his addiction to the philosophy of force, and from his comments on Matteotti, that the liquidation of this inconvenient opponent would meet with his approval. Their error was that they did not foresee that the crime would shake fascism to its foundations and that Mussolini in his dilemma would seek to disclaim responsibility by disowning the men to whom he had entrusted the intimidation of his enemies. It was a grievous miscalculation and only the vigorous intervention of the militia leaders caused Mussolini, six months later, when his position was less precarious, to adopt a new robust attitude.

VII

As the new year dawned in 1925 political observers in Rome had no inkling of what lay before them. In conversations with the British Embassy two members of the opposition, Amendola and Professor Raffaele Ricci, a friend of Salandra, expected Mussolini to resign; and on the Aventine there were signs of returning confidence. The British ambassador was bound to take note of these opinions, but he expressed the conviction that Mussolini was resolved to cling to power.

Mussolini soon proved Sir Ronald Graham to be right, for when the Chamber reassembled after the Christmas recess on January 3, 1925, he delivered a speech which opened a new chapter in the evolution of fascism. The groping attempts to find a formula for a parliamentary coalition were abandoned and he returned, or rather he was forced back, to the narrow path of purely Fascist rule. He denied that he had created a secret police or that after his conciliatory speech of June 7 he had planned a crime against an opponent whom he esteemed for his courage. He attacked the opposition for leaving parliament and the press for exploiting a dead man. He listed the steps he had taken to bring about internal peace, but in vain, for the opposition were determined to insult fascism and to raise the moral issue.

On this point he defied the opposition to prosecute him and he declared that before the Chamber and the whole Italian people he assumed full personal responsibility for all that had happened. If fascism had been only castor oil and the bludgeon rather than an expression of what was best in Italian youth, his was the fault. If fascism was an association of delinquents, he was the leader of that association. If all the acts of violence flowed from a particular historical, political, and moral climate of opinion, it was he who had created that climate.

He concluded by saying that action had at last been taken because a nation did not respect a government which allowed itself to be reviled and because the cup was now full. Eleven Fascists had been slain in the previous two months and there were definite signs of a revival of subversive activity. When two irreconcilable elements were in conflict, force was the only solution. People had believed that fascism was finished because he himself was restraining it, but the house could be certain that during the forty-eight hours following his speech the whole situation would be cleared up.

Mussolini went down to the Chamber with fear in his heart to make this violent speech. Only when he saw, to his surprise, how well it was received and how feeble was the reaction of opponents did he take the plunge into dictatorship. The murder of Matteotti was thus a turning point in Italian political life. There are some of his former associates who aver that Mussolini's character, his intolerance of opposition, and his conception of personal rule would in the long run have led fascism to dictatorship, but that he would have acted in his own time and in his own devious way. Others are convinced that Mussolini, who was as much a Socialist renegade as a revolutionary, sincerely hankered after an accommodation with the Socialists; and that a broadly based administration, such as he had undoubtedly at one time envisaged, would have assured the perpetuation of parliamentary government in Italy.

However this may be, Mussolini's speech of January 3, 1925, made reluctantly under pressure, sounded the deathknell of civil liberties in Italy. Once more he had yielded to the single-minded resolution of the extremists in his own party, and once more he had been saved by the inertia of the representatives of the other parties. During the months that followed, successive measures were taken with savage energy to abolish the parliamentary system and to create the totalitarian police state. There was no opposition. Recalcitrant political adversaries went into exile or were kept in custody on the islands. The remainder of the nation conformed. The man who for over two years had, with great skill, worked the parliamentary system and who had intended to broaden his government, soon found himself as the consequence of a fortuitous event the unchallenged dictator of Italy.

The events of 1924 also had their effect on Mussolini's outlook. Execrated by millions of Italians and deserted by many of his associates, he had passively ridden the storm awaiting the counterstroke of the opposition, which never came. His nerve had been shaken and his only thought had been to do what he could to placate parliament and public opinion. Eventually he had been pushed into aggression, and the event proved that he had little to fear from his adversaries. His experience served to increase his contempt for human nature, to bolster his self-confidence, and to convince him that he had been unduly cautious and that he could in the future work his will without much regard to the opposition or to Italian opinion. His outlook rather than his character had changed, but it was unfortunate for the Italians that their unstable and capricious leader should have undergone this experience so early in his political career.

CHAPTER TEN

The Dictator

1925–1929

I

THE country on the whole accepted Mussolini's speech of January 3 with relief. It showed that he intended to govern, and its effect was to enhance his prestige with the masses. He was helped by the circumstance that in 1925 there was a significant improvement in Italy's economic position. On the other hand, the politically conscious minority, who were attached to civil liberties, were appalled and looked with growing apprehension to the future. They all realized that a revolution had come upon them. The King, who had not been warned, expressed his displeasure to Mussolini and refused his request for a dissolution of parliament at a date to be fixed by the Prime Minister. Briand, who met Mussolini at Locarno some months later, warned him with avuncular good humor that while it was not difficult to cross the Rubicon it was difficult to recross it. So it proved, for the nation at large, a servile parliament, and an incoherent opposition had all combined to place Mussolini in an impregnable position.

The first act of the government was to mobilize formations of the militia. Within three days the Minister of the Interior was able to report that ninety-five politically suspect clubs, together with 109 groups of the "Free Italy" Association, had been dissolved. One hundred and fifty offices had been closed, 655 domiciliary searches had been made, and 111 persons had been arrested. In addition the prefects had been instructed to take vigorous action against any manifestation of antifascism and to apply the press laws more strictly. In consequence opposition newspapers were sequestrated almost daily and a number of journalists were arrested.

The Aventine opposition considered returning to the Chamber, but decided against it. Instead they issued a statement declaring that the issue was between Fascist domination and the country: "The mask of constitutionalism and normalization has now fallen. The government tramples on the basic laws of the state, arbitrarily suffocates in an unprecedented manner the free voice of the press, suppresses all right of assembly, and mobilizes the armed forces of its party while it tolerates and leaves unpunished the devastations and arson inflicted on its adversaries." Having cast this damp squib at the enemy, the opposition approached the King with the suggestion that he should dismiss Mussolini. But the King was unwilling to act. For one thing he was sick of the old parliamentary parties and claimed that the nation had hoisted Mussolini into power. More important, he was now principally concerned to preserve the monarchy and saw no sense in hazarding his crown in a conflict with the man who seemed to have the armed forces of the state at his command. Mussolini was left to work his will on the Italian people. For more than a decade he was to enjoy unlimited power and to march from one success to another. Assured of the good will of the majority of Italians, and untroubled by reverses, he was able to present to the world an impression of strength and good sense. But it was an illusory impression, for under the surface his restless spirit was chafing and he was casting about for means of realizing his far-flung ambitions.

The pace of his revolution was accelerated by a number of attempts on his life, which were exploited to justify still further encroachments on the liberty of the citizen. On November 4, 1925, Tito Zaniboni, a Freemason and a Socialist, was arrested for preparing to assassinate Mussolini from a window. He was tried together with a number of alleged accomplices and sentenced to thirty years' imprisonment. On April 26, Miss Violet Gibson, to whom reference has already been made, fired at Mussolini and wounded him in the nose. She was mentally deranged and declared that she had come to Rome with the intention of killing either Mussolini or the Pope; and it had been an accident that Mussolini had given her the first opportunity. Relations with England were good at the time, and Mussolini with a certain magnanimity gave orders that she should be quietly released. The third attempt was made by a young militant anarchist, Gino Lucetti, who on September 11, 1925, threw a bomb at Mussolini's car while he was on his way to the Palazzo Chigi. The Duce was unhurt, but four persons were injured. Lucetti was condemned to thirty years' imprisonment. On October 13, 1926, a shot was fired at Mussolini's car in Bologna. A fifteen-year-old boy, Anteo Zamboni, was lynched on the spot, but it subsequently became known that he was not the perpetrator and it was alleged that the Fascists had staged the affair for political ends. These four incidents, conveniently spaced, aroused sentiment in Mussolini's favor and created a climate of opinion in which the change from parliamentary democracy to totalitarian fascism could safely be made. Only a very few irreconcilables raised their voices in protest and they were quickly silenced.

In February, 1925, Roberto Farinacci became secretary of the party. This was a significant appointment since he set himself to destroy the party machine, to curb the power of the provincial *ras,* and so to pave the way for Mussolini's system of personal rule. The failure of the party to react to Mussolini's arrest in 1943 can be attributed largely to Farinacci, who effectively deprived it of the capacity to take any independent action at all. Moreover, as an extremist, Farinacci could be relied upon to smite the enemies of the regime without too fastidious a regard to the methods employed. In July, 1925, the well-known opposition Deputy Giovanni Amendola was so brutally assaulted by Fascists that he died eight months later from his injuries.

The Zaniboni plot against Mussolini gave the authorities the excuse for which they were looking. Because he was a Freemason and a member of the Socialist Unitary Party, orders were given to the police to occupy all the masonic lodges in Italy and the colonies. The Socialist Unitary Party was dissolved and its organ, *La Giustizia,* sequestrated. At the same time steps were taken against two of the more important opposition papers. Senator Luigi Albertini, the director of Italy's leading newspaper, the *Corriere della Sera,* was dismissed on Farinacci's orders, the shareholders liquidated the company, and the *Corriere* became a Fascist organ. The London *Times* said sadly that the end of the independent *Corriere* represented a serious loss for European civilization. The Turin *Stampa* was suspended for an alleged affront to the army, and its leading men were forcibly ejected. A large number of lesser newspapers ceased publication or were transferred into Fascist hands.

In November, 1925, Mussolini began a program of legislation which was to last until the end of 1926 and was intended to impose a Fascist imprint on Italian life. The year 1926, he declared in his monthly *Gerarchia,* was to be the Napoleonic year in the Fascist revolution, for during this period he intended to bring into force the basic laws of the new regime. He was not entirely successful in adhering to his timetable, partly because he was incapacitated for some months by the gastric ulcer to which reference has already been made. Nevertheless it was an imposing mass of legislation, which converted Italy into a police state under the personal control of the Prime Minister.

On November 26, 1925, a law was promulgated governing the activity of all associations, bodies, and institutes as well as the position of public servants. Secret associations such as Freemasonry were prohibited. All associations and institutes were obliged to give particulars of their activities and membership to the police. Any breach of this regulation by the heads of such associations was punishable by imprisonment and by the dissolution of the association; and public servants who were members of secret associations were liable to dismissal. The law was applicable to political parties.

On December 24, 1925, a law enabled the government to dismiss any public servant whose conduct within or outside his office did not fully guarantee the faithful fulfillment of his duty or which was incompatible with the general political directives of the government. The first victims of this law were a number of university professors who had defended cultural liberty at a philosophical congress in Milan.

On December 31, 1925, a decree law rendered newspaper proprietors responsible for editorial policy and created an association of journalists which virtually excluded anti-Fascists from the profession.

A law of January 31, 1926, empowered the government to deprive of Italian citizenship any citizen who committed an act abroad calculated to disturb public order in the kingdom or to damage Italian interests or prestige, even if the act did not constitute a crime. Loss of citizenship could carry with it the sequestration or confiscation of the offender's property in Italy, even if he had meanwhile become a foreign citizen. Among the first victims of this law were the well-known historian Gaetano Salvemmi and the Catholic journalist Giuseppe Donati, who had denounced De Bono for the murder of Matteotti.

A law of November 25, 1926, instituted capital punishment for attempts against the life of the King, the Queen, the Crown Prince, and the Head of the Government as well as for treason, insurrection, or incitement to civil war. Lesser penalties were laid down for anti-Fascist activities and all persons prosecuted under this law were to be brought before a Special Tribunal composed of a General Officer as president and five militia Consuls. There was no appeal and the Tribunal was instructed to act quickly and with exemplary severity.

These laws directed against liberty were accompanied by a number of laws designed to alter the constitutional structure of the Italian state. Thus on December 24, 1925, a law defined the "attributions and prerogatives of the Head of the Government and Prime Minister." Mussolini ceased to be President of the Council, or Prime Minister in the British sense. Instead he received the new title of Head of the Government and was invested personally with full executive authority, which he exercised on behalf of the King without the intervention of parliament. Another provision of the law further restricted the initiative of parliament, in that it laid down that no question could be discussed without the assent of the Head of the Government. Finally the law accorded to the Prime Minister precedence over the members of the Order of the Annunziata. A further law of January 31, 1926, enabled the government, that is to say Mussolini, to legislate by decree.

The next step was to abolish local government. A law of April 6, 1926, extended the powers of the prefects, who were appointed by the government, and they became "the highest state authority in the provinces." On July 7, 1926, the government issued a statement to the effect that they had ordered the suspension of all administrative, communal, and provincial elections.

With the law of April 3, 1926, governing the organization of syndicates and labor relations, a beginning was made with the establishment of the so-called Corporative State. Behind this façade lay a considerable degree of disorder, which was never wholly cleared up; and Mussolini, with the passage of time, handed over to others the somewhat untidy execution of the plan as soon as he had achieved his primary aim to bring labor and the employers under the close control of the government.

II

The Corporative State was based on the Fascist conception of government, that is to say, the conception of a monolithic state controlling and directing every activity, ostensibly in the interests of the nation at large. It was not an altogether novel conception. For example, in 1917 Walther Rathenau had advocated such a system:

> The state will become the moving center of all economic life. Whatever society does will be done through the state and for the sake of the state. It will dispose of the powers and the means of its members with greater freedom than the old territorial potentates; the greater part of the economic surplus will accrue to it; all the well-being of the country will be incorporated in the state. There will be an end of economic-social stratification and consequently the state will assume all the powers now wielded by the dominant classes.[1]

Nevertheless the practical application of the conception in Italy was in many respects original. The various Corporations, representing every branch of production and every profession, were created by decree of the Minister of Corporations, who also appointed their executive officers. Their functions included the arrangement of collective contracts, the organization of labor exchanges, the settlement of labor disputes, vocational training, and social welfare in the widest sense. In all these matters the government acted as umpire and final arbiter.

The work of the individual Corporations was coordinated by a National Council of the Corporations to which the government appointed certain ministers, high officials and other nominees. Its main function was to issue regulations governing the national economic life as a whole.

The most important innovation, however, was the introduction of a Law of Political Elections which based the Chamber of Deputies on the Corporative system. Under this law the election of Deputies took place in three stages: first the nomination of candidates by the occupational organization concerned, secondly the selection from among these candidates of 400 names by the Fascist Grand Council, and finally the approval of the list by the electorate. The list drawn up by the Grand Council was the only list of candidates in the field and the electorate was invited to accept or to reject it. Thus parliament became a tool of the executive and could only be termed representative in so far as its members were originally nominated by diverse sectional interests, themselves controlled by a National Council appointed by the government. It was a convenient arrangement, and the Prime Minister of New Zealand ironically remarked during a visit to Rome that its introduction in his country would spare him much work and embarrassment.

Meanwhile the last step in the liquidation of the parliamentary system was taken on November 9, 1926, when the secretary of the Fascist party proposed and carried a motion in the Chamber declaring that the parliamentary mandates, and with them the parliamentary immunity, of the Aventine opposition had lapsed. Among the members who thus lost their seats were Alcide de Gasperi and Mussolini's old Socialist enemies Claudio Treves and Filippo Turati. At the end of 1926 the Duce could look back with satisfaction on two years of notable achievement. His revolution had been completed. He had swept away all obstacles to the exercise of dictatorial power and for the first time was in control of the Fascist party. The only remaining link with the old system was the King, who still enjoyed the constitutional power to appoint and remove the Head of the Government. The dyarchy, as Mussolini termed it, was at times inconvenient, but it preserved the fiction that the constitution was being respected, and, despite some grumbling and an occasional outburst of opposition, he continued, while gradually paring away the prerogatives of the monarchy, to sustain it until his fall.

III

While Mussolini was busy at home entrenching himself in his Fascist zareba, events of importance were taking place in the field of Italy's foreign relations. During the spring and summer of 1925 negotiations were on foot under the impulse of Sir Austen Chamberlain to regularize Franco-German relations by means of a guarantee of the Franco-German frontier. Mussolini's first impulse was characteristically primitive: his concern was to extract some advantage for Italy which would redound to his prestige at home. Accordingly he sought to obtain for Italy's northern frontier the same guarantee as that which was to be given for the Franco-German frontier. When the Italian ambassador in Berlin put forward this request in Berlin, Dr. Stresemann replied dryly that this involved the German annexation of Austria, since only if the Germans extended her territory to the Brenner Pass could she guarantee the frontier. In vain Contarini, Permanent Undersecretary at the Foreign Office, sought to persuade Mussolini of the advantage of associating Italy with the treaty on the same footing as Britain. He still hankered after his guarantee, and in October, when the delegates of Britain, France, Italy, Belgium, and Germany gathered at Locarno to draft their treaty, he was still sulking. Only when it became clear that the conference was on the point of reaching agreement did he suddenly decide to participate in person.

His appearance at Locarno was dramatic, but unhappy. He had arrived by special train from Rome to Milan, by racing car to Stresa, and by speedboat to Locarno. But the local inhabitants were anti-Fascist and he was not received with the popular acclamation to which he was accustomed. On the following day he announced that he would receive the representatives of the world's press. Unfortunately the correspondents with the exception of two decided to boycott the conference as a protest against the murder of Matteotti. At the appointed hour the Duce with his massive retinue came down the hotel stairs and swept into the empty conference room. He read a short statement to his audience of two, turned on his heel, and angrily left the room.[2]

His experience in the conference room was no happier. The leader of the Belgian delegation, the Socialist Vandervelde, refused to shake his hand; and he was dissatisfied with the treaty itself, not only because his request for a guarantee had been repulsed, but because it seemed to him an instrument for the maintenance of the *status quo*. On his return to Italy his ill humor was manifested in a furious press campaign against France. Nevertheless, in a speech to the Senate of May 29, 1926, he was more concerned to defend his action than to indulge his resentment.

It would have been a colossal error not to underwrite the guarantees of Locarno. If we had not done so, we should have had no part in an agreement which constitutes the basis of the relations between the Great Powers of Europe. Secondly we should have been isolated. Thirdly we should have lost an opportunity of placing ourselves on an equal footing with England in a memorable event.

It was characteristic of Mussolini that in this matter of the Brenner guarantee, to which he attached so much importance, he should have involved himself in reckless contradiction. In his speech to the Senate of May 20, 1925, he said: "It is necessary not only to guarantee the frontier on the Rhine, but it is also necessary to guarantee the frontier on the Brenner." Nearly a year later, on February 6, 1926, Stresemann revealed to the Reichstag that the Italian government had sought a frontier guarantee; and Mussolini on the following day publicly denied it. "There is a statement in the Stresemann speech which I must deny in the most formal manner. The Italian government has not only not made but has scrupulously rejected any suggestion of the kind both before and after Locarno, since it is convinced that in the present state of affairs the most solid guarantee of the Brenner lies in the moral and material character of the treaties and of the Italian people." But three months later, speaking to the Senate on May 28, 1926, he said: "The fact that the Brenner frontier was not guaranteed is easily to be explained: the government did not insist on this because the Locarno treaties were already too complex."[3]

Whatever Mussolini may have thought of the proceedings at Locarno, to Sir Austen Chamberlain the treaty represented the culminating point of his political life. "The wonderful week is over.

I have lived such days and celebrated such a birthday as is given to no man to experience twice."[4] He invested his treaty with a mystic significance and kept a special place in his affections for all those who had been associated with him in the enterprise. He had already formed a favorable opinion of Mussolini when he had visited Rome in December, 1924, and his relations with the Duce were now to be placed on a basis of personal friendship which endured to the end. Mussolini was sensible to this attention and reciprocated Sir Austen's sentiments. The French on the other hand, having reached their accommodation with Dr. Stresemann at Locarno, had no further use for Italy and made little effort to conceal their dislike of Mussolini and the aspirations of his Fascist Italy. Characteristic of their open contempt for all things Italian was a remark by Berthelot,* to whom at a conference an Englishman observed that it would be interesting to see whether the Italian delegate turned up in a black shirt. The Italian in question was not particularly tidy or spry in appearance and Berthelot retorted in a loud voice: "It will be much more interesting to see whether he can appear in a clean shirt."

The friendship of Sir Austen Chamberlain was not only balm to Mussolini's egotistical soul, but brought solid advantages in its train. The cession to Italy of Jubaland had been effected in 1924 by the Labor government, and now in 1925 there was a settlement of the Italo-Egyptian frontier problem under British auspices and an agreement whereby Britain undertook to support Italy in acquiring a concession to construct a railway across Ethiopian territory from Eritrea to Italian Somaliland. In this climate Anglo-Italian relations remained for many years unclouded by any difference. Mussolini's restless peevishness was now directed against France, where, to aggravate matters, most of Italy's political exiles were concentrated. But he recognized that Italy alone could do nothing, and it was much too early to show his hand. His immediate policy must be to lean on Britain, to keep the international pot astir, to await some opportunity he could turn to advantage, and meanwhile to prepare his country for the coming struggle. As early as December 11, 1925, he declared to the Cham-

* M. Philippe Berthelot, Secretary-General of the French Ministry for Foreign Affairs.

ber that he considered Italy to be in a permanent state of war: "I have said, and I repeat, that the next five or ten years will be decisive for the destiny of our people. They will be decisive because the international struggle has broken out and will continue to extend; and we who have arrived a little late on the international scene cannot disperse our energies."

Another significant event in foreign affairs was the signature at Tirana on November 27, 1926, of an Italo-Albanian pact declaring that any disturbance of the status quo in Albania was contrary to the interests of the two governments, who undertook to afford mutual support for the safeguard of those interests. The treaty established a virtual Italian protectorate in Albania and was warmly welcomed by the nationalists, who had never ceased to bewail the withdrawal of Italian troops after the war. It was a success in foreign affairs which exasperated the French and Yugoslavs and which appealed particularly to Mussolini's romantically chauvinist spirit.

IV

Before leaving the pregnant years 1925 and 1926 one domestic event in Mussolini's life must be recorded. On December 29, 1925, he was married to Rachele in the Milanese church of San Pietro in Sala. It was a private ceremony and the witnesses were his brother Arnaldo and his principal private secretary Paolucci de Calboli. The religious marriage was certainly intended as a gesture towards the Vatican, but this was not its only reason. Mussolini came to believe that as the leader of the nation it was proper that he should conform, outwardly at all events, to the religion professed by his compatriots. Moreover he had his brief, recurring moments of piety and he may well have been glad to regularize his matrimonial position. Rachele, as usual, was prepared to do whatever her lord required: "Towards the end of 1925 Benito insisted on our going through the religious marriage ceremony. To me our deep attachment to each other, the fact that we had stood together as one in our stormy life, and above all our children were a firmer bond than any conventions. But I readily agreed to consecrate our union in the sight of God."

V

At the end of 1926 the period of spectacular events in Fascist Italy had passed for the moment. The opposition had been scattered, no alternative government was in sight, and Mussolini had created a situation in which it seemed that if he went there would be chaos. Many patriotic Italians, not particularly enamored of Mussolini or Fascism, openly declared that they preferred him to chaos. It was therefore not without justification that he claimed to be in power by the will of the nation, an argument invoked by the King when reproached for supporting the Duce.

The next two years were a period of consolidation, and it was a sign of the times that the firebrand Farinacci had been replaced as secretary of the party by the moderate and popular Augusto Turati. Most modern dictators attach a curious importance to clothing tyranny with a semblance of legal propriety; and it was only after he had fortified himself by the legislation of 1925 and 1926 that Mussolini felt free to take administrative steps to squeeze the Italian nation into the Fascist mold. In February, 1927, the Special Tribunal began its work and on May 26, 1927, he was able to announce to the Chamber that 698 political prisoners were safely under lock and key. One of these was De Gasperi, accused of seeking to flee abroad and sentenced to three years' imprisonment. The public services were drastically purged. In the Ministry of Foreign Affairs, according to a statement of the Stefani news agency on January 7, 1928, 82 out of 450 employees had been recently retired, while 200 who had been admitted between 1921 and 1925 were in the majority Fascists. Even sport was drawn into the net. Under a regulation of March 2, 1927, all sporting clubs were organized in thirty-two federations under the Italian National Olympic Committee, which in turn was placed under the direct control of the secretary of the Fascist party; and in October the party secretary was appointed an honorary football referee and presented with a golden whistle. In March, 1928, the Cabinet approved the dissolution of all youth organizations which did not belong to the Fascist youth body, the *Balilla*.

The injection of fascism into the machinery of government

created a novel constitutional position. Mussolini ruled Italy in two capacities: as Prime Minister and as leader of the Fascist party. But while he was currently referred to as the Duce, it was only later that he adopted the title of "Head of the Government and Duce of Fascism." It was a system to be faithfully copied by Hitler.

The new electoral law, to which reference has already been made, came before the Chamber on March 16, 1928, and was passed without debate by 216 to 15 votes. Giolitti voted against the bill and put in a written statement to the effect that he had done so because he regarded it as a violation of the constitution. On the following day Mussolini delivered his reply in the *Foglio d'ordini* of the party. He admitted that parliamentary government had been brought to an end, but it was infantile, he declared, to hark back to the constitution:

> The constitution was promulgated in 1848. Today we are in 1928. When the constitution was promulgated, Italy of Vittorio Veneto did not exist, nor Italy of the Blackshirts, nor Italy the Corporative State, nor in a word Italy of the Fascist revolution. Eighty useless years have passed in the history of a nation.[5]

The law came before the Senate on May 12, 1928, where, after a debate, it was passed by 161 to 46 votes. Among the Senators who voted against the bill were Albertini, Croce, and Einaudi. Among the majority were Gentile, Scialoia, and Marshal Badoglio.

Since the electoral law invested the Grand Council with constitutional powers, it became necessary to regularize the position of the Council, which hitherto had rested on an administrative decision of Mussolini. It now became an organ of the state, and a law laid down that its opinion must be sought in regard to all constitutional questions. Among the matters specified as constitutional questions were bills concerning the succession to the throne, the prerogatives of the Crown, the composition and functions of the Grand Council, Senate, and Chamber, and the replacement of the Head of the Government. The law elevated the Grand Council to the highest position in the state and put into practice Mussolini's system of dyarchy; the monarchy and the legislature on one hand and the apparatus of the party on the other. It was a system, Mussolini once declared, which was based on the arrangement of the matrimonial chamber with twin beds.

The King was furious and declared that the Fascists had no business to interfere with the throne. The question of the succession was already settled under the constitution, but if a party in a monarchist state now claimed to determine the succession, the monarchy as such could be said to have ceased to exist. Nevertheless, neither the King nor Mussolini wished to embark on a public quarrel; and so after an exchange of growls the difference was allowed to subside. Neither could foresee that it was the Grand Council which was to give the King a constitutional basis for the dismissal of Mussolini or that Marshal Badoglio, whom Mussolini had installed in 1925 as Chief of Staff against the best professional advice, was the man to whom the King would turn.

The law on the Grand Council duly passed through a docile Chamber and Senate, and on December 8, 1928, the twenty-seventh legislature was dissolved. It was the parliament that had buried the constitution and destroyed Italian liberty at the behest of one man; and its members, many of whom could under the new law never return, left the building with Mussolini's closing speech ringing in their ears. He told them that they would have a place in history as the creators of the Fascist revolution and that the elections which would take place the following year would have nothing in common with elections of former days or of other countries. The old Chamber had been 85 per cent Fascist; the new Chamber would be 100 per cent Fascist. Totalitarianism in such a body was not an absurdity; it was a necessity, the regime itself being totalitarian.

CHAPTER ELEVEN

The Conciliation

1929

I

WHILE in the full light of day the Fascist revolution had been bulldozing its way through the constitution, Mussolini had for two years been busily engaged on a secret enterprise which was to bring him the most resounding success of his whole career: the so-called Conciliation between Church and state.* Until 1859 the Pope had been at the same time head of the Catholic Church and temporal sovereign of the Papal States covering some 16,000 square miles with a population of over three million. Between 1859 and 1870 the territories belonging to the Pope were annexed by the kingdom of Italy and, when in 1870 the Pope's capital was occupied by Italian troops, he retired to the Vatican, a complex of buildings and gardens behind St. Peter's covering about 500,000 square yards.

The Italian government in 1871 passed the Law of Guarantees, which defined the position of the Pope and regulated the relations between Church and state. It was not an illiberal measure. The person of the Pope was declared inviolable and he was accorded

---

* For information relating to the negotiation of the Conciliation I am indebted to three informants and to the following works: Francesco Pacelli, *Diario della Conciliazone* (Vatican City, 1959); Carlo Alberto Biggini, *Storia della Conciliazone* (Milan, 1952); Daniel A. Binchy, *Church and State in Fascist Italy* (London, 1941); Arturo Carlo Jemolo, *Chiesa e stato in Italia negli ultimi cento anni* (Rome, 1948).

the honors due to a sovereign. He was allowed the use of the Vatican, the Lateran palace, and the papal villa at Castel Gandolfo; and he was authorized to maintain a personal armed guard. The Italian government undertook to exercise no jurisdiction in the Vatican and diplomatists accredited to the Holy See were to enjoy the same immunities as those accredited to the Quirinal. Moreover the Pope was to receive from the Italian state an annual subvention of 3,225,000 lire for the maintenance of his court and his diplomatic service, this being the sum allotted for the purpose in the former papal budget.

As regards relations between Church and state, the law made substantial concessions to the Vatican. For example, the bishops were relieved of the obligation to swear fealty to the King, and civil courts were to exercise no jurisdiction in the matter of sentences of ecclesiastical courts relating to spiritual and internal disciplinary affairs.

From the Vatican point of view the law, however liberal its intentions, was objectionable on one basic ground. It was not a negotiated agreement but a unilateral act which might at any time be modified or even abrogated by another Italian parliament. The very wording of the law which granted the Pope the use of the Vatican implied that it was not his property and that what had been lent to him might at some future date be withdrawn. Moreover the Pope, who had been forcibly despoiled of his temporal possessions, was not disposed meekly to accept a settlement imposed on him by the Italian government.

Consequently Pope Pius IX rejected the Law of Guarantees, repulsed the offered subvention, declared himself a prisoner, and laid formal claim to the possessions of which he had been robbed. When he died in 1878 his successor Leo XIII took the same line and continued to regard the King of Italy as a usurper. As the years passed the need for coexistence of Church and state mitigated the tension between them, but so long as no formal agreement defined their relations the quarrel persisted and Italian society continued to be grievously divided.

Towards the end of the nineteenth century two methods of breaking the deadlock were ventilated: either the internationalization of the Law of Guarantees or its replacement by an international treaty. But neither solution found favor at the time. The Vatican objected to being placed under the protection of the signatory powers and, more important, the Quirinal was reluctant to submit to any measure of foreign control or supervision, even in this limited sector, on Italian territory.

After the First World War further efforts were made to find a solution. The climate of opinion was not unfavorable. Pope Benedict was well disposed and inclined towards a settlement which might be ratified by some sort of international guarantee, although in deference to Italian susceptibilities the word guarantee would not be used. In June, 1919, there were preliminary conversations between Orlando, the Prime Minister, and Monsignor Ceretti, later Nuncio in Paris. Shortly afterwards Orlando fell and was succeeded by Nitti, who in turn embarked on conversations with Cardinal Gasparri. These had not made progress when in 1920 Nitti fell and Giolitti became Prime Minister for the fifth time. Giolitti, however, was not prepared to pursue the matter and said to his Minister of Foreign Affairs: "The conversations have been very creditable to both sides, but the best thing for the state and the Church is to continue as in the past: two parallels that get on well together without ever coming into contact."[1] Giolitti was one of those nineteenth-century liberals who believed in the secularization of the state and who considered that the functions of the Church should be confined within the four walls of places of worship and preferably on Sundays only. At the age of eighty he could scarcely be expected to change his ideas; and in his reluctance to make a move he was sustained by the King, who did not relish being branded as a usurper and was implacably hostile to the claims of the Holy See.

II

This was the unfortunate situation which Mussolini determined to bring to an end. It has been said that mutual animosity had so much diminished and the desire for an accommodation had become so evident on both sides that in any event a settlement would have been reached. But it appears doubtful whether in fact negotiations would have been brought to fruition by any of the feeble postwar governments based on tenuous parliamentary majorities and by politicians who did not wield Mussolini's exceptional authority and who were not equally resolved to succeed. In June, 1921, in his maiden speech in the Chamber he had attracted attention by the friendly terms in which he spoke of the Vatican and of the need to reach an agreement, and in February, 1922, he had shown his interest in the Holy See by going to the Piazza San Pietro on the penultimate day of the conclave in the hope of seeing the white smoke which signifies the election of a pontiff. The newly elected Pope, Achille Ratti, Pius XI, for his part, demonstrated his conciliatory intentions by coming out onto the outer balcony of St. Peter's to bless the crowd in the piazza. He was the first Pope to have done so since 1870.

When later in the year Mussolini came to power, a number of measures were progressively taken to improve relations between Church and state: the crucifix was restored in schools and law courts, the laws against blasphemy were strengthened, divorce was made more difficult, religious instruction was imparted in elementary schools, equal treatment was assured for State schools and private confessional schools, recognition was given to the Catholic university at Milan, there was official participation in religious ceremonies, the Freemasons were suppressed, the state contribution to the Church was increased, chaplains were appointed to the armed forces, and exemption from military service was granted to clerics. Mussolini even had a private conversation in 1923 with Cardinal Gasparri, the Papal Secretary of State, in which he ventilated the possibility of solving the Roman question.

He had done much to pave the way for an agreement. But in 1925 Mussolini went further and proposed the revision of Italian ecclesiastical legislation in conformity with the wishes of the clergy. The Minister of Justice, Alfredo Rocca, appointed a commission to study the matter and included in this body, with the tacit approval of the Vatican, three ecclesiastics. This step and the government measures which preceded it were all tokens of good will and as such helped to prepare the way. But of course they contributed nothing to the settlement of the basic problem, and Pope Pius XI made this very clear when on February 18, 1926, after the commission had been at work for a year, he wrote to

Cardinal Gasparri that the Church could accept no conclusion regarding Italian ecclesiastical law so long as the Roman question remained unresolved. This letter was regarded not as a challenge, but as an invitation; and both the British diplomatic missions in Rome reported rumors that the Roman question was to be reopened.

In view of the Pope's communication the work of the commission was suspended; and the Minister of Justice told the Chamber that the matter would be taken up later at an appropriate time and in a larger framework, because the Pope's letter had altered the scope of the problem and the government was obliged to take account of the fact. This statement aroused interest in the Vatican, particularly since it was followed by a verbal intimation that the Prime Minister wished the reform of Italian ecclesiastical law to be incorporated in a settlement of the Roman question. Cardinal Gasparri, while gratified at this communication, told the intermediary, Monsignor Enrico Pucci, editor of the Catholic *Corriere d'Italia,* that he could do nothing until he received something official. The government replied through the same intermediary that they must first be assured that an official approach would not be met by a rebuff. Cardinal Gasparri replied that he saw no reason why there should not be an exchange of views on the problem. Thus despite the utmost wariness on both sides a point was reached at which the initiation of conversations was envisaged. But a little time was required before intentions could be translated into deeds.

Meanwhile Mussolini optimistically determined to regard the Pope's letter as a proposal. In a long letter of May 4, 1926, to Rocco, he said that the Fascist government had repudiated the conceptions of the Liberals, as well as the principle of agnosticism in the state and the separation of Church and state, which was as absurd as the separation of the spiritual and material in man. The government had methodically restored to the nation its Catholic character, of which it had been robbed by the Liberals. It was therefore natural that the Fascist government should wish to give careful attention to the Pope's desire to see a satisfactory regulation of the relations between the Holy See and the Italian state. Mussolini concluded his letter with these words: "I have always considered the quarrel between the Church and the state baneful for both and its settlement sooner or later to be historically inevitable. If the news you receive indicates that the time is near, my heart will be filled with joy. But if it proves otherwise, we shall continue in the expectation of better times to do our duty as Italians and Catholics."

Despite Mussolini's zeal the idea of opening conversations simmered very slowly on both sides. Neither the King nor the Fascists were enamored of the idea of a reconciliation, and on the Vatican side there was a long history of enmity and suspicion to overcome. Fortunately for Mussolini the throne of St. Peter was occupied by a vigorous, self-willed pontiff in the person of Pius XI, whose authority was sufficient to overcome any hesitations there may have been among his advisers.

In fact the next step came from the Vatican, when Monsignor Luigi Haver approached a personal friend, who was a Counsellor of State, Domenico Barone, with the suggestion that negotiations might now be opened for a solution of the Roman question. On August 5, 1926, Barone made the first request for a talk, and during the month there were a number of conversations between Barone and Francesco Pacelli, brother of the future Pope Pius XII, who was entrusted by Pope Pius XI with the conduct of the negotiations.

Barone kept Mussolini informed and on August 30, 1926, addressed him a long memorandum setting forth the upshot of his conversations. The Pope, said Barone, had been apprised that Mussolini had laid down one condition: namely an explicit renunciation by the Holy See of every temporal claim against Italy. To this the Pope had replied that he was disposed to accept this demand in substance, but that the form of any declaration required careful consideration. For his part the Pope had posed three conditions:

1. The initiative must come from the Italian government. Seeing that the Church had been despoiled of its temporal power by the Kingdom of Italy, it was right that the latter should make the first move for a reconciliation.

2. The Italian government must declare that the negotiations should leave out of account the Law of Guarantees.

3. The negotiations must be conducted in the most complete secrecy.

Barone, who was at pains throughout to smooth the path, had this to say in explanation, and indeed support, of the Pope's conditions:

> 1. In practice this first condition presents no difficulty. All that is required is to charge some person, such as the writer, to begin the negotiations and to make a formal communication notifying the appointment. The Holy See would concur in terms acceptable to the Italian government and its reply could be agreed before the Italian note was communicated.
> 2. The unilateral character of the Law of Guarantees is offensive to the dignity of the Holy See. The Pope originally intended to ask that during the negotiations it should be regarded as suspended, but on further reflection decided to limit his demand to a declaration in the form suggested.
> 3. The Pope wishes the negotiations to be confined to a very limited circle: himself, Cardinal Gasparri, and Pacelli on the Vatican side and Mussolini and Barone on the Italian side.

Barone went on to say that the Pope was opposed to the intervention of foreign powers, which would be acceptable neither to the Holy See nor to the Italian government. It was contemplated that there should be two conventions: a political instrument, which would settle the Roman question, and a juridical instrument, which would make provision for the administrative arrangements between Church and state. The political convention would assign a territory to the Holy See and accord a sovereign status to the Pope. It would be the function of the Holy See to notify foreign governments and to secure their recognition of the new arrangement.

Barone concluded by saying that he was convinced that the Pope sincerely desired a reconciliation with the state and that he considered that the proposals which he had outlined constituted a satisfactory basis of negotiation.

Barone's memorandum, which extended to over four thousand words, achieved its purpose. On October 4 Mussolini in a handwritten letter headed "Rome, 4 October 1926–iv. Feast of St. Francis of Assisi," formally instructed Barone to initiate negotiations with representatives of the Holy See in order to discover on what terms the Holy See would be disposed to regularize relations between Church and state. On the same day Cardinal Gasparri addressed a letter to Pacelli, formally appointing him the representative of the Holy See for an exchange of views with Barone.

III

The way was now clear for a beginning to be made. Pacelli and Barone worked very quickly, particularly when one considers that they were obliged to consult their principals on every point. Pacelli, for example, had no fewer than thirty-one audiences with the Pope between August and December. After a month they were able to produce a first draft of the political convention in sixteen articles. They then passed to a consideration of the second convention, but in the meantime the Italian government judged the progress that had been made to be sufficient to justify lifting the conversations to a more formal plane. On December 10, 1926, the King authorized Mussolini to open official negotiations, and on December 31 Mussolini in a handwritten letter informed Cardinal Gasparri of this development.

While all was going smoothly at the conference table, events in Italy threatened to wreck the enterprise. In November the Fascists attacked Catholic establishments in fourteen cities and the Pope replied to Mussolini through Pacelli that he would not consent to open official negotiations until he received a public expression of regret and assurances for the future. On November 27 Pacelli reported that Mussolini had sent instructions to prefects and Fascist leaders to desist from violence, but he professed himself obliged to proceed with caution, since he was unable at one blow to put a stop to extreme Fascist anticlericalism.

The situation was aggravated in December when the Italian government introduced a bill under which the state claimed a monopoly of political and physical education, which was to be carried out exclusively by the *Balilla* organization, while Catholic bodies that catered to youth were to be dissolved. Pacelli was instructed to demand that the bill be suspended, and when Mussolini declined to comply the reaction of the Pope was very sharp. He spoke publicly of the menace to Christian education and denounced totalitarianism in the state. Tempers rose on both sides. Cardinal Gasparri reminded the diplomatic corps of the prescription in force since 1870 forbidding contact with their colleagues accredited to the Quirinal or with the Italian authorities and the so-called White society. On the other side the many Fascists who disliked the idea of an accommodation with the Holy See gleefully seized the opportunity to heap insults on and to threaten violence against the Church. The press was, however, under Mussolini's control and steps were taken to see that it did not exacerbate the quarrel. In this field Arnaldo Mussolini as editor of the *Popolo d'Italia* was able to play a useful conciliatory role.

On January 6, 1927, the Pope, having failed to obtain any satisfaction over the *Balilla* bill, finally instructed Pacelli to inform Barone that the negotiations must be suspended. Nevertheless, this move was more of a demonstration than a definitive breach. Accordingly, with the Pope's knowledge, some contact between the parties was maintained and drafts and counterdrafts continued to be privately exchanged, at a slower tempo and without commitment on either side. So the year 1927 passed without registering any significant progress, while constant petty incidents threatened to revive the embers of the quarrel. A Jesuit priest, Father Tacchi Venturi, who had influence with Mussolini, was used as an intermediary.

On January 21, 1928, the Pope, who was still anxious to reach agreement and who allowed himself to relent in the face of somewhat tenuous assurances transmitted through Pacelli and Tacchi Venturi, assented to the resumption of the negotiations; and he accepted the Italian government's proposal that they should henceforth become official. In February Barone was able to submit to Mussolini a further draft of the second convention with a long explanatory memorandum. In the course of the following months Mussolini and the Pope exchanged proposals and counterproposals for modifications to both conventions. The negotiations followed the course familiar to every diplomat in the sense that the process of accurate drafting brought to light divergencies hitherto concealed by vaguer verbal communications; and it was necessary either to find formulae to resolve the differences or to barter one concession against another. The Pope, who had originally claimed territory outside the Vatican including the extensive Villa Doria Pamphili, wisely agreed to be content with only the area in the Vatican proper, which he already occupied. He said later: "We are glad to see the earthly territory reduced to such minute proportions." But he was intransigent over the provisions relating to marriage and education; and he demanded that the treaty and the concordat be linked, so that if the Italian government violated or denounced the latter, the former became invalid.

By November, 1928, most of the substantial differences had been removed and the King appointed Mussolini, assisted by Barone, as his delegate charged with the task of concluding the two conventions. At the same time the Pope appointed Cardinal Gasparri, assisted by Pacelli and Monsignor Borgoncini Duca of the Secretariat of State, to represent him in the last stage of the negotiations. At this point Barone's health began to fail and he died on January 4, 1929, without seeing the fruits of his labors, but having lived long enough to ensure by his patience, tolerance, and good sense that the conventions would be brought safely into port.

From this point Mussolini was in sole charge of the negotiations. From January 8 until February 9 he met Pacelli fifteen times at his apartment in the Via Rasella. They were long meetings which lasted from 9 P.M. till the early hours of the morning. The drafts of the two conventions were closely examined and a number of modifications made. Pacelli reported daily to the Pope and Mussolini sent the texts of the amendments to the King, who on four occasions wrote to convey his congratulations on the improvements which Mussolini had been able to secure. On February 10 Mussolini was able to inform the Sovereign that the texts were virtually ready and that they would be signed on February 11. He impishly enclosed a copy of an article published in various European newspapers, in which the exiled Nitti had declared that there was no prospect, close or distant, of any agreement between Italy and the Holy See. From the tone of the letter it is clear that Mussolini was in a triumphant mood.

Under the two agreements, the treaty and the concordat, Italy recognized the sovereignty of the Holy See, while the Holy See for its part recognized the Kingdom of Italy under the Savoy dynasty with its capital in Rome and declared the Roman question solved.

The Pope received a territory, which was substantially that which he already occupied and which was to be termed the Vatican City. Under the financial convention he also received 750 million lire in cash and one billion lire in government bonds by way of indemnity. The convention recognized that this sum did not cover the value of the property taken from the Holy See and that, in limiting his demands, the Pope had taken account of the economic situation of Italy after the war. Finally the concordat regulated the administrative relations between Church and state. The most contentious articles were those relating to education and marriage. The state undertook to extend religious education from the elementary to the secondary schools and to do so through the agency of teachers and textbooks approved by the ecclesiastical authorities. As regards marriage, it was stipulated that religious marriages should be legal and the obligation of the Church was confined to the communication within five days of the documents to the civil authorities for entry in the civil register. Moreover, and this was a bitter pill for Mussolini to swallow, it was laid down that cases of nullity or of dispensations on the ground that the marriage had not been consummated should be exclusively reserved to the ecclesiastical courts.

The Pope had been ready to make concessions in regard to the size of the Vatican City, and indeed he believed that its boundaries should be reduced to the minimum essential to secure real sovereignty for the new state. He was also easy in the matter of the indemnity, but the articles on education and, particularly, marriage became a sticking point. Mussolini on January 20, 1929, wrote somewhat apologetically to the King:

> I do not conceal from Your Majesty that the most difficult obstacle to surmount in the concordat has been the article on marriage. Here the state has retreated a long way and has been virtually excluded in so fundamental a matter as the constitution and the evolution of the family. But it seems that the Holy See regards this as an essential condition of first-class importance, on which the issue of the whole treaty depends.

The two treaties were signed at the Lateran on February 11, 1929, by Mussolini for Italy and by Cardinal Gasparri for the Holy See. Mussolini made a forty-minute speech in which with fulsome eloquence he played the part of a loyal son of the Church, while

Cardinal Gasparri nodded his approval. It was a happy gathering and Mussolini returned to the Palazzo Chigi in high spirits at his success. But he admitted to his private secretary that he was not enamored of Pope Pius XI: "The fact is that we both have the mentality of the peasant." [2]

Within a short time news of the signature spread through the city and crowds came out to cheer the Pope, the King, and the Duce. While the shouts of the demonstrators were echoing in the streets the Pope was granting his usual Lenten audience to the parish priests of Rome. He gave them a short account of the treaties followed by a long and vigorous defense against "certain doubts and criticisms which have already made their appearance and which will probably increase in volume." Next day the ceremony in St. Peter's to celebrate the seventh anniversary of the Pope's coronation was the occasion for further popular manifestations. There was a general feeling that the conciliation had set the final seal on Italian unity and there could be no doubt as to the genuine enthusiasm with which the news was received.

IV

The event did not, however, create lasting harmony between Church and state. The totalitarian character of fascism and the exaggerated claims which it made on the individual were bound to lead to conflict. Moreover, misunderstandings arose from Mussolini's characteristic failure to apprehend the nature and outlook of the Papacy. Having made what he conceived to be a generous settlement, he considered that the Vatican should blindly accept and sustain Fascist policy at home and abroad not only from motives of gratitude, but also of self-interest. It seemed to him that the Church, in order to extend its influence, should wish to increase the power of the one man who could be relied upon to give effective help in the struggle against German paganism, Russian atheism, British anti-Popery, French gallicism, and Spanish nationalism. He took no account of the Church's universal character and of its position in international affairs, which made it impossible for the Pope to take sides in conflicts between Catholic or even non-Catholic nations. Nor did he recognize that the Papacy regarded the old quarrel as stemming from an act of aggression and felt under no obligation to manifest gratitude for a partial act of reparation.

The first rumbles of discord were heard on May 13 when the debate on the Conciliation took place in the Chamber. In his speech on the second day Mussolini was concerned to meet the sullen criticism of the extreme Fascists and so to place the treaties in the most favorable light. It was a long speech lasting some three hours, and it was one of his best. He opened in deliberately aggressive style with an ironical reference to the jubilation which had greeted the settlement. "After three months these ardors have naturally abated; and now I propose to make you the least lyrical and most frigid of speeches." Almost every passage which followed was calculated to enthuse the Fascist anticlerical and to mortify Italian Catholic sentiment.

Previous speakers, who had referred to Cavour's formula of "a free and sovereign Church in a free and sovereign state," were told that they were grievously mistaken, for the treaties had made no such provision. There were two sovereign entities separated by six hundred miles, even if it required only five minutes to visit the new Vatican state and ten minutes to cross its boundaries. But in the Italian state the Church was not sovereign or even free, for it was subject to Italian law and to the provisions of the concordat.

He went on to make some wounding observations on the origin of Catholicism: a religion which had been born in Palestine, but which became Catholic in Rome. Had it remained in Palestine, he declared, it would very probably have been but one of the many sects that flourished on that ardent soil, such as the Essenes, and very probably it would have perished without leaving any trace.[3] A history of the Papacy followed. There was a caustic reference to the collapse of the temporal power at the hands of Napoleon and a long account of the Roman question and of the abortive attempts to settle it. He then described the origin of his negotiations and their course. As to the result: "We have not resurrected the temporal power of the Popes, we have buried it." No territory had been surrendered and nowhere had the Italian flag been hauled down. In the field of education, the Fascist will had prevailed: "In this matter we are intractable. Education must be ours." The other provisions of the concordat were in line with similar treaties concluded by the Holy See, and he claimed, with chapter and verse to prove it, that Italy had given away nothing.

While the Catholics were aghast, the speech delighted the Fascist extremists; and the King expressed his gratification that Mussolini should have swept away clerical illusions. To the British ambassador Mussolini cynically explained that before the elections he had required the good opinion of those who were Catholics before they were Fascists. But he now thought that the emphasis should be shifted for the sake of the powerful elements in the country who were apprehensive of clerical predominance.

Of course the Pope was outraged and remarked to his intimates that he had been tricked by Mussolini.[4] The following morning he delivered a spirited reply when he addressed the pupils of the Jesuit college of Mondragone. He said that on education he was not intractable, for that was a sign of weakness, but he was intransigent. "We have no material means of enforcing our intransigence. Nor do we regret this, for truth and right have no need of material force."

On May 22 Pacelli under instructions from Pius XI told Mussolini that the Pope expected him to correct his speech when he addressed the Senate; and Mussolini undertook to do so. In the event, the speech to the Senate was conciliatory in form and made an effort to correct the modernism of his views on the origin of Christianity. In substance, however, it altered nothing. Indeed Mussolini explicitly stood by all he had said in the Chamber: "I had to clear an atmosphere which, through excess of nebulousness and sentimentality, would have ended by altering the shape of things and the character and significance of events."

Once more the Pope instructed Pacelli to protest. Mussolini replied that he had been obliged to defend himself from "ferocious attacks" made on him for having restored the temporal power of the Papacy and surrendered the Italian state to the Church. He expressed the desire, however, to give the Pope some measure of satisfaction. In particular he undertook to take the first opportunity to make a friendly gesture to the Vatican, a promise which, incidentally, was never fulfilled; and he said that if the Pope wished to make public his dissatisfaction, he himself would not only remain silent, but would allow the papal statement to appear in every

Italian newspaper. It was the old story of relations between the Italian government and the Holy See. Behind the façade of conflict there had always been even in the days of the most acute dissension a typically Italian desire to find a "*combinazione*" which would permit a practical working arrangement without any sacrifice of principle.

Once the Chamber and Senate had approved the treaties it was necessary to perform the formal act of ratification in order to bring them into force. But there was one last hurdle to be jumped, namely the Pope's insistence that the concordat should be linked with the treaty, that is to say, that a breach of the concordat should be recognized as invalidating the treaty. On this point Mussolini was resolved not to give way and the resulting deadlock is described by Pacelli as the most difficult issue of the whole negotiation. Eventually on June 6 he was able to find a formula acceptable to both Mussolini and the Pope, whereby the contracting parties undertook to observe in the letter and the spirit both the treaty and the concordat.

The Pope, however, was not prepared to allow Mussolini's speeches to pass without reply. On June 6 the Vatican newspaper published a letter from Pius XI to Cardinal Gasparri in which he declared it to be his duty to dissipate misunderstandings. He defined Mussolini's observations on the essence of Christianity as heretical and described the alleged distinction between the sovereignty of the Holy See under the treaty and the subjection of the Church to the Italian government under the concordat as a dangerous error. Moreover the effort to separate the treaty from the concordat was repugnant to the spirit of the agreements since both were indissolubly connected. He examined Mussolini's statements on the details of the concordat and in each case flatly rejected them. Finally he declared that for the future his faith lay in the help of God.

Mussolini adhered to the promise which he had given to Pacelli and made no reply. The exchange of ratifications took place the following day, June 7, 1929, at the Vatican in the presence of a large Italian delegation headed by Mussolini in diplomatic uniform. The Pope and the King exchanged telegrams and ambassadors were appointed: Monsignor Borgoncini Duca became nuncio in Rome and the Quadrumvir Cesare de Vecchi, the first Italian ambassador to the Holy See. De Vecchi had always been something of a problem child, and Mussolini was glad to kill two birds with one stone. The nomination of a Quadrumvir was a compliment to the Holy See and it was convenient to have De Vecchi in a situation in which he could be kept under close supervision.

V

Professor Binchy remarks with truth that the foreign student is faced with a formidable task when he comes to balance the gains and losses which the reconciliation brought to the Church in Italy.[5] One thing is, however, certain. The treaties brought an immense access of prestige to Mussolini, for he had solved a problem which had eluded all his predecessors. In reaching this result he had sacrificed no substantial Italian interest; and indeed so far as material things were concerned, and these were what interested the ordinary man, he could show that it was the Pope who had made the principal sacrifices. Both sides were subsequently disappointed, Mussolini because he failed to make the Pope the political vassal of the Fascist state and the Pope because he was in practice unable to secure for the Church the liberty accorded to it by the treaties. Yet in the troublous years ahead neither party was willing to push disagreement to a point which endangered the settlement.

This in effect constitutes the main justification of the treaties. In 1961 Cardinal Pizzardo, the last survivor of the transaction, with the advantage of hindsight, expressed the view that, despite the difficulties with the Fascist government and those with the postwar Christian Democratic government, he was convinced that the Conciliation had on balance brought substantial advantage to both Church and state in Italy.[6]

Mussolini himself regarded the Conciliation as his most notable success and in the evening of his life, when he had little to do except evoke memories of the past, it was the event on which he most often dwelled. In a conversation with his sister Edvige he recognized that his speech of May 14, 1929, had been a mistake. It was absurd, he admitted, to have suggested that the early Christians had received from a decadent Rome the impulse which created a dominating Church and religion. He went on to reveal his ambivalent attitude towards the Church. He thought that when he made his speech he had given expression to sentiments of envy. In the prelates he had met, however suave and indeed hypocritical, he could see the faces of the Palestinian fishermen and the image of the revolution which they had wrought. But in his own case, although he had indeed obtained power, the revolutionary ideas and the socialism of his youth had been left by the wayside. Eventually his career had met a farcical end in an ambulance and he was glad to be able from his limbo to take a dispassionate view of history. But when he contemplated the story of the eternal Catholic Church, how he envied her.[7] It would of course be a mistake to read too much into this conversation with Edvige. Mussolini always admired the Catholic Church for her authority, her continuity, her worldwide empire, and the skill of her prelates. But beneath the surface there remained until the end of his days more than a residue of that hatred for the Church and Christian doctrine which inflamed his youth.

CHAPTER TWELVE

The Halcyon Years

1929–1935

I

WHATEVER may be the verdict on the Lateran treaties Mussolini was quick to gather the first fruits of his success. He had driven forward the negotiations with one eye on the elections which were due to take place in March. The signature of the treaty in February enabled millions of Catholics to cast their votes for the Fascist list with good conscience. The government was in any event sure of victory, but Mussolini required the elections, which he termed a national plebiscite, to give him an overwhelming vote of confidence and in his own words to "demonstrate to the world that Italy is Fascist and that fascism is Italy." [1]

The Catholic organizations duly played their part. The central committee of Catholic Action called on Catholics to cooperate in the creation of the new legislature which was destined to ratify and execute the Lateran treaties; and the editor of *Civiltà Cattolica* in two articles emphasized the importance of voting in order to assure the entry into force of the treaties. In both cases nothing was said about other aspects of Fascist policy, and Catholic voters were urged to cast their votes merely to register approval of the Conciliation. But Mussolini was more concerned to obtain votes than to scrutinize the motives of the voters; and his accommodation with the Vatican brought him in effect a large number of votes which he would otherwise have not received.

Polling took place on March 24, 1929. The percentage of the electorate which voted was 89.63 per cent, an unpredictably large proportion. Mussolini's list received 8,517,838 votes, and the number who voted against it was only 135,773. It was, however, noteworthy that in the large towns the percentage of hostile votes was much greater than in the country. In Milan, for example, 23,156 votes out of a total of 412,269 were cast against the list. In conversation with Sir Austen Chamberlain at Florence on April 1 Mussolini expressed his disappointment at this result, although it was only a blemish on the bloom of a resounding victory.

With the Conciliation and the election of 1929 Mussolini reached the high plateau of his career. It was a plateau on which he was to rest for some years. They were rather dull years in his story, for they lacked the fire of his rise to power and the drama of his decline. Nevertheless they were important inasmuch as during this period he formed the habits and laid the plans which led to his ruin.

The liquidation of democracy not unnaturally brought with it a widespread political apathy. The ordinary citizen felt that he could no longer make any impact on politics, which were henceforth not a subject of discussion in the press or on the platform; and he consequently tended to dissociate himself from his rulers. In order to stimulate a disciplined interest in public affairs, the domestic measures which Mussolini deemed to be necessary were presented in the picturesque form of campaigns waged with great skill and a certain flamboyance. When the economic hurricane of 1929–31 hit Italy as hard as any other country, there was the Battle of the Lira, launched to defend with some success the national currency, at the price of wage reductions and sacrifices from the poor.

It became necessary to reduce imports, and the government fought the Battle of the Grain. There were competitions in production between provinces, and in 1933 a special decoration, a gold, silver, or bronze star, was instituted to reward successful farmers. Mussolini was photographed at the threshing machines, dancing with the peasant girls, and drawing his agricultural laborer's pay. By the end of 1933 the battle was declared to have been won. Only 179,805 quintals (a quintal is 224 pounds) were imported as against 1,091,866 in the previous year.

Closely connected with the Battle of the Grain was the *Bonifica*

Integrale, or land reclamation scheme. By October, 1933, according to government statistics, over nine million acres had been recovered all over the country: in Puglia, Tuscany, Venetia, the Po valley, and Sardinia. Of these projects the most important and the most publicized was the draining of the Pontine marshes. This enterprise, which had been begun under the pontificate of Pius VI, had been allowed to collapse for want of energy and technical capacity. The Fascist plan was to transform about 150,000 acres of malarial marsh between Rome and Terracina into small holdings, on which 75,000 inhabitants drawn from the indigent parts of Italy were planted. The work began in November, 1931, and on December 19, 1931, the Duce inaugurated the little town of Littoria in the center of the Pontine area. Soon Sabaudia and other new towns arose, roads and canals were built, public services were established, malaria was eradicated, and the insalubrious marshes became the prosperous smiling countryside that the traveler beholds today.

This was perhaps the most striking and valuable legacy bequeathed to the Italian people by Mussolini. Some of his critics have protested that he was only concerned with self-advertisement and that the money spent on the Pontine marshes could have been better spent on land further removed from Rome and easier to reclaim. There is no doubt that Mussolini was bewitched by the mystique of Rome and that he derived a special satisfaction from the foundation of the town and eventually the province of Littoria. But it seems ungenerous on this account to rob him of the credit for a technically grandiose and socially beneficent enterprise.

Mussolini's concern for Rome was less agreeably manifested by his public-works program and his reconstruction of the city. He was a man of vulgar taste, and his new buildings—Fascist headquarters, post offices, sports arenas, and government offices—reflected his passion for sheer size. Even more deplorable was his attitude towards papal Rome and its historical traditions. He was jealous of the Papacy and saw no reason to preserve its monuments and buildings. Imperial Rome was, however, another matter: "Within five years Rome must appear as a marvel to the nations of the world: vast, orderly, powerful, as it was in the times of the Augustan Empire." [2] In the same speech he undertook to open a vista of the Pantheon from the Piazza Colonna and to destroy the intermediate buildings which belonged to the "centuries of decadence." Fortunately this particular threat was never put into effect, but Mussolini achieved a singular devastation of medieval Rome which nothing can repair. For more than a hundred and fifty years travelers have complained that Rome is not what she used to be, but none are more entitled to voice that complaint than those who knew the city before and after Mussolini's day.

The most boisterous and least successful of Mussolini's campaigns was the Demographic Battle, waged in order to bring about an increase in the population. The target was a population of sixty millions by the middle of the century and Mussolini explained that in the modern world Italy with only forty million inhabitants was condemned to remain a second-rate power. Propaganda for a rise in the birthrate often reached ludicrous proportions, and one prefect aroused nationwide hilarity by assuring Mussolini in a published telegram of his resolve to make a personal contribution towards the solution of the problem.

In order to encourage marriage there was a tax on bachelors, and to stimulate fertility, prizes were awarded in each city to the most prolific women. Amongst them the champions of each province were selected; and on December 23, 1933, Mussolini himself received the winners, ninety-three women who between them had borne over thirteen hundred children. Despite these and many other inducements, which might have been devised by an American advertising agency, the birthrate did not rise. It fell from 27.5 per thousand in 1927 to 23.4 per thousand in 1934. Sceptics were apt to inquire why a nation which claimed to be short of living space should deliberately aggravate the evil. Nevertheless, the campaign, although it was ill conceived and a failure, brought incidental benefits to a society which enjoyed little social assistance from the state. At the public expense the health of mothers and children was now cared for, and an effort was made to stamp out tuberculosis.

The impact of these flamboyant campaigns was sustained by the so-called realizations, that is to say, the functions accompanying the opening of new roads, public works, land projects, and the like. It was Mussolini's practice to attend as many of these as possible, and press photographs with adulatory captions combined to create the impression at home and abroad that only in Italy were such things being done and that every achievement was the result of the personal intervention of the Duce.

II

It was necessary to call public attention to progress on the home front, for in the field of foreign affairs the years following the Conciliation were necessarily a period of stagnation. Mussolini knew that Italy was in no state to embark unaided on hazardous foreign adventures. Yet he was not prepared to settle down and meekly acquiesce in the existing international order. Sir Ronald Graham was well aware of the danger to be apprehended from Mussolini's restless spirit, and as early as July, 1925, warned his government that it would be rash to assume that Italy was inevitably yoked to the car of the Western powers and that an eventual association with Germany was not to be excluded. As relations with France deteriorated, Mussolini tended, even before the advent of Hitler, to lean more and more towards Germany. In June, 1932, Grandi warned Graham of the ominous growth of pro-German feeling,* particularly in extreme Fascist circles and in the immediate surroundings of Mussolini, who claimed that a policy of cooperation with the Western powers was a "renunciatory policy" which brought no advantage to Italy. This observation offered the clue to Mussolini's outlook.

During these intermediate years his policy was to rattle the saber intermittently, to warn the Italian people to prepare for every warlike eventuality, and at the same time to cooperate at Geneva and elsewhere, particularly with Britain. In order to keep his hands free for this dual and sometimes embarrassing role and to present a reassuring front to the outside world he appointed the conciliatory Dino Grandi to be Minister for Foreign Affairs in September, 1929. At the same time he vacated six other ministries, retaining for himself only the Presidency of the Council and the portfolio of the Interior.

---

* At about this time Goering and other Nazi emissaries were descending on Rome and attempting, not without success, to win sympathy for German National Socialism.

In 1930 the divergence between Italian foreign policy as expounded by Grandi and Mussolini's utterances became glaringly apparent. On January 21 the conference for the reduction of naval armaments met in London and Grandi declared that Italy wished to progress in a tranquil world and a pacified Europe. Nevertheless, difficulties soon arose from the Italian demand for complete parity with France. Fanned by Mussolini himself, anti-French and indeed anti-European feeling mounted in Italy. On April 17 the *Popolo d'Italia* declared: "Between one war and the next Europe is intoxicating itself with the narcotics of pacifism and democracy. The anti-European sentiment of modern Italy is not a pose, but a necessity. We are anti-European in the same way as we are against typhus, plague, and cholera."

On May 11, speaking at Leghorn, Mussolini said that he had no desire to embark on imprudent adventures. But those who might threaten Italy's independence and future did not realize to what a pitch of fever the Italian people could rise. The whole nation would form a compact mass which could be hurled against the rest of the world. At Florence on May 17 he affirmed that the Italian naval construction program would be carried out to the last ton: "Words are beautiful things, but rifles, guns, ships, airplanes are still more beautiful. When tomorrow dawns the spectacle of our armed forces will reveal to the world the calm and warlike countenance of Fascist Italy." [3]

When Grandi spoke on foreign affairs in the Senate on June 3, it was agreed between himself and Mussolini that he should reduce tension. But when he inquired of the Duce how it was possible to reconcile moderation in an official statement of Italian policy with the Duce's bellicose utterances, he was told that there was no connection between the two: "what have my speeches got to do with it? What does it matter what I say to my crowds [*la mia folla*]? Why do you think I made you Foreign Minister except to enable me to talk to them exactly as I please?" [4] The official apologists explained the discrepancy by pointing out that while Mussolini barked, he never bit; and that although inflammatory language would be dangerous from the mouth of a lesser man, the Duce could be trusted to control his people and to take care that incitement was not followed by action. This form of assurance found general acceptance, and the Italian dictator's warlike posturings were received with good-humored tolerance in which there was little element of apprehension. After all, it was said, he had done great things for Italy and, if extravagance in language was the only charge to be imputed to him, there was no serious ground for complaint.

III

During the eighteen months between the end of 1929 and the beginning of 1931 several events occurred of importance to Mussolini's domestic life. On September 3, 1929, his fifth and last child was born and was named Anna Maria after Rachele's mother. Mussolini told his wife that he was resolved to obtain a dwelling in Rome which would accommodate the whole family. Shortly afterwards, in November, the move was made from the squalid apartment in the Via Rasella to the ample Villa Torlonia. Cesira Carocci, the housekeeper, who had been engaged by Margherita Sarfatti and who for six years had played the part of domestic dragon, was discharged on pension and Rachele assumed her rightful place at the head of the household.

In the following year the problem of Edda's marriage, which had been disturbing the family for some time, was finally solved. She was an undisciplined girl and there was always the threat of an unsuitable union. There had been an Indian whom she met in Ceylon, a Jew, and an unfortunate young man, who went so far as to ask the Duce what her dowry would be. The frigid reply brought this romance to a sudden end. Nevertheless, the family felt that for safety's sake every effort should urgently be made to find an acceptable suitor. Arnaldo was consulted, and at his instance a Sicilian deputy put forward the name of Galeazzo Ciano, son of Count Costanzo Ciano.

It came as a surprise to Mussolini that his old friend had a son, but inquiries were diligently made and the outcome was satisfactory. Galeazzo, after working as a journalist and making an unsuccessful attempt to be a playwright, had entered the Italian foreign service and was well spoken of at the Palazzo Chigi. He was still only a vice-consul in China, but he was regarded as quite promising. Reports on his politics were equally favorable. He had at one time been something of a deviationist, but had outgrown this youthful aberration and was now a fervent Fascist. It was decided to transfer him from China to the Italian embassy at the Holy See so as to bring him under closer observation.

Meanwhile Edda was sent to Leghorn to make the acquaintance of her prospective parents-in-law. The meeting was a success; and in the following year, when Galeazzo had returned to Rome, she was introduced to him at the opera and was soon more than ready to fall in with her parents' wishes. One night in April, 1930, Vittorio and Bruno returned from the cinema to find the Villa Torlonia upside down. Guests were coming to dinner. Rachele told the children to put on their party clothes and added disconsolately that the whole Ciano family was coming, that is to say, the parents and Galeazzo. The prospect of entertaining three guests to a short simple meal seemed to dismay Rachele and her inexperienced maidservant.

On April 23, 1930, the day before the wedding, there was a reception at the Villa Torlonia. Over five hundred guests were invited. Ambassadors, prelates in their red silk cloaks, representatives of Roman society, and party leaders moved across the lawns amidst banks of flowers, while a quartet played classical music. It was the first and last large party given by Mussolini, and when it was over he told the boys that when they married it would be with less fuss. On the following day the marriage took place at the Church of San Giuseppe and the witnesses were Arnaldo Mussolini, Dino Grandi, De Vecchi, and Prince Torlonia. There was an enormous number of wedding presents. The Queen, the Fascist party, and the Governor of Rome sent pieces of jewelry and the Chamber of Deputies a valuable tea service. Mussolini's present to his daughter was a curious choice: a rosary of gold and malachite.[5]

At about this time Mussolini suffered three personal bereavements. On February 3, 1930, Michele Bianchi died. He had been with Mussolini since the first meeting in the Piazza San Sepolero and was the ablest of the *Quadrumviri.* Indeed Mussolini often said of him that without his resolution and leadership the March on Rome would never have taken place. He was not a man for whom Mussolini ever entertained a real affection, and indeed he was apt to view all his *Quadrumviri* with jealous suspicion. Nevertheless Bianchi represented a link with the past, he was closer to Mussolini than the other three and his disappearance left a gap.

In 1930 Sandro Mussolini, Arnaldo's son, died of leukemia. It was a heavy blow to the father, who was already in poor health, and on December 21, 1931, Arnaldo, after a heart attack, followed his boy to the grave. In Arnaldo, Mussolini lost the only associate in whom he had complete confidence and with whom he could treat without any sentiment of jealousy. He was now more lonely than ever and he brought his sister Edvige to live in Rome. Throughout the vicissitudes of his life he kept in constant touch with her, and their correspondence reveals in her a genuine respect and affection for her brother and in him a surprising degree of humanity. Proud and to all appearances self-sufficient, he clung pathetically to the last surviving companion of his childhood's days.

IV

The year 1931 was marked by a violent quarrel between Church and state, a storm which blew up suddenly and dispersed with equal suddenness. It arose from long-standing friction over Catholic Action, an organization to which Pius XI attached particular importance as a bulwark for the defense of Christian social principles. The Fascists for their part viewed with intolerance the existence of any body which impinged on the claims of a totalitarian state to the complete and individual loyalty of each individual citizen. The success of Catholic Action in attracting to its ranks not only adults but the younger generation, on whom the Fascists pinned their hopes, exacerbated the quarrel.

The smoldering fires of resentment burst into flame when, at the end of March, 1931, the *Lavoro Fascista* launched a violent attack on Catholic Action. Shortly afterwards the government banned congresses of Catholic undergraduates at Ferrara and Pavia; and on April 19 Giuriati, the secretary of the party, made an offensive speech in Milan. The Pope reacted sharply in an open letter to the Cardinal Archbishop of Milan, and in May the press under official direction attacked Catholic Action on a wide front. The premises and in some cases the members of Catholic Action were assaulted and in the streets of Rome crowds shouted "Death to the traitor Ratti." * On May 30 the police were ordered to dissolve all branches of the Catholic Youth organization and the University Federation.

The Vatican retorted the following day by suspending the mission of the Cardinal Legate to Padua for the seventh centenary of the death of Saint Anthony. On June 1 the bishops were ordered to suspend the customary processions on the feast of Corpus Christi. At a public audience the Pope gave expression to his grief at the attack on the youth and university associations and at the street demonstrations, which he described not without cause as a first sample of the fruits of an education which is the antithesis of all Christian education.

On June 3 Mussolini after a meeting of the party directorate issued an uncompromising statement to the press:

> The directorate, having examined the recent polemics provoked by the attitude, which has been proved by documentary evidence, of open or secret hostility on the part of certain sections of Catholic Action: while reaffirming its profound and unchanging respect for the Catholic religion, for its head, its ministers and its temples, declares in the most explicit manner that it is firmly resolved not to tolerate that antifascism, surviving and hitherto spared, shall receive refuge or protection under any banner old or new.

The statement ended with a call to defend the revolution, and a few days later a long defense of the government's case was broadcast on the Italian radio system.

The Pope now countered with his biggest gun. On June 29 he signed the famous encyclical letter "*Non abbiamo bisogno,*" a slashing and effective attack on the Fascist position, couched in language which Senator Vincenzo Morello described as having no parallel in papal literature. Steps were taken to ensure its safe transport to the outside world and the *Osservatore Romano* containing the text was placed on sale in Rome five hours before the usual time, thus enabling a large number of copies to be sold before the police could seize them.

The press of course subjected the encyclical to violent attack, and the party directorate described it as an appeal to the foreigner

---

* Achille Ratti, Pope Pius XI.

launched by the Vatican. The government on July 9 declared that the existing compatability between membership of the party organizations and of Catholic Action was revoked and that members of both must choose between them. Membership of Catholic Action was in no sense a religious obligation, whereas a party ticket was essential to public servants and to men in a wide range of employment. Accordingly it was not surprising that the edict should have been followed by many thousands of resignations from Catholic Action. It seemed as if the government were resolved to pursue its vendetta regardless of consequences.

Then quite suddenly, less than four months after the first shot was fired, a tacit armistice was declared. As if at a sign from the conductor's baton the strident cacophony of the press was muted, the street demonstrations ceased; and at the Vatican the Pope in the course of his audiences began to hint at an accommodation.

Several factors had combined to bring about this remarkable change. The Pope, incensed at Mussolini's behavior, had very secretly dispatched Father Tacchi Venturi with a message to the effect that if the persecution of Catholic Action continued, he would have no hesitation in excommunicating the Prime Minister. Father Tacchi Venturi reported back that Mussolini had been suitably impressed and wished to assure the Pope that means would be found of settling the dispute.[6] There were of course other grounds for moderation. The Pope had shown an unwelcome and unexpected capacity to defend himself and had ranged a significant body of foreign opinion behind the Holy See. There were many Italians both inside and outside the party who would have deplored a *Kulturkampf*, and Mussolini himself was reluctant to wreck the Conciliation, his own personal achievement. Nevertheless the threat of excommunication undoubtedly expedited, if it did not bring about, his decision to seek a truce.

In August a number of secret meetings was held. The Pope laid down one condition: any agreement must be preceded by the restoration of the Catholic Youth organizations that had been suppressed. On August 28 the government announced that the measures taken against these organizations had been revoked and on September 2 the terms of the agreement were announced. First, Catholic Action was placed under the direct control of the diocesan bishops and its members undertook to refrain from all practices traditionally proper to political parties. Second, the professional sections of Catholic Action were to have no trade-union functions but would serve only religious ends. Third, the Catholic Action youth organizations would refrain from athletic activities and would confine themselves to educational and recreational functions for purely religious ends. On September 30 the secretary of the party revoked the order declaring incompatibility between membership of Catholic Action and the party.

The settlement was a compromise. The Pope made a sacrifice in accepting a ban on those activities which would enable Catholic youth organizations to compete with the Fascists. On the other hand, he saved Catholic Action by securing the revocation of the measures designed for its destruction. With the exercise of prudence on the Vatican side and the acceptance of the new situation by the Fascists, relations between Church and state returned to normal, that is to say, to an uneasy but tolerable state of coexistence.

Peace with the Vatican was sealed by an official visit which Mussolini paid to the Pope on February 11, 1932. It was a courtesy call and, although the audience lasted for half an hour, nothing of significance was said. The point which excited public interest, and which was never cleared up, was whether Mussolini showed the customary marks of respect to His Holiness. To Emil Ludwig's inquiry Mussolini replied that he made it a practice of complying with local customs, but when Rachele asked him whether he had kissed the Pope's slipper he looked at her in stony silence.[7] In any event after the audience Mussolini paid the usual visit to the Basilica and, while photographers were kept at bay, knelt in prayer at the tomb of St. Peter. He returned to his family full of good will towards the Vatican and the person of the pontiff. Seven years were to elapse before another open quarrel broke out, this time on the issue of racial persecution.

V

Meanwhile Mussolini was glad of a breathing space, for he was now aware that a number of important international problems were pressing on him: disarmament and with it the acrimonious debate on Franco-Italian naval parity: the rise of Hitler and a new deployment in Europe; and finally, already germinating in his mind, the Abyssinian enterprise. In troubled Europe Mussolini roamed restlessly and with little purpose except as occasion offered to pick up what scraps he could in the prevailing confusion. His moves were not always unintelligent or ill conceived, but they were tactical rather than strategic and were inspired by a desire to gain short-term successes for himself rather than to plan a safe long-term policy for Italy.

In February, 1932, the Disarmament Conference met at Geneva and Grandi, who was the principal Italian delegate, put forward a comprehensive plan for the total abolition of heavy artillery, tanks, battleships, submarines, aircraft carriers, and bomber aircraft. This time the principal obstacle was the attitude of the German government, which on August 29 formally demanded the abrogation of the clauses of the Treaty of Versailles imposing unilateral disarmament on Germany.

By this date Grandi was no longer Minister for Foreign Affairs, for on July 20 Mussolini had resumed the portfolio with Fulvio Suvich as his Undersecretary, while Grandi was sent to fill the embassy in London. So sudden and unexpected was the change that Grandi's personal private secretary, who had been sent to the railway station to represent his master at the departure of a distinguished traveler, returned to the Ministry to find the Minister gone and to receive the news of the move from the office messenger. Grandi had served his purpose and, moreover, he had acquired for himself a certain international reputation, which aroused Mussolini's jealousy and suspicion. It was time to take the reins of the Ministry of Foreign Affairs into his own hands; and in London Grandi could do no harm. In the Palazzo Chigi, where Grandi's principal officials were soon posted abroad, there was the feeling that a new orientation of foreign policy was in the wind. But to the public the change was, as usual, represented as "the changing of the guard," and to Sir Ronald Graham Mussolini gave the disingenuous explanation that Grandi, who was in perfect health, was worn out after eight years as an Undersecretary and a Minister. In fact the Duce, when dismissing his Foreign Minister, had given him another explanation. "You have," he told him, "become too enamored of Geneva and the League of Nations." [8]

When the time came in October, 1932, to celebrate the end of fascism's first decade, Mussolini displayed the exuberance of a man who had overcome all doubts and hesitations and to whom success was now a matter of course. Speaking at Milan on October 25, he said that when he had predicted that fascism had sixty years before it the movement was still in its early days. "Today with a quiet conscience I tell you, this vast crowd, that the twentieth century will be the century of fascism. It will be the century of Italian power; it will be the century in which Italy will return for the third time to be the leader of human civilization, for outside our faith there is no salvation either for individuals or for peoples." In the Chamber on November 16th he repeated the claim: "In this dark, tormented, and already tottering world salvation can only come from truth in Rome and from Rome it will come."

VI

A few weeks later, on January 30, 1933, the aged Hindenburg called Hitler to be Chancellor of the German Reich. The Italian newspapers greeted the event with enthusiasm. But to Mussolini the news was not altogether welcome; and to some extent it was a surprise. In October, 1932, in a conversation with the British ambassador he had expressed the view that Hitler had definitely lost his opportunity. If he had been resolved to seize power, he should have resorted to force, but it was now too late. He predicted a monarchist restoration in Germany, a forecast which incidentally illustrated his ignorance of German affairs, and thought that this would be no bad thing for Europe since a monarch would be unlikely for some time to imperil his throne in foreign adventure.

Of course the spread of fascism abroad was in a sense gratifying; and it conduced to Mussolini's personal prestige to have deferent disciples in foreign countries. Nevertheless it seemed unlikely that an authoritarian Germany would be content for long to play second fiddle in the European orchestra and there was the danger that it would not consent to play at all. Despite his misgivings Mussolini was not prepared to antagonize the new ruler, and the Italian press gave Hitler a warm welcome.

In order to meet the situation Mussolini's agile mind devised a plan designed at the same time to bring the new Germany into a European association under his personal aegis, to weaken the influence of the League of Nations, to undermine France's system of alliances, and to satisfy Britain that Italy was pursuing a policy of European cooperation. A fumbling effort had been made by the French government at the end of 1932 to improve its relations with Italy, but it had failed partly owing to a lack of resolve in Paris, but principally because Mussolini had no desire to come to terms with France.

At this juncture Ramsay Macdonald, head of the National government in Britain, accompanied by his Foreign Secretary Sir John Simon, paid a visit to Rome on Mussolini's invitation. They arrived in March, 1933, ostensibly for an exchange of views, particularly on disarmament. But shortly before they arrived in Rome Mussolini without warning produced for their consideration the draft of a four-power pact between Italy, Britain, France, and Germany. The basis of the treaty was collaboration to keep the peace. The four powers recognized the principle that the peace treaties should be revised in accordance with the Covenant of the League of Nations; Italy, Britain, and France admitted that in the field of disarmament Germany should enjoy parity of rights, while Germany for her part undertook to exercise such rights gradually and in agreement with the three other powers. Finally the four powers undertook to adopt as far as possible a common policy in Europe and outside Europe. In a word the treaty pledged the four powers to work together and made them the guardians of Europe.

It was a realistic project inasmuch as it took into account the fact that without harmony among these particular four powers it would be difficult to preserve peace in Europe. Collective security was a myth since none of the smaller members of the League had any military strength at all; and a large number of zeros when added together still come to zero. There was therefore something to be said for a return to the Concert of Europe, whose record over a hundred years was probably more creditable than that of any other system. Nevertheless in 1933 realism was unfashionable and any proposal which seemed to question the efficacy of the system of collective security and thus the authority of the League of Nations was necessarily suspect.

There were, however, other objections to the draft treaty. In particular the French, with their Little Entente allies, disliked the reference to treaty revision, while the latter also rejected the conception of a Europe governed by a small committee of Great Powers from which they were excluded. The Soviet Union and Turkey saw in the proposed alliance an instrument which might be used against them. All these considerations rendered the French government hostile to Mussolini's initiative. Hitler favored it. In Britain opinion was divided. Austen Chamberlain and Winston Churchill described the project as inopportune, while Ramsay Macdonald, who was delighted with his trip to Rome, vigorously defended it and did all he could to bring the French to his way of thinking.

In the course of a brisk round of negotiations the treaty was much watered down and in its new form it was initialed in Rome on June 7, 1933. There was no longer any mention of treaty revision nor of Germany's equality of rights. Mussolini endured the emasculation of his project because the alternative was to admit failure and because the ceremony in Rome created a momentary illusion of success. In fact, the Four-Power Pact was ratified only by Italy and Germany, and it consequently never came into force. By that time, however, other events were engaging the public mind and the collapse of Mussolini's plan passed unobserved. The cause of four-power collaboration received a further setback when, in October, 1933, Hitler suddenly announced Germany's withdrawal from the disarmament conference and the League of Nations.

VII

These events gave impulse to Mussolini's zeal for the rearmament of Italy. In July, 1933, he once more took over the Ministry of War and in November the Ministries of Marine and Air. In compensation for loss of office at the Air Ministry Balbo was promoted to the new rank of Air Marshal and shortly afterwards was appointed Governor of Libya. Mussolini was glad to export him from Italy, for he disliked him personally and had little confidence in either his loyalty

Wide World

The March on Rome, Mussolini has ribbon across chest.

Mussolini arrives to take office after the March on Rome.

Central

King Victor Emmanuel III of Italy, as he appeared in 1939.

Wide World

Mirrorpic

Mussolini soon after taking over as Premier of Italy.

Mussolini and his son Vittorio on vacation in 1926.
UPI

UPI
Mussolini with his family on a picnic in 1927.

Mirrorpic

At the Rome Horse Show, early in the Duce's career.

Mussolini takes a horse over a jump.

Mirrorpic

Wide World

Reviewing Blackshirts in Naples.

The Fascist Directorate.

Wide World

UPI
Mussolini with high Church and State officials at the Lateran Palace.

Cardinal Gasparri and Mussolini signing the Lateran Pact.
UPI

Wide World

Keystone

Above: *Alcide de Gasperi, post-war Italian Premier.*

Below: *Gabriele D'Annunzio, poet, dramatist, novelist, and orator, he was also a man of action and an early exponent of fascism.*

Acme

Mussolini as pilot.

Wide World

Roberto Farinacci, an early, extremist Fascist Party member. So pro-German, he was not used by the Duce in the Salò Republic.

Mirrorpic

The grandiose office of the Duce in Palazzo Venezia.

On his white stallion Atlantico, Mussolini reviews a parade.

UPI

Wide World

Hitler and Mussolini meet for the first time, at Venice in 1934.

UPI

The two dictators—Germany, 1937.

Wide World

Meeting in Venice, 1937.

Keysto

Inspecting Libya in 1937, the Duce is preceded by Arabs carrying the fasces.

Acme

Reviewing a new levy of young Fascists on the Via del Impero in Rome.

UPI

A gifted orator and unscrupulous demagogue, Mussolini enjoyed haranguing his enthusiastic followers from the balcony of Palazzo Venezia.

or his good sense. Having discarded Grandi and Balbo, Mussolini was more than ever in personal control of the machinery of government since he was now in charge not only of the key Ministry of the Interior but also of the Foreign Office and three service ministries. The only important position he did not fill, and here he showed his good sense, was that of Minister of Finance.

In order further to reinforce his personal authority he dissolved parliament at the end of the year and fixed the national plebiscite for March 25, 1934. Like all modern dictators he felt the urge to be fortified by a manifestation of popular support, however illusory. In this case the election was a blatant farce. Voters were given two papers, one colored in green, white, and red with the word "*Si*" and one plain paper for those who wished to vote "*No.*" The elector placed his voting paper in the urn in the polling booth and returned the unused paper to the returning officer. It was alleged that in many cases he was pressed even to dispense with the formality of entering the booth. The result showed, as expected, an overwhelming victory for the government list. Over 95 per cent of the electorate were declared to have gone to the polls, of whom over ten millions voted for the official list and only fifteen thousand against. Once more Milan, with over five thousand adverse votes, was the town which showed the least satisfactory return. Mussolini could now return to the problem of foreign affairs.

VIII

The mirage of a four-power consortium having evaporated, Mussolini was thrown back on the same purely opportunist policy as before. He was unwilling to throw in his lot with the Western powers because they, particularly France, were antirevisionist and unlikely to help him to burst the bonds in which he conceived Italy to be constricted. Nor was he as yet ready to commit himself to Germany. Hitler represented an unknown quantity and he viewed the resurgence of German power with misgiving. The most profitable course was to keep in contact with both sides, to play one off against the other, and in the process to extract what advantage he could for Italy.

This was his mood when on April 2, 1934, he received Franz von

Papen, who was on a visit to Rome. Papen suggested that the time was ripe for a visit by Hitler to Italy and put forward as an agenda the problem of disarmament; the extension of the economic protocol drawn up at tripartite discussions in Rome; * coordination of the policy of the two governments in central Europe, and finally the Austrian problem.[9] Mussolini agreed in principle and Ulrich von Hassell, the German ambassador in Rome, when reporting this development to his government, recommended the conclusion of an agreement that the independence of Austria should not be infringed. Since in December, 1933, Hitler had assured Suvich in Berlin that the *Anschluss* was not urgent or even desirable for Germany,[10] this seemed to Hassell a safe and sensible suggestion.

After further careful diplomatic preparation and two postponements Hitler's visit was finally fixed for June 14 at Venice. Mussolini allocated the royal suite at the Grand Hotel to Hitler, while he took up residence at the Villa Pisani in Stra. This imposing monument had for some time been uninhabited, possessed no modern kitchen equipment, and was otherwise unsuitable for the purpose. Nevertheless, when these objections were raised, Mussolini angrily brushed them aside and told the responsible official that it was his business to surmount them. With the utmost difficulty furniture and crockery were borrowed from private sources and from hotels in Venice, the Villa Pisani was swept and decorated, and all made ready for the august visitors. The Duce was determined to make an impression on his German guest.

On June 13 Mussolini, accompanied by a large retinue, including Suvich, Ciano, and Starace, now secretary of the party, arrived at Stra driving his own motor car. The following morning he met Hitler at the Venice airport and took him to lunch at the Villa Pisani. After lunch the interpreters were dismissed and Mussolini closeted himself alone with Hitler for a two-hour talk, after which the guest was sent sightseeing in Venice while the host remained at Stra. The choice of the villa was not a happy one, for the Italians were so plagued by a mosquito assault that Mussolini was compelled to transfer the next day's proceedings to Venice.

---

* There had recently been an Italo-Austrian-Hungarian agreement which the Germans suspected was directed against Germany.

On June 15 the two men met again for lunch, this time at the Fort of Alberoni on the Lido, the headquarters of the local golf club. Once again there was a conversation without interpreters. It had been the intention to confer in a motorboat, but according to the officially inspired account the landscape was so "*suggestivo*" that it was decided at the last moment to hold the conversation on a rustic bench on the banks of the lagoon. Later in the afternoon Mussolini addressed a huge and wildly enthusiastic crowd in the Piazza San Marco, while Hitler watched the proceedings from a balcony in a neighboring palace. It was an opportunity to display to the Fuehrer the Duce's popularity and his mastery over the masses. The speech was intended for Venetian domestic consumption and only contained a short reference to the meeting with Hitler, which, Mussolini declared, was not designed to alter the map of Europe or to add to international disquiet, but to disperse the clouds on the horizon. On the morning of June 16 Hitler left Venice.

An official communiqué made the usual reference to the cordial spirit in which questions of mutual interest were examined, and the comments of a servile press were as fulsome as they could be. Nevertheless the visit was not a success. On the contrary, it was from every point of view a conspicuous failure. Mme. Cerruti, wife of the Italian ambassador in Berlin, described it as a collision. Mussolini had intended to show a certain condescension towards a man more than ten years junior in dictatorial rank whom he regarded as a disciple. He was not meeting one of those European elder statesmen, who induced in him a sense of inferiority, but a neophyte making his first expedition to a foreign country. He would be kind and dispense advice to a man who needed it and would receive it gratefully.

Unfortunately Hitler declined to play the role allotted to him. He talked too much and what he said was disquieting and repugnant. On Austria he was uncompromising. While he admitted that the question of the *Anschluss* was of no interest and was internationally not practicable, he gave warning of his intention to meddle in Austrian affairs. In blunt terms he demanded the withdrawal of Dollfuss and his replacement by an independent man, after which there would have to be fresh elections and the introduction of National Socialists into the government. He also expressed the wish that Mussolini should remove his protecting hand from Austria. Mussolini could only take note of this disagreeable pronouncement.

For the rest Hitler made wounding observations on the superiority of the Nordic race and the negroid strain in the Mediterranean peoples. He restated his inflexible views on German disarmament, while Mussolini deplored the fact that there was not a single real statesman in the government of England. Mussolini was, however, able to make only one constructive contribution to the conversation. At the instance of Neurath and Hassell he warned Hitler against the pretensions of the Brownshirts; he is said to have told Hitler the Tarquin story about cutting down the flowers that grow too high.[11] He also proffered advice about the folly of persecuting the churches and the Jews.[12] Hitler neither accepted nor rejected this unsolicited and unwelcome advice. He was probably thinking grimly of the fate which would shortly befall Roehm and his henchmen.

It was a meager and unsatisfactory result. All that Mussolini had secured was a half-hearted assurance that for the moment Hitler would not pursue the question of the *Anschluss*. But there were other factors which accounted for the frigid atmosphere in which the meeting took place. Hitler was shy and awkward on his first appearance in a foreign country and the disparity between the two leaders was emphasized by the difference in their appearance: the Duce in his Fascist uniform resplendent among his obedient and acclaiming crowds; and the Fuehrer ill at ease in a badly fitting suit, patent leather shoes, a shabby yellow mackintosh, and an old gray felt hat. A French journalist described him as "un petit plombier tenant un fâcheux instrument [his hat] devant son ventre."[13] To the eyes of the Venetians he might have borrowed his wardrobe from Charlie Chaplin.

A further difficulty arose from the problem of communication. Hitler had brought with him an excellent interpreter, Hans Thomsen,* but unfortunately Mussolini, who prided himself on his mastery of the German language, insisted on dispensing with any interpretation. It was not surprising that at times he failed either to

* Later chargé d'affaires in Washington and ambassador in Stockholm. A capable and experienced official, who was working in Hitler's Secretariat on loan from the Foreign Office.

understand Hitler's strange and torrential German or to render his own observations comprehensible.

Hitler left Venice with mixed feelings. He knew that he had cut a poor figure and he had little to show from his first contact with the outside world. For his poor showing he was inclined to blame his Foreign Minister, for it had been Neurath who had advised him to appear in civilian clothes, an error of judgment for which, it was said, he was never forgiven. On the other hand he was pleased with the upshot of his conversations on Austria. He believed that he had secured Mussolini's assent to the removal of Dollfuss and the participation of Nazis in the government; and in return he had only conceded that the need for the *Anschluss* was "not acute."[14] As regards the personality of Mussolini, Rosenberg reports that Hitler returned from Venice bewitched by his experience. The enthusiasm and fanaticism of the crowds were genuine, he declared. "The people stand bowed in humility before him, as before a Pope, and he strikes the Caesarean pose necessary for Italy. But all this disappears in a personal conversation, when he becomes human and agreeable."[15] It was a judgment which Hitler never felt called upon to revise throughout the vicissitudes of their long and strange relationship. Mussolini for his part formed a thoroughly unfavorable impression of his German colleague: "Instead of speaking to me about current problems, he recited me *Mein Kampf*, that boring book which I have never been able to read."[16] To his familiars he spoke of Hitler in scornful and derisive terms. Suvich told Starhemberg some days later that Mussolini had described Hitler as a buffoon.[17]

Mussolini had, however, enjoyed one satisfaction. He had from time to time been able to speak his mind; and even though he had been compelled to endure the Fuehrer's prolixity and his habit of addressing individuals as if they were a public meeting, he had at least been able to open his mouth and Neurath was able to report to his friends that the two dictators had roared at one another like bulls.[18] Despite the communiqué, which spoke of developing in the future the personal relationship so happily initiated at Venice, three years were to elapse before Duce and Fuehrer met once more. By that time Germany's power had grown to a point which justified

Hitler in requiring Mussolini—except at Munich in 1938—to listen to a monologue. This was to be his role for the remaining years of their association.

Unsuccessful though the Venice meeting was, Mussolini was not the man publicly to admit failure. The press was accordingly instructed to acclaim the event and to represent that agreement had been reached on the independence of Austria. Dr. Virginio Gayda, mouthpiece of the Ministry of Foreign Affairs, stated categorically in the *Giornale d'Italia* that Hitler had agreed that the independence of Austria was not in question and that the two countries should collaborate for a speedy return to normal political conditions in that country.

Fifteen days later Mussolini's adverse opinion of Hitler was dramatically confirmed when news reached him of the sanguinary liquidation of the S. A. leader Ernest Roehm, many of his lieutenants, and a number of politicians and civil servants. From the exultant tone in which Hitler spoke of his part in destroying these men it seemed that the flabby hand which Mussolini had shaken in farewell on the Venice airfield was stained with his victims' blood. Mussolini's antipathy to Hitler was increased. He burst into a room in which his sister Edvige was sitting, and waved a bundle of newspapers: "He is a cruel and ferocious character and calls to mind legendary characters of the past: Attila. Those men he killed were his closest collaborators, who hoisted him into power. It is as if I came to kill with my own hands Balbo, Grandi, Bottai. . . ." [19] At the same time the meeting at Venice and the massacre in Germany brought Mussolini to understand clearly that Hitler was a creature who required handling gingerly. He was not a Ramsay Macdonald nor a Stanley Baldwin.

IX

Mussolini was still simmering with displeasure at Hitler's brutality when news reached him of an event which plunged him into a flurry of rage and threw him into the arms of the Western Allies for more than a year. On July 25, 1934, Nazi thugs invaded the Austrian Chancellery and shot Chancellor Dollfuss, who was left in his office to die of his wounds. By the evening the governmental forces were in control and the revolt had failed. But two things were clear. The men behind the abortive plot were to be found in Nazi Germany, and the independence of Austria was grievously threatened.

Mussolini's prestige as well as the interests of Italy were now directly engaged. For some time he had proclaimed that he was not prepared to accept an Austro-German union. As early as 1925 he had said: "Italy would never tolerate such a patent violation of the treaties as would be constituted by the annexation of Austria to Germany.[20] As late as March 19, 1934, speaking to the Quinquennial Fascist Assembly he said: "Austria knows that she can count on us to defend her independence as a sovereign state." In private he was equally emphatic. In 1930 he told Prince Starhemberg that the day Austria was swallowed up by Germany would mark the beginning of European chaos.[21] In 1932, when undertaking to supply Austria with arms, he again assured Prince Starhemberg that an independent Austria must always be the aim of Italian foreign policy and that the Austrian Chancellor could rely on the help of Fascist Italy.[22] In 1933 in the course of a further conversation Mussolini undertook to place two million schillings at the disposal of the Austrian *Heimwehr*, and he added: "What I am doing I do because I need Austria, because I am a friend of Austria, and because I am your friend." [23]

In May, 1933, the Austrian Chancellor had visited Rome to assure himself of Mussolini's support, and in August, 1933, when the two men met again at Riccione, Mussolini categorically renewed his undertaking. The official communiqué did not lie when it affirmed their identity of views on Austria and the Danubian problem. Fortified by Italian support, Dollfuss on January 17, 1934, boldly addressed a note to the Nazi government protesting against their interference in Austrian internal affairs; and on the following day Suvich, Undersecretary at the Italian Ministry of Foreign Affairs traveled to Vienna to meet Dollfuss in Vienna. Despite this overt expression of Italian solidarity with Austria the German government rejected the Austrian protest and declared provocatively that they could not remain indifferent to a system of government which oppressed and outlawed the German elements in Austria.

By this time Mussolini was fully committed to Dollfuss, for whom he entertained a personal regard. His next step in the face of Hitler's intransigence was to secure the support of the Western powers.

At his instance Dollfuss communicated the exchange of correspondence with the German government to the governments of Britain, France, and Italy, which with very little delay issued identical statements of February 17, 1934, affirming the need to maintain the independence of Austria. Thus Mussolini had not only given Austria repeated and categorical undertakings, but he had taken the lead in forming a Western front against Hitler's expansionist ambitions. The murder of Dollfuss was a personal affront aggravated by the circumstance that on July 25, the very day on which he was assassinated, Dollfuss was engaged to leave Vienna for yet another meeting with Mussolini. At Riccione, where the meeting was due to take place, Frau Dollfuss and her children were already awaiting the Chancellor's arrival.

The news of the murder reached Mussolini while he was visiting public works in the neighborhood of Forlì. He at once abandoned his tour and drove to Riccione to break the news to the widow. He was angry and mortified. He had hoped to exercise a restraining and guiding influence on the young Germany. He also thought that in Venice he had secured at least a moratorium on Austria. He was disillusioned on both points and under his direction the Italian press launched a savage attack on the German barbarians. The Rome *Messagero* of July 28 declared that while men of good faith might be caught once, only fools would fall into the same trap twice. It was unfortunate for Mussolini that in his later dealings with Hitler he paid little attention to this truism.

Before returning hurriedly to Rome from the North Mussolini ordered a concentration of troops and aircraft on the Austrian border and dispatched a telegram of condolence to Prince Starhemberg, assuring him that the independence of Austria would be defended by Italy. He expected a similar demonstration by Britain and France. The fact that they did nothing was more than a disappointment. It confirmed his contempt for the democracies; and he resolved petulantly that he would not again attempt to pull the chestnuts out of the fire for the West. The episode was one he remembered when three years later the Austrian problem was once more on the agenda. At the same time he did not in 1934 abandon Austria nor his effort to create a Western common front.

In Berlin July 25 was a day of some confusion. At first the Nazis openly voiced their jubilation at the liquidation of the archenemy. The German official news agency issued a triumphant statement: "The people have risen in judgement on the government of Dollfuss. The inevitable has happened. The German people in Austria have risen in judgement against their oppressors, jailers, and torturers." As soon, however, as news of Mussolini's mobilization reached Hitler the brakes were suddenly applied, for he was not prepared to risk a clash even with Italy alone. He possessed no military forces capable of intervening in Austria and came to the very rapid conclusion that prudence required an immediate and indeed humiliating retreat. "We are faced with a new Sarajevo," he shouted to Papen. Theodor Habicht, the Party Inspector for Austria, was incontinently dismissed, the Nazi Austrian Legion poised in Bavaria for an incursion was halted, the fugitive murderers were surrendered to the Austrian government, the German Minister in Vienna was recalled, the German News Agency statement was withdrawn before publication, and Hitler publicly disavowed and condemned the crime. Franz von Papen, who had been called into hurried consultation, was himself appointed German Minister in Vienna, with instructions to repair Austro-German relations.

Mussolini was not deceived. In a long conversation with Starhemberg at Ostia early in August he showed more prescience than most British politicians of the day. What he had done, he declared, had been done in the vital interests of Italy. The man guilty of Dollfuss' murder was Hitler, a horrible sexual degenerate and a dangerous fool. National Socialism in Germany represented savage barbarism and it would mean the end of European civilization if this country of murderers and pederasts were to overrun the continent. In consequence it behooved them all to have done with Hitler, for otherwise he would yet set the whole world ablaze. In this sense the murder of Dollfuss might have done some good, if it brought the Great Powers to recognize the German danger and to organize a coalition against Hitler. "I cannot always be the only one to march to the Brenner. Others must show some interest in Austria and the Danube basin." [24]

The peril of the *Anschluss* was momentarily averted and public opinion in Italy and indeed elsewhere attributed the credit to Mussolini's energetic intervention. The incident not only raised his prestige, but had the effect of bringing Britain, France, and Italy closer together. On September 27, 1934, the three governments issued a further statement confirming their resolve to maintain the independence of Austria. The problem of containing Hitler was now uppermost in their minds, although it was not the only matter engaging Mussolini's attention, for, as will be seen, he was already actively preparing for his Abyssinian enterprise. His aim was to maintain a solid three-power front against German encroachment on Austria and at the same time to acquire a free hand in Africa. He saw no inconsistency in these two objectives, for he believed that Abyssinia presented no military problem and that he could return from a victorious African campaign in time to mount an effective guard on the Brenner.

X

In October, 1934, the French Foreign Minister Louis Barthou was assassinated by Croats in Marseilles at the side of King Alexander of Yugoslavia. Mussolini was of course suspected in some quarters of complicity, but his closest associates are convinced that he had no part in the crime. Indeed, when some time later the Yugoslav government applied to Rome for the extradition of certain Croat terrorists, he informed the officials of the Ministry of Foreign Affairs that he had no objection. He would scarcely have done so if he had thought that the men were in a position to make compromising revelations.

Barthou was replaced by Pierre Laval, who at once set about the task of improving Franco-Italian relations. After some preparatory work Laval came to Rome for four days in January, 1935. It was an important visit, which has given rise to much discussion and misunderstanding. The Frenchman and the Italian were pursuing two quite different aims. Laval was concerned to maintain the wobbly united front against Germany and in the process to sacrifice no substantial French interest. Mussolini, while he was prepared to join France and Britain in protecting Austria and required some French concessions to display to his people, attached prime importance to obtaining from Laval an assurance that France would acquiesce in the Italian conquest of Abyssinia.

On January 7, 1935, a series of Franco-Italian agreements was signed. In discharge of her obligations under the Treaty of London of 1915 France ceded to Italy a track of desert territory on the borders of Libya, a strip of French Somaliland, and an island in the Red Sea. In addition Italy secured some shares in the Djibouti-Addis Ababa railway and a prolongation of the special rights of the Italian community in Tunis. As regards Austria, the two governments undertook to consult one another and other governments in the event of a threat to Austrian independence. A general declaration affirmed that the matters in dispute between the two countries were settled and that the governments intended to develop their traditionally friendly relations.

Italian public opinion, which resented German conduct in Austria, welcomed the agreements. But they represented a meager harvest for Italy and Italian officials were dismayed at the extent of Mussolini's complaisance. He had, however, unknown to most of them secured from Laval a secret and verbal undertaking that France would disinterest herself in Abyssinia. The exact terms of this undertaking will never be known since there were no witnesses and both principals are dead. According to certain Italian versions Laval in conversation spoke of a free hand for Italy and there was talk of an Italian protectorate on the Moroccan model.[25] But Laval claimed subsequently that the French pledge to support Italy in Abyssinia related only to economic questions and did not cover warlike operations.[26] There is support for his contention in the account of the Laval negotiations given by Suvich to the German ambassador in Rome: "An arrangement had been made to supplement existing agreements between France and Italy in respect of economic activity in Abyssinia. This naturally related only to peaceful intentions there."

Thus it seems clear that Laval did not specifically commit France to the support of an Italian war in Abyssinia. Nevertheless there was no one better able to drop a hint, and it is almost certain that by his manner he brought Mussolini to accept an otherwise unfavorable agreement in the confident belief that he had secured his main aim.[27] Laval for his part left Rome boasting that he had drawn Mussolini into the anti-German coalition at little or no cost to France. The subsequent misunderstandings as to the nature of the

Franco-Italian exchanges in Rome were to affect Mussolini's attitude to France.

Meanwhile Mussolini displayed towards Laval a confidence which reflected a curious trait in his character. Although normally contemptuous of mankind, he was apt on occasion to place trust in individuals. He did so, for example, in the case of Hitler despite all the evidence of his ally's perfidy. It was as if he felt a childlike need to rely on someone or at least to discard suspicion in order to ward off betrayal. In the case of Laval he did not reflect that the undertaking was not as categorical as it might have been and was purely verbal; and that in any event French ministers were transient figures, whose secret engagements might be repudiated by their successors. No, he was satisfied that France was henceforth fully committed to support Italy against any objections which might be raised in Britain. He was annoyed when he was shown a deciphered telegram in which Laval gleefully informed Paris that he had secured the agreement without having to go to the limit of the concessions authorized by the French government.[28] Nevertheless, Mussolini continued to believe that so far as Abyssinia was concerned there was now no danger of any opposition from France.

On February 1, 1935, there was a Franco-British conference in London. The final communiqué among other things expressed approval of the agreements between France and Italy signed at Rome and declared that the two governments remained opposed to the unilateral abrogation of the existing obligations relating to disarmament. In the course of these exchanges the French did not reveal the undertakings, such as they were, which Laval had given to Mussolini about Italian designs on Abyssinia. Hitler, however, was never impressed by words. On March 9 Goering announced the creation of the German air force; and on March 16 Germany introduced compulsory military service and published a plan for the formation of thirty-six divisions. Despite this act of open defiance Sir John Simon and Mr. Anthony Eden visited Berlin in the hopeless endeavor to secure Hitler's assent to a scheme for a comprehensive settlement in Europe.

Mussolini regarded the British expedition to Berlin as a deplorable display of weakness. Nevertheless he was still anxious to make a forceful demonstration against Germany: "The best way to stop the Germans is to mobilize the class of 1911 . . . there is no other way of convincing them."[29] Sustained by Laval's promises, he traveled hopefully to the Franco-British-Italian conference which had been summoned to meet at Stresa. It was a fateful turning point in Mussolini's career. He hoped to achieve two aims: to contain Hitler, for which purpose he required the active support of Britain and France, that is to say, an undertaking to move against Germany if she violated Austrian independence, since he was not prepared to assume the sole responsibility for the defense of Austria; and to go forward in Abyssinia. He had been told by Grandi from London that on the first point the British would meet his wishes, but that on the second they would prove intractable. Nevertheless he believed that it would not be beyond human ingenuity to devise some tolerable settlement. Provided he obtained the substance of his requirements, he would be ready to make concessions as to the form. He would almost certainly have accepted a solution on the lines of the Hoare-Laval plan and very probably something less.[30]

There is other evidence that at the beginning of 1935 Mussolini was thinking in terms of some possibly negotiated and peaceful solution. When De Bono sailed for Africa his instructions were "to take an olive branch in his pocket." He must of course prepare for the worst, but if the Wal-Wal dispute were settled to Italy's satisfaction, he was to tell the Emperor that he had come to collaborate in the establishment of friendly relations.[31] Mussolini was still seething with anger against Germany. He could not conceive that Britain and France were not in a like mood, and that in the face of the common peril they would destroy the unity of the three powers merely in order to prevent Italy doing in Abyssinia what they themselves had done in Egypt and Morocco. It was a question of finding a mutually acceptable formula.*

The statesmen gathered at Stresa on April 11, 1935. France was represented by Flandin and Laval; Britain by Ramsay Macdonald and Simon, accompanied by Vansittart. The original intention had been for Simon to lead the British delegation with Eden to assist him. Unfortunately there was a last-minute change of plan since Eden had fallen ill on his return from Moscow, where he had flown

* According to Count Grandi, Mussolini in April, 1935, had no intention of going to war in Africa.

after the Berlin visit, and Macdonald decided that he must himself make the journey to Stresa. This alteration in the composition of the British delegation was to have unforeseen and disastrous consequences. Eden, whose courage and tenacity have never been questioned, would certainly have insisted on raising the Abyssinian problem. In his absence Simon, who resented having to take second place, resolved that if anyone were to grasp the nasty nettle, it would not be himself but the Prime Minister. Macdonald, however, was by that time at the end of his tether [32] and quite incapable of broaching so unpleasant and delicate a problem.

Other factors were at work. While Mussolini had come to Stresa with a clear idea of what he wanted, the British had made no such careful preparation and were hopelessly divided. Some foresaw that an Italian attack on Abyssinia was bound to split the fragile unity of the three powers and believed that an effort should be made to deter Mussolini or at least attenuate the scope of his designs. Others, including the forceful Vansittart, thought it essential to build a solid front against Hitler and deprecated any action which might deflect Mussolini from wholehearted cooperation with the West.[33] When this had been achieved and only then would it be safe to deal with the secondary problem. With divided counsels among the officials no effective pressure could be exercised on the two otiose ministers and neither during the six sessions of the conference nor in the lobbies did any Briton breathe a word to the Duce about Abyssinia.

In so far as the Austrian question was concerned, the outcome of the conference was equally unsatisfactory. The British government, in acordance with its traditional practice, was not prepared to undertake Continental commitments in a hypothetical case. All that was achieved was a joint resolution in which the three governments censured Germany for rearming, affirmed their loyalty to the Locarno Treaty, repeated their resolve to defend Austrian independence, and pledged themselves to cooperation in the maintenance of peace in Europe. The original draft spoke of peace in general, but Mussolini demanded and secured an amendment to "peace in Europe." This significant modification passed unobserved or at least it was not contested by the British delegation.

Mussolini subsequently gave his version of the events leading up to and including the Stresa conference. In an interview granted to

Ian Munro, Rome correspondent of *The Morning Post,* on September 11, 1935, he claimed that on January 29, 1935, he had sent an invitation to the British and French governments to discuss the Abyssinian question, but the British Foreign Office had not been prepared to do so. He had been ready to open talks at Stresa, but nothing had been done there. Finally he had inserted the word "European" into the Stresa joint resolution in order to emphasize that Africa was not covered. In these circumstances he had decided to go ahead and allow Italy to solve her African problem by herself.

There is no doubt that the fact that the word Abyssinia had not been breathed to him in the course of long negotiations covering a wide field came as a great surprise. When the conference was over Mussolini went to the station, accompanied by Grandi, to bid farewell to the British ministers. As the tail of the train disappeared from sight, he turned fiercely to Grandi: "You are a futile ambassador," he said, "you told me that on Austria the English answer would be 'yes,' and on Africa 'no.' As it happens, their answer on Austria was 'no,' and on Africa 'yes.'" [34] And he spat the word "yes" with furious emphasis.

Thus Mussolini left Stresa with the clear conviction that Britain, which was fully aware of his military preparations, attached little importance to Abyssinia. Now that Laval had signified the aquiescence of France, the way was clear. There was no call to stoop to any squalid compromise and nothing could hinder the realization of his dream. With this resolve the Duce took the first step towards the abyss.

CHAPTER THIRTEEN

The Abyssinian War

1935–1936

I

IN the year 1896, when Mussolini was thirteen years of age, the Italian army suffered a resounding defeat at the hands of the Emperor Menelik of Abyssinia. Six thousand dead were left on the field of Adowa while the remainder of the Italian army retreated in disorder over the frontier. Other European powers had previously suffered colonial reverses, but in due course they had usually been able to take steps to restore the position and no lasting damage had been done to their prestige. In Italy, however, the disaster, which had deeply impressed the young Benito, not only remained unavenged but caused a powerful and long-lived reaction against any colonial adventure whatsoever. It was a failure which rankled in the hearts of many Italians, not least in that of Mussolini.

The original entry of Italy into Africa had only been made possible by an initiative of the British government. The opening of the Suez Canal had given the Red Sea a new importance; and in order to diminish French influence in the area the British government in 1884 invited Italy to occupy the port of Massawa on the Red Sea. In 1889 the Italians captured Asmara and six months later the colony of Eritrea was constituted by royal decree. In 1895 the Italians began to advance into the Tigri province of Abyssinia with a few thousand men and in six weeks reached Lake Ashangi, 200 miles from their base. At this point Menelik moved against them with vastly superior forces, drove them back step by step, and eventually defeated them at Adowa. Fortunately for Italy, he also suffered severe losses in the engagement and was not disposed to follow up his victory. Peace was signed in 1897 and Italy was left in possession of her newly won colony.

There is no doubt that Mussolini was moved by a desire to wipe out this stain on Italian arms, but mingled with the primitive itch for vengeance was the ambition to extend Italy's overseas possessions. The mirage of a modern Roman Empire beckoned; and if he was to match the position of Britain and France in the world, he must also possess overseas territories, from which, so he argued, he could draw raw materials and to which he could export his surplus population. It is, incidentally, remarkable that both Mussolini and Hitler should have entertained the delusion that in the twentieth century raw materials were readily available only to the colonial powers and that significant numbers of Europeans could be planted in Africa. However this may be, Mussolini began very early in his career to cast covetous eyes on Abyssinia.

In this enterprise he displayed the qualities and defects of his character. On the tactical side, from the point of view of short-term success, his conduct of the operation could not have been bettered. Elasticity, opportunism, energy, resolution, and an accurate assessment of the opposition immediately confronting him, all enabled him to celebrate a veritable Roman triumph. But strategically he was completely at sea. Ignorance, vanity, and egotism blinded him to the consequences of his acts. Had he been able to foresee the cruel dilemma in which his policy would place him four years later, it is certain that he would have chosen the path of conciliation. It will be seen that Britain and France were equally at fault, but a politician who claims to be a great statesman cannot legitimately rely on the wisdom of foreign powers to rescue him from the consequences of his own folly.

At first Mussolini sought merely to acquire a special position in Abyssinia; in 1923 he joined France in sponsoring the application of the Emperor for admission into the League of Nations. The application aroused the Anti-Slavery and Aborigines Protection Society, which discovered among other things that the British Minister's butler was maintaining a large number of slaves in the legation compound at Addis Ababa. When Lord Curzon called on Sir Charles Russell to put an end to the scandal, he bravely replied that the slaves represented his butler's life's savings and that he was not disposed to strip him of them. In view of the publicity given to the continued practice of slavery and the outcry which it occasioned, the British delegation at Geneva opposed the Abyssinian application, but they were overborne by the Italo-French coalition and Abyssinia was duly admitted. The circumstances attending this transaction were very soon forgotten in Britain.

Mussolini relates that not long afterwards he began to apply his mind to ways and means of getting his foot into the Abyssinian door. Speaking in the Chamber on May 25, 1935, he said: "This problem does not date from today nor from January, 1935, but (as proved by documents, which may be published in due course) it goes back to 1925. It was in that year that I began to examine the problem. Three years later it seemed that a political treaty was the instrument best suited to assist our pacific expansion in that vast world, still enclosed in its prehistoric system and yet capable of great progress." In effect the Negus paid a state visit to Rome and in 1928 a treaty of friendship with Abyssinia was concluded, but the special position after which the Duce hankered still eluded him. The Abyssinians, more through sloth than malice, failed to fullfil their obligations under the treaty and the situation of Italy in Ethiopia was no better than that of any other power. Mussolini was disappointed and displeased. He remarked petulantly to one of his officials that his aim must be to give the Italian representative at Addis Ababa the same status as the British High Commissioner in Egypt.

Accordingly he decided on more drastic methods. After all the British had bombarded Alexandria, and the protectorate in Morocco rested on French bayonets. There could be no objection to establishing an analogous Italian system in a country which the British had recently described as unfit to be a member of the League of Nations. So, early in 1932 he dispatched the Minister of Colonies, De Bono, to Eritrea with secret instructions to examine the situation and report on the measures necessary to render the colony a suitable springboard for an attack on Abyssinia. Since it was normal for the Minister of Colonies to visit the dependencies, De Bono's mission aroused no comment in Italy or abroad. It remained a secret between himself and the Duce.

In Eritrea Mussolini did not make the mistake of trying to do things cheaply. On the contrary he was disposed to make assurance doubly sure by supplying more than the experts demanded; and he authorized the initiation of a massive program of public works: the improvement of the port of Massawa and of the railway to Asmara; the construction of a network of roads, hospitals, and airfields and the organization of an adequate water supply for an expeditionary force. A native labor corps was created and the locally recruited Eritrean regiments were raised to a strength of 60,000. These initial preparations were described as measures designed to ensure the defense of the colony against Abyssinian aggression. At the same time an organization was set on foot to undermine the loyalty of Abyssinian chieftains. If General De Bono is to be believed, the large sums placed at its disposal were not wasted: "From the very outset of the campaign there were signs of the results of this disintegrating political action. . . . It deprived our enemy of at least 200,000 men who either did not take up arms, or who, though enrolled and armed, remained inert." [1]

Early in 1933 De Bono at the Ministry of Colonies had drawn up an estimate of the forces required for a war of aggression, but nothing had been definitely settled. The international situation was in flux and the General Staff was reluctant to weaken the home front by diverting a large army to Africa. Nevertheless De Bono was sufficiently in touch with Mussolini's thinking to apply for the command in the war against Abyssinia: "The Duce looked at me hard and at once replied: 'Surely.' 'You don't think me too old?' I added. 'No,' he replied, 'because we must not lose time.' From that moment the Duce was definitely of the opinion that the matter would have to be settled no later than 1936. . . . It was the autumn of 1933. The Duce had spoken to no one of the coming operations in East Africa; only he and I knew what was going to happen." [2] It was all a foretaste of the Hitlerian technique.

In March, 1934, Mussolini gave the first public hint of his intentions. Addressing the second quinquennial assembly of Fascists, he spoke of a natural expansion and added that Italy could above all civilize Africa, a task to which she was entitled by virtue of her

Mediterranean position; and "earlier arrivals" were warned not to block her spiritual, political, and economic expansion. In July the Italian Chief of Staff, Marshal Badoglio, to whom the plan had been revealed at the end of 1933, inspected the so-called Eritrean defenses. By the end of the year the Abyssinians were becoming urgently aware of the increasing danger on the other side of the border; and their resentment was reflected in a number of incidents, which were in turn exploited by the Italians to give color to the pretense that the preparations in Eritrea were purely defensive.

II

In the climate of mutual recrimination and suspicion, and having regard to the indiscipline of the Abyssinians, it was certain that sooner or later the Italians would be given the pretext they required. In the event Mussolini did not have to wait very long, for on December 5, 1934, there was an accidental affray at Wal-Wal, a fort and watering place close to the junction of Abyssinia, Italian Somaliland, and British Somaliland. Wal-Wal was certainly on the Abyssinian side of the ill-defined border line, but the three governments whose territories converged at that point had never drawn a formal frontier line and were content to allow the nomad tribes to move freely to and from the Wal-Wal wells, which were in practice recognized as belonging to the Italian colony.

In November, 1934, Colonel Clifford, head of the British mission delimiting the frontier between British Somaliland and Abyssinia, arrived at Wal-Wal with an escort of the Somaliland Camel Corps. A number of Abyssinian tribesmen gathered round Colonel Clifford's party and their appearance caused the Italian commander at Wal-Wal to believe that he was threatened with attack. He summoned reinforcements and Colonel Clifford prudently withdrew from the area. Unfortunately his departure was the signal for the tribesmen who had attached themselves to the British party to attack the Italians at Wal-Wal and in the ensuing engagement the victorious Italian native troops suffered heavy casualties. Mussolini at once demanded an unconditional apology, a large indemnity, and a final settlement of the frontier, while the Emperor claimed that the dispute came within the terms of the treaty of 1928, under which differences were submitted to arbitration.

Mussolini was determined to make the Wal-Wal incident a test case. If the Emperor were prepared to embark on a policy of appeasement, increasing pressure could be brought to bear upon him until Abyssinia became a virtual Italian protectorate. Alternatively, force would have to be used and for this purpose it would be necessary to transport and deploy in Africa a massive army and an air force. Owing to the rains he could not move until the autumn of 1935, but there was no time to lose. He would require every day of the intervening months to make his military preparations and he was determined to finish quickly in Abyssinia since he could not afford to leave his northern frontier uncovered for long against the growing German threat.

Thus, the most important and urgent task was to organize and despatch the expeditionary force. Meanwhile the diplomats would be busy making a show of negotiation at Geneva and above all securing the acquiescence of Britain and France, on whom he was relying for support against Hitler. He was looking forward to a spectacular campaign, but he was prepared for the sake of the common front to compromise if need be. This was the mood in which he faced the dawn of 1935.

On January 7, while the Franco-Italian agreement was being signed in Rome, General De Bono was on his way to Massawa to take up his post as High Commissioner for East Africa. Shortly afterwards this appointment was made public and it was announced that Mussolini had taken over the Ministries of Colonies and Corporations. He was now in charge of seven out of the thirteen departments of state. Under his impulse the preparations for the war were energetically pushed forward. In February and March the first two divisions of regular infantry were shipped to Africa. No attempt was made to conceal these troop movements and indeed the congestion of transports in the Suez Canal was plain for all to see.

In May two further regular divisions and four Blackshirt divisions were being made ready to go. By the end of May nearly a million Italians were estimated to be under arms. Thus during the first five months of 1935 it became clear to the world that Mussolini was making preparations for an important military enterprise in Abyssinia. This is the background against which the diplomatic exchanges must be seen.

III

Mussolini, having settled with Laval, lost little time in approaching Britain. On January 29, 1935, Signor Vitetti, the Italian Chargé d'Affaires in London, officially informed the Foreign Secretary of the Franco-Italian agreement and conveyed the wish of the Italian government to harmonize British and Italian interests in Abyssinia. This was, and was recognized as, a polite intimation that British interests would be safeguarded, if Italy were given a free hand.

No indignant nor immediate answer was given to this communication. Sir John Simon merely promised to look into the matter and to reply in due course. An interdepartmental committee, appointed under the chairmanship of Sir John Maffey, reported five months later that "there were no vital British interests in Abyssinia or adjoining countries such as to necessitate British resistance to an Italian conquest of Abyssinia." This document was purloined from the British embassy in Rome and confirmed Mussolini in the view which he formed at Stresa that Britain was not really interested in Abyssinia. More than ever he was resolved to push ahead and the rhythm of his military preparations was accelerated. He was determined that victory should not be lost or even delayed for lack of resources; and he not only supplied the number of troops his generals demanded, but he sent them considerably more.

Meanwhile two events had occurred on the German front which seemed to Mussolini to furnish additional justification for his policy. On March 16, 1935, the German government proclaimed the introduction of conscription and the creation of a peacetime army of thirty-six divisions. On June 18, only three months later, Britain, without consulting France or Italy, condoned Hitler's flagrant treaty breach by signing an Anglo-German naval agreement binding the Germans not to build beyond 35 per cent of Britain's naval strength.

From the first event Mussolini drew the conclusion that he was right to make haste over Abyssinia. He must at all costs finish in

Africa before Hitler was ready in Europe. From the second event he drew two conclusions: first, that Britain was a feeble and unreliable ally; and secondly, that if the British government were ready amiably to condone on the part of an unarmed and helpless Germany a treaty breach threatening England's national security, they would be unlikely to interfere with an armed Italy, who moreover was a useful potential ally, on account of an uncivilized country in which England had no material interests. The last conclusion seemed logical enough, but the Duce was unaware that British policy is often at the mercy of sudden gusts of irrational popular emotion.

The naval agreement was damaging in another sense. Mussolini's policy had been to extract such advantages as he could from the antagonism between Germany and the Western powers. The threat to Austria had momentarily driven him into the Western camp, but this was a risk that was acceptable only if the Western powers hung together. Now it seemed that Britain had left the Western bloc in order to make a selfish deal to her own advantage; and it might even be that the naval agreement would inaugurate a new era of Anglo-German cooperation. It obviously did not suit Mussolini to be isolated in opposition to Germany, and he was already receiving disturbing warning signals from Berlin. The extreme Nazis were still smarting under Mussolini's interference in Austria, while the army, which expected an Italian fiasco in Africa, the navy, and elements in the Foreign Office all favored an understanding with England. The mood was reflected in a film, *Abessinien von Heute,* which was markedly friendly to the Emperor and was shown all over Germany. It looked as if the Germans might be turning against Italy.

Mussolini did not know, however, that Hitler was of a different mind. To the Polish ambassador he remarked that Mussolini was taking a grave risk in Abyssinia, but, although the Duce was hostile to Germany, he himself would regard an Italian defeat as a disaster, because it would constitute a blow to their common ideology.[3] This was not the sentiment of the German nation, and all that Mussolini saw was a real risk that Britain might make a separate accommodation with Germany, a fear which constantly haunted his mind. Consequently as soon as he scented a pro-British and anti-Italian wind in Berlin, he began to trim his sails. He moderated his anti-German transports and sent a new ambassador, Attolico, to Berlin in place of the notoriously anti-Nazi Cerruti. From every point of view, and particularly from the point of view of British relations with Mussolini, nothing could have been more damaging at that particular moment than the capricious and ill-considered decision to sign the naval agreement.

The British cabinet, unlike Mussolini, was only too aware of a stir in British public opinion; and they viewed accordingly with rising trepidation the ineffective proceedings at Geneva and the constant flow of Italian troops to Africa. Thus Vansittart after the Stresa conference warned the Italian ambassador that the nation worshiped at the shrine of the League of Nations and that if Italy invaded Abyssinia, no British government could control the tide of popular indignation. In May the British ambassador in Rome was instructed to beg Mussolini's help in the search for a formula which would save the prestige of the League of Nations. Mussolini gave him a stiff reply: Italy had chosen her course and nothing now could stop her assuring her own security by every possible means including war.

IV

As a last expedient the cabinet decided in June to despatch Eden to Rome with a compromise plan under which Britain would compensate Abyssinia for concessions made to Italy. Thus in return for the cession to Italy of a portion of the Ogaden province, Abyssinia would receive a substantial strip of territory in British Somaliland with an outlet to the sea at Zeila.

Eden's two meetings with Mussolini have been the subject of much ill-informed comment. It has been said that the exchanges were stormy, that the Duce insulted and dragooned his British visitor, and that the interviews created a mutual antipathy which was never subsequently dissipated. Nothing is further from the truth. The conversations were conducted with the normal courtesy attending such transactions in Western countries, and indeed Signor Guariglia comments on the calm with which Mussolini received the British proposals.[4] This is borne out by the official British and

Italian records, which are in substantial agreement. Eden and Mussolini were in no sense kindred spirits; and no dictator of the period cared for the bulldog tenacity with which Eden probed his adversary's intentions and clung to his own position. Mussolini complained to his sister of Eden's Anglo-Saxon self-possession and invincible obstinacy.[5] But such personal antipathy as there was between the two men only became a factor in Anglo-Italian relations during the period of sanctions when Mussolini savagely attacked the defender of the League of Nation's faith and Eden retorted in kind.

The first meeting between Mussolini and Eden took place at the Palazzo Venezia on June 24, 1935, ostensibly to discuss disarmament, but in reality to consider the British government's proposals, which had been communicated in advance neither to the French nor to the Italian governments. On the eve of Eden's arrival in Rome the French ambassador, who had just returned from Paris, called on Suvich to give him a reassuring account of his government's attitude.

According to Suvich's record of the conversation, Laval had expressly charged the ambassador to inform the Duce that he was faithfully adhering to the policy laid down in the Rome agreements. Neither England nor any other country would be able to disturb Italo-French friendship. Suvich asked whether Geneva would be able to disturb it and the ambassador replied that: "Laval trusts that the Ethiopian question will be settled without causing any trouble at Geneva. . . . Laval hopes too that the Italian demands will be accepted without any recourse to arms. He will do everything in his power to help us obtain what we want peacefully. I reply that I think it is not improbable that the Negus will accept our demands peacefully. In conclusion, the ambassador affirms that on the Ethiopian question France is for us."[6] The fact that Laval laid emphasis on a peaceful solution did not in Mussolini's eyes diminish the value of his assurance of support.

It was thus in a confident mood that Mussolini received Eden on the following day. In his opening statement Eden said that England was concerned about the Abyssinian conflict because of its repercussions on the League of Nations, since an Italian stand against Geneva would provoke a strong reaction which would disturb the good relations between the two countries, with very disagreeable consequences. In order to find a way out the British government wished to make the following proposals to the Italian government. Britain, aware that Abyssinia attached importance to access to the sea, had resolved to cede the bay of Zeila with a corridor linking the port to Abyssinia in return for considerable concessions to Italy. These concessions would be the cession of the province of Ogaden, economic concessions, and other privileges to be determined.

Mussolini at once declared the proposal to be unacceptable on three grounds. First, because it would make Abyssinia a maritime power, thereby increasing her prestige; secondly, because England would appear as the protector of Abyssinia; and finally, because Italy could not accept the cession of territory through the mediation of third powers. Moreover the proffered concessions fell far short of Italy's aspirations. The Italian government had already expended a billion lire and a considerable effort, for which they intended to exact the liquidation of the Ethiopian question. They were not prepared to remain any longer under the threat of an attack at a time when they might be engaged elsewhere. The only acceptable peaceful solution would involve the cession to Italy of all the territories which were not racially a part of Ethiopia, in addition to control over the central nucleus. A solution by war would involve the removal of Abyssinia from the map.

When Eden expressed his disappointment and repeated that the difficulty arose from Abyssinian membership of the League, Suvich interjected that France also adhered to the League, but adopted a different attitude to the Abyssinian question. At this point Eden retorted that, according to the account he had himself received from Laval, the French promise of a free hand to Italy referred only to the economic field. According to Eden's record, Mussolini at once contested this interpretation:

> Signor Mussolini replied that might be, so far as a written document was concerned, but since he had yielded to France 100,000 Italians in Tunis, and received in return half a dozen palm trees in one place and a strip of desert, which did not contain a sheep, in another, it must be clear that he had understood that France had disinterested herself in Abyssinia. I contested this, telling Signor Mussolini that when Monsieur Laval had

described in Geneva his interview with Mussolini, he had insisted that France had only given a free hand to Italy in economic matters, and that he had added to Signor Mussolini: "*vous avez les mains fortes. Faites attention,*" making it clear that French goodwill did not apply to other than economic enterprises. At this, Signor Mussolini flung himself back in his chair with a gesture of incredulous astonishment.[7]

It was clear from this interview that there was little hope of reconciling the divergent views of the two governments. Nevertheless Eden did not give up. After all, there were many imponderables: the extent of the Emperor's determination to resist, the degree of support which France would give Italy, and the danger attending a breach in the Stresa front and a collision with England for the sake of Abyssinia. All these factors gave rise to the hope that reason might yet prevail and that means might be found of devising a compromise. Accordingly, Eden, before breaking up the interview, made a last effort to shift the Duce. He urged Mussolini with all the eloquence at his command not to embark on an adventure, the end of which no man could foresee. He emphasized that Britain could not abandon the League of Nations and begged Mussolini not to force their two countries into open conflict. Mussolini replied that he also would deeply regret any disturbance of the old Anglo-Italian amity, but that he was now too far committed to withdraw. He had spent an astronomical sum in Eritrea and he could not bring back his vast army without firing a shot and with little or nothing to show for the effort Italy had expended. Eden besought Mussolini to come to no definite conclusion that night, to ponder over what he had said, and to give a definite answer on the morrow. On this note Eden and Mussolini parted, to meet again at luncheon when Mussolini readily agreed to another meeting. But the omens were not good and Eden noted that there had been "a gloomy fatality about his temper which I fear it may be beyond the power of reasoning to modify."

The second meeting took place at five o'clock on June 25. Both parties went over the same ground and Mussolini once more demanded the cession of all territory except the provinces belonging to Abyssinia in the pre-Menelik era, with control over the remainder, such as Britain or France exercised in Egypt or Morocco. In the face of Mussolini's refusal to yield an inch, Eden asked for a private meeting and received the same answer, namely that a stage had been reached which made it quite impossible for Italy to abandon her Abyssinian enterprise. Eden had shown the utmost persistence, but he now had no alternative but to express his disappointment and to express the pious hope that a peaceful solution might yet be found before it was too late. He was too experienced a diplomatist not to recognize that on the basis of the proposals he had brought with him there was no prospect of a deal.

Eden's visit to Rome, far from resolving the deadlock, only crystallized it. On his return to London it was impossible to avoid statements in Parliament, and the publicity given to them and to the circumstances of his abortive mission alerted public opinion, which in turn stiffened the attitude of the government. Mussolini was not insentitive to this development and launched an anti-British campaign in the press. Relations between Italy and Britain deteriorated and the prospect of a negotiated settlement began to fade.

V

Nevertheless the British government did not altogether abandon hope. The story of the next three months is the story of distraught diplomats, with their endless scurrying hither and thither in a frantic search for a formula to save the peace. There was an abortive effort to secure arbitration of the dispute under the Italo-Abyssinian treaty of 1928. In August representatives of Britain, France, and Italy met in Paris, but within three days Mussolini had rejected the Anglo-French proposals. At Geneva in September a committee of five—Britain, France, Poland, Spain, and Turkey—presented another, more complicated plan, which Mussolini described as unacceptable, since he was not a collector of deserts. As the weeks passed and the date fixed for the invasion approached, Mussolini became more truculent and arrogant, while the Western powers were principally concerned, by a series of moves designed to gain time, to create the impression of activity and, to quiet those who were stridently demanding the intervention of the League.

By September, however, it was clear that little hope remained of averting war. All through the summer, under cover of the fruitless negotiations, troops had been pouring into Africa. Already General De Bono had at his disposal, poised for the attack, five regular divisions, five Blackshirt divisions, two native divisions, and a considerable air force. At the same time second-line divisions were being formed in Italy to replace those mobilized for service in Africa. It was a formidable military effort.

Sir Samuel Hoare and Laval took advantage of the Assembly of the League of Nations in September to survey the melancholy prospect and to lay their plans. Laval was prepared to cooperate, but only on condition that there was no war with Italy and no breach of the Latin front against Germany. The two Foreign Secretaries agreed that, since they must avoid provoking Mussolini into open hostility, any economic pressure should be cautiously applied and nothing done, as Laval put it, to drive Mussolini into the German camp. This was easy to say, but as will be seen, France and Britain did in effect drive Mussolini into the German camp, without doing anything to weaken him or to diminish the value to Hitler of his new ally.

Laval's version of his agreement with the British Foreign Secretary was subsequently given to the French Chamber of Deputies on December 28, 1935.

> On September 10 I had some conversations with Sir Samuel Hoare and Mr. Eden. We were convinced that our first effort at conciliation had failed and that hostilities were going to begin almost immediately. . . . We found ourselves instantaneously in agreement upon ruling out military sanctions, not adopting any measure of naval blockade, never contemplating the closure of the Suez Canal—in a word ruling out everything that might lead to war.

On the following day, September 11, 1935, Sir Samuel Hoare endeavored to translate his understanding with Laval in a statement of policy to the Assembly of the League. It was a speech which he had most carefully prepared and which was intended to emphasize that collective security, if it was to be effective, must be comprehensive. Greatly to his surprise, as he returned from the rostrum to his seat in the body of the hall, he was greeted with loud and universal acclamation. His statement had been completely misunderstood, partly because it was not free from a certain disingenuousness, but principally because the euphoria in which the Assembly and indeed the democratic world elected to live caused his carefully formulated reservations to be ignored. "In conformity with its precise and explicit obligations," Hoare declared, "the League stands and my country stands with it, for the collective maintenance of the Covenant [and at this point he paused, regarded his audience for a moment, and repeated the word "collective"] in its entirety, and particularly for steady and collective resistance to all acts of unprovoked aggression." This was the passage which caught the ear of the Assembly and little attention was paid to the warning that Britain would do no more than France or any other country. "If the burden is to be borne, it must be borne collectively. If risks for peace are to be run, they must be run by all. The security of the many cannot be ensured by the efforts of a few, however powerful they may be."

Encouraged by Hoare, a succession of speakers followed in the same vein and the outcome of the debate was an impressive demonstration of League solidarity against the Italian aggressors. It seemed to the delegates in the atmosphere of Geneva that no country would dare to affront world opinion, so cogently expressed and backed by so powerful an array of force. They did not then foresee that some of the states there represented would decline to apply even the most innocuous economic sanctions and that of the remainder none would be prepared to turn the screw to the point of risking war.

In Rome Mussolini was undeterred. As early as May 18, 1935 he had written to De Bono:

> I have made it understood that we shall not turn back at any price. . . . It is absolutely indispensable not to alter the date—October—which we have fixed for the beginning of the eventual operations. . . . You must make sure beforehand of victuals and ammunition for at least three years, and also, however absurd it seems, because there are formal conventions in existence relating to the passage of the Suez Canal in peace and war, one must expect difficulties in respect of its passage. In the House of Commons there has been even talk of closing the Canal. One must always make ready for the most pessimistic and difficult eventuality.[8]

In September Mussolini adhered to the resolve which he had formed in May. On September 26 the Emperor of Abyssinia, who had throughout pinned his faith in the League, formally requested the despatch of observers to establish the facts in regard to the Italian aggression, which was now clearly imminent. Two days later he appealed to the Council of the League to take precautionary measures and he announced general mobilization to ensure the defense of his country. On October 2 it was reported that Italian troops had violated the frontier and a decree of mobilization was published in Italy. From his Roman balcony Mussolini addressed an enormous and enthusiastic crowd:

> A solemn hour is about to strike in the history of the Fatherland. . . . Not only is an army marching towards its objective, but forty million Italians are marching in unison with the army, all united because there is an attempt to commit against them the blackest of all injustices, to rob them of a place in the sun. . . . With Ethiopa we have been patient for forty years. Now enough! . . . To sanctions of an economic character we will reply with discipline, with our sobriety and with our spirit of sacrifice. To sanctions of a military character we will reply with acts of war.[9]

Early on the following morning, two days before the date originally fixed, the vanguards of three Italian army corps crossed the frontier and began the invasion of Abyssinia.

VI

It will be convenient to pause at this point to recapitulate and to examine the motives which led Mussolini to this momentous decision. While it is true that a man's conduct is conditioned by habits of thought and action formed over a period, it is also undeniable that no single act contributed more directly to Mussolini's downfall than his invasion of Abyssinia.

The official Italian reasons for the so-called liquidation of the Abyssinian question were two. First, it was necessary to protect the African colonies from Abyssinian aggression, which might at any time be launched, particularly when Italy was militarily committed in an already storm-tossed Europe. Secondly Italy needed both room for her expanding population and a source for raw materials which could be paid for in her own currency. These motives were, however, not sufficient to decide the issue and to enable Mussolini to overcome the opposition of his civil and military advisers, who were reluctant to drain the country's financial resources and to weaken Italy's strength in Europe. Other considerations came into play.

There was of course the burning desire to erase the shame of Adowa. The British ambassador reported that during the early months of 1935 a visitor was almost certain to find on the desk in Mussolini's room in the Palazzo Venezia some book or other which referred to that battle or to the campaign. Secondly there was the ambition to raise Italy to the position of a Great Power; and a symbol of that status was an overseas empire. Hence the recurring references to the situation of Britain and France in Egypt and Morocco, respectively. Thirdly there was jealousy of the upstart Hitler, who would shortly be able to deploy his newly found strength. Italy must use the intervening months to make her display of military power. Fourthly, obsession with the glories of the former Roman Empire impelled him to renew them under the standards of fascism. Finally, he may have been attracted by the prospect of diverting public attention away from the internal economic difficulties which beset every poor country, and towards external adventure with its accompanying excitement and glory.

All these motives exercised a strong pressure on the headstrong Mussolini, but they might not have been decisive had he not at the same time miscalculated the attitude of France and Britain. He was never shaken in his conviction that Laval had in fact given him a free hand in Abyssinia; and he believed that in the last resort Britain too would acquiesce. He was warned by Sir Eric Drummond in May and by Eden in June that the British government, if compelled to choose between the League and the old Anglo-Italian friendship, would inevitably choose the former; and many similar warnings were given to Signor Grandi in London. But Mussolini preferred to believe that *The Daily Mail* and *The Daily Express,* which supported the Italian thesis, registered the heartbeat of the nation. Here he was sustained by his intuition, which told him that no British government would wreck the Stresa front for a barbarous African territory in which they had no interest. In a speech on October 2, 1935, Mussolini said that he declined to believe that "the real British people, which has never had any dispute with Italy, is disposed to take the risk of plunging Europe into a disaster in order to defend an African country, universally branded as a country without a trace of civilization."

In the final analysis intuition was overlaid by emotion. He had a profound hatred of and contempt for the Abyssinians. He could not bring himself to treat Abyssinia at Geneva or elsewhere on an equal footing. Nor could Italy as a Great Power come before the League as a suppliant. Accordingly the only course was for Italy to settle her accounts with Abyssinia and settle them directly and without delay. As the weeks and months of 1935 passed, he became more and more involved in a military enterprise and less and less inclined to sacrifice his military investment to a peaceful settlement. He knew that when the rains ceased, he must strike or abandon the use of force for another year. He decided to strike.

This is not the place to examine the foreign policy of the Western powers, but it must be said that their attitude contributed to his calamitous decision. The best chance of inducing Mussolini to compromise over Abyssinia lay in demonstrating that the Stresa front would otherwise be broken and that the maintenance of an effective Stresa front was essential to Italian security. This latter proposition Mussolini was conditioned to accept. The murder of Dollfuss had inflamed him against Germany and he was beginning to be frightened of Hitler. But, before committing himself to an anti-German coalition, he required to be assured that his partners would be stout and could be relied upon to stand up to Hitler. Unfortunately he received no such assurance. When Dollfuss was murdered and Italy mobilized, neither France nor Britain moved. In March, 1935, when Germany proclaimed her rearmament, the protest which emerged from Paris and London was purely formal. Within a few weeks British ministers were in attendance on Hitler at Berlin and in June Germany's treaty violation was condoned by the signature of the Anglo-German naval agreement. It is not surprising that in the light of these events Mussolini should have come to the conclusion that the Stresa front had little value for Italy and that it was not worthwhile making concessions in Abyssinia to secure its perpetuation.

VII

While negotiations had been going on in Geneva and military preparations pushed forward in Rome, the British government had been taking precautionary measures. Early in September the Mediterranean fleet was despatched to the eastern Mediterranean and a number of units of the Home fleet were sent out to reinforce it. These naval moves provoked a violent reaction in Italy, and the possibility of war became the one topic of conversation. It was said, doubtless not without official inspiration, that it would be better to go down fighting than ignominiously to surrender before a show of force. In the resulting electric atmosphere the possibility of an unprovoked attack by Italy on Britain (in the jargon of the day, this was described in official documents as "the mad-dog act") seemed less remote.

If there was uncertainty in London, the Duce was equally tormented by doubts. At times he was inclined to believe that Britain was reluctant to break with Italy and would in the last resort negotiate an acceptable agreement. At others he feared that the British plan might be to exhaust Italy by sanctions and then to launch a sudden attack. This inner conflict was to some extent resolved when, on September 23, 1935, a formal assurance was given to Mussolini that the British naval measures were purely precautionary and defensive. Mussolini accepted the assurance more readily than he might have done had he not purloined from the embassy documents revealing deficiencies in the battleworthiness of the fleet; and tension was momentarily reduced. There was even some talk of a simultaneous reduction of the strength of the British fleet and of the Italian army in Libya. Nevertheless Mussolini, sustained by the King, continued from time to time to drop dark hints that Italy would react with force to any excessive pressure by the League. It appears certain now that he had no intention of putting such threats into effect, but it is equally certain that in France and Britain the fear subsisted that he might, if sufficiently provoked, commit the mad-dog act. It was a test of nerves, and in this contest Mussolini won.

Another circumstance which favored him was the disarray

among the Western powers. Laval was resolved not to take extreme action against Italy, while in Britain, on whom the leadership at Geneva devolved, opinion was hopelessly confused and divided. Here there were, broadly speaking, four currents of opinion. The extreme pacifists opposed any action which would lead to war. The extreme imperialists sympathized with Mussolini's colonialist ambitions and saw no reason to interfere. The pragmatists, a party of which Vansittart was the leading spokesman, argued that Europe was approaching its supreme ordeal, a confrontation with Hitler. Nothing must be done to weaken the Stresa front or, still worse, to drive Mussolini into Germany's arms. The majority of the nation favored effective League of Nation sanctions, without considering too closely the possible consequences. Sir Winston Churchill was the interpreter of these sentiments, when on September 26, 1935, he said in the House of Commons:

> The whole country, indeed the whole Empire is, I believe, ready to support His Majesty's government in making its contribution to the authority of the League of Nations in accordance with the obligations into which we have entered. Our duty and our vital interest in peace compel us to take our share and do our part in the workings of that great international instrument, which seeks to establish the reign of law among nations and ward off the measureless perils of another world struggle. If the League of Nations is now found capable of preventing a colonial war in Africa without broadening it out into a general European war, that will be an immeasurable gain to the safety of all countries. I trust that France will realize how vital to her own security in the future it is for the League of Nations to emerge successful from this decisive test.

Of course, if the pragmatists had had their way and then displayed the requisite firmness in dealing with Hitler, it might have been possible to acquire Mussolini for an effective anti-German coalition. If the sanctionists had had theirs, Mussolini would have been struck down and could have brought no aid and comfort to Hitler. As it turned out, thanks to divided counsels, neither of the two courses was adopted. It is against the background of sloth in Paris, confusion in London, and general fear of a mad-dog act by Mussolini that the complicated diplomatic transactions during the last months of 1935 must now be viewed.

VIII

Under Eden's vigorous leadership the Council of the League acted with commendable energy and speed. By October 7 a committee of six powers had reported to the Council that Italy was guilty of a violation of the Covenant, and for the first time the Council defined a member of the League as an aggressor in terms which obliged every member to proceed to sanctions. With three dissentients the Assembly of the League endorsed the findings of the Council and on October 11 appointed a coordination committee to deal with the application of sanctions.

So far so good. Only eight days had been spent in getting the cumbrous machinery of the League into motion, but, as so often happens, agreement in principle was followed by certain difficulties arising from its application in practice. The coordination committee recommended five relatively modest proposals: that the arms embargo against Abyssinia be raised and a similar embargo imposed on Italy; that all loans, credits, and other financial transactions with Italy be prohibited; that an embargo be placed on all goods from Italy; that an embargo be placed on certain goods going to Italy, but specifically excluding oil and several other primary materials; and finally that there be mutual economic support and compensation for those states adversely affected by the sanctions.

Even these mild measures were only partially applied. Four member states—Austria, Hungary, Albania, and Paraguay—refused to take any action. Several other members failed to apply the various sanctions, while it proved impossible to secure a full measure of cooperation from the United States or Germany. Moreover the date fixed for the application of these sanctions, November 18, gave the Italians time to accumulate considerable stocks.

In Italy the announcement of these steps was received in official quarters with some relief, since it had been feared that oil sanctions and the closure of the Suez Canal might bring the whole Abyssinian enterprise to a grinding halt. Nevertheless the government was quick to take the opportunity of beating the patriotic drum; and the Fascist Grand Council denounced the sanctions as an iniquity, "a plan to suffocate the Italian people economically" in order to prevent it realizing its ideals. This propaganda fell on fertile soil, for the Italians were only too ready to remember the sense of grievance under which they had suffered after the First World War and to believe that the rich, powerful nations were determined to exclude them from access to the good things of the world.

The indignation of the people was nurtured by the government, which organized the boycott of foreign imports and proclaimed the need for economic independence. The financial burdens imposed by the war would in any event have required domestic restrictions, and it was convenient to ascribe to sanctions the sacrifices and shortages which the nation had to bear. The war widows and mothers collected precious metals for the war effort, and married women offered their gold wedding rings in exchange for iron rings. In Rome the Queen, standing in the rain on the marble platform of the War Memorial, was the first of 250,000 women in the capital to throw her wedding ring into the flaming brazier. Similar ceremonies were held in countless towns and villages up and down the country, while a strident press whipped up patriotic fervor combined with hatred of the sanctionist powers. Mussolini's propaganda campaign was entirely successful, for whereas public opinion had originally been lukewarm or even hostile to the war, the nation was now welded together in a common determination to resist external pressure. Even some of the political exiles such as the Socialists Professor Arturo Labriola and Mario Bergamo rallied to the national cause. Passive opponents of the regime such as Orlando, Croce, Senator Albertini, and the dramatist Sam Benelli also voiced their support of the war.

In Geneva on the other hand the semblance of solidarity between the majority of the member states concealed a profound difference between the two governments, who wielded power and on whom rested the responsibility for leading the League through its fiery test. The British government stood for the application of such sanctions, including those on oil as would frustrate the aggressor. The French government was concerned to find a settlement of the dispute by conciliation and in the meantime, while saving the face of the League, to embark on no measures likely to prejudice a negotiation. Thus, as will be seen, the proposals for an oil embargo and for conciliation became inextricably intertwined.

The question of imposing an oil embargo was first raised on October 19, 1935, in the so-called Committee of Eighteen, a subcommittee of the Coordination Committee. On November 6, the committee formally adopted a proposal to embargo oil, coal, pig iron, iron, and steel, but by December 12 only ten member states had notified the Secretary-General that they were willing to put this recommendation into effect. This hesitation was due not only to natural prudence, but to Laval's agile and skillful maneuvers. He not only succeeded in postponing from November 25 to December 12 a meeting of the Committee of Eighteen called to expedite the application of oil sanctions, but he cleverly prepared the ground for conciliation in a debate on November 2 in the Coordination Committee. His plan was to put off oil sanctions until he had created a climate of opinion in favor of a compromise.

During the debate in the Coordination Committee the Belgian representative said:

> In the circumstances, does it not seem right that efforts towards conciliation should, from this moment be placed under the auspices and within the framework of the League itself? Since the responsible leaders of two great countries have already devoted a large part of their time and their talents to this task, why should the League not entrust to them the mission of seeking, under its auspices and control and in the spirit of the Covenant, the elements of a solution which the three parties at issue—the League, Italy, and Ethiopia—might find it possible to accept? If the suggestion were to meet with the approval of the members of this Assembly, I think that the moral position of the League would be still further strengthened and that the chances of peace would be increased.

In the minutes of the Coordination Committee it was recorded that the Committee took note of the desire expressed by the Belgian delegate.

Laval had achieved his aim and it is clear that Hoare believed that he had received a mandate to seek a compromise. "This proposal," he telegraphed home, "was warmly supported by most of the other speakers and opposed by none. It was clear that it represented the unanimous sense of the meeting." [10] This then was the genesis of the Hoare-Laval plan.

Meanwhile in Rome and in Paris the way had been prepared

for a possible compromise. During the month of October there had been a number of soundings and exchanges between the Vatican, the Italian government, and the French and British diplomatic missions on the subject of a solution which would partition the Ethiopian Empire between Italy and Abyssinia. It was felt that Mussolini, having avenged Adowa and occupied a considerable tract of Abyssinia, would now prove more amenable. On the British side emphasis was laid on the importance of submitting any solution to the League of Nations; but in London there was no objection in principle to a negotiated compromise, and a British Foreign Office official, Mr. Maurice Peterson, was sent to discuss the matter at the Quai d'Orsay.

There was a pause for the British general election on November 14, 1935, which returned Mr. Baldwin to office, but on November 21 the conversations on the official level were resumed in Paris and within a short time sufficient progress had been made to justify an early meeting. On December 6, 1935, Hoare in a speech in the House of Commons claimed that he had consistently followed the double line approved by the League. That was to say, Britain had taken her full part in collective action under the Covenant while continuing her efforts for a peaceful settlement. "The world urgently needs peace. We and the French, acting on behalf of the League and in the spirit of the League, are determined to make another great effort for peace. We have no wish to humiliate Italy or to weaken it. . . . Cannot we lay aside the suspicion and concentrate in the immediate future upon finding a basis of settlement." It was a clear warning of what was in the wind.

It was on this note that Hoare, a sick man on his way to a much needed holiday in Switzerland, stopped in Paris for conversations with Laval. The outcome of two long meetings on December 7 and 8 was the famous plan, which recommended the cession to Italy of eastern Tigre, substantial rectifications of the frontiers between Abyssinia on the one hand and Eritrea and Italian Somaliland on the other, and an outlet to the sea for Abyssinia. The total territory to be ceded to Italy was greater than that which the Italian army had already conquered. The British and French governments were, moreover, to use their influence at Addis Ababa and Geneva to obtain in southern Abyssinia a zone of economic expansion and settlement reserved for Italy. Finally the plan was to be submitted to the three parties to the dispute: Italy, Abyssinia, and the League of Nations. Steps were taken to make the necessary communications in Rome, Geneva, and Addis Ababa; and Hoare, having completed this transaction and apparently quite unaware of the stir which it would cause, left Paris for his Swiss holiday.

Before dealing with the fate of the plan it may be useful briefly to describe what had happened in the meantime to the campaign in Abyssinia. Thanks to the withdrawal of the Abyssinian troops from the frontier areas and to the thorough preparations made by the propaganda of the Italian political officers, the initial advance was rapid and spectacular. Adowa was captured within three days and by November 8, 1935, General De Bono had occupied Makalle, some eighty miles from the border. There De Bono proposed to stop, for on logistic grounds he did not believe that it would be safe to attempt a further advance until he had consolidated his gains and improved his communications.

Mussolini was, however, not prepared to wait. The application of economic sanctions might be extended to oil and other essential products, and he was still obsessed by the need to disengage in Abyssinia sufficiently quickly to enable him to face the growing might of Germany in Europe. He was still four hundred miles from Addis Ababa and could afford to lose no time. He accordingly recalled De Bono on November 16 and sent out in his place Marshal Badoglio with instructions to bring the campaign to an end during the coming year.

These events undoubtedly impressed Hoare, who in Paris acted under the conviction that nothing could now save Abyssinia except a compromise, which Mussolini would prefer to the obvious risks attending a war to a finish waged in the teeth of the concerted opposition of the League. This was not, however, the view of public opinion in Britain. Here events moved fast. On December 9 certain French opposition newspapers had made a partisan disclosure of the Hoare-Laval plan and the London press followed with critical and at times violently hostile comment. In snowball fashion indignation mounted against the offer of a premium on aggression and two damaging debates in the House of Commons showed clearly how opinion was moving. Sir Samuel Hoare, against his doctor's orders, returned posthaste from Switzerland on December 16. After two days of feverish consultations it became clear that the British nation would have none of the so-called peace plan and on December 8 Hoare resigned,* ten days after he had initiated the ill-fated agreement in Paris. The whole project was now dead and it only remained to give it formal burial. The Emperor, still pathetically placing his reliance on the League, formally rejected it on December 19, while on the previous day the Council of the League, while thanking the British and French delegates for their communication, politely put it on the shelf. It is idle to speculate on the course which events would have taken, if the Hoare-Laval plan had been regarded in Britain as an acceptable solution, but there is evidence that, although it fell short of his original demands, Mussolini would have accepted it as a basis of negotiation. On December 18 the Grand Council met and that same evening Guariglia on Mussolini's instructions drafted the following statement for publication in the newspapers of December 19:

> The Grand Council, meeting in the evening of December 18 to examine the appeal addressed to the Duce by the governments of France and England, expresses its sincere appreciation of the friendly spirit inspiring the communication made by the two governments with the object of finding a solution to the Italo-Ethiopian conflict. It notes the explicit declarations of the British and French governments defining these proposals. It decides to consider the verbal proposals as a possible basis of negotiation, leaving it to the government to formulate the necessary reserves designed to safeguard the rights of the nation.[11]

Mussolini subsequently told the French ambassador in Rome that on December 18 he had signed a document recommending to the Senate the decision endorsed by the Grand Council.

During the night, however, news reached Mussolini of Hoare's

---

* When Hoare resigned Mussolini instructed Grandi to ascertain at once who the successor would be. Italy's relations were not such as to permit a direct inquiry and Grandi was at a loss. In the evening an Italian radio program to which he was listening was interrupted to announce Eden's appointment. Grandi immediately telephoned Mussolini at the Villa Torlonia. "I have just been informed [which was true]," he said, "that Eden is to be Foreign Secretary." "I congratulate you," was Mussolini's reply, "on having secured this early intelligence."

resignation and he at once suspended publication of the statement. On the following morning he instruction the Italian delegation at Geneva to thank Laval for the efforts he had made, but to explain that the Italian government must now suspend judgment until the situation could be clarified. Thus the last chance was lost of maintaining a united front against German aggression. The only alternative open to the Western powers was to rely on the League and collective security, a policy which demanded the imposition of effective sanctions on Italy regardless of the consequences. In the event Britain and France fell between two stools, opening the door, as Hitler had foreseen, to the conquest of Austria and to the subsequent acts of force which led fatefully to the Second World War.

The collapse of the Hoare-Laval plan was received in Berlin with a sigh of relief. When the Polish ambassador saw Hitler shortly after the public announcement of the plan, he found him greatly excited,[12] and his attitude was reflected in the German press, which denounced the "plot against the League of Nations." But a few days later Hoare's resignation and the British repudiation of the proposals created a new and favorable situation for Germany. Mussolini was now definitely separated from the Western powers, the prestige of the League was shaken, France and Britain were at loggerheads, the world had been treated to a damaging display of irresolution by the democratic governments, and Hitler was encouraged to believe that he could embark on a policy of aggression without much risk.

From the wreck Laval salvaged something, the postponement of the proposal to impose oil sanctions. When on December 12 the Committee of Eighteen had met, he had secured the adjournment of the debate on oil sanctions on the ground that the Paris agreement was in course of submission to Italy, Abyssinia, and the Council of the League. Thus the steam was taken out of the initiative and it was never possible subsequently to revive it with any prospect of success, for British public opinion while resolved in an outburst of indignation to bring Hoare to his fall, was not prepared to draw the logical conclusion and to insist on policies which might involve the country in a war with Italy. Moreover as time passed Italy was able to lay in stocks of oil and it gradually became clear that, in view of the speed of the Italian advance, the end of the war would come before oil sanctions could exercise any effective influence on the military operations.

IX

The way was now clear for Mussolini. Provided he could secure a quick victory in Abyssinia, he no longer had anything to fear from Britain or the League. Marshal Badoglio, spurred by a stream of imperatives from Rome, lost no time in poising his forces for the offensive. The first advance was launched on January 12, 1936, and a brilliant campaign followed which, in the space of four months, brought about the flight of the Emperor and the capture of Addis Ababa on May 5. The King was only reflecting the views of the nation when he recognized the part which his Prime Minister had played by the immediate award of the Grand Cross of the Order of Savoy, the highest Italian military decoration. He had been offered the title of Prince, but had refused it.

On May 9, 1936, Mussolini, from the balcony of the Palazzo Venezia, proclaimed to a delirious crowd the annexation of Abyssinia and the assumption by the King of Italy of the title of Emperor of Abyssinia. It was the moment of his life in which he savored his greatest triumph. He had avenged Adowa and wiped out the Italians' sense of inferiority. He had conceived the enterprise and launched it against the advice of his experts. He had personally supervised every move and seen to it that sufficient troops and material were made available to the commander-in-chief. He had accurately assessed the strength and resolution of the forces arrayed against him at Geneva and on the battlefield. With fewer hesitations than those which attended other crises in his life he had deliberately run great risks. As Winston Churchill put it:

> To cast an army of nearly a quarter million men, embodying the flower of Italian manhood, upon a barren shore two thousand miles from home, against the goodwill of the whole world and without command of the sea, and then in this position embark on what may well be a series of campaigns against a people and in regions which no conqueror in four thousand years ever thought it worth while to subdue, is to give hostages to fortune unparalleled in all history.[13]

Finally, Mussolini had by his drive and will power overridden the hesitations of his military commanders, and delivered to his people a complete victory in the shortest possible space of time.

As he stood upon the balcony surveying the swaying crowds and hearing the rhythmic cry of "Duce, Duce," he knew that he was celebrating the triumph of one man. He knew also that, possibly for the first time, he was enjoying the unqualified admiration and support of the whole Italian nation. What he did not realize was that he was living his last day of glory and that henceforth his star would begin to set.

X

He was soon faced by the aftermath of the Abyssinian war and the many problems which it created. In March, 1936, Hitler had taken advantage of the breach in the Stresa front to hazard the occupation of the Rhineland and from that moment the threat to Austrian independence became acute. In Paris elections had, in May, 1936, thrown up a Popular Front government under Léon Blum, with whom Italy would find it hard to do business. In Britain resentment was still simmering and was likely to frustrate any attempt the government might make to place relations with Italy on a better footing. Yet Mussolini was still anxious to keep his hands free to commit himself to neither side and with his customary opportunism to extract as occasion arose what advantage he could from the European conflict. When, a year later, Mussolini spoke in Berlin, he declared that the Axis had been born in 1936. This was only true inasmuch as he himself coined the word in 1936. In fact Italo-German relations were fluid and Mussolini was still watching with dislike and apprehension the growing giant in the north. Almost his first act after the Abyssinian war was to seek to repair his bridges with Britain.

On April 23, 1936, Mussolini issued instructions that press attacks on Britain were to cease. He followed this move by a veritable bombardment of Britain with conciliatory messages. Thus on April 29, 1936, Grandi, on instructions from Rome, assured King Edward VIII that Italy desired a complete resumption of the old political collaboration between the two countries. On May 4 Grandi told

Eden that Mussolini wished to reconstitute the Stresa front as soon as possible; and on May 26 Grandi came back to the Foreign Office to express Mussolini's wish for collaboration on a Locarno basis. He added significantly that there was no question of any closer relationship between Italy and Germany.

In Rome Mussolini was holding similar language to the British and French ambassadors; and indeed to the latter he gave the impression that he was more favorably disposed to Britain than to France. In an interview given to *The Daily Telegraph* on May 28, he said: "Not only is an Anglo-Italian rapprochement desirable, but it is necessary, and for my part I will do everything which lies within my power to bring it about."

In making these protestations Mussolini may have been moved by the fear that a rearmed Britain would seek revenge for Abyssinia,[14] but he was also anxious not to be forced into too close an association with Germany. When in the spring of 1936 Prince Starhemberg visited Rome, Mussolini spoke to him of Germany's increasing power and showed that he was uneasily aware of the advantage which Hitler was drawing from Italy's conflict with the Western Powers. So far as Austria was concerned, the situation was manifestly deteriorating. On May 12, 1936, Prince Starhemberg, in order to appease the Germans, was forced to resign; and two months later the Austrian Chancellor, Schuschnigg, signed a *modus vivendi* with Germany. Schuschnigg had given Mussolini previous notice of his intention to perform this further act of appeasement; and Mussolini, while repeating the formal assurance that nothing would ever alter Italy's determination to defend Austrian independence, had signified approval. He had no alternative. The Stresa front had been broken, Germany's power had increased, and Italy had neither the resources nor the will to act alone in halting Hitler. The obvious course was to incline once more towards the West.

Nevertheless, as Mussolini well knew, there were formidable obstacles to a resumption of friendly relations, particularly with Britain, where in some quarters there was no disposition to forget and forgive, while on the Italian side national pride demanded an early end to sanctions and what was more difficult, early recognition of Italy's Ethiopian empire. More important, the overwhelming military victories in Africa had aroused in Mussolini a sense of exaltation which made him increasingly difficult to deal with. Ciano was probably reflecting his master's views when on June 12, 1936, he told the British ambassador that Italy was now the military equal of any power in Europe.

The Duce was no longer disposed to listen to counsels of prudence or indeed to accept advice from any quarter. A species of palace government now ruled Italy. The press was brought under even tighter control and received from the Ministry of Culture and Propaganda the most detailed instructions as to the handling of news. Nothing was too insignificant to escape its attention, as the following example will show:

June 28, 1935: "No publication of photographs of Carnera * on the ground."
April 27, 1936: "Resume the campaign against flies."
June 18, 1936: "In regard to the death of Gorky no article, no comment, no biographical tendency. Publish the fact without observations."
December 26, 1936: "No notice ever to be taken of Einstein." [15]

The influence of the monarchy, which in the past had played its part, was now lost to Italy. The King and Queen by their support of the Abyssinian war had so identified themselves with the Fascist system as to deprive the throne of any power to intervene in the conduct of affairs. Mussolini, without any restraining hand, basking in his immense personal prestige and drunk with adulation, felt that nothing was beyond him. He had tasted blood in Africa and was itching to grasp the first opportunity of displaying his strength to his countrymen and to the world. At this crucial moment, on June 9, 1936, he appointed Galeazzo Ciano to be Minister for Foreign Affairs. It was a fateful decision.

In all the circumstances it would have been difficult enough for Mussolini to find any basis for Anglo-Italian collaboration, let alone the easy relationship, which existed during Grandi's tenure of office. But an event occurred which finally wrecked any chance of an accommodation with the Western powers. The inconsequent frivolity with which Mussolini darted off on a new course illustrated the instability of his foreign policy. It also illustrated his lack of judg-

* Carnera was the Italian heavyweight boxing champion.

ment and his propensity to garner the easy fruits of an ephemeral success without much regard for the ultimate consequences. His reason told him not to place himself in Hitler's power, but he could not resist the temptation to reach for the crown of another military victory. In consequence, encouraged by Hitler, he embarked on an adventure which estranged him from the Western powers, still further exhausted his country's military and financial resources, and drove him step by step into that closer association with Germany against which his instinct rebelled.

BOOK III

Decline

CHAPTER FOURTEEN

The Spanish War and German Entanglement

1936–1939

I

ON July 18, 1936, General Franco from Morocco staged a military revolt against the Spanish Republican government and civil war broke out. As usual, personal predilections played their part in influencing Mussolini's conduct. He disliked democratic governments, but he had learned to live with the old, established democracies in Britain and France. In Spain, however, the situation was very different. There the democracy was of very recent growth, and the Spaniards had ventured to alter their system at a time when he had publicly declared that democracies were on the way out. It was something of an affront.

In consequence Mussolini was temperamentally disposed to eye with favor the establishment of a totalitarian government in Spain. There was the further consideration that such a development would increase his power in the Mediterranean and correspondingly diminish the influence of France. As early as February, 1934, Spanish representatives of the Right had approached Mussolini and there had been a meeting in the Palazzo Venezia at which it had been agreed in principle to furnish arms and money to a right-wing revolutionary movement.[1] At this stage Mussolini was not concerned with the danger of communism in Spain, for he was still on tolerably good terms with the Soviet government.

The months of 1934 passed without any revolutionary outbreak in Spain, and in 1935 Mussolini was too preoccupied with Abyssinia to give much thought to the matter. But when in 1936 the war in Africa was over and Franco's revolution began, he was in a mood to entertain an appeal for help. It was not long in coming. Franco at once requested twelve aircraft and Mussolini after a little hesitation agreed to send them on condition that their activities were confined to escorting the troop transports of the invading force.

At the Palazzo Chigi neither Mussolini nor Ciano thought fit to consult their professional advisers or to heed the advice of the King, who was opposed to the adventure. They seem to have been moved by the fear that the Republican government would soon collapse before Franco's onslaught and that, if Italy was to draw credit from the affair, no time was to be lost. On July 29, 1936, two Italian aircraft made a forced landing in French Morocco and the fact was made known to the world. Thereafter prudence was discarded and the extent of Italian aid progressively increased. The restrictions on the use of the aircraft were soon removed and a volunteer infantry force, ill prepared and without adequate arms or training, was rushed to Spain. Like a man who allows a finger to be drawn into a machine, Mussolini found himself dragged into a massive intervention in a long, costly, and profitless struggle, which was eventually to rob him of all liberty of movement.

Hitler showed himself a better judge of the situation. He welcomed the Spanish revolt, not on any sentimental or ideological ground, but simply because it promised to further his own plans. His policy was to give Franco a modicum of help, enough to garner credit for himself and to ensure that the Republicans did not win, but not enough to bring the war to a speedy end. His aim was to prolong the civil war in the hope that Spain would become the focus of trouble, that attention would be drawn away from his machinations in central Europe, and that Italy would gradually become embroiled with the Western powers and so gravitate towards Germany.

Hitler achieved his purposes, for at the moment when the withdrawal of sanctions threatened to bring about an improvement of Western relations with Italy, the disputes arising from the Spanish war began once more to fan the embers of dissension. In December, 1936, the German ambassador in Rome reported hopefully:

> The role played by the Spanish conflict as regards Italy's relations with France and England could be similar to that of the Abyssinian conflict. . . . The struggle for dominant political influence in Spain lays bare the natural opposition between Italy and France; at the same time the position of Italy as a power in the western Mediterranean comes into competition with that of Britain. All the more clearly will Italy recognize the advisability of confronting the Western powers shoulder to shoulder with Germany.[2]

Nearly a year later, on November 5, 1937, while Mussolini was becoming hopelessly bogged down in Spain, Hitler was cheerfully telling his generals that "a hundred per cent victory for Franco was not desirable from the German point of view. Rather we are interested in a continuance of the war and in keeping up the tension in the Mediterranean."[3]

It was in accordance with this policy that German aid to Franco was limited to an air force unit, the so-called Condor Legion, and to the supply of weapons with technicians who used the Spanish battlefields as a profitable proving ground. Mussolini, on the other hand, who desperately desired an early victory, was remorselessly driven to raising his stakes until Italy was on the point of exhaustion. By the year 1937 he had despatched to Spain some seventy thousand troops as well as large quantities of aircraft, arms, and equipment. It was a cruel burden on a country which had just emerged from an African campaign; and the prolongation of the war was a bitter disappointment. But it never occurred to Mussolini that he was merely playing the part of Hitler's pawn.

During the two years which followed the outbreak of the Spanish Civil War Mussolini was involved in four different, but inextricably intertwined, diplomatic affairs. These were the effort in London, Paris, and Rome to draw a line under the Abyssinian adventure; the negotiations flowing from foreign intervention in Spain; the gradual eruption of German violence towards Austria; and finally Hitler's design to forge an Italo-German alliance. From none of these affairs did Mussolini or the Western powers emerge with much distinction. In every case the man who drew profit from each transaction was Hitler. He knew what he wanted and where he was going, while Britain and France found it impossible to make up their minds whether or not to take the steps required to reach an accommodation with Italy; and Mussolini in a similar uncertainty allowed himself to be pulled towards the European war for which he knew that his country was not ready.

In the midst of these urgent and fateful preoccupations he was in every sense diverted by a love affair which lasted for the rest of his life. In the autumn of 1936 he resumed and regularized his liaison with Clara Petacci, who was now separated from her husband and was living with her family in a flat in the Via Spallanzani, overlooking the gardens of the Villa Torlonia. He telephoned to her every day and eventually installed her in his private apartment in the Palazzo Venezia. There she arrived at about three o'clock every afternoon and waited patiently for the appearance of her lord. He may have found refreshment in the company of this ardent, submissive young woman, but he admitted to his biographer Ivon di Begnac that Italian public opinion would not approve and that he was running a political risk.[4] From now on he seems to be stumbling towards his destiny, only making intermittent efforts to retrace his steps.

II

The liquidation of the Abyssinian war, even if it had left no residue of rancor, was not an easy matter. The first step was taken on July 4, 1936, when the Assembly of the League of Nations made the formal decision to lift the sanctions imposed on Italy. It was generally agreed at Geneva that no useful purpose would be served by prolonging the shameful farce, but the problem of the recognition of the new Italian Empire, on which Mussolini set particular store, presented greater difficulty. Abyssinia was still, in theory, a member of the League and the fallen Emperor was stalking its corridors. So, in September, 1936, when the Assembly met and Abyssinian delegates presented themselves, it was decided to admit them. Only Austria, Hungary, Albania, and Ecuador voted against the motion. The outcome of the debate might have been less unfavorable to Italy, but for the events which were concurrently taking place in Spain.

There most of the leading countries in Europe were becoming involved on one side or another. Germany and Italy supported Franco, while Soviet Russia and France were supplying arms and equipment to the Republican government. Russia was obviously concerned to prevent the establishment of another Fascist government, while the Popular Front in France was on ideological grounds equally opposed to a Franco victory. M. Léon Blum told the Chamber of Deputies that in the eyes of France there was only one legal government in Spain.[5] On the other hand France was not prepared to push intervention to the point of provoking a European war.

The British government sat uneasily on the fence. Ostensibly it favored the legally elected government, but there were elements in the Conservative government and in the country which viewed with distrust the intervention of Russia and the emergence in Spain of an extreme left-wing, or even Communist, government. Moreover there was in Britain, as in France, a desire to do everything possible to localize the war.

The upshot of these conflicting aims was the establishment of the Nonintervention Committee, which held its first meeting in London on September 9, 1936. Among the twenty-six nations represented on the Committee were Russia, Italy, Germany, France, and Britain. Hitler was prepared to join because he did not judge it expedient at that moment to play the role of a disturber of the peace and because his purpose was to prolong the civil war. Mussolini joined because he was convinced that with the aid which Italy had already furnished, Franco must win within two or three months, unless massive help were given from some outside source to the Republicans. But he had no intention of tying his own hands. The German chargé d'affaires in Rome reported that the Italian government was obviously reserving freedom of action for all contingencies, and equally obviously had no intention of abiding by the declaration of nonintervention.[6]

So it proved. As the war dragged on, the scale of Italian intervention gradually grew and with it the rift between Italy and the Western powers. The original militia volunteers were gradually reinforced by infantry formations drawn from the army, the arrival of which in Spain could not be concealed. The Spanish Republican government protested at Geneva, but in the Nonintervention Committee the French and British representatives, exacerbated though they were, affected to regard the reports as exaggerated because they feared that they might otherwise be called upon to take military action against Italy and Germany.

Mussolini, encouraged by this display of pusillanimity in London, abetted by Ciano, and driven by the need to score an early victory in Spain, became more and more reckless. In June, 1937, he began to give publicity to the Italian effort. Reports of the embarkation of Italian troops at Naples, casualty lists, and news of military successes appeared in the press. Worse still, Italian submarines made attacks on British and other shipping. The Ciano diaries reflect the frivolous satisfaction with which the Italian government viewed these dangerous acts of piracy.[7]

For once London and Paris reacted sharply. Under the auspices of Britain and France a naval conference, at which Italy and Germany refused to take part, was held at Nyon in Switzerland on September 9, 1937. In a short time agreement was reached to establish an international naval patrol, which was authorized to attack piratical submarines and aircraft. Mussolini was annoyed, but since he was fundamentally as reluctant as France or Britain to be drawn into a general war, he had no alternative but to suspend piracy. It was an example of the efficacy of stout measures against the dictators.

The constant wrangles in the Nonintervention Committee, the indignation aroused by Italian piracy, and the evident bad faith of Mussolini throughout these transactions all combined to prevent any amelioration of Anglo-Italian relations. Hitler, who had been watching these developments with malicious satisfaction, was quick to seize the opportunity to draw Mussolini closer to Germany; and the British government in turn, alarmed by this development, began to make ill-timed advances to Italy. It might appear that in this situation Mussolini was favorably poised between two powerful contestants for his favor. In reality, with the arrogance of a man who cannot see the dangers threatening him, he became in 1937 virtually committed to Germany. Admiration for Hitler's ruthlessness and fear of German power confirmed him in this course; and in Ciano, who was later to be so anti-German, he found a ready agent to hand. The two Italians only realized when it was too late that Hitler had with diabolical skill played upon their vanity, their vacillations, and their fears to entice them step by step into the net of a formal Italo-German alliance.

II

Hitler's first move had been made on June 29, 1936, when the German ambassador brought Ciano a message, offering to recognize the Empire whenever the Duce should consider the time ripe; and on July 25 the German government suppressed the legation in Addis Ababa.[8] It was a gesture to which Mussolini was particularly susceptible and it paved the way for further advances. On September 23 Hans Frank, Hitler's Minister of Justice, who was on a visit to Rome, was received by Mussolini. Frank, who was one of the more presentable Nazis and who had doubtless been selected on that ground, was well briefed.

He brought with him a cordial invitation for Mussolini to visit Germany and suggested that Ciano should in the meantime go to Berlin to prepare the way. He assured the Duce that the Fuehrer's interest in Spain was purely ideological, since he regarded the Mediterranean as an Italian sea. This led naturally to a survey of the Bolshevik conspiracy and the need for close cooperation between Italy and Germany in the common battle against communism. Frank was sufficiently tactful not to press for any concrete decision, and indeed Mussolini undertook no commitment. But the seed had been well sown, and in October Ciano duly left for Berlin.[9]

After a preliminary conversation with Neurath and a round of entertainment in the capital, Ciano traveled to Berchtesgaden for his first interview with the Fuehrer, on October 24, 1936. Hitler, who was an excellent actor and could deploy a certain gawky charm, set out to captivate his guest. He referred to Mussolini as the leading statesman in the world, to whom none might even remotely compare himself. In a long monologue he spoke flatteringly of Fascist maturity and of Italy's rise to the stature of a Great Power. He declared that he, as Fuehrer of National Socialist Germany, could only reach an understanding with another Fuehrer, who by the most fortunate accident was a Latin. The Germans and the Latins complemented one another; and Italy, which in the past had been deprived of military glory through the incompetence of her princes and governments, was now destined to be the companion in arms of the greatest military power in modern history.[10] With these honeyed words he held out the alluring prospect of an Italo-German coalition against bolshevism and against the Western democracies.

Ciano, in order to make quite certain that Hitler should entertain no lingering aspirations towards an understanding with Britain, communicated to Hitler two documents, purloined from the British embassy in Rome: a circular from Eden on the German danger and a despatch in which the British ambassador in Berlin described the German government as a government of dangerous adventurers. Hitler reacted in a satisfactorily violent manner. "According to the English there are two countries in the world today which are led by adventurers: Germany and Italy. But England too was led by adventurers, when she built her empire. Today it is governed merely by incompetents." For the rest, Hitler assured Ciano that there was no need to fear England. German and Italian rearmament was proceeding much more rapidly than it could in Great Britain. In three years Germany would be ready, in four years more than ready.[11]

During this long conversation there was no mention of Austria, but when it was over Hitler received the members of Ciano's suite in the sitting room of the Berghof, with its enormous window overlooking the Alpine valley leading to Salzburg. Slowly he led the Italian party to this point of vantage, while uniformed servants arrived with telescopes for the guests. At the end of the valley it was possible to discern the town of Salzburg, and Hitler pointed out the buildings of the archiepiscopal palace. The rasping and implacable voice continued: "And so I am compelled to look at my German motherland, Salzburg, through a telescope."[12]

Ciano left the Berghof dazzled by the warmth of his reception and by the prospects so amiably held out before him by the Fuehrer. A secret protocol had been prepared by the Italian and German Foreign Offices before the visit and it had been signed by Neurath and Ciano in Berlin. It provided for cooperation over a wide field:

a new Locarno pact, the League of Nations, Spain, Austria, the Danubian states, Abyssinia, and the common recognition of the Japanese puppet state of Manchukuo.

The text of the protocol was not published, although it was referred to in a speech delivered by Mussolini in the Piazza del Duomo in Milan on November 1, 1936:

> The Berlin conversations have resulted in an understanding between our two countries over certain problems which had been particularly acute. But these understandings, which have been sanctioned in fitting and duly signed agreements, this Berlin-Rome line is not a diaphragm but rather an axis, around which can revolve all those European states with a will to collaboration and peace.

These words were music in the ears of Hitler, who felt that he could now safely turn his attention to his dark designs in central Europe. For Mussolini it was the beginning of servitude, for he had forged and put onto his leg the first shackle. It was a mistake not to have taken note of the ominous words: "In three years Germany will be ready," but he was a man who looked only to the present and paid little heed to the future. For the moment the association of Italy on ostensibly equal terms with powerful Germany ministered to his vanity and to his instinctive dislike of liberal-democratic systems of government. It did not occur to him that he would soon be relegated to the role of junior partner, if the word "partner" can be at all accurately applied to the part which he was to play.

IV

Hitler's success was followed very soon by a fumbling effort on the part of the British government to repair the damage which had been done in Berlin. It was a fumbling effort because in contradistinction to Hitler, who with his singleness of purpose knew exactly what he wanted, the British cabinet could only bring a divided mind to the problem. Some members, headed by Chamberlain, were resolved to appease Mussolini, almost at any cost, while others believed that a limit must be set to the complaisance with which Italy was treated. The outcome was a policy which lacked conviction and which in all the circumstances was bound to fail. It would have been wiser and more dignified to allow Mussolini to follow his own course, without giving him the comforting illusion that, if Hitler proved too exacting a partner, he could always at the moment of his choice switch back to an arrangement with the West. It was an illusion which he cherished for some years, when he vacillated between sudden decisions to stand shoulder to shoulder with Hitler and the prudent impulse to evade, and eventually escape from, the clutches of the German alliance.

Towards the end of 1936 Anglo-Italian conversations were opened and resulted in the signature of the so-called Gentlemen's Agreement on January 2, 1937. It was largely designed to assuage British fears of an Italian foothold in Spain and it recognized freedom of entry into and transit through the Mediterranean. Both governments disclaimed "any desire to modify, or as far as they were concerned to see modified, the *status quo* as regards national sovereignty in the Mediterranean." In the House of Commons, on January 19, 1937, Eden explained that:

> This declaration is neither a treaty nor a pact, but it marks, we hope, and believe, the end of a chapter of strained relations. It marks no departure in policy by His Majesty's government. It neither calls for nor embodies any concession from us, neither of course does it involve any modification of any of our existing friendships. But that this declaration has been of service to an appeasement in the Mediterranean there can be no manner of doubt.

The cold terms of this guarded statement reflected the divided counsels in the cabinet and were not calculated to evoke a warm response in Rome, where Mussolini was still awaiting the British recognition of his empire. The invitation to the Negus to attend the Coronation of King George VI added to his displeasure.

On May 17, 1937, Mr. Neville Chamberlain became Prime Minister. He was obsessed by a sense of mission to conjure away the threat of a European war and was convinced that his best course was to turn his back on the past. There must be a new deal in foreign policy, and his first task must be to make friendly overtures to the two dictators. On July 19, 1937, Eden made a speech reflecting the importance which the British government attached to a better understanding with Italy. In July and August there was an exchange of correspondence in which Chamberlain assured Mussolini of his friendly sentiments, and Mussolini replied by reciprocating these and reaffirming that he had no territorial aspirations in Spain. Chamberlain's move had come at a favorable moment, for Mussolini, despite the appearance of resolution given by his reckless conduct in Spain, was not at all happy at his growing isolation and dependence on Germany. That summer an American visitor, Mr. Lamont, had found Mussolini in a confused state of mind and completely perplexed as to the course he should take in international affairs. He had even asked Mr. Lamont what he thought he should do.[13]

When Mussolini wrote to Mr. Chamberlain that he had no territorial aspirations in Spain, he may have meant it, but three months later he was to give Ribbentrop a different picture of his designs. In the course of a conversation in Rome on November 6, 1936, he said:

> It is a fact that we have established at Palma a naval and an air base; we keep ships permanently stationed there and have three airfields. We intend to remain in that situation as long as possible. In any case Franco must come to understand that, even after our eventual evacuation, Majorca must remain an Italian base in the event of war with France; that is to say, we intend to keep all the installations ready there so as to be able in a few hours to bring the island of Majorca into effective play as one of our Mediterranean bases.[14]

If Mussolini had been taxed with insincerity, he probably would have replied that his letter to Chamberlain truthfully reflected his intentions, whereas his conversation with Ribbentrop was designed to impress his Axis partner. He was always concerned to give the Germans the impression that he did not fall behind them in ruthlessness and nerve.

However this may be, Chamberlain accepted Mussolini's assurances at their face value, and the British ambassador in Rome was authorized to tell the Italian government that Britain was ready to open conversations in September with a view to concluding a treaty of friendship. At this juncture Chamberlain's moves were halted by the mutual ill-feeling arising from Italian piracy in the Mediterranean. There was not much logic in combining submarine attacks on British shipping with dalliance with Chamberlain. But Mussolini was not a logical thinker, he was doubtful about his attitude to

Britain, and he was in any event determined to use every means which lay to hand in order to bring the Spanish war to an early end.

V

While on the British side the approach to Italy was only half-hearted, it was equally true that Mussolini did not do much to ease Chamberlain's path; and in 1937 he made two expeditions which were not calculated to endear him to British hearts. In March he paid a twelve-day visit to Libya, in the course of which he opened the new strategic highway along the coast through Tobruk to the Egyptian frontier. It was a road with which many thousands of British soldiers were to make a close acquaintance four years later. In Tripoli at a much publicized ceremony he was presented with the sword of Islam and spoke of Fascist Italy's intention to "show her sympathy towards Islam and towards Moslems throughout the world." In view of Italy's modest position in the Mohammedan world Mussolini's pretension to be the protector of Islam seemed ridiculous, but it was none the less displeasing to the powers with Arab dependencies. The resentment aroused by this theatrical gesture was increased by the subsequent establishment of a wireless station at Bari, which transmitted anti-British broadcasts in Arabia.

The second journey which was calculated to alarm and ill dispose the West was Mussolini's triumphal progress through Germany in September, 1937. Hitler, who boasted openly that he knew how to corrupt any man, had accurately assessed the character of his Italian colleague and no trouble or expense was spared to accord to Mussolini the honors due to a Head of State, which he was not, and to display the resources of Nazi Germany in all their might.

On September 23 Mussolini left Rome accompanied by Ciano; Alfieri, the Minister of Press and Propaganda; Starace, the party secretary; and about a hundred officials, journalists, and subordinate staff. At Munich he was met by Hitler, who remained at his side for the duration of the five-day visit and fussed incessantly about the welfare of his guest. Precautions were to be taken lest he catch cold and the unfortunate head of protocol was bombarded with questions as to the flowers placed in the Duce's room; whether a certain picture, which was to have been taken away, had in fact been removed; whether the curtains were too dark; whether the train stops were sufficiently long to afford a proper night's rest; whether the supply of veal was satisfactory; and so on.

At Munich, after seeing the Brown House and Hitler's apartment, Mussolini attended a lunch with the *Alte Kämpfer* of the Nazi party and the Munich program ended with a parade of the Labor Service, the Hitler Youth, and Party formations. For hours the Königsplatz resounded to the stamp of marching German boots and Mussolini's suite noted, some with dismay, the look of admiration which he bestowed from the reviewing stand on this manifestation of German power. It was the first occasion on which he had seen anything of the kind, and it left an indelible impression on his mind.

That evening a special train took the dictators from the seat of party headquarters to impressive military maneuvers in Mecklenburg. Here there was an unrehearsed interlude when an over-zealous conducting officer loudly announced, before he could be silenced, in the presence of the British military mission, but not of Mussolini, that it was the intention of his commander, before launching his attack, to drench the enemy with gas.[15]

On the following day there was a visit to Krupp's works at Essen, where Mussolini saw the resources of the giant enterprise fully extended in the production of artillery, tanks, and every conceivable engine of war. Once more Mussolini was visibly impressed by the discipline of the workers and the scale of the operation, which he seemed to attribute to the genius and the personal intervention of his host.

The first three days in Germany represented a useful indoctrination, but the culmination of the visit was the welcome accorded to the Duce in the capital. Never before in German history had Berlin witnessed such a display. A special railway station had been prepared on the outskirts of the city, near the Olympic Stadium. There the two dictators arrived in their separate special trains from Essen; and elaborate measures had been taken with true German thoroughness to ensure that for the last few miles of the journey the two trains should run side by side, thus signifying the parallelism of the two revolutions.

Just before the arrival, which was punctual to the second, Hitler's train shot forward, so as to enable him to be on the platform to greet his guest. The state drive was equally well stage managed. From the station at the Heerstrasse the broad straight road leading into the center of the city had been decorated with thousands of German and Italian flags. Four rows of white illuminated pylons, bearing golden eagles and Nazi and Fascist emblems, had been erected in Unter der Linden, while the houses in this street and in the Wilhelmstrasse had been literally covered with giant German and Italian flags, which hung alternately down the façade. It was estimated that 55,000 square yards of bunting had been woven for the decoration of these two streets.

In this setting vast crowds were assembled to greet the Duce. Nearly a million spectators were brought in by special trains from the provinces, and work in Berlin ceased at 4 P.M. on the day of the arrival so as to enable the local population to be present. The following day was declared a public holiday. The most stringent security precautions, in which Hitler showed a personal interest, were taken to protect the Duce. S. S. formations from every part of Germany, some 60,000 strong, lined the route, in places three or four deep. The S. A. was conspicuously absent, but the police were reinforced by detachments from Saxony; while plain clothes men in large numbers moved among the crowd and in their rear police dogs lurked and armed launches patrolled the distant Spree. As the procession passed, the crowd dutifully gave Mussolini the prescribed roar of acclamation. The Duce, standing up in the car with Hitler on his left, was obviously delighted with his reception. To one spectator who had known him in his heyday he was no longer the youthful, spry, and ardent figure who had captivated the visitor to Rome. He had coarsened. He was fat and bald, and presented the visage of a dissolute Roman emperor of the decadence.

On the following day, in order to comply with Mussolini's wish to meet the masses, a mammoth demonstration had been organized on the Maifeld, adjoining the Olympic Stadium. From four o'clock in the morning a crowd of some eight hundred thousand men and women, carrying their rations for the day, had been conveyed to the city's outskirts and marshaled before the official tribune. Some twelve hours after the initiation of the gigantic trek Hitler and Mussolini made their appearance. After an introduction by Hitler,

Mussolini addressed the crowd, in German, in a speech which he had carefully prepared. Unfortunately, in the excitement generated by the grandiose spectacle afforded by the countless thousands in his audience, he began to speak faster and faster so that his words became almost completely unintelligible; and the ample gestures and facial contortions, which normally accompanied his oratory, seemed comic rather than illuminating.

He declared that his visit was not a normal diplomatic episode, but a manifestation of solidarity between two revolutions sharing a common purpose. While professing his desire for peace, he uttered a warning that it would be fruitless to attempt to divide Italy and Germany. It was part of Fascist ethics to be loyal to one's friends and to march with them to the end. Henceforth one hundred and fifteen million souls would be indissolubly united and the gigantic manifestation on the Maifeld would bear witness of this truth to the world.

In the midst of Mussolini's speech the darkening skies suddenly opened and torrential rain fell on the Maifeld. Soon the script in front of the Duce was no more than a sodden rag, and the downpour on the microphone and loudspeakers still further distorted an already incomprehensible oration. Nevertheless he managed to struggle to the end, when the patient crowds, soaked to the skin, gallantly attempted to drown the noise of the rainstorm with the sound of the German athems. On the following day after a military review Mussolini left Berlin.

While nothing could have exceeded the outward magnificence of the reception given to Mussolini, the German people were not impressed by their new ally. The cynical Berliners, although they had enjoyed the show, were heard to mutter that since the Allies had carried Italy in the First World War, it seemed only fair that Germany should now assume the burden. Officials spoke in equally contemptuous terms and an illuminating example of the attitude of the German army was given by the behavior of the officer in charge of the British military mission to the German maneuvers. The mission, which had been taken to see the demonstration on the Maifeld, found itself unable in the confusion caused by the cloudburst to reach its cars. But the conducting officer had no hesitation in quickly bundling his British charges into the transport allotted to the Italian military mission, leaving Marshal Badoglio with his suite stranded in the rain.

Nevertheless the purpose of the display so lavishly organized in Germany was not to persuade the German people of the value of the Italian alliance, but rather to impress the Duce. Here Hitler was completely successful, though there was little time for any serious conversation and the immediate political gains were meager. They were summarized in a circular to German diplomatic missions abroad:

> An early end of the Spanish Civil War and the reconstruction of Spain is urgently desired by both parties; the interests and potentialities of Italy will have due preference here. Quite generally Italy will not be impeded by Germany in the Mediterranean, whereas on the other hand, the special German interests in Austria will not be impaired by Italy. However, it is entirely correct that, as Mussolini has publicly stated, the Rome-Berlin axis is not directed against other countries and that therefore nothing was discussed or agreed upon which Austria could consider dangerous or infringing upon her independence.[16]

While Mussolini had avoided any specific Austrian commitment, he was manifestly intoxicated by the spectacle of so much power and fascinated by the man who was plainly resolved to wield it. Here was an ally whom it would be profitable to join and whom it would be dangerous to cross. From that moment Mussolini fell under Hitler's influence. It was an influence which sometimes waned under stress, but which could always be revived when the two men met.

V

Mussolini returned to Rome determined to imbue the Italian people with the virtues of toughness and discipline, which he had so much admired in Germany. As an earnest of his intentions he announced that the goose step would be adopted by the armed forces under the title of the *"passo romano."* The King objected, less because he thought the innovation ridiculous, but because he distrusted the Germans. Mussolini was, however, not in a mood to defer to his sovereign: "It is not my fault if the King is half size. Naturally he won't be able to do the parade step without making himself ridiculous. . . . But a physical defect in a sovereign is not a good reason for stunting, as he has done, the army of a great nation. People say the goose step is Prussian. Nonsense. The goose is a Roman animal—it saved the Capitol." [17]

Such manifestations of Germanophilic ecstasy in Rome smoothed Hitler's path and it was not long before he was able to gather the fruits of his newly won ascendancy. Within three weeks Ribbentrop, then still ambassador in London, appeared in Rome with a proposal that Italy should now join the Anti-Comintern Pact, which had been concluded the previous year between Germany and Japan. Mussolini at once agreed and Ribbentrop returned to Rome on November 6, 1937, for the formal ceremony, which converted the bilateral agreement into a tripartite pact. As a sop to Mussolini's vanity there was a supplementary statement to the effect that Italy had been considered "an original signatory" together with Germany and Japan. It was a further step towards bringing a still slightly hesitant Mussolini within the fold of a German alliance. On December 11, 1937, Italy withdrew from the League of Nations and within twenty-four hours the official news agency in Berlin announced that a return of Germany to the League would never again be considered.

Thus by the end of 1937 in the Anglo-German competition for Mussolini's favors the resolute Fuehrer emerged as the clear victor over his vacillating adversary. Whereas the half-hearted British advances had made little impression on the Duce, Hitler had registered tangible and important successes. The ground had been sufficiently prepared to enable him to embark on new adventures. No opposition, he declared to his generals on November 5, 1937, to the removal of Czechoslovakia or Austria was expected on the part of Italy.

Since 1936 Hitler had made use of the providential diversion created by the Spanish Civil War to undermine the position of the Austrian government and to condition Mussolini to acceptance of the *Anschluss.* The Austro-German agreement of 1936 in theory recognized Austria's independence, but in practice gave Germany the opportunity to interfere in Austrian internal affairs on the ground that the agreement was not being observed. In September, 1936, Papen was recommending to his government "continued patient, psychological treatment with slowly intensified pressure, aimed at changing the regime." In 1937 Nazi activity was increased. Constant bombing incidents and massive Nazi demonstrations shook the government's authority. German agents were insinuated into positions in the ministries, the police, and even into Schuschnigg's organization, the Patriotic Front. Soon nobody knew who could be trusted and the demoralization of the whole Austrian system grew apace. By the end of 1937 it was being fatalistically said in Vienna, even by the most resolute opponents of nazism, that the Austrians themselves were incapable of effective resistance to German penetration. The only hope, and it was a tenuous hope, lay in foreign intervention.

Meanwhile a succession of Nazi envoys, taking advantage of the improvements in Italo-German relations, had been visiting Rome. In the course of their conversations and of similar conversations on German soil the question of Austria was always raised; and while the German spokesmen never revealed to Mussolini the brutal truth in regard to Hitler's intentions, they led him skillfully to tacit and passive acceptance of the inevitable. It was clear to him in his periods of pro-German enthusiasm that he could not thwart Hitler in Austria and at the same time enjoy the friendship of the world's mightiest power. So he continued to declare for Austrian independence, but hoped pathetically and against all the evidence that something might still turn up to rescue him in his dilemma.

On January 23, 1937, Goering and Mussolini had a long conversation, in the course of which Austria was discussed. Goering complained that the Austrian government was not fulfilling the agreement of July 11, 1936, and in particular was persecuting the pro-German element; and he asked Mussolini to advise Schuschnigg to be more conciliatory. In the course of his remarks he let fall the observation that the *Anschluss* must come and would come. Mussolini allowed this statement to pass, probably because he did not understand it, but when it came to be translated by Dr. Paul Schmidt, he energetically shook his head. Nevertheless it was Schmidt's impression that he was only making a gesture and that he was in fact resigned to the inevitable.[18]

Mussolini undertook to make representations to the Austrian government in the sense desired by Goering. In doing so he must have been aware that he was taking the first step down a slippery slope, but the Spanish war had ranged him so far on Germany's side and the conversation with Goering had been so friendly that it was difficult to refuse. To reward him for his complaisance, Goering gave him an assurance that in Austria there would be no surprises.[19]

By November 6, 1937, the day of the signature of the tripartite Anti-Comintern Pact, Mussolini had almost reached the bottom of his slippery slope. In the course of a long conversation Ribbentrop, in his usual hectoring manner, pointed out that in the grand policy of Rome and Berlin, Austria now represented an element of secondary importance and that it would be necessary at a certain moment to settle it. This time Mussolini did not even shake his head. On the contrary, he seemed only too anxious to fall in with German wishes. After all, he said, Austria was a German country and he was tired of mounting guard over Austrian independence. Italian interest was not so lively as it had been, partly because their eyes were now directed on their imperial destiny and partly because of Austria's cold and negative attitude towards Italy. The best course would be to allow events to take their course and to abide by the existing Italo-German understanding that nothing would be done without previous exchange of information.[20] He could not have given a clearer intimation that, so far as Italy was concerned, Germany was free to go ahead; and Ribbentrop, convinced that he had personally made a diplomatic conquest of the first order returned hotfoot to Berlin to impart the glad tidings to the Fuehrer.

VII

Events now moved fast. The German pressure on Austria was increased and on February 4 Papen was dismissed from his post as German minister at Vienna, while Ribbentrop was appointed to succeed Neurath as Foreign Minister. It was an ominous signal that the period of intrigue was over and was to be followed by a policy of force. On February 12 Schuschnigg was enticed to Berchtesgaden, ostensibly to discuss the better implementation of the agreement of July 1936. There he was bullied by Hitler and a group of German generals into signing a seven-point agreement which virtually spelled the end of Austrian independence. In the course of this somber interview Hitler, who showed himself at his worst, remarked that no one in the world would interfere with his designs: "With Mussolini I am in the clear; my ties of friendship are very close. England? England will not lift a finger for Austria. . . . And France? Two years ago when we marched into the Rhineland with a handful of battalions, I took a grave risk. If France had marched then, we should have been compelled to withdraw. . . . But now it is too late for France." [21]

As was to have been expected, the Austrian Chancellor returned to Vienna to find his position considerably shaken. Emboldened by this development, the local Nazis began to run amok; and they were encouraged to do so by the stream of demands, far exceeding the bounds of the Berchtesgaden agreement, which began to pour from Berlin on to the Austrian government. By the end of February Schuschnigg was at the end of his tether and decided to embark on the desperate expedient of a plebiscite. He communicated this decision to Mussolini through the Austrian military attaché and received a message in reply to the effect that, if Austria stood firm, German pressure would diminish; and in the meantime he would be well advised to abandon the idea of the plebiscite. Schuschnigg was, however, not to be deterred and on March 9, 1938, he publicly announced that a plebiscite on the independence of Austria would be held on Sunday, March 13.

Hitler decided to strike before an unwelcome vote could be registered. Nevertheless, despite all the favorable reports from Rome, he was still not quite sure what Mussolini's attitude would be. He was possibly uneasy at his own failure to abide by the undertaking to do nothing in Austria without prior consultation. So at the last moment he made an effort to appease his ally. At about midday on Friday, March 11, 1938, only twelve hours before the invasion of Austria, Prince Philip of Hesse * telephoned to the Italian embassy in Berlin that he was charged with bearing an important and urgent letter to Mussolini. It was a long, disingenuous, and propitiatory message:

* Married to Princess Mafalda, daughter of the King of Italy. He was arrested on September 8, 1943, and placed in the Flossenbürg concentration camp.

> In a fateful hour I turn to you, Excellency, to inform you of a decision, which the circumstances have seemed to demand and which cannot now be changed. . . . In recent months I have seen with growing anxiety how, little by little, between Austria and Czechoslovakia a relationship has been growing up which we could with difficulty allow in peacetime, but which, in the case of war being imposed on Germany, would cause the gravest menace to the safety of the Reich. In the course of this rapprochement the Austrian state has begun to barricade and fortify all the frontiers. The purpose of this can only be (1) to bring about the Restoration at a given moment, (2) to operate even against Germany, if necessary, the weight of a mass of at least twenty million people.

Hitler went on to say that in this situation he was determined to restore law and order in his homeland, but he begged Mussolini to consider this step only as one of national self-defense and he addressed to his new ally a personal appeal:

> In a critical hour for Italy I proved to you the steadfastness of my sympathy. Do not doubt that in the future there will be no change in this respect. Whatever the consequences of the coming events may be, I have drawn a definite boundary between Germany and France and now draw one just as definite between Italy and us. It is the Brenner. This decision will never be questioned or changed.[22]

As the German tanks rolled towards the Austrian frontier, Hitler waited with growing impatience to the reply from Rome. He had sufficient respect for Mussolini's intelligence to know that he would not be taken in by such a farrago of nonsense and the question was whether in the interests of the Axis he would condone the German breach of faith. It was a critical moment, for Germany had overstepped her strength and was not in a position to meet strong, concerted measures by Britain, France, and Italy.

At 10:25 P.M. Prince Philip of Hesse telephoned to the Reich Chancellery: "The Duce accepted the whole thing in a very friendly manner. He sends you his regards." A flood of relief swept over Hitler. It was a moment he never forgot and his expressions of gratitude bordered on hysteria:

> Hitler: "Then please tell Mussolini I will never forget him for this."
> Hesse: "Yes."
> Hitler: "Never, never, never, whatever happens. . . . As soon as the

Austrian affair is settled, I shall be ready to go with him, through thick and thin, no matter what happens."

Hesse: "Yes, my Fuehrer."

Hitler: "Listen, I shall make any agreement—I am no longer in fear of the terrible position which would have existed militarily in case we had got into a conflict. You may tell him that I thank him ever so much; Never, never shall I forget."

Hesse: "Yes, my Fuehrer."

Hitler: "I will never forget, whatever may happen. If he should need any help or be in any danger, he can be convinced that I shall stick to him whatever may happen, even if the whole world were against him." [23]

Hitler need not have worried, for Mussolini had already written off Austria, since he was realist enough to know that he could not have his German cake and eat it. It was, of course, a tiresome episode and Hitler might have gone through the form of consulting him, but short of reconstituting the Stresa front, which he was not prepared to do, there was no alternative but to put the best possible face on it. To Ciano he remarked that one ambiguity had been removed from the map of Europe; and in the Grand Council replying to Balbo's criticism of Germany, he said: "If we had eight million Italians on our frontiers, we should do just the same. At least I should." [24]

Although Mussolini elected to bask in Hitler's effusive expressions of thanks and to pretend that he had not suffered a painful reverse, his pride was wounded and he was disturbed by the outbreak of irridentist propaganda in South Tyrol, which naturally followed the annexation of Austria. A month later he was using language to Ciano very similar to that of 1935: "These Germans will compel me to swallow the bitterest pill of my life. I mean the French pill. . . . If the Germans behave well and are obedient Italian subjects, I shall be able to encourage their culture and their language. If, on the other hand, they hope to move the frontier post one single yard, they must learn that it can't be done without the most bitter war, in which I shall combine the whole world into a coalition against Germanism. And we shall crush Germany for at least two centuries." [25]

The Italian people, unaware of the successive steps by which Mussolini had sold the Austrian pass, were shocked by the extent of Hitler's victory. Not since the murder of Matteotti in 1924 had any event so damaged Mussolini's popularity and prestige, for it was plain for all to see that the roles of the Fascist dictators had been reversed and that the Duce was now the junior partner. A flood of anonymous letters, protesting against the *Anschluss*, poured into the Palazzo Venezia and the Palazzo Chigi.[26]

Mussolini was obliged to conceal his misgivings and to make in the Chamber an apology, which was lame and unconvincing:

> To those more or less official circles beyond the Alps, which ask why we did not intervene to "save" the independence of Austria, we reply that we had not assumed any obligation of the kind, either direct or indirect, written or verbal.
>
> The Austrians, I feel bound to state, have always had the comprehensible modesty not to ask for the use of force to defend the independence of Austria, for we should have answered that an independence which needed the help of foreign troops against the majority of the nation no longer deserves the name.

He went on to say that it was better to accept than to oppose the inevitable and to assure his audience that they had nothing to fear from Germany. The Axis had proved itself, and "the two nations, whose unification has been parallel in time and method, united as they are by an analogous conception of the politics of living, can march forward together to give our tormented continent a new equilibrium." [27]

Another fatal step had been taken towards German captivity. In boys' adventure stories the reader despairingly beholds the hero committing one monstrous folly after another, to place himself eventually in the power of the villain. So it was with Mussolini; only there was to be no last-minute escape.

VIII

Nevertheless Mussolini, always tormented by doubts and indecisions, was at the beginning of 1938 not so satisfied with his own position as he affected to be; and he decided without much conviction to pick up the broken threads of the Anglo-Italian negotiations, an enterprise in which he found Chamberlain to be a ready partner. His attitude to Britain was fluid, to say the least, for on December

21, 1937, he was discussing with Ciano the possibility of a surprise attack on the British fleet as soon as the Spanish war was over.[28] Yet at the beginning of February he sent Chamberlain a friendly message through the widow of Austen Chamberlain, and on February 16, 1938, Ciano was pressing Grandi to expedite the conclusion of an Anglo-Italian agreement:

> To-morrow, should the *Anschluss* be an accomplished fact, should Greater Germany by then press on our frontiers with the weight of its whole seventy million, then it would become increasingly difficult for us to reach an agreement or even talk with the English, since it would be impossible to prevent the whole world interpreting our policy of rapprochement with London as a journey to Canossa under German pressure.[29]

The Anglo-Italian negotiations were no more real in 1938 than they had been in 1937. In Britain opinion continued to be divided. While Chamberlain enjoyed the support of the majority of the cabinet and had been relieved by Eden's resignation on February 20, 1938, of a dissident colleague, he was inhibited by the residue of anti-Italian sentiment in the country and by the feeling that so long as Italy continued to intervene in Spain there could be no basis of agreement. In Rome Mussolini, still under the impression of his visit to Germany, had in his heart decided to commit himself to Germany. It may seem strange that in these circumstances he should have professed to attach importance to an immediate agreement with Britain. But, despite his bellicose gestures, he was afraid of a war for which Italy was not prepared, he distrusted the Germans, and he wished to enjoy the illusion that he still possessed some liberty of movement. Hence he instructed Ciano to press on with the negotiations, while at times disclaiming much interest in the outcome. It would be difficult to imagine less favorable auspices for an accord.

Nevertheless the negotiations, begun in February, proceeded laboriously over the period of the *Anschluss* and culminated after many difficulties in the signature on April 16, 1938, in Rome of an Anglo-Italian agreement. It was a comprehensive series of documents, which covered all the points at which Anglo-Italian interests touched. The agreement of January 2, 1937, on freedom in the Mediterranean was confirmed; and annexes contained agreements regarding the Middle East, the exchange of military information, and the renunciation by both parties of hostile propaganda.

The most important provision deferred the entry into force of the agreement until the undertakings of Britain to recognize the empire in Abyssinia and of Italy to withdraw the volunteers from Spain had been fulfilled. In the event, seven months were to elapse before these conditions were met and by that time the agreement had lost any significance it may ever have possessed. Mussolini's comment on the entry into force of the agreement in November revealed his state of mind: "All this is very important, but it does not alter our policy. In Europe the Axis remains fundamental." [30]

This observation reflected the true state of his mind, which at the time was almost wholly absorbed with the preparations for Hitler's state visit to Rome in the following month. It was a matter to which he gave his personal attention, for he was as anxious now to impress Hitler as Hitler had been to impress him.

IX

Meanwhile a minor domestic disagreement had clouded Mussolini's relations with the King. It was a wholly unnecessary dispute and would never have arisen if Mussolini's judgment had not been blinded by his victory in Abyssinia, by the exaltation of his visit to Germany, and by his wild itch to match the Fuehrer in power and strength. On March 30, 1938, Mussolini made a speech in the Chamber in praise of the armed forces, his object being to dissipate the deplorable impression created by his apology for the German occupation of Austria. The scene was carefully set. The Chamber was packed and the deputies awaiting the Duce's arrival spent the time singing "*Giovinezza*" and other Fascist songs. When Mussolini did appear, he was received with an organized ovation, which continued throughout his speech. As soon as he had finished Costanzo Ciano rose to introduce, without any previous notice, a law creating the new rank of "Marshal of the Empire." This new rank was simultaneously conferred, under the law, on the King-Emperor and on Mussolini. The law was passed without debate by acclamation; and it was rushed to the Senate where it was approved, again without debate, the very same day.

The King was as angry as he could be. He had not been warned of a measure to which he attached importance and which he believed to have been deliberately sprung on him as a surprise. As Supreme Commander of the armed forces, he resented being put on the same military footing as Mussolini; and he wondered if the law were not designed to open the way to Fascist control of the army. Finally he regarded the law as outside the competence of the Chamber and therefore unconstitutional. Accordingly when Mussolini called at the Quirinal to obtain the royal signature to the law, he met a frigid reception. "This law," the King said testily, "is another mortal blow at my sovereign prerogatives. I could have given you any other rank as an expression of my admiration, but to put me on the same footing as yourself places me in an impossible situation, because it is another flagrant violation of the constitution of this kingdom." The King went on to say that the Chamber was not competent to take such initiatives and that but for the imminent international crisis, he would have abdicated rather than submit to such an affront.[31] Having made his protest, the King reluctantly allowed the matter to drop. But resentment did not altogether die away either in the Quirinal or the Palazzo Venezia. To Ciano, Mussolini said: "I am fed up. I do the work and he does the signing.[32] The episode illustrated Mussolini's inconstancy. He was not prepared to strike down the monarchy, and indeed his policy was to sustain it. But he could not bring himself to refrain from an act of self-glorification which was quite unnecessary and was calculated to impair his relations with the monarch.

X

Very soon, however, all eyes were directed on the Fuehrer's visit which had been most carefully prepared in the Reich and in Italy. Walter Schellenberg of Reinhardt Heydrich's secret police department flew ahead to prepare the security measures. His men drove repeatedly along the route which Hitler was to take and searched all the houses overlooking it. Over six thousand suspects were arrested by the Italians, and in order to supplement these and other precautions, Schellenberg placed eighty of his best detectives at key points while others were assigned to banquets and functions. In addition five hundred of the best linguists in Heydrich's service were selected and despatched to Italy as tourists. They were organized in cells of three on the Russian model and their mission was to report any suspicious circumstance and to collect intelligence on the state of public opinion. It was the first case of significant Nazi infiltration into Italy.[33]

On the Italian side the preparatory work lay in the hands of Ciano, under close supervision by the Duce. Along the railway line houses were freshly painted and appropriate slogans displayed. In Rome a new station was built near Saint Paul's Outside the Walls so as to permit a triumphal drive into the city. Starace, who was a good stage manager, was in charge of the various parades and of the welcoming crowds. The streets were festooned with banners, Fascist symbols, and Nazi swastikas.

In the midst of these bustling preparations for the great day Ciano was obliged to address himself to the problem of rising tension between Germany and Italy. The Anglo-Italian agreement had not been well received in Berlin and moreover there was growing agitation in the Italian Tyrol. The Austrian Nazis were convinced that Hitler intended to liberate their brethren and found confirmation in Hitler's Reichstag speech of March 18, when he referred to three and a half million Germans who were not yet free. The Italian chargé d'affaires in Berlin twice made representations to Goering on the subject.[34] On the first occasion Goering disclaimed any knowledge of or responsibility for propaganda or incidents in South Tyrol. On the second occasion he gave an assurance that Hitler would abide by his undertaking to respect the Brenner frontier and he let fall a suggestion that a transfer of population might be expedient. In any event it was a problem which could usefully be discussed by the two leaders when they met in Italy. With this meager result Ciano had to be content.

Hitler arrived at the San Paulo station on May 3, 1938, accompanied by an enormous suite, including Ribbentrop, Goebbels, Hess, Himmler, Frank, Sepp Dietrich, General Keitel, and a troop of uniformed journalists. On the platform to greet him were the King and the Duce. From the dictator's point of view it was regrettable, but according to the rules of protocol inevitable, that Hitler should be the King's guest in Rome. Hitler, who had been led to believe that Mussolini ruled Italy, was surprised and disgusted to find, on descending from his train, that he was received by the King surrounded by his generals, while Mussolini stood respectfully at a distance. Outside the station Mussolini disappeared and Hitler, in reply to an inquiry, was told that the Duce would not be taking part in the procession to the Quirinal. The King, who disliked the Germans in general and the Nazis in particular, was also ill humored and his annoyance was increased when Hitler entered the royal horse-drawn carriage and seated himself first. The crowds along the route showed little enthusiasm, and as the doors of the Quirinal closed behind them, the German party found themselves in novel and uncongenial surroundings. There were no longer any Blackshirts to be seen, only gentlemen of the Court with their frigid, impeccable manners, wearing the Cipher of the House of Savoy in their buttonholes. Himmler was heard to mutter: "This place smells of catacombs."

Hitler spent six nights in the Quirinal and disliked every minute. He resented the coolness displayed to him by the sovereign, and continued to complain that it was the Duce who should fill the first place in the state. It was an opinion which he and his suite did not hesitate to voice to Mussolini himself. Moreover Hitler criticized the palace as being melancholy, uncomfortable, and having the character of an ancient museum. He objected to being conveyed in a carriage, and was heard to inquire petulantly when the House of Savoy would hear of the invention of the automobile. But he was particularly unfavorably impressed by the Court, which he described as reactionary and anti-Fascist.

His recollection of the Quirinal never ceased to rankle. Years afterwards he said to his familiars at table: "It is always painful to me, when I meet the Duce in Italy, to see him relegated to the rear rank, whenever any of the Court entourage are about. The joy is always taken out of the reception he arranges for me by the fact that I am compelled to submit to contact with the arrogant idlers of the aristocracy." [35] The unreliability of the Italian King and his Court was always the excuse he proffered, when in subsequent years he was reproached for not keeping his ally informed of his intentions.

The King, for his part, found Hitler repugnant and said to all and sundry that he was a psychophysiological degenerate who took stimulants and narcotics. In order to support this thesis, he spread the story that Hitler had turned the palace upside down by demanding the attendance of a chambermaid in the middle of the night, on the ground that he could not sleep unless he actually saw a woman remake his bed. It proved impossible to find a maid in the palace at that late hour and one was eventually produced from a neighboring hotel. The attitude of the King and Hitler's complaints about the monarchy and the Court had the effect of still further impairing the relations between the Quirinal and the Palazzo Venezia. They remained correct, but something of the old warmth had gone. In his irritation Mussolini spoke of the monarchy as a brake on the Fascist regime.[36]

Another discordant note was struck by the Vatican, whose newspaper, *L'Osservatore Romano,* demonstratively made no reference to the visit. Pope Pius XI marked his displeasure by closing the Vatican museums and retiring to his country residence at Castel Gandolfo. There on May 3 at his customary audience to the newly wed he voiced his regret that the banner of another cross, which was not the cross of Christ, should that day have been raised in Rome.[37]

In other respects the visit was a success and achieved its aim, which was to impress Hitler and to offer a range of entertainment exceeding anything which had been provided in Berlin. There were parades and the new *passo romano* was displayed. Cynics said that while Germany had given Italy the *passo romano,* Italy would give Germany the *passo Brennero.* Peasants danced in the Villa Borghese in their various provincial costumes and visits were paid to historic monuments.

It was all Mediterranean rather than Wagnerian, but Hitler was enchanted by all he saw and his enthusiasm for Rome, together with his desire to flatter the Duce, found expression in his speech at the Palazzo Venezia banquet on May 7. He spoke of the "Roman state" created by Mussolini and promised that the frontier of the Alps, raised by nature between the two peoples, should forever be inviolable. Their friendship would assure a prosperous future to both Rome and Germany. The identification of the new Italian state with Rome was of course delightful to Mussolini, and few were disposed pedantically to question the definition of the frontier as the Alps rather than the Brenner.

On May 5 the day was spent in Naples, where an imposing naval review had been prepared. The highlights of the performance was the spectacle of a fleet of submarines submerging and then surfacing simultaneously at every point of the compass on the glassy sea. Hitler, who possessed virtually no navy but prided himself on his knowledge of naval matters, both envied and admired the sleek lines of battleships and cruisers arrayed for his inspection; and he returned to Germany with the conviction that, whatever might be the state of the army, Italy had something of value to contribute at sea.

On May 9 Hitler left Rome for Florence and Mussolini accompanied him. Liberated from the custody of the King, Hitler became quite genial and was loud in praise of the city and its surroundings. The enthusiastic reception given him by the inhabitants, in contrast to the behavior of the crowds in Rome, contributed to his good humor, and when in the evening Hitler boarded his train to return to Germany, there was an affectionate farewell. As they shook hands, the Duce said: "Henceforth no force will be able to separate us," and the Fuehrer's eyes filled with tears.[38]

XI

During all the junketing during the six days of the visit there was once again little opportunity for political conversations. The problem of Czechoslovakia was broached in a very general way and Hitler gathered that Mussolini was content to leave him a free hand. His assessment of Mussolini's attitude was perfectly correct, for it is plain from Mussolini's domestic conversations at the time [39] that he attached no importance to Czechoslovakia. It was characteristic of his ephemeral outlook that he was unable to apprehend the danger of a global conflict or to foresee that within four months Hitler's designs would place Italy in a precarious and embarrassing position.

Ribbentrop was annoyed that so little time had been left free for political discussions, for he had come to Rome armed with a memorandum tabling the topics of conversation: Austria; Axis solidarity; bolshevism as the common enemy; cooperation with likeminded states and relations with France and England; Spain; Japan and the Far East. There was also another matter to raise, which he hoped would represent a personal diplomatic triumph: a proposal for a German-Italian military alliance.[40] It seems that the decision to offer this alliance was probably taken at the end of March, 1938, in the first flush of Hitler's joyful reaction to Mussolini's acceptance of the *Anschluss.*

There was no opportunity to ventilate the topics listed in the memorandum, and the interpreter Schmidt noted that Mussolini and Ciano were at pains to evade any serious discussion.[41] But at Naples Ribbentrop was able to hand to Ciano a draft treaty of alliance together with a secret protocol laying down the terms of Italo-German military cooperation. Ciano was noncommittal, but that evening he noted in his diary: "The Duce intends to make the pact. We shall make it, because he has a thousand and one reasons for not trusting the Western democracies. I myself thought it better to postpone it, in order not to create difficulties for Chamberlain just before the meeting of the League Council, at which he is to launch the recognition of the Empire." [42]

On the tactical issue Mussolini was at one with his Foreign Minister, and when the parties had returned to Rome Ciano handed to Ribbentrop a counterdraft, correctly described by the German State Secretary as resembling rather a peace treaty with an enemy than a pact of loyalty with a friend. It was a plain rejection of the German proposal and Ribbentrop, who saw his dream of a resounding success fading, was extremely angry. There was a brief and violent altercation in which Ribbentrop pressed his point with his usual tactless persistence, but Ciano was not to be moved and merely retorted with a smile: "The solidarity between our regimes has been so clearly manifested during the last few days as to render a formal treaty of alliance superfluous." [43] Hitler was wise enough not to press the matter further, for he knew that events and a little patience on his part would bring Mussolini into his net. Thereafter the German ambassador in Rome was instructed to drop the matter for the time being and Ribbentrop, mastering his mortification, told the Italian ambassador that it was not of decisive importance.

Hitler could afford to wait; and his judgment was justified, for almost exactly a year later he brought the Italians to the table in Berlin to sign a treaty which was substantially the same document that Ciano had rejected in Rome.

If Ribbentrop was smarting under a sense of personal failure, Hitler had every reason to be satisfied with the impact which his visit had made on Mussolini's mind. He felt that any coolness which might have arisen from his Austrian adventure had been dissipated, and that he could now safely embark on new enterprises without bothering to repair the crockery which the *Anschluss* had broken in Rome. As always, personal contact with the Fuehrer had aroused in the Duce confidence in the future of the Axis and the desire to exhibit himself as another man of blood and iron. It was only in association with Hitler that he could realize his own ambitions and enjoy the opportunity of displaying the ruthless nerve which he so much admired in the German dictator and of which he knew uneasily that he was at times painfully deficient. This was made clear in a speech which Mussolini delivered at Genoa on May 14, 1938, only five days after Hitler's departure.

It was an aggressive speech which caused some consternation in London, where Chamberlain was relying on the Anglo-Italian agreement to reduce tension and to bring about an improvement in Franco-Italian relations. Mussolini spoke of the collaboration between the two revolutionary powers as destined to make its imprint on the century; and after an angry and gratuitous reference to sanctions he declared that there could be no return to Stresa, since much water had flowed under the bridges between 1934 and 1938. After a perfunctory reference to the Anglo-Italian agreement, he made a violent attack on France. There was, he continued, little prospect of a Franco-Italian accord, because in Spain the two countries were on the opposite sides of the barricades. It might be that the democratic powers were not preparing an ideological war, but if they were to do so, the totalitarian powers would make common cause and march together to the end. Not many months were to elaspe before events proved how little these brave words reflected his policy and intentions. Nevertheless they fulfilled their immediate purpose, which was to impress Hitler. How irresponsible and capricious Mussolini was in Genoa, is revealed by Ciano:

It is a very strong, anti-French speech. The crowd hisses France, laughs ironically at the agreement with London. I have compared the speech as he delivered it with the draft he had prepared. . . . The draft was entirely different—the attack on France was lacking, he was more polite towards the English, and less definite in promises towards Berlin. He was carried away by the crowd. Good. Now we must await reactions from Paris and London. Then we shall see what the tone of the negotiations can be, if indeed they are going to continue.[44]

XII

Another manifestation of Axis solidarity which followed Hitler's visit was the extension to Italy of Germany's racial theories. Until then the Jewish community had presented so social problem, for there were only forty-seven thousand * of them in Italy, as against over six hundred thousand in Germany, and they made relatively little impact on the national life. It has been said that Mussolini nourished ill-informed resentment against the Jews and derived his prejudice from the pages of Nietzsche. In the matter of anti-Semitism Mussolini was as inconsistent in his utterances as in any other matter; and it would be easy to find throughout his career evidence of hostility towards the Jews. For example, as a young man he had written that "the inversion of moral values has been the principal work of the Jewish people";[45] and as late as September, 1937, he was aping the Germans in speaking of America as "a country of Jews, the forces which disintegrate civilization. . . . The races playing an important role will be the Italians, the Germans, the Russians, and the Japanese. Other countries will be destroyed by the acid of Jewish corrosion."[46]

On the other hand condemnations of anti-Semitism abound in Mussolini's speeches, writings, and conversations; and he was in 1933 and 1934 particularly severe on Germany's racial policies. On March 30, 1933, he instructed the Italian ambassador in Berlin to make personal representations to Hitler about the German racial policy. There was an unpleasant interview and Hitler refused to yield an inch,[47] but Mussolini continued to do what he could to

* The census of 1938 showed 47,252 Jews, of whom only 37,203 professed the Jewish faith.

secure an amelioration of the situation of the Jews in Germany.

In his personal relationships he showed no sign of racial bias. The two women who exercised the greatest influence on him were Jewesses, Angelica Balabanoff and Margherita Sarfatti; a Jew, Aldo Finzi, held office in his first cabinet and another, Guido Jung, was his Minister of Finance for many years. There were also Jews in the Fascist parliament and in many leading positions in the state and party. At least five Jews were present at the foundation of the Fascist party in Milan on March 23, 1919. All Mussolini's surviving collaborators who have been questioned on this point are unanimous in declaring categorically that he entertained no racial prejudice whatsoever against the Jews. He was, however, opposed to Italian, as against international, Zionism on the ground that it was calculated to provoke a conflict of loyalties.

The explanation of Mussolini's change of heart must be sought elsewhere. He was above all an opportunist; and until 1935, when he was opposing Hitler's aspirations in Austria, expediency coincided with his inclinations, and he had every reason to maintain good relations with the West and to avoid friction with the Jews. At that time he was at pains to demonstrate that fascism with its Latin humanity was superior to Nazi barbarism.* The Abyssinian war, however, brought about a deterioration of the relations between fascism and international Jewry, which condemned the Italian aggression; Italy moved towards Germany and began, moreover, to court the Arabs. After Mussolini's visit to Berlin and Hitler's visit to Rome it was no longer a case of emphasizing the difference in the character of the two regimes, but of demonstrating their identity.

The decision to introduce racial measures into Italy in 1938 was entirely Mussolini's and there is no evidence that he was at any time under pressure from Hitler.[48] His decision is to be attributed principally to his recognition of Italy's changed alignment in Europe. He became convinced that in order to cement the new alliance he must eliminate any difference in the policy of the two

* Speaking to Prince Starhemberg, he said: "Fascism is a regime which has its roots in the great cultural traditions of the Italian people. . . . National socialism on the other hand is savage barbarity." (Starhemberg, *op. cit.*, p. 170.)

countries. There were also the itch to emulate Hitler and the feeling that he owed it to his new ally to prove his own ruthlessness by a racial gesture, even if it were somewhat limited in scope. Other minor contributory factors were pressure from his own pro-German extremists and the belief that he must toughen the Italian people. He was always concerned to transform the Italians into a race of warriors; and it was characteristic of him that in this process he should have invoked principles and ideals which were the negation of any principle or ideal.

At the beginning of 1938 certain newspapers, particularly the extremist *Tevere,* embarked on a deliberate anti-Semitic campaign, but the first official warning shot was fired on February 16, when the *Informazione Diplomatica* published a statement [49] categorically denying that the Italian government entertained any intention of taking political, economic, or moral measures against the Jews. The sting was, however, in the tail of the document, which declared that the Fascist government reserved the right to watch the activities of recent Jewish immigrants and to ensure that the influence of the Jews in the national life was not out of proportion to their numbers.

In July, 1938, two months after the Fuehrer's visit, a number of scholars published under the auspices of the Ministry of Culture a manifesto, in the drafting of which Mussolini took a hand,[50] defining the Fascist position in relation to the racial problem. It was an absurd document couched in turgid, pseudoscientific language, and possessing a distinctly German flavor.[51] It declared that there was a pure Italian race, that it was time that the Italians declared themselves to be racists, that Jews did not belong to the Italian race, and that the purely European characteristics of the Italians should not be altered in any way. Starace and Farinacci were all enthusiasm for the new dogma, and a sumptuous anti-Semitic review was brought out, entitled *La Difesa della Razza.*

The manifesto was soon followed by concrete measures against the Jews. It is true that these fell far short of the action taken in Germany, but they constituted a clear violation of the undertaking given in February. On August 3 the Minister of Education prohibited the entry of foreign Jews into Italian schools. On September 1 a decree law, introduced by Mussolini himself, forbade foreign

Jews to be domiciled in Italy, Libya, or the Aegean islands. Those who had come from abroad after January 1, 1919, were to leave within six months, and those who had acquired Italian citizenship after that date were deprived of it. This was a cruel blow to the many refugees from Nazi persecution. On September 2 under another decree law Jews were removed from the teaching staffs in state schools and from all scientific literary or artistic bodies. On October 6 the Grand Council imposed further disabilities on the Jews.[52] No Italian would be allowed to marry a Jew; and Italian Jews were forbidden to join the Fascist party, own or direct enterprises employing more than a hundred persons, own more than 123 acres of land, or serve in the armed forces.

In contrast, however, to the German practice, Jews were defined as persons both of whose parents were of the Jewish race, or who were born of a Jewish father and a foreign mother, or who, although born of a mixed marriage, professed the Jewish religion. It was also laid down that a wide range of persons should be exempted from the provisions of the racial laws. These included the families of those who had fallen in war or had volunteered or had won the war cross, and the families of those who had joined the party in the early days or those who had fallen or suffered in the Fascist cause, or who had rendered special services to the state.*

Buffarini-Guidi was sent to San Rossore, the royal summer residence in Piedmont, to secure the King's assent; and he returned with his errand accomplished to Mussolini's satisfaction. But the King was unhappy about the business and subsequently remarked: "I do not understand how a great man like him can import these racial fashions from Berlin into Italy. Yet he must understand that if he falls into the German rut, he will range against himself the Church, the bourgeoisie, and the army high command."[53]

The Pope, however, was not as amenable as the King. Addressing students of the Propaganda Fide college, he emphasized that racism was foreign to the Italian tradition and that he regretted that Italy should have imitated Germany; and in a series of further

* The number of families that benefited from this provision was 3,502. (De Felice, *op. cit.*, p. 421.)

speeches at Castel Gandolfo he tartly denounced exaggerated nationalism. Mussolini reacted sharply. Ciano was instructed to warn the Nuncio that, if the Pope continued in this vein, a clash would be inevitable, since the Duce regarded the racial question as fundamental.[54] Father Tacchi Venturi was summoned to receive an ultimatum, and to Ciano, Mussolini said: "If the Pope continues to talk, I will tickle up the Italians and in less than no time I will turn them into anticlericals again." [55] As usual, Mussolini's words bore little relation to his deeds, and, as usual, the quarrel with the Vatican was tacitly allowed to drop.

The new laws came as a shock to public opinion. According to a party report from Turin, Catholic circles openly condemned the anti-Semitic policy of the government, and their reprobation in time provoked "a general feeling of solidarity with the Jews, which was manifested on every possible occasion." [56] In Milan Cardinal Schuster wrote a pastoral letter deprecating racism, while from Trieste the revulsion of the public caused the anti-Semitic Starace to advise the local federal secretary to apply the law with caution.[57]

Mussolini was quite aware that his policy would affront the Christian sense and the natural tolerance of the Italian people. He knew also that it was not a policy which could be defended on any moral or rational ground. Nevertheless he was profoundly irritated by the opposition of the public, and he was particularly sensitive to the charge that he was merely following the German lead. To a group of federal secretaries from North Africa he angrily declared: "To say that fascism has imitated anyone or anything is simply absurd.[58] It was, however, clear to everyone that he was in fact aping the Germans, and this circumstance made the policy even more unpopular than it would otherwise have been. All the resources of Fascist propaganda were deployed in vain to present the issue in a more favorable light, but Mussolini could only note with rage in his heart that he had failed to overcome the obduracy of his people.

XIII

Altogether Mussolini was in an abnormally excitable, irritable state in that summer of 1938. He knew that in the European race

Hitler was pulling away from him; and the effort to maintain an outward confidence and serenity was imposing a severe strain on his nervous system. He was becoming more and more exercised at the drawn-out Spanish war and he vented his spleen on Franco. He "used violent language about Franco for letting the victory slip when he already has it in his grasp." [59] Five days later Ciano records that: "The Duce is angrier than ever with Franco for his flabby conduct of the war. He is afraid there may be some very serious surprises. " 'Put on record in your book,' he said to me, 'that today, August 29, I prophesy the defeat of Franco. Either the man doesn't know how to make war or he doesn't want to. The Reds are fighters—Franco is not.' " [60] It was an observation which, as so often, reflected no credit on Mussolini's reputation as a soothsayer.

Mussolini's sense of frustration and irritation, which was described by some as incipient insanity, was also visited on the French and on the Italian bourgeoisie. At the end of May he had instructed the party to create a "wave of Francophobia to liberate the Italians from the last shackle of servitude, that of Paris." [61] In July he was raging against the enervated and defeatist Italian bourgeois class, which after the Anglo-Italian agreement was hoping for peace through an understanding with the Western democracies. Ciano noted that:

> Mussolini is very angry with this section of the bourgeoisie. . . . He talks of a third wave, to be set in motion in October, with the support above all of the masses, workers, and peasants. He intends to introduce the concentration camp, with more severe methods than those used in the present form of police detention. A first hint of the turn of the screw will be given by a bonfire of Jewish, Masonic, and pro-French literature. Jewish writers and journalists will be banned from all activity. . . . Henceforth the revolution must impinge on the habits of the Italians. They must learn to be less "sympathetic," in order to become hard, relentless, and hateful—in fact, masters.[62]

It was language which echoed the dogmas preached on the other side of the Alps in Nazi Germany.

The Germans, taking advantage of Mussolini's mood of nervous excitement, continued to keep up a gentle and continuous pressure. There was a succession of visits to Rome by Nazi notables, and on

June 19, 1938, Ribbentrop, in a conversation, in the course of which he dropped dark hints to the Italian Ambassador about German intentions in Czechoslovakia, renewed the offer of a military alliance. In order to make the proposition more attractive he assured the ambassador that in the event of a conflict arising from German action in Czechoslovakia the alliance would not be operative.[63] This time he was able to register a satisfactory degree of progress. The answer was no longer "No," but "Not yet." Ciano was instructed to telegraph the acceptance of a visit by Ribbentrop to Como, during which the matter would be "discussed in all seriousness." Meanwhile public opinion would have to be prepared and the Germans told that the alliance would be concluded as soon as it ceased to be unpopular.[64]

XIV

Within a very short time the relations between the Axis powers were to be put to the test with an urgency which very gradually absorbed all Mussolini's attention. Ever since the *Anschluss* Mussolini had been aware that the next victim on Hitler's list was likely to be Czechoslovakia, but he affected to believe that no Italian interest was involved and that in any event Hitler would find some means of gaining his ends without resort to war.

In May, 1938, there was a European flurry over Czech mobilization against Germany and the killing of two Sudeten Germans, but Mussolini opined that the situation was not so alarming as many people thought;[65] and on May 26 the German ambassador was informed that Italy was not interested in the fate of Prague. At the same time Mussolini, convinced that he would not be called upon to honor his pledge, boldly declared to Ciano that if war broke out, he would immediately enter the struggle on the side of the Germans.[66] His optimism was founded partly on his growing habit of wishful thinking and partly on the more solid basis of documents stolen from the British embassy, which indicated clearly that the British wanted peace almost at any price. Warnings from the Italian ambassador in Berlin that Hitler was bent on military action in Czechoslovakia were discounted as alarmist.

Nevertheless, as the weeks passed and evidence of German intentions accumulated, Rome became more and more uneasy; and the ambassador in Berlin was importuned to find out exactly what Hitler proposed to do. He was uniformly unsuccessful. Although a definitive plan was in the German files, neither Ribbentrop nor the State Secretary, Weizsäcker, gave the unfortunate Attolico the information he was soliciting. On August 3 Weizsäcker merely advised the ambassador to take his leave before the end of September, while a fortnight later Ribbentrop deliberately threw dust in his eyes. In reply to Attolico's questions, Ribbentrop said that if the Czechs provoked Germany again, Germany would march. This could be tomorrow, in six months, or perhaps in a year. Nevertheless the German government, if the situation deteriorated or as soon as the Fuehrer made his decision, would inform the Duce as soon as possible. On September 4 Ciano, in despair, instructed Attolico to demand from Hitler exactly how things stood, since he could not allow the Italian public to think that its rulers had again been taken by surprise, as in the case of the *Anschluss*. Still there was no answer from Berlin, and Mussolini was left in the humiliating position of having to make such deductions as he could from the Fuehrer's public statements. Ciano consoled himself by reflecting that the German attitude left Italy liberty of action in any eventuality.

The Nazi party congress took place at Nuremberg from September 6 to 12 and there at last in a flow of hysterical abuse of Beneš, Hitler revealed his sinister design. Within a few days German S. S. formations were operating across the Czech border and there was now no doubt in men's minds that Europe was standing on the brink of the abyss. But Mussolini continued to hope that the storm would blow over and on September 13 Ciano recorded: "Telegraphic reports from Prague about the ultimatum delivered to Beneš by Henlein after yesterday's incidents. I speak to the Duce. He agrees that the situation is very serious, but thinks that Beneš will end by accepting the ultimatum. 'Swallowing pills is what democracies are made for.' "[67]

In order to bring maximum pressure on Beneš, Mussolini decided to advertise his solidarity with Germany. On September 13 he drafted a statement for the *Informazione Diplomatica* in which he claimed that only a radical solution, on the basis of self-determination, could put an end to the Czech crisis. He followed this up on September 15 with an open letter to Lord Runciman, the British mediator at Prague, sustaining the German case and urging him to propose to Beneš a plebiscite not only for the Sudeten Germans, but for all nationalities who asked for it.

When news reached Mussolini that Chamberlain was flying to Germany, he became more than ever convinced that Hitler would prevail. To Anfuso he said: "As soon as Hitler sees that old man, he will know that he has won the battle. Chamberlain is not aware that to present himself to Hitler in the uniform of a bourgeois pacifist and British parliamentarian is the equivalent of giving a wild beast a taste of blood." He went on to say that Czechoslovakia was only a beginning. Not only would Hitler not stop, but he would insist on a total revenge for Versailles, person by person and nation by nation; and he concluded: "It is better that it should happen with us rather than against us." [68]

It was with this thought in mind that on September 18 Mussolini made a speech at Trieste in which he pledged his support to Germany and once more demanded a plebiscite. While he still professed to hope for peace, he told his audience that if it came to war, Italy knew where she would stand. From the Duce's propaganda campaign Hitler deduced, not unreasonably, that Italy was giving him a blank check; and any chance which Mussolini might have had of exercising a moderating influence was irretrievably lost. In September, 1938, Mussolini, as always, was something of a gambler.

He seems to have been strangely detached and almost like a man in a dream during the days in which the crisis deepened, until on September 27 Mr. Chamberlain's initiative was seen to have failed and Europe stood on the threshold of war. On September 25 he assured Prince Philip of Hesse that, should the conflict become general, Italy would place herself by the side of Germany immediately after the entry of England into the war.[69] Yet he did nothing, as if some inner voice told him that he would not have to redeem his pledge. Germany's military preparations were far advanced and on September 24 news had been received of general mobilization in Czechoslovakia. In England units of the fleet were being concentrated, and from France came news of military measures which fell little short of total military mobilization. The Rumanian Minister informed Ciano that his country was under strong pressure to allow the passage of Soviet troops.[70] On September 26 there were bad tidings from Spain, where Franco, in his exposed position, thought it prudent to announce his intention of opening negotiations with Britain and France in order to make a declaration of neutrality.[71] Throughout these hectic days, while the rest of Europe was in a turmoil, Mussolini maintained his Olympian calm. It was not until 11 P.M. on September 26 that he spoke to Ciano of ordering mobilization on the following day.[72] Even then, only the sketchiest measures were taken, and, had war then broken out, Italy would have been the one country concerned which had taken no effective precautionary measures whatsoever. In Paris the German military attaché was already complaining that the Italians were doing absolutely nothing to pin down French troops on their frontier, and that Mussolini seemed to be abandoning his ally in a crucial hour.[73] In Rome the German military attaché told his Yugoslav colleague, with whom he was on particularly friendly terms, that the German ambassador and his whole staff were convinced that Italy had no intention of siding with Germany in the event of a general war.[74]

Meanwhile Mussolini continued to hope that Hitler would obtain all he required by peaceful means without placing Italy in a dilemma. It may seem strange that a man who in 1934 and 1937 evinced alarm at Hitler's rise, should in 1938 have viewed with equanimity the aggrandizement of German territory and power. But he was now bewitched by a mirage and was in no mood to reflect on the consequences of his policy. It is impossible to say whether he would in fact have hurled himself recklessly into the fray, for at times he seemed to recoil from his own bluster; but, as it happened, the dice on this occasion ran kindly for him. At the eleventh hour, when, on the morning of September 28, it seemed certain that Hitler would open hostilities that afternoon,* Chamberlain came to the rescue with a request that Mussolini should intervene to save the peace.

---

* On September 27 Berlin warned Rome that "the day is tomorrow." Ciano, *Diary, op. cit.*, entry for September 27, 1938.

At 10 A.M. on September 28 the British ambassador telephoned to ask Ciano for an immediate interview. He recalled the guarantee given by Britain and France that the Sudetenland be transferred to Germany and urged that the Duce should intervene with Hitler. There was now no time to lose, and Ciano hurried to the Palazzo Venezia. Mussolini agreed at once, and at 11 A.M. telephoned to Attolico instructing him to inform the Fuehrer that, while in any event Italy would be at his side, the Duce recommended that the beginning of hostilities should be delayed for twenty-four hours pending further consideration.

The Chancellery was in a state of tumult that morning. In the passages and anterooms swarmed orderly officers, experts, party chiefs, generals, and State Secretaries, who had arrived with their ministers for consultation with the Fuehrer. There were no formal conferences, but Hitler moved from room to room, delivering to anyone who was prepared to listen a monologue embodying his appreciation of the situation.

Into this scene of disorder Attolico hurled himself, hatless and breathless, at about 11:30 A.M. To his dismay he found that Hitler was at that particular moment closeted with the French ambassador, who was attempting valiantly, but without much visible success, to persuade the Fuehrer that he could obtain all he required without going to war. But Attolico was not prepared to wait. An orderly officer was despatched into Hitler's room to announce that the Italian ambassador had come on an urgent mission. Hitler at once went out, but before he had crossed the threshold, the still breathless ambassador began to shout: "I have an urgent message for you from the Duce." He went on to explain that the British government had solicited Mussolini's mediation and he conveyed the message which he had been instructed to deliver. After a moment's hesitation Hitler replied: "Tell the Duce that I accept his proposal." Joyfully Attolico scuttled back to the embassy to telephone the happy outcome of his mission. Meanwhile Chamberlain, unaware of what had happened in Berlin, at 11:30 despatched a further message to Mussolini and Hitler: "I am ready to come to Berlin at once to discuss arrangements for transfer with you and representatives of the Czech government, together with representatives of France and Italy if you desire. . . . I cannot believe that you will take responsibility of starting a world war which may end civilization for the sake of a few days' delay in settling this long-standing problem."

The British ambassador in Rome communicated this message immediately to Ciano and once more Mussolini was on the telephone to Berlin in order to instruct Attolico to propose a four-power meeting, that is to say a conference, but without the Czech representative suggested by Chamberlain. At about 12:30 Sir Nevile Henderson was with Hitler, conveying Chamberlain's message, when once more Attolico intruded with his second communication from the Duce. Again Hitler left the Western ambassador to confer with his ally, and again he accepted the Italian proposal, this time on condition that Mussolini should attend the conference, which might be in Frankfurt or in Munich at Mussolini's convenience. A further telephone call to Rome elicited the information that Mussolini accepted the condition and selected Munich. For the third time that day Attolico appeared at the Chancellery to inform Hitler of Mussolini's acceptance. At about 3 P.M. invitations were despatched to Rome, London, and Paris to a conference at Munich on the following morning.

The news was received with enthusiasm all over the world. In the streets of London, Paris, Rome, and elsewhere happy crowds greeted the lifting of the cloud and eagerly tore the newspapers from the vendors' hands. Roosevelt sent his congratulations to Chamberlain in a telegram of two words: "Good Man." The Assembly of the League of Nations passed a resolution welcoming the efforts for peace which had been made outside the framework of the League. Except for the protests from Prague and criticism from a small section of the British House of Commons only two dissenting voices were heard. In his peace message of September 29 the Pope spoke of the gentle and heroic Czech martyr St. Wencelaus in terms which were plainly intended to convey that he was referring to the impending martyrdom of the Czech people. In Moscow the Soviet government condemned the transaction and foretold that the powers engaged on the dismemberment of Czechoslovakia would live to rue the day.

Of the four leaders who were about to meet at Munich, only Mussolini had any reason for unalloyed satisfaction. Hitler, while he had ostensibly gained his point, was angry at the interference with his plan, which envisaged the conquest of the whole of Czechoslovakia. Daladier had abandoned his ally, and both he and Chamberlain had manifestly made a craven surrender to the threat of force. Mussolini on the other hand was enjoying the best of both worlds. He had earned Hitler's thanks for his blustering support of Germany's case, his bluff had not been called, and now he was being hailed as the man who had saved the peace. For a short time he could escape the hateful role of Germany's vassal.

So he traveled to Munich that night in the best of humors. At the dinner table with Ciano he launched a lighthearted attack on the British:

> "In a country where animals are adored to the point of making cemeteries and hospitals and houses for them, and legacies are bequeathed to parrots, you can be sure that decadence has set in. Besides, other reasons apart, it is also a consequence of the composition of the English people. Four million surplus women. Four million sexually unsatisfied women, artificially creating a host of problems in order to excite or appease their senses. Not being able to embrace one man, they embrace humanity." [75]

Early the following morning Hitler met Mussolini at Rosenheim, halfway between the frontier and Munich. It was a courtesy, designed to demonstrate to the world that he held the Italian Duce in special regard, but it was also an opportunity for a useful preliminary indoctrination. The two dictators traveled together to Munich in Hitler's train, and on the way the Fuehrer unrolled the maps of Czechoslovakia and of Germany's western frontiers in order to illustrate his lecture. It was a procedure to which Mussolini was to become accustomed in the following years. While Hitler stood on one side of the table in front of his maps, and Mussolini stood obediently on the other, the German oracle spoke.

The Siegfried line had been completed, and Germany no longer feared attack. If the democracies were so imprudent as to attack, no time would be given them, for German troops would be launched in a "certain direction" and the campaign would be decided before the democracies had even completed their mobilization. "I have no need to mobilize. The German army stands ready and asks only to be allowed to realize my aims." He begged the

Duce to believe that he would not sacrifice the life of a single German, if he did not know that delay would be fatal to the future of the whole German nation. Only timely action could forestall encirclement by the democracies. He praised his own fortifications and in a flow of technical jargon demonstrated with the aid of his finger on the map, how he would destroy the Maginot line.

The train rolled on towards Munich, and Hitler continued to talk. The topic was war, and Hitler spoke as if it had broken out and as if he were directing operations from the train. He explained that he intended to liquidate Czechoslovakia as she then was, because she immobilized forty of his divisions. It was good that all this should happen while the Duce and he were still young and full of vigor. To this tirade Mussolini gave no sign of assent, but he listened attentively. Only as the train was approaching Munich did Mussolini take advantage of a slight pause in the Fuehrer's lecture to inquire, as if it were in an afterthought: "And what about Czechoslovakia. What are your minimum demands?" Hitler looked at Ribbentrop, who produced a sheet of paper with the words: "Here are the minimum German demands. If France and England can induce Beneš to accept what the Fuehrer has been demanding for so many months, the government of the Reich is not opposed to reaching an agreement."[76] On arrival at Munich shortly afterwards, Mussolini examined the document, and he eventually laid it before the conference as a basis of discussion put forward by himself.*

Of all conferences Munich was the most disorderly. There was no chairman, no agenda, and no agreed procedure. At times all four representatives were speaking at once, at others the meeting broke up into islands of separate conversations. As the day wore on and night began to fall, more and more people invaded the conference chamber until it began to assume the appearance of a

* There is a widely diffused story to the effect that in order to prevent Hitler constantly stepping up his demands, Goering, Neurath, and Weizsäcker elaborated in the course of September 27 some draft German proposals, which were transmitted through Attolico to Mussolini, who in turn produced them as his own, to Ribbentrop's annoyance. It is alleged that in the meantime Ribbentrop had drafted a more extreme document and was only foiled by Mussolini. Boris Celovsky in his book *Das Münchener Abkommen von 1938* (Stuttgart, 1958), p. 462, effectively demolishes this story.

waiting room at a railway station on the eve of a holiday weekend. Ambassadors could be seen running with drafts and counterdrafts to the typists' room. Owing to lack of preparation, the telephone system in the building had broken down, and the delegations found it quicker to send messages by car to their hotel offices than to attempt to telephone. Finally, at the moment of signature, it was discovered that the pompous inkstand contained no ink.

In this hurly-burly Mussolini showed to the best advantage. He was the only one of the four who was not wholly dependent on the interpreter; and he enjoyed the deference which was demonstratively paid to him by the Fuehrer. Hitler's attitude was dictated partly by his genuine respect for Mussolini and partly by his dislike of the whole business. He was content to sit brooding angrily, while Mussolini assumed the principal role in an affair in which the Fuehrer desired to play no part. For all his previous belligerence, Mussolini was throughout determined to do all he could to ensure that the conference should not break down; and he made no effort to conceal his relief and satisfaction at the outcome.

XV

Mussolini's return to Italy was a triumphal progress. At every station, at every grade crossing, and even along the railway lines crowds, many of them on their knees, had gathered to acclaim him. On the station platform at Florence the King, who had journeyed specially from his country seat at San Rossore, was standing in order to add his personal congratulations to the applause of the nation. It was the brief Indian summer of Mussolini's life. More than six years remained, but never again was he to sniff the aroma of success. Yet he was not wholly satisfied. As he entered Rome that bright autumn day, he inveighed against the Italians for their love of peace. It would be difficult with a pacifist nation behind him to retain Hitler's esteem or to carry conviction with those warlike gestures to which he was now addicted. Besides, he despised pacifists and resented any suggestion that the Italians were not a warlike people. When the Italian secret service reported the Belgian ambassador as having said that the Italians did not want to fight, Mussolini was indignant. He immediately despatched to the ambassador four copies of a book on the African war with an anonymous note couched in these terms: "There is reason to believe that you say the Italian people do not like war. They have, however, fought four victorious wars in a quarter of a century." [77] This communication, which must have surprised the ambassador, represented a novel departure from the normal diplomatic practice. This was not the only occasion on which Mussolini used anonymous letters to vent his spleen. When he heard that the new British ambassador, Sir Percy Loraine, had said disagreeable things about Italy, he arranged for anonymous letters to be sent to him, containing carefully chosen insults and equally carefully chosen press clippings with photographs of the Italian armed forces.[78]

The meeting of the four powers at Munich led directly to a complicated series of diplomatic transactions in Berlin, in the course of which Mussolini lost any advantage which he might have gained by his successful intervention. It was the Germans who ruthlessly carried the day on every contentious issue arising from the implementation of the Munich agreement.

Meanwhile there had been a conversation in the Fuehrerbau with Chamberlain in which it had been agreed to bring the Anglo-Italian agreement of April, 1938, into force on the basis of the recognition of the Empire by Britain and the withdrawal of ten thousand Italian volunteers from Spain. Within six weeks negotiations were satisfactorily concluded, and on November 16, 1938, the agreement became effective with the presentation of the British ambassador's new credentials addressed to the King Emperor. It was at the same time arranged that Chamberlain and Halifax should pay a visit to Rome in January, 1939.

Reports were already reaching Rome of Hitler's dissatisfaction with the Munich settlement, and Italy's interests required that the impetus given at Munich to four-power collaboration should be maintained for as long as possible. Unfortunately any profit which Mussolini might have drawn from the Anglo-Italian agreement was dissipated by the unbridled attacks which he elected at the moment to launch against France. These culminated on November 30 in an uproar in the Italian Chamber of Deputies when Ciano's speech was greeted by shouts of "Tunis, Corsica, Nice, Savoy." The Duce was delighted and on the way from the Chamber to the

Palazzo Venezia remarked to Ciano: "That is the way to pose a problem and to set a people in motion." At the Grand Council he announced his intention at some convenient opportunity of taking Albania, Tunisia, and Corsica, of moving his French frontier to the line of the Var, and of annexing the Ticino, since "Switzerland has lost her cohesive force and is destined one day, like so many little countries, to be disrupted." [79]

These excesses naturally caused a sharp reaction in France, where students organized demonstrations demanding the annexation of Venice and Sicily. In Britain they were a source of embarrassment to Chamberlain; and from Germany, where Hitler was completely indifferent to Italian claims, there were complaints that Italy was prejudicing German efforts to secure from France a free hand in the East. Ribbentrop, who was in Paris, sent for the Italian ambassador and told him somewhat roughly that the French Minister of Foreign Affairs had expressed surprise that one member of the Axis should be attacking France at a time when the other partner was seeking to conclude a pact of friendship. "I shall not hide from you," Ribbentrop continued, "that Italian policy is prejudicing that of Germany. Nevertheless I told the Minister that one should not attach too much importance to what was happening in Italy, since Italian claims can only be regarded as an expression of the exuberance of a young people." [80]

Mussolini was understandably annoyed, and he had another ground for complaint when, in the matter of the Italo-German arbitration of the Hungarian-Slovak frontier, the Germans espoused the cause of the Slovaks against Italy and Hungary.[81] The Germans were already beginning to treat him in the offhand and patronizing manner which was to characterize their future relationship. Nevertheless Mussolini was obliged to stomach these indignities, for he knew that Italy alone could not hope to realize his ambitious program of territorial aggrandizement. The Western powers stood for the maintenance of the *status quo,* and, if he were not to waive his claims, it was only in association with his large, powerful, and aggressive northern neighbor that the maps of Europe and Africa could be redrawn. The Germans were aware of all this and showed little delicacy or tact in trading on their knowledge.

At Munich Ribbentrop had discussed the advantage of a military alliance between Germany, Italy, and Japan, and he handed a draft text to Ciano. He soon followed up this necessarily cursory conversation by arriving in Rome on October 27, 1938, to discuss the matter further. It was an important conversation, and from it Ciano derived the conviction that Ribbentrop wanted war. "He does not name the enemy or indicate the objectives. He wants war in the course of the next three or four years." [82]

Ribbentrop exposed at length the reasons for which the Fuehrer, after some previous hesitation, thought that the moment was now ripe to conclude a military alliance. As a result of the Munich crisis, the Axis powers were masters of the situation, for they could not be attacked. All their energies could now be directed against the Western democracies. The Duce replied that there had been an irreparable break between the two worlds, and he agreed that within a few years there would be war between the Axis and the Western powers. Unfortunately, however, although public opinion favored the Axis, it was unprepared for a military alliance. The upper ranks of the army were reserved in their judgment, the middle classes still looked to London, and the conflict between nazism and Catholicism was a cause of coolness, which would evaporate if an understanding in religious affairs could be reached in Germany. A little time would be needed to allow the idea of an alliance to mature amongst the masses.

Nevertheless, Mussolini assured Ribbentrop that the alliance was a sacred pledge to be respected and fulfilled in its entirety. When the time was ripe for its conclusion, it would be necessary to lay down its objectives. It must not be a purely defensive alliance, since no one was thinking of attacking the totalitarian states. Instead Italy wished to make an alliance in order to change the map of the world, and it would be necessary to fix the objectives and the conquests to be made.[83]

The prospect of an early war held out by Ribbentrop should have alarmed Mussolini, but he was now so far committed that he accepted it with fatalistic resignation. On the following day he drafted a written reply to the Germans, confirming his approval in principle of an offensive as well as a defensive alliance, although the date of its entry into force would have to be postponed.[84] With this success Ribbentrop had every reason to be content. He knew that he now had only a very little time to wait.

As the year 1938 closed, the last year of peace in a Europe which for so long had led the world, the ledger showed an alarming increase in the credit balance of Germany and a corresponding diminution in that of the Western powers. So far as Italy was concerned, Mussolini had, against the inclinations of his people, irrevocably espoused the German cause. Deaf to reason and to the feeble, ill-timed, and ill-considered appeals which were to reach him during the following year from the West, he was no longer to be deterred. It would have been better for Italy and the world, if he had been struck down in 1936, while there was still time.

CHAPTER FIFTEEN

Prelude to War

1939

I

DESPITE the aggravation of Franco-Italian relations caused by the shrill demands of Fascist spokesmen and the press, Chamberlain made no move to cancel his visit to Italy. He preferred to cling to the fiction that the Italian government was not responsible for these public manifestations, and he told the House of Commons that the terms of the Anglo-Italian agreement of April, 1938, regarding the maintenance of the *status quo* in the Mediterranean covered Tunis and Corsica. Accompanied by Lord Halifax, he duly arrived in Rome on January 11, 1939. He was given a sympathetic reception by the people, who welcomed the opportunity of demonstrating their desire for peace. Mussolini was courteous. There was an official dinner and a visit to the opera, where Mussolini in deference to the susceptibilities of his guests wore evening dress rather than uniform.

Nevertheless, the visit and the political conversations were completely unproductive. Mussolini declared that he required no mediation or intervention in Franco-Italian relations. He thought that once the Spanish Civil War was over, it might be possible to conclude an agreement; and Chamberlain could only wish him success. On Germany Mussolini expressed his confidence in Hitler's pacific intentions and in the sincerity with which he professed to desire only the annexation of purely German territories. From these flabby and meaningless exchanges Mussolini derived the impression that Chamberlain was concerned to maintain peace, almost at any price. It would have been wiser for the Britons to have emphasized that Britain stood shoulder to shoulder with France, was resolved to call a halt to Nazi aggression, and possessed both the will and the means to do so. A lecture in the Hitler manner on Franco-British military strength and on current plans to increase it would certainly have given cause for reflection.

As it was, the visit merely confirmed Mussolini's decision, which, as will be seen later, he had just taken, to sign a military alliance with Germany. "These men," he said, speaking to Ciano of Chamberlain, "are not made of the same stuff as the Francis Drakes and the other magnificent adventurers who created the Empire. These, after all, are the tired sons of a long line of rich men, and they will lose their Empire." [1] Pacifism was, however, not the only reproach he leveled at Chamberlain. He sensed, quite correctly, that the British were less concerned to win the friendship and support of Italy than to detach her from Germany. It was an attitude which wounded his pride and made him more than ever resolved to take his revenge on the democracies.

In order to demonstrate his loyalty to the Axis, Mussolini, while Chamberlain was still in Rome, gave the German ambassador a sight of the written record of the Anglo-Italian conversations. He received little credit in Berlin for his candor, since the Germans, unaccustomed to the idea of confidence between allies, merely deduced that he must have been concerned to conceal some transaction with the English. They were not, however, unduly worried, for they knew that Mussolini was now within their grip and that it was no longer necessary to treat him with consideration.

II

Indeed he was soon to receive a further blow from his ally. At the beginning of March, 1939, the Italian ambassador in Berlin began to have the uneasy feeling that something was afoot. It was an indefinable sensation, familiar to all foreign residents in Berlin, which might be likened to the malaise of a sailor when a hurricane is approaching. On March 9 the ambassador asked to see Ribbentrop, but he was not available. The following day Attolico attended a Nazi ceremony and noted that Hitler was wearing the face of his grand occasions. He approached Weizsäcker, but was unable to extract any information from him; his lips appeared to be sealed. On March 11, having failed once more to obtain an interview with Ribbentrop, he telephoned to Kassel, ostensibly to inquire after Princess Mafalda, but in reality to find out whether Prince Philip of Hesse was at home. He was told that Hesse had been summoned urgently to Berlin and he knew at once that his worst suspicions were confirmed. The winged messenger was obviously on the way to perform his customary ritual task.

Shortly afterwards Attolico learned that his Hungarian colleague had suddenly left Berlin for Budapest. He made a third request to see Ribbentrop and when he was eventually received, all he was told was that the situation in Czechoslovakia was very grave and that in consequence the German government had authorized Hungary to occupy sub-Carpathian Ruthenia. Attolico knew that this could not be the end of the story, but he pleaded in vain for further information; Ribbentrop turned a deaf ear to his tart observation that this was no way to treat an ally.

Meanwhile Rome was celebrating. Pope Pius XI had died and on March 12, 1939, Cardinal Pacelli was crowned under the title of Pius XII. Mussolini was still strangely optimistic. On March 10 he observed to Ciano that the Germans were a military, but not a warrior, people. "Give the Germans a great deal of sausage, butter, beer, and a cheap car, and they will never want to risk their skins." [2] It was on March 15, while the festivities following the papal coronation were still in full swing, that news was received in Rome of the rape of Bohemia and Moravia.

Hesse duly arrived with the usual message from the Fuehrer. It was on this occasion a verbal message only, to the effect that he had acted because the Czechs would not demobilize, because they continued to keep their contacts with Russia, and because they maltreated Germans. Ciano noted that such pretexts might be good for the propaganda of Dr. Goebbels, but that they should not be advanced to the Italians, whose only fault was excessive loyalty to the Germans.[3]

Hitler's brutal annexation of Bohemia aroused the utmost indignation in Italy. Reports poured into the Palazzo Venezia, from the police and from Fascist party offices, emphasizing the anti-German sentiments of the people, without distinction of region or social class. Telegrams from the Italian missions abroad spoke of universal disgust at Germany's cowardly action. The former German ambassador, Hassell, heard from friends in Italy that "feeling against us there is almost the same as in 1934." [4]

Mussolini was as upset as any Italian. He declined to allow any references in the press to Hitler's message. "The Italians would laugh at me; every time Hitler occupies a country he sends me a message." He was also disturbed at the breach of Hitler's assurance that he did not wish to annex one single Czech. He had credited Hitler with sincerity on this issue, but after what had happened in Prague, could any weight be attached to those German declarations and promises which more directly concerned Italy? Ciano describes the Duce as "sullen," "unhappy and depressed," and "worried and gloomy"; and when in his diary he referred angrily to the humiliation of the Italian people, it was really of the humiliation of the Duce that he was thinking.[5]

From Berlin Attolico sounded a warning note. The diplomats representing Germany's neighbors, he reported, were profoundly shaken and were anxiously inquiring who was likely to be the next victim. Italy should draw the necessary conclusions from the events of the last few days. The German government with one stroke had annulled the agreements of Munich and Vienna, without any regard for the principal architect of these treaties and her only potential ally. If the two countries were to march together, it was essential that the rights and obligations of each partner should be clearly defined and that Hitler should categorically declare his intentions. Only then could one begin to discuss a treaty of alliance, a meeting between Ciano and Ribbentrop, a visit by Goering to Rome, and other manifestations of Axis solidarity.[6]

It was an unpleasant moment, and, as usual in the face of a crisis, Mussolini was for a time undecided. Ettore Muti, who had not seen him for two months found him tired and aged by many years. He was afraid that the Croats might proclaim their independence and place themselves under German protection. In such an event, he said, he would have either to fire the first shot against Germany or be swept away by a Fascist revolution. On March 19 he ordered a concentration of troops on the Venetian border; and Ciano warned the German ambassador that Italy could not tolerate any intervention in Croatian affairs. Two days later the German government gave Ciano the most explicit assurances on the point, but Mussolini only wondered gloomily whether he could place any trust in Hitler's word. In his bewilderment he considered the advisability of delaying the projected despatch of troops to Libya and of coming to an agreement with France through London. On March 19 he opined that it was now impossible to present to the Italian people the idea of an alliance with Germany. "The very stones would cry out against it." The King fed Mussolini's resentment, spoke of Germanic insolence and duplicity, and referred to the Germans as rascals and beggars, contrasting their behavior with the straightforwardness of the British.

Sober reflection, however, swung Mussolini back to a more realistic appraisal of the situation; and he was obliged to temper his anger. As Mario Donosti put it, the serpent he had nourished in his bosom had become so large that he had neither the strength to strangle it nor the courage to throw it out.[7] He told Ciano that Prussian hegemony in Europe was now established and that Italy had no alternative but to accept the German trick with as much good grace as she could muster. On March 21 he spoke to the Grand Council of the need to adopt a policy of uncompromising loyalty to the Axis. Balbo, who was the only Fascist chieftain who was never afraid to speak his mind, derisively accused Mussolini of licking Germany's boots. Mussolini angrily remarked to Ciano after the meeting that Balbo would always remain the democratic swine, who was once the orator of a Ferrara Masonic lodge.[8]

On March 25 Mussolini received through the German ambassador a letter in which Hitler fulsomely expressed his friendship and admiration for his ally. It was a flattering tribute to the achievements of fascism, but Mussolini still retained something of his resentment and told Anfuso, who brought him the letter, that in his speech to the Fascist militia on the following day he would speak of France in moderate terms and had ordered Starace to ensure that there should be no anti-French demonstrations. Nevertheless, the speech, which he delivered on March 26, was an aggressive statement of pro-Axis policy. The second Czechoslovak crisis was now a closed episode. Once again Italy had been forced to toe the line and Hitler was fortified in his conviction that in his future enterprises no trouble from Rome need be apprehended.

III

The gloom induced by events in central Europe was lightened by happy news from Spain. On March 28 Madrid fell to Franco's forces, Valencia was captured on March 30, and with the occupation of these and other cities the Spanish Civil War came to an end. Every building in Italy was beflagged and crowds poured into the streets to acclaim the Duce. The victory in Spain was the event for which Mussolini was waiting, in order to deliver his reply to the German occupation of Prague.

For some time Mussolini and Ciano had been itching to bring off a stroke in the Hitlerian manner; and Albania, which was already virtually under Italian control, was the obvious selection. In May, 1938, Mussolini told Ciano to warn Ribbentrop that Italy regarded Albania as a "family matter," the phrase which the Germans used for Austria and the Sudetenland. Ciano noted: "The Duce declares that he is ready to go into Albania at once, even at the cost of setting fire to the European powder barrel. He is already making the necessary military preparations." [9]

In October, 1938, the Italian minister in Tirana was able to assure Ciano that his preparations were going ahead so rapidly that it might be necessary to advance the timetable. He envisaged the fomentation of riots against the Albanian government, the descent from the mountains of tribes in Italian pay, an appeal to Italy to intervene, the offer of the throne to the King Emperor, and annexation. He guaranteed to bring all this about at a month's notice.[10] It only remained to fix a date for the operation.

Smarting under the seizure of Prague, the Italians thought that Hitler could appropriately be paid back in his own coin and that they could recover some of their lost prestige in Albania. On March 15, 1939, Ciano put the definite plan to the Duce, who authorized the preparation of local revolts in Albania and ordered the navy to hold a squadron ready at Taranto. On the following day, however, he had changed his mind. He was now afraid of upsetting the balance in Yugoslavia and said that the Albanian operation must be postponed. On March 23 the news from Spain was better, and Mussolini once more decided to move in Albania. He himself drafted an Italo-Albanian agreement, which virtually permitted Italy to annex the country. The idea was to present this document to King Zog and, failing immediate acceptance, to undertake the military seizure of Albania. For this purpose four Bersaglieri regiments, an infantry division, air force detachments, and a naval squadron were concentrated in southern Italy. With the fall of Madrid on March 28 Mussolini finally made up his mind. He was sitting at his desk in the Palazzo Venezia, while the crowds outside were acclaiming the victory; and pointing to an atlas open at the map of Spain, he said to Ciano: "It has been open in this way for almost three years, and that is enough. But I know already that I must open it at another page." [11]

By the end of March news reached Rome that King Zog was making difficulties about the draft agreement. More disturbing, the Italian minister, Jacomoni, reported misgivings about the condition of the Italian expeditionary force, and Badoglio sent the Duce a written criticism of the plan of operations. But Mussolini was now determined to go ahead and Good Friday, April 7, was fixed as the date for the landing. It seems strange that Mussolini, who was ordinarily so sensitive to opinion around him, should have selected this particular date, but he was in an agitated mood, anxious to get the business over without further delay and unwilling to defer to Christian susceptibilities.

The actual invasion of Albania provided evidence of Italy's unreadiness for war. There was a lamentable shortage of equipment and the only explanation proffered by the military was to the effect that the army's resources had been dissipated in Abyssinia and Spain. So ill-found was the expeditionary force and so inadequate the military plan, that it was said that if King Zog had possessed a competent fire brigade, the Italian army must have been hurled back into the sea.[12] Fortunately for Mussolini the landing was virtually unopposed, but the subsequent military operations were attended by confusion, which nearly brought disaster in its train.

The force commander, General Guzzoni, had received categorical instructions to march on Tirana as soon as possible, and not to delay his advance on any pretext whatsoever. Nevertheless as the day of April 7 passed and no news was received in Rome that Guzzoni had yet covered the short distance from the coast to the capital, anxiety began to mount. Eventually in the course of the afternoon the infuriated Duce received from Bari a telephonic explanation of the delay: the march on the capital had been halted because King Zog had despatched envoys, accompanied by the Italian military attaché at Tirana, to meet the Italian troops.

The time lost in these fruitless parleys might have had the most serious consequences. King Zog had fled with the whole of his family in the direction of the Greek frontier, leaving the city to the mercy of the mob. By the evening the prisons had been opened and armed bands were roaming the streets, sacking and plundering as they went. It looked as if the Italian legation, for the defense of which no preparations had been made, might be attacked at any moment. At about nine o'clock in the evening Jacomoni telegraphed that he had burned his codes and that he was awaiting an assault at any moment, since the crowds were then looting the palace of the Queen's sister, on the other side of the street. Shortly afterwards it seemed that all was lost, for the radio station at Rome intercepted an S. O. S. from the legation, which the overexcited radiotelegraphist had sent out under the false impression that the mob was breaking down the front door.

Fortunately for Mussolini no news of this harlequinade leaked to the public and as the night wore on, the situation at Tirana began to improve. Towards midnight Jacomoni was able to report that armed volunteers were seeking to restore order, that the mob had withdrawn from the precincts of the legation, and that one of his officials, who had made a reconnaissance, had returned with the news that the situation was calmer. The Ministry of War confirmed that the crisis was over, that a column of Bersaglieri was now advancing and hoped to reach Tirana in the early hours of the following day. Moreover, the airfield at Tirana was already in the hands of the troops.

Encouraged by these developments, Ciano, who should have been attending to the diplomatic aspect of the enterprise, decided to pay a lightning visit to the seat of war. On his return the following day he was faced by the problem of the future status of Albania. It was characteristic of the thoughtless frivolity of the Mussolini-Ciano regime at the Palazzo Chigi that the military operation was launched before any plans had been made for the administration of the country.* After a meeting on April 9 with officials, which lasted only half an hour, Ciano saw Mussolini and proposed a union under a common Crown. That is to say, each country would preserve its own institutions and the only link would be the King. Ciano smugly observed that the advantage of this solution would be that, while it would give Italy possession of Albania, it would not look like aggression.[13]

Mussolini approved, but as the days passed Ciano's project was gradually whittled down until nothing at all was left of Albanian independence. The country was to become a province of Italy under the administration of Italians, who knew nothing of its customs and traditions. On April 15 a party of sad Albanians arrived at Rome to attend the ceremony at which, on the following day, they were formally to offer the Albanian crown to King Victor Emmanuel. When Ciano spoke to the Duce about their state of mind, he replied airily that he would talk to them about their national independence and sovereignty in such a manner as to send them home reassured.[14] Unfortunately any such assurances were so incompatible with the facts that they failed to bring any comfort, even to the simple and primitive delegates from the Albanian mountains.

Abroad, although there was an initial feeling of revulsion against the choice of Good Friday for an act of aggression, the rape of Albania brought Mussolini no unpleasant conseqeunces. The German government, which had been previously informed, expressed its satisfaction and conveyed its congratulations on the success of the enterprise; and Ribbentrop magnanimously told Attolico that any Italian victory represented an accession of strength to the Axis. In Paris the episode was viewed with weary indifference. In London, where Italy might have been arraigned for a breach of the April, 1938, agreement by altering the *status quo* in the Mediter-

* For a moment Ciano toyed with the idea of taking the Crown of Albania himself (Susmel, p. 139).

ranean, there was at first a strong protest and a request for assurances, particularly in regard to the position of Greece. Nevertheless on April 9 in conversation with the Italian chargé d'affaires Lord Halifax merely criticized the irresponsibility with which Italy disturbed the waters as soon as they showed any sign of a calm. He was told in reply that the Great Powers should not oppose Italian dynamism, which was not directed at their own vital interests, and that Albania would give Italy a useful field of activity, where she would do no harm to anyone. The matter was tacitly allowed to drop. The conscience of the world was becoming dulled to the progressive liquidation of small independent European countries. Only where Africans or Asiatics were concerned was it still possible to arouse any sense of guilt.

IV

With the Albanian enterprise safely out of the way and with the conviction that his prestige at home had been enhanced by this success and by the victory in Spain, Mussolini felt able to take up the question of the German alliance. On January 1, 1939, he had taken the decision to transform the Anti-Comintern Pact into a formal tripartite alliance, and a letter to this effect had been despatched to Ribbentrop on January 3. Mussolini wished the treaty to be signed before the end of the month, and the reason for this haste was that he considered a clash with the Western powers more and more inevitable, and that in consequence he wished to effect a military alignment in advance.[15] Attolico was now in favor of this move, not because he was pro-German, but because he thought it safer to define Italy's obligations rather than to undertake vague open-ended commitments.

Ribbentrop immediately produced drafts of a tripartite political pact and a secret military convention, which were despatched to Rome on January 6. Unfortunately, despite German assurances to the contrary, Japanese ardor for the alliance had by this time cooled; and on February 8 the Duce, exasperated by Japanese hesitation, favored an immediate Italo-German alliance without the participation of Japan. In March the Italians proposed staff conversations and those duly took place at Innsbruck on April 5 and 6. General Keitel led the German delegation and General Pariani the Italian. The German General Staff was always inclined to treat the Italians with reserve, and no attempt was made to discuss operational plans or a concerted conduct of a European war. General Pariani merely emphasized the unreadiness of Italy as the result of the Abyssinian and Spanish campaigns, and said that the existing deficiencies could not be repaired before 1943. Nothing was said about the Italian invasion of Albania, which was to take place within a few hours. General Keitel, for his part, took note of the Italian statement and reassuringly declared that the German armed forces were also in the process of development. Both sides were equally concerned to deceive the other, and there was no indication that either party expected shortly to be engaged in a common war. So inauspicious were the staff conversations that Mussolini was prepared to shelve the German alliance for the moment, and to wait at least until he had dealt with Albania.

On April 16 Goering arrived in Rome to attend the ceremony of the presentation of the crown of Albania to the King of Italy, and Ciano was disturbed by the aggressive tone of his remarks about Poland. It reminded him unpleasantly of the tone used in previous years about Austria and Czechoslovakia.[16] Mussolini, however, far from seeking to dampen the bellicose ardor of his visitor, retorted that he wished to settle accounts with France; and in order to create an impression of readiness for war mounted a blackout and anti-aircraft exercises in Rome. Unfortunately, shortage of antiaircraft guns made it impossible to simulate a strong defense and field artillery was brought into the city to make the requisite noise.[17]

Ciano's misgivings were shown to be justified when, a few days later, Attolico reported from Berlin that he regarded German action against Poland as imminent. The news did not dismay Mussolini. He may have thought, or at least hoped, that Hitler would have his way in Poland, as he had done over rearmament, the Rhineland, Austria, and Czechoslovakia. In any event he remained resolved to go on with the alliance. His policy was to upset the existing international order; he could not risk being isolated between a rampaging Germany and the conservative democracies; and so both ambition and fear counseled him to bind himself to the most powerful military state in the world. Nevertheless, like a man who has sold

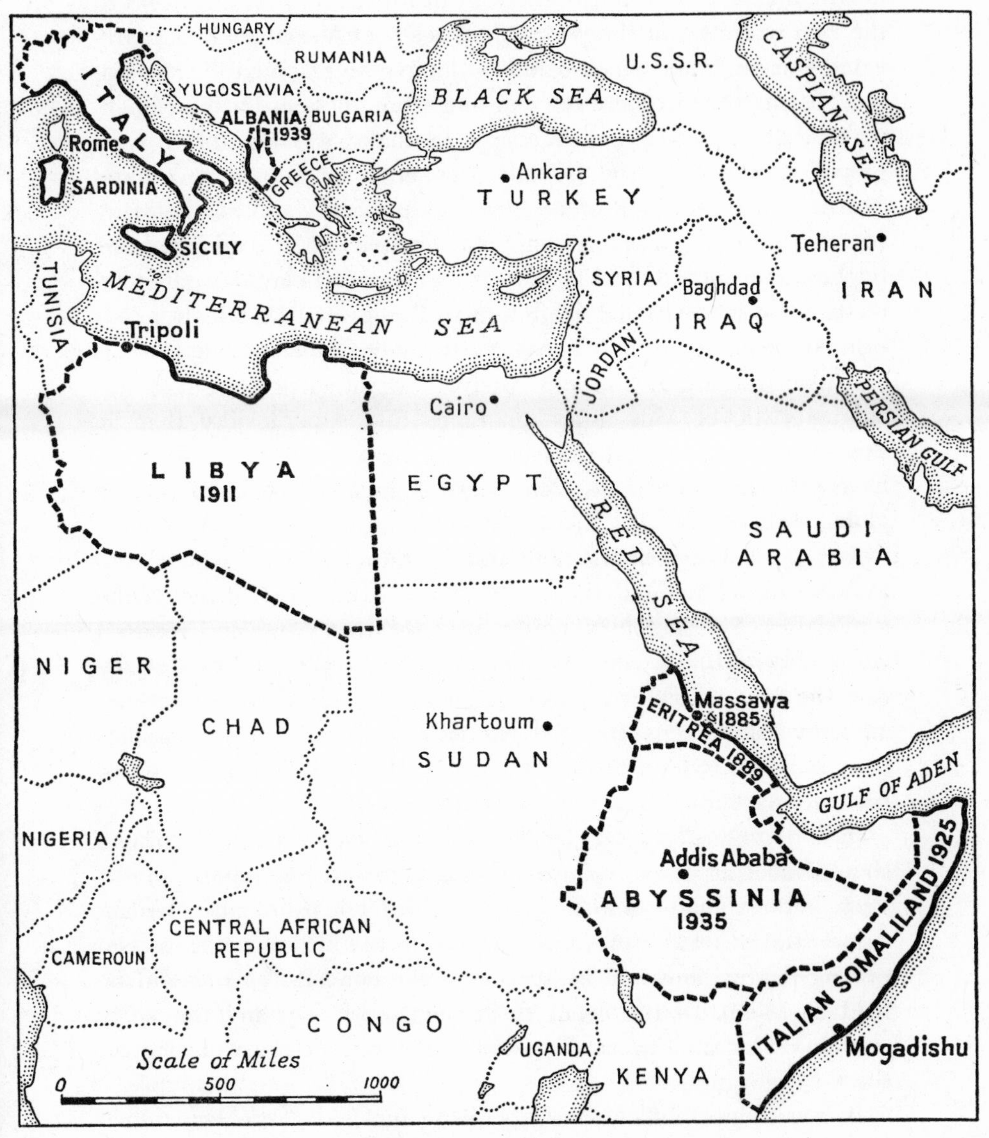

The Italian Empire in 1939.

himself to the devil, he was concerned to put off the day of reckoning as long as possible.

He prepared a memorandum for communication to the Germans in which he recognized that war was destined to break out between the rich nations and the poor. The Treaty of Versailles had aggravated the problem, which could no longer be resolved by negotiation. It was a choice between war and strangulation. But he emphasized that it would be necessary to make a long and careful preparation for the struggle. Italy, weakened by the Abyssinian and Spanish wars, required some years of peace and could not be ready before 1943 to embark on a long and terrible war. He adduced one further, somewhat trivial argument in favor of delay. He intended to stage an international exhibition in Rome in 1942, which would bring in enough foreign currency to enable him to complete his war preparations. Exhibitions rarely show much profit, but it was characteristic of Mussolini's ignorance and superficiality that he should have argued that the earnings of his Rome exhibition would have any significant impact on Italy's financial capacity to wage a global war.

A copy of the memorandum was sent to Badoglio, who claims to have told Mussolini that, with the exception of the navy, the armed forces were totally unprepared for war. Mussolini retorted that sufficient funds would be placed at his disposal and that in any case the date of 1943 was purely an indication and did not represent an irrevocable commitment.[18] He was not prepared to alter his memorandum, which formed the basis of Ciano's instructions for his meeting with Ribbentrop at Milan on May 6.

It had originally been decided that the two Foreign Ministers should meet at Como for a general discussion, but reports in the French press that Como had been selected because anti-German demonstrations would have taken place in the birthplace of fascism provoked Mussolini into insisting that the conversations should be held at Milan. In the event the federal secretary and the party machine were able to assure a more than satisfactory welcome for the German guest.

In accordance with his instructions Ciano laid particular emphasis on Italy's requirement of three years of peace and preparation. Ribbentrop was on his best behavior. Never again was he to be so easy, so amiable, and accommodating. He was prepared to go even further than Ciano, and he volunteered that Germany was also convinced of the need for a period of peace, which should be not less than four or five years, although of course she could be ready for war much sooner. In order to give verisimilitude to this assurance, he told Ciano that in regard to Poland the Fuehrer was determined to follow the path of conciliation. His policy was to allow the matter to mature, while remaining ready to react sharply if the Poles passed over to the offensive. On Russia Ribbentrop made some observations which might have alerted Ciano to Hitler's plans. Any favorable occasion, he said, must be seized to promote the accession of Russia to the totalitarian bloc. While professing to agree that the greatest discretion should be shown, he insisted on the need to improve the relations between the Axis and the Soviet Union. There is nothing to show that Ciano grasped the significance of this change of wind.

So far as the military alliance was concerned, Ribbentrop proposed to submit within a few days a draft treaty, which might form the basis of discussion. He suggested that signature might take place in Berlin as soon as possible and in the most solemn manner.[19]

It was all most satisfactory; and Ciano took advantage of an adjournment for dinner to telephone a full account of the conversation to the Duce. Mussolini was delighted and quite unexpectedly ordered Ciano to secure German assent to the immediate publication of the news that a formal Italo-German alliance had been agreed on in Milan. He might have been less impetuous had he known that a month previously, on April 3, Hitler had issued a directive to the armed forces, "Case White," instructing them to make ready for the annihilation of Poland: "Preparations must be made in such a way that the operation can be carried out at any time from September 1, 1939, onwards."[20] The fatal date lay less than four months ahead.

Ciano was not best pleased at Mussolini's haste, but had no alternative but to obey. Ribbentrop, who still hankered with his customary obstinacy after his original proposal for a tripartite pact, somewhat reluctantly undertook to consult the Fuehrer by telephone and received instructions to close at once with the Italian offer. Hitler had obtained exactly what he wanted. The exclusion of Japan was convenient, for it would facilitate the approach which he hoped to make to Russia, while the timely announcement of an Italo-German alliance might scare the Western powers, and so enable him safely to come to grips with Poland. On May 7 a joint statement was issued to the effect that the conversations had once more established the complete identity of views of the two governments, and that it had been decided formally to define the relations between the Axis powers in a political and military treaty.

Mussolini had now recovered complete confidence in his ally and was content to leave the drafting of the treaty to the Germans. On May 13 the text was handed to Ciano, who exclaimed, as well he might: "I have never read such a pact; it contains some real dynamite." [21] It was virtually the same text as that which the Italians had rejected the previous year. Only two modifications of the original draft were made at Mussolini's request: the first reduced the indefinite duration of the treaty to a period of ten years, and the second, at Attolico's suggestion, provided for a sentence in the preamble asserting that the existing Italo-German frontier was fixed for all time.

In all other respects the German draft, which bound Italy to Germany in every conceivable circumstance, was obediently swallowed by Mussolini. It is true that Article II imposed on each ally the obligation to consult, but Article III gave Hitler the escape clause he required: "If it should happen, against the wishes and hopes of the contracting parties, that one of them becomes involved in warlike complications with another Power or with other Powers, the other contracting party will come to its aid as an ally and will support it with all its military forces on land, on sea, and in the air." Article V bound the allies not to conclude a separate armistice or peace. There was not even the conventional protection afforded by a clause to the effect that the treaty only came into force in the event of aggression by an enemy. So ardent was Mussolini to place his head in the noose which Hitler had prepared for him, that the treaty was never subjected to the scrutiny of the other members of the government or of the political and legal experts of the Palazzo Chigi. It was decided to sign forthwith.

Historians have proffered various explanations of Mussolini's extraordinary conduct. It has been said that he was exasperated by allegations in the foreign press that Germany was so unpopular in Italy that he could not impose an alliance on the people. He was also believed to be disturbed by news of an Anglo-Turkish pact, which he regarded as directed against Italy; and he was certainly in a nervous mood of contempt for and resentment against the Western powers. Finally, he was on the lookout for another success to feed into the insatiable maw of his propaganda machine. All these considerations doubtless played their part, but there was one more important impulse driving Mussolini. Like an impatient speculator, who rushes into the market without waiting to take advice, he instinctively felt that he could no longer afford any delay in linking his fortunes with those of Nazi Germany. Speaking to the Grand Council on February 4 he had explained that Italy could not continue to be imprisoned in the Mediterranean:

> "The March to the Ocean. Which Ocean? The Indian Ocean linking across the Sudan and Libya to Abyssinia; or the Atlantic Ocean across French North Africa? In the first, as in the second hypothesis, we find ourselves face to face with Anglo-French opposition. To brave the solution of such a problem without having secured our backs to the Continent would be absurd. The policy of the Rome-Berlin Axis therefore answers the historical necessity of a fundamental order." [22]

If this program were to be realized, he must not let slip the possibly fleeting opportunity of a German alliance.

On May 20, 1939, Ciano left for Berlin, where he was given the reception of a conqueror. The pylons bearing the Italian and German flags together with the Fascist and Nazi party emblems, which had been used for Mussolini's visit, were fished out of the warehouse and erected in the streets. Along the route formations of the Hitler Youth were drawn up in their thousands to cheer and to wave Italian flags. In the evening there was a banquet, and on the following morning in a setting of great magnificence and in the presence of Hitler and his Court, the treaty, shortly afterwards christened the Pact of Steel by Mussolini, was solemnly signed by the two Foreign Ministers.

Ciano was enchanted and gleefully noted in his diary that nothing had been changed in regard to the agreement reached in Milan. Ribbentrop had repeated Germany's interest in an intention to ensure a long period of peace—at least three years. It is true that in the intervening fortnight the period of truce had contracted from "four to five years" to merely "three years." But it would have been pedantic in the joyful euphoria of the signature to have called attention to the trivial discrepancy.

In the chorus of mutual admiration in Berlin there was only one discordant note. Goering had for some time coveted the collar of the Annunziata, and had been put off on the pretext that the King of Italy was unwilling to confer it on a foreigner. It may be imagined with what rage and mortification he regarded the unexpected bestowal of this high decoration on Ribbentrop during the festivities connected with the signature of the pact. He had tears in his eyes when he saw the collar around his colleague's neck, and was only pacified when Ciano promised to try and obtain another collar for him.

V

The alliance was not popular in Italy, and Ciano on his return to Rome ruefully noted in his diary that outside Fascist circles, which gave him a warm reception, it was better liked in Germany. The King observed that as long as the Germans had need of Italy they would be courteous and even servile, but at the first opportunity they would reveal themselves as the rascals they really were.[23] Mussolini was, however, more than satisfied at the outcome of Ciano's expedition and deluded himself that he had signed an alliance with an equal, whereas Hitler knew that he had acquired a vassal. Intoxicated by his success, Mussolini gleefully seized the first opportunity to show that he would have no further truck with the Western powers. On May 27, when the new British ambassador, Sir Percy Loraine, paid his initial call, he gave him an icy reception, and inquired whether in view of the British policy of encirclement the agreement of April 16 retained any value. On May 31 he told Ciano that he had no intention of easing relations with France.

Nevertheless, although he was prepared to bluster and to assure all and sundry that Italy would march with Germany in every conceivable circumstance, the shocking state of Italy's military preparedness caused him recurring nagging anxiety. On May 30 he despatched General Ugo Cavallero to Berlin with a memorandum for Hitler, in which he repeated that he required three years in which to make the necessary moral and material preparations for the inevitable war. Militarily, Italy needed this period of peace in order to establish herself in Abyssinia, Libya, and Albania, to re-equip the army with artillery, to commission six battleships under construction, and to transfer a number of war industries from the north to the south.

General Cavallero, who was the Italian representative on the permanent mixed commission set up under Article IV of the Treaty of Alliance, spent ten days in Berlin and received from his German colleagues no sign that they dissented from or did not accept the Italian thesis that war must not be allowed to break out for at least three years. The German silence was therefore read in Rome as consent; and Ciano felt justified in assuring Mussolini that the German alliance carried with it no immediate danger for Italy.

Until he had decided to give credence to Ribbentrop's undertaking in Milan Ciano had been extremely disturbed at the prospect of being dragged into an early war. On April 29 he noted in his diary that the Italian divisions had merely the strength of regiments, that there was a shortage of ammunition, that antiaircraft and antitank weapons were lacking, and that the artillery was obsolete. "There has been a good deal of bluffing in the military sphere and even the Duce has been deceived—a tragic bluff." But Mussolini seemed indifferent and was doing nothing to remedy the situation. "His attention seems to be devoted to matters of drill; there is trouble if the 'present arms' is not done correctly, or if an officer does not know how to do the goose step, but he seems little concerned about the real weaknesses." [24]

While Mussolini was basking in the illusion that he had gained his point and that Germany had agreed to a period of peace, Hitler was making active preparations for an early war. He had now so effectively isolated Italy from the Western powers that he had no reason to pay the slightest regard to his ally. Events were soon to prove the accuracy of King Victor Emmanuel's assessment of the Germans.

On May 23, the day after the signature of the Pact of Steel, Hitler held a war council in the Chancellery and outlined his plans. Germany, he declared, required space which could not be acquired without invading other countries or attacking other people's possessions. There was no question of sparing Poland, and Germany must take the decision to attack Poland at the first suitable opportunity. There was a long dissertation on the prospects of isolating Poland and on the character of a war with the British, whom he described as the driving force against Germany. But the conclusion was uncompromising: "The idea that we can get off cheaply is dangerous; there is no such possibility. We must burn our boats. It is no longer a question of right or wrong, but of life or death for eighty million human beings." There was one final consideration: "Secrecy is the decisive prerequisite for success. Our objectives must be kept secret from both Italy and Japan." [25]

By the end of May German preparations for war were making good progress. Weapons of all kinds were flowing from the production lines in the giant armament factories, the military staffs were polishing their plans, and men were gradually being called up for summer training. On June 22 General Keitel signed orders for the execution of the "Case White" plan and a concealed mobilization. On the political front also Hitler was beginning to pave the way. In the greatest secrecy and without informing his ally he was groping towards an understanding with the Soviet Union.

VI

Meanwhile, in Rome Mussolini and Ciano, blissfully unaware of the storm about to break over their heads, were busily engaged on the trivia of adventurous Fascist diplomacy. Mussolini was considering the fomentation of a Croat revolt and the proclamation of an independent state in confederation with Rome.[26] There were negotiations in Berlin over the Alto Adige, in the course of which the Germans gave the Italians a measure of satisfaction. They could afford to do so, for Hitler knew that very shortly the European order would be in the melting pot. Mussolini was also concerned to enlarge the scope of the alliance with Germany and to draw in Japan, Hungary, and Spain, for he was anxious not to remain alone in the boat with Hitler. In all these transactions he behaved as if he had plenty of time.

He was particularly keen to receive compensation for his effort on Franco's behalf in the Civil War and to bring Spain into the Axis. In June Serrano Suñer paid a long visit to Italy and gave satisfying expression to his friendly feeling for Italy, although he was reserved about Germany because of his Catholic susceptibilities. Nevertheless he warned his hosts frankly that Spain was not in a fit state to wage a war and that an alliance would be premature. In July Ciano traveled to Madrid and found Franco civil, amiably professing his intention of following an Axis line, but firmly resolved not to submit to any entanglement. He declared that for some time he must continue to maintain tolerable relations with France, principally in order to recover the wealth exported by the Reds. Moreover Spain's requirements went further than the two or three years of peace stipulated by Italy. She must have at least five years and even that figure seemed to many observers optimistic.[27]

Ciano returned from Madrid with empty hands. The prospect of an agreement with Russia confirmed Hitler in his opinion that it would be untimely to press a reluctant Japan to join the alliance. The accession of Hungary without Spain or Japan would be of little significance. Mussolini's plans for the extension of the alliance had collapsed almost as soon as they were made; and he was left alone with Hitler to face the crisis which was approaching with ever-lengthening strides.

VII

The first storm signal was hoisted on June 17, 1939, when Dr. Goebbels at Danzig made a violent speech accusing Poland of suppressing the rights of the German population of the city. This was the language which had been leveled at Dr. Schuschnigg and Beneš; and it aroused a shudder of apprehension throughout the capitals of Europe, but not in the Palazzo Venezia, where Mussolini sat secure in the secret assurances prodigally dispensed by Ribbentrop. Attolico, however, took a different view and at once sought an interview with the State Secretary, from whom he requested, basing himself on the Pact of Steel, a clear statement of Hitler's intentions. He was told that there had been no new development in the Polish question and that the Fuehrer had taken no decision for an immediate solution of the problem of Danzig.[28]

During the weeks which followed, Attolico continued to send urgent warnings, and to suggest a meeting between Hitler and the Duce, or at least a meeting between the Foreign Ministers in the hope that Italy might exercise a moderating influence. But Mussolini and Ciano remained optimistic. On July 4 Ciano noted that nothing dramatic was in the offing. On July 22 he considered that Attolico had lost his head and on July 28 after a conversation with the Duce he wrote: "This ambassador has done good work, but now allows himself to be taken in by the war panic." [29]

On July 7 Sir Percy Loraine brought Mussolini a personal message from Chamberlain calling attention to the dangers ahead and appealing to him to use his influence to attenuate the German claims on Danzig. Mussolini was glad to take the opportunity of giving the British envoy a sharp answer: "Tell Chamberlain," he said twice, "that if England is ready to fight in the defense of Poland, Italy will take up arms with her ally Germany."

Mussolini was now in an increasingly difficult situation. He considered himself to be the architect of the Pact of Steel, and he was at pains to demonstrate to the world his unshaken loyalty to the alliance and his confidence in Hitler. Hence his aggressive reply to the British ambassador. But as the weeks of July passed, he began to entertain intermittent doubts and to lapse into his normal state of indecision. At the beginning of July Attolico was instructed to see Ribbentrop and make an effort to ascertain the real intentions of the German government. He was no more successful on this than on previous occasions. Nevertheless Mussolini and Ciano, although disturbed, were still unaware of the imminence of the danger. Consequently Ciano informed Attolico that while he was disposed to accept his proposal for a meeting with Ribbentrop, he considered that the date to be suggested to the German government should be one not before the first of September.

When this instruction was received in Berlin, Ciano was away in Spain, and Attolico replied in a tart personal letter addressed to Anfuso, Ciano's principal private secretary. The fact, he said, that a date in September had been suggested, demonstrated that, despite all his warnings, Rome remained unaware of the gravity of the situation. War was already at the gates. The Germans had no intention of awaiting Italian permission before launching this attack on Poland. The military preparations were complete and the propaganda orchestra was approaching the end of its symphony. It looked as if the end of August was the date fixed for the blow; and accordingly, if it was desired to act, something must be done at once rather than in six or eight weeks.

After communicating with Ciano by telegraph, Anfuso showed the letter to Mussolini, who recognized the need to have an early confrontation with the Germans. As soon as Ciano returned to Rome, Magistrati * was summoned from Berlin to a meeting which took place at the Palazzo Venezia on July 22. As the situation became more threatening, the Duce's ardor for war was slowly ebbing away, although he was careful not to reveal this. Instead, remembering his Munich success, his mind was moving towards the idea of an international conference. Why, he inquired of Ciano and Magistrati, should not the two dictators, accused as they always were of desiring war, sponsor a practical peace plan, such as a conference between Italy, Germany, France, Britain, Poland, and Spain? Mussolini knew that Hitler and Ribbentrop would dislike the proposal and might even accuse him of wishing to default on his obligations. So he briefed Magistrati carefully. There was no question of Italy backing out of the alliance: "Whenever Germany finds it necessary to mobilize at midnight, we shall mobilize at five to twelve." On the other hand there were good tactical grounds for not plunging into war at the moment. A war of nerves suited the Axis better; a conference would enable Danzig to be transferred to Germany; if the others refused to confer they would place themselves in the wrong; and according to his information, Poland, France, and Britain were in earnest and intended to fight. Finally Mussolini made it plain that he would not move without Germany's prior agreement.[30]

Armed with these instructions, Magistrati, together with Attolico, repaired to Fuschl, near Salzburg, on the following day to see Rib-

* Count Massimo Magistrati, Ciano's brother-in-law, was the able Counsellor of the Italian Embassy in Berlin and played a prominent part in the mission's conduct of affairs.

bentrop and secure his assent to a conference. It was not a successful expedition. Ribbentrop, speaking in English and at great length, undertook to consult Hitler, but pronounced very definitely against a conference. Germany, he argued, could not afford to give any impression of yielding or of weakness, particularly since the Western powers were in a state of some confusion and the United States was embarking on neutrality legislation. The Poles had behaved extremely badly, but it seemed likely that one day they would come to their senses and accept the German demands. In any event he could give an assurance that the Fuehrer agreed with Mussolini that a general conflagration was undesirable. Hitler was a hundred per cent certain that he could isolate Poland and was firmly resolved to avoid any course of action which might lead to international complications. This was the third occasion on which Ribbentrop had promised that there would be no war; and the two Italians were suitably impressed. Ribbentrop had prefaced many of his sentences with the words: "I will tell you very frankly." But his frankness did not extend to revealing at that stage what was on foot between Germany and Soviet Russia.

Foiled in their main objective, the Italians proposed an early meeting with Hitler on the Brenner frontier, but Ribbentrop excused himself with the specious argument that it would be a mistake to provoke speculation in the enemy camp. If a meeting were to take place, it could not be allowed to end in a banal statement. Ribbentrop was sufficiently informed of his master's intentions to know that Italian intervention would not be tolerated.

Three days later, on July 27, the military order for the German seizure of Danzig was drawn up. On July 31 Hitler, who on tactical grounds had delayed a definite reply for as long as possible, pronounced against a meeting with Mussolini. Meanwhile more disturbing intelligence was coming in from Berlin. The Italian military attaché reported concentrations of forces and troop movements on the Polish frontier and Attolico's alarmist bombardment continued. At the beginning of August there was a violent Polish-German altercation over the threatened expulsion of Polish customs officials from Danzig. Ciano, who had throughout professed optimism and had deprecated Mussolini's proposal for a conference, because he believed that the West would collapse, now began to take fright. On August 6 he discussed the position with Mussolini. "We agree in feeling that we must find some way out. By following the Germans we shall go to war, and go to war in the most unfavorable conditions for the Axis, and especially for Italy. Our gold reserves are reduced to almost nothing, as well as our stocks of metals, and we are far from having completed our economic and military preparations. If the crisis comes, we shall fight if only to save our 'honor.' But we must avoid war." [31] Mussolini must then have regretted his impetuous decision to sign an offensive alliance; and a series of diplomatic transactions followed (there were five meetings with the Germans in seven days), which were designed to free Italy from the trap.[32]

Ciano proposed, and Mussolini agreed, that he should have an early meeting with Ribbentrop. Once more Mussolini prepared for his envoy a memorandum, designed to convince the Germans that it would be folly to embark on war. In 1939, he argued, the Axis would have no more than an even chance of victory, whereas in three years the odds would be four to one. He reverted to the idea of a conference and Ciano, cured of his previous facile optimism, now warmly endorsed it.

The fateful meeting took place at Salzburg on August 11. For the first time Ribbentrop showed his hand and mulishly declined to be moved by Ciano's arguments. He admitted that in previous conversations he had always spoken of two or three years' preparation, but he claimed that new situations had arisen which would probably precipitate events. The impression he left with Ciano was of an unreasonable, obstinate determination not to modify his views or even discuss them. Having failed to secure his main objective, Ciano sought to obtain some information on Germany's plan of action, but Ribbentrop refused to reply. When Ciano pointed out that the imminence of the crisis had not been brought in any way to the attention of the Italian government and had even been denied in recent conversations with Attolico, he blandly replied that he was not in a position to give particulars of what was about to happen, because all decisions were still locked in the Fuehrer's impenetrable bosom. The Italian record of this long and often acrimonious conversation, which lasted ten hours, ends gloomily: "I left him [Ribbentrop] with the profound conviction that he intends to provoke the conflict and that he will oppose any initiative which might have the effect of solving the present crisis peacefully."[33] More than four years later, in his prison cell at Verona, Ciano wrote:

It was at his residence at Fuschl that Von Ribbentrop, while we were waiting to be seated at the dinner table, told me of the German decision to set a match to the European powder keg. This he told me in much the same tone that he would have used about an inconsequential administrative detail. "Well, Ribbentrop," I asked, as we were walking together in the garden, "What do you want? The Corridor or Danzig?" "Not that any more," he said gazing at me with his cold metallic eyes. "We want war." I felt that the decision was irrevocable, and in a flash I saw the tragedy that threatened humanity.[34]

Ciano was not only gloomy, he was angry, frightened, and mortified. He was angry at having been made to look a fool, frightened at the yawning chasm to which Ribbentrop had blithely led him, and mortified at the Germans' ill-concealed disdain for Italy. "I am becoming aware," he writes, "of how little we are worth in the opinion of the Germans. The atmosphere is icy. . . . During dinner not a word is exchanged. We are distrustful of each other."[35] Ciano was never to recover from the shock administered to him by Ribbentrop at Salzburg.

On the following day he traveled the few miles to Berchtesgaden for a conversation with the Fuehrer. Hitler was more tactful and civil than his Foreign Minister, but, so far as the substance was concerned, Ciano soon found that the outlook was as bleak at Berchtesgaden as it had been at Salzburg. Indeed Hitler allowed himself to be a little more specific than his Minister of Foreign Affairs. In an interminable monologue he described for Ciano's benefit the strength of Germany's military position, the weakness of her enemies, the grounds on which he must attack Poland, and his certainty that he could localize the war. He then raised his sights to a wider perspective and spoke with pleasurable anticipation of an Axis war against Britain and France, which should be waged while the two great men were still young enough to lead their respective countries. As a special bait to Italy he advised the Duce to liquidate Yugoslavia as soon as possible; and here his voice rose with excitement.

Ciano, aghast at what he had heard, complained that no indication had ever been given by Germany either at Milan or later in Berlin that the situation was so grave. On the contrary Ribbentrop had stated that, in his opinion, the Danzig question would be settled in due course. He then proceeded stoutly to give chapter and verse for Italy's material unpreparedness and inability to conduct a war; and he pleaded for a postponement of the conflict. But Hitler brushed all this aside with the observation that German action against Poland would not in fact provoke a general conflict and that in consequence he would not have to ask for Italian help "according to the existing obligation."

As a last expedient Ciano ventilated the idea of issuing a joint statement, of which a draft had previously been concocted by Mussolini, holding out the hope that means would be found of resolving in a peaceful way the disputes which were disturbing the political life of Europe. The Germans, who were concerned to secure the support of Italy merely in order to bring the maximum pressure to bear on the Western powers, were not disposed to agree; and Ribbentrop had on the previous day suggested a statement merely emphasizing the identity of views of the two Axis powers. Nevertheless Hitler, possibly because he felt that he must not drive Ciano too far at one stage, decided to postpone until the morrow a final decision on the communiqué; and he closed the three-and-a-half-hour meeting with a repetition of the thesis, which it had already taken him a long time to expound.

Just as the Italians were about to return to Salzburg a dramatic incident was staged. The door opened and Walter Hewel, Ribbentrop's liaison officer at the Chancellery, entered the room to whisper something to his chief, who in turn informed Hitler that a report had just come in to the effect that Stalin was prepared to receive the German Minister of Foreign Affairs to sign a pact of non-aggression. No trace of any such telegram from Moscow has been found in the German documents, and indeed it is certain that a firm invitation from the Soviet government was only received several days later. The Germans were probably relying on a conversation, in which the Soviet chargé d'affaires in Berlin had guardedly spoken of the possible German-Soviet discussions and were anticipating events in order to impress Ciano. Nevertheless the Italians, despite the warnings of their ambassador in Moscow, had never credited the possibility of a German-Russian accord, and Ciano turned a sceptical eye on the German maneuver.

He returned to Salzburg that night in a mood of blank despair. The relations between the Axis partners were now such that he kept his airplane under special guard on the Salzburg airfield for fear of sabotage. In the gloomy discussion, which took place between the Italians at their hotel in Salzburg, Attolico begged Ciano to regard Italy as freed from the obligations of the alliance. But Ciano declined to take any decisive step without Mussolini's assent; and the only conclusion reached was that it would be better to issue no communiqué. The Germans would not accept the pacific Italian version and the Italians could not risk a statement emphasizing that they were completely at one with Germany.

On the following morning, before the meeting with Hitler, Ciano conveyed this view to Ribbentrop; and Hitler at once agreed: "The door would thus remain open for all parties, no one would be committed, and no project would be prevented." For the rest, Hitler was even more categorical than on the previous day. After ranting against the Western powers, whom he described as "misers on their heaps of gold, wallowing drunkenly in their riches," he spoke again of his resolve to crush Poland. Ciano's comment in his diary was: "In his gestures the man reveals even more than he did yesterday his wish for immediate action."

If Hitler was more decisive, Ciano for his part made little effort on the second day to swim against the tide. According to the Italian record, when Hitler asked him whether he had anything to say, he replied that he was waiting to hear the Fuehrer's decisions. Schmidt relates, and the German record confirms, that Ciano folded up completely and merely said to Hitler that he had been proved right so often, that it was possible that on this occasion his appreciation of the situation was correct.[36] He did, however, pluck up courage to inquire when the operation would begin. Hitler replied that, while no final decision had yet been taken as regards the date, Poland's political attitude must be clarified by the end of the month at latest, for Germany on military grounds could afford to wait no longer. All military preparations had, however, been made and, should the operation have to be launched as the result of a serious incident, it could take place at any minute. On the other hand it might be necessary to wait a little for a suitable pretext; but the last date for the opening of hostilities was the end of August.[37] At last Ciano knew the horrid truth; at best the cataclysm was only eighteen days away.

Ciano left Germany in a rage. Apart from the peril to Italy, his vanity was wounded. He had prided himself on his position as Minister of Foreign Affairs of a Great Power; he had enjoyed diplomatic transactions, in which he had played the role of an equal speaking to equals; and now the Germans had declined to pay the slightest attention to his representations, and had made it plain that they regarded him as a not very satisfactory vassal. His mood is reflected in his diary: "I return to Rome completely disgusted with the Germans, with their leader, with their way of doing things. They have betrayed and lied to us. Now they are dragging us into an adventure which we do not want. . . . The alliance was based on promises which they now deny; they are traitors, and we must not have any scruples in ditching them."[38] From this moment he remained anti-German to the end.

Mussolini was torn in two directions. He also was angry with the Germans and was terrified of war, since he still did not believe that the Western powers would stand aside. On the other hand he felt, and here he was sustained by Starace, Alfieri, and General Pariani, the Undersecretary of War, that Italy was in honor bound to march with Germany. With his usual vehemence he expressed totally contradictory views several times a day. On occasions he professed to agree with Ciano that he had no alternative but to remain neutral. On others he wished to instruct Attolico to confirm to Ribbentrop that in spite of everything Italy would enter the war if the Western powers did so. It was not only a sense of honor which impelled him, but fear of Hitler's vengeance. There was also the consideration that the democracies might give in, in which case he would require some of the booty. All in all, Mussolini during those mid-August days was tortured by doubts and indecisions; and Ciano struggled in vain to bring him definitely to his own way of thinking.

Meanwhile Attolico was not inactive. On his return to Berlin from

Salzburg he angrily reported a further breach of faith by the Germans. Hitler, having agreed at Berchtesgaden that there should be no public statement, had authorized his Ministry of Foreign Affairs to publish a unilateral communiqué declaring that at Salzburg the two Ministers had reached complete agreement in their examination of the situation and in the line of policy to be followed. Attolico urged that in the face of this barefaced attempt to compromise Italy, Mussolini should inform Hitler in writing that in his view the conflict could not be localized and that he was therefore resolved to stand aside. In Rome Grandi, Bottai, and others were urging the Duce to denounce the Pact of Steel.

Mussolini was not prepared to accept this advice, but he summoned Attolico for a conference, which took place on August 17. Here Mussolini took the view that loyalty required Italy in every circumstance to make common cause with the Germans. Ciano and Attolico wrestled with him, apparently in vain. Eventually Mussolini began to draft documents, setting forth the Italian point of view: first a letter to Hitler, then a memorandum, and then again a letter. But since he did not know exactly what he wanted to say, being torn between fear of war and fear of seeming afraid, the process of drafting was not conspicuously successful. It was eventually decided to tear up the drafts and to despatch Attolico with verbal instructions to call the attention of the German government to the incalculable consequences of their policy, but without any statement of Italian intentions.[39]

Attolico, accompanied by Magistrati, saw Ribbentrop at Fuschl on August 18. It was a very stormy interview, which achieved precisely nothing. The two Italians returned wearily to Munich, where Ribbentrop telephoned to tell them that the decisions adumbrated to Ciano had now been definitely taken. In other words, Hitler had resolved to conclude a pact with the Soviet government. On the following day they were summoned back to Salzburg to receive further clarification. On this occasion the interview took place not in the idyllic surroundings of Ribbentrop's castle at Fuschl, but in a Salzburg hotel, the Oesterreichischer Hof. Fortified by instructions, which he had received from Hitler overnight, Ribbentrop was more rigid than ever and told them severely that Germany could no longer tolerate Polish provocation, that Hitler remained convinced that he could localize the war, but that, even if the conflict became general, victory was certain.

Attolico replied firmly that in these circumstances he must reserve the position of the Italian government, which did not share the German appreciation of the situation, and indeed profoundly disagreed with it. As the argument proceeded, Ribbentrop became extremely heated and Magistrati, who had been asked by Ribbentrop to leave the room, heard angry voices from his lonely post in the corridor. He was summoned back by Attolico, who asked Ribbentrop to repeat an allegation that the Italian embassy in Berlin was unreliable and defeatist, an accusation to which the ambassador replied with all the passion of a southern Italian.[40] Ribbentrop sulkily withdrew the charge, but the altercation marked the end of any tolerable relationship between Attolico and Ribbentrop, who eight months later was to demand and obtain his recall.

Attolico traveled from Munich to Rome and on August 20 attended a conference at the Palazzo Venezia with Mussolini and Ciano. Mussolini on that particular day was in one of his pro-German moods, and argued that it was too late to go back on the Germans and that Italy could not afford to expose herself to a charge of cowardice. He once more stubbornly favored an immediate communication to the Germans stating Italy's intention to enter the war. The British government had that day made an appeal to Mussolini to contribute to a peaceful solution, and Ciano used this move as a pretext for delay. So nothing was decided that night, but the omens were unfavorable and Attolico left the Palazzo Venezia "discouraged and overwhelmed with grief." [41]

On the following day, August 21, Ciano returned vigorously to the charge. He had, he told Mussolini, gone to Salzburg in order to adopt a common line of action, but had found himself faced by a *Diktat.* It was the Germans who had betrayed the alliance in which Italy was to have been a partner, not a servant. "Tear up the Pact. Throw it in Hitler's face and Europe will recognize in you the natural leader of the anti-German crusade." He proposed that he should be sent to Salzburg to speak to the Germans as they should be spoken to. "Hitler will not tell me to put out my cigarette as he did Schuschnigg." [42]

Mussolini, who was apt to be impressed by the last man he had seen, agreed to seek a further meeting between Ciano and Ribbentrop, although he made it clear that he did not wish to break up the Axis for the time being. A telephone call was put through to Ribbentrop, who replied that he was unable to give an immediate answer because he was awaiting an important message from Moscow. At half-past ten that night he telephoned that he would prefer to see Ciano at Innsbruck rather than at the Brenner Pass because he was to leave later for Moscow to sign a political pact with the Soviet government.

Although the Germans had not concealed from the Italians their intention to seek an accord with the Soviet Union, they had not kept their ally informed of the detailed course of the latest negotiations; and the news that an agreement would be signed forthwith came as a bombshell. A fresh situation had been created, which required consideration. The Italians telephoned to Ribbentrop that the projected meeting had best be postponed until after his return from Moscow. There was at the back of their minds the alluring prospect of snatching some advantage in Croatia and Dalmatia.

On the following day the German ambassador asked to see Mussolini. At once he jumped to the conclusion that the Germans were on the point of asking him to declare his intentions. It seemed to him that Hitler's master stroke in Moscow had placed Germany on the winning side and that he must be in a position to tell the ambassador that he had already spontaneously taken his decision. He immediately drafted a personal telegram to Hitler: "As soon as you cross the frontier, I shall be at your side"; and the draft was delivered to the Minister of Foreign Affairs with instructions for urgent despatch. Ciano, however, gave orders that it was to be held up, saying that if Mussolini made inquiries, he should be told that the delay was due to encoding. He could safely rely on Mussolini's ignorance of administrative matters to put forward so lame a pretext. Some hours later Mussolini telephoned to Ciano to ask whether the telegram had gone, and on being told that it had not, heaved a sigh of relief and said that it was to be stopped.

It happened that the German ambassador, far from putting a pistol at Mussolini's head, had come merely to inquire what Italy would require in the way of arms and supplies to enter the war. In view of this mild and tentative approach, Mussolini had suddenly altered course and decided not to commit himself. The cancelled draft telegram was prudently placed with Ciano's private papers and subsequently disappeared.[43]

VIII

Meanwhile in Berlin Hitler was preparing for his war. On August 22 he called a military conference at the Chancellery and in a long, rambling discourse explained to his generals why he had decided to strike at once. There were, he explained, two personal considerations: his own personality and that of Mussolini. The Duce's existence was decisive. "If something happens to him, Italy's loyalty to the alliance will no longer be certain." The Western powers were weak and would probably not fight, while Germany was at the peak of her power. Russia was no longer a potential enemy. "The way is open for the soldier, now that I have made the political preparations." The only danger now was a proposal for mediation. The order to march would be given later, probably for the morning of August 26. On the following day, August 23, General Halder noted in his diary: "Y day definitely set for the 26th. No further orders."[44] That evening, after a three-hour meeting in the Kremlin, Ribbentrop signed the German-Soviet pact.

In Rome on August 23 Mussolini, still seeking for himself an honorable way out, authorized Ciano to present to the British ambassador a proposal for the preliminary cession of Danzig to Germany, followed by negotiations and a peace conference. It was a hopeless proposal, for it afforded Poland no guarantee of her future security. Mussolini must have realized that the plan would not extricate him from the trap and he soon relapsed into belligerence. That very evening Ciano found him warlike. "He talks of armies and attacks. He received Pariani, who gave him good news about the condition of the army. Pariani is a traitor and a liar."[45]

At Berchtesgaden Hitler was on August 23 receiving Sir Nevile Henderson, who came with a letter in which Chamberlain warned the Fuehrer that whatever the nature of the German-Soviet agreement, Britain would stand by Poland. Having made the position clear, Chamberlain again appealed to Hitler to seek a peaceful solution of his dispute with Poland and offered his good offices to secure it. Hitler, who was excitable and uncompromising, declined to be moved and merely replied that Germany, if attacked by England, would be found prepared and determined. Weizsäcker telephoned from Berchtesgaden to Ciano to inform him of "Hitler's harsh answer to the British ambassador"; and Ciano noted in his diary: "Another hope is gone." In another diary General Halder was writing that night: "There will be no more orders regarding Y day and X hour. Everything is to roll automatically."

On August 24 there was a pause. Hitler was confidently expecting some sign of withdrawal by the Western powers under the impact of the German-Soviet Pact and Mussolini was helplessly waiting on events. Ciano traveled to see the King at Sant'Anna di Valdieri, ostensibly to thank him for the collar of the Annunziata, which had recently been conferred on him, but in reality to discuss the situation. He found the King as anti-German as ever and strongly in favor of neutrality, for in his judgment Italy was in no condition to wage war. The army was in a pitiful state, the frontier defenses were insufficient, the officers were incompetent, and the equipment obsolete. To all this must be added the state of mind of the Italians, which was distinctly anti-German. Ciano left the King fortified in his opposition to Mussolini's romantic bellicosity.

August 25 was the decisive day. It saw Mussolini turning and squirming, while he floundered in the hopeless attempt to reconcile the dictates of reason and the interests of his country with the desire to cut a good figure with his ally. During the previous night Ribbentrop had telephoned to Ciano that the situation was becoming critical because of Polish provocation, and he was evasive when the suggestion of a meeting was put forward. Worse still, Ciano was warned that during his absence the Duce's attitude had become furiously warlike.

This was the state of mind in which Ciano found him that morning. "I make use of the King's opinions in order to dissuade him, and I succeed in getting him to approve a communication to Hitler, announcing our nonintervention for the time being, pending a reexamination of our position and until such time as we have completed our preparations for war." Ciano returned to his Ministry with a lighter step than he had entered the Palazzo Venezia, but his satisfaction did not last long, for within a very short time Mussolini had changed his mind again. He could not bear to be accused of behaving as Italy had done in 1914 and was afraid of Hitler. Ciano was summoned back to the Palazzo Venezia to be told by Mussolini that he wished to intervene at once. "It is useless to struggle," he notes, "I submit and go back to the Palazzo Chigi, where consternation takes the place of the harmony that had reigned before." [46] Mussolini ordered a mobilization decree to be prepared for that evening.

The afternoon brought a dramatic change in the situation. Hitler remained convinced that the cowardly Western powers, confronted by the German-Soviet Pact and a solid Rome-Berlin Axis, would at the last moment retreat. But it was important, in order to produce this result, to obtain a satisfactory definition of Italy's attitude, about which disquieting reports were circulating. There was speculation in the foreign press on Italy's neutrality and reliable information from Rome, which pointed to the hesitations of the Duce and the possibility that Italy might repudiate her obligations under the Pact of Steel.

On August 20 Magistrati had called on Weizsäcker at the Foreign Office and told him that since Germany had not consulted Italy in accordance with the terms of the alliance and had elected to treat the dispute with Poland as an exclusively German problem, Germany was thus dispensing with Italy's armed assistance. Accordingly, if the Polish conflict developed into a general war, Italy did not consider that the prerequisite of the alliance existed.[47] On August 23 a further warning was received from Mackensen, the German ambassador in Rome, who reported that the Italian government took the view that, if Germany attacked Poland, she would violate the Pact of Steel, which was based on an agreement to refrain from war until 1942. The Duce, Mackensen added, was sure that the Western powers would intervene, and the United States as well after a few months. Thus while Germany remained on the defensive in the West, the French and British "would descend on Italy with all the forces at their disposal. In this situation Italy would have to bear the whole brunt of the war in order to give the Reich the opportunity of liquidating the affair in the East.[48] To

Hitler this report rang true in view of Ribbentrop's adverse comment on the attitude of Ciano and his own knowledge of the anti-German sentiment of the House of Savoy. The only hope was Mussolini, in whom Hitler still placed trust.

With these considerations in mind, Hitler on the morning of August 25 drafted a long personal letter to Mussolini, to whom he affected to open his heart.[49] He explained why he had decided to conclude a pact with Russia and why he had omitted to keep his ally fully informed. He had been unable, he claimed, to foresee the scope of the conversations or to entertain any certainty in regard to their success. In any conflict the benevolent attitude of Russia was now assured, Rumania would not dare move, and Turkey would be obliged to revise her policy. In short, the successful negotiations with Russia had created a new situation and represented an enormous gain to the Axis. Having thus attempted to fortify Mussolini, he went on to utter a warning that the attack on Poland might take place at any moment, though he carefully refrained from giving his ally the exact date, which he had already fixed. He concluded by appealing for Italy's understanding, without specifically asking for her help, which under the terms of the alliance was to be automatic.

The text of the letter was telephoned to Mackensen with instructions to deliver it at once and ask for an immediate answer. Mussolini received the ambassador in the presence of Ciano at about three o'clock on the afternoon of August 25. Mussolini knew that the sands were running out, and, faced by the need to take a decision, could not bring himself to give a negative reply. According to a report despatched by Mackensen late that night, Mussolini, after carefully reading Hitler's letter twice, declared that he was in complete agreement about the pact with Russia and assured the ambassador that "he stood beside us unconditionally and with all his resources." [50]

As soon as Mackensen had left the room Ciano began once more to wrestle with Mussolini. Fastening on the passage of the letter in which Hitler merely asked for understanding, Ciano at last persuaded Mussolini to despatch a temporizing answer. After expressing his "complete approval" of the pact with Russia, agreeing that the situation of Rumania and Turkey had changed for the better, and assuring Hitler that he understood the German attitude towards

Poland, he came to the less agreeable part of his communication:

> As for the *practical* attitude of Italy in case of military action, my point of view is as follows:
>
> If Germany attacks Poland and the conflict remains localized, Italy will afford Germany every form of political and economic assistance which is requested of her.
>
> If Germany attacks Poland,* and the latter's allies open a counterattack against Germany, I inform you in advance that it will be opportune for me not to take the *initiative* in military operations in view of the *present* state of Italian war preparations, of which we have repeatedly and in good time informed you, Fuehrer, and Herr Von Ribbentrop.
>
> Our intervention can, nevertheless, take place at once if Germany delivers to us immediately the military supplies and the raw materials to resist the attack which the French and English would predominantly direct against us. At our meetings the war was envisaged for after 1942, and by that time I would have been ready on land, on sea, and in the air, according to the plans which had been concerted.
>
> I am furthermore of the opinion that the purely military measures which have already been taken, and other measures to be taken later, will immobilize in Europe and Africa considerable French and British forces.
>
> I consider it my bounden duty as a loyal friend to tell you the whole truth and inform you beforehand about the real situation. Not to do so might have unpleasant consequences for us all. This is my view, and since within a short time I must summon the highest governmental bodies,† I beg you to let me know yours.[51]

This letter was very quickly drafted and was telephoned to Berlin at about five o'clock. Meanwhile Hitler had been awaiting the Duce's reply with rising impatience, inquiring from time to time why it had not yet come. His petulance was understandable since the attack on Poland was scheduled to open in less than twelve hours. Eventually at about six o'clock Attolico arrived at the Chancellery to deliver the letter. It could not have arrived at a worse moment, for news had just been received that Britain had signed a mutual-assistance pact with Poland against German aggression, and, according to Schmidt who was present, it struck the Fuehrer

* In the German version this reads: "If Poland attacks."

† In fact the Cabinet did not meet until September 1 and the Grand Council until much later.

like a bombshell. He told Attolico that he would answer the Duce's letter at once and curtly dismissed him.

As Schmidt was accompanying the ambassador out of Hitler's study, General Keitel entered the room. A few minutes later the General emerged and shouted to his adjutant: "The order to advance must be delayed again." There was considerable excitement and disorder in the Chancellery and Schmidt overheard the Fuehrer complaining that "the Italians are behaving just as they did in 1914." Halder described the Fuehrer as considerably shaken (*ziemlich zusammengebrochen*). Nevertheless Hitler was not prepared to give up his war, and he made a last effort to neutralize Britain by making a comprehensive proposal to guarantee the British Empire, and to bring Italy in by a friendly inquiry as to her requirements.

At half-past nine that same day Mackensen appeared again at the Palazzo Venezia bearing a second letter in which Hitler mildly inquired what arms and raw materials Italy required and within what time, in order to meet the attack which France and Britain were likely to launch against her. He concluded by thanking the Duce from his heart for the military measures already taken by Italy, which he noted with great satisfaction. There was no recrimination, no note even of disappointment.

At ten o'clock on the morning of August 26 Mussolini held a meeting of the service chiefs to draw up a list of Italy's requirements. It was not a modest bill and, as Ciano put it, "it is enough to kill a bull—if a bull could read it." It included seven million tons of petroleum, six million tons of coal, two million tons of steel, one million tons of wood, and about half a million tons of fourteen other products. In addition Mussolini demanded one hundred and fifty antiaircraft batteries with ammunition and a quantity of machinery listed in a paper previously handed to General Keitel.

To accompany the list, Mussolini drafted a letter which must have made his intentions painfully plain:

> Fuehrer, I would not have sent you this list, or else it would have contained a smaller number of items and much lower figures, if I had had the time agreed upon beforehand to accumulate stocks and to speed up the tempo of autarchy.
>
> It is my duty to tell you that unless I am certain of receiving these supplies, the sacrifices I should call on the Italian people to make—and I

know that I should be obeyed—could be in vain and compromise your cause along with my own.[52]

Mussolini, with his customary wishful thinking, was still hankering after a negotiated settlement; and he concluded his letter with an assurance that if Hitler thought that there was any possibility of a solution in the political field, he was ready, as before, to afford full support and to take any initiative which might be considered useful.

This letter was telephoned to Berlin at about noon on August 26. Attolico, who delivered it personally to Hitler, took it upon himself to add that all material on the list must be in Italy before the beginning of hostilities, and that this demand was decisive. This was manifestly a ludicrous condition, since obviously some sixteen million tons could not be delivered in a few hours or even days. He later explained to Ciano that he had acted deliberately in order to discourage the Germans from meeting Mussolini's requests.[53]

The tempo of the exchanges between Duce and Fuehrer did not diminish. To those who have had experience of important diplomatic transactions under pressure it is clear that both men must have been under considerable strain, particularly Hitler, on whom the burden of his timetable was weighing. In all the circumstances the tone of his third letter, which was telephoned at about 3 P.M. on August 26 was remarkably calm. There was still no sign of impatience or dismay. He told the Duce that he could meet Italy's demands in coal, steel, and timber, and could despatch at once thirty antiaircraft batteries, but he was unable to supply seven million tons of oil or the required quantity of copper and nickel. Since, however, the Italian ambassador had stipulated that all deliveries must be completed before hostilities, a condition which on technical grounds it was impossible to fulfill, he could only take account of Italy's situation and beg the Duce to pin down Anglo-French forces "by active propaganda and suitable military demonstrations such as you have already proposed to me." He concluded by announcing that he was resolved on war, whatever the attitude of Italy or the Western powers.

As neither France nor Britain can achieve any decisive result in the West, and since Germany in consequence of the agreement with Russia will have all her forces free in the East after the defeat of Poland and possesses undisputed air supremacy, I do not shrink from solving the Eastern question, even at the risk of complications in the west.[54]

This letter was delivered to Mussolini by Mackensen at about 5 P.M. and at 6:45 Mussolini telephoned a reply in which he made a further despairing appeal for a peaceful settlement.

I believe that the misunderstanding into which Attolico involuntarily fell has been cleared up immediately in accordance with my instructions. That which I asked of you, except the antiaircraft batteries, was to be delivered in the course of twelve months. But even though the misunderstanding has been cleared up, it is evident that it is materially impossible for you to help me to fill the large gaps which the wars in Ethiopia and Spain have created in Italian armaments.

I will therefore adopt the attitude which you advise, at least in the initial phase of the conflict, thereby immobilizing the maximum Franco-British forces, as is already happening, while I shall speed up military preparations to the utmost possible extent.

Mussolini was only too painfully aware that, having posed for a generation as a warlord, he was cutting a poor figure before his more robust partner; and he sought to express his anguish. "I leave it to you," he continued, "to understand my state of mind at being compelled by forces outside my control to withhold from you my active support in the hour of action." Disclaiming any taint of pacifism, he concluded again by appealing for negotiation:

I venture to insist anew, and not from my considerations of a pacifist character foreign to my nature, but by reason of the interests of our two peoples and our two regimes, on the advantage of a political solution, which I regard as still possible in a form which will give full moral and material satisfaction to Germany.[55]

It was now plain to Hitler that he had failed in Rome, and he became resigned to being left in the lurch by Mussolini. In his reply, which he despatched shortly after midnight, he did not bother to refer to Mussolini's plea for peace, but repeated that he intended to go ahead alone. At the same time he made an effort, which must have cost him something, to spare his ally's susceptibility. He still held the Duce personally in high regard and, besides, he might need Italy later. So the letter, though hard in substance, was in tone as conciliatory as it could be in the circumstances:

I have received your communication on your final attitude. I respect the reasons and motives which led you to take this decision. Indeed in certain circumstances it can nevertheless work out well.

In my opinion, however, the prerequisite is that, at least until the outbreak of the struggle, the world should have no idea of the attitude Italy intends to adopt. I therefore cordially beg you to support my struggle psychologically with your press or by other means. I would also ask you, Duce, if you possibly can, by demonstrative military measures, at least to compel Britain and France to tie down certain of their forces, or at all events to leave them in uncertainty.[56]

Having made this request, Hitler sought to infuse his own optimism into his partner. He repeated that, should a major war break out, the issue in the East would be decided before the Western powers could score any success. Then in the winter, or at latest in the spring, he would attack with forces at least equal to those of France and Britain. The blockade would not be effective and the danger to Italy would diminish, not increase, with the prolongation of the war. He concluded with a plea for Italian labor. "In specially commending to your generosity this request of mine, I thank you for all the efforts you have made for the common cause." [57]

This fourth letter arrived in the early hours of August 27 and the German ambassador did not bring it round till nine o'clock in the morning. Mussolini replied at once by assuring the Fuehrer that the world would not hear of Italy's decision until after the war had broken out. This promise, as will be seen, was not to be kept. After a somewhat boastful account of his military measures—seventeen divisions, twenty-seven Alpine battalions, and the frontier guards concentrated on the French frontier and ten divisions in Libya—he also promised that everything possible would be done by his propaganda machine to emphasize Italian support for Germany. This undertaking was observed for a few days, but on September 1 Mussolini, fearing that the Western powers might take him at his word, issued an instruction to the press: "Abandon the motif of English responsibility, even in the headlines." Finally, Mussolini promised to send as much Italian labor as he could spare and expressed his desire to keep in close contact, in order to coordinate the policy of the two countries.[58] Of course nothing was further from Hitler's mind than any close collaboration, as Mussolini might have guessed from past experience. He was soon to receive further confirmation of the fact in even more brutal fashion.

Earlier in the day, when discussing Hitler's letter with Mackensen, Mussolini had repeated in forceful terms that he still "believed it possible to gain all our objectives without resort to war"; and had said that he would again advert to this aspect in his written reply. But in fact he did not. His tattered pride revolted at the prospect of another snub. Mussolini's fourth reply to Hitler closed the correspondence and appeared to have settled the matter. But it did not bring any peace or satisfaction to Mussolini's soul. Never before had he been so distraught, so uncertain, so ill-tempered and unhappy.

Ciano's diary for the five remaining days of August describes Mussolini's volatile mood. His reason told him that he had taken the right decision, but he rebelled helplessly with every fiber of his being against inaction in the hour of battle. "The Duce is now quite calm, as he always is after he has made a decision. He does not want to utter the word 'neutrality,' but it is this frame of mind that he has definitely reached. He even begins to hope that the struggle will be hard, long, and bloody for others, for he sees in this a possibility of great advantage for us." He was suspicious of the Germans and resented Hitler's offer to guarantee the British Empire. He resented Hitler's unwillingness to consider a negotiated settlement, and Ciano, as ever, records his master's views. "Hitler is acting in this fashion for fear that intervention on the part of the Duce will settle the crisis at the last moment, as was done last year at Munich. This would have the effect of raising his prestige, of which Hitler is jealous."

On August 29, Mussolini was no longer calm. "The Duce is restless. He would like to do something. Certain articles in the English press, which speak of the necessity for Italian neutrality, have had a bad effect on him. Meanwhile, he sets down a series of military and civilian measures, which in my opinion need not be taken at this time." On August 30 Mussolini was convinced that the Germans were about to march.

Naturally the idea of a neutrality imposed on us weighs more and more upon him. Not being able to wage war, he makes all the necessary preparations, so that in case of a peaceful solution he may be able to say that he would have waged it. Calls to arms, blackouts, requisitions, closing of cafés and amusement places. . . . All this carries with it two grave dangers: one, external, since it would cause London and Paris to believe that we are preparing to attack, and hence induce them to take the initiative in moving against us; the other internal, because it will alarm the population, which is more and more openly anti-German.

On August 31 two final efforts were made in Rome to stave off the war. In the morning Ciano informed Halifax by telephone that the Duce could only intervene with Hitler if he were in a position to bring a fat prize: Danzig. Mussolini was still so completely out of touch with his partner that he did not know that Hitler was uninterested in Danzig and was only concerned to destroy Poland. Halifax asked Ciano to bring pressure on Berlin to establish direct contact with Poland, and later telephoned that the proposal to cede Danzig was unacceptable.

Having failed over Danzig, Ciano with the Duce's concurrence proposed to the British and French ambassadors an international conference on September 5, for the purpose of reviewing the contentious clauses of the Treaty of Versailles. Halifax undertook to submit this proposal to Chamberlain, but the day passed without any answer; and at 8:20 P.M. the central telephone office in Rome informed the Palazzo Chigi that London had cut its communications with Italy. "Here then," Ciano comments bitterly, "are the consequences of the measures taken in the last few days, or better, the consequences of too much publicity about the meager results of the too many measures taken in the last few days."

The Duce, who had been breathing fire for the last few days, was now brought up with a sudden jerk. His bellicose gestures had created a situation in which he might be attacked at any moment by Britain and France. This was a risk he was not prepared to face and, despite his categorical undertaking to Hitler, he authorized Ciano to inform the British ambassador that same evening of August 31 that Italy would not enter the war.

IX

On September 1 news was received that the German armies had entered Poland. The reluctant decision to remain neutral had been irrevocably taken the previous day under the pressure of fear and advice from every quarter, but the Duce early in the morning telephoned personally to Attolico urging him to "entreat Hitler to send him a telegram, releasing him from the obligations of the alliance. He does not want to seem perfidious in the eyes of the German people, nor in the eyes of the Italian people, who, to tell the truth, do not show too many scruples, blinded as they are by anti-German hatred." [59]

In the expectation of favors to come, and also because he was moving to the conviction that he would not require Italian help for the moment, Hitler sent a prompt and satisfactory reply:

> I thank you most cordially for the diplomatic and political support which you have been giving recently to Germany and her just cause. I am convinced that I can carry out the task assigned to us with the military forces of Germany. I therefore believe that in these circumstances I shall not need Italian military aid. I also thank you Duce for everything which you will do in future for the common cause of fascism and national socialism.[60]

Three hours later, at about 12:45 P.M., Hitler sent Mussolini a further message designed to put the blame for the war on Polish intransigence and to discourage any further attempt at intervention. If the Polish government, Hitler declared, had entertained even the slightest desire to solve the dispute amicably, they could have done so at any time: "For this reason, Duce, I did not wish to expose you to the danger of assuming the role of mediator." [61]

Despite all the evidence that Hitler would resent any further interference from Rome, the danger of mediation seemed to Mussolini preferable to the ignominy of neutrality. So, despite the publication of Anglo-French notes, warning Germany that the Western Allies would go to war unless the German troops withdrew from Poland, Mussolini made a last attempt to launch his proposal for a conference. At ten o'clock on September 2 Attolico handed the following communication to the German State secretary:

> For purposes of information, Italy wishes to make known, naturally leaving any decision to the Fuehrer, that she still has the possibility of getting France, Britain, and Poland to agree to a conference on the following bases:
>
> 1. An armistice, which leaves the armies *where* they now are.
> 2. Convening of the conference within two or three days.

3. Settlement of the Polish-German dispute, which as matters stand today, would certainly be favorable to Germany.

The idea, which originally emanated from the Duce, is now supported, particularly by France.

Danzig is already German, and Germany has already in her hands pledges which guarantee her the greater part of her claims. Moreover Germany has already had her "moral satisfaction." If she accepted the proposal for a conference, she would achieve all her arms and at the same time avoid a war, which even now looks like becoming general and of extremely long duration.

The Duce does not want to insist, but it is of the greatest moment to him that the above should be immediately brought to the notice of Herr Von Ribbentrop and the Fuehrer.[62]

There was a flutter in Berlin, caused by Ribbentrop's contention that the Duce's proposals could not be reconciled with the Anglo-French warnings, which had the character of an ultimatum. While Attolico in Berlin was busy gathering satisfactory assurances from the Western ambassadors that no ultimatum was intended, in Rome Mussolini's last effort was being frustrated by the unbending attitude of the British government. At 2 P.M. Ciano, in the presence of the British and French ambassadors, informed Bonnet and Halifax by telephone of the latest developments. Bonnet effusively thanked Ciano for his efforts for peace, but Halifax, though confirming that no ultimatum had been intended, expressed his personal view that Britain could not accept the Italian proposal for a conference unless the German army withdrew from Poland. He undertook, however, to inform Ciano of the decision of the British cabinet on the point.

At 7 P.M. the blow fell. Halifax telephoned that Britain accepted the Duce's offer on condition that Hitler withdrew his troops to the German frontier. Even Mussolini and Ciano now realized that the last hope of a compromise had been extinguished and that there was no alternative but to allow events to take their course. At 8:50 P.M. on September 2 Attolico informed Ribbentrop that Britain declined to enter a conference on the terms proposed by Mussolini, but demanded the withdrawal of German troops from Danzig and Polish territory. In the circumstances the Duce now considered his mediation proposal as having lapsed. Ribbentrop received this communication with the silence of contempt.[63] In Rome that night Ciano noted in his diary: "The last note of hope has died. . . . The Duce is convinced of the necessity of remaining neutral, but he is not at all happy. Whenever he can, he reverts to the possibility of action. The Italian people, however, are happy about the decisions taken."

On the following day, September 3, Britain and France declared war on Germany. That evening at about nine o'clock Hitler despatched his last message to the Duce. It was again a friendly message, but it contained a veiled threat. After thanking Mussolini for his last attempt at mediation, which was rendered fruitless by England's determination to go to war, he went on to predict that Poland would quickly collapse. But he was also aware that the struggle would be one for life and death, though his faith in ultimate victory was as firm as a rock. Then came the advice to the Duce:

You kindly assured me recently that you believe you can help in some fields. I accept this in advance with sincere thanks. But I also believe that, even if we now march down separate paths, destiny will yet bind us one to the other. If National Socialist Germany were to be destroyed by the Western democracies, Fascist Italy would also face a hard future. I personally was always aware that the futures of our two regimes were bound up, and I know that you, Duce, are of exactly the same opinion. . . . Please accept once more my thanks, Duce, for all the support you have given me in the past, and which I ask you not to refuse me in the future.[64]

Having delivered this warning, Hitler a few minutes later entered his special train and sped to his war headquarters in the East.

The message was delivered to the Duce by Mackensen the following morning. According to Ciano,

the Duce expressed full solidarity with Germany, and this is what he really feels. He gives in to my suggestions momentarily, but later, as is his way, returns to his former ways. He is convinced that France does not want, and cannot fight this war . . . and he is still dreaming of heroic undertakings against Yugoslavia . . . forgetting completely what our situation really is. . . . At times the Duce seems attracted to the idea of neutrality, which would permit us to gather economic and military strength, so that we could intervene effectively at the proper moment. But immediately afterwards he abandons this idea. The idea of joining the Germans attracts him.[65]

Mussolini's pro-Germanism, however, could not be relied upon for very long. Five days later he was complaining of German conduct in Hungary, and Ciano noted that after an interview in which the Hungarian minister in Rome had referred to German designs on Trieste, the Duce was shaken and advised the Hungarians to reject German demands for the right of passage through their territory. When the minister had left, Mussolini violently attacked the Germans, but adds Ciano, "he wishes to be prudent, since a German victory cannot be completely discounted." On the following day, when Mussolini saw Attolico, who reported that German public opinion was becoming increasingly hostile and that there was talk of Italian treachery, the Duce was indignant and wanted to publish Hitler's telegram releasing him from his obligations. There was also trouble over the Alto Adige, when the Germans announced that they would postpone until the end of war the repatriation of the Germans. Once more the Duce was indignant; and Attolico and Ciano noted with satisfaction "the change in Mussolini's psychology." [66] But they were very much mistaken if they imagined that he would remain for very long poised in the same position.

Mussolini was ashamed of his inglorious posture, afraid of Hitler, and tortured by the thought that he might be missing a chance of picking up some cheap loot. All this was very bitter, but he was also mortified to feel that his position at home had been shaken. The Duce, who for years had been proclaiming Italy's might and boasting of all he had done to strengthen the armed forces, was now compelled to admit that of all the major European powers Italy was the only one that was in no position to go to war. Moreover, Italy was now for the first time excluded from the councils of Europe. Germany was parleying with Russia and might come to any agreement behind Italy's back regarding the future of Poland and the Balkan states, while Britain and France were busily concerting to hatch their plans. From the convulsion a new Europe would emerge. At a time when this tremendous drama was being played, Italy was compelled to stand silent, unseen and ill-considered in the wings, watching the others strutting on the stage. It was on this world stage that the old trouper was determined by hook or by crook to appear at the earliest opportunity.

CHAPTER SIXTEEN

The Bitterness of Neutrality

1939–1940

I

AFTER the outbreak of war Mussolini never ceased for nine long months to bemoan the fate which condemned him to inactivity in what seemed likely to become the world's most extensive and important conflict. His irritation was aggravated by the satisfaction with which his people greeted his proclamation of neutrality, or rather of nonbelligerence, as he chose to put it. Any manifestation of craven pacifism was apt to arouse his resentment; and when the stock market rose, when foreign orders were placed in Italy, and when Italian shipping flourished, he was not impressed. "The Duce takes an interest in all this," Ciano noted sadly, "but not a great deal as yet." [1]

At first he looked for escape from his predicament in an early compromise peace. On September 6 Ciano reports him as "still believing that the opportunity of entering the game will shortly present itself." On September 8 Mussolini saw in the occupation of Warsaw "some possibility of a rapid conclusion of the conflict." On September 14 Ciano in a letter to Lord Halifax spoke of the Duce's intention to do all he could, not only to prevent an extension of the conflict, but to bring it to an end as soon as circumstances permitted.[2] On September 23 the German State Secretary noted that on three recent occasions the Italian ambassador had urged a generous peace offer.[3] Mussolini's ill-founded hopes were, however, finally dissipated when Chamberlain on October 12 made it clear to the House of Commons that he was not to be seduced by the bogus offer of peace held out to him in Hitler's Reichstag speech of October 6. Mussolini, after reading Chamberlain's speech, regretfully concluded that "every possibility for an understanding has now disappeared." [4]

Mussolini could no longer take refuge in illusions and was obliged to face facts. For a time, and at intervals, he allowed himself to be possessed by anti-German sentiment. The behavior of the Nazis in the Alto Adige continued to cause friction, and since the Russo-German partition of Poland affronted Italian sentiment, the Italian embassy in Berlin was instructed to show the utmost liberality in the issue of visas to Poles and Jews.[5] This and other manifestations of anti-Germanism could only be justified on the assumption that Germany would lose the war, and this was the view that he affected to take. Thus on October 3 he was sceptical about a German victory and thought that Britain and France would hold firm. Besides, on that particular day he did not wish the Germans to win; and Ciano noted: "He is somewhat bitter about Hitler's sudden rise to fame. He would be greatly pleased if Hitler were slowed down, and, hoping this, predicts that it will come about." [6] On November 9 Mussolini felt some embarrassment at having to draft a telegram congratulating Hitler on his escape from the attempt on his life in the beer cellar at Munich. "The Duce has tried hard to compose a telegram expressing his delight that peril has been avoided. He wanted it to be warm, but not too warm, because in his opinion no Italian feels any great joy over the fact that Hitler has escaped death—least of all the Duce." [7] Two days later Ciano discussed with him reports of an impending German invasion of Holland and Belgium. Ciano observed that they had received no information from Berlin and that in fact Hitler and Ribbentrop had always specifically excluded an attack on the neutrals for moral and technical reasons.

But, considering what has already happened, anything is possible. Mussolini does not believe that such an attack will be made, but he admits that if it did take place, Germany would be totally discredited, and that in Italy there would be a great wave of hatred for Germany, which would have to be taken into account. The Duce in these last few days, probably because of the situation in Alto Adige, expresses himself as more and more anti-German.[8]

On November 20 Mussolini was encouraged by reports of a crisis in Bohemia, which he thinks might retard or prevent an offensive in the West. "For Mussolini, the idea of Hitler waging war, and, worse still winning it, is altogether unbearable. He gives instructions to our consul at Prague to advise the Bohemians to side with the Communists." [9] Italo-German relations were subjected to still further strain when, on November 30, 1939, Russia attacked Finland. There were anti-Russian and anti-German demonstrations throughout Italy, and Ciano took advantage of the climate of opinion to show Mussolini a report by an Italian resident in Posen on German atrocities against the population. "The Duce was indignant; he advised me to see to it that by indirect channels the American and French newspapers get the contents of the report. The world must know." [10]

II

Mounting public indignation against Germany enabled Ciano to secure Mussolini's approval of a speech in the Chamber which, as Ciano put it, was designed to "destroy or at least undermine our relations with Germany, which are materially worsening." [11] The speech was delivered on December 16. It contained a review of events between the wars, in which Ciano's observations were completely in accord with Axis philosophy: the folly of the Treaty of Versailles, which was described as the root cause of disequilibrium in Europe; disparaging references to the League of Nations, which offered only the illusion of security; a tribute to Italo-German cooperation, which constituted the best guarantee of peaceful evolution; criticism of the attitude of the Western powers. But having, as it were, formally discharged his obligations to his partner, Ciano made a two-pronged attack on German policy.

He first recalled the circumstances in which Italy, at Germany's request, signed the Anti-Comintern Pact. The object of this treaty, he declared, had been to consolidate the anti-Communist system and to prepare the way for a closer collaboration in every sector of the signatories. Italy's accession to the Pact had been the logical consequence of the consistent policy of Mussolini, who had been the first man in the world to denounce the peril of bolshevism and to combat it not only in the streets in Italy but on the battlefields of Spain.

Having thus implicitly condemned the Russo-German accord, Ciano then proceeded to outline the events immediately preceding the war and to claim that Germany had been guilty of a breach of faith towards her ally. At his meeting with Ribbentrop in May, he said, it had been agreed that, while Germany and Italy must forcibly repel any attack by their enemies, they must make every effort to preserve peace in Europe for a long time in order to complete their internal reconstruction and their military preparations. The period of peace required by the two allies had been defined as three years by the Italians and four or five years by the Germans; and it had been agreed that during this period neither government would raise any question calculated to arouse controversy.

It was on these premises that the Italo-German alliance had been signed in Berlin on May 22; and the declarations accompanying the signature had emphasized the intention of the parties to maintain peace in Europe. Shortly afterwards the Polish crisis had arisen, and at Salzburg in August, Italy had proposed the issue of a joint statement to the effect that it was still possible to reach a settlement through normal diplomatic channels. But in the course of long conversations Hitler and Ribbentrop had explained why Germany was no longer ready to endure the delays which diplomatic negotiations would involve. It was true that Hitler had expressed his desire to limit the conflict, but Italy for her part had informed the German government that she desired a peaceful solution or, at least, a localization of the war.

Ciano concluded with a defense of the Italian policy of neutrality. "It is universally recognized," he said, "that it is the realistic attitude of Italy which has hitherto prevented the extension of the war; and it is towards our country that the eyes of all states are turning, who wish to safeguard, together with their own interests, the peace of the world." With the neutral states, in particular with Yugoslavia, Greece, Bulgaria, Switzerland, Latin America, and

Japan, Italy shared a community of interests. "Fascist Italy will continue to follow events with vigilant interest, ready, if this is possible, once more to make her contribution towards the pacification of the world, but also firmly resolved inflexibly to safeguard her interests, her land, sea, and air communications, her prestige, and her future as a Great Power." [12]

Ciano was pleased with his speech.

> My speech was a great success, even if everybody did not discern the subtle anti-German poison which permeated it. . . . They tell me that the German ambassador listened to it in silence, and at times was not able to conceal his disappointment. Good. During the evening I saw Sir Percy Loraine, who is highly satisfied and pays me compliments. . . . If it was difficult formerly to persuade the Italians to march side by side with the Germans, it is impossible now despite their pledged word, since they know the whole truth and what is happening behind the scenes. Everybody knows and understands that Germany has betrayed us twice. . . . They consider my speech to be the real funeral of the Axis.[13]

In Berlin the Germans were far from pleased, and Ribbentrop was reliably reported to the Italian embassy as being in a state of fury. He objected in particular to Ciano's revelation that it had been agreed in Milan to keep the peace for three years and that the Germans had even spoken of four or five. The fact that Italy had asked for three years' grace, he said, would convince the enemy that she had no contribution to bring to German strength; while the German talk of a four- or five-year period of preparation would convey the impression that the Reich was bluffing.[14] The State Secretary reflected his master's views when he dryly took note of Magistrati's plea that the speech had in fact been pro-German; and he retorted that the French, the British, and the neutrals had placed a different interpretation on Ciano's words. Hitler, however, was not to be provoked, since he still attached importance to the Italian alliance and remained determined to draw Italy into his impending conflict with the Western Powers. So on December 28, 1939, Ribbentrop, while expressing surprise at the extreme anti-Russian attitude of Italy, and demurring at Ciano's account of their prewar conversations, told the Italian ambassador calmly that he did not attach any importance to the matter.[15] It was not often that Hitler showed patience, but with Mussolini he was content to bide his time.

III

Still under the momentum generated by Ciano's speech, Mussolini on January 3, 1940, addressed a very long letter to Hitler, in which he set forth his views on current affairs.[16] It was in substance a criticism of certain aspects of German policy and a warning. Never again was he to speak so frankly and so sharply to his partner. After assuming full responsibility for Ciano's speech, he concentrated on the main burden of his complaint, namely the German understanding with Russia.

You will not be surprised if I tell you that the German-Russian agreement has had painful repercussions in Spain. The Civil War is too recent. The earth which covers the dead—yours and ours and the Spanish—is still fresh. Bolshevism is a memory that obsesses Spain and the Spaniards; with their passionate and fanatical logic they do not understand the tactical necessities of politics. It is clear that what Germany and Italy have lost during the last few months in Spain has been won by the French and the British.

In a further passage on Russia Mussolini claimed to recognize that expediency required the neutralization of Russia since "Ribbentrop's efforts towards nonintervention by the French and the British were not realized." After this dig at the German Foreign Minister, Mussolini went on to deliver his warning.

But I, a born revolutionist, who has not modified his way of thinking, tell you that you cannot abandon the anti-Semitic and anti-Bolshevist banner, which you have been flying for twenty years and for which so many of your comrades have died; you cannot renounce your gospel, in which the German people have blindly believed. It is my definite duty to add that a further step in your relations with Moscow would have catastrophic repercussions in Italy, where the anti-Bolshevik unanimity, especially among the Fascist masses, is absolute, solid, and indivisible.

Mussolini went on to suggest that the solution of Germany's space problem lay in Russia with her vast expanse of territory and sparse population. Germany's task in essence was to defend Europe from Asia. "Until four months ago Russia was world enemy number one; she cannot have become, and is not, friend number one. This has profoundly disturbed the Fascists in Italy and perhaps also many

National Socialists in Germany. The day when we shall have demolished bolshevism we shall have kept faith with our two Revolutions."

Flowing from his observations on Russia came comment critical of the German attitude to Finland and Poland. Fascist Italy, he said, was well disposed towards brave little Finland, and thousands of volunteers had presented themselves at the Finnish legation in Rome and the consulates. As regards Poland, he claimed that British propaganda in Italy was successfully making capital of the treatment meted out to the Polish population.

A people which has been ignominiously betrayed by its miserable politico-military governing class, but which—as you yourself chivalrously recognized in your Danzig speech—fought courageously, deserves a treatment which does not give occasion for hostile speculations. It is my conviction that the creation of a modest, disarmed Poland which is exclusively Polish, liberated from the Jews—for whom I fully approve your project of gathering them all in a large ghetto in Lublin—can no longer constitute any threat to the Greater Reich. . . . Unless you are irrevocably resolved to prosecute the war to a finish, I believe that the creation of a Polish state under the German aegis would be an element that would resolve the war and constitute a condition sufficient for the peace.

So far as the war itself was concerned, Mussolini expressed himself in a somewhat pessimistic vein. While he did not believe that the Western powers would ever be able to compel Germany, "assisted by Italy," to capitulate, it was not certain that France or Britain could be brought to their knees or even divided. Moreover the United States would not permit a total defeat of the democracies. Now that Germany had secured her eastern frontiers, was it worth while to risk all, including the regime, to hasten the fall of a fruit which must of necessity be harvested by the new forces of Europe.

Having delivered himself of these pungent, and almost unfriendly, criticisms of German conduct, Mussolini concluded his letter with an assurance of Italy's active military preparations, of the value to Germany of her neutrality, and of her fidelity to the alliance.

This important letter marked the culmination of the anti-German sentiment which permeated Italy and infected Mussolini himself during the first four months of the war. But it would be a mistake to suppose that Mussolini himself was consistently anti-German even during this period. On the contrary, Ciano's diary and the memoirs of Anfuso, his principal private secretary, show Mussolini as constantly chafing under the yoke of neutrality and intermittently relapsing into pro-Germanism. Ciano states that his attitude "has always been vacillating and fundamentally he is still is favor of Germany." [17]

IV

Mussolini at intervals kept repeating that a great nation could not eternally remain neutral without losing face, and that some day it should prepare to intervene. In October he was eagerly telling the German ambassador, whom he was always anxious to impress, that his military preparations were well advanced and that in the spring he would be able to give help rather than receive it; and to Ciano he complained that the Italians "after having heard my warlike propaganda for eighteen years, cannot understand how I can become the herald of peace, now that Europe is in flames." As the weeks passed he became more and more restless. "He feels that he is out of this great struggle and in one way or another he would like to find a way to get into it." [18]

Anfuso paints a similar picture of Mussolini's attitude.

> In those ten months, up to May, 1940, I always found Mussolini in the state of mind of a man who, having decided not to enter the game, is nevertheless determined to get into it as soon as he has gathered his strength. . . . The motive of "*Treue*" [loyalty] agitates him. I still see Mussolini in that period as a virile recluse held down by chains. His outbursts are frequent; his assessment of Italian military potential realistic, but obscured by the distorted image of the Italian "happy warrior."

German successes pleased him in so far as they justified his Axis policy, but saddened him because they were not Italian.[19]

While Mussolini was wrestling indecisively with the conflicting claims of reason and emotion, Hitler was calmly resolved to seize every opportunity to persuade the Duce to enter the war. He had an exaggerated opinion of the value of the Italian navy, and for psychological as well as material reasons he wanted Italy on his side in the conflict against France and Britain. He was displeased at Mussolini's lack of faith in German prowess, and the obvious remedy was to attempt to inspire the Italians with his own confidence in a German victory and at the same time to threaten that if Italy stood aside, she could expect no share of the spoils. Moreover, he was always at pains to emphasize that in the last resort a German defeat would spell the end of Mussolini and his Fascist party. From the outset the pressure was severe and continuous.

On September 30, 1939, Ribbentrop had telephoned to propose a meeting between Hitler and Mussolini at Munich, or a visit by Ciano to Berlin, or a meeting between himself and Mussolini on the frontier. Mussolini had no desire to see Ribbentrop, and a meeting with Hitler might place him in a predicament. It was accordingly decided that Ciano should go to Berlin. Ribbentrop, to whom the Italian decision was communicated by telephone, said that the matter was urgent and that Ciano must leave that very evening. The Germans were now in the habit of making peremptory demands on their ally without much consideration for Italian dignity or convenience; and Ciano submissively hurried to Berlin without any idea of what the Germans intended to propose, but determine to safeguard his liberty of action.

His conversation with Hitler took place in the Chancellery the following day. Hitler, a consummate actor, was at his best that morning, radiating serenity and confidence in the approaching triumph of German arms. For more than two hours he spoke to the fascinated Ciano without the aid of a note and without a pause to draw breath. The Polish campaign, he said, had now reached its victorious conclusion and Germany was ready to turn on the West. He would offer Britain and France peace, but if they refused, as seemed likely, he would strike with a vigor and ruthlessness of which they had no conception. Now was the favorable moment to act. The Western powers were weak, morally and materially; and there was no risk of a two-front war, for he had neutralized Russia, with whom he was resolved to live in peace. "If Germany and Italy went into the battle together, England and France would be so completely crushed that many of the still unsettled problems would be solved once and for all."

At this decisive moment, the Fuehrer emphasized, the Italians must realize that not only the future of Germany, but also that of

Italy, would be at stake in a final conflict with Britain and France. He was himself convinced that Germany would emerge triumphant, but a defeat of Germany would at the same time mean the end of Italy's great aspirations in the Mediterranean. In making his appeal, Hitler was tactful enough not to invoke the alliance or to make reproaches about Italian neutrality. He could not, however, refrain from remarking that Britain would not have signed her treaty with Poland, if she had not previously learned what Italy's attitude would be. This, incidentally, was a reproach constantly leveled at the Italians during the succeeding months. But he was prepared magnanimously to agree that in the first phase of the war Italy's neutrality had proved to be advantageous to the Axis alliance. He made it clear, however, that in the second phase he expected Italy on grounds of enlightened self-interest to intervene actively at his side.[20]

For a time Hitler's blandishments, though they unsettled Mussolini, remained without effect. Ciano, while he was impressed with Hitler's confidence and mastery of his subject, opined that "the game will not be as simple as he believes."[21] At the end of October the secretary of the Fascist party, Starace, was dismissed and replaced by Ciano's nominee Ettore Muti, who incidentally proved a disastrous choice. Alfieri was translated from the Ministry of Propaganda to the Vatican embassy, and there were other changes in the government, which became what was popularly termed the "Ciano Cabinet." It seemed that Ciano and his policy of neutrality were now in the ascendant. Hitler was accurately informed of what was happening in Italy, and told his generals on November 23 that only the Duce and his Fascists favored action. Nevertheless he knew his man well enough to believe that he could eventually enfold him.

> Much depends on Italy, above all on Mussolini, whose death can alter everything. Italy has great goals for the consolidation of her empire. . . . As long as the Duce lives, so long can it be calculated that Italy will seize every opportunity to reach her imperialistic goals. However, it is too much to ask of Italy that she should join in the battle before Germany has seized the offensive in the West.[22]

Hitler's solicitude for Mussolini's life was probably prompted by reports from Rome that his health was beginning to wilt under the strain, and that he was showing signs of increasing instability. But the turn of the tide duly came for Germany at the beginning of 1940, not long after the despatch of Mussolini's unpleasant letter of January 3, 1940. Two factors contributed to Mussolini's change of heart: well-authenticated reports of an impending German offensive in the West and increasing irritation over the action of the British government in tightening their blockade measures. The emphasis in the Palazzo Venezia gradually changed. From January to May it was no longer a policy of neutrality with intermittent relapses into pro-Germanism, but a policy of intervention at the earliest possible moment with intermittent relapses into neutralism and anti-Germanism.

V

By the middle of January the British and French ambassadors were expressing to Ciano their concern at the attitude of the Duce, and at the meeting of the Italian cabinet on January 23 all his shafts were aimed at France and Britain, who "could no longer win the war." He told his ministers that Italy could not remain indefinitely neutral, since that would compel her to play second fiddle in Europe. He looked forward to intervention in the second half of 1940 or early 1941, and spoke of terror bombing of France and acquiring control over the Mediterranean.[23] He became increasingly irritable and inveighed against the pacifism of the Italian people. "We must keep them disciplined and in uniform from morning till night. Beat them and beat them and beat them"; and "Have you ever seen a lamb become a wolf? The Italian race is a race of sheep. Eighteen years are not enough to change them. It takes a hundred and eighty, and maybe a hundred and eighty centuries." This was not the language he held to the Germans, to whom he depicted his Italians as happy warriors, ardent for battle.[24]

Mussolini's changing mood was soon reflected in the press and in his policy. The newspapers, and in particular Mussolini's *Popolo d'Italia,* which had hitherto been instructed to report the war impartially, now began to attack the French. British requests for military supplies were rejected, and on February 22, 1940, he concluded an agreement with the Germans committing himself to deliver copper, hemp, and other raw materials, of which there was already a shortage in Italy. Although there were still occasional outbursts against the Germans, Mussolini more and more often emphasized to his familiars his belief in German victory.

He was thus not disposed to give Sumner Welles' peace mission the same favorable reception which he would have accorded it in 1939. When on February 26 he received his American visitor, his manner was guarded and cool. In reply to a question, he said that a compromise peace might be concluded if no time were lost, but that if a real war broke out, any hope of negotiation would be killed for a long time to come. For the rest he spoke bitterly about Britain and emphasized his resolve to obtain the satisfaction of Italy's claims.

Welles noted, as he could not have failed to do, the difference of outlook between Ciano and Mussolini, but he left Rome not without hope that the Duce might still be induced to restrain the Fuehrer. His principal impression was one of surprised dismay at the declining health and vigor of the Duce, whom he had pictured as active and animated. "The man I saw before me seemed fifteen years older than his actual age of fifty-six. He was ponderous and static rather than vital. He moved with an elephantine motion; every step appeared an effort. He was heavy for his height, and his face in repose fell in rolls of flesh. His close-cropped hair was snow white." [25]

The visit of the peacemaker only served to increase Mussolini's irritation. On March 1 the British added fuel to the flame by announcing that as from that day German coal would be seized on the high seas as an article of contraband. Mussolini himself dictated the concluding phrases of the note of protest, which was "harsh and threatening." [26] On March 7 he angrily told Ciano that the British would be inexorably beaten and "you should get it into your head." Ciano was somewhat shaken, for this was the first occasion on which Mussolini had attacked him personally.[27]

VI

The scene was thus set for another effort by the Germans, who were watching Mussolini's vacillations as closely as were the

French and British. Prince Philip of Hesse had in February been sent to Rome with a suggestion for an early meeting with the Fuehrer, but on March 8 the German ambassador suddenly notified Ciano that Ribbentrop would arrive in Rome on March 10, bringing with him Hitler's belated reply to the Duce's letter of January 3. Ciano telephoned at once to Mussolini, pointing out the inadvisability of a meeting at a time when the coal blockade threatened to embroil Britain with Italy, but the Duce was not impressed and Ciano had no alternative but to reply to the ambassador that Ribbentrop's visit would be welcome. He accurately forecast the consequences.

I dread the Duce's contact with the Germans. In these last few days his hostile attitude towards the Allies has become more pronounced. The thought of war dominates him, and it will dominate him even more, if the offensive on the western front begins. Inaction will then go against the grain of his aggressive temperament. In the circumstances, Ribbentrop will need no great power of oratory to urge on the Duce a course which he, the Duce, desires with all his soul.[28]

Ribbentrop arrived in Rome on March 10, accompanied by a suite of thirty-five, including Clodius, his economic adviser, Gaus, his senior legal adviser, two hairdressers, a doctor, a masseur, and a gymnastics instructor. At the meeting with Mussolini he duly presented Hitler's reply. It was an exceedingly long letter, of about four thousand words, in which Hitler rebutted Mussolini's insinuation that Germany would not have attacked Poland if she had not miscalculated the attitude of Britain and France. The fact was that the Western powers were determined to destroy Germany, and Hitler, quite apart from the intolerable provocation of Poland, was convinced that it was wise to deal with Britain and France before his relative strength declined. As it was, the German armed forces were now poised for victory against the untrained and ill-equipped British and the demoralized French armies. There was also a long passage in which Hitler disingenuously defended his policy toward Russia, which had renounced world revolution; and he explained why he had liquidated Poland and why he had no cause to champion Finland's interests.

Against this background, Hitler cunningly held out his bait.

There were no recriminations about the past, no suggestion that Italy had not been a loyal ally. On the contrary, "I fully understand, Duce, your attitude and your decision in August of last year. . . . I also share your view, Duce, that under the conditions which then prevailed it was probably even a good thing that Italy was not immediately drawn into the war on our side." Having thus pandered to Mussolini's pride, he proceeded to play upon his ambition.

I believe, Duce that there can be no doubt that the outcome of this war will also decide the future of Italy. If that future is viewed in your country merely as the continued survival of a modest European state, then I am wrong. But if that future is conceived as a guarantee of the existence of the Italian people from the historical, geopolitical, and general moral viewpoints, that is, according to the criteria of your people's right to existence, Duce, then you will some day be confronted by the same opponents who are fighting Germany today. I know full well, Duce, that you yourself do not think differently on the subject.

Hitler concluded his letter by repeating that he understood and appreciated Mussolini's attitude. Nevertheless, sooner or later, however events developed, it would prove impossible for Italy to escape the clash of arms. When that time came, "your place will then more than ever be at our side, just as mine will be at yours." In order to follow up this appeal, and conscious of his personal ascendancy over Mussolini, Hitler proposed an early meeting, "since there are many things which can be explained only in lengthy discussions." [29]

When presenting the letter to Mussolini, Ribbentrop took some pains to stroke Mussolini's anger against Britain by telling him that the Fuehrer was incensed at the latest measures to block the shipment of coal to Italy by the sea route. "He viewed these measures as an outrageous attempt of the plutocratic democratic states to strangle Italy economically." Germany was able and willing to supply the entire coal requirements of Italy and would make proposals for solving the transport problem. For the rest, he repeated Hitler's defense of the Russian pact, brought evidence of Western hostility to Fascist Italy, and emphasized his conviction that the British and French armies were moving towards the greatest disaster of their histories.

Mussolini listened to Ribbentrop with some reserve. In reply to the statement that Soviet Russia had renounced world revolution, he inquired sarcastically whether Ribbentrop really believed that; and as regards the evidence of Western hostility produced for his inspection he acidly replied that the documents contained nothing new, since he had always known from the outset that the democracies disliked authoritarian systems. Nevertheless he was careful not to rebuff his German visitor and he closed the conversation by saying that he would give thought to all the points raised and that he believed that the Fuehrer was right.[30]

On the following day Mussolini and Ribbentrop met again. It was a fateful interview, for it soon became clear that in the intervening twenty-four hours Mussolini, for no apparent reason, had passed from guarded scepticism and uncertainty to bellicose resolution. Schmidt describes him as having become suddenly warlike.[31] He told his astonished visitor that Italy would enter the war at the proper time and fight on the side of Germany. After grandiloquently enumerating his achievements in the way of rearmament, he said that the question of timing was extremely delicate, for he should not intervene until his preparations were complete, so as not to become a burden to his partner. In any event Italy was in no position financially to sustain a long war.

This reservation came as something of a blow, and Ribbentrop sought to extract from Mussolini a firm statement of the date fixed for Italy's entry into the war, but all he could obtain was a reply to the effect that a moment would come when a definition of Italy's relations with France and England, i.e., a break with these countries, would occur. Nevertheless Ribbentrop, after the uncertain and indeed inauspicious outcome of the first meeting, had every reason to be satisfied with his day's work. The previous night he had telegraphed to Berlin that he had been unable to obtain any clue as to how the Duce's mind was moving; and he had an uneasy feeling that Sumner Welles might have stimulated Mussolini's unfortunate predilection for a negotiated peace. Now he could go home with the Duce's definite, if qualified, promise in his pocket. In order to clinch the bargain, he proposed an early meeting with Hitler at the Brenner Pass for some date after March 19. This was readily agreed to and an unusually cordial session ended with mutual compliments and assurances to the effect that Italy and

Germany were tied by a common destiny.[32] There was, however, on the German side no reference to the impending attack on Norway and Denmark.

VII

As usual, the hour of decision was followed by misgivings; and on the following day Mussolini pressed for the German record of the conversation, ostensibly because it might contain some error, but in reality because he feared that he had gone too far in his commitment to enter the war.[33] The Italian press was instructed to be cautious, to give an account of Ribbentrop's engagements in Rome, to reproduce some foreign and particularly German comment, but not to depart from the line hitherto taken in any "sober comment" which might be offered.[34]

Yet, despite momentary misgivings, Mussolini knew in his heart that there was now no retreat; and Sumner Welles, who returned to Rome on March 16, was quick to note the change.

> He did not seem to be laboring under the physical or mental oppression which had seemed so obvious during my first conversation with him. . . . He seemed to have thrown off some great weight. Since that time I have often wondered whether, during the two weeks, which had elapsed since my first visit to Rome, he had not determined to cross the Rubicon, and during Ribbentrop's visit had not decided to force Italy into the war after Germany's all-out offensive commenced.[35]

Meanwhile on March 13 Ribbentrop, still fearful of Welles, had telephoned to ask that the Brenner meeting should be brought forward to March 18. At first Mussolini exploded: "These Germans are unbearable; they don't give us time to breathe or to think matters over," but, as usual, he soon tamely agreed. During the intervening days Mussolini looked forward to the meeting with a mixture of pleasurable excitement and apprehension. He wanted to join in the war, and so far as the meeting was likely to advance that end, it was welcome; but at the same time he was afraid of being dragged in prematurely. He knew that as soon as the German offensive began his position would become more difficult; and he hoped against his better judgment that he might dissuade Hitler from his Western offensive. "The prospect of an imminent clash, in which he might remain an outsider, disturbs him and, to use his words, humiliates him." He even spoke of obtaining from Hitler a document in the shape of a communiqué, which would give him latitude to stay out. When Ciano warned him that Hitler would get more out of him than Ribbentrop had been able to do, he partly agreed, but insisted that he could not decline the offer of a meeting. In so far as he could make up his mind without knowing to what pressure Hitler would subject him, it was his intention to intimate that he would fight, but that he must determine the moment.

VIII

It was snowing on the Brenner when Mussolini arrived on the morning of March 18, and he waited for the Fuehrer "with anxious elation." He was already under Hitler's spell and Ciano noted that "recently he has felt more and more the fascination of the Fuehrer. His military successes—the only successes that Mussolini really values and desires—are the cause of this." [36]

When Hitler arrived at the frontier, the two dictators repaired to Mussolini's train, a cheap concession by the German to the Italian's vanity. It was the first time they had met since Munich, and Hitler was in the best of tempers. But, as usual, he regarded a conference as an occasion for a monologue and Mussolini for a long time was not given an opportunity to speak. It was the old story, repeated at wearisome length. Hitler was never afraid of being a bore and he believed in endless repetition as a means of convincing the doubter and beating down the resistance of his victim. So Mussolini was treated to the usual discourse on the power of the German army and air force, and on the certainty of early victory over France and England. He had, Hitler emphasized, reached a satisfactory agreement with Russia, and, since there was now no conflict of interests between the two countries, he had resolved to maintain forever friendly relations with the Soviet Union. Moreover Stalin had thrown overboard the old Jewish-internationalist bolshevism in favor of Slav nationalism.

When he came to the position of Italy, Hitler was once more cautious and tactful. He declared that he had not come to the Brenner to ask for anything, but merely to explain the situation.

If Italy was content with a second-rate position in the Mediterranean, then she need do nothing more; if on the other hand she desired to be a first-class Mediterranean power, she would always find England and France across her path. It was for the Duce on the basis of the facts to take his own decisions. He must, however, point out that the destinies of Germany and Italy were indissolubly linked. The victory of Germany would be the victory of Italy; and likewise the defeat of Germany would spell the end of the Italian Empire. He claimed to be a realist and would not wish the Duce to do anything which ran counter to the interests of the Italian people, for, unlike the English, he did not expect other nations to snatch his chestnuts out of the fire.

With this display of ruthless self-confidence, combined with courteous consideration for his ally, Hitler achieved his purpose. Mussolini, when he was at last able to open his mouth, hastened to assure the Fuehrer that he hated the Western powers and that Italy's entry into the war was inevitable. The great problem, however, was the date, and Italy would have to be very well prepared, since her financial position did not allow her to wage a protracted war. In an effort to secure a postponement of the German offensive, he asked whether delay would endanger Germany. He believed not. In three or four months he would have completed his military preparations, and would not be in the embarrassing position of seeing his comrade fighting while he himself was limited to making demonstrations.

In reply Hitler made it clear that he was not prepared to postpone his attack. But, he suggested, it might be possible to intervene more cheaply than by means of a frontal attack on France's Alpine border. A strong Italian force of some twenty divisions with German troops could well advance along the Swiss frontier towards the Rhone valley in order to turn the Franco-Italian mountain frontier from the rear. Once the enemy had been effectively smashed in northern France, the moment would come for Italy to intervene actively, not at the most difficult point, but elsewhere. To this proposition the Duce assented gladly. It was just what he wanted to hear; and he replied that "once Germany had made a victorious advance, he would intervene immediately . . . when the Allies were so shaken by the German attack that it needed only a second blow to bring them to their knees." But "if Germany's progress was slow, the Duce said that then he would wait." [37]

Hitler was so confident of victory in northern France that he was not unduly disturbed at Mussolini's reservation nor at the evidence of his ally's pusillanimity. He had received Mussolini's promise to enter the war under conditions which he knew he could meet, and he was satisfied. Mussolini on the other hand would have liked to have cut a somewhat better figure, and felt that the meeting had not quite come up to expectations. He "resented the fact that Hitler did all the talking; he had it in mind to tell him many things, and instead he had to keep quiet most of the time, a thing which, as dictator, or rather the dean of dictators, he's not in the habit of doing." [38] He would have been still more annoyed, had he known that Hitler, while purporting to lay bare his plans, had also deliberately concealed from him the first move in his western war: the occupation of Norway and Denmark.

Hitler must have thought that he had made an impression on Mussolini, for he lost no time in following up his idea of an Italo-German offensive in southern France. At the beginning of April the German military attaché in Rome was summoned to headquarters at Zossen and instructed to submit to the Italian General Staff a proposal for the despatch of twenty to thirty Italian divisions to southern Germany. These, together with the German Seventh Army, were to cross the Rhine and advance through the Belfort gap. The plan was duly put to Marshal Graziani and General Roatta, who merely replied that in existing political conditions they could not entertain such a proposal.[39] The clumsy effort to take the Italian citadel by storm had failed.

It was, however, only a momentary failure, and as the days passed it became clear to everyone in Rome that on the Brenner Mussolini had fatally committed himself to Hitler. In fact on March 31 Mussolini had sent a memorandum to the King speaking of the inevitability of war "parallel to that of Germany to obtain our objectives." [40] The French ambassador inquired at the Palazzo Chigi whether he must now consider that the die had been cast; and Ciano was unable to reassure him. Mussolini's language became more and more pro-German and his attitude began to influence many Fascist leaders. On April 2 Ciano reports a "violent turn of the wheel in the direction of war"; and in the Council of Ministers that day Mussolini forecast that the war might begin at any moment. "He speaks of a Mediterranean empire and of access to the ocean. He believes blindly in a German victory and in the word of Hitler concerning our share of the booty." Rumors began to circulate that Mussolini intended to dismiss Ciano from the Ministry of Foreign Affairs.[41]

IX

Thus the situation in Italy was already developing in a manner entirely satisfactory to Hitler, when he delivered his first stroke against the West. At two o'clock in the morning, April 9, a secretary of the German embassy arrived at Ciano's house with a letter from the ambassador asking to be received at seven o'clock. It was to be a repetition of the comedy to which the Italians were now becoming accustomed. At half-past six the ambassador, "pale and tired," appeared with news that the German attack on Norway and Denmark had been launched. They then went together to the Duce to deliver a written message from Hitler: "The usual letter, in the usual style, announcing what he had already done." Mussolini merely said: "I approve Hitler's action wholeheartedly. It is a gesture that can have incalculable results, and this is the way to win wars. The democracies have lost the race. I shall give orders to the press and to the Italian people unreservedly to applaud this German action." The ambassador left in high fettle.[42]

Mussolini, for once, was sincere in welcoming Hitler's initiative. If the attack proved a success, conditions would be created which would enable him to intervene without much risk. If, on the other hand, Hitler was held up in Norway, the dreaded offensive in the West might be postponed or even abandoned; and Italy would be justified in remaining out of the war. He was excited at the new prospects opening before him, and as soon as the German ambassador had left, he began to talk of Croatia. "His hands fairly itch," wrote Ciano. "He intends to quicken the tempo, taking advantage of the disorder that reigns in Europe. But he didn't go into details, except to say that he is convinced that an attack against Yugoslavia will not lead France and Britain to strike at us." [43]

Hitler was assiduous in keeping up the pressure. On April 11 the German ambassador brought a second message from the Fuehrer; and Mussolini replied enthusiastically that from the following day the Italian fleet would be ready, while preparations on sea and land were proceeding apace. On April 20 a third message from Hitler arrived and this was followed by further letters on April 28 and May 4. These letters were, says Ciano, of meager importance, but "Hitler is a good psychologist, and he knows that these messages go straight to Mussolini's heart."

As the campaign in Norway developed and it became clear that the Germans were winning, Mussolini became more and more bellicose and irritated at his monarch's prudence.

> The King would like us to enter only to gather up the broken dishes. I hope that they will not break them over our heads before that. And then it is humiliating to remain with our hands folded while others write history. . . . To make a people great it is necessary to send them into battle, even if you have to kick them in the pants. . . . And if we do not take advantage of this occasion to pit our Navy against the French and British forces, what is the use of building 600,000 tons of warships? Some coast guards and some yachts would be enough to take the young ladies on a joy ride.[44]

The Germans, sensing Mussolini's growing enthusiasm for war, judged the moment opportune for a demand that Attolico should be removed from the post of ambassador to Germany. They had for a long time regarded him, and rightly, as a determined opponent of Italian intervention; and his presence in Berlin was not only a hindrance but a source of personal irritation to the impetuous Ribbentrop. Against all normal diplomatic precedent they named Alfieri and Farinacci as successors who would be welcome. Mussolini immediately acquiesced without demur, and Attolico was transferred to the Vatican, while Alfieri was appointed to Berlin in his place. It was an unpleasant portent.

In Rome rumors that Italian military operations were imminent began to multiply, and Ciano received anxious inquiries from the French, British, and American embassies. In this situation the French Prime Minister, Paul Reynaud, decided, somewhat inadvisedly, to address a personal appeal to Mussolini. On April 24 the

French ambassador called on Ciano with a sealed letter, in which his Prime Minister sought to play on the dictator's sentiment. After referring to a published telegram in which Mussolini had expressed to Hitler his desire to see Germany victorious, Reynaud went on:

I do not want to try in this letter either to supplicate or to threaten you. The essential virtue, which we should possess, is to understand and to tolerate one another. . . . It is as vital for Italy as for France that a balance of power should be maintained in Europe. Without this, no peace, no prosperity can be lasting. What are the disagreements which have been able to arise between us during the last four years beside this fundamental fact? It is not too late to try and bridge this broad ditch which seems at present to separate us. Your frankness and my own should try to link a traditional regime like ours and a new regime like yours; each would, thereby, be reinforced in the future by the dissipation of this distrust of its neighbor. . . . It will not be possible to say that France and Italy came to blows on the battlefield without a thorough discussion and a meeting on the part of their leaders. A war between us, and our people would feel the same as we do, would be a sacrilege against our common heritage and against the sacrifice of those who lost their lives at Bligny. In these days when peace is so much more difficult than war, I offer you the more difficult.[45]

Reynaud's appeal to Mussolini's better nature would have been doomed to failure in any circumstances. The only effective deterrent was fear, induced by evidence that the Western powers possessed the will and the capacity to strike back at Germany. The course of the campaign in Norway pointed the other way and the only effect of the letter was to evoke in Mussolini an outburst of arrogance. It was with almost sadistic exultation that he drafted his answer. "A cold, cutting, and contemptuous letter," Ciano described it, "I tried to make the letter less harsh, at least in form, but my efforts had meager results."[46] On April 26 Mussolini's reply was despatched:

I hasten to reply to your letter of April 22, which was handed to me on the 24th through your ambassador in Rome. First of all, may I term as unjustified the reason which inspired your message, namely the telegram in which I expressed a wish for a German victory. This should not come as a surprise to you, nor make you forget that Italy is and means to stay the political and military ally of Germany in adherence to the Treaty of

May, 1939, a treaty which Italy, like all nations, who cherish their honor, intends to respect.

Your remarks on the relations between democracy and fascism and the need for a European balance of power would require developing at length, and this is not the place to do so.

You seem in one passage of your letter to allude to the possibility of a meeting between us. I must, to my deep regret, decline such an offer. You will have no difficulty in understanding the reason for this.[47]

On May 1 the United States ambassador brought a message from the President, warning Mussolini not to enter the war. Mussolini was now in a mood to reject with contumely any pacific advice, and he personally drafted an answer to Roosevelt, "cutting and hostile, in which he arrives at the conclusion that if the Monroe Doctrine has force for the Americans, it must also have force for Europeans."[48]

Meanwhile in Berlin signs were multiplying that the German offensive would be launched at any moment. On April 27 Ribbentrop summoned the diplomatic corps to the Chancellery, and it was feared that his purpose might be to announce the invasion of Holland and Belgium. However, he merely announced that documents recently captured proved that it had been the intention of the Western powers to occupy Norway; and the Dutch and Belgian ambassadors left the building, heaving a sigh of relief at their brief reprieve. On April 30 Goering told the Italian military attaché that the decisive stroke would be delivered in France, after which England would give way. But he offered a solemn assurance that the Duce would receive at least a fortnight's notice of a German offensive on the western front.[49]

In London there were reports in the Foreign Office that Mussolini intended to enter the war on May 1 or 2. On May 8 Sir Percy Loraine, who had returned to Rome after a period of sick leave in England, remarked to Ciano that the possibility of war with Italy had reappeared. Ciano replied that Mussolini stood by his pact with Germany and would come to his decision at his own time and in his own way. For the moment Italian policy was unchanged, but he could not say for how long—"perhaps two months, perhaps four, perhaps six, maybe even two years." He hinted that Mussolini's attitude would be determined by what happened when the real war began. Meanwhile he would discuss trade matters, but would resent and reject any attempt to bribe him away from his obligations to Germany.[50]

The reports from Berlin of Hitler's military preparations still further excited Mussolini's martial ardor, and he was no longer seeking to postpone the German offensive. On the contrary, he was now at pains to impress the senior partner with his own zeal for the fray. Accordingly, on May 1 he despatched a message informing Hitler that the feeling of the Italian people was now decisively against the Western allies. "I have ordered the 1916 class to be called up on May 15, and further personnel will subsequently be called to the colors, so that by the summer we shall have two million men ready." [51] On the following days Ciano reports Mussolini as exultant and impervious to reason. "He contemptuously dismisses the possibility of warships being sent into the Mediterranean, convinced as he is that the Allies will never take the initiative against us. The news from Norway literally exalts the Duce, who, with ever increasing emphasis, affirms his certainty of a German victory." [52] Hitler now had Mussolini in the right frame of mind. It only remained to deliver the military blow, which would have the effect of pushing him the last few inches over the brink.

X

On the night of May 10 Ciano dined at the German embassy. It was a dull, boring evening and nothing was said about the situation. But, as the party broke up after midnight, Mackensen warned Ciano that he might have to disturb him during the night about a communication that he expected from Berlin. At four o'clock in the morning the ambassador duly turned up at Ciano's house with a large file of papers, which could not have arrived in the interval; and together they went off to see the Duce.

At that early hour there were no officials on duty at the Villa Torlonia, and it was Irma, the dark maidservant from Romagna, who introduced the party into the Duce's study. Mussolini opened the Fuehrer's sealed letter and began carefully and silently to peruse the pages in which Hitler explained the grounds on which he had been obliged to invade Holland and Belgium, and invited the Duce to make the decisions he considered necessary for the future of his country. After looking at a number of papers annexed to Hitler's letter, Mussolini told the German ambassador that he was convinced that France and Britain had been preparing to attack Germany across Holland and Belgium, and he entirely approved Hitler's action. He would answer the Fuehrer's letter on the following day, but in the meantime he could say that he was certain that the German army would triumph and that Italy stood at her ally's side. He would have liked to have said more, but the Fuehrer was aware of his position: he was threatened by Britain, and although much had been accomplished, there was still much to do. He sent his good wishes on the success of an enterprise on which depended the destiny of the two countries.

After Mackensen had left, Mussolini spoke to Ciano of his belief in a rapid German victory and of his intention to intervene.[53] On the following day Mussolini was less bellicose and more disposed to wait, probably because of reports from his General Staff on Italy's military prospects, as well as because of his propensity to recoil from his own decisions. Nevertheless, two days later he was once more in full cry. "Some months ago I said that the Allies had lost the victory. Today I tell you that they have lost the war. We Italians are already sufficiently dishonored. Any delay is inconceivable. We have no time to lose. Within a month I shall declare war. I shall attack France and Great Britain in the air and on the sea. I am no longer thinking of taking up arms against Yugoslavia, because it would be a humiliating expedient." [54]

The triumphant march of the German armies across Holland, Belgium, and northern France seemed to confirm Mussolini's judgment, and it brought a number of Italians into the interventionist camp. It also stimulated the Western leaders to make another attempt to keep Italy out of the conflict. On May 16 Sir Winston Churchill addressed the following letter to the Duce:

> Now that I have taken up my office as Prime Minister and Minister of Defense, I look back to our meetings in Rome and feel a desire to speak words of goodwill to you as Chief of the Italian nation across what seems to be a swiftly widening gulf. Is it too late to stop a river of blood from flowing between the British and Italian peoples? We can no doubt inflict grievous injuries upon one another and maul each other cruelly, and darken the Mediterranean with our strife. If you so decree, it must be

so; but I declare that I have never been an enemy of Italian greatness, nor ever at heart the foe of the Italian lawgiver. It is idle to predict the course of the great battles now raging in Europe, but I am sure that whatever may happen on the Continent, England will go on to the end, even quite alone, as we have done before, and I believe with some assurance that we shall be aided in increasing measure by the United States, and indeed by all the Americas.

I beg you to believe that it is in no spirit of weakness or of fear that I make this solemn appeal, which will remain on record. Down the ages above all other calls comes the cry that the joint heirs of Latin and Christian civilization must not be ranged against one another in mortal strife. Hearken to it, I beseech you in all honor and respect, before the dread signal is given. It will never be given by us.

Although Mussolini "appreciated the tone of the letter," [55] he was in no mood to parley, for he was now itching for action. Accordingly his response was hard, although, as Churchill remarked, it had at least the merit of candor.

I reply to the message you sent me, in order to tell you that you are certainly aware of grave reasons of an historical and contingent character, which have ranged our two countries in opposite camps. Without going back very far in time I remind you of the initiative taken in 1935 by your government to organize at Geneva sanctions against Italy, engaged in securing for herself a small space in the African sun without causing the slightest injury to your interests and territories or those of others. I remind you also of the real and actual state of servitude in which Italy finds herself in her own sea. If it was to honor your signature that your government declared war on Germany, you will understand that the same sense of honor and of respect for engagements assumed in the Italian-German Treaty guides Italian policy today and tomorrow in the face of any event whatsoever.[56]

From this moment the British government entertained no doubt of Mussolini's intention to enter the war at the first favorable opportunity. The French, however, were obsessed by the idea that it might still be possible to buy him off with offers of significant territorial concessions. There was an Anglo-French exchange of views, and in the face of a firm British refusal to make any further approach the French decided a few days later to put forward an offer of their own, which Mussolini treated with disdain. "He was not interested," said Ciano to the French ambassador, "in recovering any French territories by peaceful negotiation. He had decided to make war on France." [57] A further appeal by Roosevelt was brushed off with similar harshness.

Meanwhile the situation of the Allies in the battle of France was deteriorating rapidly. On May 28 the King of the Belgians capitulated; and by the end of the month the evacuation at Dunkirk was in full swing. At last Mussolini made up his mind to fix a date for his declaration of war. On May 30 he despatched the following letter to Hitler, who on May 13, 18, and 25 had sent him enthusiastic progress reports on the battle.

> Once more I thank you for the messages which you sent me and in which I found the information concerning the courage of the soldiers of the different armies particularly interesting. In the meantime I have received news of the capitulation of Belgium and I congratulate you on this. I have delayed my reply to you for some days because I wanted to announce to you my decision to enter the war as of June 5. Should you consider that I ought to wait a few days longer for the sake of better coordination of your plans, you will tell me so; the Italian people are, however, impatient to be at the side of the German people in the struggle against the common foe.

Mussolini went on to boast of his military preparations: seventy divisions standing to arms, and his navy and air force already on a war footing. He intended to assume the supreme command of the armed forces and he assured Hitler that he was in a position to form another seventy divisions. Finally, in a passage which reads oddly in the light of after events, he emphasized the importance of not extending the conflict to the Balkans, from which he would have to draw supplies which had hitherto come from beyond Gibraltar.[58]

Hitler was enchanted. Although his generals attached little importance to the participation of Italy, he himself had sufficient confidence in Mussolini's boastful accounts of Italy's military prowess to believe that plans had already been laid to deliver a telling blow against France and Britain in the Mediterranean. He was soon to be disillusioned, but for the moment he looked forward eagerly to the presence of an ally on his southern flank. He replied the following day that he was profoundly moved. "If there could still be anything which could strengthen my unshakable belief in the victorious outcome of this war, it was your statement. . . . The mere fact of your entering the war is an element calculated to deal the front of our enemies a staggering blow." He asked Mussolini, however, to put back his date by three days. He wished to complete the destruction of the French air force, and he feared that Italy's entry might bring about a regroupment, which might frustrate his plan.[59]

Mussolini reluctantly complied, and in a further letter to Hitler of June 2 agreed to postpone his date until June 10, when he would declare war. Hostilities, he added, would begin on the following day. Once more he undertook not to extend the war and promised to include in his speech on June 10 a statement to the effect that the undertaking extended to the Danube and Balkan countries, including Greece and Turkey.[60] On the same day, however, the German ambassador asked for an interview and told the Duce that Hitler had changed his mind and would welcome an earlier intervention. By that time, however, troop movements were in progress and it would have been dangerous to declare war until they had been completed. It was therefore decided to adhere to June 11 as the day for opening hostilities.

The King was informed of the decision, but there was no consultation with either the cabinet or the Grand Council. Indeed Mussolini seems to have been at pains to keep some of his principal lieutenants in the dark. As late as May 29 he saw Grandi and told him that the issue of the French campaign was far from decided, and that in fact the Germans, as a result of Weygand's appointment, would shortly reel under a counterstroke as they had done in 1914 on the Marne. Four days later, on June 2, he assured Balbo that Italy would not enter the war, and the Governor returned to his colony in Libya with the comforting conviction that he would not be called on to make any urgent military preparations. When it came, Italy's declaration of war on the side of a traditional enemy affronted the sentiment of the nation as well as the good sense of military and political advisers. It was manifestly the responsibility of one man; and when things began to go badly and hardships pressed, it was not surprising that resentment should have been concentrated on the person of the Duce.[61]

As the few remaining days passed, Mussolini's impatience rose. His outlook was like that of young British officers in 1914 who, believing that the war could not last long, feared that it might be over before they could get to the front. He had no idea what the Italian armed forces would or could do when war was declared; nor was he mortified at having to rush to the aid of the victor. He was simply itching to enter the fray.

On June 10 Ciano summoned the French and British ambassadors in order to inform them of Italy's decision to declare war. Sir Percy Loraine calmly inquired whether he was to consider the intimation as advance information or as a formal declaration of war. On being told that it was the latter, he left the room with dignity without saying a further word. The French ambassador, when his turn came, could not resist a parting shot. "The Germans are hard masters. You too will learn this," he said to Ciano before leaving the Palazzo Chigi for the last time.

That evening Mussolini from the balcony of the Palazzo Venezia announced to the Italian people and the world that Italy would be at war the following day.

> An hour marked by destiny is striking in the sky of our country [he shouted], the hour of irrevocable decisions. We are entering the lists against the plutocratic and reactionary democracies of the West, who have always hindered the advance and often plotted against the very existence of the Italian people. . . . At a memorable meeting in Berlin I said that, according to the laws of Fascist morality, when one has a friend, one goes with him to the very end. We have done this and will do this with Germany, with her people, with her victorious armed forces.

There was no surprise, and little enthusiasm either for war or for friendship with the Germans; and Ciano closed his dairy for that fateful day with the words: "I am sad, very sad. The adventure begins. May God help Italy."

CHAPTER SEVENTEEN

War

1940

I

MUSSOLINI was aware that in the Axis enterprise he was the junior partner. But he sought to blur this unpleasant fact, and to claim an illusory parity with Germany, by concocting the theory of the "parallel" war, that is to say a war which would be fought separately by the two allies, each in his own sphere of influence. Thus Hitler would look after the northern theatre, while he himself would be responsible for conducting independent operations in the Mediterranean basin. The German generals, who attached little importance to Italy and were reluctant to impart their military secrets to their ally, found this arrangement convenient. They were confident of being able to win the war by their own efforts; and the less they had to do with Italy the less likely it was that they would be called on to supply to the southern theater resources which they would have preferred to keep under their own hands.

The consequence was that on the outbreak of war there was no real Italo-German military coordination, and each ally sought to keep the other in ignorance of his own plans and intentions. The first misunderstanding occurred immediately after Italy's entry into the war, when Hitler was surprised and disillusioned at Mussolini's inactivity. He subsequently explained in the hearing of the German military attaché in Rome that, when Mussolini had declared that he could not postpone his declaration of war to a date later than

June 11, he had himself assumed that an Italian operation had been prepared against Corsica, Tunis, or Malta, which could not safely be deferred on grounds of military secrecy. When therefore Mussolini had announced from the balcony of the Palazzo Venezia that he would be in a state of war at six o'clock on the morning of June 11, it seemed reasonable to suppose that something would happen. In fact, to Hitler's disappointment, no move had been made. It reminded him, he observed sarcastically, of the procedure in the Middle Ages, when the cities exchanged messages of defiance without doing anything about it.[1]

II

Meanwhile the Germans had entered Paris on June 14, and it became plain for all to see that the dissolution of the French armies and of French resistance was imminent. It seemed to Mussolini that the operations in France might cease and indeed that the war might be over before he had had an opportunity of distinguishing himself on the battlefield. He accordingly ordered Marshal Badoglio on June 15 to launch an offensive on the French Alpine front on June 18. Badoglio demurred on the grounds that communications in the Alps were poor and that he would require twenty-five days to regroup his troops, which had taken up purely defensive positions, for an offensive. Mussolini, however, insisted that he would not be able to put forward his demands on France—Nice, Corsica, and Tunis—unless he had taken part in the battle, and that the attack must take place on the stipulated day. Moreover, he demanded that the motorized "Littorio" division, of which he was inordinately proud, should be thrown in. In deference to his wishes the division was hurriedly moved by train from the valley of the Po to the Alpine foothills, where it served only to block the movement of the Alpine division which was already deploying for the attack.

Mussolini's four-day campaign, which began after the French had asked the Germans for an armistice on June 17, was spectacular only in its failure. Although enjoying enormous numerical superiority and fighting a beaten foe, whose government had already solicited an armistice, the army group commanded by the Crown

Prince was only able to occupy the frontier towns of Modane and Briançon, and was finally held up in the streets of Mentone. It was a sorry business and Mussolini vented his annoyance on the Italian people, who never wanted the war and who from the first day to the last regarded it as "Mussolini's war." On June 21, the third day after the attack had been launched, Ciano noted:

Mussolini is very humiliated because our troops have not made a step forward. Even today they have not succeeded in advancing and have halted in front of the first French fortification which put up some opposition. . . . Mussolini is taking it out on the Italian people: "It is the material that I lack. . . . A people who for sixteen years have been an anvil cannot become a hammer within a few years."

Thus it was that a deflated Duce was obliged to travel empty-handed to Munich in order to discuss armistice terms. He looked forward to the meeting with understandable distaste and during the journey discussed his tactics with Ciano.

The Duce is an extremist. He would like to go so far as the total occupation of French territory and demand the surrender of the French fleet. But he is aware that his opinion has only a consultative value. The war has been won by Hitler without any active participation on the part of Italy, and it is Hitler who will have the last word. This naturally disturbs and saddens him. His reflections on the Italian people and, above all, on our armed forces are extremely bitter this evening.[2]

While the Germans gave the Italians a warm welcome, the substance of the conversations was completely unsatisfactory. Ciano found the usually bellicose Ribbentrop in a strangely pacific and magnanimous mood. It was the Fuehrer's intention, he was told, to impose on France armistice terms which would not be so severe as to invite rejection and lead to the establishment of a Pétain government in England or Algeria. In particular he was concerned about the French fleet, which could not be seized and which, sooner than pass into enemy hands, would sail to England or America. So far as England was concerned, the Fuehrer did not desire the destruction of the British Empire, which he believed to constitute a valuable element of stability in the world. All he asked was that England should withdraw from some of her positions and bow to the facts; and feelers had already been put out confidentially through the Swedish legation. When it came to a discussion of Italian claims on France, which Ciano defined as Nice, Corsica, Tunisia, French Somaliland, and possibly an outlet in North Africa on the Atlantic Ocean, Ribbentrop was sympathetic, but noncommittal. It was clear that the Germans, for all their courtesy and friendliness, cared little about the satisfaction of the Duce's ambitions. When the surprised and disillusioned Ciano inquired flatly whether Germany preferred peace or the prosecution of the war, Ribbentrop without hesitation replied: "Peace." [3]

In his conversation with Mussolini, Hitler was equally cautious and once more emphasized the importance of not acting in such a manner as to allow the French fleet to fall into the hands of the British or to drive the French government to flee to England or North Africa. He rejected Mussolini's demands for the Italian occupation of the Rhone valley and the demilitarization of Corsica, Tunisia, and Djibouti. He even refused to agree to joint armistice negotiations with the French, for he would not forego his plan for a Franco-German confrontation at a very historic spot, which, incidentally, he declined to divulge. He did, however, promise that his armistice with France would not come into effect until the French had concluded one with Italy. Except for this meager concession Mussolini had obtained nothing, and he inquired twice whether he was being refused his share of the booty because he had entered the war too late.

There was of course a fundamental conflict of interest between Germany and Italy. Hitler would have liked to reach some agreement on his own terms with England so as to free his hands in the West before marching against Russia. Moreover, the French were to be treated with some consideration since the emergence of General De Gaulle as a leader of resistance to tyranny presented an obvious danger. If France and Europe rallied behind De Gaulle, England's will to fight would be fortified, with the consequence that the war would be prolonged. With these considerations in mind, Hitler was not prepared to be embarrassed by Italian claims which were not justified by Italian performance. According to Roatta's notes, based on Mussolini's verbal account, the Fuehrer gave the clear impression that "he wishes to conclude in the shortest space of time peace with England. He only referred vaguely to offensive action against her and in completely hypothetical terms."[4]

Mussolini left Munich angry and frustrated. He even nursed the hope that the Germans might be punished for their arrogance.

Mussolini is very much embarrassed. He feels that his role is secondary. He reports on his conference with Hitler, not without a tone of bitterness and irony, and he concludes by saying that the German people have, in themselves, the germs of a collapse because a formidable internal clash will come that will smash everything. In truth, the Duce fears that the hour of peace is growing near and sees that unattainable dream of his life, glory on the field of battle, fading once again.

Ciano on the other hand was not displeased at the prospect of seeing a German peace offensive come to the rescue of Italy from the predicament in which the Duce had placed her. From all that Hitler said it was clear to Ciano that he wished at act quickly to end the war. "Hitler is now the gambler, who has made a big scoop and would like to get up from the table, risking nothing more. Today he speaks with a reserve and a perspicacity which, after such a victory, are really astonishing. I cannot be accused of excessive tenderness towards him, but today I truly admire him.[5]

On June 22 the Franco-German armistice terms were signed at Compiègne. Two days later the Italian armistice was signed at the Villa Incisa on the Cassian road near Rome. In deference to German requirements all that Mussolini attempted to secure was the occupation of what his troops had conquered—a few acres of French territory—together with the demilitarization of a fifty-kilometer strip along his European and North African frontier with France. In these painful circumstances he judged it prudent not to attempt to emulate the Fuehrer's behavior at Compiègne. There was, he ruled, to be no theatrical display, the meeting would take place almost secretly, and the press would be instructed to give it no publicity.[6]

III

The guns in France were silenced, but Mussolini's troubles were only just beginning. For weeks he was obliged to wait for Hitler's decisions. Would the Fuehrer make peace with England, or alternatively would he be able to invade England? While these grave matters were being pondered in Berlin, he was obliged to stand impotently on the sideline, oppressed by manifold fears which alternated with moments of insensate optimism. He was concerned that France might be slipping into the German camp and that thus Italy might be defrauded of her booty. He offered to participate in the German attack on Britain, an offer to which Hitler did not deign to reply. He wondered anxiously whether the Germans had captured documents in Paris which might compromise him. He spoke of landing on the Ionian Islands, of dismembering Yugoslavia, and of the early capture of Alexandria, an operation which Badoglio describes as easy and safe.[7]

Although in theory Mussolini was still waging his parallel war, everything really depended on Germany.

On July 7 Ciano arrived in Berlin to discuss the next moves with Hitler. Once more he was received with the utmost cordiality, but the conversation did little to throw light on Hitler's intentions, probably because Hitler had as yet formed no idea as to how, if at all, he was to bring the war to an end. They discussed France, and the Fuehrer, while defending his armistice terms, pleased his visitor by saying that eventually she would have to pay and pay dearly. As regards the attack on England, the problem was difficult and delicate, and he was unable to express a view until a study by the General Staff had been completed. He was thinking of making a peace gesture which would have some psychological and propaganda value, but had not yet come to any decision in the matter. Nor was he yet in a position to give a reply to the Duce's request to participate in the operations against England. It was all very vague, but Ciano thought, and rightly, that Hitler and Ribbentrop were in a more belligerent frame of mind than they had been a fortnight earlier in Munich.

There was also some talk about impending Italian operations in North Africa and Ciano mentioned difficulties with Greece. Hitler rashly and disingenuously replied that the Mediterranean and the Adriatic were purely of Italian concern, and that he would give a blanket approval to anything that Mussolini judged fit to do. But he did warn Ciano against premature intervention in Yugoslavia, which might upset the Russians and bring about an undesirable extension of the conflict.[8]

On July 13 Hitler addressed a long letter to Mussolini, declining the offer of an expeditionary force on the ground that logistic difficulties would arise from the supply of two different armies. It was a reply that much annoyed Mussolini, but he was encouraged by an intimation that Hitler, in the face of British refusal to listen to reason, had decided to launch his attack. "I have," Hitler wrote, "made to Britain so many offers of cooperation, and have been treated so shabbily, that I am now convinced that any new appeal to reason would meet with a similar rejection." [9] Three days later Hitler issued to his commanders a directive for the preparation of a landing operation against England. Its code name was to be "Sea Lion" and preparations were to be completed by the middle of August.

Nevertheless, on tactical grounds Hitler did eventually decide in his Reichstag speech of July 19 to launch a last appeal for peace.

> In this hour I feel it to be my duty before my own conscience to appeal once more to reason and common sense in Great Britain as much as elsewhere. I consider myself in a position to make this appeal, since I am not a vanquished foe begging favors, but the victor, speaking in the name of reason. I can see no reason why this war should go on.

There was no indication at all of his peace terms; and the British press and the B.B.C., without prompting from the British government, rejected out of hand any idea of a parley.[10]

The news of the quick British reaction soon spread around Berlin and caused universal disappointment among the Germans. But Mussolini was not so sure. He described Hitler's speech as much too cunning. "He fears that the English may find in it a pretext to begin negotiations. That would be sad for Mussolini, because now more than ever he wants war." [11] The Duce, as Churchill subsequently wrote, "need not have fretted himself. He was not to be denied all the war he wanted." [12]

Ciano, who had been to Berlin to hear the Reichstag speech, saw Hitler on the following day. He was told that England would certainly collapse under the first blows which Germany would deliver. Meanwhile it was of the utmost importance that peace be preserved in the Balkans. In other words, Hitler withdrew the blank check that he had carelessly handed to Mussolini a few days previously. After a few words of perfunctory praise for the Italian war effort, which in fact had amounted to nothing at all, Hitler closed the interview by undertaking to write to the Duce, or preferably to see him at the Brenner Pass, as soon as he had made his plans for the next phase of the war.[13] Ciano returned to Rome once more without much idea of what the Germans intended to do. It was characteristic of the Axis partnership and fortunate for its enemies that neither ally was at any time willing to open his heart to the other. From this state of affairs Italy, as the junior partner, suffered the most, although Mussolini was able on occasion by way of retaliation to present his friend with an unpleasant surprise.

As the summer weeks passed the war seemed to stand still. Britain was anxiously girding herself for the invasion which did not take place, while in Italy there was little sign of war. Except for the formations in Albania and Africa, the main bulk of the army stood idle at their home stations. Mussolini was reviewing cavalry divisions at Udine and there was an international horse show at Merano, in which a German team took part. It was a frustrating situation for Mussolini, who constantly, but vainly, pressed his reluctant generals to undertake an early offensive against Egypt. On August 4 the Duke of Aosta did begin a halting invasion of British Somaliland, which was not to be seriously defended, but in Libya, Marshal Graziani sturdily refused to move. Mussolini was still laboring under the fear that the war might at any moment be brought to an end by some Anglo-German accommodation and that he might have to appear at a peace conference without a single territorial pawn and without a single feat of arms to his credit. In his feverish search for new theaters of war he spoke to Ciano of attacking Yugoslavia, and on August 12 there was a conference at the Palazzo Venezia at which impending action against Greece was discussed.[14] On August 16 a communication was made to the Germans to the effect that Italian differences with Greece could be resolved in September by exploiting incidents provoked from Rome.[15]

These pipedreams were quickly shattered when Ribbentrop, who had been warned by the Italian military attaché of Italian designs on Yugoslavia, at once summoned the Italian ambassador and told him sternly that every effort must be made against Britain, because there and there alone would the issue be decided. Accordingly any plan to attack Yugoslavia must be abandoned and any action against Greece would be unwelcome in Berlin. As Ciano put it, "it is a complete order to halt all along the line." [16] The Italians meekly complied, and within twenty-four hours a submissive reply was sent to Berlin, agreeing that the conflict with Britain must take priority over all other considerations. The ambassador was to assure the Fuehrer that no action would be taken against Yugoslavia, while the Greek dispute would be handled by diplomatic means and Italy would confine herself to reinforcing the troops in Albania by a few divisions.

On August 29 Ciano, who was on his way to Vienna for a joint Italo-German arbitration of a territorial dispute between Hungary and Rumania, stopped at Berchtesgaden to see Hitler. The invasion of England was still hanging fire, and Hitler explained that massive preparations were essential: the assembly of ships and landing craft, the deployment of heavy artillery on the French coast, and the destruction of the Royal Air Force. Although Hitler continued to express the utmost confidence in the outcome, it seemed to Ciano that the Germans envisaged the prolongation of the war beyond the winter. All this was scarcely surprising, but Ciano apprehended for the first time on the German side a significant distrust of the Soviet Union, which was described as ready to exploit any complications in order, with the complicity of Bulgaria and Yugoslavia, to drive to the Dardanelles, the Aegean, and even the Adriatic.[17]

September came, and still the world held its breath awaiting the clash of arms. The Battle of Britain was in full swing, but Hitler was beginning to recoil from the hazard of an invasion and to turn his eyes in the direction of the Soviet Union. Italy had been in the war for nearly three months and Mussolini was becoming more and more impatient for action. Graziani was told that if he did not launch his attack without further delay, he would be replaced. He undertook to comply, but, as Ciano noted, "never has a military operation been conducted so much against the will of the commanders." [18]

Eventually on September 13 the Italian army began to cross the Egyptian frontier. The British made a planned, fighting withdrawal and by September 17 the Italians had advanced sixty miles to Sidi Barrani, where they were to spend the next three months. Mussolini was "radiant with joy. He has taken the entire responsibility of the offensive on his shoulders, and he is proud that he was right." [19] His joy was short-lived, for two shattering blows were soon to fall upon his unsuspecting head.

IV

Meanwhile in Berlin the refusal of Britain to collapse in the face of her hopeless prospects and under the hail of a merciless air bombardment was evoking annoyance and dismay. Hitler, under the influence of his generals, also was thinking of circumventing his problems by opening new theaters of war; and on September 19 Ribbentrop appeared in Rome to ventilate two proposals: first, the signature of a tripartite alliance between Germany, Italy, and Japan, which would reinforce the isolationist elements in America; and secondly, the entry of Spain into the war, which would lead to the capture of Gibraltar. Mussolini gladly embraced both proposals, but took the opportunity to revert to his designs against Greece. While he admitted that the principal aim must be to defeat England, the Greeks, he said, represented for Italy what the Norwegians represented for Germany before the action of April. It was therefore necessary to proceed with the liquidation of Greece, all the more so as, when the Italian army advanced into Egypt, the English fleet, unable to remain at Alexandria, would seek refuge in Greek ports.[20]

The Tripartite Alliance was duly signed on September 27 in Berlin with the usual inflated ceremony, and on October 4 Hitler arrived at the Brenner Pass to insure that Mussolini remained in tow. Although expressing his customary buoyant optimism about the outcome of the war, which he described as "already won," Hitler conveyed to the Italians in a multitude of words that he had for the time being abandoned the idea of invading England and had elected to rely on the effects of air bombardment. When, however, he came to Spain, it became clear that he was no longer quite so enthusiastic about enlisting Franco's aid. Two factors had contributed to this change of heart. On September 22 Franco had rejected a German request for naval bases in Spain, and his Foreign Minister, who had recently been in Berlin, had been unsympathetic, difficult, and dilatory. His demands had seemed to the Germans quite excessive, for he required not only considerable supplies of material but the cession of a large tract of French North African territory.

Hitler explained that the satisfaction of this latter demand might provoke two unfortunate consequences: the occupation by Britain of the Canaries and the accession of the French Empire in North Africa to the cause of De Gaulle. It was worth noting, he added, that the French had recently committed acts of hostility towards Britain, and one could not exclude the possibility of eventually drawing France into an anti-British continental coalition.

Mussolini agreed as to the danger of an immediate undertaking to cede French Morocco to Spain, but he was not prepared to abandon the prospect of bringing Spain into the war. He accordingly proposed that Serrano Suñer, who was waiting in Rome, should be told that the Axis powers were in agreement as to the satisfaction of Spain's claims on England and also on some territorial adjustment in Morocco, which must be determined when peace was signed. Moreover Italy and Germany were prepared to furnish the greatest possible material aid. All this might be more fully discussed at a meeting with Franco. The Fuehrer declared himself in agreement with Mussolini's proposal.

Finally Mussolini vaingloriously dilated on his plans for the conquest of Egypt. The first phase, he declared, would shortly be followed by an advance to Mersa Matruh, while the third phase would carry the Italian army to Alexandria and the Nile Delta. The Fuehrer offered the help of specialized German units, but Mussolini had the pleasure of being able to reply that he did not need them, at least before the final phase.[21] So far as he was concerned, it had been a satisfactory meeting, for it had shown that Germany was in no better posture than Italy, and for the first time he had been allowed an insight into the Fuehrer's plans. "Rarely," said Ciano, "have I seen the Duce in such good humor and good shape as at the Brenner Pass today." On the way back to Rome Mussolini was bursting for action. He spoke of dismissing Muti, the secretary of the party; of spurring Graziani to accelerate his offensive; and he rampaged against the King as being the only defeatist in the country.[22] His generals were, however, not so ardent; and both Graziani and Badoglio opined that it would be madness to attempt any further operation in Libya until November at the earliest. The Duce was furiously helpless.

V

The stalemate made it all the more important to seduce Franco, and on October 23 Hitler, not in the best of tempers, traveled all the way to Hendaye on the French frontier to meet the Spanish dictator. He was under the impression that he could propel Spain into the war on his own terms and he was resolved not to make any written promise to cede French colonial possessions. He still hoped to induce France to open hostilities against England and told Ribbentrop that, if the Spaniards obtained any concessions in writing, "with these talkative Latins the French are sure to hear something about it sooner or later." Besides, if such an agreement with the Spaniards became known, the French colonies would probably go over to De Gaulle.[23]

When the meeting with Franco took place, Hitler began, as usual, with a glowing account of his military position. England was beaten, though she would not admit it; but if she lost Gibraltar, she could be expelled from the Mediterranean and from Africa. He accordingly invited Franco to come into the war in January, 1941, when Gibraltar would be taken by the same special units which had captured the Eben Emael fort at Liège. The prize he offered was Gibraltar and there was a vague mention of colonial territories in Africa.

For the first time Hitler met a man who was blandly impervious to every argument. The meeting lasted nine hours, and at the end of that time Franco was as resolved not to be lured into the war as he had been at the beginning. His tactic was, with quiet courtesy and an impenetrable expression, to pose conditions which he must have known were unacceptable: rectification of the Pyrenees frontier, the cession of French Catalonia, which lay north of the

Pyrenees, and of Algeria from Oran to Cape Blanco and virtually the whole of French Morocco. Moreover he raised innumerable material and political difficulties. Spain needed several thousand tons of wheat immediately and he inquired whether Germany was in a position to deliver this. He required a large number of heavy guns and antiaircraft artillery. He must protect his long coastline from the British navy and take into account the certain loss of the Canaries. Finally he declared that it was not consistent with national pride to accept Gibraltar as a present; the fortress could only be taken by Spaniards. As regards the war, he discounted Hitler's hopes of early victory over Britain and declined to believe that German armored units from Gibraltar could clear the British out of Africa. "To the edge of the great deserts, very possibly," he said, "but central Africa would be protected against major attacks by land by the desert belt, in the same way that an island is by the open sea. As an old African campaigner I am quite clear about that." Finally, as a sop to the Germans, Franco undertook to consider accession to the Tripartite Pact. It was a meaningless gesture, which did little to veil the failure of the Fuehrer's pilgrimage.

To a man like Hitler, who was accustomed to impose his will on helpless satellites, the conversation was frustrating in the extreme. "Rather than go through it again," he later told Mussolini at Florence, "I would prefer to have three or four of my teeth out."[24] Ribbentrop, reflecting his master's mood, cursed the "Jesuit" Suñer and the "ungrateful coward" Franco, who owed Germany everything and now refused to join her.[25] In his rage Hitler sullenly resolved for the time being to exclude Franco from his calculations and to abandon any further attempt to solicit Spanish aid. His irritation was understandable and wiser counsels were shortly to prevail.

On the following day Hitler met Pétain at Montoire, with the object of drawing France also into the war. Once more there was the customary opening monologue, in which Hitler assured his listener that England was beaten, but, he said, every European country would suffer from the prolongation of the war, and it would be in their joint interest to form a Continental community with the object of shortening its duration. What position, he asked, did the French government propose to adopt? Pétain, who throughout the interview was reserved and laconic, replied vaguely that, while he accepted collaboration in principle, ways and means must be studied. Hitler, however, continued to press him, and finally inquired what France would do if she were again attacked by England, as at Oran. Pétain, who understood the implication, at once answered that his country had suffered too much to engage herself in a new conflict. It was a rebuff and, as he left Montoire on his way back to Germany, Hitler made no effort to conceal his disappointment.

VI

Meanwhile an event occurred which was to have unpleasant consequences for the Axis. In June the Soviet Union had addressed an ultimatum to Rumania demanding the immediate cession of Bessarabia and northern Bukovina. Under the agreement between Berlin and Moscow, Rumania east of the Pruth fell in the Russian zone of influence; and so the Germans, although much disturbed, had no alternative but to advise the Rumanian government to yield. Hitler was at least relieved that his rich sources of oil and food had not been cut off by a total Russian occupation of the country. As suspicion of Russia grew in Berlin, so did determination to safeguard the oil wells. On September 20 Hitler issued a top-secret directive ordering the despatch of so-called military missions to Rumania to protect the oil district and to prepare the deployment of troops against Russia in case war with the Soviet Union was forced on Germany.[26] At the beginning of October German troops began to enter Rumania, ostensibly at the invitation of General Antonescu, but in reality to occupy the oil district.

The news of this move, made without prior consultation, by an ally who had sternly discountenanced any initiative in the Balkans and who was not prepared to allow Italy to be associated with the protection of the oil wells, aroused Mussolini's indignation. "Hitler always faces me with a *fait accompli.* This time I am going to pay him back in his own coin. He will find out from the papers that I have occupied Greece. In this way the equilibrium will be re-established."[27]

Mussolini at a meeting of his war leaders in the Palazzo Venezia on October 15 took the final decision to attack Greece. In the light of after events his wide-flung objectives seen unrealistic and quite out of the range of his ill-prepared and ill-found army standing in Albania. They were to seize the Ionian islands and Salonika and subsequently to occupy the whole of Greece, "in order to put her out of action and to assure that in all circumstances she will remain in our politico-economic sphere." The date fixed for the operation was October 26. Marshal Badoglio pointed out that twenty divisions would be required, whereas only nine infantry divisions and one cavalry division were available, but Mussolini, to whom Ciano, Jacomoni, and the army commander in Albania, General Visconti Prasca, represented that the enterprise presented little difficulty, brushed the Marshal's misgivings aside: "I shall send in my resignation as an Italian if anyone objects to our fighting the Greeks." [28] The Marshal was, however, able to secure a postponement of the date by two days.

On October 19 Mussolini drafted a letter to Hitler, which was not despatched until October 22 and not delivered in Berlin until October 24. He informed the Fuehrer that he had decided to put an end to delays and to strike at Greece very soon, but he was deliberately vague as to the date because, as Ciano noted, he was afraid that "once again an order might come to halt us." As a further precaution Badoglio was categorically instructed not to inform the German military attaché of the coming attack. The gist of Mussolini's letter was immediately conveyed by the German Foreign Office to Hitler and Ribbentrop, who, in their respective special trains, were returning from France after their unsatisfactory conversations with Franco at Hendaye and Pétain at Montoire. Hitler, in the hope of deflecting Mussolini's purpose, instructed Ribbentrop to telephone from the next station to suggest an immediate meeting, ostensibly to report on the interviews with Franco and Pétain. Mussolini proposed Florence on October 28, but Hitler arrived too late, for as he stepped onto the festively decorated platform from his special train on the morning of that day he was greeted by an exultant Duce with a smile of self-satisfaction and the words: "Victorious Italian troops crossed the Greco-Albanian frontier at dawn today." [29] Ribbentrop, voicing Hitler's views, had on the way to Florence angrily described the invasion of Greece as a crazy scheme and predicted that the Italians would never get anywhere in the autumn rains and winter snows. But, once he was faced with the accomplished fact, Hitler controlled himself remarkably well and, during the friendly conversation which ensued at the Palazzo Pitti, gave no sign of his resentment.

Far from giving Mussolini a truthful account of his failure at Montoire, Hitler was only concerned to dispel Italian suspicions of German policy towards France and to blur the fundamental conflict of interest between the two countries. He told him that, while Laval was "a dirty democratic politician who is moving towards us merely to save himself," Pétain had made an excellent impression. It was, he continued, now clear that the struggle between Vichy and De Gaulle was genuine, and French solidarity with the Axis would be of great importance not only from a military, but also from a psychological, point of view. Nevertheless he twice solemnly declared that he would sign no peace treaty with France if all Italy's requirements were not previously satisfied, requirements to be regarded as extremely modest and certainly less than the French expected.

As regards Spain, he had found Franco a brave man, who must have become leader by sheer chance, but he was no organizer and Spain was in a state of great confusion. The Spaniards had no conception of their position and were putting forward unacceptable demands, quite out of proportion to the contribution which they could make. He had, however, been able to secure agreement in principle on Spain's accession to the Tripartite Alliance; and with this sterile face-saving device the two dictators were obliged to be content.

Greece was not mentioned except at the beginning of the conversation, when Hitler expressed his solidarity with the Italian enterprise and offered to place at the Duce's disposal his parachute divisions, which might be used for the occupation of Crete.[30] His forbearance did not, however, signify that he was reconciled to Mussolini's behavior. He knew that the Italians had, at a difficult moment for the Axis, committed a capital error, which must prejudice their position in the Mediterranean. As Schmidt records, he "went north again that afternoon with bitterness in his heart. He had been frustrated three times—at Hendaye, at Montoire, and now in Italy. In the lengthy winter evenings of the next few years these long, exacting journeys were a constantly recurring theme of bitter reproaches against ungrateful and unreliable friends, Axis partners, and deceiving Frenchmen." [31]

Mussolini on the other hand returned to Rome in high spirits to await news of victory from the Greek front. He was to be disappointed, for it soon became clear that things were going very badly indeed. Within a few days the initial assault was repulsed and the Greeks passed to the offensive. At once the whole Italian position was threatened, and during November and December a flow of bad tidings poured into Rome. At the end of November Badoglio resigned as Chief of Staff and was replaced by General Count Ugo Cavallero. It did not prove a happy choice, for Cavallero, though a first-class organizer, proved excessively subservient to his German allies.

It was not, however, only from Albania that bad news arrived. The British were able to improve their position by the occupation of Crete, Lemnos, and other islands, while on November 11 Admiral Cunningham launched a devastating blow against the main Italian fleet based on Taranto. The battleship "Cavour" was sunk, two battleships, the new "Littorio" and the "Duilio," were seriously damaged, and havoc created in the dockyard. On the following day the undamaged units of the Italian fleet left their base and the balance of naval power in the Mediterranean had been decisively altered. The sudden reversal of Axis fortunes was a portent, noted by Franco in Spain and by other neutral governments.

VII

Hitler's immediate reply was not given on the battlefield, but at the conference table. On November 20, at a ceremony in Vienna attended by Hitler, Ribbentrop, and Ciano, Hungary acceded to the Tripartite Pact and it was arranged that Rumania and Slovakia should do so shortly afterwards. It was an insignificant gesture, since these countries were already German vassals, but it was all that the Axis could manage at the moment. On the way to Vienna Ciano stopped at Salzburg for conversations with Hitler and Ribbentrop. The Fuehrer was pessimistic and reserved, although in his report to the Duce, Ciano emphasized that he was not "displeased" or inclined to recriminate over Greece. But, in expressing the view that Italy had landed the Axis in a dangerous predicament Hitler did not mince his words; and he admitted that he had come to Florence in the hope of persuading the Duce to postpone his invasion until the following spring. It was only when he heard that the operation had actually begun that he had judged it useless to raise the matter.

The point which disturbed Hitler most was the prospect that the British would establish air bases in Greece, from which they would be able to attack the Rumanian oil fields. This was a threat which must be firmly parried and he proposed to concentrate troops in Rumania and later to march across Bulgaria into Greece. He could not, however, do this before the middle of March, and he hoped that the Italians would be able to deliver a simultaneous blow on their Albanian front. He also hoped that Mussolini would be able to pursue his operations against Egypt and he declared his readiness to despatch a formation of new Stukas to Libya.

It was, however, on the diplomatic front that Hitler made his most interesting contribution. He thought that the time had come to draw Yugoslavia on to the side of the Axis, where she could play an advantageous role in the attack on Greece. He accordingly proposed a pact with Yugoslavia based on three points: an Axis guarantee of Yugoslavia's frontiers, cession of Salonika to Yugoslavia, and demilitarization of Yugoslavia's Adriatic coast. When Ciano replied that he thought that the Duce would accept such a pact, the conversation took on a more cordial tone and the Fuehrer was in the best of tempers at the prospects opening out before him. "If that is so," he said to Ciano, "I am sure that we can have Yugoslavia on our side and the Greek business will turn out to be a major Axis success. Yugoslavia will have Salonika, Bulgaria an outlet to the sea, Italy the remainder of Greece. England, when she has lost Greece and Egypt is threatened, will be virtually chased out of the Mediterranean." [32]

When Hitler said good-by to Ciano at Vienna he handed him a sealed letter for Mussolini and added: "From this city of Vienna, on the day of the *Anschluss,* I sent Mussolini a telegram to assure him that I would never forget his help. I confirm it today, and I am at his side with all my strength." [33] Ciano says that he had two big tears in his eyes. What a strange man!

Hitler's very long letter, which was intended to follow up the conversation with Ciano, did not make pleasant reading. He commented tartly on the damaging psychological and military effects of the Greek campaign, and told the Duce that no remedial military action could be taken before March, 1941. Meanwhile the Italians should seek to reach at least Mersa Matruh, which would bring Alexandria and Suez within air range, after which a successful offensive could be mounted against Egypt also in the spring. Air attacks should also be mounted on the British Mediterranean fleet; and for this purpose he suggested the withdrawal of the Italian air units serving on the western front and the despatch to Italy of German bombers. On the political front he proposed that Spain should be induced to intervene immediately, that the German troops should be further reinforced in Rumania, and that Yugoslavia should be brought into the Axis.[34] Quite apart from Hitler's censure of the Greek enterprise, the letter was an intimation that Germany intended to take control in the Balkans, an area which Mussolini had hitherto regarded as his own under the theory of the parallel war. "He really smacked my fingers," was Mussolini's rueful comment to Ciano.[35] There was, however, no alternative but to accept all Hitler's proposals, although in his reply Mussolini did make the condition that Yugoslav troops should not come into action until the Italians had dealt Greece a first blow.[36] It was a childish attempt to retain some vestige of his self-respect.

On December 6 Marshal Milch arrived in Rome to arrange for the despatch of German air force units to Italy, and he brought with him a further letter from the Fuehrer announcing that he had begun his approaches to Belgrade. For the rest the letter was not particularly encouraging. Hitler was plainly exasperated at the continued equivocations of the Spaniards and was beginning to wonder whether Vichy hostility to De Gaulle was in fact genuine.

This communication crossed one, equally gloomy, which the Italian ambassador had hurried back to Berlin to deliver. On December 4 the Duce had received from General Ubaldo Soddu, the commander in Albania, an alarming telegram reporting that the situation could no longer be retrieved by force of arms and that consequently a political solution must be sought. To Ciano, Mussolini said: "This is grotesque and absurd, but it is a fact. We have to ask for a truce through Hitler." [37] He railed against his generals and the Italian people: "If, when I was a Socialist, I had had a knowledge of the Italian middle class, not purely theoretical reading from Karl Marx, but practical, based on experience such as I have now, I would have launched a revolution so pitiless that, by comparison, the revolution of Comrade Lenin would have been child's play." [38]

Alfieri, who happened to be on sick leave in Rome, was hurriedly summoned to the Palazzo Venezia, where he found the Duce plunged in the depths of depression. His face was drawn, his eyes were swollen, and he had not shaved for two days. It was decided that Alfieri should fly to Berlin without delay in order to appeal to Hitler for help. When the unfortunate ambassador subsequently asked Ciano for more specific instructions, the reply he received was symptomatic of the panic and disorder reigning in Rome. "Any assistance, so long as it's prompt," said Ciano. "The situation is such that the despatch of a few airplanes, a few guns, a few battalions may make all the difference." There was no need to be specific.[39]

Alfieri's airplane was compelled by bad weather to make a forced landing in Venice and he did not see Ribbentrop until December 7. In view of the haste with which he had left and the sketchy instructions he had received, it was not surprising that the representations of the inexperienced and somewhat incompetent ambassador should have made a bad impression. He first asked for a diversionary military operation by German troops in Rumania and, when Ribbentrop rudely replied that this would be ridiculous, he begged that Germany should compel the Bulgarians to mobilize. This request was also summarily dismissed. Finally Alfieri asked for direct military and material aid. But when Ribbentrop inquired exactly what aid was needed, Alfieri could only reply that he had no idea; all he had received were verbal instructions from Ciano to solicit "immediate aid." [40] Ribbentrop, who was at his best on these occasions, retorted icily that the ambassador would do well to be better briefed by his government. For good measure he added that the present disasters could be ascribed to the fact that the

Italians had elected to ignore the Fuehrer's warning not to attack Greece.

On the following day Alfieri saw Hitler. It was another unpleasant interview, for the Fuehrer was in the worst of tempers and not only complained aggressively of the Italian decision to attack Greece, but criticized the bearing of the Italian troops. Any units, he declared, that failed to do their duty should be brought before a special tribunal and summarily dealt with. He advocated the use of "barbaric means, such as the shooting of generals and colonels who abandoned their positions and the decimation of troops." After administering this reproof Hitler did undertake to despatch as many transport planes as the Albanian airfields could accommodate and he asked for a very early meeting with the Duce.[41] With this meager result the Italians had to be content.

VIII

Mussolini's appeal to Berlin might have been more strident and coherent had he known that within a few days he was to suffer a further grievous blow. On December 9 the British launched a powerful attack on the Italians at Sidi Barrani. To the Italians, who had been thinking of advancing themselves on Mersa Matruh in God's good time, the news came "as a thunderbolt" and Ciano wrote that telegrams from Graziani confirmed that "we have had a licking." [42] But the magnitude of the disaster was then still veiled. Sidi Barrani fell on December 10, Bardia on January 4, and Tobruk on January 7. Within a month the British desert army had advanced over two hundred miles and captured 113,000 prisoners and over 700 guns. Already on December 12 a catastrophic telegram arrived from Graziani, who spoke of withdrawing to Tripoli. Mussolini was severely shaken and spoke gloomily to Ciano of the "real defeat in Libya."

These events still further damaged Italy's standing in Berlin, where Hitler began to use a more peremptory tone. When on December 19 Alfieri presented a letter from the Duce, specifying what material aid he required, Hitler replied that he would provide aid. But he immediately qualified his undertaking by two wounding observations. He would not send raw materials, but only finished products of the type and quality determined by German economic experts; and as a counterpart Italy would have to send labor to Germany on an unprecedented scale.[43] This interview not only registered Italian vassalage, but it paved the way for the German occupation of Italy. It was the end of the "parallel" war and of any vestige of control by Italy of her own destiny. From now on hordes of German so-called economic experts, and secret agents posing as such, swarmed into Italy and began to interfere in every aspect of Italian affairs. To the economic experts were added a large number of military, who arrived to prepare the way for the despatch of an armored corps and air formations. In his diary Simoni noted gloomily that the Germans no longer believed that material aid to Italy would save the day. They would have to take command, and if necessary occupy the country, as they had already done in Rumania.[44]

On December 31 Hitler addressed a long letter to Mussolini wishing him a happy new year, and magnanimously pointing out that the fortunes of war were bound to ebb and flow. There was no longer any talk of immediate victory, although there was no sign of any loss of confidence in the final issue. But he admitted that Franco, impressed by recent events, was still stubbornly refusing to intervene and that the Axis must abandon the hope of being able to march through Spain in the immediate future. "I fear," he wrote contemptuously, "that Franco is committing here the greatest mistake of his life."[45] After the war Goering, in his prison camp in Luxemburg, was to declare to the author that it had been Hitler's greatest mistake not to seize Gibraltar and North Africa, with or without Franco's consent.[46]

The year closed gloomily for the Axis. Neither country wanted a long war and, while it was difficult to see how Britain could win, it was equally difficult to see how the war could quickly be brought to an end, particularly after Hitler's failure to involve Spain and Vichy France. The longer the war continued, the more uncertain its course, and the shadows of America and Russia loomed over the future.

For Mussolini it had been a bitter experience. In June the prospect had been alluring and it had seemed certain that his intervention would quickly bring him the fruits of victory without risk and little effort. Then had come the abortive campaign against France,

German pressure to abate his claims, and the catastrophic campaign in Greece. In his last year at Salò he constantly harped on the humiliation of his failure in Greece. In the Mediterranean his fleet had been mauled; in Africa he was faced with the loss of Abyssinia, Eritrea, and Somaliland; and now the campaign in Libya, which was going from bad to worse, might involve the total loss of Italy's last foothold on the African continent. He had been compelled to crawl to Berlin to solicit aid, with the consequence that he had lost his liberty of action and was now, if he wished to survive, at Hitler's mercy.

At home morale and the prestige of the regime had reached its lowest point. It is true that in 1942 and in subsequent years Italian fortunes still further declined, but in the public attitude there was then an element of resignation compounded with the hope of an end to the war. But as the year 1941 closed, the nation was reeling under the shock of successive and unexpected disasters; and there was no lead from the top to rally them, for the Duce and his principal lieutenants were distraught and divided. On November 26, 1940, Ciano noted in his diary that "the ushers at the Palazzo Venezia were given instructions to show leading Italians into different rooms in order to prevent a general brawl."

It was a bleak prospect with which to open the new year. As it happened, both the years 1941 and 1942 were to bring a series of striking successes to Axis arms, and the enemy was to be extended almost to breaking point. But they were to be all German triumphs, to which the Italians contributed little; and gradually Italian dependence on Germany grew until in October, 1941, Mussolini was forced to admit to Ciano that Italy would become the most important confederated province of Germany. "We have to accept these conditions because any attempt to rebel would result in our being reduced from the position of a confederated province to the plight of a colony. Even if they should ask for Trieste tomorrow as part of the German *Lebensraum,* we would have to bow our heads."[47] Already at the end of 1940 Mussolini knew in his heart that he had lost all hope of bringing the war to an honorable end, and for the next thirty months only the Fuehrer's magnetism, exercised at constant meetings, and the optimism which he was then able to infuse, sustained the Duce in the struggle.

CHAPTER EIGHTEEN

The Thorny Path

1941

I

THE year 1941 opened with an unpleasant episode, which brought home to Mussolini his total dependence on Germany. During December it had occurred to the distraught Duce that he might improve his position by making approaches to Russia, partly in order to receive economic aid, of which he was desperately in need, and partly to reduce tension in the Balkans. The Italian move was favorably received by Molotov, who dined at the Italian embassy on December 13, and subsequently produced a memorandum requiring an Italian guarantee that the *status quo* in the Balkans and the Dardanelles should not be altered without Russia's previous consent. The Italians signified that they were agreeable in principle, but Ciano, rather late in the day, judged it wise to inform the Germans of what was afoot.

It was unfortunate for the Italian ambassador in Berlin that he was obliged to make this communication to the German government at a moment when Ribbentrop was already upset by the recent death of his father. The interview was stormy, and Ribbentrop made it plain that Italy had no business to be meddling in the Balkans, an area which, incidentally, in Mussolini's palmy days had been recognized in Berlin as Italy's sphere of influence. Ribbentrop, after a visit to the Berghof, returned with categorical instructions that Mussolini was to cut off all further parleys with the Russians. The order was immediately obeyed, the Russians were displeased, and all hope of economic aid from the Soviet Union disappeared. It was a cruel rebuff.[1]

The sorry tale of Italian disasters had caused the Germans to press throughout December for an early meeting between Hitler and Mussolini, but it had been impossible to fix a firm date, since Mussolini was understandably reluctant to face a meeting "burdened by these numerous failures, until they have been at least in part redressed." [2] It was eventually decided that the encounter should take place at Berchtesgaden on January 19, and Mussolini left Rome "frowning and uneasy."

He need not have been afraid, for Hitler, following his usual tactics, gave him a cordial welcome. There were no "condolences in the air—condolences that Mussolini feared." Instead the Fuehrer quickly got down to the business of fortifying his ally with a two-hour talk on the Axis prospects and the tasks ahead. In the course of long sessions, which lasted two days, he unfolded his plan to invade Greece and explained why it would be imprudent to attempt a landing in England. He expressed his misgivings about Russia, though he was careful not to reveal that he had already taken the decision to attack her. Finally, he came to his most important topic, Spain. He said that the uncertain attitude of France made it essential to bring Spain into the war. Unfortunately his extensive preparations to capture Gibraltar had been frustrated by Franco's hesitation, which he attributed to the influence of Serrano Suñer and the Church. He asked the Duce to use his personal influence with Franco and emphasized that he was prepared to give the material aid of which Spain stood in need. The Duce, after some hesitation, agreed to undertake this commission and, in view of the urgency of the matter, promised to see Franco toward the end of the month. Hitler's monologues, his display with maps and statistics of Germany's military might, and his patronizing friendliness to his ally had all combined to irritate the Duce. To Ciano he remarked: "This is torture. I can hardly wait to go." [3] Nevertheless he had been impressed and, according to Ciano, he returned to Rome "elated, as he always is after a meeting with Hitler." There had, after all, been no recriminations, no excessive demands; and Hitler's buoyancy had convinced him that the tide would shortly turn. Ciano, however, was not so satisfied and was particularly upset by an observation from Ribbentrop to the effect that he saw no possibility of the war ending before 1942. "And how about us?" he wrote in his diary that night.[4]

II

In order to prepare the way for Mussolini's interview with Franco, Hitler on February 6 sent a strongly worded letter to the Spanish dictator.

> About one thing, Caudillo, there must be clarity; we are fighting a battle of life and death and cannot make any gifts. . . .
>
> The entrance of Spain into this struggle has certainly not been conceived of as exclusively to the benefit of German and Italian interests. . . . Spain will never get other friends than those given her in the Germany and Italy of today, unless it becomes a different Spain. This different Spain, however, could only be the Spain of decline and final collapse. For this reason alone, Caudillo, I believe that we three men, the Duce, you, and I, are bound together by the most rigorous compulsion of history, and that thus we in this historical analysis ought to obey as the Supreme Commandment the realization that, in such difficult times, not so much an apparently wise caution as a bold heart can save nations.[5]

Mussolini approached his conversation with Franco in a mood of weary defeatism. In conversation with Anfuso he remarked that the Germans would never understand the Spaniards, and that it was clear that Franco was not at the moment willing to make common cause with the Axis; and he added bitterly that if the Italian army had occupied Greece according to plan, Spain would have quickly forgotten Hitler's equivocations.[6] After all, Spain was in a position very similar to that of Italy in September, 1939, and Mussolini from his own experience found it difficult not to sympathize with Franco's resistance to German pressure, particularly since, unlike Italy, Spain was not bound to Germany by any treaty obligation.

On February 12 Franco met Mussolini at Bordighera. It was a strange interview, for Mussolini, who never showed much moral courage in tackling an unpleasant conversation, seemed more concerned to spare, and indeed agree with, his guest rather than bring pressure to bear on him. After an opening statement, which might have been modeled on a Hitlerian monologue and in which he professed his faith in an Axis victory, Mussolini very gingerly broached the delicate topic of Spain's participation. He explicitly disclaimed any intention of putting forward a request, but emphasized that, although he shared the Caudillo's view that Spain could not stay out, the date and the manner of her intervention must be a matter for the sole decision of the Spanish government. He added lamely that Hitler, who had a great personal regard for the Caudillo and who was ready to furnish all possible aid, was only asking that German troops be allowed to capture Gibraltar.

Franco had little difficulty in dealing with this feeble gambit. He repeated that Gibraltar could only be captured by Spanish troops, and he tabled a number of complaints against the Germans who, he declared, had shown no comprehension of Spain and her aspirations. In the first place, Germany was pandering to France, Spain's principal enemy. Secondly, Spain, if she were not to starve, must have wheat and she had legitimate territorial demands to put forward. On none of these points had Hitler been willing to give him firm and satisfactory assurances.

The Duce made little effort to reply. On France he was, of course, in agreement, but he claimed that Hitler had abandoned the idea of an alliance with her. On the other two points, he merely inquired whether he was correctly interpreting the Caudillo's mind in stating that Spain would enter the war when two conditions had been fulfilled: the despatch of wheat in sufficient quantity and the acceptance of her colonial aspirations. Franco replied affirmatively, but added a qualification: the entry of Spain into the war depended more on Germany than on Spain herself. The sooner Germany came to her aid, the sooner Spain would lend her support to the cause of world fascism. The Duce pursued the matter no further, and was content to close a very long conversation by saying that he would report to the Fuehrer.[7] From the record of the conversation and from Serrano Suñer's account,[8] it would have been impossible to apprehend that to Mussolini in his desperate situation the entry of Spain into the war was at least as important as it was to Hitler. His attitude was detached and he seemed to wish to confine his role to that of honest broker. Indeed, he subsequently said to Anfuso that he could not find it in his heart to blame Franco, although it would have been difficult for Italy to have followed his example.[9]

Four days later, Franco, emboldened by his success at Bordighera, sent Hitler a firm reply stating that it was impossible to fix a date for Spain's entry into the war on account of the economic position and Germany's failure to deal with it. Without referring to the Italian collapse in Libya he went on to observe sarcastically that, if the capture of Gibraltar would improve Italy's position, it was equally true that the closure of the Straits of Gibraltar could not be decisive unless the Mediterranean were simultaneously closed to Britain at Suez. If this latter operation could not be undertaken, Spain was not in a position to bear the burden of a long war. Finally, he reminded Hitler of the limited agreement reached at Hendaye, which, he said, had been indeterminate and lacking in precision. In the intervening months developments had left the circumstances of October far behind and their understanding had become outmoded.[10] It was the end of the dream of Spanish intervention, and Hitler conceded defeat. "The long and the short of the tedious Spanish rigmarole," he wrote to Mussolini, "is that Spain does not want to enter the war and will not enter it. This is extremely tiresome, since it means that for the moment the possibility of striking at Britain in the simplest manner, in her Mediterranean possessions, is eliminated." It was a failure of German diplomacy, of which Ciano, who had also suffered from Hitler's overbearing methods, was painfully aware. "If Spain falls away," he wrote, "the fault rests in great part with the Germans and their uncouth manners in dealing with Latins." [11]

III

The collapse of the Spanish negotiations came at a bad moment for Mussolini, for elsewhere the shadow of failure fell across every Italian enterprise. In Albania it had proved impossible to launch a counteroffensive. In Libya, Benghazi fell on February 6 and the whole of Cyrenaica passed into British hands. Farther to the south the Italian Empire was beginning to crumble. By the end of February Italian Somaliland had been lost, and operations had been begun which led to the capture of Eritrea and to the return of the

Emperor of Abyssinia to his capital on May 5. "We have lost our empire, while the French still retain theirs," was the Duce's bitter comment.

The prestige of the Fascist system at home and abroad had sunk and discontent was rife. Donna Rachele was much disturbed. In conversation with Ciano she expressed her alarm at the way things were going. "She thinks that the barometer indicates stormy weather and she affirms that everything and everybody blames the Duce." Even the starlings were deserting the Villa Torlonia. "They are flying to the trees of the Villa Savoia where the King lives." [12] Mussolini, although from time to time displaying "serenity," as Ciano described it, was beginning to suffer in health under the strain. His temper became short and his judgment clouded; and when Ciano left Rome for three months at the front in consequence of an order that ministers and party leaders should go on active service, his farewell interview with the Duce was far from cordial. "He made certain observations which he might well have omitted." [13]

The despatch of Fascist leaders to the front was a typical piece of window dressing for which there was no justification. In the midst of a critical situation ministries and party offices were handed over to subordinate officials by the departing incumbents who possessed no military qualifications and who, in any case, were to be away for so short a period as to have no impact on events. Ciano went to Bari where, in the relative comfort of a hotel, he commanded an air force group. Most of the others were, however, sent away from the fleshpots of Rome to the squalor of the Albanian front. They went unwillingly, for they knew that in that theater of war there were no laurels to be gained. In the mud, rain, and snows of Albania was first nurtured the hatred of the Duce and the ensuing conspiracy which were later to bring about his fall.[14]

IV

However, the fortunes of war were soon to undergo a change. On February 29 the Bulgarian government, which had previously agreed to allow the passage of German troops for the attack on Greece, acceded to the Tripartite Pact; and four days later the Regent of Yugoslavia was summoned to the Berghof, where after the usual threats he was offered Salonika and a territorial guarantee which was obviously directed against Italy. Unable to resist the German pressure, the Yugoslav Prime Minister and Foreign Minister, without saying a word to anyone, crept to Vienna where, in the presence of Hitler, Ribbentrop, and Ciano, they signed the Tripartite Pact on March 26. As soon as the news became known in Belgrade, the government was overthrown, the youthful Peter was declared king, and the leader of the military dissidents, General Simovic, became Prime Minister.

Hitler's rage was unbounded and he at once issued orders that the attack on Russia, timed for May 15, should be postponed by a month and that Yugoslavia should be crushed with merciless harshness. At dawn on April 6 Belgrade was attacked from the air and German troops streamed across the Yugoslav and Greek frontiers. On April 13 Belgrade was captured and on April 23 the Greek armies capitulated. The British expeditionary force of some 50,000 troops was for the greater part successfully evacuated from Greece. Towards the end of May Crete fell to a German airborne invasion; and in Iraq a revolt under Rashid Ali placed an additional strain on British resources.

In Libya Rommel on the last day of March had struck at the British forces, weakened by the despatch of troops to Greece. In twelve days he had recaptured almost all of Cyrenaica, invested Tobruk, and reached Bardia. Within a few weeks the British position in the eastern Mediterranean had crumbled and Hitler was in a position to follow up his successes and to deliver a blow which might have proved fatal to the enemy whose destruction he had recently defined as the primary aim of Axis strategy. Fortunately for Britain Hitler had changed his mind. The attack on Russia, now fixed for June 22, must take precedence, and only after it was over would it be possible to consider the problem of launching an offensive on the Suez Canal and ousting the British from the Middle East and the Persian Gulf. With this disastrous decision Mussolini was not concerned, for he was never informed nor even consulted.

Mussolini's satisfaction at the more favorable turn of events was tempered by the fact that he had been obliged to seek aid from Hitler, a circumstance which humiliated him as much as defeats in the field; and, secondly, by the behavior of the Germans, who made it clear that they intended to be the sole masters in Greece and who moreover were tiresomely interfering in his plans to create an Italian kingdom in Croatia. On June 10, the anniversary of Italy's entry into the war, Ciano found him in a furiously anti-German mood.

It is of no importance [Mussolini said] that the Germans recognize our rights in Croatia on paper, when in practice they take everything and leave us only a little heap of bones. They are dirty dogs, and I tell you this cannot go on for long. I do not even know if German intrigue will allow Aimone, Duke of Spoleto, to ascend the Croatian throne. Besides, I have been thoroughly disgusted with the Germans since the time List made an armistice with Greece without our knowledge, and the soldiers of the Casale division, who are natives of Forlì and hate Germany, found a German soldier at Ponte di Perati barring the road and robbing us of the fruits of victory. Personally, I've had my fill of Hitler and the way he acts. These conferences, called by the ringing of a bell, are not to my liking; a bell is rung when people call their servants. And besides, what kind of conferences are these? For five hours I am forced to listen to a monologue which is quite fruitless and boring. . . . For the moment there is nothing to be done. We must howl with the wolves. Today at the Chamber I will cajole the Germans, but my heart is full of bitterness.[15]

Mussolini was quite right. In the situation in which he had placed himself and his country he had no alternative but to tag along behind, painful and humiliating though it might be. Two days after his outburst to Ciano, Churchill, addressing a gathering of Dominion High Commissioners and Allied Ministers, spoke of "Hitler, with his tattered lackey Mussolini at his tail and Admiral Darlan frisking by his side."

Mussolini's annoyance with Hitler led him to view with some satisfaction any discomfiture of his ally. Thus, when at the beginning of May, Hess flew to Britain and Ribbentrop hurried to Rome with disingenuous explanations, he told Ciano that he regarded the affair as a tremendous blow to the Nazis and added that he was glad of it because it would damage German prestige, even with the Italians.[16] While Hitler was preparing his stroke against Russia, there were other episodes which showed that Britain was far from finished, and that the war was likely to last a long time. On May 27 the German battleship "Bismarck" was sunk, on June 15 Wavell launched an offensive, with very limited success, against Rommel in the desert; and on June 8 operations were begun by Anglo-French forces in Syria, which brought that country under Allied occupation within a month. This was a notable success, which materially improved the British position in the Mediterranean.

The course of events prompted Hitler on May 31 peremptorily to demand a meeting on the morrow or the day after; and Mussolini reluctantly, but obediently, repaired once more to the Brenner Pass. It was an inconclusive interview, at which Hitler spoke for hours of his intention to win the war against England with his U-boats, of Hess, of the loss of the "Bismarck," and of the situation in the Balkans. As usual, his manner was friendly, but the Italians were unable to glean anything of his intentions; and he said no word about his plans for the campaign against Russia which had already been unfolded to the Rumanian General Antonescu and which were the subject of excited conversation in official circles in Berlin. Indeed Ribbentrop told Ciano categorically that rumors of operations against Russia were "devoid of any foundation or at least exceedingly premature." There had been, he explained, Russian troop concentrations on the German frontier and all the Germans had done was to reply with an equally imposing concentration. He did not think that Stalin would commit the folly of attacking Germany, but, if he did so, the Russian army would be smashed. Ribbentrop added shamelessly that his major preoccupation was that war would interrupt the flow of Russian supplies, which were being delivered at a satisfactory rate.[17]

A fortnight later, a week before the first shot against Russia was fired, Ciano met Ribbentrop at Venice to discuss the accession of Croatia to the Tripartite Pact. On the way to dinner in a gondola Ciano asked Ribbentrop about the many rumors of an impending aggression against the Soviet Union. He was given a reply which he had already received on a previous occasion in another context. "Dear Ciano, I cannot tell you anything as yet because every decision is locked in the impenetrable bosom of the Fuehrer. However, one thing is certain: if we attack, the Russia of Stalin will be erased from the map within eight weeks." The Italians were by now becoming so accustomed to German lies that they attached no importance to German statements; and when Mussolini returned to Rome from the Brenner meeting, he remarked to Ciano: "I would not be at all sorry if Germany in her conflict with Russia lost many feathers." [18] He did not reflect that the opening of a new front would preclude any major effort either against the British Isles or, more important, in the Mediterranean.

V

It was accordingly no surprise when, at three o'clock in the morning of June 22, the German chargé d'affaires appeared in order to deliver to Ciano the long ritual letter from the Fuehrer explaining why he had found it necessary to invade Russia.[19] If he was not surprised, the Duce was once again annoyed at the manner in which he had been treated. "I do not disturb even my servants at night," he grumbled to Ciano, "but the Germans make me jump out of my bed at any hour with the least consideration." [20] Nevertheless there was nothing to be done but to express understanding and approval. His principal concern was to secure some share of the glory which, he felt sure, would attend the Axis arms in Russia; and he insisted, although the Germans were manifestly reluctant to accept it, on the despatch of an expeditionary force of three infantry divisions and one cavalry division under the command of General Giovanni Messe. To Messe he said: "We cannot count less than Slovakia and other minor states. I must be at the side of Hitler in Russia, as he was at mine in the war against Greece." [21] The troops were hastily assembled and the spearhead passed through Vienna on July 13. Simoni, who accompanied the German ambassador in Berlin to inspect them, noted that they were dirty, ill-equipped, and likely to make a bad impression.[22] It was what Ciano feared when he wrote:

> At Verona, Mussolini reviewed the first division on its way to Russia. He telephoned to say that it was perfect. Be that as it may, I am concerned about a direct comparison between our forces and the Germans. Not because of the men who are, or may be, excellent, but because of their equipment. I should not like to see us play the role of a poor relation yet again.[23]

At first things went very well in Russia and at the end of August Mussolini joyfully accepted the Fuehrer's invitation to pay a visit to the eastern front. On August 25 the two dictators met in Hitler's headquarters in the dark forest at Rastenburg, and Mussolini's aim was to secure Hitler's assent to a substantial reinforcement of the Italian expeditionary force. In the train on the way to East Prussia he explained to Anfuso that a significant Italian contribution was essential. It was in Russia that Hitler intended to win the war, and "if we are absent, the circumstance that I was the first to combat communism will count for nothing against the fact that the Italians were not in Russia. That is why our participation is of capital importance."[24] Once again Mussolini was making the mistake of believing that victory was around the corner and that the Italians, however unprepared, must put in an appearance on the battlefield before it was too late. Bemused by Hitler, he became a willing accomplice in a plan which reprieved the British in the Mediterranean, dispersed the Axis forces, and eventually opened the soft underbelly of Europe to his foes.

The meeting with Hitler was not a success. Mussolini was depressed at the recent death of his son Bruno in an air accident, and he failed to obtain satisfaction on the point to which he attached importance. The Fuehrer, while thanking him for his offer of troops, spoke of logistic difficulties and could only with difficulty be persuaded to give further consideration to the matter. In reply to Mussolini's complaints against France, the Fuehrer merely said that nothing could be done until after the end of the Russian campaign. For the rest, Hitler spoke with bitterness about Franco and expressed his conviction that he would annihilate the Russian armies. When this task had been accomplished, he would deliver the final blow against England by invading the island.[25]

On the following day Hitler accompanied Mussolini on a tour of the eastern front. They flew to Field Marshal von Kluge's headquarters at Brest Litovsk and later visited Rundstedt in the Ukraine. Resting troops were inspected and Mussolini was given an opportunity to see an Italian division. After lunch in the open air Hitler left his guest with Rundstedt in order to chat with German soldiers, who had been eagerly watching the great men at their meal. Such was Mussolini's sense of inferiority that he immediately took umbrage, and complained of a deliberate slight. To Alfieri he said: "Hitler might have taken me with him when he went to speak to the troops, instead of leaving me with old Rundstedt. Did you notice how unsoldierly the Fuehrer looked when he was among his men?" [26] On the return flight, however, he wiped out the affront by insisting, to Hitler's dismay, on piloting the airplane, a performance which he demanded should be recorded in the communiqué.

The visit closed with an incident which still further ill disposed the Duce. Largely at the instance of the Italians it was decided that the communiqué should give prominence to the conception of the "European New Order," and to the resolve of the dictators to eradicate bolshevism and to establish peaceful collaboration among the European nations. The purpose was to reply to the Atlantic Charter of August 12, 1941, and to give an attractive ideological complexion to the war aims of the Axis powers. Otto Dietrich, Hitler's press chief, warmly welcomed the proposal and took part in the process of drafting a suitable statement; but Ribbentrop, probably because the idea had not originated with himself, was lukewarm and even hostile. Eventually a text was elaborated, which was approved by Hitler, and it was agreed that the communiqué should be published as soon as Mussolini reached Italian territory. His train, however, made an unscheduled stop at Klagenfurt,* close to the Italian border, where a telephone message was received to the effect that Ribbentrop had had second thoughts and was not prepared to allow the publication of the agreed communiqué. For once Mussolini revolted. He refused to discuss the matter with the Germans on his train and instructed Anfuso to reply that the text could not be altered since it had already been given to the Italian press; he would not proceed any further on his journey until the matter was settled to his satisfaction. In the face of Mussolini's unusually robust attitude, Ribbentrop, under Hitler's instructions, capitulated on the understanding that a few verbal amendments should be made to the text. It was said that his objections had stemmed from the circumstance that in the communiqué Keitel's name had appeared before his own. However this may be, the episode of the communiqué, the offense taken by Mussolini at Hitler's conduct while chatting to

* In some accounts the incident is said to have occurred at Villach, some twenty miles away.

the troops, and Mussolini's own revenge in the aircraft, illustrated the childish triviality and the stresses attending the meetings of the Axis leaders.[27]

In their train on the way to Rome the Italian party was visibly depressed.[28] Mussolini still believed in an eventual German victory over Russia, but he was coming back from Rastenburg with empty hands and, from all he had seen on the eastern front, he had derived the uneasy conviction that it would be a long, bloody war waged against a strongly nationalist Russia, to whom was allied an undefeated Britain.

VI

The value of the European New Order as a propaganda card appealed to Hitler, and when Ciano saw him in October he was impressed by the enthusiasm with which the Fuehrer seemed to have embraced the idea.

> In the past [Ciano wrote to Mussolini], we have seen in turn the flowering and decline of a series of slogans which are born in the mind of the Fuehrer and are repeated all the way down to the lowest-ranking of his collaborators. Now the fashionable slogan is that of "European solidarity." Europe—the Fuehrer said—besides being a geographical expression is a cultural and moral concept. In the war against bolshevism the first signs of continental solidarity have shown themselves. . . . When Russia is defeated, and under the leadership of Germany in the north and of Italy in the south, Europe will be able to organize herself politically and economically, and constitute the grand union destined to create the barrier to the real danger of tomorrow, American imperialism. This is what the Fuehrer expounds; and this is what all those hear him repeat.[29]

It sounded very well, but Hitler had no intention of putting these principles into practice, not even where Italy was concerned. In September Ciano received a report on the maltreatment of Italian laborers in Germany, who were not only being beaten but set upon by trained watchdogs. "These things," said the Duce angrily, "are bound to produce a lasting hatred in my heart. I can even wait many years, but in the end I shall square this account. I will not permit the sons of a race which has given to humanity Caesar, Dante, and Michelangelo to be devoured by the bloodhounds of the Huns." It was agreed that Ciano should raise the matter at an early meeting with Ribbentrop.[30]

When Ciano saw Hitler and Ribbentrop at Rastenburg on October 25, he received little satisfaction. All Hitler would say was that such incidents were inevitable, and that one should dramatize neither the failure of individual Italian workmen nor conflict between them and the Germans. After all there were still in the working classes a number of anti-Fascists and anti-Nazis who had every interest in sowing discord between the two allies.

On the other point which Ciano was instructed to raise, namely a larger Italian participation in the Russian war, Hitler was guarded but a little more forthcoming. He said that after the Caucasus had been traversed it would be possible to employ Italians in a climate more suitable to their circumstances. Meanwhile the despatch of Alpine divisions to the Caucasus might be considered, and he suggested that the two General Staffs might have consultations on the subject. For the rest, Hitler treated Ciano to the usual, immensely long dissertation on the impending collapse of Russia and his plans for the future. Ciano was impressed by Hitler's confident vigor, and, although he had failed in his mission, he reported complacently to the Duce that his reception had been most cordial and that never had he found on the German side so much comradely interest in Italian affairs. This, he concluded, must be placed on the credit side.[31]

A month later Ciano was back in Germany, this time to attend a demonstration in Berlin of the new European solidarity invoked by Hitler. Representatives of Italy, Spain, Hungary, Rumania, Slovakia, Croatia, Bulgaria, Finland, and Denmark, together with those of Japan and Manchukuo, had been invited to renew the Anti-Comintern Pact, and Ciano in his diary accurately depicted the position: "The Germans were the masters of the house, and they made us all feel it, even though they were especially polite to us. There is no way out of it. Their European hegemony has now been established. Whether this is good or bad is neither here nor there, but it does exist. Consequently, it is best to sit at the right hand of the master of the house. And we are at the right hand." [32]

In a long report to Mussolini Ciano emphasized the particular consideration shown to himself and the tributes paid in public to the person of the Duce. So far as the future of the New Order was concerned, the German indifference to the fate of other European countries was cynically revealed by Goering, when reports of impending famine in Greece were discussed.

We cannot worry unduly about the hunger of the Greeks [he said]. It is a misfortune which will strike many other peoples besides them. In the camps for Russian prisoners they have begun to eat one another. This year between twenty and thirty million persons will die of hunger in Russia. Perhaps it is well that it should be so, for certain nations must be decimated. But even if it were not, nothing can be done about it. It is obvious that if humanity is condemned to die of hunger, the last to die will be our two peoples.[33]

Ciano concluded his report to the Duce with an account of the impressions he had gathered in Berlin. There was less traffic to be seen, more wounded, and many fewer party uniforms on the streets. The people had shown no interest in the ceremonies; and whereas the square in front of the Chancellery had previously been filled by an applauding crowd, on this occasion it had been deserted. Faith in victory was high, but there was no outward sign of enthusiasm, probably because the certainty that it would be a long war was not calculated to evoke any joyful manifestation. Nevertheless, Ciano concluded, none of the persons he had met seemed shaken or even disturbed about the future. In fact both Mussolini and Ciano were now by force of habit becoming reconciled to the idea of a protracted global conflict.

VII

Within a few days an event was to occur which should have made it even plainer to Mussolini that the war would indeed be long and the issue more problematical. On December 3 the Japanese ambassador called at the Palazzo Venezia quite unexpectedly to announce that negotiations with the United States had been abortive, and that war was likely to break out at any moment. In consequence, the Japanese government, invoking the pertinent clause of the Tripartite Pact, asked that Italy should declare war immediately after the opening of hostilities and should sign an undertaking not to conclude a separate peace with either the United States or the British Empire.

In point of fact the Tripartite Pact only bound Italy to assist Japan in the event of an attack on her by some other Power. But Mussolini was in no mood to stand on the letter of the treaty, and without much reflection he gaily undertook to meet both Japanese requests.[34] He had in the past criticized Hitler for not grasping the importance of America, but now he seemed not only ready but anxious to see the might of the United States ranged against the Axis. As soon as the ambassador had left, he expressed to Ciano his satisfaction at the Japanese communication and added: "Thus we arrive at the war between continents, which I have foreseen since September, 1939." [35] Four days later the Japanese attacked Pearl Harbor and on December 11 Italy declared war on the United States. The news was given to the Italian people from the balcony of the Palazzo Venezia by the Duce in a short, aggressive speech. It is difficult to account for the lightheartedness with which he viewed this dangerous extension of the conflict. But things were going so badly in Russia and Libya that he may have been ready to clutch at any straw.

In the Russian winter the German troops, unprepared for the ordeal before them and suffering untold hardships from the cold, had been halted; and on December 6 they were subjected to a counteroffensive which but for Hitler's resolution might have led to a general retreat and a disaster. At first, Mussolini characteristically allowed his pique to get the better of him, and Ciano noted in his diary on December 20 that "Mussolini is satisfied with the way the war is going in Russia. He talks about it openly. The failure of the German troops cheers him." But five days later Alfieri reported from Berlin that the disasters on the Russian front had gone farther than was desirable for Italy. "The Duce," wrote Ciano, "who in the beginning underestimated the problem, now affirms that it is serious and that perhaps it will have further consequences." [36]

Nevertheless Mussolini had not lost confidence in an eventual German victory in Russia, and he was still eager to reinforce his troops on the eastern front. In October he had wanted to despatch some fifteen or twenty divisions, but owing to shortage of equipment the number was reduced to six and it was later agreed that in addition three Alpine divisions should be sent to the Caucasus. Now, with the King's consent, he proposed that the new Italian army should be commanded by the Crown Prince. It was not a proposal acceptable to the Germans, and Hitler in his rancor against the House of Savoy replied that he would sooner do without Italian troops than agree.[37] It was accordingly decided to entrust the command to General Italo Garibaldi and to begin the troop movement in the spring of the following year. The Germans might have done better to take the Crown Prince, for Garibaldi turned out to be a recalcitrant Germanophobe.

Closer home, and consequently more disturbing, were the reverses being inflicted in the same month of December on the Axis forces in Libya. On November 18, just as the Axis forces were preparing to resume their march on Egypt, General Auchinleck had unleashed his offensive and after hard fighting had relieved Tobruk on November 29. In this battle Rommel's army had lost 33,000 men, and in view of his shortage of supplies due to the incessant air and sea attacks on his communications he had no alternative but to order a general retreat. By the middle of December Cyrenaica was cleared for the second time; and Rommel was reported in Rome to be thinking of breaking into Tunisia in order to evade capture.[38] These events plunged Rome into gloom.

In an effort to extricate himself from his Libyan difficulties Mussolini insisted, against professional advice, on writing a long letter to Hitler pointing out that the problem of supplying the Axis armies was critical and advocating the occupation of Tunis, with or without the consent of the Vichy government.[39] Unfortunately the Fuehrer was not prepared to accede to this proposal, on the ground that it would upset the French; and Mussolini had no alternative but to comply with his master's wishes.

In this mood of angry frustration he directed his ill humor at the Church and at the religious convictions of his people. "Mussolini," Ciano wrote, "has again attacked Christmas. He is surprised that the Germans have not yet abolished this holiday, which only reminds one of the birth of a Jew who gave the world debilitating and devitalizing theories, and who especially contrived to trick Italy through the disintegrating power of the popes. He has prohibited newspapers from mentioning Christmas, yet you only have to look out of the window to see that the people remember it and love it just the same."[40] Mussolini was becoming more and more remote from the masses, who only wished to disassociate themselves from his war.

He was also becoming out of touch with realities. The man who eighteen months previously had declared that Italy could not stand a long war was now calmly envisaging a war lasting at least four or five years.[41] He was enveloped in a blanket of fatalism. The dream of glory on the battlefield had faded and he could only rely on the Germans to save him. Despite his occasional tantrums there was now no alternative but to follow obediently in Hitler's wake and to hope that on the day of victory he might receive some reward for his loyalty. In one particular respect he was wiser than his ally. His instinct told him that Russia would not be as easily overthrown as Hitler affected to believe; and he was already beginning to toy with the idea of a separate peace between the Axis and the Soviet Union. It was an idea which, during the coming months, he was to endeavor without success to impress on his fellow dictator.

CHAPTER NINETEEN

Defeat

1942–1943

I

THE year 1942 opened darkly. The Germans were still retreating in Russia, while in Libya the situation of the Axis forces remained precarious. In Zagreb there were anti-Italian demonstrations, and Italo-German relations were deteriorating under strain and mutual dissatisfaction at the conduct of the war. Mussolini was complaining of Hitler's folly in attacking Russia, while the Germans were attributing their military failures to the weakness of their ally. Thus, General Arthur Schmidt in an interview with a correspondent of *The Daily Herald* disclosed that he had been obliged to surrender in Libya because he was in command of Italian troops.[1] There was also friction between the Italian civilian population and the ever-increasing number of German soldiery, who were apt to behave as conquering invaders. Another cause of resentment was the continued ill treatment of Italian nationals in Germany and occupied territory. In February, for example, the Italian consul general in Prague reported that the deputy Reich Protector was treating Italians, if not worse than the Czechoslovaks, certainly not much better. Mussolini, although not prepared to lodge a violent protest, was indignant. "I much prefer the yellow people," he said to Ciano, "even if the Japanese were to spread as far as the Persian Gulf." [2]

More serious still, under the weight of war weariness and of food, coal, and other shortages, public dissatisfaction and opposition to the Fascist regime was beginning to come into the open. There were many arrests of anti-Fascists, Fascist office holders were expelled from the party or arrested for defeatism, and the Chief of the *Carabinieri* reported that the country had lost faith in the party, which was no longer an element in the national life.[3] Mussolini's reaction was to abuse the Germans for not fulfilling their commitments to send supplies to Italy. "Among the cemeteries," he said, "I shall some day build the most important of all, one in which to bury German promises. They have delivered nothing, or almost nothing, of what they promised"; and he added with childish pettishness: "So I have persuaded Cavallero not to ask for the antitank guns and the antiaircraft guns for our divisions going to Russia. I prefer to take the risk of taking twelve batteries from the Rome defenses." He also castigated the Italian bourgeoisie, whom he was sorry not to have exterminated in 1911.[4]

The disaffection spread to men in high places. Bottai was in league with dissident Fascists and Grandi was not afraid to remark to Ciano that he wondered how he had been able to disguise himself as a Fascist for twenty years. The Minister of the Royal Household, Duke Pietro d'Acquarone, was in touch with dissident generals and even Ciano himself added his voice to those of the malcontents. Serrano Suñer, who visited Rome in the spring of 1942, noted that Ciano was violently critical of the Fascist party and, for the first time, spoke ill of Mussolini. In particular he talked of the scandal caused by the Duce's relations with Clara Petacci; and when Suñer retorted that his own life was not above reproach, he replied: "It is of no consequence to run after a number of women. What is grave and scandalous is to devote oneself assiduously to one woman, and that is the case of Mussolini." [5] Even Buffarini, the servile Minister of the Interior, told Felix Kersten, Himmler's Finnish doctor, that Italy sooner or later would have to make a separate peace; and he advised Kersten to leave "those cold-blooded Germans" and settle in Rome.[6]

Early in 1942, the Duce attempted to rally the Fascist party by means of a tour in the provinces. It was to be his last tour, and he reverted to the language of his early campaigns before the March on Rome. It aroused the usual enthusiasm among his packed audiences, but on his return to Rome he realized that he had achieved little or nothing. In the personal system of government which he had established the party counted for little, and in the face of military reverses and economic hardships he was unable in his condition of lowered vitality to stop the rot. To the party directorate he confessed: "I have no longer any doubt in regard to lack of discipline, sabotage, and passive resistance all along the line. The regime is exhausting itself, wearing itself out, and literally consuming scores of comrades in the party organizations and the ministries, and we are almost back where we were." [7]

Reports of crumbling morale in Italy caused concern in Berlin and at the end of January Goering arrived for a six-day visit to Rome, in order to discuss Italian reinforcements for the Eastern front, an attack on Malta, and in general, to infuse some optimism into the Italians. The visit was not a success, for Goering was more concerned to enjoy himself than to discharge his mission. Ciano found him bloated and overbearing. "He said nothing that is especially worthy of mention." At dinner two days later, he talked of little else but the jewels he owned; and when he left Rome he was wearing "a great sable coat, something between what motorists wore in 1906 and what a high-grade prostitute wears to the opera. If any of us tried a thing like that, we should be stoned in the streets." [8]

II

As reports of Italian disaffection continued to reach him, Hitler judged it wise to take an early opportunity of exercising his personal ascendancy over his wavering ally. At the end of April, 1942, the Italians were summoned to Germany; and, as Ciano put it, "this is a meeting that was desired by the Germans, and for which, as usual, they have given no indication of an agenda." On April 28, Mussolini and Ciano left Rome for Salzburg, this time to foregather for two days at Schloss Klessheim, a former residence of the prince-bishops of Salzburg and now used as a guesthouse.* On the following day, Ciano was received by Ribbentrop while Mussolini and Hitler conferred alone with an interpreter. In neither room, although there

* After the war Schloss Klessheim was used as a hotel for American officers, and the author stayed there in 1952.

was much discussion of forthcoming operations, was anything of consequence said or decided. There was the usual talk of the inevitability of German victory and speculation on the possibility of a peace move from Britain. To Mussolini, Hitler admitted that disaster in Russia had only been averted by his own resolution, backed by a few generals and the valor of the troops.[9] Once again Mussolini was given no opportunity to speak, nor does he seem to have sought one. His performance on the battlefield scarcely entitled him to raise his voice, and he was by now angrily resigned to following in Hitler's wake.

The gloom attending the conference at Klessheim is well reflected in Ciano's diary.

> There is much cordiality, which puts me on my guard. The courtesy of the Germans is always in inverse ratio to their good fortune. Hitler looks tired . . . I see for the first time that he has many gray hairs. Hitler talks with the Duce, I talk with Ribbentrop, but in two separate rooms, and the same record is played in both. . . . But what of tomorrow? What does the future hold? On this matter Ribbentrop is less explicit. An offensive against the Russians in the South with the oil wells as a politico-military objective? When Russia's sources of oil are exhausted, she will be brought to her knees. Then the British Conservatives, and even Churchill himself, who after all is a sensible man, will bow in order to save what remains of their mauled Empire. . . . But what if the British, who are stubborn, decide to continue? What course must be followed to change their minds? Airplanes and submarines, says Ribbentrop. We turn back to the 1940 formula. But this formula failed then and was put in the attic. Now they pull it out again, and, after dusting it thoroughly, they want to offer it to us again.

Not only was the conference barren, but the Italians were obliged to listen with an appearance of civility to Hitler's endless monologues. "Hitler talks, talks, talks, talks. Mussolini suffers—he, who is in the habit of talking himself, and who, instead, has to remain practically silent. . . . The Germans, however, dreaded the ordeal less than we did. Poor people. They have to endure it every day, and I am certain there isn't a gesture, a word, or a pause which they don't know by heart. General Jodl, after an epic struggle, finally went to sleep on the divan. Keitel was yawning, but he succeeded in keeping his head up. He was too close to Hitler to let himself go as he would have liked to do." Nevertheless Mussolini, despite everything, was satisfied with the visit and came away fortified by the injection of robust optimism which Hitler had been able to administer. To Ciano, the Duce remarked that the mauled German military machine would make a new effort and must attain its goal.[10]

The only immediately impending military operation which was discussed in any detail at Klessheim was the capture of Malta, for which the Italians had been pressing for some time. They were distraught at the heavy losses inflicted on their convoys by the units of the British fleet based on Malta; * and particularly since the Germans were not prepared to allow them to improve their position by the seizure of Tunis, they came to the not unreasonable conclusion that they could not hope to win a decisive victory in Libya until Malta had been eliminated.

In March, Admiral Raeder had at last been able to secure Hitler's grudging consent to the project and in April the German High Command signified its willingness to afford military support. A German parachute division was earmarked to cooperate with the Italian parachute division already in training at Viterbo; and at Klessheim it only remained to make the final arrangements for the operation, which received the code name "Hercules." The German generals stated that an early offensive in Libya was essential and that the German air force would be too fully committed to undertake an attack on Malta, but it was eventually agreed that Rommel should launch his attack at the end of May, that he should halt on the Egyptian frontier, and that "Hercules" should take place at the latest during the July full moon.

The agreement reached between the German and Italian commanders was approved by Hitler and Mussolini. Nevertheless Hitler remained sceptical about the whole business. The battle of Crete had been a close-run thing, and he was reluctant to embark on another hazardous enterprise in conjunction with the Italians, in whom he had no confidence. He even affected to believe that it would be wise to leave Malta in British hands and so inflict heavy losses on

* In October, 1941, 63 per cent of Rommel's supplies and reinforcements were sunk.

the British convoys and their escorts. It was only with some difficulty that he was induced to give his formal consent.

III

On May 26, 1942, Rommel duly passed to the attack. The battle lasted three weeks and on June 17 Rommel was able to report that he had defeated the enemy and was regrouping for the assault on Tobruk. On June 21, Tobruk fell. Together with 33,000 prisoners the Germans captured more than 10,000 cubic meters of gasoline and sufficient supplies for 30,000 men for three months. Their immediate logistic problems had been solved, and on the following day Rommel signified his intention of destroying the remaining British forces before him and opening the road to Egypt.

Hitler now saw a welcome opportunity to shelve "Hercules" and in a letter to Mussolini strongly urged this course.

> Destiny has offered us a chance which will never be repeated in the same theater of war. . . . So far I have always had every defeated enemy followed as far and as completely as our forces allowed. . . . The British Eighth Army is practically destroyed. In Tobruk, whose port installations are almost intact, you possess an auxiliary base, Duce, which is all the more important since the British themselves have built a railway from there almost as far as Egypt. If the remnants of the British army are not now followed by every soldier to his last breath, the same thing will happen which deprived the British of success when, within a very short distance of Tripoli they suddenly stopped in order to send troops to Greece. . . . Therefore, Duce, if in this historic hour, which will not be repeated, I can give you a piece of advice straight from my eager heart, it would be: "Order operations to be continued until the British forces are completely annihilated. . . . The goddess of fortune passes only once close to warriors in battle. Anyone who does not grasp her at that moment can very often never touch her again." [11]

Mussolini was unable to resist this appeal. Bewitched at the prospect of capturing Egypt, and trusting Hitler's military genius, he readily gave his assent in the face of protests from his own Chief of Staff. So there was agreement to stake all on the invasion of Egypt and to postpone "Hercules" until September. As it happened, it was later found necessary to throw the Italian and German parachute divisions into the land battle and the enterprise against Malta was finally abandoned. With this decision the Italians lost their last hope of securing their vital communications with Africa.*

Mussolini was now determined to extract from the African victory as much personal glory as he could. He saw himself wielding the Sword of Islam and riding a white horse through the streets of Cairo. It would be a day of Italian rather than of German triumph. Accordingly he arranged with Cavallero that, as soon as it was certain that the army had begun an advance which would take it to the Canal, he should despatch a telegram containing the single word "*Tevere.*" The telegram containing the code word arrived on June 27, but Mussolini was delayed for two days by a cyclone, and when he reached Africa on June 29 Rommel had been halted at Alamein. The visit was inauspicious from the start. The second aircraft carrying some of the suite crashed, and Mussolini's barber was killed. The troops, impressed by this disaster and depressed by the check to the advance, concluded that the Duce must have the evil eye. Later Mussolini was to describe his trip as the turning point: "The wheel of fortune turned on June 28."[12] "The hinge of fate" was Sir Winston Churchill's description of this period.

Nevertheless hopes still ran high, and the Italians began to prepare for the administration of conquered Egypt. On July 2, Mussolini telegraphed to Ciano, instructing him to propose to the Germans that Rommel should be the military commander, while the principal civilian officer should be Italian. On the following day Hitler replied that he agreed, so far as Rommel was concerned, but that he would defer an answer about the Italian Commissioner and about the problem of German representation in the civilian administration.[13] It was an unsatisfactory reply, and the Italians were ill disposed still further when Hitler promoted Rommel to the rank of marshal, thus giving him seniority over the nominal Commander-in-Chief in Libya, the Italian General Ettore Bastico. The Italian counter was to promote Bastico and Cavallero, since the latter obviously could not be passed over. There was also friction because, the Italians alleged, the Germans had seized all the booty and were

* In *The Rommel Papers* (London, 1953, p. 203) Rommel criticizes the failure of the Axis to capture Malta. But for reasons explained in Liddell Hart's introduction the book is not accurate in every detail; and the evidence shows that Rommel was as keen as Hitler to press on into Egypt.

behaving insolently to their allies, even to the extent of not giving way on the road to Italian generals. Mussolini was also enraged because during his whole visit Rommel did not see fit to pay his respects.

It was in this atmosphere of mutual recrimination that Mussolini without ever visiting the front wandered disconsolately for three weeks in the Libyan desert behind a now stagnant battle line. He inspected troops and hospitals, and he waited. Eventually on July 20 he could wait no longer and he left Libya, but before doing so he instructed Bastico to prepare a defensive position in the rear on a line east of Bardia, an order which could not be carried out because Rommel insisted on moving every available unit forward to the front. The self-appointed Commander-in-Chief of all the Italian forces no longer counted for anything.

On his way home Mussolini called at Athens, where the economic position was giving rise to anxiety in consequence of the depredations of the German army of occupation. Greece was nominally in the Italian sphere of influence, but the Germans behaved as if they were in sole control and without reference to the Italian civil representatives levied occupation costs and other contributions on a scale which threatened to plunge the country into bankruptcy. After seeing the Greek Prime Minister and Finance Minister, who had threatened to resign, Mussolini addressed a letter to Hitler pointing out that unless Germany made a serious effort to rescue the Greek economy, the government would collapse, with serious consequences for the Axis. It was the last occasion on which he ventured to speak his mind to Hitler; and the reply he received not only infuriated him, but once more showed him clearly how meager was his influence. Hitler retorted blandly that Greece was responsible for her own ruin and had no right to bewail it. All he would agree to do was to despatch an official to Rome to study the problem with Italian experts.

IV

On July 21 Mussolini returned to Rome a broken man. He looked ill and complained of intolerable gastric pains; and when he retired for a brief spell it was rumored that he had cancer, that he was dying. Bottai described him as aged and devastated by repressed anxiety.[14] A number of doctors were called in, but they differed with one another. Dr. Aldo Castellani, a specialist in tropical diseases, diagnosed amoebic dysentery. When the patient showed no sign of improvement and had lost forty-two pounds in weight, Castellani called in Professor Cesare Frugone and together they diagnosed the reappearance of the old ulcer with the added complication of an acute attack of dysentery. A course of injections was prescribed, but in November a third consultant, Dr. Arnaldo Pozzi, suspended the injections.

For the rest of the year, despite all the doctors could do for him, Mussolini continued to suffer severe pain, to the point that he was sometimes unable to transact business. Even the now hostile Bottai admired his fortitude. But the fact was that medicine could bring him no more than temporary relief. He was suffering not from any organic disease, but from a nervous collapse brought on by an accumulation of humiliations and frustrations. The visit to Libya had been the last straw. Not only had it been physically exhausting and a bitter disappointment, but it had robbed him of his last hope of escaping from the net which was slowly closing around him. He could only vent his impotent rage on the Germans. To Ciano he said: "The people are now wondering which of the two masters is to be preferred, the English or the Germans." [15]

But worse was to come. Thanks to the failure to subdue Malta, the Italian convoys were under increasing enemy pressure and in August only half the gasoline shipped in Italian ports was safely landed in Africa. Nevertheless Rommel decided to resume the offensive and on August 30 he struck again. Within a few days he was back in his original position and the last hope of conquering Egypt had vanished. There was even some discussion of retiring to the Egyptian frontier and, if Mussolini is to be believed, he favored a withdrawal.[16] But Hitler was fundamentally opposed to surrendering a yard of conquered ground, and, as usual, his will prevailed. In September Rommel passed through Rome on his way to Germany on six weeks' leave; and Mussolini, who did not believe that Rommel would ever return to Africa, found him physically and morally shaken.[17]

The autumn lull on the Libyan and Russian fronts disturbed

public opinion and another wave of pessimism swept over the country. Official reports from Germany and the Balkans were uniformly discouraging, the situation in Greece was rapidly deteriorating, and Fascist leaders of both wings, such as Farinacci and Bottai, were complaining of the failure of the party to still the ever-louder murmurs of popular discontent, aggravated by growing indignation at the proceedings of the Petacci family.* It was a moment which required strong leadership. But Mussolini, wracked by pain and disillusioned by events, was in no state to supply the need. Completely isolated, for he rarely showed himself after his return from Libya, he sank into a fatalistic apathy, from which he only occasionally aroused himself with ever-diminishing zest to cope with the problems before him. Bottai found him

> gray, ashy, with sunken cheeks, troubled and tired eyes, and his mouth revealing a sense of bitterness. . . . The man seems not so much ill as humiliated, sad and unable to struggle against his advancing years. It is distressing to one who has loved him and who, despite all still loves him. One would like to take his hands and speak to him. But he is no longer the man he was. The road to an exchange of confidences has been barred. Even to ask after his health arouses his suspicion.[18]

The nation and its leader awaited the next blow with resignation. "Our state of mind," wrote Ciano on September 28, "at the beginning of the winter is what, on the worst showing, we might have expected at the end." On October 23 Montgomery fell on the Axis forces at Alamein and by November 5 their front had collapsed. The news evoked no great surprise since, as Ciano remarked, for some time past a sense of irrepressible fatalism had taken possession of the Italians. All Mussolini could do was to whistle to keep up his courage. The loss of Libya, he affected to believe, would represent some advantage, "because this region has cost us our merchant fleet and we can better concentrate on the defense of Italy itself." [19]

V

Two days later Ribbentrop telephoned at half-past five in the

* In particular there had been a notorious scandal caused by illicit traffic in gold on the part of Marcello Petacci with the complicity of the Minister of the Interior and the representative in Madrid of the Minister of Foreign Exchange.

morning to impart the news of the Allied landings in Morocco and Algeria. According to Princess Bismarck, wife of the counsellor at the German embassy, the Germans were "literally terrified by the blow, which is very severe and, above all, unexpected." In Italy there was equal consternation. General Amé, head of the Intelligence Service, told Ciano that the situation was grave, since Italy would become the point of attack in the Allied offensive against the Axis; and he added that the morale of the army was "sensationally low." Although Mussolini put a brave face on things, he was to write later:

> In Italy the moral repercussions of the American landing in Algiers were immediate and profound. Every enemy of fascism promptly reared his head; the first of the traitors, minor figures, even though some were National Councillors, emerged from the shadows. The country began to feel the strain. As long as only the English were in the Mediterranean, Italy, with Germany's help, could hold firm and resist, though at the cost of ever greater sacrifices; but the appearance of America disturbed the weaker spirits and increased by many millions the already numerous band of listeners to enemy radio.[20]

Less than a year had elapsed since Mussolini had joyfully welcomed the attack on Pearl Harbor and the entry into the war of the United States.

During the night of November 8 Ribbentrop telephoned again, this time to demand that either the Duce or Ciano should travel at once to a conference at Munich. Mussolini was awakened, but declined firmly to obey the summons. He was not feeling well enough to face the ordeal of a meeting with Hitler under the shadow of defeat. So Ciano left Rome at once and met Hitler the following night.

Hitler had previously been toying with the idea of an alliance with France, which might have encouraged the French to fight in Algeria, but when he saw Ciano, he had changed his mind and was resolved on the total occupation of Vichy France, Corsica, and a bridgehead in Tunisia. On the following day, November 10, Laval arrived in Munich. After a preliminary talk with Ribbentrop in which he rejected a formal alliance, he was admitted to Hitler's presence, and after a long exchange of views was informed of the decision. "Vous voulez gagner la guerre," he retorted, "pour faire l'Europe, mais faites donc l'Europe pour gagner la guerre."[21] But it was only a token protest, and, although he made a brilliant plea for France, he was soon advising the Germans to go ahead without consulting Marshal Pétain, since he could not himself assume the responsibility of yielding Tunis and Bizerte to the Axis. It was decided that the Italians should occupy Corsica and a strip of southern France to the Rhone valley, while the Germans occupied the remainder of the country. The necessary orders were issued at half-past eight that night and carried out without incident. "I thought," wrote Ciano, "that there would be some gesture of opposition, at least for the honor of the flag. But nothing of the kind. Only the French navy made it known to us that the fleet would remain loyal to Vichy, and that it does not want the occupation of Toulon by the Axis. The Germans agreed and also, willy-nilly, the Duce, who, however, does not trust their word of honor and thinks that some day we shall wake up to find the port of Toulon empty."[22]

On November 11 the first German formations landed in Tunis. They were followed by a stream of German and Italian reinforcements until nearly a quarter of a million troops with a considerable armored force had been poured into the bridgehead. It would have been wiser to have strengthened Rommel before the disaster, and once this opportunity had been lost, to have used these resources to defend Italy and stem the Russian advance. In the event all that was achieved was to delay by a few months the loss of North Africa at the cost of the surrender of a vast and invaluable army. In this insensate undertaking Mussolini was a ready accomplice, since he was less interested in making the best military dispositions than in ensuring that Italy on prestige grounds should not stand aside in an area which he regarded as falling within the Italian sphere of interest.

On November 27 Hitler, without any previous consultation with his ally, decided to occupy the port of Toulon. For once a German lightning stroke was not entirely successful, for the French were able to delay the German entry into the base until the crews had scuttled the ships. One battleship, two battle cruisers, seven cruisers, twenty-nine destroyers and torpedo boats, sixteen submarines, and eighteen other vessels sank at their moorings. Hitler had failed in his design, but he had at least ensured that the French fleet should never pass into the hands of the Allies; and Mussolini was consoled at the thought that a future naval rival in the Mediterranean had now been eliminated.

Symptomatic of the decline in the Axis fortunes was a first effort by the Vatican to have Rome declared an open city. On December 4 the Cardinal Secretary of State handed the Italian ambassador a note stating that the Holy See had recently urged the Allies not to bombard Rome from the air. The British minister had, however, retorted that Rome was the seat of government, housed Italian and German military headquarters, and possessed airfields, war industries, and a railway station which was a nodal point of military communications. The Holy See accordingly invited the Italian government to consider moving from Rome those objectives which might be defined as military. The Italian government in reply undertook to evacuate the military headquarters; and Mussolini at first actually agreed to transfer himself in his capacity as Commander-in-Chief outside the city. But it was easier to give the undertaking than to carry it out. The Germans refused to move at the behest of the Vatican, and on further reflection Mussolini regretted his impulsive submission to the demands of the enemy. So, for the time being, the project fell to the ground.

The war was now going so badly, and the Germans were becoming so suspicious of the Italians,* that Goering was despatched to Italy on a further rescue operation, this time to push the Italians into a total mobilization of their resources. Once again his intervention failed of its purpose, and Rommel, who accompanied him, complained that all he had achieved was to

> put their backs up without having any hope of getting anything put right. . . . Many Italians felt very deeply that the Axis was a sham and consequently believed that in final victory we would have scant regard for their interests. It was generally felt that if Tripolitania were lost, Mussolini would be threatened by a political crisis in Italy. His position may have been further weakened by Goering's sudden heavy-handed

* On November 10, 1942, Kersten noted: "Himmler has informed me that the Italians would make a separate peace. The traitor Ciano has sold Italy to the Allies. . . . 'You may be sure Herr Kersten that the day is coming when the Fuehrer will have Ciano hanged.' " (Kersten, *op. cit.*, p. 160.)

behavior. A great many Italians had had enough of the war, and were considering how best they could get out of it.[23]

VI

Hitler now felt the need for another conference with his ally. He was not prepared to go south and, since the Duce was not well enough to face either the monologue or the long journey, it was decided that Ciano should travel to East Prussia. Before he left Mussolini gave him precise written instructions on the need to make peace with Russia, a subject which was now occupying his mind. On November 6 he had raised it with the German military attaché; on December 4 he had repeated his advice to Goering; [24] and on December 15 he complained to Bottai of Ribbentrop's obstinacy about the decisive Mediterranean front and referred to the expediency of a settlement with Russia.[25]

Now he instructed Ciano to advise the Fuehrer urgently to come to an agreement with Russia, or at least retire to a shortened defensive line in the east. The following year, so the instructions ran, would see the peak of the Anglo-Saxon effort, and the greatest possible number of troops should be made available for Africa, the Balkans, and even the West. At his headquarters on December 18 Hitler spurned this unsolicited advice. He was not prepared to parley with the Russians or to retreat; and he fell back on the old story—there was still no doubt that he could win the war on all fronts.

It was not an exhilarating gathering.

The atmosphere is heavy [wrote Ciano]. To the bad news there should perhaps be added the sadness of that damp forest and the boredom of living in collective barracks. . . . When I arrived no one tried to conceal from me or from my colleagues the uneasiness over the news of the breakthrough on the Russian front.* There were open attempts to place the blame on us. Hewel, who is very close to Hitler, had the following conversation (in English) with Pansa. Pansa: "Had our army many losses?" Hewel: "No losses at all. They are running." Pansa: "As you did in Moscow last year?" Hewel: "Exactly!" The atmosphere engendered by this exchange of feline amenities was not improved when Keitel ad-

* The Russians had pierced the German line north and south of Stalingrad and had isolated the German VI Army.

mitted that in 1939, when the Germans were committed to three years of peace and when Cavallero arrived bearing a warning letter from Mussolini, the Germans had in fact, unbeknown to their allies, already decided on the war against Poland, even to the setting of the date.[26]

Ciano returned to a Rome where the atmosphere was no less oppressive than it had been in the sodden forest of Rastenburg. Defeatism was in the air, the economic position continued to deteriorate with ever-greater shortages of foodstuffs and raw materials, the Allies were stepping up their air attacks on Italian towns, and public war weariness and irritation were growing. Opposition groups were getting together and clandestine leaflets were in circulation. There was more talk of discarding the Fascist regime and with it the German alliance; and Senise, the Chief of Police, was discussing ways and means with Acquarone and the King's household. On the government side, although the Duce's health had improved, only spasmodic efforts were made to react. Mussolini spoke of breaking with the Petaccis, but found himself unable to do so when it came to the point of taking the decisive step. The home front was crumbling as completely as were the battlefronts in Africa and Russia. The people only wanted one thing, an end to the war and that as soon as possible. Colonel Dollmann, Himmler's representative in Rome, anxious to be ready for every eventuality, was reporting to Berlin that

> everyone who studies and watches must over and over again, in connection with the Duce's health, be confronted with the thunderously dark question: What is going to happen if it leads to a catastrophe here? . . . Italy as an ally stands and falls militarily with the fate of North Africa and the political future of the Axis is and remains bound up with the life of the Duce. If Germany wishes to think of the Alliance beyond the lifetime of the Duce, then a weighty and most delicate problem arises: in which direction must channels of contact already explored and established, and which are secure for the future, now be built up?[27]

The deteriorating situation at home and abroad brought on a recurrence of the Duce's nervous gastric ailment. The Duce spent Christmas in bed at the Villa Torlonia and on January 11, instead of paying his weekly visit to the King, packed up and retired to La Rocca delle Caminate. Dr. Frugoni was inclined to think that he might be suffering from cancer, but after a consultation with Dr. Domenico Cess-Bianchi the two doctors came to the conclusion that it was a case of chronic gastric ulcer, provoked by nervous tension.[28] There is no doubt that the effort to present a brave public face to the world had added to the strain.

Meanwhile the cabals were becoming active in Rome. On January 8 Ciano lunched with Bottai and Farinacci, two dissidents on opposite wings of the party. "They are exasperated," wrote Ciano that night. "Bottai, speaking of the loss of Libya said, 'At bottom we have achieved another aim. In 1911 Mussolini declared, let us get out of Libya. He has kept his word, thirty years too late.' " In his diary Marshal Caviglia spoke of the rumors circulating in Rome: that Cavallero was almost openly preparing to succeed Mussolini and that Grandi, Bottai, and Farinacci were among the candidates for the succession.[29] These intrigues were duly brought to the Duce's notice by party headquarters and by Buffarini, who visited La Rocca for the purpose. But, for the moment, he took no action except to telephone to Ciano to inquire whether he had in fact lunched with Bottai and Farinacci.[30]

VII

Mussolini returned to Rome for a meeting of his Cabinet on January 23, 1943. The war situation was continuing to deteriorate. Tripoli had been evacuated, the German armies in Russia were reeling under fresh disasters and alarming reports had been received from the Italian diplomatic representatives in Hungary and Rumania. But Mussolini was not prepared to bow to the storm or to lend an ear to those who were advising him to extricate himself from the German alliance. He resolved on two steps: to pin responsibility for defeat on the military and to remove unreliable elements from the government.

On January 31 he informed the King that he had appointed General Vittorio Ambrosio to replace Cavallero as Chief of Staff and on February 5 he sent for his son-in-law, who in his diary records the conversation. "On entering his office, I notice that he is very embarrassed, and I grasp what he is trying to tell me. 'What would you like to do at the moment?' he begins, and then adds in a low voice that he has changed the whole government. . . . I choose the embassy to the Holy See. It is a place of rest, which, however, holds many possibilities for the future." Later that day the Italian radio announced the composition of the new government. The Duce became Foreign Minister with Bastianini as Undersecretary. Bottai was dismissed from the Ministry of Education and Grandi from the Ministry of Justice, although he remained President of the Chamber. Mussolini also dismissed Buffarini, who had been involved with the Petaccis, from the Ministry of the Interior, which he took over himself. Other casualties were the Ministers of Finance, Public Works, Communications, Corporations, and Popular Culture. The last two posts had been held by Renato Ricci and Alessandro Pavolini, two veteran *Squadristi,* who were to reappear at Mussolini's side in the last phase. In almost every case the public announcement was the first intimation which ministers received of their dismissal.

The transaction was characteristic of Mussolini's methods. To Giuseppe Gorla, the retiring Minister of Public Works, Grandi explained that it had only one significance: "In order to liquidate Ciano and Buffarini all the ministers were dismissed as a wrapping round the removal of the two elements which he wanted to get rid of." This was the explanation which Mussolini himself advanced to Gorla: "You should know that, in a first moment you were exempt, but then I had to make the change to give the measure wider character." [31] This was, however, not the whole story, for Mussolini was also concerned to distract public attention and to show that he was still in control. This was Bottai's explanation. "What has Mussolini been trying to do. . . . To distract people from the great interrogation marks of the hour. . . . And then, to show his power over men." [32] So far as relations with Germany were concerned, the removal of Ciano, Grandi,* and Bottai were reassuring, but Berlin must have been disquieted by the German ambassador's report,

* Hitler took a particularly adverse view of Grandi. When Grandi visited Berlin as Minister of Justice, he was received by the Fuehrer, who in the course of conversation asked him who, in his opinion, were the greatest Germans of recent times. Grandi imprudently and unthinkingly replied, "Bismarck and Stresemann." On hearing the word Stresemann, Hitler immediately rose and terminated the interview, without even waiting for the usual photograph to be taken.

which spoke of Mussolini's decision to act in the face of the loss of the Italian people's will to resist.[33]

A fortnight after these events Ribbentrop asked the Duce to receive him to discuss certain important current questions. The purpose of the visit was twofold: to make it clear that Hitler was not prepared to consider a political settlement with Russia and to raise an issue on which the Germans and Italian military had for a long time been at loggerheads. Briefly, in Yugoslavia the Italians regarded Tito as the main enemy, and were prepared to cooperate with Mihajlović and the Cetniks, who were also opposed to Tito. The fact that Mihajlović had received arms and assistance from Italy's enemy, Britain, was not in their view relevant. The Germans, on the other hand, favored the impartial liquidation of all irregular forces in Yugoslavia. The impending loss of North Africa and the possibility that the Allies might thereafter land in the Balkans rendered a solution of Italo-German differences a matter of urgency. It was a problem which was now becoming something of an obsession to Hitler.

Ribbentrop arrived in Rome with a very long letter from Hitler, sixty pages of typescript, which was to form the basis of his instructions.

> I regard the situation [Hitler wrote] in the Balkan peninsula itself with the gravest concern. . . . If a landing takes place tomorrow, Duce, anywhere in the Balkans, then Communists, followers of Mihajlović, and all the other irregulars will be in accord with one thing: launching an immediate attack on the German or Italian armed forces. . . . It is high time we exterminated this movement, if we do not want to incur the risk of being stabbed in the back the moment the Anglo-Saxons land in the Balkans.

Ribbentrop began by disabusing Mussolini of the idea that it would be possible to make peace with Russia. The Fuehrer was about to mount a new offensive in the east and was resolved to paralyze Russian offensive power, for he did not believe that a political settlement was possible. He then surveyed the position of the neutrals and the prospects in the Mediterranean, thus leading up to his main theme, the liquidation of the Cetniks. Here he met surprising resistance on the Italian side. General Roatta, commanding the Italian Second Army in Croatia, argued that the Cetniks were serving a useful purpose; Bastianini contested the thesis that the groups would come together in the event of invasion; and Mussolini observed that no effective method of fighting the partisans had yet been found.

On the following day the meeting was resumed. But although some semblance of agreement was reached, the fundamental difference remained. All the Italians would consent to do was to accept a vague commitment to disarm the Cetniks after they had served their purpose or after an Allied landing in the Balkans. With this the Germans had to be content, though Ribbentrop in conversation with Alfieri on February 28 "expressed emphatically his astonishment at the activities of the Italian High Command," where "there were tendencies which one could not exactly describe as Fascist." [34] The Germans were no longer winning the war and, however deep Mussolini's loyalty to the Axis, the Italian generals were now not prepared to accept dictation from their unsuccessful colleagues in the German High Command. There was a strong anti-German sentiment abroad. As a letter from Russia put it: "Among the officers of both higher and lower rank, a general feeling of rancor and distrust against the Germans as responsible for every mistake is generally predominant here. A dangerous anti-Fascist spirit lurks and creeps." [35]

It was characteristic of the Germans that Italian recalcitrance should have driven them to concessions which subservience would never have won. Ribbentrop agreed to the publication of an official communiqué defining in glowing terms the aims of the Axis New Order, with its ideals of liberty for all peoples and active collaboration between the nations; and the *Völkische Beobachter* printed an Italian commentary about the Duce's peacemaking career. More important, Hitler, though in desperate need of foreign labor, agreed that the Italian workers in Germany should be allowed to return home.

These concessions, however, did little to reconcile Italian opinion. On March 6 open demonstrations began at Fiat's, followed by a massive strike, which was only brought to an end by the payment of 300 lire to all workmen. There was also an outbreak of trouble in Milan.

With these events as a background Mussolini on March 6 despatched his reply to Hitler's letter.[36] Under pressure from Ambrosio he spoke of the need to hold Tunisia and to obtain increased German aid for the purpose.

We must remain in Tunisia, whatever the cost. . . . I am convinced that we must resist on the Mareth line. But in order to resist, and perhaps even counterattack, our forces must be provisioned; and above all guns, tanks, and gasoline must reach them. . . . To obtain all this, Fuehrer, I will never tire of repeating it: the Axis air forces in the Sardinia, Sicily, Tunisia zone must be at least equal to the enemy aviation.

On the two points which Hitler had raised, Mussolini's reply was not entirely satisfactory. In Croatia the local Italian commanders had been instructed to cease arms deliveries to the Cetniks, who would be disarmed after the Communist partisans had been dealt with. On Russia Mussolini questioned the wisdom of Hitler's policy: "I wonder whether it is not too risky to repeat the struggle against the boundless space of Russia . . . while the Anglo-Saxon peril is mounting in the West." In these words were reflected the mounting anguish with which the Italians viewed Hitler's preoccupation with the eastern theater, which would absorb his resources and leave Italy naked. For years they had besought the Germans to regard the Mediterranean as the principal theater, and time was now running short.

On his return from Rome Ribbentrop had duly conveyed to Hitler his misgivings about the attitude of the Italian generals; and this report together with information from other quarters on the Italian domestic situation caused Hitler once more to demand an urgent meeting with the Duce. Meanwhile Mussolini, with a surprising access of optimism in the face of military reverses in Africa and massive casualties to his convoys, had conceived an ingenious plan to reverse his fortunes. If only Russia could be disposed of and Axis forces concentrated in the Mediterranean, it would be possible to destroy the Anglo-American forces in North Africa by holding Tunisia and seizing Gibraltar and the Balearics. This plan was unfolded to Hitler in a letter of March 26. "The Russian chapter must therefore be liquidated in some way or other. On that day we can put out our flags, as victory will definitely be within our grasp. . . . What I propose to you is a bold move, but you have given too many proofs of your audacity for this not to interest you." [37]

These babblings were not to be taken seriously and Bismarck, the German counsellor in Rome, realistically forecast the Duce's attitude at the coming summit meeting: "I do not foresee, on the part of Mussolini, any particular embarrassing request. His fleet does not exist, his army is problematical. His future is even more so. He feels himself to be weak. . . . I can say, since I have seen the minutes of the talks between Mussolini and Hitler, that the Duce has never taken the initiative and never raised general questions as to the political line to adopt." [38]

VIII

On April 6 Mussolini entrained for Salzburg, accompanied by, among others, Ambrosio, Bastianini, and Dr. Pozzi. During the journey he was again attacked by gastric pains and he made up his mind that at Klessheim he would eat alone. On arrival at Salzburg he was manifestly in bad shape and Hitler begged him to submit to the attentions of his own quack doctor, the notorious Professor Morell. But Mussolini refused; and to Alfieri he said: "If you want to know the name of my illness, I can tell you—convoys." [39]

There are no records of Mussolini's private conversations with Hitler, but from the statements of survivors of this Klessheim gathering it is clear that the meeting was as abortive as any of its predecessors. According to Schmidt, Mussolini did plead for an understanding with Russia. It seemed, he is alleged to have said, that it was impossible to conquer Russia, and that consequently the best course was a compromise peace in the east so as to obtain a free hand in the west.[40] But Hitler was not prepared to listen, and Mussolini was in no physical or moral state to insist. According to Simoni, it was necessary to suspend the talks for a whole day because Mussolini was not well enough to take part.

The conversations on other levels were equally barren. With Ribbentrop, Bastianini vainly tried to advance his plan of a charter for the Axis New Order. The Germans were not impressed with a proposal put forward by Mussolini to mount an operation against Gibraltar, for which they had no forces available; nor were the military able to reach any conclusions regarding the coordination of the Axis war effort. The fact was that the aims of the two allies were now more widely divergent than ever. The Italians wished to free themselves from the German alliance and to get out of the war, failing which they advocated a standstill in the east, the withdrawal of Italian troops from Russia, and the concentration of Axis forces in the Mediterranean. Mussolini had promised Ambrosio and Bastianini to take this line. The Germans, under Hitler's impulse, were resolved to smash Russia, to give the eastern front the first priority, and to deny Italy the military aid she was seeking. The German High Command was not prepared to coordinate their military plans, and on the political side Bastianini's plan to rally the smaller nations under the umbrella of a New Order was viewed with some suspicion. What if Italy, Hungary, and Rumania were to get together to seek the negotiated peace for which their peoples were obviously longing? The Germans were unwilling to yield on any point and the conference at Klessheim marked the end of the last vestige of Axis collaboration. It also marked a decline of Mussolini's prestige among his own people. Despite careful briefing and considerable pressure from his advisers, he had failed to make the slightest impact on the Fuehrer.

Nevertheless Mussolini, as usual, returned to Rome in better heart. According to Goebbels, the Duce had been really restored to his old form after the four days at Klessheim, and the Fuehrer, by applying every ounce of nervous energy, had pushed him back on the rails. "When he got out of the train, the Fuehrer thought he looked like a broken old man; when he left again, he was in high fettle and ready for anything. . . . The Duce understands clearly that there can be no further salvation for him except to win or die with us." [41] In this view he was becoming more and more isolated, for his associates, who had no part in the decision to enter the war, were not inhibited by any sense of responsibility for its outcome.

IX

In Rome criticism of the Duce's conduct of the war was mounting. On April 16 Ambrosio told General Puntoni, head of the King's military household, that he was not in agreement with the euphoria of the Duce. Italy had obtained nothing at Salzburg, for Germany was only thinking of her own interests without regard to those of Italy, which were now decisively compromised.[42] Events soon confirmed Ambrosio's judgment, for a frantic appeal by Mussolini to Hitler on April 30 for air reinforcements to save Tunisia fell on deaf ears. The fact was that the Germans were being so hard pressed in Russia that they were obliged to write off Tunisia. A minute of May 2, written in the Italian Foreign Ministry, spoke of the exacerbation of criticism directed at the head of the government. "For some days with the increasingly critical situation in Tunisia, unfavorable comments at the expense of the Duce and Marshal Kesselring have been openly and violently expressed, and with a significant solidarity between generals and admirals, to such a point as to give rise to a suspicion that a 'common attitude' between the leaders of the armed forces is under way." [43] Anfuso, who was on a visit to Rome from Budapest, found an odor of conspiracy in the air. "After two decades of fascism, Rome was plotting." [44]

In this situation Mussolini, under the stimulus administered by Hitler, made his last spasmodic effort to prop up the home front. On April 14 he dismissed the Chief of Police, Carmen Senise, replacing him by Renzo Chierci, an old faithful and companion of Balbo from Ferrara. Three days later he appointed Carlo Scorza, another old party member, to succeed the young Vidussoni as secretary of the party. On May 3 he addressed the new party directorate in a speech described as "a supreme appeal to the whole structure of the nation to strengthen our resistance"; and on May 5 the Duce addressed a vast crowd of enthusiastic supporters from the balcony of the Palazzo Venezia. "I hear," he shouted, "vibrating in your voices the proclamation of your old and incorruptible faith. The bloody sacrifices of these hard times will be recompensed by victory, if it is true, and it is true that God is just and Italy immortal." It was the anniversary of the entry of Italian troops into Addis Ababa and the last occasion on which he was to speak from that balcony.

These measures were, however, quite ineffective. The people wanted an end to the war and the party was wholly discredited. A police report spoke of the growing public dissatisfaction: "The party has in twenty years lost the confidence and esteem of even its own followers, because of the excessive robberies of the bosses and the patent injustices which have been committed. . . . Enormous progress has been made by communism, which is undermining all branches of production."[45] Even the party extremists were disillusioned, for they called in vain on Mussolini to take the draconian measures which he had himself demanded from the parliamentary government of Italy in the dark days of Caporetto. Words had lost their magic and the only thing which might have rallied the nation was victory on the battlefield.

Instead, on May 8 Tunis and Bizerte fell, and five days later at Cape Bon the remnants of the Axis forces in North Africa laid down their arms. It was a blow which, the Germans had been warned, was likely to prove fatal to the Fascist system.

The event brought Hitler face to face with new problems. So long as the Mediterranean war was being fought in Africa he could afford to regard it as a secondary theater. He had been warned by the German military attaché that the Italian army, which had been virtually destroyed in Greece, Russia, and Africa was in no state to parry an invasion of metropolitan territory; and he might now be obliged to "take over the Italian positions with German forces, and keep—and this point was the decisive consideration—the war as far away as possible from the heart of Europe and thereby from the frontiers of Germany."[46]

Relations between the Axis partners were, however, not such as to enable rational plans to be coordinated. While Hitler still continued to repose full confidence in the person of the Duce, he mistrusted, and rightly, the Court, the Italian High Command, the dissident Fascists, the bureaucracy, and the people. The Italians on the other hand were aware that the Germans had no regard for Italian interests and recoiled from a German occupation of their country. Thus, when early in May the Germans offered three divisions for the defense of Italy and on May 9 increased the number by two, Mussolini churlishly replied that three divisions would alter nothing; and he rejected the offer of the two additional divisions, asking instead for air reinforcements.

On May 12 Hitler despatched Admiral Doenitz to Rome. He found Mussolini "well, optimistic, composed, very frank, sincere, and amicable." It was one of Mussolini's qualities of leadership that he could assume in times of danger and stress, albeit at the cost of strain on his nervous system, an appearance of stoical calm. There was also an element of instinctive optimism. Events had so often come to his aid in the past that they might be expected to do so again. Nevertheless, despite his amiability and the gravity of the situation, Mussolini made it clear to Doenitz that he was still opposed to the despatch of five German divisions to Italy. Kesselring reported to the Fuehrer that Mussolini's attitude proved that the Italians wanted to remain masters in their own house.[47]

This and other reports from Rome confirmed Hitler in his suspicions; and the German General Staff began to lay plans for the contingency of Italy's withdrawal from the war. Under the code names "Alaric" and "Konstantin" countermeasures were prepared for the occupation of Italy and the assumption of Italy's military responsibilities in the Balkans. Transport arrangements were made for three S. S. divisions to be moved, if necessary, to the Italian border and for the transfer of armored divisions from the east.

The mutual mistrust between Berlin and Rome was still further aggravated by the revival of their dispute over the Balkans. By means of an ingenious deception * the Germans had been led to believe that feint attacks would on launched on Sicily and the Dodecanese, while the main thrusts would be against Crete, the Peloponnese, and the Italian mainland. The prospect of an Allied landing in the Balkans drove Hitler to a frenzy and on May 19 he addressed a long, furious letter to Mussolini,[48] complaining of the conduct of the Italian High Command.

It is not a question of the problems of the High Command, nor of the [Italian] Second Army, nor of the Governor of Montenegro, but of the common struggle for our future destiny. . . . By exercising truly angelic patience I have frequently and repeatedly succeeded in arriving at real collaboration in the conduct of war in this region. But my efforts have failed in the face or repeated sabotage—I must use this hard word—of the agreements reached on operations.

Unless communications in Yugoslavia were safeguarded, there would be a disaster and he must ask the Duce to give instructions to conform, not only in the letter, to the existing agreements.

---

* Under the code name "Mincemeat" a corpse in British officer's uniform, bearing false operational plans, had been planted on the Spanish coast.

When delivering this letter on May 20 Kesselring took with him also an invitation to an immediate conference with Hitler. It was not a prospect which Mussolini viewed with relish, and he replied evasively. Instead he despatched a placatory answer to Hitler's fulmination. After making a few legitimate debating points, he yielded to Hitler's demands. The Governor of Montenegro had been ordered to clarify the situation regarding all those who were or would be enemies, for the Axis could not risk rebel zones in the rear when an enemy landing in Greece might be imminent.[49]

The remaining weeks before the final blow fell were spent in unedifying, muddled, and unprofitable wrangles between the Italian and German commands on the subject of ground and air reinforcements for Italy. The fault did not lie wholly with the Germans, for they simply did not possess the resources with which to meet their commitments in Russia, the Balkans, the West, and the Mediterranean.

During much of this time Mussolini was out of action, owing to a severe attack of his gastric complaint. On May 26 he retired to the Rocca, where on May 30 he was so ill that he was thought to be dying.[50] A week later, he returned to Rome for a consultation with his doctors, who prescribed a course of injections and a period in bed. Rintelen, who saw him then, described him as no longer the old Mussolini, but as a statesman bent by illness and tortured by doubts.[51]

Meanwhile the conspirators were busy. On May 15 the King had drafted three memoranda setting forth his views [52] and concluding with the words: "One must think seriously of the possible need to detach Italy's armed forces from those of Germany, whose internal collapse might come without warning, as happened to Imperial Germany in 1918." By the end of the month Acquarone, who was the moving spirit in the Palace, had established contact with surviving politicians of the pre-Fascist era, whom the King was ready to consult. On June 2 the King saw Bonomi, who advocated a military government headed by Ambrosio, Caviglia, or Badoglio; and later he received Marcello Soleri, a former minister of the pre-Fascist era. On June 7 Soleri met Acquarone, who told him that the King had decided not to intervene unless there were some new political or military event.

The King took a similar line with Grandi when he received him on June 4. "The moment will come," he told Grandi. "I know that I can count on you. Leave your King to choose the opportune moment and in the meantime help me to obtain the constitutional means." [53]

The King's hesitations were rational. There were two factors to be taken into account. If Italy were suddenly to loose herself from Germany, she would risk vengeance at the hands of the barbarous dictator in the north. The tidiest and safest solution would be for Italy to withdraw from the war with Hitler's knowledge and consent. Such a solution might not be altogether to Germany's disadvantage, so the Italians ingenuously argued. Instead of frittering away resources in Italy which she could ill spare, Germany would be able to concentrate on the defense of the Reich. Such reasoning took no account of Hitler's character. But in any event it was clear, even to the most optimistic Italian, that only one man could bring Hitler to give his assent. So long as there was any hope of securing this assent it would be folly to discard the Duce.

The second consideration was one which weighed heavily with the King. He had always been a stickler for constitutional propriety, and, as he had indicated to Grandi, he was waiting for a vote in the Chamber or in the Grand Council to give him the mandate to intervene. So he decided to wait on events, and he did not have long to wait.

X

On June 11 the fortified island of Pantelleria, with a garrison of twelve thousand men, surrendered to the Allies without a struggle. The commander, Admiral Paresi, sought Mussolini's permission to capitulate on the grounds of lack of water and superior enemy strength; and the Duce, probably because he was incapacitated by illness, at once tamely agreed. "It was astonishing," wrote Rintelen, "that the Duce, without further inquiry, should have ordered the surrender." [54] In fact there was no shortage of water on the island. Two days later Lampedusa fell, and the Allies had acquired their springboards for the assault on Sicily. But still the Axis,* bemused

* Unbeknownst to Hitler, the Spaniards had let Mussolini into the secret.

by Operation Mincemeat, were in doubt as to where the blow would fall.

On the night of July 9 the Allies landed in Sicily. Events soon bore out Mussolini's police reports of disaffection on the island. The astonished British troops beheld, painted on the walls of houses, the inscriptions *Viva Stevens; Viva il Colonello Stevens.** The Italian troops were no longer ready to die for Mussolini, and only the desperate resistance of the German units held up the Allied advance. At the naval base of Augusta the admiral blew up the batteries and surrendered without firing a shot. Already on July 12 Bastianini was telephoning to Alfieri in Berlin to solicit the reinforcement of the air force. "We cannot hold on any longer in Sicily." This appeal was followed up the same day by a personal message from Mussolini to Hitler making the same urgent request, but without any mention of army reinforcements. This conspicuous omission was explained by Rintelen, who reported that "the opposition to a further spreading of German forces throughout Italy comes from the Duce himself. The reasons for this are probably the following: the maintenance of Italian prestige in the country itself; the excessive economic burden through having many German troops; a considerable overestimation of battleworthiness of Italian troops.[55]

The Germans were now in a dilemma. Disgusted as they were by the Italian performance in Sicily, they were reluctant to commit further troops to inevitable destruction in the island. On the evening of July 12 Rintelen delivered to the Duce an insulting message from the Fuehrer to the effect that if the Italians did not intend to fight, he would send no further troops to Italy.[56] On the other hand, they could not afford to allow the Fascist system to collapse. As Alfieri put it in a private letter to Bastianini of July 12, "one has the impression that she [Germany] intends to aliment the heroic Italian resistance with limited concessions." [57]

German misgivings would have been confirmed had they read a minute of July 14 to the Duce in which Ambrosio described the fate of Sicily as sealed. The causes of the disaster were the result

---

* Colonel Stevens, a former military attaché in Rome, was the celebrated broadcaster in the B.B.C. Italian Service.

of three years of war, begun with scanty means, during which the country's few resources had been dissipated in foreign fields. He concluded by saying that, if it proved impossible to prevent the constitution of an Allied second front, it would be for the highest political authorities "to consider whether it would be expedient to spare the country further sorrow and ruin, and to anticipate the end of the struggle, seeing that the final result will undoubtedly be worse in one or more years.[58]

Even without a sight of this minute, Hitler moved with the utmost caution. In his written reply to the Duce's appeal he spoke of modest land and air reinforcements, but sternly demanded Italian cooperation in Sicily and measures to insure that the Italian troops should fight. But on July 15 when Kesselring delivered Hitler's reply, he took the line that the Fuehrer was now opposed to sending equipment and troops to Sicily until supplies of ammunition, gasoline, and rations could be assured. The defense of the lines of comunication in Calabria was more important.[59]

It was an extraordinary situation between allies bound by ideological ties and in a moment of common peril. According to a staff officer's diary, Ambrosio, who was present when Hitler's letter was delivered, was aghast at the contemptuous tone used by the Germans and astonished that Mussolini should have tolerated it.[60] If Germany were unwilling to furnish aid, it seemed hopeless to go on struggling; and he advised the Duce to reply to Hitler in this sense. Mussolini was, however, not prepared to accept such extreme advice and drafted a moderately worded answer, in which he claimed that the Italian authorities had done all they could to cooperate with the Germans and that the Italian forces were resolved to defend the island to the last. He concluded with a dig at German egotism: "The sacrifice of my country cannot have as its principal aim the delaying of a direct attack on Germany"; and he suggested that the time had come to examine the situation together in order to meet the interests of both countries.

Meanwhile Scorza, in his efforts to rally the country, had conceived a plan to despatch Fascist leaders on a speaking tour of the provinces. Preliminary conversations between them had disclosed that all, in a greater or lesser degree, were alarmed at the situation into which Mussolini's system of personal government had led them;

and they demanded that Mussolini should receive them before their departure for the provinces, in order that they should have an opportunity of making their feelings plain. It was reminiscent of the visit of the officers in December, 1924, after the murder of Matteotti.

On the afternoon of July 16 Scorza and fourteen orators (Grandi and Federzoni had declined to come from Bologna and Ciano was allegedly indisposed) presented themselves to a reluctant Duce, who "turned his head to us, one by one, slightly aslant as if he wanted, by looking at us sideways, at the same time to defend himself and to penetrate our intentions." [61]

Farinacci asked that the Grand Council should be summoned so that those present should be put in a position to assume total responsibility with the Duce. Bottai put the case more coherently. It was essential, he said, that the constitutional organs of fascism should be allowed to govern. "We are asking that the regime puts its apparatus in working order again. We are not here to ask that your powers or power should be diminished or to divide or fragment your responsibilities. We are here to share those responsibilities." [62] When the speakers had finished, Mussolini curtly announced that he would summon the Grand Council, and he dismissed them without another word. He later confirmed that he had not cared for this meeting:

> All the speakers, or nearly all, insisted on the necessity of convening the Grand Council, if only to enable me to inform the members of the highest assembly and the regime of certain facts which could not be given to the general public. At the end of this discussion, which, not having been prepared, revealed nothing but a sceptical frame of mind all round, I announced that I would convene the Grand Council in the second half of the month.[63]

At Rastenburg, where gloomy reports from Rome were flowing in, Hitler was wrestling with the intractable Italian problem. The High Command was itching to take over Italy, but this assumed an imminent collapse, and Hitler favored caution. After all, "without the Italian army we cannot defend the whole peninsula. In that case we would have to withdraw to a relatively short line," a move which Jodl pointed out would have very serious repercussions in the Balkans. Hitler closed the proceedings by saying that unless it proved possible to effect a radical change in Italy—and by this he meant invigoration of the government and regeneration of the army—it would be pointless to throw in additional German troops, thus engaging Germany's last reserves.[64]

With these objects in mind Hitler instructed the German ambassador on Sunday, July 18, to transmit an urgent invitation to an immediate summit conference. He was prepared to come to Italy, and the meeting might last three days. The Duce at once agreed, and a meeting was fixed for the following day at Senator Gaggia's sumptuous villa at Feltre near Venice. It was unfortunate for the Italians that they should not have received longer notice, since, although Hitler knew exactly what he wanted to achieve, viz., control of Italy under the nominal authority of the Duce, Mussolini's advisers required some time in which to brief their ailing and vacillating chief. They were united in wishing him to explain frankly to the Fuehrer that Italy materially and morally was at the end of her tether, and that ways and means must be found of releasing her from the war. Most of them were also agreed that if for any reason Mussolini failed to make the position plain, he would have to go. General Hazon, commander of the *Carabinieri,* had been drawn into the conspiracy, which in the early days of July had made so much progress that the removal of Mussolini seemed to present no insuperable practical difficulty.

There was, however, no opportunity to make any preparations for the conference, since Mussolini left Rome by air at once for Riccione, accompanied only by his private secretary and doctor and without a word to any of his advisers. It may seem strange that Mussolini should have approached with so little preparation what was perhaps the most important meeting of his life. But he had lost the habit of taking advice and he was in a curious mood of resignation, with moments of unreasoning optimism. He knew in his heart that his advisers were right; but, as always, he recoiled from an unpleasant interview. So he shut himself up. As Bastiniani said to Alfieri, he "no longer gave any sign of his feelings. He now maintained an inscrutable silence, and it was impossible to divine his thoughts."[65]

XI

On the morning of July 19 the participants at the Feltre conference began to foregather. Ambrosio and Bastianini arrived by train at Treviso, where they were met by Alfieri, who had flown from Berlin. They agreed that Mussolini must be persuaded to make a firm stand and, if it were not too late, free himself from his commitments. When Mussolini landed at 8:30 A.M. on the airfield at Treviso, Alfieri told him that the Germans were showing great anxiety about the situation in Italy; and Bastianini intervened to report that on the journey from Rome he had tried to ascertain from Mackensen and Rintelen whether Hitler intended to place the Italian armies under German command. Mussolini reacted with satisfactory annoyance to this suggestion, but before the matter could be pursued Keitel, followed by Kesselring, arrived on the airfield and presented himself to the Duce.[66] Further private conversation between the Italians became impossible, but Keitel in an aside to Rintelen was able to tell him that the object of the conference was: "All power in the hands of the Duce, removal of the influence of the Royal House, German reinforcements in Italy, and control by the German High Command." [67]

Punctually to the minute the Fuehrer's aircraft landed. The two dictators greeted one another cordially enough, but, as Rintelen noted, there was no longer quite the same atmosphere as at previous meetings. "Over the airfield lay a leaden weariness which could not be solely attributed to the heat." Hitler immediately announced that he must return home that very afternoon, and he added curtly that the available time must be used to the best advantage. Nevertheless during the train journey to Feltre and in the car to the villa only trivialities were exchanged. Mussolini was reluctant to grasp the nettle, and Hitler was less concerned to provoke a discussion than to lay down the law. Ambrosio, who traveled with Keitel, did attempt to draw the German, who only replied: "The two leaders will discuss all these matters themselves." So two precious hours were wasted.

The formal session began in the big drawing room of the Villa

Gaggia at eleven o'clock. Hitler was supported by Keitel, General Warlimont, Rintelen, and Mackensen. In order to mark the military character of the meeting neither Ribbentrop nor any member of his Ministry attended. On the Italian side were Mussolini, Ambrosio, Bastianini, and Alfieri.

Once the assembled delegations were seated in a circle, Hitler treated them to a monologue, which lasted for two hours. At noon the cascade was halted for a few minutes, while Mussolini's secretary entered the room with the news that Rome was at that moment being subjected to a violent air attack. It was a frightful blow to Mussolini, but Hitler seemed resentful of the interruption and, without a word of commiseration to his friend, at once took up the threads of his discourse. It was a measure of Hitler's ignorance of Italian psychology that he did not at once grasp that the bombardment of Rome was of capital significance. The Anglo-Americans had revealed their power and had dramatically provided to the dissident elements welcome evidence that the West was strong enough and close enough to afford protection against German vengeance.

Hitler went on to say that some of his generals had advocated withdrawals on operational grounds, but he was resolved not to surrender an inch of conquered territory and to hold the war as far away from Germany as possible. Moreover he must keep his hands on all the sources of raw materials which were essential to the total war which he was determined to wage. There were in Germany also some people, principally in bourgeois circles, who wished to end the war and to leave to a later generation the decisive conflict with Russia. He rejected this advice, for Germany would not in three hundred years possess a man like himself who was capable of solving this problem. He would sacrifice his time and personal comfort to the task of bringing about a settlement in his own lifetime. He promised his audience a turning point in the submarine war and the very early use of two potent secret weapons against the British.

So far as the Italian theater of war was concerned, he made a wounding attack on the Italian conduct of the war. The troops had not fought, the High Command had failed, the civil administration was weak, and defeatism was rampant. The sternest measures were now required. He was now in two minds as to what should be done in Sicily, and in a long, rambling dissertation he made it clear that, if the Italians were not prepared to do battle, he was not prepared to help them. The Italian demand for 2,000 aircraft was unrealistic and, moreover, the war would be won in the first place by men.

The Fuehrer's harangue was not translated, so that most of it passed over the heads of the Italian delegation. Mussolini, who never uttered a word except when he was informed of the air attack on Rome, sat "cross-legged on the edge of his armchair, which was too large and too deep, and listened patiently and impassively, clasping his hands on his knees." He seemed unmoved, except that he sometimes shifted his position and nervously passed his right hand over his face.

Occasionally he put his left hand behind his back and pressed it against a spot that must have been causing him pain—a spot in the vicinity of his stomach ulcer. From time to time he heaved a deep sigh, in the manner of a man who is forced to endure a tedious and interminable monologue, gazing with a weary resigned expression at Hitler, who, in a voice that grew more strident every minute, continued imperturbably to pour forth a stream of reproaches and recriminations.[68]

Schmidt describes the session, in which Mussolini was "properly put on the mat," as one of the most depressing meetings at which he ever took part.[69] He reports that Mussolini was so upset that he was unable to follow what was said; and Alfieri describes the Duce as struggling towards the end to conceal his distress.

The period of his crucifixion was mercifully brought to an end by a member of Hitler's staff, who came in to whisper to his master that it was one o'clock and time for lunch. The two dictators were to lunch alone; and in the brief interval the Italian advisers, who only knew that Mussolini had not spoken, made a last appeal to him to approach Hitler with a view to seeking a way out. Alfieri told him that he would never have a better opportunity of speaking frankly to his friend and ally;[70] and, according to Bastianini, the outspoken Ambrosio delivered an ultimatum to get out of the war in fifteen days.[71]

Mussolini wearily invited his persecutors to sit down.

Can you suppose [he said] that I have not long been tormented by this problem? My apparent indifference marks an intense agony of spirit. For the sake of argument, suppose we were to make a separate peace. It looks so simple. . . . Are we prepared to obliterate at a single stroke twenty years of fascism? . . . It's so easy to talk about a separate peace. But what would be Hitler's attitude? Can you believe that he would allow us to retain our liberty of action? [72]

This was precisely what the advisers hoped and what they wished the Duce to secure from his friend. The conversation was interrupted by Mussolini's private secretary, who came to take him away to his private lunch with the Fuehrer.

At lunch, according to Mussolini's account, Hitler repeated that the submarine offensive would be resumed with new means, and he sought to stiffen Mussolini with the assurance that by the end of August the new secret weapons would be launched on London, which would be razed to the ground in a few weeks.[73] According to Admiral Maugeri, who later accompanied him to the island of Ponza, Mussolini claimed that he had at Feltre once more advised Hitler to make peace with Russia.[74] But, whatever else may have been said in the short time available, there was no ventilation of Italy's main problem. Soon it was time to go, and the two dictators embarked on the return journey to Treviso.

In the train, according to Mussolini's subsequent account,[75] he told Hitler that Italy was in danger of succumbing under the onslaught of two empires, that tension was high, and that the African campaign would have taken a different turn if the Axis had possessed superiority or even parity in the air. Hitler replied that the defense of Italy was of the utmost importance to Germany; and in the course of a friendly conversation he undertook to send further reinforcements for the defense of the peninsula. But although Mussolini, according to Rintelen, had promised Ambrosio to describe Italy's desperate situation to Hitler, he apparently only did so in the context of a request for further German help. He could not bring himself to admit that Italy was unable to continue the struggle.[76]

In a neighboring railway carriage Keitel and Ambrosio were conducting a less friendly conversation. Keitel made it brutally plain that the Italians could expect no reinforcements unless they accepted German conditions:

(1) From the tactical point of view: increase of forces to form a strong defensive line. The Italians to supply two divisions and the Germans two.

(2) From the operational point of view: the assurance of supplies and the creation of powerful defense in Calabria and Apulia.

(3) From the organizational point of view: measures to give the military full control in southern Italy. This was total war and all civil activity must be placed under the command of the Italian Seventh Army. To facilitate this task the Germans would set up a liaison staff with the Seventh Army.[77]

It was obvious to Ambrosio that acceptance of the two last conditions meant a considerable degree of German interference in Italy's internal affairs, and he curtly replied that, as to measures of a general character, the decision must rest with the Duce. When he pointed out that an adequate air force was required, Keitel retorted: "Only after everything has been directed in the sense of the above three points can all the necessary material be sent to this sector." [78] It was an ultimatum. According to Rintelen the atmosphere was frosty. Ambrosio was "reserved and monosyllabic," and protested once more that the Italian High Command was not allowed to dispose freely of the German divisions committed in Italy.[79]

At five o'clock the two dictators took leave of one another at Treviso airfield. According to Alfieri they looked calm and satisfied. On parting from Hitler Mussolini said: "Ours is a common cause, Fuehrer"; and to Keitel he remarked: "Send everything we require as quickly as you can and remember that we are in the same boat." [80] Despite the Fuehrer's apparent cordiality the communiqué for publication the following day was frigid: "Yesterday in a locality in northern Italy the Duce and the Fuehrer met. Questions of a military character were examined."

When the Fuehrer had disappeared into the sky and Mussolini turned to board his own aircraft, the advisers approached him on the runway. But Mussolini forestalled them. "I had no need to approach the Fuehrer in the way you suggested," he said. "This time he promised *faithfully* to send all the assistance we ask for"; and turning to Ambrosio, he added: "Of course our requests must be reasonable and not astronomic." [81]

For once a meeting with the Fuehrer had failed to exhilarate the

Duce. Nothing had been decided, and Mussolini returned to Rome afflicted by the news of the air bombardment of the city and oppressed by the sense of his own failure. His advisers were equally depressed. To Bastianini, Ambrosio exclaimed: "Did you hear what he said to Hitler after my warning of this morning? He asked him again for that war material which they will never send. He still deludes himself. . . . He is mad, I tell you, mad."[82] The conspirators had been relying on General Hazon to take action in the event of the collapse of the Feltre talks. His death in the air attack on Rome complicated the problem and added to the gloom. It would be necessary now to make other arrangements for the removal of the Duce.

BOOK IV

Fall

Fox

Another view of Mussolini from the famous balcony of the Palazzo Venezia.

Wide World

Carlo Sforza led the opposition to Mussolini in the first years of his power. A leading anti-Fascist, he became Foreign Minister in 1947.

Dino Grandi held a succession of high posts in the Fascist regime. It was he who led the revolt that caused Mussolini's downfall.

Wide World

UPI

Il Duce *in a typically dramatic gesture while addressing his men.*

One of Mussolini's personal foibles was his over-emphasis on youth and vigor. Here he is with his son Romano skiing at Terminillo.

Acme

Acme

The Munich Conference, 1938. Left to right, Neville Chamberlain, Édouard Daladier, Adolf Hitler, Mussolini, and Galeazzo Ciano.

Wide World

Italian Foreign Minister Ciano reviews an honor guard at Berlin in 1939.

Ciano and German Foreign Minister Ribbentrop meeting in Berlin.

Keystone

Keystone

Marshal Rodolfo Graziani, leader of Italian armies in North Africa. He later became Minister of War in the Salò Government.

Wide World

Surrounded by his body guard, Mussolini gives the Fascist salute during a parade celebrating the 125th anniversary of the Carabinieri.

Keystone

Bruno, Mussolini's son, killed in an airplane crash during World War II.

Wide World

Italo Balbo, a famous aviator, was Governor-General of Libya. He was shot down mysteriously by Italian forces near Tobruk.

UPI

Mussolini, Hitler, and Ciano meet at the Brenner Pass in 1940.

Acme

Shortly after abortive attempt on Hitler's life on July 20, 1944, the Fuehrer receives a visit from Mussolini.

Wide World

A smiling Mussolini is flanked by Fascist Party Secretary Ettore Muti on his left and, on his right, Marshal Pietro Badoglio, who was appointed Premier by the King on Mussolini's fall.

K

Otto Skorzeny, leader of the special German force that rescued Mussolini.

Vorld

Mussolini enters a German airplane after his rescue from the Italians.

Donna Rachele Mussolini, the Duce's wife.

Keystone

Angelica Balabanoff, Socialist acquaintance of Mussolini.

Wide World

Wide World

ra Petacci, Mussolini's tress, who died at his .

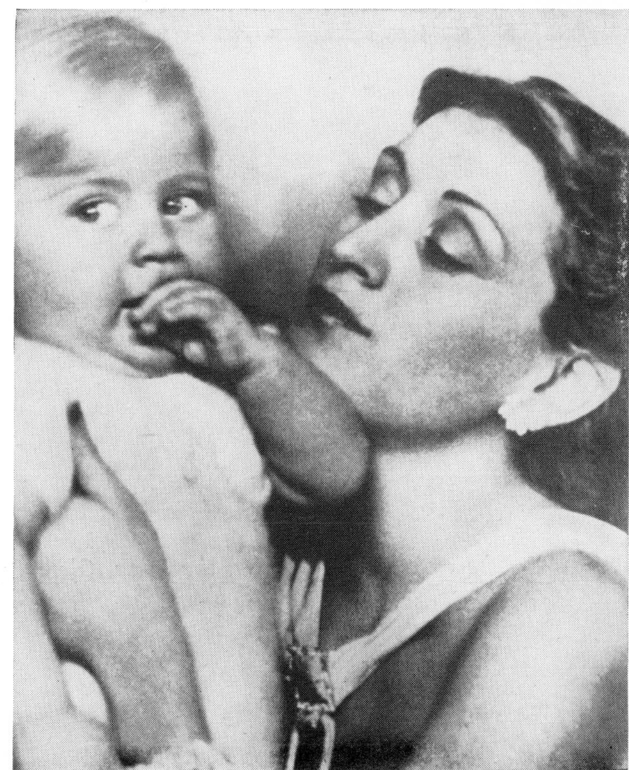

Keystone

la Mussolini, the Duce's ghter, wife of Galeazzo no.

UP

The end: Achille Starace, the Duce, Clara Petacci.

CHAPTER TWENTY

The Palace Revolution

1943

I

THE disconsolate Italian party returned to Rome from Feltre to face the consequences of Hitler's ultimatum and Mussolini's refusal to present the Italian case. On the afternoon of July 20, a few hours after the arrival of the special train in Rome, Rintelen appeared at the Palazzo Venezia to demand the Duce's answer to Keitel's three points.[1] Although it was clear that acceptance meant ultimate German control of Italy, without the slightest assurance that adequate German reinforcements would in fact be despatched, rejection would have involved a German disengagement and the collapse of the Italian front. So, although Ambrosio proffered his resignation, the Duce accepted the German terms. It was a grudging acceptance. Both Mussolini and Ambrosio, says Rintelen, had dark looks; and some days later he reported to Berlin that "in all authoritative military and political circles since the conversations of July 19 exists the overriding doubt whether Germany is in a position to give sufficient aid to Italy in her defensive struggle against invasion."[2]

The German plan was to avoid excessive commitments in Italy and to buy time so as to enable a suitable defensive line to be prepared as far away as possible from the homeland. This could only be done by taking control, but so far as outward appearances were concerned Hitler, on personal as well as domestic political grounds, attached importance to the preservation of fascism and the maintenance in office of the Duce. On this latter point he was reassured by his reports of developments in Rome.

On July 21 Farinacci, accompanied by Marshal Cavallero, called at the German embassy to give Mackensen an account of the internal political situation. He described the representations of the party leaders and told the ambassador that the Grand Council would meet before the end of the week. The conversation left Mackensen with the comforting impression that the more active members of the party had persuaded Mussolini to summon the Grand Council, in order to introduce the sweeping measures required to invigorate the Italian war effort.[3] He must have reported in this sense to Berlin, for Goebbels noted in his dairy:

> In the course of the day we received confidential information that a certain change was taking place in Italian domestic politics. Led by Farinacci, the Old Guard Fascists have requested the Duce to call a meeting of the Fascist Grand Council. At this meeting, according to Mackensen, the Duce is to be requested to initiate more energetic policies. He is to be persuaded to get rid of the burden of holding so many offices so that he may regain his initiative and strength for guiding the over-all policies and the war effort of Italy.[4]

Misled by Mackensen, the Germans were content to allow events to take their course, and no particular preparations were made to meet a crisis. Indeed it was decided that the preliminary alert for operations "Alaric" and "Konstantin" should be called off.

The complacency of Berlin was shared by Mussolini. There had been intercepted telephone conversations, and warnings had reached him from Angela Curti, a former mistress, Ottavia Dinale, an old friend, Buffarini, Farinacci, Scorza, Chierci, Rachele, and many others. To all of these he turned a deaf ear. He was confident in his own ability to handle the situation and he placed implicit trust in the King.

The way was thus left free to the conspirators, if the term may be applied to men of widely divergent views, some of whom did not know exactly what they intended to achieve. As Anfuso put it, "each character donned his mask and came onto the stage."[5] There is reason to believe that after the fiasco at Feltre the King, who for a long time had been brooding over the problem, resolved to liquidate Mussolini and conveyed the decision to Ambrosio.[6] When Mussolini saw the King on July 22 he found him frowning and nervous. The war, the Sovereign declared, could not go on much longer. The discipline of the troops had broken down and the Germans would betray Italy. There was no alternative but to explain to the Germans the Italian dilemma.[7] To General Puntoni the King said: "I tried to make the Duce understand that it was his person . . . which prevented an internal recovery. . . . He did not understand or did not wish to do so. It was as if I was talking to the wind." [8]

Grandi, after consultations with Federzoni in Bologna, arrived in Rome with a draft motion, which he intended to sumbit to the Grand Council. It demanded the revival of all the existing organs of government: Grand Council, Cabinet, Parliament, and Corporations; and it proposed the assumption by the King of the command of the armed forces. He was determined not to be accused of conspiracy and he proceeded, quite openly, to canvass support for his motion.

On the morning of July 21 he saw Scorza and gave him a copy of the draft. According to Grandi's subsequent account, Scorza later in the day sent him a promise of support.[9] However this may be, Scorza later in the morning showed the draft to Mussolini. "I read the document," Mussolini wrote (a long one of more than three pages), "and handed it back to Scorza, declaring that the document was inadmissible and contemptible. Scorza put it back in his briefcase and did not insist further. It was on that occasion that Scorza made me a rather ambiguous speech in which he spoke of a 'shocker' or rather 'supershocker' which might be in store, a speech to which I did not attribute great importance." [10]

After seeing Scorza, Grandi called on Federzoni, where he found Bottai. "We all three thought alike. There was no need of discussion." [11] Steps were also taken to draw in Ciano, who had returned to Rome from Leghorn and who spent some time with Grandi and Bottai discussing the draft. Later, Ciano brought Alfieri to Grandi's office and persuaded him to give his support, while Federzoni secured the accession of De Vecchi and De Stefani. Others who had signified approval were De Bono, Suardo, and Bastianini. In the short time available good progress had been made and at no time was there any attempt to throw a cloak of secrecy over the proceedings. Not only Scorza but Farinacci were kept fully informed. Indeed, when Farinacci saw Grandi on July 24, he purported to agree to everything in the draft except full powers to the King.[12]

In order that everything should appear to be above board Grandi sought an audience with Mussolini. He was received during the evening of Thursday, July 22, and found in the waiting room Marshal Kesselring, who was due to be received after Grandi and was on the Duce's engagement list for an interview lasting an hour and a half, whereas Grandi had only been allotted a quarter of an hour. As it turned out, Grandi stayed for an hour and a half.*

According to Grandi, Mussolini listened to him quite affably,† while he urged that it was the Duce's duty to divest himself spontaneously and legally of dictatorial powers so that the people could freely express their will. The war, he said, was lost and the best service fascism could now render was to divert the wrath of the Allies from the nation to the regime. When he had finished, Mussolini, who had listened patiently, without interrupting, replied: "You would be right and the solution of putting everything into the hands of the King would be acceptable, if the war were lost. But in fact it is about to be won, because within a few days the Germans will launch a weapon which will transform the situation. . . . For the rest we will talk calmly of all this at the session of the Grand Council next Saturday."[13] In his memoirs Mussolini merely states that Grandi came to give him a volume relating to the proceedings on the nonintervention committee. He "touched on various points, but said nothing of what was to come."[14] There is, however, no doubt that Mussolini was in possession of Grandi's draft motion and it seems certain from Zamboni's account and from Bottai's subsequent conversation with Grandi[15] that the latter did in fact give Mussolini a clear indication of the attitude he intended to adopt in the Grand Council. It was in line with Mussolini's mood

* Grandi's version. According to the Germans, the interview lasted three-quarters of an hour (Deakin, *op. cit.*, p. 426).

† Mario Zamboni, a National Councillor and a close friend, who accompanied Grandi, described the atmosphere as bad tempered. (Deakin, *op. cit.*, p. 426.)

of remote detachment that he should have paid no attention to the warning. Indeed he remarked happily to Kesselring, who saw him immediately after Grandi had left: "Do you know Grandi, who has just been with me? We have had a good talk and are in general agreement. He is completely loyal to me." [16]

So confident was Mussolini that when Grandi, "at a certain point" suggested postponing the Grand Council—"a clever move to look like an alibi"—he replied that it was essential to clarify the position. The date had been fixed, the invitations had been issued, and of all the organs of the State the Grand Council was the most suitable for reviewing the problems of the war.[17]

While Grandi and his associates were working for the resignation of the Duce and his replacement by themselves at the head of a constitutional government, the generals in the persons of Ambrosio and Castellano and the Court in the person of Acquarone were independently planning the arrest of the Duce. The circumstance that Grandi's motion might give the King the constitutional pretext he required provided an additional stimulus to their hurried preparations. General Angelo Cerica, who had been appointed commander of the *Carabinieri* on the death of General Hazon, was drawn into the plot, as was General Giacomo Carboni, who had been given command of a motorized corps being formed near Rome, ostensibly to defend the capital against the Germans. Senise was to return as Chief of Police; and it was decided that while the *Carabinieri* under Cerica should, in concert with Senise, undertake the arrest of Mussolini and certain dangerous party leaders, Carboni and the army should be responsible for dealing with any intervention by the Germans or the Fascist militia.[18]

By July 24 preparations were sufficiently advanced to enable Acquarone and Ambrosio to call on Badoglio with the intimation that the King had decided to remove Mussolini and to appoint him head of the government. That evening Grandi sent Zamboni to Acquarone with a letter to the King enclosing a copy of his motion and explaining that it represented an attempt to restore the constitution and the prerogatives of the Sovereign. "We," Grandi concluded, "are about to perform our duty"; and he was confident that the King would save the country.[19] Thus the stage was set for the meeting of the Grand Council the same evening. Of all those who were concerned in the affair only Mussolini and the German ambassador seem to have been unaware that an acute and dangerous crisis was impending.

In his memoirs Mussolini wrote: "I intended the meeting to be a confidential one in which everyone would have the chance of asking for explanations and receiving them; a sort of secret committee. In expectation of a long discussion, the Grand Council was convened for 5 P.M. instead of the usual hour of 10 P.M.[20] Mussolini left the Villa Torlonia as if he were going to a routine meeting of the cabinet or the Grand Council. Rachele, whose instinct was surer, urged him to arrest the dissidents without further ado, but he confidently shrugged off her premonitions. The other members of the Council, clad by order in their black "Saharan" shirts, gathered at the Palazzo Venezia in a mood of anxious trepidation. Grandi had been to confession, had left behind him a last letter to his wife and children, and had taken the precaution of bringing with him two hand grenades. He found the Palazzo Venezia full of militiamen in the courtyard, the corridors, the stairs, and even the apartments. A chill ran down his spine and Bottai whispered to him that it had been a mistake to have revealed everything to the Duce. "This," he said, "is our end."[21] As the Councillors assembled in the Chamber, Grandi took a last opportunity to canvass support for his motion.

II

Shortly after five o'clock Quinto Navarra, the Chief Usher, bearing Mussolini's briefcase, entered the Chamber followed by the Duce, wearing the uniform of the Supreme Commander of the Militia. He thus distinguished himself from the others, who were wearing black bush shirts. Scorza called the usual greeting: "Salute the Duce," and all present shouted the reply: "We salute him." Mussolini, without deigning to look at anyone, seated himself in the embroidered armchair on the raised dais at the head of the table, arranged his papers, and, after Scorza had called the roll, began to speak.

It was a curious speech, for while he defended his conduct at great length, he did so without passion or conviction.[22] The war, he said, had reached an extremely critical stage, and what had at one time seemed impossible, namely, the invasion of the homeland, had now come to pass. In this situation the heterogeneous elements hostile to the regime were closing their ranks and had even provoked symptoms of demoralization in certain Fascists. "At this moment I am certainly the most disliked or, rather, loathed man in Italy"; and this in a sense was understandable.

The sharpest criticism was aimed at those responsible for the military conduct of the war. But he, the Duce, had never wanted the Supreme Command. That had resulted from an initiative by Marshal Badoglio; and here Mussolini read out three documents to prove his point. He had never, he affirmed, directed military operations. Only once had he, in Cavallero's absence, intervened, namely, on the occasion of the victorious sea and air battle off Pantelleria on June 15, 1942. When he fell ill in October, 1942, he had thought of giving up the Command, but did not do so because it seemed wrong to abandon the ship in a storm. So he postponed doing so until after a sunny day, which had not yet appeared. "I think there is nothing further to be said on the question of command."

Another contentious point was the degree of aid from Germany. Without any reference to his many fruitless appeals to Hitler or a single word on the meeting at Feltre, he declared baldly that "we must admit in all fairness that Germany has met us generously and substantially"; and he quoted a long string of figures representing the total German deliveries of raw materials since 1940. In addition 1,500 antiaircraft guns had been provided in response to Italian requests. All this must have sounded unconvincing to men who were aware of Italy's vain requests for unconditional air and armored support. But Mussolini concluded this chapter of his address with the claim that the figures he had cited gave the lie to the "thesis of the defeatists, according to which the Germans had not given Italy the necessary help."

He then went on to say that "another point of the capitulationists is that 'the people's heart is not in the war.'" But the people's heart had never in history been in any war—in 1917 less than in the present war.

There is therefore no need to be overcome by these psychological fluctuations. . . . This is the moment to tighten the reins and to assume the necessary responsibility. I shall have no difficulty in replacing men, in turning the screw, in bringing forces to bear not yet engaged, in the name of our country whose personal integrity is today being violated. In 1917, some provinces of the Veneto were lost but no one spoke of "surrender." Then they spoke of moving the government to Sicily: today, if we must, we shall move it to the Po valley.

In conclusion Mussolini turned to the terms of Grandi's motion, which constituted an appeal to the King. The Sovereign could in that event do one of two things. He could ask the Duce and the regime to carry on. Or he could accept the invitation embodied in the motion and, in accordance with the wishes of reactionary, anti-Fascist, and pro-Anglo-Saxon circles, seize the opportunity to liquidate the regime at one blow. "Gentlemen, beware. Grandi's motion may place the very existence of the regime in jeopardy." [23]

The Duce's opening statement had lasted for nearly two hours. When he had finished, there was a moment's uneasy silence. His halting and disingenuous argument had failed to take with him a single member of the Council. "A disastrous speech," was one muttered comment.

Marshal De Bono followed, and contented himself with a brief defense of the army against accusations of sabotaging the war, while the other surviving Quadrumvir, De Vecchi, made a speech, the purport of which does not seem to have been understood. Mussolini records him as having taken issue with De Bono in an attack on the defeatism of many officers,[24] while he himself claims to have defended the army and to have blamed Fascist education and the political appointments of senior officers.

After this ineffective curtain raiser Grandi rose to speak in a tense and sultry atmosphere. He began by saying that not the army but the dictatorship was responsible for the disaster and that the Italian people had been betrayed from the day on which Italy had been Germanized and blindly cast into the arms of Hitler. It was the Duce who had plunged them into a destructive war without regard for the honor, the sentiment, and the interests of the nation. He read the text of his resolution demanding the restoration of all the organs of the state and the transfer to the King of the effective command of the Armed forces.

He then launched a long, bitter attack on Mussolini's system of personal rule, which had wrecked fascism and brought about the loss of the war. The Duce might accept responsibility, but the Grand Council was also responsible. His own motion sought to create a national front and to enable the King to assume his proper functions. He criticized the activities of the party under Starace and Scorza; and in his peroration he reminded Mussolini of his own slogan in the distant days of 1924: "Let the parties perish, let our own Fascist party perish, so that the Nation may live." In order to defeat the Germans in the First World War, Italy had sacrificed 600,000 lives. Today they once more had the Germans on their soil, and Italian mothers were shouting from the housetops that Mussolini had assassinated their sons.[25] Grandi's philippic had lasted nearly an hour and seemed to arouse no feeling in Mussolini, except that he intervened to deny that he was execrated by Italian mothers, and on another occasion he interjected sarcastically: "Tonight we can also debate that the revolution is finished."[26]

Bottai followed in general support of Grandi, and Ciano confined himself to a statement of the circumstances in which the Pact of Steel was signed against Hitler's undertaking not to raise matters which might lead to war until 1942. "We are not the betrayers, but the betrayed." It was for this factual intervention followed by his vote that he was eighteen months later condemned to death.

Farinacci then rose and submitted the text of his motion which emphasized solidarity with Germany, included the party in the list of state organs to be reactivated, and called on the King to assume the Supreme Command. He demanded the resignation of Ambrosio, an inquiry into the military leadership, a single Axis High Command, and a unified politico-military direction of the war. He concluded with a savage attack on Grandi for provoking the crisis of fascism while the enemy stood on Italian soil.

After a speech by De Marsico, Minister of Justice, in favor of Grandi's motion, Mussolini announced that the party secretary had proposed an adjournment until the following day. Grandi immediately protested that, while they were chattering, hundreds of soldiers were dying. "The destiny of our country is in our hands. Let us go on until we vote." After all, he reminded Mussolini, the Grand Council had been kept up all night in 1927 to discuss the Charter of Labor. Mussolini hesitated a moment, looked round the table, and then said: "As you will."

Federzoni then spoke for Grandi; and Bignardi, Secretary of the Confederation of Agricultural Workers, made an indeterminate intervention on the subject of the morale of the rural community. It was now nearly midnight, and at this point Mussolini, who after seven hours of debate was becoming exhausted, called for a fifteen-minute recess and retired to his study, ostensibly to read the latest reports from the battle front. He was joined by Scorza, Galbiati, and Alfieri, while he sat at his desk quietly sipping a glass of milk and spooning the sugar into his mouth. Alfieri took advantage of the opportunity to urge Mussolini once again to persuade Hitler that Italy could do no more; and he was coldly dismissed. Buffarini, who came in subsequently, urged Mussolini to arrest the lot, and was told to keep calm. Outside the remaining Councillors were waiting anxiously. Some of them were expecting arrest or even sudden death at the hands of the militia. Others were timorously calculating the outcome of the debate. Grandi was busy whipping up support for his motion.

Nothing untoward happened, however, and at the appointed time Mussolini returned to reopen the session. From this moment the debate became even more ragged and untidy. Albini spoke of the internal situation, and Bastiniani once more pleaded for a negotiated end to the war. Galbiati spoke strongly against Grandi, and Mussolini, in a rambling statement, intervened for the second time. He spoke of the enrichment of certain party bosses and with reference to the proposed transfer of power to the King, put the question: "It is then a matter of knowing whether I accept to be beheaded"; and he concluded with the cryptic statement: "And what is more, I have in my head a key which will resolve the war situation. But I will not say what it is." [27]

Scorza, whose attitude was regarded by both sides as equivocal, then rose to put forward his own motion which called for new methods and reforms, and for the revival of the constitutional organs, but did not envisage the transfer of the command to the King. By this time the restless and exhausted Councillors were beginning to drift, even while speakers were on their feet, into the adjoining rooms where a refreshment table had been set up. Alfieri emphasized that the Germans were only concerned to use Italy as a bastion for the defense of German territory. A solution must be found and only the Duce could find it by means of a direct approach to Hitler.

Bottai spoke again, more excitedly according to Mussolini,[28] in an executive attempt to pull together the threads of a disorderly discussion. Grandi after a few words then handed his motion to Mussolini with the names of the nineteen signatories. It was now half past two in the morning and the debate had lasted nearly ten hours. According to Alfieri, Mussolini put the paper in front of him "with affected indifference"; [29] and then "without another word or gesture and in a relaxed and resigned manner" [30] he called on Scorza to put the motion to a vote. A different version is given in one of Grandi's accounts, where Mussolini is described as having looked round the table and as having said slowly and calmly: "I have allowed you all to speak and each of you has expressed his opinion. I could have prevented you and had you all arrested. I did not and I shall not do so. But there are some of you who seem to wish to get rid of me." He went on to recall his long years of service and to express the conviction that the King and the people were behind him. But, when he realized that he was not making an impression, he concluded more loudly: "Yes the King is still in favor of me. I have never had friends, but the King is my friend, and I wonder what those who oppose me tonight will think tomorrow." [31]

In obedience to Mussolini's instructions Scorza rose and, putting Grandi's motion [32] to the vote, began to call the roll. Nineteen voted for the motion, seven, excluding Mussolini, voted against. Suardo, who during the session had labored under deep emotion and had signified that he withdrew his support of Grandi, abstained. Farinacci voted for his own motion, although it was never put to the vote.* According to Grandi, Mussolini, while the vote was being taken sat glowering, with contracted jaws, but with a certain air of detachment. When the vote was completed, he looked at the assembled Councillors one by one in the face and stood up. "You

* These voted:

For Grandi's motion: Grandi, Acerbo, Albini, Alfieri, Balella, Bastianini, Bignardi, Bottai, Cianetti, Ciano, De Bono, De Marsico, De Stefani, De Vecchi, Federzoni, Gottardi, Marinelli, Pareschi, Rossoni.

Against: Biggini, Buffarini, Frattari, Galbiati, Poverelli, Scorza, Tringali-Casanova.

have provoked the crisis of the regime," he said, "the session is closed." Scorza was about to give the "Salute to the Duce" when Mussolini checked him, "No, you are excused." [33] He withdrew to his study, while the Councillors dispersed, many of them without knowing exactly what they had done or what would be the consequence. Gottardi, who was almost stone deaf and was attending his first Grand Council meeting, heard nothing of the proceedings and voted for Grandi because, since Mussolini had put the motion to the vote, it seemed reasonable to assume that he approved it.

In his study Mussolini had some desultory conversation with some of those Councillors who had supported him at the meeting. There was talk of the constitutional powers of the Grand Council, and the Duce was urged to arrest his opponents. But Mussolini was scarcely interested and gave no indication of what was passing through his mind.

It is curious that he should so passively have faced a crisis which threatened his political and even his physical life. He might have reacted more sharply had he not been feeling wretchedly ill. Some months later, speaking at Gargagno to the futurist Marinetti, who also suffered from ulcers, he said:

> You only can understand me, because you have experienced the effects of our ailment. On the night of July 24 I was feeling very ill. Two hours before the wretched meeting of the Grand Council I had a violent attack. . . . I spoke without enthusiasm in a low voice. I was very much troubled by the strong light of the electric lamps, and I turned half away with my hand before my eyes. After my statement the discussion started. I seemed to be assisting at my own trial. I felt as if I were in the dock and at the same time a spectator. I suffered physical pain from the ulcer, but my brain was very lucid. I distinctly heard Grandi's ruthless indictment, but all energy in me was suddenly drained away. You know that this is one of the results of our ailment: it totally saps all energy while conserving a lucidity which I could describe as completely transparent.[34]

This account, given by Mussolini, is borne out by others present at the session. They saw him wincing from the pain, putting his hand to his back, as if to press it away; and they noted with amazement the calm and indifference with which he listened to his accusers. Buffarini described him as wrapped in distant thought, disembodied, and in a different world. "It seemed to me as if he had covered his head with a toga, like Caesar under the dagger thrusts of Brutus and the conspirators." [35]

Nevertheless illness is not the only explanation of Mussolini's behavior, which was not wholly out of character. He knew in his heart, or rather, more accurately, in a compartment of his head, that his accusers were right and that he had failed at Feltre. A few days later he was to admit in captivity: "We must throw off the German yoke. We have a right to tell them that we have been at war for three years and more, lost our mercantile marine and almost all our fleet, and had a large number of towns destroyed. They won't help us. There is nothing else to be done." [36] There was really no answer to Grandi and the others, and Mussolini knew it. Besides he had always disliked unpleasant interviews, and now with failing health, a certain weariness of office, discouragement over the issue of the war, and an increasing sense of detachment, he was less than ever inclined to confront his critics. As Grandi put it, he accepted their blows almost with humility.

Behind this curtain of helpless defeatism other thoughts were coursing through his mind. There was the straw to which he was always clutching: Hitler's promise of secret weapons and a dramatic turn in the Axis fortunes. Moreover, he was confident of the King's support. He had always been able to turn events to his own advantage, and so long as he had his Sovereign behind him, there was always the possibility of an advantageous "*combinazione*," the exact nature of which must be worked out. Night might bring counsel and in the meantime with his customary secretiveness he would not reveal himself even to his closest associates. He dismissed the little gathering in his study and with Scorza returned to the Villa Torlonia. It was three o'clock in the morning.

III

Rachele, who had been waiting all night in a fever of apprehension, ran into the garden to meet Mussolini. His haggard face told her what she wanted to know and she blurted out the question: "You've had them all arrested, I suppose?" "No, but I will," he murmured in reply. She followed him into the study. He looked worn out, and asked her to telephone the Supreme Command and find out whether there had been any air raids or alerts. Rachele already knew that there had been alerts at Milan, Bologna, and many other towns, but she did as she was told. Mussolini was enraged when the Supreme Command replied that all was quiet, and he said sadly to his wife: "There's nothing more I can do; they are set on my ruin. I am afraid my orders do not count any more." [37] They went wearily to bed.

The day of Sunday, July 25, dawned hot and sultry. The city of Rome lay in ignorance of the momentous events of the previous night. The morning newspapers published the Italian war communiqué admitting the fall of Palermo and the German communiqué giving the same news in guarded terms. There was talk of bitter fighting and of the sinking of enemy transports. For the rest the public were informed that an organization had been formed for the recovery of lost children, that mineral water would cost more, and that the race meeting at Villa Glori had been canceled.

Meanwhile, unknown to the population, events were moving fast. In the early hours of the morning Acquarone had called on Grandi to ascertain the outcome of the session of the Grand Council. After some discussion he put to Grandi the pertinent question: how would Mussolini now react. "I would not be surprised," said Grandi, "if he considered the voting tonight as a trump card in the disengaging maneuver which he intends to carry through on his own with Hitler. The only thing which would astonish me would be to see him oppose any decisions of the King." [38] After reporting at the royal villa Acquarone joined Ambrosio at his headquarters, and shortly afterwards they both carried to Marshal Badoglio the signed royal decree appointing him Prime Minister. Thus, there were, for a short time, two Prime Ministers in Italy. The Marshal was in a nervous, restless mood and told his family not to go out, but to put a bottle of champagne on ice. The task of the three men was now to put into operation the existing plan for the arrest of Mussolini. The Grand Council vote had precipitated things, and it might be necessary to move more quickly than they had anticipated.

Mussolini, who was perhaps more disturbed than he had allowed to appear, had slept badly and woke early that morning. When his doctor, Arnaldo Pozzi, appeared at the Villa Torlonia to give him his customary injection, Mussolini was already up. But he refused the injection on the ground that his blood was much too agitated. Nevertheless he was determined to show that he intended to behave as if nothing abnormal had occurred. He ordered his car and drove to the Palazzo Venezia.

I went to my office, as I had done now for nearly twenty-one years, and arrived there about nine o'clock. . . . Scorza did not appear, but telephoned to say that "the night had brought wisdom, and some were beginning to have qualms." "Too late," I answered. Indeed, a little later Cianetti's famous letter arrived, in which he bitterly repented of having voted for Grandi's motion. . . . It was that letter—to which I made no reply—which later saved the writer's life.[39]

Mussolini then tried to summon Grandi, to "ask him why, when he came to see me on Thursday [July 22] . . . he had asked and even beseeched me not to summon the Grand Council. An alibi or a maneuver?"[40] It is not clear why Mussolini wished to see Grandi, but it is possible that he had it in mind to include him in the *combinazione* which was to be proposed to the King. Grandi, however, was not to be found and it was said that he had gone to the country.

At eleven o'clock Albini, the Undersecretary of State at the Ministry of the Interior, presented himself for his usual daily report. Mussolini asked him why he had voted for Grandi's motion, and he replied in some confusion that while he might have been guilty of an error of judgment no one could doubt his devotion to the Duce. "As he left the room, his livid face revealed him as a self-confessed traitor."[41]

Shortly afterwards Mussolini instructed his secretary to telephone to General Puntoni to ask for an audience with the King at five o'clock that afternoon. It had been his practice to report to the King every Monday and Thursday morning, but under the pressure of the Grand Council vote he was seeking to anticipate the normal audience by a few hours. According to Mussolini's account, he intimated that he would come in civilian clothes,[42] but another version states that General Puntoni, when confirming the appointment, added that it was the Sovereign's wish that he should not appear in uniform, a circumstance which aroused Rachele's suspicions as to the King's intentions.[43]

The next visitor was General Galbiati, who had spent a sleepless night embodying his views in a memorandum. In this somewhat hysterical paper, reflecting the shock and disarray caused by the Grand Council's defection, he made a number of proposals, which Mussolini attentively read. He advocated calling a meeting of the party directorate or a joint meeting of federal secretaries and militia consuls. He recommended alternatively that he should be sent to Germany to concert with Himmler for the joint establishment of a new defense system; or that a Mussolinian army should be formed, commanded by himself, to continue the war at the side of the Germans.

Galbiati anxiously awaited the Duce's verdict on his paper, but Mussolini, apparently paralyzed by indecision, did not open his mouth. He held the document in his hand, surveyed it, and placed it on the table. Then he shifted the photograph of his son Bruno and held it up to the light. There was an oppressive and embarrassing silence, broken by Galbiati, who volunteered that Grandi's disappearance was ominous and that the best course would be to arrest the dissident nineteen. Finally Mussolini roused himself. He would not hear of it, he said. After all Grandi's absence was probably due to his sense of shame, especially if he knew that defections had already begun. Cianetti had retracted, Albini had apologized, and soon all of them would be coming around to declare that they had voted in the confident belief that they were acting in the Duce's interest. Secondly, "In a few hours I shall go to the King and examine the position with him. Measures against a particular person must be preceded by his first being replaced in the office which he holds. It is a question of ministers and undersecretaries whom I cannot change without royal assent. And then there are the Collars of the Annunziata, whom I cannot treat in the same way as an ordinary citizen." [44]

None of these arguments was calculated to carry conviction, but Mussolini was not in a mood to take a decisive step, and any excuse was good enough to justify inaction. His plan was to feel his way, as he had done in other difficult situations, before the March on Rome and after the murder of Matteotti, without consulting his henchmen and relying on his intuition. If he refused to be put off balance by the events of the previous night, if he continued to display a calm indifference, he could rely on the King to agree to some arrangement which would enable him to maintain himself at the head of affairs.

As if to prove that his normal routine was not to be upset by a minor domestic squabble, Mussolini did not cancel a long-standing appointment made for noon on July 25 by the new Japanese ambassador. Bastianini introduced the ambassador who, in the name of his Prime Minister, asked for information on the military and political situation in Europe. Mussolini complied with good grace, speaking clearly and lucidly. He said that he approved Japan's policy in the Far East because he considered that when it was no longer possible to deal with events by the force of arms alone it was necessary to fall back on political means. He had tried to convince his friend Hitler of the truth of this observation, but in vain. Speaking of Italy, he emphasized the serious lack of material with which to conduct the war and said that in the following week he would take energetic steps to persuade the Fuehrer to suspend hostilities on the eastern front. If the Reich could reach an accommodation with Russia, it could bring its whole military strength to bear on the Mediterranean. He asked the Japanese ambassador to convey these views to his Prime Minister and to urge him to support Italy's representations. There was no other way out. Circumstances in Italy were such that she would very shortly be unable to continue the struggle and would be compelled to consider a political solution.

When the ambassador took his leave Mussolini shook him warmly by the hand and renewed his request that the Japanese Prime Minister should help him to convince Hitler. Italy had no other course open to her.[45] Bastianini stayed behind to discuss current affairs and there was no reference to the proceedings of the Grand Council or to the afternoon appointment with the King at the Villa Savoia. It had been arranged that Goering should pay a courtesy visit to Rome on July 29 to present the Fuehrer's good wishes on the occasion of the Duce's birthday, but Mussolini informed Bastianini that he did not consider the moment suitable for such formalities and that he had therefore asked Goering to come on July 27. Bastianini was to instruct Alfieri (the Italian ambassador to Germany), if he had not already returned to Berlin, to remain in Rome since he would be required to be present at the interview with Goering. He probably had it in mind to use Goering's visit to ventilate the ideas which he had exposed to the Japanese ambassador. They represented, so far as he could see, the only way out of his predicament.

There was no sign that Mussolini was not confident that he would continue to be Prime Minister and he exerted himself to give an impression of self-possession and poise. Nevertheless he acted and moved and spoke as if he were in a trance, and seemed still to be a prey to the sensation of the previous night that he was now only a spectator and not an actor; and this caused him to exhibit a certain cold detachment and worried malaise.

Before going home to lunch, Mussolini summoned Galbiati to accompany him to the districts which had suffered badly in the air attack of July 19. On the way Mussolini reverted to the Galbiati memorandum. The members of the Grand Council, he said, were cowards who accused him of having usurped their functions or of having called on them too late. Galbiati ingratiatingly replied that they were cowards who should be locked up and Mussolini retorted: "They have sniffed the contrary wind, and felt the approaching storm, as happens with certain species of animals, and they fool themselves into creating an alibi. It never occurs to these pusillanimous creatures that when he who raised them up on his own shoulders is no longer here, they will feel pretty miserable in the mortal dust." [46] Galbiati asked whether Germany would send reinforcements and Mussolini was reluctant to discuss the subject. Sicily, he said, had given an unfortunate occasion to draw comparisons between the two allied armies. Someone at Feltre, after making disparaging remarks about Italy, had inquired of him in an offhand manner against whom it was proposed to use all the weapons for which he was asking. It was all very depressing.

At San Lorenzo, to the surprise of the onlookers, Mussolini left his car, chatted for a few minutes, distributed money, made some written notes, and drove away. He was well received and, as usual, contact with the masses seemed to have stimulated him. To Galbiati he said that no action which might complicate matters should be taken against the party riffraff. That afternoon he would settle matters with the King. When Galbiati asked him how he stood with the King, Mussolini replied: "I have never done anything without his complete agreement. For more than twenty years I have been to see him once or twice a week. I have consulted him on every matter of state and even private questions. He has always been solidly with me."[47] At about three o'clock Galbiati left Mussolini's car as it entered the Via Torlonia by the side entrance in the Via Spallanzani.

At the Villa Torlonia, Mussolini ate without appetite a little soup and stewed fruit. "An oppressive sultriness weighed on things and people. It sank down on Rome from a motionless sky." He spent some time talking to Rachele, to whom he once more expressed his confidence in the King. But she was not to be reassured, and in vain begged him not to go to the audience, from which, she told him, he would never return.[48]

While the Duce was deluding himself about his impending audience, Acquarone was busily engaged in advancing the preparations for the arrest. Together with Ambrosio, Castellano, Carboni, and Cerica the final plans were drawn up. It had already been agreed that the *Carabinieri* should make the actual arrest, while Carboni should take over the Rome garrison. Two junior *Carabinieri* officers were selected and briefed, and orders were issued that all *Carabinieri* units in Rome should be confined to barracks on the pretext that their new commander intended to pay a visit of inspection. Thus a reserve would be immediately to hand to meet an emergency such as a revolt by Mussolini or a move by the Fascist militia.

The plan envisaged the use of a motor ambulance and a detachment of fifty *Carabinieri* in a truck. The ambulance would be parked in the drive of the Villa Savoia, not far from the front door, while the truck and the detachment would be hidden from view in the garden behind the house. In order to avoid any risk of an incident in the streets, the conspirators favored making the arrest in the grounds of the villa. The Queen, who always exercised a strong influence over her husband, objected that to capture the Prime Minister in the royal residence would be an act unworthy of a Sovereign and an abuse of the laws of hospitality. Eventually, at the last moment, under pressure, the King gave his reluctant and ill-tempered assent to the arrangement.

As the afternoon wore on the news of Mussolini's reverse at the hands of the Grand Council began to be bruited about in Rome. Fascist nabobs lunching in a restaurant in the Piazza Colonna were overheard discussing the session and at the house of Ivanoe Bonomi a few prominent anti-Fascists had gathered to discuss the implications of a Badoglio government. But in the provinces all was still normal. The usual Fascist Sunday functions were in progress, troops were being sent on normal leave, and the movie houses were showing newsreels depicting Mussolini at a public function surrounded by applauding crowds.

IV

As five o'clock approached all the actors were preparing to walk on. The ambulance and the truck took up their appointed stations. Mussolini was assembling the papers he would require: the Act constituting the Grand Council, Cianetti's letter of retraction, and other documents proving that the resolution of the Grand Council had no binding force. "I thought," he wrote, "the King would withdraw his delegation of authority of June 10, 1940, concerning the command of the Armed Forces, a command which I had for some time past been thinking of relinquishing." His mind was completely free from any forebodings.[49] Just before he left for his appointment Scorza telephoned to say that Graziani would accept the appointment of Chief of Staff in succession to Ambrosio; and Mussolini cheerfully undertook to summon Graziani after the audience.

In the Villa Savoia the King was nervously putting the finishing touches to his own arrangements. To General Puntoni he said, "As I do not know how the Duce will react, I would ask you to stand by the door of the drawing room where we shall retire to talk. You can then intervene if need arises." [50]

Shortly before five o'clock Mussolini's car entered the main gate of the royal villa, which had been opened in anticipation of his arrival. He was accompanied by his private secretary, De Cesare, while the three cars carrying his detectives and escort remained, as was the usual practice, outside. He noticed "reinforcements of *Carabinieri,* but that did not seem out of the ordinary." [51] To the end he was able to convince himself that all would be well. As if to confirm this impression, the King, in Marshal's uniform, was waiting for him in the doorway. Together they went up to the drawing room.

The conversation did not, however, take its predicted course. Mussolini began to give an account of the military situation and dwelled for some time on the session of the Grand Council, emphasizing that its role was purely consultative and that in consequence its vote could have no constitutional significance. He tried to appear calm, but his hands were shaking and he found it difficult to hold steady the notes between his fingers. The King, who was not disposed to argue, intervened to say that it was useless to go on. Italy was defeated, army morale had collapsed, and the Alpine regiments were singing a song, which the King recited in Piedmontese dialect, to the effect that they would no longer fight for Mussolini. At the moment the Duce was the most hated man in Italy, without a friend except the Sovereign, who would insure the safety of his person.

The King went on to say that in this situation he must require the Duce's resignation, and he told him that he had already appointed Badoglio to be head of the government. When Mussolini attempted to argue that the King was taking a grave decision which would have disastrous consequences, he was cut short, and General Puntoni through the door heard the King repeating several times: "I am sorry, I am sorry, but the solution could not have been otherwise." [52] The audience was over. The King accompanied Mussolini to the front door, where he said goodby. "On the threshold," Mussolini recorded, "he shook me by the hand with great warmth." [53] The interview had passed off without incident, and Mussolini seemed ready to accept his Sovereign's decision.

While the audience was in progress Mussolini's chauffeur had been lured into the porter's lodge on the pretext that he was wanted on the telephone. There he was seized and incarcerated till all was over. The ambulance was backed in such a manner as to make it convenient for Mussolini to enter it at the rear, and the two *Carabinieri* officers took up their positions.

As Mussolini, accompanied by De Cesare, emerged from the villa he was confronted by one of the two *Carabinieri* officers who said to him: "His Majesty has charged me with the protection of your person." When Mussolini retorted that this was unnecessary and made for his driverless car, the officers declared that he was under orders: "No, Excellency, you must come in my car." Mussolini said nothing further, but followed meekly to the rear door of the ambulance, where he hesitated. Three *Carabinieri* noncommissioned officers were drawn up on the near side of the door, while three plainclothes policemen were posted on the other side of the ambulance. The officer, supporting Mussolini by the elbow, helped him to mount the steps and sat down beside him. The second officer and De Cesare went to the front, and the three *Carabinieri* and the three policemen then entered the ambulance. It became a somewhat overcrowded vehicle.

The doors were shut and the driver made off at high speed through the hot, deserted streets. In the city everything still appeared normal. The band of the antiaircraft militia was giving its customary outdoor Sunday concert and the police band was playing in the Pincio. The police, who always guarded the Duce's route whenever he was at large, were standing in the torrid heat, anxiously awaiting the end of the audience. Eventually a car passed down their ranks and someone leaning from the window told them that they could go home since the Duce was not returning to the Palazzo Venezia. Mussolini had not yet grasped what had happened to him, and still thought that "all this was being done, as the King had said, in order to protect my person." [54]

In a short time the ambulance arrived at the Podgora *Carabinieri* barracks in Trastevere. In the courtyard Mussolini alighted and was taken to the officers' quarters, where he was lodged under an armed guard. Shortly afterwards he was removed for safety's sake to the barracks of the *Carabinieri* cadet school in the Via Legnano. That evening he was visited by a doctor and refused medical attention, but he chatted quietly and dispassionately about the situation. The new government, he said, was a good administration, which would continue the directives of their predecessors. There might be pacifist demonstrations in the Po valley, which would be easily suppressed, for the Italian people were superficial.[55] The doctor left him and he remained shut up in the Colonel's office. While he was assured that it was only a question of protecting him, he saw the sentries outside the door and, for the first time began to wonder whether after all he was not in captivity. What possible danger could there be in a barracks containing two thousand *Carabinieri* cadets? [56] He refused all food and at eleven o'clock turned out his light.

CHAPTER TWENTY-ONE

Imprisonment and Rescue

1943

I

OUTSIDE the barrack walls the twenty-one-year-old Fascist movement had soundlessly collapsed like a soap bubble in the breeze. In the evening the party secretary, who alone had the means of calling the party out to the defense of the Duce, visited General Cerica and was told that Mussolini was under arrest. Scorza was released on parole against an undertaking to issue an immediate instruction that there was to be no bloodshed. The telegrams were duly sent, but whether or not on Scorza's orders has never been cleared up. In any event Scorza went immediately into hiding, and the party remained quiescent.

Similarly Galbiati, who might have called out the Fascist militia, threw in the sponge without a struggle. After frenzied confabulations and in the face of the measures taken by the army, he telephoned to Albini at the Ministry of the Interior: "I request you to inform whoever at this moment is responsible for the government that the militia remains faithful to its principles, which are: to serve the Fatherland in the joint names of the King and the Duce." [1] At midnight he received a message from Badoglio instructing him to hand over his command to a soldier, General Armellini. He immediately complied. Thus the transfer of power had taken place without loss of life. The various militia units in the country made no move, and the only disorder was caused by about a hundred militiamen, who were quickly disarmed in the streets of Rome. As the day closed the communications centers and other key points were safely in the hands of the military.

At 10:45 P.M. the Italian radio broadcast the text of three messages announcing the Duce's resignation, the appointment of Badoglio, the assumption of the Supreme Command by the King, and the continuance of the war at the side of Germany.[2] In London the news was picked up by the monitoring service of the B.B.C. It was at once incorporated in the three news bulletins of the European Service which at the moment were on the air; and in a short time it had circled the globe.

In the streets of Rome amazed and excited crowds thronged the streets. Fascist emblems were destroyed and a concourse of people marched on the Quirinal to acclaim the Sovereign. The news that the war would go on did little to damp the general enthusiasm. It was thought, and not erroneously, that Badoglio was maneuvering for position. It would be peace at last.

Of the formerly active party leaders nothing was heard or seen. Many were arrested without incident. Of the others, Manlio Morgagni, director of the Stefani news agency, committed suicide; Alessandro Pavolini, editor of the Rome *Messagero,* of whom more will be heard, disappeared after asking that the salary due to him should be paid to his wife; Farinacci fled to the German embassy, whence he secured air passage to Germany. In the early hours of the morning Host Venturi, the former Minister of Communications, walked the streets "to see whether the party had made any move. Everything was deserted and complete calm reigned." [3] Later Mussolini was to liken the conduct of his followers to the behavior of the disciples on the Mount of Olives. But if anyone was to blame, it was not the party disciples but Mussolini, who for a decade had deliberately so devitalized the party that it was incapable of any spontaneous movement. He had made himself the mainspring of the system, and when he broke it ceased to function.

At one o'clock on the morning of Monday, July 26, the commanding officer came into Mussolini's room and told him that General Ernesto Ferone of the General Staff had arrived with a message from Marshal Badoglio. Mussolini rose and went into the next room where he was handed an envelope addressed in the Marshal's hand to "Cavaliere Sig. Benito Mussolini":

The undersigned Head of the Government wishes to inform Your Excellency that what has been done in your regard has been done solely in your personal interest, detailed information having reached us from several quarters of a serious plot against your person. He much regrets this, and wishes to inform you that he is prepared to give orders for your safe accompanying, with all proper respect, to whatever place you may choose.

Mussolini, after reading this missive, immediately dictated his reply to General Ferone, who wrote it down on a piece of paper.

1. I wish to thank Marshal Badoglio for the attention he is according to my person.

2. The only residence at my disposal is Rocca delle Caminate, whither I am prepared to go at any moment.

3. I wish to assure Marshal Badoglio, if only in remembrance of the work we have done together in the past, that not only will I raise no difficulties of any sort, but I will cooperate in every possible way.

4. I am glad of the decision to continue the war together with our allies, as the honor and the interests of the country require at this time, and I express my earnest hope that success will crown the grave task which Marshal Badoglio is assuming by order and in the name of His Majesty the King, whose loyal servant I have been for twenty-one years and shall continue to be. Long live Italy! [4]

It would have been difficult to have drafted a more acquiescent and submissive answer. The fact was that Mussolini, conscious of and overwhelmed by his own failure, was in a mood to abdicate; and he could think of no better solution than to retire quietly to political obscurity in his native Romagna. He was thus not in a position to censure his followers, as he subsequently did, for their various acts of abdication. But, as has already been observed, Mussolini was never prepared to apply to himself the standards which he exacted from others.

There is no reason to believe that Badoglio's offer was other than sincere. Unfortunately, according to a reliable version, security objections began immediately to present themselves. In particular the Fascist prefect of Forlì strongly advised against the move on the ground that the people of Romagna had broken loose and that no display of force could guarantee that Mussolini would not be lynched by his infuriated fellow countrymen.[5] So it was decided at the last minute to send Mussolini to the Ponza archipelago, and to entrust the operation to Admiral Franco Maugeri, the head of Naval Intelligence. Mussolini was, however, not informed of this change of plan, and continued for two dreary days in the *Carabinieri* barracks impatiently to await the departure for his beloved homestead.

II

Eventually at seven o'clock on the evening of July 27 the *Carabinieri* were alerted, a convoy of cars entered the barracks, and Mussolini was told that the order to leave had come. He still believed that he was being taken home, but soon through a split in the blinds of the car he perceived that he was being taken south. In reply to a question he was told that the orders had been changed. At Gaeta the cars stopped and Mussolini was handed over to Admiral Maugeri, who was awaiting him on the wharf and who escorted him to the corvette "Persefone."

Shortly before dawn the vessel weighed anchor and proceeded to the island of Ventotene, where a police inspector went ashore to see if the island could provide a suitable residence. He returned with the bad news that there was a German garrison on the island, and Admiral Maugeri decided to proceed to Ponza, a well-known penal settlement. Among the political prisoners on the island at the time were Tito Zaniboni, who was alleged to have tried to shoot Mussolini in 1925, and his old friend Pietro Nenni, who had been imprisoned with him at Forlì during the war in Tripoli. On this occasion, however, they did not meet and Nenni was shortly afterwards set free.

On the way Mussolini had some conversation with Admiral Maugeri. He seemed resigned to his fate, but complained of the ungenerous behavior of the Badoglio government. After all he had shown magnanimity in 1922 when he had left his former political opponents at liberty, and had even made Facta a senator. Besides it was all pointless, for he no longer constituted a danger to anyone. "What are they afraid of? I am politically defunct." [6]

He also attempted to justify himself and to put the blame on Hitler for the misfortunes of the Axis. It had been, he said, a capital error to attack Russia and the Germans had never grasped the importance of the Mediterranean theater. Moreover, the mistake having been made, Hitler had declined to retrace his steps; and Mussolini proceeded to give a varnished account of the conversations at Salzburg and Feltre.

I advised Hitler to come to an agreement with Russia and latterly to do so at any price, giving up everything he had conquered, the Ukraine included. . . . It was no good. . . . At Salzburg * I told him: "We can't get back into Africa again, the Italian islands will be invaded; there is only one last hope, and that is to make peace with Russia and switch your whole potential over to the Mediterranean. You can't help us, not because you don't want to, but because you cannot do so until you have made peace with Russia." The talk at Feltre did not go off well. . . . As usual, none of the questions on the agenda were dealt with at all, but only quite different ones. I repeated my old theme peace with Russia. Impossibility of the Germans giving us any substantial aid.[7]

The corvette anchored off Ponza and once again the police officers made a reconnaissance, this time with a satisfactory outcome. So Mussolini was landed and lodged in a small, bare dwelling which had housed the Abyssinian Ras Imeru. There he passed ten Spartan, uneventful days. On July 29 he celebrated his sixtieth birthday and Goering sent him a telegram of congratulation, which was duly delivered. According to his own account,[8] he spent his time in solitude, translating Carducci's *Odi barbare* into German and reading Giuseppe Ricciotti's *Life of Jesus,* which he later left as a gift to the parish priest.

Misfortune and solitude caused Mussolini for a brief period to turn his thoughts to religion. To his sister Edvige he wrote on August 31 that he had begun after forty years to approach his religion.

A parish priest of excellent repute busied himself over this. Then I went away and his labors were interrupted. In any event in one of the files which I kept close to the lamp in the Palazzo Venezia and which I have asked for in vain, there is in my handwriting a testament—May, 1943—which says: "Born Catholic, Apostolic, Roman, so I intend to die. I do not want funerals and funeral honors of any kind." I bring to your knowledge that this is my wish.[9]

* April 7–10, 1943.

On August 5, just before he left Ponza, he wrote to the parish priest to ask that a Mass should be said for his son Bruno, "killed in air combat over Pisa." * The letter ended with a phrase which expressed his weary disillusionment: "Through Ricciotti's work [*The Life of Jesus* referred to above] Italy may perhaps have achieved pre-eminence in another field." [10]

His letter to Edvige also expressed a calm, even dignified, resignation. "Think of me sometimes. I do not repine at all and am prepared to defend myself. If not men, time will do me justice, and will distribute the burden of responsibility." In a second letter he wrote: "I get the war communiqués and other sporadic and occasional news. But I only require to know what is indispensable. I do not even want the newspapers. . . . I believe that after this month is over my peregrinations will come to an end and that—once the anger of my Romagna people has been placated—I shall be allowed to go to the Rocca, and there peacefully await the end of my life, which I hope will come soon." [11]

Resignation was also reflected in the historical jottings which he made at Ponza. "When a man and his organism collapse, then the fall is irretrievable, particularly if the man is over sixty"; and "I am able to arrive at two conclusions: that my system has collapsed, and that my overthrow was final." One single day of victory, the day which he called the "day of sunshine," would, he said, have restored the situation, as was shown by the enthusiasm with which rumors that the Sicily landing had failed were greeted by the people. But the day never came.[12]

On August 1 some of Mussolini's effects arrived and he was able for the first time since his arrest to enjoy a change of clothes. He also received a letter from his wife and some much-needed money. On August 2 he had a recurrence of his gastric trouble, but he soon recovered and was able to bathe.

On August 6 the Badoglio government, fearful of a German attempt to rescue Mussolini, decided to move Mussolini to the more secluded island of La Maddelena, a small naval base off Sardinia. The operation was again entrusted to Admiral Maugeri, who arrived at Ponza in a destroyer late that night. In the early hours

* He was in fact killed in a training flight.

of the morning Mussolini and the members of his escort were embarked. Maugeri found him looking bolder, less flaccid, and with a better color. When the admiral explained to him that the Germans might be planning to rescue him, he flared up: "That," he replied, "is the greatest humiliation which could be inflicted on me. And do they really think that I might go off to Germany and try to seize the reins again with German aid? Ah no, I should think not."[13] A little later he was to write: "I had never nourished any hope of being liberated by Italians, even Fascists. . . . From the very beginning I felt sure that the Fuehrer would do everything to try and rescue me."[14]

In general, Maugeri found him not only better in appearance but rather less submissive than he had been ten days previously, when he was still suffering from the shock of his sudden dismissal. The days of fascism, Mussolini declared, would be regretted; and a note of vindictiveness had begun to creep into his comments on the conduct of leading Fascists. Scorza had played an ambiguous role; Ciano was scornfully described as a "truly wretched creature"; and Farinacci was "incorrigible." The impression left on the Admiral was that Mussolini no longer felt "politically defunct," as he had described himself on the journey to Ponza.[15]

On La Maddelena, Mussolini was lodged in a villa built by an Englishman and providing relatively comfortable quarters. "A senior officer's room" was the comment of the local admiral, as he supervised the installation of the Duce. Once again, Mussolini was virtually cut off from the outside world. He was allowed to write some family letters and to receive a surprise gift from Hitler, a splendid complete edition of Nietzsche's works in twenty-four volumes with a signed dedication. Accompanying it was a letter from Marshal Kesselring: "The Fuehrer will consider himself happy if this great work of German literature gives you a little pleasure, Duce, and if you will consider it as an expression of the Fuehrer's special attachment to you."[16]

III

On August 18, after he had been ten days on the island, a German aircraft flew so low over the house that Mussolini was able to see the pilot's face. Not long afterwards he was not surprised to be told that he would be leaving. At 4 A.M. on August 28 he was embarked in a Red Cross seaplane and flown to Lake Bracciano, north of Rome, where he was met by a *Carabinieri* officer and a police inspector. A journey by motor ambulance took him to an inn close to the starting point of a funicular railway leading to the Gran Sasso, a ski resort in the Apennines. After a week it appeared to the *Carabinieri* officer and the police inspector that the Germans were taking a suspicious interest in the place. A German military car sought to approach the funicular station and a German aircraft made several reconnaissance flights over the inn. Mussolini's guardians decided on September 6 to move him to the Campo Imperatore Hotel on the mountain top, which had been cleared of its summer guests. Mussolini was reluctant to move and inquired whether the funicular was safe, adding: "Not for my sake, because my life is over, but for those who accompany me."

In the hotel he was given a luxurious apartment on the second floor, and he settled down again to the regular, monotonous existence of a prisoner. According to the manageress of the hotel [17] he neither read nor wrote, but sat with a thoughtful expression on his face, whenever he saw that he was being observed. He ate in the dining room, listened to the wireless, played cards, and chatted endlessly with the police inspector and other members of his guard. They noticed, as Admiral Maugeri had done, that he was critical of Hitler's Russian war and of his former political associates. One of his favorite topics was his own betrayal, and his resentment was principally directed against Ciano, Grandi, Farinacci, and various generals and admirals. Although he had one mild gastric attack, his health seemed to improve in the keen mountain air. He spoke of skiing as soon as snow fell; and the whole party settled down to a long stay on the mountain. Some of the policemen had already brought up their skis and winter sport equipment.

The Germans, however, had other ideas. In the intervening month both Hitler and Badoglio had been playing for time and jockeying for position. Hitler, although maddened by Italian treachery, was prudently reluctant to push Badoglio into the arms of the Allies before he himself was fully ready to take over Italy, while Badoglio, for his part, was determined not to bring things to a head until he had made his arrangements with the Allies.

Nevertheless on one point Hitler made up his mind at once. As early as July 27 Otto Skorzeny, commander of a special S. S. Commando unit, was summoned to Rastenburg and selected to lead an operation for Mussolini's release. The details were to be worked out by Skorzeny in concert with General Student in Rome and a small circle of German officials. An elaborate game of hide-and-seek followed, the Italians always one step ahead of the Germans. There were many false trails, and Skorzeny lost much time following them up. Thus a German officer was sent to reconnoiter Ventotene, but in the meantime Mussolini had been moved to La Maddelena. He was traced there by the German Chief of Police in Rome, who intercepted a letter from Edda Ciano to her father. Skorzeny attempted to confirm this report and was in the aircraft which Mussolini saw flying low over his house, but any doubt which remained was finally resolved when an officer, sent to make a reconnaissance, returned with the information that he had seen Mussolini. Urgent measures were taken to organize an operation, but before they could be put into effect news reached the disconsolate Germans that Mussolini had left La Maddalena for a unknown destination. At the beginning of September Skorzeny was back where he started.

The first days of September saw two events, the first of which presented Hitler with an immediate problem, while the second was not to have an impact on events for some considerable time. On September 8 the Italian radio announced the surrender of the Badoglio government to the Allies, and three days later the Germans seized Rome. On September 3 the National Liberation Committee, composed of all parties, was formed in Rome. It was this Committee which later was to give its impetus to a fratricidal war of unexampled bitterness and ferocity.

Skorzeny was, however, not concerned with either of these events, and he continued with singleminded pertinacity to track down his quarry. There were false alarms, but eventually reliable intelligence pointed to Gran Sasso, and preparations were put in hand. The circumstance that Badoglio had capitulated added both to the urgency and the difficulty of the operation. On September 8 Skorzeny undertook an aerial reconnaissance of the mountain, which seemed to show that close to the hotel there was a small flat patch on which gliders might be landed. It was accordingly decided that, while one party seized the funicular station at the bottom of the mountain, twelve gliders should land a hundred and twenty men under Skorzeny's command to capture the hotel. In order to confuse Mussolini's *Carabinieri* guard, an Italian officer, General Soleti, was at the last moment forced into accompanying the expedition.

IV

On September 12 the funicular station was occupied without incident and shortly afterwards, at about two o'clock, the gliders, which had been launched from the German airfield at Pratica di Mare, were released over the Gran Sasso. Unfortunately the flat piece of ground seen on the photograph turned out to be a stiff slope; and one glider crashed badly, seriously injuring its occupants, while three others failed to land. Nevertheless eight gliders, carrying a sufficient force for the purpose together with the invaluable Soleti and the commander, made a successful landing some two or three hundred yards from the hotel.

Mussolini at his window was a spectator of the extraordinary scene. The first man to appear was General Soleti, followed by a German officer who was pressing a gun into his ribs. He ran forward, calling on the *Carabinieri* not to shoot, while Mussolini, leaning out of his window, was shouting the same instruction in Italian and in German. As it happened there was never any danger of bloodshed. Some of the *Carabinieri* fled down the mountainside, while the remainder allowed themselves to be overrun.* Within a few minutes the garrison had capitulated and Skorzeny was in Mussolini's room. The Duce looked aged and ill, an impression intensified by the fact that he was unshaven and that his usually smooth head was covered by short stubbly hair.

According to Domenico Antonelli,[18] manager of the hotel from September 11, Mussolini was told that his family had been taken to Vienna and that he could join them that same day, but he replied that he would prefer to go to Rocca delle Caminate. The German

* It seems that in consequence of events in Rome, Senise, the Chief of Police, had instructed the police inspector in the hotel to be "prudent," that is to say, not to offer armed resistance to any German incursion.

plan, however, laid down categorically that the Duce should be taken back to the air base in a Storch aircraft which had landed with the gliders; and Skorzeny was obliged to insist that there should be no modification of this arrangement. The Duce somewhat reluctantly agreed to comply.

Some time was spent preparing for the departure, and at about half-past four Mussolini emerged from the hotel, dressed in a long overcoat and a dark pork-pie hat, looking less like a dictator than a seedy actor. He shook hands with the hotel staff, advanced with a "youthful elastic step" towards the Storch and, after a moment's hesitation, climbed in. Skorzeny, who was a large heavy man, insisted on accompanying him. His own weight constituted an additional risk to the Duce, but he knew that the take-off would be hazardous, and he was not prepared to face the Fuehrer alive after a fatal accident to the Duce.

Under its excessive weight the Storch lurched forward over the uneven ground, pushed its nose over the edge, and for a time looked as if it must plunge to destruction. At the last moment the pilot was able to right the craft and to set course for Rome. Skorzeny noticed that Mussolini looked pale and shaken, but no word was spoken. It had been a close thing.

On arrival at Pratica di Mare, Mussolini was transferred to a comfortable Heinkel aircraft and flown to Vienna, still under the escort of Skorzeny. It is not clear why he was taken to Vienna, when his family had been flown by Hitler's order from Forlì to Munich the previous day. In any event he arrived safely at Vienna airport shortly before midnight and was taken, still with Skorzeny, to the Hotel Continental. It had been a long, physically and emotionally exhausting day and he was so worn out that he had no thought but to go to bed. When the elated Fuehrer telephoned shortly afterwards, Mussolini replied that he was tired and sick and would first of all like to have a long sleep. He added that on the following day he wanted to visit his family in Munich.

Goebbels was doubtful whether the Duce was capable of playing a useful role, and he was realistic enough to see that his elimination would carry many practical advantages. It would enable the Germans to do what they thought fit in Italy without any inhibitions, to annex Italian territory and wipe the slate clean, whereas "a regime under the leadership of the Duce would presumably fall heir to all the rights and duties incident to the Three-Power Pact. A rather distressing prospect." Hitler, however, was looking forward to meeting Mussolini and was determined, if only on ideological grounds, that he should be restored to power. National Socialism had in a sense sprung from fascism, and Hitler was obsessed by the idea that the collapse of fascism might set an unfortunate example before the Germans.*

On September 13 Mussolini arrived at Munich, where he was met by Rachele and members of his family. She had expected to find him exhausted, but his "deathly pallor" gave her a shock. Together they spent a domestic evening in the former Karl palace, placed at their disposal by the German government. Rachele busied hereslf about her man and prepared a bath, of which he was greatly in need. "He had not had a change of clothes for some time and his socks were sticking to his feet." Husband and wife sat up together exchanging information and listening to the news from Italy given out by Fascist broadcasts from Munich. It was late when they went to bed.[19]

V

On the following day, September 14, Mussolini left for Hitler's headquarters. He was no longer the Duce of fascism, traveling in his own train with his suite, to meet his ostensible equal amidst the ritual pomp which normally attended such gatherings. He was now a lonely fugitive in a German aircraft dependent on the resources and good will of his hosts. He was, after six weeks, hopelessly out of touch with affairs and he had no plans for his own future. There was certainly in his demeanor no trace of resolution to recover his lost position. The man who throughout his life had been ready to sacrifice all for power, now seemed ready to relinquish it for the sake of peace and quiet.

Hitler received him with warmth. "The mutual greetings," wrote Goebbels, "were exceptionally cordial and friendly. The Fuehrer awaited him outside his bunker with the Duce's son Vittorio. Hitler

* Goebbels wrote: "The Fuehrer invoked final measures to preclude similar developments with us once and for all." (Diary entry for September 11, 1943.)

and Mussolini embraced after their long separation." * It was a deeply moving example of loyalty between men and comrades." [20] The two men withdrew for a private conversation which lasted two hours. †

Later that evening Mussolini received a small group of faithful Fascists, who had been gathered together by the Germans at Rastenburg in the hope that they would form the core of a new Fascist administration. It was not a satisfactory meeting, for the henchmen were expecting strong leadership which was not forthcoming, while Mussolini was disconcerted at their ardor. He was clearly not sure of himself and gave the impression that he considered himself out of the picture or at least wished to remain so. When Pavolini reiterated the need for a leader, Mussolini replied: "At this moment I cannot take any decisions. I lack too many elements to form a judgment. Let us see tomorrow." [21] But it was Hitler who was to take the decision for him.

Next morning there was another conversation with Hitler; and Goebbels has left a secondhand account of what passed between them.

The Fuehrer told me in detail about the Duce's visit, which had stirred him deeply. The Duce's personality did not impress him as powerfully this time as at their earlier meetings. The main reason may be that the Duce now came to the Fuehrer without any power and that the Fuehrer accordingly looked at him somewhat more critically. The Duce has not drawn the moral conclusions from Italy's catastrophe which the Fuehrer expected. He was naturally overjoyed to see the Fuehrer and to be fully at liberty again. But the Fuehrer expected that the first thing the Duce would do would be to wreak full vengeance on his betrayers. He gave no

---

* It was in fact less than two months after the disastrous meeting at Feltre.

† There is no record of the Hitler-Mussolini conversations of September 14 and 15. Professor Wiskemann relies largely on the account in *Il Memento,* said to be based on notes left by Mezzasomma, Minister of Propaganda at Salò, and other Neo-Fascists. But Tamaro (I, 560) baldly declares this version to be apocryphal. Goebbels gives the version he obtained from Hitler; and Anfuso (p. 326 ff.) that which he obtained from Mussolini, which differs radically from that of Mezzasomma. There is a less reliable secondhand account in Carlo Silvestri's *Mussolini, Graziani e l'antifascismo,* summarized in Pini and Susmel, IV, 325. It is, however, possible to reconstruct what passed. There is no doubt that Hitler was determined to put Mussolini back into the saddle under German protection; and Mussolini, though he hankered after a quiet life, soon saw that he had no alternative but to comply.

such indication, however, which showed his real limitations. He is not a revolutionary like the Fuehrer or Stalin. . . . The Fuehrer had the greatest difficulty in convincing him that at least Grandi was a deliberate traitor to the Fascist party. . . . I have never before seen the Fuehrer so disappointed in the Duce as this time. The Fuehrer now realizes that Italy never was a power, is no power today, and will not be a power in the future. Italy has abdicated as a people and as a nation.[22]

Hitler's assessment of Mussolini's frame of mind was perfectly correct, and he spoke frankly and tartly. "What is this sort of fascism which melts like snow before the sun?" he inquired. "For years I have explained to my generals that fascism was the soundest alliance for the German people. I have never concealed my distrust of the Italian monarchy; at your insistence, however, I did nothing to obstruct the work which you carried out to the advantage of your King. But I must confess to you that we Germans have never understood your attitude." [23] Nevertheless, according to the version given by Mussolini to Anfuso, Hitler, on the assumption that the Duce would play his allotted role, was ready to promise that Italy would not be made to suffer for Badoglio's behavior. "The war must be won," Hitler said, "and once it is won, Italy will be restored to her rights. The fundamental condition is that fascism be reborn and that the traitors be brought to justice." Conversely, of course, if Mussolini refused to comply, as at one time he showed signs of doing, Hitler would have to treat Italy as the enemy she was. The country would be occupied and German officials sent to govern it.[24]

It seemed to Mussolini that, as a corollary, a new army must be raised, but on this point Hitler was reserved; and indeed the issue was to constitute a constant source of friction during the months ahead. On the subject of criminal proceedings against Ciano and the other Fascist traitors Hitler did not press his guest too hard at this early stage. Having made his point, he said: "I understand, Duce, your family feelings." [25] But, as part of his program, he intended to see in due course that the delinquents should be made to pay for their crime.

The upshot of the conversations was summarized by Goebbels:

He [Mussolini] has arranged for the Fuehrer not to return to Italy for the present. He wants to establish his temporary seat of government some-

> where in southern Germany. All our political and military measures remain intact; the Fuehrer has insisted that no change be made. The Duce intends first to build the Fascist party. . . . As the crown of this work he then proposes to call a constitutional convention. Its task would be to eliminate the House of Savoy. The Duce is still somewhat hesitant about taking this action as he is of course aware of the strong ties between the Italian people and the Royal House and knows that these ties cannot be severed lightly. . . . On the whole I am very glad that the Fuehrer has stuck to his original intentions. Obviously, sentimental, emotional considerations no longer influence him.[26]

The "original intentions," of which Goebbels spoke so smugly, had not been fully revealed to the Duce.* On September 10 Hitler had decided to set up a political and military system in Italy which would take effective control of the country and which would bring under its wing any future Fascist administration. The two frontier provinces of Venezia Giulia and Alto Adige (South Tyrol) were virtually annexed and placed under two Nazi *Gauleiters,* Friederich Rainer at Trieste and Franz Hofer at Innsbruck. Hofer was the man whose irredentist activities during Mussolini's heyday had more than once aroused angry protests from Rome, and his appearance on Italian soil in the mantle of authority was as wounding to Italian pride as the German occupation of Trieste.†

It is not difficult to explain why Mussolini so readily lent himself to Hitler's plans. Hitler had been very outspoken and there was, Mussolini soon perceived, no chance of his being allowed to go into peaceful retirement; and, quite apart from any satisfaction which his rehabilitation brought him, it seemed prudent to take on German terms what had been offered. He knew Hitler well enough to realize that, if thwarted, he might exact a terrible vengeance; and

---

* On this point there is some divergence of testimony. But the evidence (see, for example, Rahn, p. 235) seems to show that while dark hints were thrown out Mussolini was not informed of the details. As Hitler made clear in *Mein Kampf,* he believed in the gradual demoralization of his victims.

† The Berlin political wits had long foreseen Hitler's descent on Trieste. The story they told was to the effect that in 1933 Hitler gave a Jew who had befriended him 10,000 marks to emigrate to Vienna. In 1938 the Jew, rendered penniless by the *Anschluss,* was given another 10,000 marks to emigrate to Prague. A year later he was again on Hitler's doorstep. "Here," said the Fuehrer, "is 10,000 marks for the last time. But one word of advice: "don't emigrate to Trieste."

he saw himself in his new position as a buffer between his own people and the barbarian Germans. His was not a wholly ignoble character, and there was in him a streak of genuine patriotism. Indeed at times during the ensuing months he seemed to show less concern for his own future than for that of the Italian nation; and it comforted him to feel that, like Pétain at Vichy, he was able to save his compatriots from the worst excesses of the occupying power.

Thus Mussolini lost no time in doing what was required. That very evening after his second talk with Hitler on September 15 an official communiqué issued in Rome announced that "Benito Mussolini has today reassumed the supreme direction of fascism in Italy." This was followed by four orders of the day,[27] appointing Pavolini provisional secretary of the "Fascist Republican party," reinstating the authorities dismissed by Badoglio, instructing the party to support the German army and to investigate the conduct of members in relation to the *coup d'état* and the capitulation, and reconstituting the Fascist militia. Under two further orders Renato Ricci was appointed commander of the militia, and officers of the armed forces were absolved of their oath of allegiance to the King.

So the conversations between Fuehrer and Duce had produced concrete results. The Fascist party and its leader had been restored, and the solidarity between the two regimes had been reaffirmed. From Hitler's point of view this constituted a useful political façade. But in fact, nothing was ever to be the same again, for Hitler, although he retained a personal regard for Mussolini, now viewed him and the Italians with suspicion and contempt. In conversation with Goebbels, he said that, while he had no proof, he thought it possible that at one time it might have been Mussolini's intention to desert Germany. In another context he spoke of annexing all Venetia and incorporating it in the Reich in a "sort of loose federation."

Goebbels, after his talk with Hitler, probably reflected his master's views when he wrote: "In any case we must begin to write off the Duce politically. However much we may like him personally, and however valuable the services which he rendered to us, there must be a limit somewhere, especially when the interests of the Reich are involved. . . . He [Mussolini] is no longer his old self, and one can no longer count on him firmly as a political factor, especially since he no longer has any power." [28]

VI

On September 17 Mussolini left Rastenburg by air for Munich. He was feeling a little better, probably because he had shed responsibility and was no longer tortured in the same way by indecision and anxiety. He had been examined at Hitler's instance by Professor Morell, who found no symptoms of any dangerous ailment, but diagnosed only a circulatory disturbance and overworked and disordered bowels—"the typical ailment," as Goebbels remarked, "of a modern revolutionary politician, from which we all suffer to some extent." Morell found no sign of syphilitic infection,* and expressed the conviction that, although the Duce's nervous complaint was in an advanced state, it could be cured completely.

Nevertheless Mussolini was still in bad condition, and Anfuso was shocked when he saw him at Munich for the first time after his fall. His collar hung loosely around a wizened neck, his eyes stared from an emaciated head, he had shrunk. He looked like an unshaven tramp. But what brought home to Anfuso the extent of the dictator's fall was less his appearance than the change in his manners. "He shook me warmly by the hand and invited me to sit down." [29] To Rahn he gave the impression of a tired, beaten man, well aware of the hopelessness of his position and evidently longing to bury himself in the quiet of a peaceful library.[30]

In Bavaria Mussolini, since he could not be exposed to the danger of bombing in Munich, was quartered with his family at Hirschberg Castle near Weilheim. Anfuso, the only senior diplomat to rally to the new regime,† had come to join him in Germany and, as he put it himself, "ended by taking on the duties of usher, secretary, and telephone operator." [31] There was no contact with the outside world except through a German telephone line, an S. S. liaison officer was posted in the house, the military guard was German, and behind

---

* A well-known Italian doctor told the author that this was in fact the case.

† Many others, including two of Mussolini's former private secretaries, had been approached. But all had refused.

them all stood the rigid figure of Baron Doernberg, head of the Protocol Department of the German Foreign Office.

One of Mussolini's first visitors was Ciano, who had imprudently fled to Germany and whom he received at Edda's request. According to Ciano's statement at his trial, he saw the Duce three times. The exact dates of these interviews cannot be fixed, but it is clear that Ciano, supported by Edda, sturdily defended himself against charges of treachery. He appears to have done so with some success, not only according to his own subsequent version, but according to the account which reached Berlin. On September 23 Goebbels wrote in his diary: "Edda Mussolini has succeeded in completely reversing the Duce's opinion of Ciano. Immediately upon her father's arrival in Munich she had a long talk with him, which resulted in a reconciliation between the Duce and Ciano. Ciano has again been accepted into the good graces of the Duce. That means that this poisonous mushroom is again planted in the midst of the new Fascist Republican party." It seems that Mussolini had so far been won over that he was toying with the idea of appointing Ciano once more to be Foreign Minister and mentioned it to Rahn.[32]

He also received a number of lesser party men who had gathered at Munich to see him, among them the militia General Ferruccio Galbi, one of the old Milan *Squadristi,* whom he had known in the early days of fascism. To Galbi he expressed regret that he had not originally liquidated the monarchy. He was, he declared, a Romagnolo and therefore a republican by birth. He had always remained one, even in 1922 when he formed his first government. But fascism was then too young and too unprepared to risk an upheaval. He could have done it after the Abyssinian victory, when his prestige stood at its highest, but he had been reluctant to profit from the sacrifices of the nation and to seem to be furthering his own ambitions. He had always remained a Socialist, an adherent of pure unmaterialistic socialism, which served only the interests of the nation.[33]

Rancor against the King and nostalgia for the socialism in which he had grown up and which he had betrayed was bringing him back to the Socialist fold. In the months which remained to him he was constantly to harp on this theme; and two of his favorite companions were a Socialist journalist, Carlo Silvestri, and a former

Communist, Nicola Bombacci, who followed him to the end.

On September 18 Mussolini made a broadcast to Italy on the wavelength of Radio Munich.[34] He sounded flat and tired to begin with and Rachele, who was with him, doubted whether many of his listeners would have recognized his voice. But he improved as he went on, and at the end was satisfied with his performance.[35] After speaking of the events of July, he went on to give the first indication of his reversion to republican socialism. Italian traditions, he declared, were more republican than monarchist; and it was the republicans rather than the monarchists who had fashioned the unity of Italy. "The state which we wish to set up will be national and social in the highest sense of the word: that is, it will be Fascist, thus going back to our origins." The policy would be to take up arms again at the side of Germany, Japan, and the other allies; to reorganize the armed forces around the militia; to eliminate the traitors at home; to annihilate the parasitic plutocracies; and to make labor the theme of the national economy and the basis of the state.[36]

The socialist complexion given by Mussolini to his regime was later to arouse misgivings and anger in Berlin. But the first reaction of the sceptical Dr. Goebbels to Mussolini's whole performance was more than favorable. His broadcast, he wrote, was "clear, determined, and of high quality. . . . He spoke quite coolly, realistically, and without exaggerated pathos. His arguments were effective and convincing. . . . The Italian Fascists will draw new hope and fighting spirit from this speech." [37]

Mussolini returned to his isolation at Hirschberg to await developments, which had been taken out of his hands and entrusted to Rahn, assisted by Pavolini. Rahn, the German ambassador, in fact played the role of a Prime Minister in a satellite state, while to Mussolini were allotted the functions of a constitutional sovereign. Rahn with Pavolini had gone to Rome to see what could be done to put the Fascist militia on its feet and to scrape up a government over which Mussolini was ostensibly to preside.

In neither enterprise were they at first at all successful. The fact was that fascism had failed,* and the formula was no longer able

* Biggini, who had voted for Mussolini at the Grand Council, advised Pavolini against resurrecting fascism. (Tamaro, II, 5.)

to arouse any popular enthusiasm. Ricci had been unable to secure more than a handful of recruits for his militia force, and it was not surprising that in this climate it should have been even more difficult to find suitable men ready to face the hazards of office in Mussolini's new government. On September 22 Rahn telegraphed to Berlin: "Regrettable weakness and incoherence of Fascist elements in Rome. Many of those followers of the Duce under consideration for ministerial posts are still hesitant. Ricci has not so far succeeded in recruiting members for the militia. I therefore think it necessary to proceed at once with the proclamation of the new Fascist Republican government." [38]

On the following day at noon the composition of the administration was made public. It was not an impressive list. After much intrigue, in which Farinacci had taken part, the key Ministry of the Interior was entrusted to the German candidate, Guido Buffarini-Guidi. He was a lawyer from Pisa, who before July 25, 1943, had been Undersecretary at the Ministry of the Interior. He was the most agile and gifted of Mussolini's new recruits. A contemporary described him as "an extraordinarily ductile man of ardent intelligence and vivid imagination. He was an incomparable tactician, a real Fouché with something of Talleyrand. He knew men and the art of dealing with them, and, although he was somewhat disorderly and inclined to promise more than he could perform, he knew how to maneuver and to keep himself afloat." [39]

So far as the rest of the government was concerned, it had proved impossible to secure a Minister of Foreign Affairs, and Mussolini accordingly was given the portfolio, with a reluctant professional as Undersecretary in the person of Count Serafino Mazzolini, who had been earmarked in 1942 to be chief civilian officer in a conquered Egypt. The third important civilian ministry, the so-called Ministry of Popular Culture, in effect the Propaganda Ministry, was entrusted to the young and almost unknown Fernando Mezzasomma. Nonentities or men with tarnished reputations on the list were: Antonio Tringali-Casanova, Minister of Justice; Pellegrini-Giampetro, Minister of Finance; Silvio Gai, Minister of Corporative Economy; Edoardo Moroni, Minister of Agriculture; Carlo Biggini, Minister of Education; Giuseppe Peverelli, Minister of Communications; and Francesco Barracu, who was to play a role in the last days, as Undersecretary in the cabinet office. In order to give the list some appearance of weight and respectability, Rahn by means of threats and flattery induced Graziani to accept the post of War Minister, with two Undersecretaries, an admiral and an airman, whose war exploits had made them popular heroes. On the afternoon of September 23 Rahn telegraphed triumphantly to Berlin: "Reconstruction of the government completed at noon. . . . I was only able to persuade Graziani to enter the government one minute before the publication of the communiqué." [40] That evening Mussolini, who had been kept in touch with developments by telephone, gave his formal approval to the list and left Munich by air for Forlì. The last stage in his career was now about to begin.

CHAPTER TWENTY-TWO

Vengeance

1943–1944

I

MUSSOLINI arrived at Forlì in a German aircraft, wearing a militia uniform without any decorations or emblems of rank and in a black shirt which Anfuso had lent him. He was met at the airport by the two men who henceforth were to be his German guardians: Rahn, his political preceptor, and General Wolff, commander of the S. S. in northern Italy, his military and security adviser. In order still further to emphasize the Duce's complete dependence on Germany a detachment of the *Leibstandarte* Adolf Hitler had been despatched for guard duties at La Rocca.

Propped up by the Germans, Mussolini's first task was to give some semblance of reality to a government which existed only in name. But the prospects were discouraging, and on September 26 he opened his heart to Rahn, who reported to Berlin that "despite the optimism which he stimulated in the presence of his colleagues, the Duce felt bound to tell me that his first impression was that Italy was in a chaotic state, like a punchdrunk man who has completely lost his bearings." Mussolini went on to say that he recognized that Germany must have sole leadership in the conduct of the war, and his task would be to maintain law and order in the rear of the German armies. But he must have the means of doing so, that was to say, control of the administration, economics, and finance. For the Germans to continue interfering capriciously would not serve German interests, since it would be "meaningless to create a government which did not govern, to lay down regulations without having the means to enforce them, and to reorganize an administration which no longer had anything left to administer." [1] This was a line of argument which Mussolini was to repeat with wearisome insistence during the months to come.

It was, however, agreed that Mussolini should hold an early meeting of his Cabinet, issue a government program, and then leave for the seat of government. On this latter point there was a difference of opinion. Mussolini would have preferred to return to Rome, if only because he realized that only in Rome could he recover some of the influence and independence which he had lost. The Germans, however, were not prepared to assent on several grounds. After negotiations with the caretakers who had been left in the capital and with the representatives of Mussolini, it had been decided to declare Rome an open city. Moreover, it was not certain for how long Rome could be held. But, more important, the Germans were determined that Mussolini should not recover any measure of independence, and that he should remain under their tutelage in some spot conveniently close to the German frontier. It was accordingly made quite clear to him that Rome was not acceptable.

The Duce had no alternative but to comply, and, with an eye on *Gauleiter* Hofer's depredations in the Alto Adige, he disingenuously suggested Merano or Bolzano. This proposal naturally found no favor at Rastenburg; and without further reference to Mussolini Rommel, who was commanding in the North, and Wolff were summarily instructed to find a suitable place close to their respective headquarters at Belluno and Verona.

The new cabinet held its first meeting at La Rocca on September 27 and at once announced that as a result of the declaration of Rome as an open city, the government intended to establish itself "in another place near the General Headquarters of the Armed Forces." There was to be an early Constituent Assembly which would determine the character of the new state, and in the meantime the Duce would assume the functions of Head of the State.

In a statement to his new cabinet Mussolini spoke of the need to prosecute the war and of his attitude to those who had given support to Badoglio. It was not his intention, he declared, to take measures against all those who in a moment of infantile aberration had thought that a military government was calculated to restore liberty or against those who, having always been opposed to fascism, had declared themselves as such after July 26. But there was another category of persons who would not escape severe sanctions, namely those who for years had held high office, who had received honors and rewards, and who in the day of trial had passed over to the enemy. They were responsible for the disaster into which the nation had fallen. Special tribunals would judge these cases of treachery.[2]

That evening Mussolini drafted a letter to Hitler to report progress and to plead once more for an end to German interference in Italian internal affairs.

As you will have seen, the Fascist Republican government has held its first sitting and issued statements about its program which have made a good impression. It is the figure of Marshal Graziani which gives character to the government and arouses vast hopes and sympathies.

If we want to reconstruct the civil life of the country, the new government I have formed must have the necessary autonomy to govern, that is to give orders to the civil authorities subject to it.

The Republican government, which I have the honor to lead, has only one desire and aim—to see that Italy resumes her place in the war as soon as possible. But to reach this supreme result, it is essential for the German military authorities to confine their activity to the military sphere only and, for all the rest to allow the Italian civil authorities to function.

If this is not accomplished, both Italian and world opinion will judge this government incapable of functioning, and the government itself will fall into disorder and, even more, into ridicule.

I am sure, Fuehrer, that you will realize the importance of the points which I have put to you, and the gravity of the problems which I have to face, and their solution is not only an Italian, but a German interest.[3]

To this communication Hitler made no reply. He had no intention of ceasing to interfere in Italian affairs. Thanks to his own resolution and to the fumbling of the Allies he had extricated himself very creditably from what might have been a most dangerous predicament. He had little confidence in Mussolini and none in the Italian people. He did not even want to see the constitution of an Italian republican army, and, when asked by his generals for his views on this point, he replied disdainfully: "Germany is no longer interested in an Italian army because her relations with Italy are too strained as the result of the events of last September and are bound to remain so. The organizing of Italian military units would therefore demand the greatest caution and watchfulness." [4] Henceforth Hitler would treat Italy as occupied territory, and allow Mussolini only the minimum of liberty required to enable him to play the limited rôle allotted to him. As Goebbels put it: "We must now proceed very coolly and realistically. . . . We must use fascism as far as possible." [5] There was no room for sentiment and German interests must be the only consideration, but of this Mussolini was as yet only dimly aware.

Hitler was not the only man to show reserve towards the new government. On German instructions the Axis satellites—Rumania, Bulgaria, Croatia, Slovakia, and Hungary—recognized it, and Japan followed suit. But that was all. Not one of the neutrals, not even the Vatican, would enter into diplomatic relations with Mussolini and his tattered regime. The bitterest blow was Franco's blunt refusal to extend more than *de facto* recognition. Mussolini, the Caudillo told the German ambassador, was only a shadow and was unlikely anyhow to live long. There were few decent Italians behind him and he was now a mere appendage of Germany. When the ambassador reminded Franco of Mussolini's prompt recognition of his government in 1936 he made no comment.

In an atmosphere of frustration engendered by a consciousness of his own difficulties and by the absence of any governmental machinery Mussolini spent seventeen empty days at La Rocca. He read the newspapers assiduously and began to give thought to the establishment of a new Fascist Republican press. The old journalist was back on familiar ground. Giorgio Pini, who had taken over Grandi's newspaper *Il Resto del Carlino,* was sent for and offered the post of director of the *Corriere della Sera.* Pini found the Duce lucid and understanding, but lacking his old fire. "He seemed like a man withdrawn into himself, and absorbed in continuous, solitary reflections on what had recently happened to him and to Italy." [6]

Mussolini did not, however, revive the *Popolo d'Italia,* which had been suppressed by Badoglio. He was too proud to risk submitting his old newspaper to German censorship and interference. "I can," he said, "and must sacrifice myself in this tragic situation, but not my newspaper. For thirty years it has been a flag, and flags must fly freely."[7]

On October 5 he told his new private secretary, Giovanni Dolfin: "Tomorrow or the next day I shall move to the place which has been selected for my headquarters. I still do not know where it will be located. It is somewhere on the western shore of Garda." Four days later he obediently left La Rocca by car for Gargagno on Lake Garda, accompanied by Renato Ricci and by Vito, Arnaldo Mussolini's son, who was to work in an additional private secretariat organized by Vittorio Mussolini.

II

The residence chosen by the Germans for the Duce was the Villa Feltrinelli, an ornate, medium-sized house faced with pink marble in a small park on the bank of the lake about a mile north of Gargagno. Here, at first, Mussolini was obliged to establish his residence and his office. Although Garda is perhaps the most beautiful of the Italian lakes, Mussolini was never happy there. He disliked lakes, which he described as an unfortunate compromise between rivers and the sea. Moreover, he objected to his isolation. The governmental area of the so-called Salò Republic was cordoned off by the Germans, and access was made so difficult that even his own private secretary found it hard to reach Gargagno from La Rocca. The various ministries, staffed by a small number of volunteers scraped together in Rome, were scattered over the countryside. The Ministries of Foreign Affairs and Popular Culture were at Salò, the Cabinet Office at Bogliaco, the Interior at Maderno, Armed Forces at Desenzano, Education at Padua, while Public Works was as far away as Venice.[8]

Closer at hand than most of his ministries were Mussolini's German guardians. Rahn was at Fasano, and Wolff at Gardone and later at Desenzano. On Mussolini's doorstep, in a house adjoining the Villa Feltrinelli, lived Colonel Jandl, the German liaison officer. A detachment of the *Leibstandarte* Adolf Hitler performed guard duties at the villa and served an antiaircraft gun mounted on the roof. Whenever he left the villa by car, he was accompanied by a German motorized escort, although he did later insist that he should also have an Italian escort and that Italian sentries should also be on guard around the house. All communications were in the hands of the Germans and telephone calls could only be made through a German field telephone exchange.

In his first report [9] Colonel Jandl claimed to have the Duce under satisfactory control. A German staff officer was living in the Villa Feltrinelli, and "this affords me the best opportunity of keeping myself apprised of happenings inside the villa, the visitors received, and the opinions current in the immediate neighborhood of the Duce, and of informing the interested German quarters should the need arise." Colonel Jandl saw the Duce every day, gave him orally such military information as he judged expedient, and used his conversations with Mussolini and other visitors in the waiting room as a basis for his intelligence reports.

Mussolini's health was also in the hands of Germans: an army doctor Zachariae, provided by Hitler on Morell's recommendation, and a physiotherapist Horn, suspected of being an S. S. agent, who gave him daily massage. As in the case of the escort and the sentries, appearances were kept up by the addition of an Italian, Dr. Baldini, assistant to Professor Frugoni.

Dr. Zachariae had already arrived at Gargagno and was on the doorstep to welcome Mussolini. He found his patient pale, yellow, and very thin. Mussolini complained of severe gastric cramp, which prevented sleep, but denied any syphilitic infection, which, he said, had been the subject of rumors designed to defame him. Indeed a blood test at Rastenburg had been negative, but Zachariae diagnosed a secondary anemia, a wasted abdomen, a dry skin, and an enlarged liver. Reflexes, heart, and lungs were normal. In short, "a very ailing man, who has bravely borne atrocious pain for nearly four years." The doctor prescribed a course of treatment which in fifteen days had relieved the pain and reduced the liver.[10] Two months later Jandl was reporting that the outward appearance of the Duce and his capacity for work had improved.*

Two rival phantom governments were now established in Italy, neither of which commanded any public support. In the south the

---

* Deakin, *op. cit.*, p. 610. This is confirmed by inhabitants of Gargagno and Salò who told the author that when they saw Mussolini on his outings, he looked strong and fit.

Badoglio government had on October 13 declared war on Germany, thereby winning the title of cobelligerent, but marking its complete subservience to the Allies. In the north the Salò Republic was only too plainly in the hands of the Germans. The issue could only be fought out on the battlefield, and the people, crushed between the contending armies, were principally concerned to see an end to war on Italian soil.

In this uncomfortable situation, and with the mists and rains of autumn descending on the lake, Mussolini settled down to his dreary life at Gargagno. He soon established an office in the neighboring Villa delle Orsoline, away from the noise, family squabbles, and petty intrigues of his home; and there he spent the whole day in a pathetic attempt to maintain the appearance of governing. His time was, broadly speaking, spent on three separate activities: relations with Germany, an endeavor to ward off the most oppressive exactions; domestic affairs, the organization of his party, the creation of a new Socialist system, the reconstruction of his army, and restoration of some semblance of order; and endless conversations in which he dwelt on the past and peered into the future, like a man who has lost interest in the present. As the hopelessness of his position impinged itself on his mind, he tended more and more to divest himself of responsibility, and to retreat into a world of his own. But at the outset there were many problems facing him and he addressed his mind, as best he could, to their solution.

III

The behavior of the Germans all over Italy was a constant source of friction. Officials from the Todt organization and the German Ministry of Labor were swarming over the country pressing Italian civilians into service in Germany. The army demanded what they wanted without regard to Italian rights and susceptibilities. Hordes of advisers on every conceivable subject invaded the ministries and public offices to give instructions which were often impracticable and contradictory. But there was one area in which the Italians were particularly sensitive: the provinces conquered from Austria in 1918. Here the Germans had installed themselves. *Gaulieter* Hofer was ruling the Alto Adige and *Gauleiter* Rainer, Trieste, while German troops were occupying Zara, Fiume, Spalato, and Cattaro. The Italian garrisons of these places had been disarmed and removed to Germany as prisoners of war.

All this was more than Mussolini could bear, and Anfuso, who had been appointed ambassador in Berlin, was instructed to ask for an official denial of a Reuters report that Germany had annexed the Italian provinces of Bolzano, Belluno, and Trieste. Rahn tried to arrange an accommodation, and at a meeting with the two *Gauleiters* suggested that the annexation should be disguised and made the subject of a friendly settlement. But worse was to come. It was soon reported that the system of the so-called operational zones in the Alto Adige and Trieste might be extended to Piedmont, where the partisans were becoming dangerously active, and Rahn reported that the situation in the Alto Adige and Trieste constituted the most severe political and psychological burden for the Duce. The announcement of a new operational zone would endanger the very existence of the Fascist government and only serve enemy propaganda. "The Italian government," he pleaded, "gives way to all necessary military supervision and control measures requested from the German side. I regard the setting up of the new operational zone, in present conditions, as unnecessary and harmful, and advise strongly against it." [11]

The German government, however, paid no attention to either Mussolini or Rahn, and on October 10 an order was issued, under Hitler's instructions, establishing German military government in northern Italy.

At the beginning of November Mussolini sent Vittorio to Germany to see what he could do. In a conversation with Ribbentrop he represented that the conduct of the German military was calculated to create the impression that the Duce was merely the agent of the German government. For example, the Duce had nominated prefects only to be overridden; he had no channel of communication with the prefectures except through German army links; the Fascist newspaper in Brescia had been confiscated by the Germans. The Duce asked that the Germans should deal only with the Italian government and not directly with the population. The present situation weighed heavily on his father, whom he had left in a very depressed state of mind.

Ribbentrop was unsympathetic and hectoring. The German army, he claimed, had found no organized Italian administration in being and their requirements in the frontier provinces were dictated by the needs of war. Draconian measures were now required. Many Italian officials were unreliable. All Hitler's measures were designed to be for, not against, the Duce; and good relations depended on the purging by Mussolini of the Italian administration. On the following day Anfuso in a letter to the Duce confirmed that the Germans were implacably resolved not to give an inch, so long as they mistrusted the will and capacity of the Fascist Republican government. "They especially emphasize," he reported, "that we have not taken up a more energetic position against defeatism and compromise inside the country"; and he concluded hopefully: "Evidently everything will be clearer when the Republican army begins to fight." [12]

German suspicion of Mussolini's administration was nurtured by neo-Fascist exiles in Germany, among them Giovanni Preziosi, an unfrocked priest and virulent anti-Semite, whom even Mussolini described as repulsive. In Berlin he shouted from the housetops that Mussolini's government was packed with Masons and pro-Semites who could not be trusted, and he compiled a special memorandum for the Fuehrer, "who is the only person who can break this circle." Goebbels seems to have been impressed, for he noted in his diary that Preziosi had been to see him and that "his report on the situation in Fascist Italy gave much food for thought. He even criticized the Duce very severely and blamed him for not having followed the right line in his treatment of Jews and Masons. That, he said, was the reason for his fall." [13]

In this climate Mussolini was obliged to recognize bitterly that there was nothing to be obtained for the moment from the Germans, although he was to raise the same issue later in different contexts. He turned his attention to domestic affairs.

IX

His first task was to organize his new state, and, as has been seen, his original intention had been to convene a revolutionary Constituent Assembly. But on closer examination this idea presented many practical difficulties. For one thing, as an internal memorandum put it, "the fact that a good part of the national territory is now removed from the possibility of control by the Fascist government raises the problem as to whether or not it is opportune to convoke urgently the Constituent."[14] Secondly, he had no clear idea of the exact shape to be given to his future republic, no novel situation in his experience. There were many contending elements inside and outside the party to be placated, and he decided on a compromise solution: to test opinion by means of a party congress, at which a manifesto would be debated, in much the same way as in Britain the government lays a White Paper and takes the opinion of the House in the course of debate. He did not intend to participate in the congress, but entrusted the conduct of affairs to Pavolini, the party secretary.

In the preparation of the manifesto he was assisted by Pavolini and by Nicola Bombacci, a former leading Communist, who had come to join him at Gargagno. Bombacci was a simple, good-humored soul who readily lent himself to the Duce's impulse to move to the Left. He was given an office in the Ministry of the Interior and, when he was not gossiping with the Duce, occupied himself with plans for social reform.

During this phase Mussolini was subjected to humiliating interference by Rahn, who reported to his superiors that the manifesto had been drawn up with his cooperation and that he had been obliged "to tone down the originally very sharp Socialist tendencies in the interests of maintaining private enterprise in war production, and further to strike out a section inserted by the Duce on the preservation of territorial integrity."[15]

In its final form the manifesto[16] contained eighteen points. A Constituent Assembly would be convened to declare the dissolution of the monarchy, to proclaim the social republic and to nominate its head, who would be elected every five years. Sovereign power would reside in the citizens and no citizen could be held under arrest for more than seven days, save by order of the judicial authorities. The failure of the former electoral system and the partial failure of too rigid an authoritarian regime called for a new "mixed system" of electoral machinery. The party would be responsible for the political education of the people and would be the custodian of the revolutionary idea. Membership would not be a condition of office or employment. The religion of the republic would be that of the Catholic Church, but all other religions not in conflict with the law would be respected. Members of the Jewish race would be foreigners and regarded for the duration of the war as enemy nationalists.

In foreign policy the republic's aim would be the unity and independence of the fatherland and recognition of the need for the living space required by its forty-five million inhabitants. Moreover it would seek the realization of a European Community and a Federation of all nations subscribing to the following principles: the elimination of the long-standing British intrigues on the Continent; the abolition of the capitalist system at home and the struggle against the world plutocracies abroad; the exploitation for the benefit of European and native peoples of the natural resources of Africa, with complete respect for those peoples, in particular the Moslem peoples, who, like Egypt, were already national entities.

In social matters, private property would be guaranteed by the state, though public services and, in general, war industries would be in the hands of state-appointed bodies. In agriculture the private enterprise of the landowner would only be tolerated in so far as it was justified by performance. The State would be responsible for an adequate housing program. The trade unions would be amalgamated in a General Confederation of Labor, and all the social legislation introduced by the Fascists during the past twenty years would remain in force. The Charter of Labor would be the starting point for a further advance.

In an article distributed to the press on November 13 Mussolini described his manifesto as meeting the needs and aspirations of the working classes. "Fascism, liberated from so much tinsel which has slowed its march and from the too many compromises which were forced on it by circumstances, has returned to its revolutionary origins in all sectors, and particularly the social one." [17] In Turin the secretary of a Fascist Syndicate, speaking to workmen, lauded Russia and assured his listeners that in Italy also the plutocrats would soon be liquidated and socialism introduced.[18] Elsewhere the manifesto gave rise to the expression of Marxist Socialist sentiments; and later Mussolini was to tell Carlo Silvestri that at Verona he had effected his reconciliation with democratic socialism.[19]

The congress met on November 14 in the large hall of the Castelvecchio at Verona. The proceeding mirrored the confusion reigning in the minds of all Italians at that juncture, and party spokesmen were repeatedly interrupted by hecklers, raising their voices against Clara Petacci and Buffarini, calling for socialist policies, and putting forward the most extreme and ill-considered demands. On only one issue was there any degree of general agreement. The sense of the gathering was against a policy of internal reconciliation and there was vociferous approval of the establishment of a Special Tribunal to try the traitors, in particular Ciano.

In his concluding speech Pavolini spoke of the "warmth of disorderly faith" expressed by the Congress and undertook that its proceedings would be carefully considered by Mussolini. He made a special note of the Congress's desire to see a Special Tribunal set up.[20] In the prevailing atmosphere of general bewilderment and perplexity there was no difficulty in securing the endorsement of the manifesto by acclamation.

To Dolfin, Mussolini gave his own assessment of the proceedings. "It was a complete and utter mix-up. A lot of confused chatter, and few precise and clear ideas. The most odd tendencies appeared, including Communist ones. One man even demanded the outright abolition of private property! We really could ask ourselves why we have fought communism for twenty years. . . . And not one, not one I say, of all those who have a sack full of ideas to wave around, comes to me and asks me to fight. The fate of the Republic will be decided . . . at the front and certainly not at congresses."[21]

In this sentence Mussolini revealed the gulf between himself and the Italian people. He knew that his future, and indeed his life, now depended on a German victory, and he recognized that, so long as he possessed no army, he could not hope to exercise the slightest influence over Hitler. Consequently he was resolved as a matter of the first priority to erase the stain of Badoglio's betrayal, to raise an Italian army, and place it in the front line. But unfortunately the Italians no longer had the slightest zest for battle at Germany's side.

The congress of Verona registered another important difference between the Duce and his followers. Mussolini was in a mood to break with fascism as it had developed during his twenty-one years of power. He was disillusioned by the party's failure to react against his arrest, he recognized that his regime had been infected by corruption, and was compromised in the eyes of the people, and his mind was moving back towards the republican socialism of his youth. Moreover, as Hitler had noted with displeasure, he was now temperamentally reluctant to take the strong measures which the Germans regarded as essential. All these considerations and the advice he received from men like Silvestri and Bombacci inclined him towards a policy of internal reconciliation.

He was supported by a minority of former Fascist officeholders. Thus the federal secretary of Venice, Eugenio Montesi, who had been imprisoned by the Badoglio government, published a manifesto affirming the need for fraternity between all Italians without distinction of party. The federal secretaries of Pisa and Verona took a similar line; and Mussolini's new Minister of Education, Biggini, allowed the notoriously anti-Fascist rector of the University of Padua to remain at his post, because he wished the university to be an instrument of national reconciliation.[22]

This tendency was, however, vigorously combated by Farinacci and Pavolini, who wanted a return to the old totalitarian system, but in a more intransigent, rigid, and ruthless form. In an instruction to party officials of October 5 Pavolini wrote that in the matter of relations with anti-Fascists it was mistaken to echo the views expressed by certain party members in the first days of the national reconstruction. He recalled what Mussolini had said at the first cabinet meeting, but added that this should not be interpreted to justify general appeals for "universal embraces." A few days later Mezzasomma, another extremist, instructed the press not to continue to publish pusillanimous appeals for pacification. The Fascists of Milan, Pavia, Turin, Arezzo, and other cities declared against any collaboration. "To the wall" was the daily slogan of the Fascist radio at Munich, and the cry was taken up by the extremists in Italy, where the organ of the Milan *Fascio* wrote: "He who talks of forgetting or refers to appeasement and the universal embrace, commits the crime of treason towards his country and a second betrayal of fascism. . . . This is not the hour of the pen, but of the sword."[23]

It was this irreconcilable spirit which was reflected at the congress of Verona. From his distant villa on Lake Garda Mussolini, with rising anxiety and with a sense of his own impotence, supinely watched the rising tide of fratricidal strife, in which excesses on both sides only served to steel the resolution of the combatants and to exacerbate the conflict. He compared himself sadly to Napoleon on the island of Elba, where the emperor held court and received the honors due to his rank, but wielded no power. Rather than yield meekly to the party leaders and their German backers he might have threatened to withdraw from public life. Indeed this was at one time suggested to him by his old friend, Ottavio Dinale,[24] but he was mortally afraid of German reprisals and he preferred to allow things to take their course. It was not the first occasion on which he had been obliged to bow to his extremists, and he was too weary to seek now to impose his will.

In Ferrara the federal secretary was shot, and Pavolini despatched a gang of *Squadristi* from Padua who seized and assassinated eighteen known anti-Fascists, among them a senator. Similar incidents took place in many other towns. Mussolini remarked to Dolfin: "Italy today is under the law of the jungle, that is to say, of wild beasts." The circulation of clandestine newspapers increased and strikes broke out at Turin and Milan. In the turbulence generated by these events, both the trial of the so-called Fascist conspirators and its outcome became inevitable.

Mussolini was, as always in a crisis, torn by conflicting emotions. The whole business hinged on Ciano, who would be the principal prisoner and who evoked the particular hatred of Pavolini * and his henchmen. But Mussolini was not convinced of Ciano's guilt and he could not fail to be moved by the entreaties of Edda, his favorite child. In a country where family feeling is strong he was reluctant to send his son-in-law to the gallows, and in general he deprecated the growth of internecine conflict. "I do not believe, and as you know, I have never believed that the condemnation of these men

* Before the war Pavolini had been a close friend and familiar of Ciano.

can help the country or the re-establishment of our internal situation. The future will prove me right."[25] His own resentment against the men who had brought about his fall would probably have not been sufficient to overcome these inhibitions, but he was under strong pressure from his own people both to exact vengeance and to make a revolutionary gesture. Moreover, he knew that the Germans, as Hitler had made clear, would judge him pitilessly for any display of weakness. He felt that he had no alternative but to go forward. If Anfuso is to be believed, he hoped that at the last moment some way out might be found.[26]

V

On October 13, 1943, the Council of Ministers had decided to constitute a Special Tribunal, and the decree establishing it declared its purpose to be the trial of those members of the Grand Council who had voted against the Duce.

The *coup d'état* of July 25 [the preamble stated] has faced Italy with the greatest betrayal in recorded history. A sinister plot involving the King, certain generals, party leaders, and ministers, who more than any others had derived advantages from fascism, struck the regime in the back, creating disorder and confusion in the country at the agonizing moment when the enemy was setting foot on the soil of the Fatherland. The treachery of the King can be left to the judgment of the people and of history; it is, however, only right that the treason of those who violated not only their duty as citizens but also their oath as Fascists should be severely repressed.[27]

The members of the Tribunal were to be "Fascists of proved loyalty" and the examining magistrate appointed to the new court was Vincenzo Cersosimo, who had held the same position on the original Special Tribunal appointed in 1926 after the four attempts to assassinate Mussolini. As Rahn subsequently reported, the members of the court were in fact "men who are proven and fanatical Fascists of the old guard, and most possess the highest war decorations, and in Pavolini's view they will offer the guarantee that particularly in Ciano's case the death sentence will be pronounced."[28]

The president was Aldo Vecchini and the other eight members were extremists selected for the purpose by Pavolini.*

At the beginning of October Ciano was still in Germany, while Edda had traveled to Italy to do what she could on his behalf with her father. She had suffered a nervous breakdown and been sent to a clinic near Parma, while Ciano, unconscious of his danger, was, it seems, encouraged by his interview with the Duce to nurse hopes that he might even receive office in the new government. In any event he telephoned to Anfuso in Berlin to seek permission to return to Italy. But before the matter could be taken any further the Germans intervened, and on October 17 he was informed that in view of the establishment of the Special Tribunal he would be sent back to Italy.

On October 19 he was flown from Munich to Verona, accompanied by an S. S. escort and a certain Frau Beetz,† a secret agent, who had been secretary to the German police chief in Rome and who had been allotted to Ciano ostensibly as interpreter, but in reality to trace Ciano's diary and private papers. On arrival at Verona Ciano was arrested and lodged in the Scalzi prison. There he was placed under special S. S. guard, while Frau Beetz, who seems to have become very attached to her charge, continued to keep him under surveillance.

Of the remaining eighteen members of the Grand Council who had voted for Grandi's motion five, Gottardi, Pareschi, Marinelli, Cianetti, and De Bono had been arrested in Rome. These men, with the exception of De Bono who was placed under house arrest in a dwelling at Verona, were now brought to join Ciano in the Scalzi prison. Grandi had fled to Lisbon, while the others had disappeared.

Having put the machinery of the Special Tribunal in motion, Mussolini characteristically suffered from misgivings, and nothing further was done until November 24 when, on Pavolini's proposal, the cabinet gave formal approval to the constitution of the Special

---

* Of these nine men Domenico Mittica was shot later by partisans in Turin and Vito Casalnuovo was shot at Dongo. The remainder disappeared in the general confusion at the end of the war.

† Her real name was Frau Hildegard Berger. She was married to an air force officer and was given the pseudonym of Felicitas Beetz or Frau Beetz. She now lives quietly at Bonn.

Tribunal. Mussolini was not the only one to entertain doubts about the project. Tringali-Casanova, the Minister of Justice, had died of a heart attack on October 30 and his successor, Piero Pisenti, a conscientious lawyer, was fundamentally opposed to the conception of special tribunals. Nevertheless it proved impossible to resist outside pressure, and all were carried away on the tide of violence which was engulfing the country.

The first procedural step was the "instruction" or preparation of the case by the examining magistrate. To assist him Mussolini placed at his disposal his own personal files and instructed the Minister of Justice to make a preliminary study of them. Pisenti replied that there was no proof of prior collusion between the members of the Grand Council, Badoglio, and the monarchy. His verdict was not surprising, since in fact there had been no collusion. The terms of Grandi's motion had been made known to Mussolini two days before the session, to the King an hour after the session had begun, and to the generals only when it appeared in the newspapers. Only a few of those who voted for Grandi wished to terminate the dictatorship, but even these had made no plans for the future government of the country. Others had simply cast their votes because they believed that the King should be more closely involved in the prosecution of the war. A few voted blindly because it seemed that Mussolini would not have put the motion to the vote unless he had approved it. Finally, the members of the Grand Council were constitutionally entitled to express their views, and the exercise of this right, implicitly recognized by Mussolini when he convened the Council and put the motion to the vote, could not properly be said to constitute treason.

All these considerations were known to Mussolini and he made no effort to dispute the justice of Pisenti's verdict. Indeed he had admitted to Dolfin that the whole prosecution was questionable, since the fact that he had agreed to put Grandi's motion to the vote showed that he accepted the possibility that it might be approved.[29] But to Pisenti he retorted: "You see in the trial only the juridical aspect. As a jurist you judge by other standards. I have to look at it from a political angle. *Raison d'état* submerges every other contradictory consideration. Henceforth one must go through to the end."[30]

Mussolini had now made up his mind. When giving Cersosimo his final instructions, he said to him: "I know you to be an incorruptible and competent man. Act, as always, according to your conscience. I have nothing more to say to you." To the president of the tribunal he said two days later that he was to do his duty without regard to any personal considerations. He explained himself to his private secretary, when he told him that no intervention could any longer put a halt to the course of events. "In me the crisis was finally resolved the other night. So far as I am concerned, Ciano has been dead for some little time. He would never be able to move about in Italy, to appear in public, or have a name. Whoever therefore voted for Grandi's motion will be condemned." [31]

On December 14 Cersosimo began his "instruction" in the Scalzi prison. At first the S. S. guard refused him access to Ciano's cell, but as a result of the intervention of Frau Beetz he was eventually allowed to interrogate the prisoner. From Ciano and the other five accused he was able to elicit very little of value to the prosecution. All protested their personal devotion to the Duce and categorically denied complicity in any plot. Unfortunately for them it was becoming clear to all concerned that the rules of evidence were unlikely to play much part in the trial. Indeed so satisfactory was the intelligence reaching Germany that Hitler judged it safe to stand aside, and Ribbentrop wrote to Rahn: "For your personal information . . . the Fuehrer has stated that the trial of Ciano [in the minds of the Germans the Verona trial was not a trial of anti-Fascist conspirators, but of one man, the anti-German Ciano] is exclusively a matter for the Duce, and that on our side no pressure whatever shall be exerted in favor of a condemnation." Rahn was able to reply the following day that Pavolini was convinced that "the three-day trial, which would open on January 8, would end not only with the death sentence, but its immediate execution." Later, on December 30, he reported that the Duce, despite pressure from all the members of the family excepting Rachele, had decided as head of the family and of the state finally to disinterest himself from Ciano's fate, and had completely handed over to Pavolini the mounting of the trial. Pavolini saw to it that the judges were informed of Mussolini's attitude.[32]

In his cell in the Scalzi Ciano, although he may have secretly hoped for some last-minute reprieve, was preparing himself for death. On December 23 he addressed a last letter to the King, which was smuggled out of the prison. "Your Majesty," he wrote, "may I, now that the last hours of my life have come, send you a message expressing my devotion." He went on to explain that he had spent two months under S. S. guard awaiting a verdict which could only be described as premeditated assassination. The monarchy, he affirmed, was in no wise responsible for the war. "One man—one man alone—through his insensate personal ambition, his thirst for military glory, condemned in his own mouth, has deliberately led the country to the abyss." He concluded by informing the King that he had arranged for his diary to be published as soon as possible after his death and requesting royal protection for his family.[33]

As the date of the trial approached, a last, desperate attempt was made with the collusion of Frau Beetz to save Ciano. On December 28, 1943, Frau Beetz called on General Harster, head of the German Security Service at Verona, with the proposal that Ciano's life should be bartered for his diary and other papers. Harster telegraphed to Kaltenbrunner at Berlin and the same day received a favorable reply signed by Himmler and Kaltenbrunner. Harster believed that Himmler had been actuated by the hope of finding in Ciano's papers material which would be damaging to Ribbentrop.

Full instructions from Himmler followed shortly. The operation was to receive the code name "Operation Count." Two S. S. men, described as specialists in such enterprises, would be immediately despatched to Verona. Disguised as Fascists they would enter the prison and with the connivance of the S. S. guards, who would put up a token resistance, remove the prisoner. Thus the operation would appear to Hitler and everyone else as having been mounted by the Fascists. Ciano, once liberated, would be flown to Hungary; and on his safe arrival Edda Ciano would hand over the diary and other papers.

A few days later Harster traveled to Innsbruck to meet Kaltenbrunner, who informed him that the plan had been somewhat modified. Himmler now required Ciano to prove his good faith and to hand over some of the documents before his liberation. Frau Beetz procured Ciano's assent and an intermediary, the Marchese Pucci, was despatched to Rome with Frau Beetz to remove the papers from their hiding place.

On January 7, 1944, the S. S. specialists, two tall, strong Dutchmen, arrived by air at Verona; and it was agreed that the operation should take place on January 7. At Rome Pucci had entered into possession of all Ciano's papers: the diary, sixteen volumes of records of conversations, a file entitled "Germany," and a file containing the papers assembled for his last diplomatic mission. Six volumes of the conversations were handed over to Frau Beetz for transmission to Harster, while the remainder of the documents were kept by Edda in safe custody. Kaltenbrunner accordingly telegraphed to Harster that the operation could go forward; and Frau Beetz was instructed to inform Edda Ciano that she should await her husband at 9 P.M. on January 7 at the 10 kilometer stone on the Verona-Brescia road. She was to bring a substantial sum of money with her.

Everything seemed to have been satisfactorily arranged, but on the afternoon of January 6 Hitler telephoned personally to Harster instructing him peremptorily to cancel "Operation Count." It fell to Frau Beetz to break the news to the prisoner and later to Edda. It was a bitter blow and on the following day Ciano made his will in favor of his wife and children. He also wrote a letter to Edda telling her, as a last expedient, to address threatening letters to Mussolini and Hitler; and he advised her to flee to Switzerland with the diary. Frau Beetz undertook to deliver the letter. General Harster remarked of her that she seemed less concerned to serve German interests than to help the prisoner.[34]

On the evening of January 7 Hitler, through the German embassy in Fasano and for reasons which are difficult to explain,* sent a message to Pavolini asking that the trial should be postponed; and Rahn who was in Germany had telephoned to support the request. †

---

* According to Dolfin, Mussolini suggested that the German initiative might be connected with an impending intervention on Ciano's behalf by Hungary or Spain. Or, alternatively, Hitler might have been moved by motives of friendship and a desire to spare the Duce pain. (Tamaro, II, 352.)

† Rahn, according to his statement to Deakin, had flown to Germany to urge Hitler to allow Ciano to escape to Switzerland. But Hitler repeated that the matter concerned Mussolini alone, and that there must be no German interference. It is odd that Hitler should at the same time have himself intervened with Pavolini.

Mussolini, however, was now not prepared to be shifted from his position, and he categorically refused to agree to any postponement. From every quarter Ciano's hope of reprieve was now being successively blocked.

VI

On January 8, 1944, the trial opened in the Castelvecchio in Verona in the same hall in which the party congress two months earlier had tumultuously demanded Ciano's head. Strong security forces were on duty: police under Mussolini's old Roman police chief Caruso and *Squadristi,* some of whom threatening openly to lynch the prisoners if the court did not convict them. The seats reserved for the public were occupied by stalwart local Fascists who could be relied upon to evince no sympathy for the accused. The Germans took pains to be inconspicuous, and only four observers, including Frau Beetz, attended the proceedings.

At about nine o'clock the six prisoners were brought in. Marinelli looked downcast and confused, but the others were calm. They had been allowed to choose a defending lawyer, but not to call witnesses. In Ciano's case it had been impossible to find anyone to undertake his defense, and it became therefore necessary to nominate a lawyer. The nine members of the tribunal, attired in black shirts, sat on a raised dais facing the public with the prisoners on their right and press and cameras to their left.

The first prisoner to be examined was Marshal De Bono, who appeared wearing military uniform and all his decorations. He denied any previous collusion with the King, referred to his services to fascism and his devotion to Mussolini, and emphasized the advantage of calling for national unity and entrusting the command of the armed forces to the King.

Pareschi, the former Minister of Agriculture, took the same line. The motion for which he had voted and which had been the subject of discussion at the Council merely dealt with the transfer of the military command to the King. "It never passed through my mind," he declared, "that the Duce should leave office." [35]

Cianetti, after referring at length to his Fascist past, claimed that he might have been foolish, but that he had acted in good faith. All he had wanted to do was to relieve Mussolini of responsibility for the war. Later he had understood the nature of the trap into which he had fallen, and he had written to the Duce offering his resignation, begging forgiveness, and asking to be sent as a combatant to the front.

Gottardi stated that he had acted in the belief that the morale of the nation was shaken. "Since it emerged from the Duce's own account at the Grand Council that the army did not want to fight, I thought that, if the Crown took a direct part in the fortunes of the war, perhaps the army would be able to recover." He also thought it would be a good thing to disassociate Mussolini from the conduct of the war at a time when it was taking a bad turn. As to the charge of conspiracy, it was the first occasion on which he had ever attended a meeting of the Grand Council, he did not even know the other members of the Council, and he had never seen Grandi's motion until it had been produced at the session. Poor Gottardi, who had been so innocently overjoyed to become a member of the Grand Council, had quite obviously not known what he was doing.

Equally pitiable was the case of Marinelli, who was deaf and had heard nothing of the proceedings at the Council from the bottom of the table, thirteen places removed from that of Mussolini. When invited by the President of the Court to say what had passed between himself and the other members of the Council before the session, he replied with conviction that he had been at Rovigo at the time in question and had never discussed the matter with anyone.

The last prisoner to be heard was Ciano, who admitted that he might have made an error, but energetically disclaimed treason. He had only wanted to muster the national forces from the King down to the humblest citizen, and in his mind the position of the Duce had been beyond discussion. The fact that the Duce had been given the text of Grandi's motion long before the session was evidence that there had been so conspiracy.

After the prisoners those who had not voted with Grandi were called. Scorza,* Suardo, Galbiati, and Frattari gave oral evidence, while Farinacci, Biggini, and Buffarini submitted written deposi-

* Scorza was under arrest at Padua and was subsequently tried and acquitted for his part in the so-called conspiracy.

tions. Nothing that they said was of any help to the prosecution's effort to establish that there had in fact been a conspiracy. Galbiati was allowed to stray into a disquisition on the events of July 26 and to explain why he did not mobilize the militia in support of Mussolini.

The court adjourned at six o'clock. It had not been a satisfactory day, for it had become clear that there had been no collusion between the Grand Council on the one hand and the King and the generals on the other. Moreover, it had even been impossible to prove that there had been any conspiracy or cooperation among the members of the Grand Council themselves. It might have been a different story if Grandi, Bottai, and Federzoni had been in the dock, but with the exception of Ciano and possibly De Bono the representatives of the Grand Council who appeared at Verona were miserable, second-rate figures incapable of conspiracy. There is evidence that even Vecchini, the president, was shaken by the failure of the prosecution to make a case.[36]

On the following day, Sunday, January 9, the proceedings took a more favorable turn. When the court opened at nine o'clock the judge read a document, the existence of which had not previously been made known. It was a statement signed by Marshal Cavallero after his arrest and interrogation by General Carboni, Badoglio's head of military intelligence. This document had been included among the papers extracted from Mussolini's files for submission to the tribunal. It had presumably been found by the Germans in Rome after September 8, 1943, and subsequently handed over to Mussolini.

In his statement [37] Cavallero described his part in the military intrigue against Mussolini from the time the Duce fell ill in November, 1942. Even after he had ceased to be chief of staff he had remained in touch with conspiring officers. "The problem of the removal of [the Duce] . . . at least from the military command, continued to occupy me. It was my view that, when Tunisia had fallen, it would be the moment to clear up the situation." The plan had been to entrust the military command to the King, who would declare a state of war throughout Italian territory, when all powers could be handed over to the army. "The rest would follow automatically." At the beginning of July, the statement continued, Ambrosio came to see Cavallero, who told him that the head of the new government would certainly be Badoglio, and that in the meantime he, Cavallero, would place himself at Ambrosio's orders for any eventuality.*

There was nothing in the Cavallero memorandum to show that any of the accused had been privy to the military intrigue. Nor was the authenticity or veracity of the statement tested or examined. Nevertheless it was eagerly accepted by the court as proving that Mussolini had been the victim of a large-scale conspiracy; and the prisoners were reproached for proposing to transfer power to the King and the military clique. What, asked one of the judges, were the accused aiming at when they sought the transfer of military powers to such traitors? De Bono answered that the whole Grand Council was against the General Staff and broadly speaking against all the generals, but these men "had twenty years of fascism on their shoulders and could not therefore all be traitors." Ciano retorted: "I voted for Grandi's motion because I wanted to commit the monarchy, and force it out of its nebulous state, by making the King take over the Supreme Command." [38] The bench, however, was able to score one small debating point when the presiding judge asked whether De Bono or Ciano had used their position as Collars of the Annunziata to intercede with the King after Mussolini's arrest. Neither was able to explain convincingly why they had done nothing.

It now fell to the public prosecutor to deliver the final speech for the prosecution. He was obliged to make bricks without straw and he elected, understandably, to rest his case on the Cavallero statement, which, he alleged, had proved the existence of an extensive plot. Having established this point, he went on to argue that there had also been a political conspiracy in the Grand Council and he demanded the death penalty for all the nineteen men who had voted for Grandi's motion. He concluded his speech with a flamboyant sentence in the revolutionary style addressed to the accused: "Thus I have thrown your heads into Italian history; perhaps my own also, but in order that Italy may live."

* It was the knowledge that these transactions would have to come to light which led to Cavallero's suicide soon after the statement was written.

The afternoon of January 9 and the following morning were devoted to the six speeches for the defense. The lawyers concerned were anxious not to compromise themselves, and, while they argued that there had been no premeditation or treasonable intent, their effort was somewhat perfunctory. At one point the president raised the hopes of the accused by suggesting to one lawyer that he would do well to lay more emphasis on the legal aspect.[39] But Vecchini was in fact merely concerned to give an impression of judicial impartiality. The only lawyer to make any impression was Cianetti's counsel, who was able without risk of offense to make some play of his client's letter of retraction and repentance.

The court retired at 10 A.M. to consider its verdict. Led by the militia general Montagna, four members of the tribunal wished to save De Bono, Gottardi, and Cienetti. For a time they were able to enlist the support of a fifth judge, who would have assured them a majority. The extremists, however, by means of threats and appeals to revolutionary conscience, eventually carried the day, and the odd vote was cast in favor of the death penalty for all except Cienetti, who was to be sentenced to thirty years' imprisonment.[40]

Shortly before 2 P.M. the court returned to deliver its verdict.[41] The prisoners heard it with composure, but with surprise, shared by the public prosecutor, who stated later that he had expected the court to show greater discrimination among the accused. Only Marinelli, who was deaf, was unaware of his fate; and he turned to Ciano: "And for me, what have they decided?" "Death, as for the rest of us," was Ciano's reply; and Marinelli collapsed in a faint.

The prisoners were conveyed back to the Scalzi prison, where they signed a petition to the Duce for a reprieve. Ciano at first refused to sign, but eventually agreed under pressure to do so in order not to prejudice the position of the others.

The hours which followed were a period of the utmost confusion, in which Edda Ciano made her last desperate effort and the extremists sought a means of rejecting the prisoners' appeal without referring it to Mussolini.

Edda Ciano had decided to flee to Switzerland with the Ciano papers, but before leaving Verona she arranged with an accomplice to push the following three letters under Frau Beetz's door.[42]

Letter to the German Military Commander in Italy.

General,

For the second time I have relied on the word of the Germans with the result which you know. This time it is enough. If what I was once promised is not done, I will unleash the most frightful campaign against the Axis and make use of all the evidence which I possess and all I know. My conditions: within three days from the moment these letters are handed over by Frau B., my husband must be in front of the military station in Berne, and accompanied only by Frau B. between ten o'clock in the morning and five o'clock in the afternoon. If this is carried out in complete loyalty, we will retire into private life and no more will be heard of us.

Frau B. will be handed the diaries by my husband on the same day. I enclose two letters on the same subject to the Fuehrer and to the Duce. Forward them immediately together with a copy of this letter.

Letter to the Fuehrer.

Fuehrer,

For the second time I believe your word, and for the second time I have been deceived. Only the fact that our soldiers have fallen side by side on the battlefields has hitherto restrained me from going over to the enemy. If my husband is not released on the conditions which I have specified to your general, no further consideration will hold me back. For some time the documents have been in the hands of persons who are empowered only to make use of them if anything should happen to my husband or to me, my children, and family. But if, as I hope, my conditions are accepted and we are left in peace in the future, you will not hear from us again.

I am grieved to take this step, but you will understand.

Edda Ciano.

Letter to the Duce.

Duce,

I have waited until today for you to show me the slightest feeling of humanity and friendliness. Now it is enough. If Galeazzo is not in Switzerland in three days according to the conditions which I have stipulated to the Germans, I shall make merciless and clearly documented use of all that I know. In the opposite case, if we are left in peace and security . . . you will hear no more of us.

Edda Ciano.

Edda Ciano reached Switzerland safely that day and the news of her successful escape reached Ciano the same night through a friend who visited him in the Scalzi prison. Her letter was transmitted by Frau Beetz through General Harster and General Wolff and was delivered to Mussolini during the night. According to Wolff, Mussolini telephoned to him at about five o'clock on the morning of January 11 to inquire whether he should intervene; and Wolff answered that he could offer no official opinion, but that privately he was against interference.[43] In any event Mussolini did nothing.

Meanwhile Pavolini was desperately hunting for someone willing to reject the prisoners' appeal and confirm the death sentences. Since the Special Tribunals acted under military law, he addressed himself in the first place to General Piatti dal Pozzo, the local district commander. The general, however, firmly declined to have anything to do with the business and pleaded incompetence to deal with a political verdict. Pavolini, accompanied by the public prosecutor and Cersosimo, then drove to Brescia to see the Minister of Justice, Pisenti. The latter had been consistently opposed to the trial and was in no mood to be helpful, but in the course of an excited and disorderly exchange of views he offered to accept the appeals for clemency and transmit them to the Duce. But this was what Pavolini was determined to avoid. "It is absolutely necessary," he shouted, "to leave Mussolini right out of it."[44]

Night had fallen and the party drove disconsolately to Maderno to interview the Minister of the Interior, who suggested to Pavolini that he should apply to the senior militia officer in Verona, Consul Vianini. The Consul at first proved equally reluctant, and declared himself ill in bed. He was, however, eventually summoned to the prefecture at Verona, and after much argument and a telephone call to Ricci he reluctantly agreed to sign the rejection of the appeals and to order the execution. It was now nearly six o'clock on the morning of January 11 and Pavolini had spent sixteen hours carrying his point.

In the Scalzi the chaplain, Don Chiot, had spent the night ministering to the prisoners, who had been allowed to leave their cells and mix together. At first the S. S. guards had refused him access, but on the intervention of Frau Beetz he was allowed to hear confessions and give communion. At about nine o'clock the public prosecutor with other officials appeared with the news that the appeals had been rejected and that the sentence would be executed forthwith. The prisoners were handed over to the Chief of the Province of Verona, and the S. S. guard, which had been posted to guard Ciano, was withdrawn.

The final scene matched the disorder and squalor of the events which preceded it. It is described in a report by an S. S. officer who was instructed to attend at the Scalzi prison and witness the execution.[45]

> The final arrangements passed in sordid confusion. Judges, police officials, and armed guards began to throng the prison. The condemned men were thrust into their cells and manacled. An untidy procession, headed by Don Chiot, filed into the courtyard, Ciano was cursing loudly, and Marinelli in a state of collapse. At De Bono's instance Ciano quieted, and turning to the chaplain, said: "we have all made mistakes, and we are all swept away by the same gale. Tell my family that I die without rancor against anyone. . . ."
>
> I accompanied the Chief of Province and his retinue in the prisoners' vehicle to the scene of the execution, a shooting range in the Forte San Procolo, a suburb of Verona. . . . The firing squad consisted of a detachment of militia, some twenty-five men strong. The execution took place in the following manner. The criminals were made to sit back to front on a chair, i.e., with the back of the chair facing forwards so that their own backs were exposed to the firing squad. Their hands were tied to the back of the chair. In the case of Marshal De Bono, who was farthest away from where I was standing, I gathered from his headshakings and reluctance that he was refusing to be bound and only agreed to it after some persuasion. The only prisoner who caused trouble was again Marinelli, who had to be bound by force by several people and shrieked and moaned the whole time. The others maintained a calm demeanor. The firing squad took up their positions in two rows fifteen paces behind the prisoners, their small Italian rifles loaded and at the ready. . . . Just before the order to fire was given one of the condemned men, either Gottardi or Pareschi, shouted: "Long Live Italy! Long Live the Duce!" After the first salvo four of the prisoners fell to the ground, taking their chairs with them, while one remained sitting on his chair quite unaffected, to judge from his posture. From the distance at which I was standing I could not make out whether he had been kept erect by sheer equilibrium or whether he had been hit at all.

The men lying on the ground had been so inaccurately hit that they were writhing and screaming. After a short embarrassed pause a few more shots were fired from the ranks of the firing squad at the man still on the chair and the others on the ground. Finally the cease fire was given, and the men were finished off with pistols by the commander of the squad and a few other militiamen. When Ciano's death and that of all the other prisoners had been confirmed I left the place of execution.

Two significant items were omitted from the S. S. officer's report. As a special precaution, the Germans had brought an additional firing squad to the rifle range. They took up station close to the Italian squad, which was thus placed on notice that no dereliction of duty would be tolerated. As soon as the execution was over, a German officer examined Ciano's body to ensure that there had been no last-minute substitution.[46]

Throughout these days Mussolini, although he maintained an outward calm, was prey to growing agitation. He received constant progress reports from Verona, and when during the afternoon of January 10 he grimly received the news of the verdict, he sought to justify himself to Dolfin. Grandi and the others, he declared, had known exactly what they were doing, although he admitted that De Bono, probably, and Gottardi, certainly, had not understood the implications of the vote. "The real culprits have escaped. If I vanquished myself by this extreme step, it is because I hope, as I have been given to understand from every quarter, that it will be useful to the country. I have never had a lust for blood."[47]

VII

During the weeks which followed the execution Mussolini was unable to dismiss the matter from his mind. He sought information on every detail, he interviewed in turn the director of the prison, the chaplain Don Chiot, the militia general Montagna, and other witnesses; and he went over the subject endlessly with Dolfin and Mazzolini. His thoughts clearly rested with Ciano and Edda rather than with the four admittedly innocent men whom he had sent to their death. He even sought to defend Ciano. To Mazzolini he declared that at the Grand Council Ciano had merely spoken of foreign policy and of the German practice of informing their ally in the middle of the night of events which had already taken place; and he described as malicious inventions the stories that Ciano had corruptly enriched himself.[48]

His attitude was summed up in an exchange of letters four months later with Serrano Suñer, who wrote to him in May, 1944, deprecating the political error of Ciano's death. On June 11 Mussolini replied: "I have sometimes thought that the end of Count Ciano would have particularly saddened you, and this I understand. In the many agitations of my life, what happened at Verona has been the most dramatic chapter. Sentiment and *raison d'état* have sharply collided in my spirit." [49] It was characteristic of Mussolini's amoral nature that he should have emphasized the violence done to his family feeling rather than to his sense of justice.

In his anguished search for self-justification Mussolini may have received some consolation from a long despatch in which his ambassador in Berlin described the repercussions of the trial in Germany.[50] Anfuso reported that the Germans had not expected such severity and concluded: "There can be no doubt that the Verona trials have revealed here that Republican Italy has cut its link with the past, and intends to be near to Germany always in every way." In Italy the effect was momentarily to strengthen Mussolini's position with his party extremists, and at the same time to exacerbate internal strife. In Milan the public sentiment was described to him as disastrous, while in Rome people spoke of the condemned men as martyrs and of Mussolini as a butcher. Ciano was reported to have won in death an esteem which he never enjoyed in life. Mussolini in conversation with his familiars made no attempt to deny that he had made himself unpopular; and when he was told that it was rumored in Rome that he was no longer alive, he retorted sadly: "They may be right." [51] His impotent resentment against the Germans increased and he was driven more and more into himself and into the world of fantasy in which he spent much of his time at Gargagno. Skorzeny, who visited him in June, found that he had gone downhill. He did not seem to be addressing himself with much zest to his political problems and spent much of his time in meditation. On his return to Germany Skorzeny reported that the Duce was no longer the active head of a state, but had become a political philosopher.[52]

The breach with his favorite child, which was never healed, continued for a long time to be a source of affliction. He tried to re-establish relations with her through Don Guisto Pancino, a priest in a mountain parish who had made her acquaintance in an Albanian hospital; and he authorized the removal of Ciano's body from Verona for burial at Leghorn, in accordance with the dead man's wishes. In May Father Pancino took to Switzerland an affectionate letter in which Mussolini gave Edda the family news and asked her to write. The reply was uncompromising. After thanking him coldly for the concession over Ciano's body, she concluded: "I shall be the wife of a traitor and a thief.* And I shall be extraordinarily proud of it. I carry the ensanguined name of my husband with pride; it is an honor. And that goes for you and for your slaves and for your masters." [53]

In July Mussolini tried again; and Father Pancino was despatched with another affectionate letter in which he pleaded for understanding. But Edda was still not ready for reconciliation. "Thank you," she replied, "for sending me the Father with my remaining effects. I do not know what to say to you. So far as I am concerned the injustice and the cowardice of men, including yourself, have inflicted so much suffering on me that I am now incapable of further suffering. I only pray that everything will finish soon." [54]

Mussolini's susceptibility to his environment and his contact with Don Pancino revived his interest in religion. There were long talks on religious matters, and he publicly declared his attachment to the Catholic faith. "We are Catholics by conviction," he said to a delegation of priests, representing a Catholic newspaper, "I am a Catholic by conviction, because I believe that Catholicism is the religion which possesses a doctrine capable of resolving all the problems of life, individual and social, national and international; and in the conflict between the spirit and materialism it sustains and desires the primacy and the victory of the spirit." [55] But when Don Pancino urged him to return to the sacraments of the Church, he replied:

* A reference to the allegation that Ciano had illicitly enriched himself.

"Let us wait a little, Father Pancino. There is time, there is time." He gave the priest the impression that he did not yet regard his cause as lost or feel that the end was approaching.[56] In fact he had a mere nine months to run.

CHAPTER TWENTY-THREE

The Salò Republic

1944–1945

I

IF Mussolini really thought that the Verona trial would improve the position of his government, he was quickly disillusioned. So long as he could place no forces in the field, he could not hope to recover any standing in the Axis alliance; and there was now little prospect of raising, training, equipping, and marshaling an army for battle. By March, 1944, the total number of men in the army was only 130,639,[1] a force inadequate to deal even with the growing partisan threat. There was not much prospect of raising any larger force since the Germans were competing for Italian manpower and obstinately refusing to release even the equipment which they had taken from disbanded Italian units. There were in Germany large numbers of interned Italian soldiers, on whom Mussolini might have drawn, but Hitler declined to free them on the ground that they were unreliable. The fact was that the Germans, while anxious to preserve Mussolini as a political figurehead, were opposed to the creation of an independent Italian administration with its own armed forces.

Moreover, it was impossible to make rational use of even the small available forces, since the members of the Salò government fought ceaselessly among themselves for control; and Mussolini was unwilling to come down definitely on the side of one of the contending parties. While this situation lasted, and Mussolini remained wholly in the hands of the Germans, who interfered in every detail of internal administration,* it was manifestly impossible to invest the regime with sufficient prestige and authority to enable it to function. In 1944 the situation deteriorated rapidly. Intrigues at Lake Garda multiplied, relations with Germans became more tense, and Mussolini without conviction or hope could only make fumbling efforts to grapple with his problems. His ingrained habit of playing one man off against another only added to the confusion attending the proceedings of his phantom government.

He soon decided to drop for the moment his project for an army and to concentrate on the structure of his republican system, a sphere in which he was not so dependent on the Germans. Here expediency and inclination coincided. The old Fascist system, now described as one of compromise with the monarchy and bourgeoisie, was discredited. The delegates at the Verona congress had echoed the sentiments of the old *Squadristi* and demanded a new deal. The Salò Republic, without a constitution, without a past, and without encumbrances could make a fresh start. In the struggle with the monarchist Badoglio government for the allegiance of the Italian people, Mussolini would raise the standard of socialism.

In doing so he not only assuaged his resentment against the monarchy, which had betrayed him, the bourgeoisie, which had sabotaged his war, and the plutocracies, who were fighting him; but he had the satisfaction of returning to the ranks of a party after which he had throughout his life intermittently hankered. It was a theme to which he constantly reverted in his conversations at Gargagno, when he even referred to Soviet Russia with respect and regard. Speaking to Dolfin, he said that, whatever the issue of the world conflict, Italy after her voluntary exit from the war was bound to be "cracked like a nut. It will be a question tomorrow for the Italians to choose a protector. In that eventuality, which now seems certain, I should not, as an Italian citizen, hesitate a moment to choose Stalin." A little later he praised Stalin's political ability in proclaiming a new Europe in which all the liberated countries could play an autonomous part, and he continued: "It is

* Rahn even demanded to be consulted before prefects were appointed.

clear that 95 per cent of the Italians, if they were called upon freely to determine their future destiny, would opt for Stalin."[2]

After some preliminary sparring between rival claimants Mussolini decided to entrust the task of socialization to a new Ministry of Corporate Economy, to which he appointed Angelo Tarchi. On February 12, 1944, the cabinet accepted a decree, which in its preamble[3] defined its aim as designed to "accompany action on the battlefield with an affirmation of a political idea"; and realize the Mussolinian conception of a higher social justice, a more equal distribution of wealth, and the participation of labor in the life of the nation. The last article of the preamble envisaged the extension of the system to other countries and spoke of "a new order, which would give the nations the opportunity of constructing their future and of conquering their rightful place on the international plane after the victory of the Axis." It was a conception wholly divorced from reality.

The decree itself,[4] entitled "Legislative Decree for the Socialization of Enterprises," laid down that in all enterprises with a capital of over one million lire or employing more than a hundred persons, management committees would be formed under the chairmanship of the director of the enterprise and composed of an equal number of representatives of the investors and management on the one hand, and of employees on the other. The director would have a vote. The workers' representatives would be elected from a special panel, an arrangement which would enable the government to exercise control and ensure that no undesirable elements infiltrated into the management committees. The director with his management committee would be answerable to the state for their conduct of affairs. There were also similar provisions for state-owned industries.

Rahn and his fellow Germans in Italy were much disturbed at this development,* of which he was informed by Tarchi two days before the cabinet meeting. He demanded to see the text of the decree, and, when this was refused, he lodged a protest against

* After the war the Christian Democrat government of Federal Germany gave the workers the right to equal representation on the boards of certain industries under the "*Mitbestimmungsrecht*" law.

such unilateral action on the part of the Italian government. He claimed that radical legislation must affect German interests in the Italian arms industry as well as labor relations in the operational zones and elsewhere. In the circumstances the advance agreement of the Germans should be obtained. Otherwise, "the Italian government must in future expect to see the publication and enforcement of cabinet decrees prevented by the Germans."

Mussolini, while he insisted on going ahead with his plan, was prepared to make a concession to the Germans. In a letter to Rahn of February 10 he declared that the new law would be approved and published forthwith. Nevertheless "its publication will not mean that it will be applied immediately. I hope that this method of procedure will be enough to re-establish a calmer apprehension of the situation and such as to convince everyone that in war ideas are the best allies of weapons. Forty years of political experience give me the right to make such an affirmation." [5]

Rahn could only refer the matter to the Fuehrer, who replied through Ribbentrop that the social and economic measures taken in Italy were a matter for the Duce to determine, though he did not think they would prove a great success. The question of a swing to the Left hardly came into it, since the swing had already occurred to such an extent that if the German troops were withdrawn the whole edifice would collapse.[6] With this directive Rahn had to be content. Nevertheless the local German representatives in Italy continued to obstruct the implementation of Mussolini's socialization measures, and in fact they were never fully put into effect.

From the point of view of internal propaganda he was equally unsuccessful. Even in the Fascist Party there was no unanimous support for the decree. Some, including Pini, were favorable; others, while admitting that it might have some propaganda value, regarded it as impracticable, while a section led by Farinacci was openly hostile and declared that no social program could be launched until the war was won. Some of the industrialists, possibly because they were concerned to improve labor relations, gave the plan cautious approval, and the managing director of Fiat went so far as to tell Rahn that the law would be welcomed by all those who, rising above private interests, saw in the new social program a means not only of reconciling capital with labor but of asserting the personality and the initiative of the individual.[7]

The big disappointment, however, was the attitude of the working classes, which regarded the operation with suspicion as a mere gambit of Fascist propaganda. The Communist agitators in the factories were quick to exploit the prevalent scepticism and at the beginning of March large-scale strikes broke out in Milan and Turin. The German reaction was swift. On Hitler's orders 20 per cent of the strikers were to be deported to Germany and put at Himmler's disposal for labor service. These measures achieved the desired result and the partisan Action Committee soon ordered a return to work, but the episode revealed not only the growing strength of the resistance movement, but the total failure of the Salò government to win the allegiance of the workers.

Mussolini's subsequent efforts to bring the law into force finally collapsed in the face of the continued opposition of the Germans and the apathy or open hostility of the workers. In a letter to Mussolini one of the Fascist syndicate leaders frankly exposed the gloomy truth:

> The masses refuse to accept anything from us . . . the workers assert there will be no nationalization. . . . They think German influence has been decisively negative, and such as to postpone the solution of the problem at least until after the war. . . . This has the effect of heaping on to us their contempt, as they said we were not in good faith and hold that the announcement of nationalization was the *n*th expedient to draw into our orbit the few mugs who still give us any credit. In brief, the workers consider nationalization as a mirror to catch larks, and they keep well away from us and the mirror.[8]

The whole operation had proved a damp squib.

II

By March Mussolini, in his isolation on Lake Garda, disappointed at the progress which his government had made, and ever more resentful of German behavior, felt that he could get no further with Rahn and that he must have a heart-to-heart talk with the Fuehrer. Apart from the aftermath of the Verona trial, which still weighed on him, the failure of his social experiment, and the endless squabbles and dissensions of his lakeside existence, there were several problems on his mind. First and foremost, there was the matter of the so-called operational zones, where Italian civil authorities had been expelled and the *Gauleiters* were behaving like viceroys. His rage and mortification were increased by reports that he was believed to have agreed to the arrangement. Then there was the question of raising and eventually expanding an Italian combatant army. Here little or no progress had been made during the six months of his government's existence, though its fate depended on an early solution. Finally there was the need to put a stop to German interference in the Italian administration and economy. On all these points only the Fuehrer could give him satisfaction.

At the end of March Rahn reported home that the Duce was angling for a meeting with the Fuehrer. He gave an accurate account of the points which Mussolini wished to raise, and he bravely recommended not only that Mussolini should be received, but that he should not be sent away with entirely empty hands. "It is in our real interest," he wrote, "to back up somewhat more the Italian feeling of independence, and to mitigate the ever-recurring depressive tendencies of the Duce by certain personal or practical satisfactions." The Fuehrer agreed with pleasure that a conference with Mussolini should be held towards the end of April.

Before leaving Italy it occurred to Mussolini that he would do well to take advantage of his visit to inspect elements of the four Italian divisions then under training in Germany. It would draw public attention to their existence and afford a welcome change from the miasma of Lake Garda. But, aware of Hitler's objections to the reconstitution of an Italian army, he put out a gingerly feeler, explaining to Rahn that his wish was not a *sine qua non,* but that he would be grateful before leaving to know whether such a visit would be agreeable to the Fuehrer. His modest request was at once granted, and on April 16 Rahn telegraphed that the Duce proposed to give Hitler a detailed report on the military and political situation in Italy. Two days would be enough, and "the Duce asks that the meeting should be confined to business, and attaches value to having his meals as far as possible alone." [9] He was already sufficiently humiliated and was in no mood to endure the panoply attending previous gatherings.

The first session of the conference took place on the morning of April 22 in the now familiar setting of Schloss Klessheim. Hitler's advisers included Ribbentrop, Keitel, Rahn, and Wolff, while Mussolini had brought with him Graziani, Mazzolini, and two Italian representatives from Berlin, Anfuso and his military attaché. In contradistinction to the normal proceeding at such conferences it was Mussolini, who, speaking in German, opened the proceedings with a long statement. After referring to the confusion reigning in Italy when he had taken over, he referred to the fate of the Italian troops interned in Italy and claimed that the morale of his people would be raised if the situation of the military internees could be improved. He then took up the question of the operational zones. But on both issues he weakened his case by admitting that the action of the Germans had been necessary at the time. Graziani was disappointed and noted later: "He was not incisive, and did not know how to speak clearly, particularly in front of Hitler." [10] Had Graziani been present at previous meetings with the Fuehrer he would have known that Mussolini was displaying his normal form.

Mussolini went on to give a pessimistic account of the standing of his republic in the eyes of the Italian people, and to urge that it was in the German interest to sustain him. After all, the republic since September 8 had made a significant contribution. Sauckel had requested a million workers, Goering had asked for two hundred thousand Italians for his antiaircraft batteries, Kesselring for sixty-two thousand. He was ready to supply these, but the Italian people must be given the impression that the Italian government was independent and that there was certain fields in which it had complete control.

At Mussolini's request Graziani then intervened to make a statement on the difficulties besetting an Italian Minister of War. He had no resources with which to build up an army, and even the telephone and telegraph lines were in German hands; there was the problem of obtaining loyal officers; there were not enough police to enforce the call-up of conscripts. The war against the partisans, in which ten or twelve battalions were engaged, was important for the prestige of the government, but whereas the partisans were well armed and equipped, the Republican forces were poorly armed and lacked transport. There were no longer any uniforms in the depots for the new recruits. When Graziani had finished, there was some inconclusive discussion on the partisan war and the meeting adjourned for lunch.

In the afternoon Hitler attended a domestic military conference, and the talks with Mussolini were not resumed until five o'clock. It was now Hitler's turn, and he dwelt at length on his difficulties. His allies had not borne their share of the burden, and circumstances had compelled him to take stern measures in Italy and Hungary. The decision, however, would be fought out in the West, and he pointed out that there were points of strife between the members of the unnatural coalition arrayed against him. On this hopeful note the conference again adjourned.

On the following morning, April 23, the Fuehrer dealt more specifically with the Italian situation, and what he had to say brought little comfort to Mussolini. Anfuso records that he had never heard Hitler express himself so brutally.[11] He complained bitterly that he had based his plans on the personality of the Duce, only to find that both the man and his regime had disappeared overnight. Turning to the Germans present, he asked dramatically whether it were conceivable that anything of the sort could happen in Germany.

As regards the position of the interned Italian troops, he complained of a Communist movement in Linz which obtained its support from Italians interned there; and he went on to allege that these subversive men enjoyed the protection of the Italian embassy in Berlin. "Believe me, Duce, whatever you may do for them will only earn you disillusion." It was only because of the unreliability of the Italian army that he had been obliged to take emergency measures to intern them. The consequence had been the imposition of fresh burdens on the German people, who rightly demanded that the Italians should at least be put to work. Even so the behavior of the Italian workers had left much to be desired. Some of them were Communists, and they compared unfavorably with French workers in Germany.

As regards Mussolini's request for a new Italian army, he emphasized the difficulty of finding arms; the Germans must have priority and "every German rifle must go to the front." Moreover, the Italians, he repeated, were unreliable. If out of the 600,000 soldiers interned, 200,000 should volunteer for active service, they would only be doing so to improve their lot. He wished to provide the Duce with the nucleus of a reliable military force, but the soldiers must be determined to fight for the Duce like a Roman legion; and he made it clear that he regarded this an unlikely contingency.

Hitler was equally intransigent over his requirements in the operational zones, which he described as essential to the safety of the German army in Italy. "Under no circumstances should a crisis be allowed to occur in the rear areas. A gradual abandonment of the necessary military measures in those zones was dependent on strengthening the Fascist system. This process, however, was dependent on the Duce, and it was of extreme importance that he should remain in good health." There was no reference to German interference in Italian internal affairs, which effectively impeded any strengthening of the regime. He concluded with a vague assurance that he would do his best for the military internees, and sort out the younger, more reliable men, in order to supply the Duce with "the yeast, the germ from which the future Italian army would be developed."

At the final session in the afternoon both men sought to attenuate the asperity of the earlier discussions. Mussolini declared that he would be satisfied if the military internees remained in Germany, and he only asked for better conditions. He also agreed that his divisions should continue to be reconstituted in Germany and that the units should be fewer and more reliable. Finally he offered to call up the 1914 class for Sauckel and the 1916 and 1917 classes for Goering; and to call up twenty classes for service in labor battalions. Hitler, for his part, repeated that he would rely on the Duce. If Rahn forwarded the Duce's wishes, he would see that they were fulfilled, or if this proved impossible, he would say so frankly.

That evening the Fuehrer and the Duce met alone over the dinner table. There is no record of their conversation, but it seems that Hitler must have reverted to the old theme of the secret weapons and the inevitability of final victory. Anfuso noted that "when they parted company Mussolini confided to me that Hitler's affirmations as to the outcome of the war had seemed to him devilishly optimistic." [12]

III

From Klessheim Mussolini traveled to Grafenroehr camp to inspect the 600 officers and 12,000 men of the San Marco division under training. Excited by their tumultuous welcome, he delivered a fighting speech quite in his old vein. "Beyond the river Garigliano," he shouted, "are the encampments not only of the cruel, cynical Briton, but of the American, the Frenchman, the Pole, the Indian, the South African, the Canadian, the New Zealander, the Moor, the Senegalese, the Negro, and the Bolshevik. You will have the joy of opening fire on this medley of bastard races and mercenaries, who in invaded Italy respect nothing and no one."[13] With the cheers of the troops still ringing in his ears he returned refreshed to the vernal landscape of Lake Garda. Thanks to the ministrations of Dr. Zachariae his health was now much improved, and he seemed more serene and optimistic. "He regained confidence in himself and the future of the Fatherland," Mazzolini wrote in his diary.[14] It proved, however, to be only the flicker of a dying fire. In the summer months to come each week brought further disastrous tidings.

On June 4 Rome fell and the Allied armies began to sweep up the peninsula. On July 3 they captured Siena, Arezzo on July 16, and by July 19 they had reached Leghorn on the Mediterranean and Ancona on the Adriatic. The loss of Rome, although not unexpected and to some extent discounted, shook the Republic and was a bitter personal blow to Mussolini. It was the city on which he had always pinned his hopes and lavished his affection. He ordered three days of national mourning and issued a proclamation to the Italian people. This reverse, he declared, should not weaken their resolve. "Soldiers to arms, workers and farmers to work! The Republic is threatened by the plutocracies and their mercenaries of every race. Defend it." In an article in the *Corrispondensa Repubblicana* he wrote that he was afflicted by the thought that black troops were passing under the arches and on the streets which had been built to exalt the ancient and modern glory of Rome.

The Italians who have not lost their sense of honor, the Italians who do not intend to remain under the burden of shame, the Italians who are not resigned but wish to rebel against adverse fortune will eventually in their love of Rome and Italy be united in hatred of and vengeance against the enemy. Garibaldi's cry: "Rome or death" will now become the order of the day, the supreme duty of all true Italians.[15]

These stirring words fell into space. There was no echo.

On the contrary, as the territory of the Salò Republic contracted, there was an exodus from the threatened towns of Fascist authorities, who streamed northwards like wild game in front of a forest fire. There were mass desertions from Italian army units under German command and the military police and the Republican Guard began to melt away, usually with their arms. When the Allies landed in Elba, the Italian garrison with bands playing went over to the enemy, an episode which to the Germans seemed to justify their complete lack of confidence in Italian troops. Pavolini, referring to conditions in the province of Lucca, reported to Mussolini that it was "difficult to imagine the state of abandonment, of weakness and squabbling, and contradictory errors."[16] There was widespread criticism of the leadership.

From the other battlefronts the news was equally depressing. The Germans had manifestly failed to repel the Anglo-American landings in Normandy; and in the East they were still in retreat. The circle was fast closing around the Third Reich.

IV

It is not surprising that in this climate there should have been a collapse of the Republic's authority and an accession of strength to the partisans. By June, 1944, the number had risen ominously. According to figures compiled by Mussolini's own army staff the strength of the rebel forces was estimated at 82,000, an increase of some 27,000 over the preceding season.[17] From Piedmont, General Montagna reported that "the rebels, who already control almost the whole of Piedmont, will finish by taking it over completely." In Liguria and in Vincenza, Verona, and Treviso the situation was described as grave. In Milan, according to the commander, it was precarious. All the military police posts in the province were closed and one night a thousand partisans had been able to enter the city.

Altogether in June there were some 2,200 engagements with the rebels.

Mussolini's most pressing task was to mobilize his tenuous resources in order to check the partisan movement before it could engulf him. On June 21 he authorized a decree establishing the so-called Black Brigades, new units composed of *Squadristi* and based on the party. On June 25 he instructed Graziani personally to coordinate all military action against the outlaws; and on June 27 he wrote to the Marshal: "The organization of the movement against the partisans . . . must be such as to strike people psychologically and rouse enthusiasm in our unified ranks. It must be the 'March of the Social Republic against the Partisans' (*La Vendée*)." [18]

Picturesque imagery made little appeal to Graziani, who proceeded to set forth his views in a long memorandum which he handed to the Duce. He first summarized the causes of the Republic's failure: the war was popularly believed to be lost; communism was spreading; the continued employment of men like Buffarini, Pavolini, and Ricci aggravated the prevailing distrust of fascism; German interference and the maintenance of the operational zones undermined the prestige of the Republic; the German recruitment of Italian manpower was unpopular and was driving men into the partisan ranks. It was "a grave error to impose the Goering-Sauckel program on Italy at such a time. The Germans have no conception of Italian psychology, as is simply shown by their treatment of the military internees"; there had been a total failure to reconstruct the army. Only four battalions had been sent to the front and, apart from the four divisions training in Germany, there were no other soldiers, only workmen; in practice the Republic only controlled the plain of the river Po. "All the rest was virtually in the hands of the rebels."

After this gloomy, but realistic, catalogue Graziani listed the military and political measures required by the situation: an end to the German levy of forced labor; reconsideration of the position of the military internees; propaganda for army recruitment; liberty of action for the Republic; German equipment of the military volunteers; reorganization of the party, involving the removal of those figures who were tainted by the past; reorganization of the Republican Guard.[19]

The problem of translating plans into effective action was complicated by two factors, internal dissension and German obstruction. Among the party bosses there was no mutual confidence and each, with Mussolini's tacit encouragement, intrigued against his fellow for this or that illusory preferment. It was all reminiscent of the conduct of an exiled government on foreign soil. The Germans, for their part, saw no virtue in an Italian army or in according any liberty to the Salò Republic. There was continued interference, to the point that they even censored some of Mussolini's press articles.

There were endless talks between Graziani and German representatives, and eventually Kesselring informed the Italians that he had recommended the despatch to Italy of two of the Italian divisions training in Germany, which would be used against the rebels. Graziani pointed out that many of the troops concerned had not been home for years. If allowed to go home, they might never return; and if refused leave, they would desert. It was agreed that before the troops returned to Italy Mussolini should pay them a visit in Germany, using his talent to bring them to a proper way of thinking. This trip would afford the opportunity of a further meeting with the Fuehrer; and the particular points to be raised were the position of the internees, on which nothing had been done since Klessheim, and the employment of the Italian divisions training in Germany.

V

Mussolini and his party left Gargagno on July 15 in a special train provided by the Germans and under the care of the German Head of Protocol. The following three days were spent traveling from camp to camp to inspect the troops. Once again he made the now familiar speeches and was received with the utmost enthusiasm; and the transient optimism with which this experience filled him seemed to infect his Italian companions. At Gargagno he was never tired of telling his visitors that he was the best hated man in Italy. The martial spectacle of troops in review order and the welcome which the young warriors gave him recalled his days of glory and banished from his mind the heartsearching and the gloom of his lonely ruminations on the lakeside.

It was consequently in a mood of some exaltation that he embarked on the long train journey from Sennelager to Rastenburg, where he was due to arrive at 3 P.M. He was about to have his last and most dramatic meeting with the Fuehrer.

As the train approached its destination, it halted suddenly, to the suprise of the Italians who were accustomed to meticulous punctuality in the German arrangements for the Duce. The doors and windows were sealed and blacked out, and from Doernberg's agitation it was clear that something serious had occurred. After an hour the train advanced slowly and drew up at Goerlitz station. On the platform Hitler, accompanied by Ribbentrop, Himmler, Bormann, Keitel, and Doenitz, stood to greet the guest. The appearance of the two dictators symbolized the crumbling fortunes of the Axis: Hitler, pale, his right arm in a sling and, despite the summer heat, wearing a large black cloak; Mussolini, sallow, his cheeks fallen in, a shrunken, almost humble, figure.

Hitler advanced to Mussolini's coach and said: "Duce, an infernal machine had just been let off at me." Although outwardly calm, Hitler was in a state of considerable suppressed excitement. He had no idea of the extent of the conspiracy, no reports from Berlin. There were orders to be given and plans for vengeance were racing through his mind. Mussolini's visit could not have come at a more inconvenient moment. Nevertheless he accompanied the Duce to the encampment at Rastenburg and, after a brief private conversation with Himmler, led the Italian party to the scene of the outrage. Here in a torrent of eloquence he described the explosion and gloried in his escape. "Having now escaped death so miraculously," he concluded, "I am more than ever sure that the great destiny I serve will transcend its present perils and that all will be brought to a triumphant conclusion." [20]

Mussolini was aghast. He had a morbid dislike of death and, despite his ability to display courage in an emergency, an ingrained fear of assassination. As he surveyed the shattered and still smoldering conference room, it seemed incredible that anyone should have survived. He was impressed by the Fuehrer's self-confidence, and readily agreed that though the outlook might seem bad, after the miracle they had witnessed it was inconceivable that their cause should meet with misfortune.[21] Nevertheless he would not have been human had he not nourished a secret satisfaction at the thought that he was no longer the only dictator to have been the victim of a palace revolution. To Barracu he later said exultantly: "The days of humiliation are over. It is not only Mussolini who is beset with traitors." [22]

The tea party which followed had the quality of a macabre gathering of criminal lunatics. Hitler sat moodily apart, sucking brightly colored lozenges prescribed by Professor Morrell, and only intervened once to rise and noisily call down bloody vengeance on the heads of the conspirators. Mussolini was silently engrossed in the problem of his forthcoming conversation. The table talk was supplied by the German nabobs, who after tendering formal congratulations to Hitler on his escape began to quarrel among themselves in front of their embarrassed Italian guests. Mutual recriminations over the conduct of the war were bandied about the room, and at one point Goering was seen to be threatening Ribbentrop with his Marshal's baton. "I am still Foreign Minister," Ribbentrop shouted back, "and my name is *von* Ribbentrop." [23]

The party was mercifully broken up to enable the meeting with Mussolini to begin. There was much for Hitler to do, and he was anxious to rid himself of the Italians as soon as he decently could. His conventional war survey was weary and perfunctory. He spoke of problems of supply, the new secret weapons which would incinerate London, the need for additional manpower. He must have Italian volunteers for antiaircraft batteries to protect the factories. If these were not forthcoming, he would have to draw on the Italian divisions. But if volunteers presented themselves, not only two but all four Italian divisions could go home and with, say, four German divisions, constitute an army under Graziani's command. In Italy Kesselring would fight a delaying action as long as possible. Meanwhile energetic steps would be taken to recover German superiority in the air. They could look to the future with confidence. The events of that day had reinforced his conviction that "Providence tested men and gave the palm only to such as pursued their path undismayed and undeterred by difficulty."

In his statement, which in the special circumstances he undertook to keep as short as possible, Mussolini agreed that the disposal of two Italian divisions could be settled between Keitel and Graziani.

In any event the return of the other two divisions would create an excellent impression in Italy. He then produced a memorandum on the military internees which had been drafted in the train, and said that he would like to receive a present from the Fuehrer on this subject. Hitler hurriedly read the paper and said that he concurred in Mussolini's proposals. His mind was centered on developments in Berlin, from which messages were constantly coming in, and Italian affairs seemed remote and relatively unimportant. Meanwhile Keitel, under Graziani's pressure, had reluctantly agreed to the return of all four Italian divisions. Mussolini had, on paper, for the first time emerged from a meeting with Hitler with the comforting feeling that he had secured all that he had set out to obtain.

At seven o'clock Hitler went down to the station to speed his guest. For the last time the two dictators gazed into one another's eyes as they said goodby. "I know," said Hitler, as they parted, "that I can count on you, and I beg you to believe me when I say that I look on you as my best and possibly only friend I have in the world." [24]

VI

As Mussolini's career drew to a close, the occasional shafts of sunlight which penetrated the clouds became shorter and less warming. The hopes of an amelioration in his situation, with which he had returned from Rastenburg, soon evaporated. The first two divisions duly returned from Germany at the end of July and were formed with three German divisions into an Army Group "Liguria" under Graziani's command, ostensibly to deal with an Allied landing on the northwest coast or an attack coming through the Alpine passes from France. In fact the Army Group was deployed against the partisans, and Mussolini's dream of seeing an Italian army in the front line was never realized. The fate of the other two divisions continued to be the subject of constant, bitter wrangling with the Germans.

The ineffectual stuggle against the partisans was waged with diminishing success. All over the country murderous assaults on Germans or on prominent Fascists, followed by savage reprisals, multiplied. In Milan on August 9 a German truck was attacked and, as a reprisal, the Germans ordered the execution of fifteen political prisoners. The were shot by an Italian detachment and their bodies were exposed in the Piazzale Loreto, the scene of the original outrage.

The episode aroused much public indignation and Mussolini in a long letter to Rahn of August 17 lodged a protest in unusually strong terms.

According to an official report [he wrote], the execution in the Piazzale Loreto took place in circumstances attended by violence and a disregard of normal procedure. The fifteen persons were removed from the truck at the corner of the Piazzale Loreto and instructed to stand with their faces to the wall of a building under construction. It appears that the victims had no idea that they had been condemned to be shot and, since they were clothed in overalls, believed that they were being conscripted for labor in Germany. As soon, however, as it became clear to them that their last hour had come, they were overcome by an access of despair and attempted to flee in various directions. The execution squad, surprised by this development, began to open fire with a machine-gun volley, which immediately killed everyone almost at once, but with mortal wounds in various parts of the body. *Some of the corpses consequently presented a horrifying appearance. One of the victims was able to flee, though gravely wounded, and climbed to the first floor of a house,* but on reaching the landing fell dead in a lake of blood, and was carried away to be placed on the heap of the other corpses.

At eight o'clock in the morning a request was addressed to General Tensfeld of the S. S., resident in Monsa (who had ordered the execution), that permission should be given for the removal of the bodies, but the reply was negative; and it was only at 6 P.M. that it was possible to take them to the mortuary. During the whole day there was a considerable crowd round the heap of corpses. They evinced their horror and many fainted, especially the women. The execution and the circumstances surrounding it have created in the whole population an extremely painful impression, with expressions of increased hostility towards the Germans, although all are united in condemning the vile assailants who massacre passers-by, as they did in the Viale Abruzzi. Among the working masses agitation continues and expressed itself yesterday in the temporary suspension of work in certain industrial establishments. During the night the streets of the city were strewn with leaflets issued by the so-called "Committee of National Liberation for Upper Italy." I enclose a specimen of one of them.

For good measure Mussolini called attention to a long series of German excesses in many other parts of the country; and he concluded:

It is necessary to give the twenty-two million Italians of the Po valley the impression that there is a Republic, a government; and that such government is considered as an ally and its territory not as *war booty,* twelve months after it has been officially recognized by the Reich. We must not give the least justification to those who regard us—in so far as we are your allies—as traitors.*

Despite all Mussolini's protests German interference continued, and towards the end of August he was driven to writing a letter to Goebbels,† not without sarcastic undertones, calling attention to the notorious German manpower crisis and suggesting that it would be helpful to reduce the staffs of the many German administrative offices in Germany. At the end of the month Mussolini was at the end of his tether and, according to Mazzolini's diary, told his cabinet in accents of the deepest bitterness that he proposed to inform Rahn that he must be placed in a position to function, or he would resign.[25]

Meanwhile the situation on all battlefronts was deteriorating further. On August 15 the Allies landed on the southern coast of France and, meeting little resistance, pushed northwards to link up with Eisenhower's forces. On August 25 Paris was liberated and by the middle of September virtually all France and Belgium were in Allied hands. On the eastern front the Russians were advancing along the whole line, and Rumania and Bulgaria had seceded from the Axis. Nearer home Field Marshal Alexander's armies, having captured Florence, were standing on August 25 on the line Pisa-Pesaro, only some 150 miles away. It seemed as if they might at any moment sweep through the Gothic line into the Lombardy plain.

It became urgent to consider the preparation of an Alpine redoubt in which to make a last stand. Three areas came under

---

* For this letter I am indebted to Mr. Donald Curry, who found it in Florence during the advance in 1944.

† After the July plot Hitler had entrusted Goebbels with the task of mobilizing the resources of the nation for war. Text of letter in Deakin, *op. cit.*, pp. 726, 727.

consideration: the Valtelline north of Como; the mountains on the border of the Alto Adige and Austria; Friuli and Carnia in the northeastern corner of Italy. There were conversations with the Germans and Rahn opted for Friuli, discarding the Valtelline because "men are men, and after a little while the solution of internment in Switzerland will flatter even the stoutest and you will remain alone with a handful." [26] Pavolini favored the Valtelline and opposed the Alto Adige on the ground that they would be under the tutelage of *Gauleiter* Hofer. Among Mussolini's remaining followers there seems to have been little enthusiasm for a last stand anywhere. In any event the idea of establishing an exile government in Germany was rejected and on September 17 the Duce set up a committee under Pavolini to study the whole problem. It was characteristic of the Salò government that nothing further was done.

It is perhaps fair to say that the matter lost its strident urgency when the Allies, after advancing some forty miles from the positions held in August, halted for the winter just south of Bologna. In the course of these operations Forlì and the Duce's beloved Rocca were captured. The house was destroyed by the invading troops and sacked by the local inhabitants. Edvige Mussolini, who lived in the neighborhood, had been safely evacuated in August and lodged in a small hotel close to Salò.

Encouraged by the unexpected winter respite, Mussolini in November sent his son Vittorio with a letter to Hitler,[27] pointing out that it was essential to wrest the initiative from the enemy, and that the only front on which this could be done was in Italy, where quite modest reinforcements could reverse the tide of war. Unfortunately Hitler was not in a position to reinforce anywhere at the moment, and in any event his confidence in Italy was so shaken that he could not contemplate committing further resources to the defense of the country.

VII

The winter clamped down on Lake Garda. In those dreary surroundings he had little to do, and his life was plagued by domestic troubles and growing dissension with the Germans. In October

Clara Petacci, who had been imprisoned by the Badoglio government and subsequently released by the Germans, had been brought to Lake Garda by the S. S. General Sepp Dietrich and installed under S. S. protection in a villa at Gardone, ten miles from Gargagno. There she was visited from time to time by Mussolini and remained in constant communication with him by telephone and letter.

At last Rachele could bear the presence of her rival no longer. She first induced the head of the police to make a search of Clara's villa and remove photostats of letters from Mussolini. She then arrived in person, accompanied by Buffarini, to demand that Clara should leave the area. There was a scene between the two women and Clara is said to have fainted under the stress of the conflict. She refused, however, to give way and Rachele in an access of rage attempted to poison herself on her return to the Villa Feltrinelli. Mussolini, unable to face his angry wife, prudently decided to spend that night and the following night at his office in the Villa delle Orsoline. The episode prejudiced the position of Buffarini, who had attempted to ingratiate himself with both women, and it correspondingly strengthened the hands of those who had been urging Mussolini to discard his Minister of the Interior. As a preliminary step, Mussolini on October 24 announced the appointment of Giorgio Pini as Undersecretary of the Ministry of the Interior. It would in any event have been difficult to have made large-scale changes in the government, for the prestige of the regime was so low that men of any standing were now unwilling to be associated with it.

As the military strength of Germany declined, so the relations between the Axis partners at every level became more ragged. It was a vicious circle. The Germans argued that they could not afford to give the Salò government a free hand until it could show that it was capable of influencing the masses; and Mussolini retorted that he could not exercise authority so long as he was seen to be in German leading strings. In this debate Rahn and Ribbentrop imprudently suggested that it would be a good thing if the Duce were to show himself more and to speak to his people. In his mood of angry frustration Mussolini decided to accept this ill-considered advice, which offered him a means of shaking off the

German stranglehold. On December 9 he told his cabinet that he intended to make a public speech in Milan and also to transfer his government from Garda to the city.

In order to prevent any last-minute German intervention he kept his plan secret, and he merely instructed Pavolini to make preparations for a Fascist demonstration in the Piazza San Sepolcro. On the evening of December 15 the Fascist radio announced that an exceptional event would take place in Milan on the following day. On the morning of December 16 Mussolini appeared before a handpicked audience in the Lyric Theater. In was his first public appearance in Milan since 1936, and his speech was his first public statement since his fall. It was also to be the last speech he was ever to deliver.

After an account of the treachery which had brought about the Italian collapse he claimed with curious complacency that 1944 had seen even more infamous betrayals, since Rumania, Bulgaria, and now Finland had gone over to the ranks of the enemy. "It is time to tell our Italian, German, and Japanese comrades that the contribution made by Republican Italy to the common cause since September, 1943—in spite of the temporary reduction of the territory of the Republic—is far superior to what is commonly believed." The following year would see an intensification of the war effort. Meanwhile the Fascist party would return to its first principles, and a significant start had been made in the work of social reform. He lured his audience with promises of secret weapons, spoke of the difficulties and dissensions in the enemy camp, and concluded with a peroration calling for national unity and sacrifice. The speech was received with great acclamation, but Pini was obliged to admit that although it was read with vigor it lacked "the magical nuances of his free improvisations" and was not one of his best efforts.[28]

On December 17 and 18 Mussolini fulfilled a number of public engagements in Milan and was given a roaring welcome wherever he went. He had not altogether lost his capacity to move the masses, and his short stay in Milan gave him another fugitive injection of courage. There was, however, no further talk of changing the seat of government and he returned quietly to his captivity in

Gargagno. The visit to Milan had proved another damp squib. To a friend who congratulated him on the trip he replied with a bitter smile: "What is life? Dust and altars, altars and dust." [29]

For the remaining four months of his life Mussolini withdrew into the shadows. There was nothing he could now do to exercise the slightest influence on the course of events. In February he at last dismissed Buffarini and appointed Paolo Zerbino to the Ministry of the Interior, a move which aroused the anger of the Germans. There were also the routine exchanges of views with Rahn and his staff in an atmosphere of mounting irritation and mutual suspicion. The Germans were ever on the watch for signs of another Italian betrayal, and Mussolini, with the fate of Trieste and the Alto Adige constantly before his eyes, was fearful of every German move. He did not, however, know that Rahn and Wolff with Himmler's consent were already engaged in a complicated series of intrigues designed to secure the surrender to the Allies of the German armies in Italy, an arrangement which would have left the Duce and the Salò government high and dry.

Having nothing to do and taking less and less interest in current affairs, Mussolini devoted much of his time to conversations. These talks have no historical importance, but, with the reservation that his words could never be accepted at their face value, they are of some interest as throwing light on his character and outlook.

His favorite theme was the return to socialism. Here he was not only "coming home," not only taking vengeance on the monarchy and the bourgeoisie, but he was nourishing the hope that he might find a place in history by establishing a form of socialism which would endure in postwar Italy. To Giovanni Freziosi, the lunatic Fascist racist, for whom incidentally he entertained a mixture of hatred and contempt, he one day exposed his ideas.

During the life of the Republic I wanted to see the problems of capital importance, such as socialization, tackled. I am an old Socialist. . . . I have not deluded myself that it would be possible in a short time to bring to completion so complex a social program. But I wished to teach the Italian proletariat what were its rights. I did intend to achieve this result some twenty years ago, but by other means, because I regarded a compromise as possible. But in fact if one wishes to progress, one must burn all one's boats behind one. All of them. At the end of this war, if we are defeated, Italy will find herself exactly in the situation of 1919, and in some respects worse off. And the question will then be: to become the advance post of the Anglo-Saxon plutocracies against the Slav world, or to be the Mediterranean sentinel of the latter against the former. With my projected social reforms I wanted the Italian proletariat to understand what should be its goal, whatever the result of the war. . . . If I have to disappear, the inheritors of power in Italy must be the Socialists.[30]

In other conversations he meandered through the past, admitting that he had made errors, but seeking to justify the decisions he had taken. In particular, he claimed that he had no alternative but to enter the war, for the loss of which he blamed the Germans, who had never taken his advice, not even when he told them to make peace with Russia while there still was time. After all Italy had been fighting to secure her elementary rights, the others to maintain the privileges of caste and class. Peering into the future, he predicted a cosmic conflict between America and Russia; and with a certain rancor he looked forward to the relegation of Britain to the rank of a second-class power.

There were also moments when he frankly recognized his failure. To Franceso Coppola he said that Giolitti was the only statesman Italy had known; and when Coppola demurred, he replied: "I am not a statesman. I am a poet and a little mad." Discussing his foreign policy with Bombacci, he gave a frank explanation of the motives which had caused him to align himself with Germany.

Hitler's Germany was Fascist: immense gatherings, dazzling parades, an epic atmosphere of vitality and military glory. All this blinded me, I must admit it. I also loved the life which was mystical and heroic, the conquests, the glory. I thought that my future lay with the Axis. I wished to convert a nation of artists into a warrior people. . . . I forgot that I was a statesman and I disregarded the fate of millions of men.

In most of these long conversations he revealed the instability of his character by constant contradictions and by asseverations which bore no relation to the truth. Only occasionally did he "lapse into sense," as Dryden said of the poet Shadwell. The need for a united Europe in the postwar world was, for example, one of the themes on which he spoke with foresight and acumen.* To a journalist, Spampanato, he said:

You will see that the Americans will forget their old inferiority complex in relation to England, and then they will not this time return to isolation, as they did after the other war. They will pursue a world policy. . . . America will not seek friendship or alliance with this or that nation, but with Europe. Moreover a united Europe, prosperous and strong, will prove to be the best of clients.[31]

By March, 1945, although he was able to maintain a stoical fortitude in public and although he may still have entertained fleeting hopes of some saving miracle, he had abandoned the struggle and was becoming resigned to his fate. He opened his heart to Maddalena Mollier, wife of the German press attaché, in an interview, which, he stipulated, was not to be published until after his death. To her he declared that he was no longer a subject of interest since he was no longer alive. "Death has become a friend, who no longer frightens me. Death is a gift from God to those who have suffered too much." He spoke of his mistakes and told Frau Mollier that he was ready to pay for them with his life.

I have never made a mistake when I followed my instinct, only when I obeyed reason. . . . I am responsible as much for the things I did well, which the world will not be able to deny me, as for my weaknesses and my fall. . . . I am finished. My star has set. I work and exert myself, though I know it is all a farce. . . . Perhaps I was destined only to point the way to my people. I should have rested content on a firm, secure basis. But have you ever known a prudent calculating dictator?

He spoke with affection of the Italian people and told his interviewer that he could now only passively await his destiny. To a question about the Verona trial, he replied that Galeazzo's death was also predestined, and he concluded bitterly: "Since that January morning I have been dying slowly. The agony is atrociously long. I am the captain of a ship in a storm. My ship has broken up or I am floating on a piece of wreckage in a tumultuous sea. It is

* Many of these conversations were recorded by the various parties; and although they may not be textually accurate, they all paint the same picture of Mussolini and his outlook. An account of many of them appeared in twelve installments in the *Corriere D'Informazione* from February 25/26 to March 11/12, 1946, under the title "Mussolini si confessa."

impossible to act or to save the situation! No one hears my voice and I now withdraw into silence. But one day the world will listen to me." [32] Mussolini always had a sense of the theater, but during those March days he was at times not far from moral collapse.

VII

Nevertheless, he did not altogether intend to abandon himself to his destiny, as he had led Frau Mollier to believe. He had always been the supreme opportunist, and he embarked on plans which had for some time been maturing in his mind to shake off the Germans and to take an initiative with the Socialists in the National Liberation Committee. There was also the possibility of doing a deal with the Western Allies. After all Churchill, whose esteem he had won in the old days, could not be so foolish as to wish to open the doors of Europe to the Bolshevik hordes. The local Germans, themselves bent on treachery, were watching Mussolini like hawks to see that he did not embark on a similar enterprise.

Cardinal Schuster, the Archbishop of Milan, had written to the Duce in February urging the Duce not to attempt a last stand in the city; and this seemed a useful peg on which to hang a proposal to the Allies for a purely Italian surrender. In March Mussolini sent his son to the Cardinal with a memorandum [33] embodying suggested terms of an agreement designed to insure an orderly transfer of power and to spare the country a civil war. The Cardinal undertook to submit the proposals to the Allies through the nuncio in Berne, but the reply, when it came, was completely discouraging: "It has come to the knowledge of the Holy See that the Allies do not intend to enter into negotiations, and insist on unconditional surrender."

In order to strengthen his hand, Mussolini at the same time appointed Anfuso to the Undersecretaryship at the Foreign Ministry, rendered vacant by the death of Mazzolino on February 23. Anfuso arrived in Salò from Berlin on March 26, and gave a gloomy account of Italo-German relations. He had had an unsatisfactory farewell conversation with Ribbentrop, who had told him that both the Fuehrer and himself were disturbed at the Socialist tendencies of the Duce. Such a policy, he declared, represented an effort to pander to European socialism and was in line neither with National Socialism nor with the Fuehrer's conception of a New Europe. Anfuso's efforts to bring the conversation back to a review of the war and its current problems failed; and Ribbentrop could only continue to asseverate that he objected to socialism of an English brand which was not National Socialism.[34]

Of more immediate importance, however, was Anfuso's verdict that the Third Reich was crumbling. The abortive December offensive in the Ardennes had represented the last ray of hope. Now each Nazi chieftain was independently seeking a way out by means of a separate peace, and even Ribbentrop was putting out feelers in Spain and Sweden, while Himmler purported to favor a peace with Russia. Only Goebbels still seemed determined to pursue the war. Anfuso was aware that Wolff was engaged on intrigues in Switzerland, but he did not believe that they presaged a German surrender and the abandonment of the Salò Republic.

Mussolini for his part told Anfuso of his proposals to the Allies made through Cardinal Schuster. Together the two men during the early days of April explored still further the possibilities of independent Italian peace moves. Mussolini recognized that, having regard to the military situation for which he bitterly blamed Hitler, the moment was inauspicious. But his optimism and capacity for self-deception led him to nurse the hope, almost to the end, that he might yet be called upon to play a role in the western European conflict with bolshevism. Hence the desperate search for an Italian solution. It was, however, clear that effective moves could not be made under German surveillance in Gargagno, but only in Milan where, moreover, it would be possible to make personal contact with the Cardinal and, if necessary, with members of the Committee of Liberation. He had not yet abandoned his idea of some accommodation with the Socialists.

Another factor which rendered the move more urgent was the military position and in particular the opening on April 9 of the Allied spring offensive in Italy. In Germany on April 12 the western Allies crossed the Elbe and were only sixty miles from Berlin. The Russians stood in force on the Oder thirty-five miles east of the city. As the armies surged forward, it became clear that there was not much time. Either a political solution must be found, or, if this failed, preparations must be made for the last Alpine stand.

Pavolini was already in Milan scratching together what forces he could, a few hundred men from one place and another. The area north of Como, which was to constitute the Alpine redoubt, was infested by partisans, whose activities compromised the plan. On April 5 Pavolini reported to the Duce that he hoped to clean up the whole Como province by April 30, and by that date to have brought the available forces up to 5,000 men. Pini, who paid a visit to the area, returned with a similarly optimistic report.

Pavolini's forecast, the impulse to seek a political solution independently of the Germans, and the Allied spring offensive all combined to bring Mussolini to the resolve to move without further delay to Milan.

On April 14 Mussolini held his last formal meeting with the Germans at Gargagno. On the German side Wolff and Rahn attended together with the new Commander-in-Chief Vietinghof and his Chief of Staff, while Mussolini was supported by Graziani and Anfuso. Mussolini explained at length the plans he had made to defend the Valtelline, and when he asked the Germans for their opinion, they offered no objection. The truth was that they regarded the whole discussion as academic, since they hoped very shortly to sign their own instrument of surrender. So far as the future was concerned, both sides were fencing for position. Mussolini was thinking of his impending departure for Milan in search of an Italian solution. Wolff, who must have apprehended what was in Mussolini's mind, pointedly asked him not to treat with the Allies through Cardinal Schuster, since a second Badoglio betrayal would be fatal for relations with Germany; and he undertook in any negotiations on which he might himself embark to look after Italian interests. He declared himself opposed to the projected move to Milan, and Mussolini promised not to carry it out.

During this inconclusive conversation the Germans reported that Ribbentrop had asked for Anfuso's urgent return for consultations in Berlin. Anfuso, who was the only man in Mussolini's entourage with the knowledge and ability to penetrate German designs, feared that it was Rahn and Wolff who wanted to "remove him from the Duce at such a delicate moment in order to have their hands more free." Nevertheless Mussolini yielded and Anfuso left the following day. However, he never reached Berlin but found himself marooned with the remainder of the Berlin diplomatic corps at Bad Gastein under the guardianship of the German Head of Protocol. He made a last attempt to rejoin his chief by car from Bad Gastein, but was held up at Riva on the north end of Lake Garda and thus escaped by a few hours the fate of Mussolini's other followers.

Despite his promise to Wolff, Mussolini summoned his cabinet at Gargagno on December 16 to announce the imminent move of the government to Milan. Rahn made a last effort to dissuade him and suggested a move with the German embassy to Merano, a few miles south of the Brenner Pass. But Mussolini was itching to discard the Germans and replied that, if the war were lost, he intended to die on Italian soil. When Rahn argued that Milan was a trap, he answered that he could always break out to the Valtelline.

The last days at Gargagno were spent in a haze of detachment. He described himself as becoming more a spectator than an actor in the great drama which was unfolding around him. One day in the Villa della Orsoline he had found one of his associates in conversation with a young man, whom he introduced to the Duce as his son. "What is he doing?" inquired the Duce. There was an uneasy pause, and the young man said defiantly: "I am a partisan." "Quite right," Mussolini replied, "I should be doing the same if I were your age." [35]

There were farewell talks with Don Pancino, Father Eusebio, a well-known military chaplain, Dinale, and Gioacchino Nicoletti, a prefect who had, in contrast to the extreme Fascists, supported Mussolini's policy of domestic reconciliation. To all these men he expressed the conviction that his end was near. When Dinale concluded his last interview with the words *"au revoir,"* Mussolini replied: "No. I have no illusions left. It is goodby." It was true that his reason told him that all was finished, but his sense of opportunism and his experience of past crises led his instinct to cling to the hope that something might yet turn up to save him.

He also sent for his sister Edvige and advised her to move to Milan with her family. The end of the war was approaching and when it came she was to address herself to Churchill if she required protection. Churchill's gift of historical objectivity suggested that he also possessed a measure of generosity. As for himself, his course was run. He said goodby to her and quoted Hamlet, "The rest is silence," and added, "I have for some time been ready to enter into that great silence." She was never to see him again.[36]

Before leaving Gargagno Mussolini carefully sorted his private papers. The most important files were put aside to be transported with him, and the remainder taken out in a boat and sunk in the lake. The truck containing the files was subsequently lost, to Mussolini's distress, during the flight from Milan to Como.

Having settled his affairs as best he could, Mussolini without further ado left Garda behind him. On April 18 his German escort was informed that he would be leaving for Milan at 7 P.M. and would be returning in two or three days. The elaborate game of deception played by both sides was continued to the end. In the garden of the Villa Feltrinelli he said farewell to Rachele. Clara Petacci, however, was determined to follow her man and left her villa at Gardone that evening for Milan, accompanied by her S. S. guardian, Lieutenant Franz Spoegler.

The Duce's convoy, with its escort under the command of Lieutenant Birzer, left Gargagno punctually and arrived safely at about 9 P.M. at the Milan prefecture, a large palazzo in the Via Monforte, where Mussolini took up his residence. The last act of his life was now to begin. It was to be attended by the confusion, diminishing hopes, and helplessness which had marked the Salò Republic from its inception.

CHAPTER TWENTY-FOUR

The End

1945

I

MUSSOLINI spent seven phantom days in Milan.* Gathered round him, an untidy throng in his anteroom, were a miscellaneous collection of men who represented the tattered remnants of Italian fascism: Pavolini; Zerbino; Graziani; Tarchi; Ricci; Barracu; Farinacci; Mezzasomma; Pisenti Liverani, the Minister of Communications; the prefect of Milan Ugo Bassi; the federal secretary of Milan Costa; General Montagna; General Nicchiarelli of the Republican Guard; General Diamanti, the military commander of Lombardy; Mussolini's new private secretary, Luigi Gatti; and his son, Vittorio. On the fringe of this official party were a number of personal followers including the faithful Bombacci, Carlo Silvestri, and a number of old *Squadristi*.

Outside the Duce's office German S. S. sentries still mounted

* The period from Mussolini's arrival in Milan to his end has been the subject of a large number of inaccurate accounts. Colonel Valerio has written three different contradictory stories, to which no credence can be given. The main facts can, however, be established. I have relied principally upon Deakin and in a lesser degree on Tamaro, Pini, who was in Milan with Mussolini, Rahn, and Cardinal Schuster. There is also an excellent account by the two Dongo partisan leaders Pier Luigi Bellini delle Stelle and Urbano Lazzaro, of which a refurbished version was published in *Epoca* in December, 1960. Their long, circumstantial story stands up to scrutiny and I have made some use of it. I found the inhabitants of Dongo reticent. All I could get out of them was a shake of the head and the asseveration that those were *"brutti tempi."*

guard. Within there was confusion of purpose. No one knew what to do and each man sponsored his own plan. Buffarini favored escape to Switzerland and a proposal to fly to Spain was discussed, but Mussolini categorically declined to seek safety in any foreign country. Graziani advocated a military surrender by direct negotiation with the Allies. In the background remained the only project on which here had been any degree of previous agreement: the Valtelline redoubt. But it soon became clear that not all those present in the prefecture were prepared to follow Mussolini on that forlorn hope.

The days passed in ceaseless interviews and discussions. In the hubbub Mussolini found time to give a long interview to a journalist, in the course of which he sought, somewhat incoherently, to defend himself; and he predicted a third world war between Soviet Russia and the capitalist democracies. In particular he claimed that he had had no alternative but to undertake the Salò Republic. "I was physically ill. I could at least have asked for a period of rest." But the consequence would have been catastrophic. The Germans had every right to regard themselves as betrayed and to install themselves as the masters of Italy. "They would not have hesitated to appoint their military government of occupation. What would then have happened? Scorched earth, shortages of provisions, mass deportations, sequestrations, occupation currency, forced labor. Our industry, our artistic, industrial, and private properties would all have become war booty." * Not ambition or lust for power, but love of his country had led to his decision, only taken after deep reflection.

On April 20, when Mussolini heard that Bologna had been cut off, he gave instructions that his scattered government offices should be disbanded and that only those indispensable officials who would be required in the Valtelline should concentrate in Milan. The same day Rahn paid his last visit to the Duce in order to persuade him to return to Gargagno, but Mussolini, having at last liberated himself from the Germans, steadfastly declined to entertain the idea. Rahn found him calm and even cheerful, as if he wished to confirm

* This interview was given to G. C. Cabella, former director of the *Popolo di Alessandria* on the night of April 20. The text, corrected by Mussolini, was published in 1948 in Rome under the title *Testamento politico di Mussolini.*

one of his favorite aphorisms: "In the hour of danger a man becomes gay." But his expressive eyes reflected the dark clouds of the impending disaster and of his tragic fate. On the desk lay an open book: a German edition of the poetic works of Noericke. Mussolini smiled and said: "Yes, that is all that remains to us." There was no political discussion, and Rahn made no reference to the German negotiations for surrender, which seemed then likely to reach an early conclusion. He returned to Lake Garda to await events.

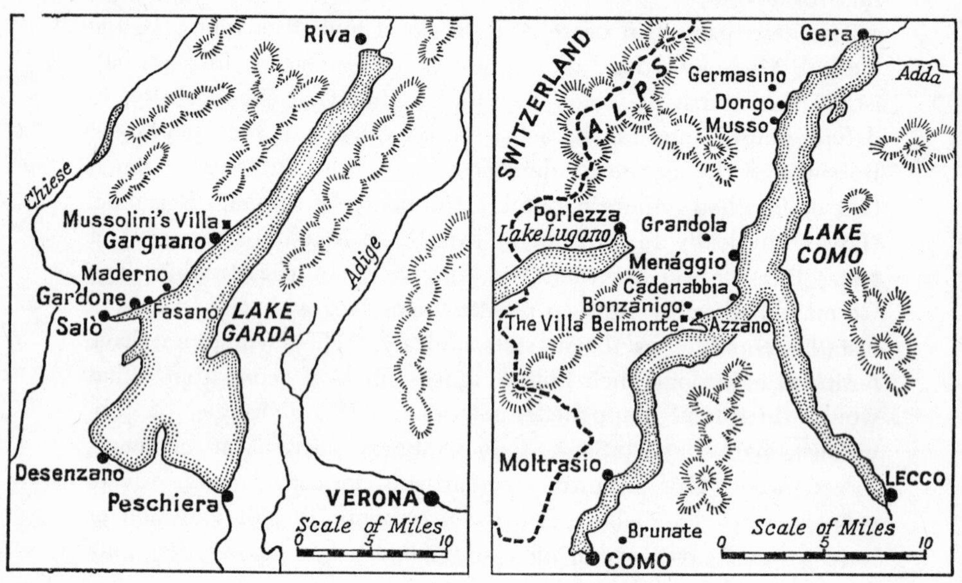

Maps of Lake Garda and Lake Como areas.

The rest of the day was spent in a disorderly discussion of ways and means of establishing contact with suitable elements of the Liberation Committee with a view to avoiding an outbreak of civil strife when the final crash came. Each man had his own idea of the best channel of communication, and no concerted action was devised or put in motion. They all ignored the passions aroused by the partisan war, and seemed unable to grasp that it would be difficult to find a single member of the Liberation Committee ready to treat with them on any but the most oppressive terms.

On Saturday April 21 Bologna was captured by the Allies, and the anti-Fascists ran amok in the district. Among the victims slain that day was Arpinati, the former Fascist chief in Bologna, who had declined to join the government of the Salò Republic. In Milan Mussolini held a meeting with such members of his government as were available. Graziani reported on the collapse of the German front in Italy, where the enemy were crossing the Po. In Germany the Russians were at the gates of Berlin. If anything were to be done it must be done quickly; and Mussolini reverted by instinct and inclination to his old idea of an accommodation with the Socialists. He had at hand, in Carlo Silvestri, an agent eminently suitable to his purpose.

On the following day, April 22, he sent for Silvestri, to whom he explained that it would be wrong for the Republic to make agreements with delegates of the conservatives or with the invading Anglo-Americans. In the last resort, however, they should favor the transfer of power to the Republican and Socialist partisan forces. A letter was drafted by Silvestri setting forth the conditions under which Mussolini was prepared to disappear after handing over to the Socialists the city and those Republican forces which would be required to maintain order.[1] It is not known by what channel or to whom exactly this communication was addressed. In any event it was rejected with contempt by the Socialist group in the Liberation Committee. Their political representative, Sandro Pertini, wrote subsequently: "When I was told that Mussolini had arranged to send a letter addressed to the Socialist party in which he offered to surrender himself and those with him, I immediately sent an answer . . . that the letter must be given no consideration at all."[2]

April 23 passed in a flurry of indecision. The news from the front continued to be bad. Parma had fallen, Genoa had been taken over by partisans, and everywhere Fascists were being hunted down and massacred. Buffarini continued to urge the Duce to flee to Switzerland, but he with equal obstinacy clung to the idea of the Alpine redoubt, although no practical steps had been taken to organize a final stand there. It had become an automatic reflex. Later in the day he visited Clara Petacci, who had just refused to accompany her parents to Spain, because, she said, her destiny was irrevocably linked with his. He also telephoned to Rachele instructing her to leave at once for Monza, which she reached at dawn the following morning.

That same day at Gargagno Rahn at last revealed to Mellini, the principal private secretary at the Ministry of Foreign Affairs, the design which the Germans had for so long been nurturing. Even now it was "a jealous secret" not to be confided to the Duce. Secret negotiations, he said, with Field Marshal Alexander were about to come to fruition. The agreement, he added, perfidiously, would avoid a massacre and save Mussolini, who would be useful in the coming struggle with bolshevism. He hoped very shortly to be in a position to lay before the Duce concrete and satisfactory proposals. Mellini for some extraordinary reason felt bound to secrecy, and, when later he spoke to Mussolini on the telephone, merely said that there was nothing special to report, but that Rahn would be coming to Milan in a day or two with an interesting communication. The Duce did not seem to attach any importance to this information.[3] In fact Rahn never came to Milan and Mussolini remained in ignorance of German intentions. The fact that the Germans now seemed to be putting up little or no resistance to the Allies did not arouse his suspicions.

April 24 was another day of anxious and febrile expectation, with the clouds of disaster rolling ever closer. The Allied troops were still advancing and their fighter planes were machine-gunning streets in the center of Milan. In the city an extraordinary situation was developing. Around Mussolini in the prefecture were gathered heterogeneous Republican detachments, some of which had flowed in from the surrounding countryside. Alongside was the Liberation Committee, with its armed bands, attempting to function as an alternative government, while the Germans remained huddled in their barracks, ready to repel attack from any quarter, but unwilling to intervene. Into this sea of rapidly growing confusion dropped a last lunatic message from the Fuehrer: a telegram despatched from his bunker in Berlin.

The struggle for existence or nonexistence has reached its climax. Using huge forces and materials, bolshevism and Judaism have engaged themselves up to the hilt to assemble their destructive forces on German territory, to precipitate our continent into chaos. Nevertheless, with their obstinate scorn of death, the German people and all the others who are animated by the same sentiments will fling themselves to the rescue, however hard the struggle, and with their incomparable heroism will change the course of the war at this historic moment which will decide the fate of Europe for centuries to come.[4]

Whatever Hitler might say, Mussolini could see for himself that the German troops in Italy were showing no ardor for battle. If he were to extricate himself, he would have to rely entirely on his own wits and exertions. Unfortunately he was now possessed of very little mental or physical resilience. Under the strain of the last few days his health had again given way, and at moments he felt inclined to give in. But there was always the Valtelline, and before he retired there a last attempt must be made to reach some agreement in Milan.

In the course of April 24 Silvestri informed Mussolini that the Socialists had rejected his approach. He accordingly agreed that Zerbino and Montagna should continue to make advances through other independent channels. It seemed a bleak prospect, and Mussolini spent an anxious disturbed night, telephoning constantly for news of the military situation.

The following day, April 25, his last in the city from which he had sprung to power, dawned inauspiciously. When the government offices opened few officials presented themselves and it was seen that many of the police had melted away. The prefect Bassi reported that in the afternoon a general strike would be called in Milan. There was an agitated debate on the general situation in the prefecture. Pisenti and many others favored staying in Milan, but Mussolini adhered to his Valtelline plan. He decided to make for the redoubt up the western shore through Como, rather than through Lecco on the opposite bank; and instructions were issued by radio that Republican detachments on the way to Milan should be diverted to Como. Rachele and her children were instructed to leave Monza at once for the Villa Mantero close to Como.

II

At this point Cardinal Schuster and the Milan Curia once more crossed Mussolini's path. For some time the Cardinal had hoped to play the part of mediator in arranging the surrender of the German forces, and to this end he had established contact with the Germans and the Liberation Committee. Wolff and his associates, however, while ready to keep open the channel with the Curia as a form of reinsurance, were otherwise engaged in promoting through Mr. Allen Dulles, the American secret service agent in Switzerland, a direct negotiation with the Western Allies. As the front began to disintegrate, the Liberation Committee and the Cardinal became impatient, but all their efforts to bring the Germans to the conference table in the Archepiscopal Palace failed. The stage was thus set for an attempt to negotiate with Mussolini instead of with the Germans.

On April 24 a Milanese industrialist, Gian Riccardo Cella, who had previously been in touch with Zerbino, had approached Achille Marazza, a lawyer and Christian-Democratic member of the Liberation Committee, with proposals for negotiations through the mediation of the Cardinal. Early on the morning of April 25 he received a favorable reply and rushed with it to the prefecture.

According to Cella's account, he was able to persuade Mussolini to attend a meeting with representatives of the Liberation Committee in the afternoon at the Archbishop's palace. Graziani and Montagna, who had independently been conducting negotiations with a representative of the Bonomi government to concentrate the Republican forces in the triangle Milan-Como-Lecco until the arrival of the Allies, were told to break off the talks in view of this latest development. Rumors of a German capitulation were now beginning to circulate, but in reply to a telephone inquiry Wolff's local representative assured Silvestri that they were devoid of any foundation.

It is not clear what Mussolini hoped to achieve under the Cardinal's auspices. It is likely that he was simply allowing events to take their predestined course. To Frau Mollier he had described himself as a mariner floating helplessly in tumultuous seas on a spar; and to a journalist he had said: "I will go where destiny sends me." [5] He was becoming more and more apathetic. In any event no preparations were made for any coherent negotiation; and it seems that to the end he was still vainly hankering after an accommodation with the Socialists, for he was heard to say in the anteroom: "I only regret that now that Mussolini no longer exists, hatred still persists of the institutions created by him. I should like to entrust the Republic to republicans and socialists, and not to monarchists and reactionaries." With Silvestri's help he filled two large pouches with documents which he might require at the meeting and prepared to set forth.

He was collected in the afternoon from the prefecture in an old limousine provided by the Cardinal and was accompanied by Zerbino, Bassi, Barracu, and Cella. At the last moment Lieutenant Birzer, who had been entrusted with the Duce's person, managed to squeeze himself into the car; and a little later Graziani, who had been left behind at the prefecture, was instructed to join the party.

On the partisan side preparations had been equally disorderly. The Liberation Committee had been expecting a meeting with the Germans, but in the face of the new situation it was necessary to convene a meeting to authorize the Committee's representatives to treat with the Duce on the basis of unconditional surrender. In consequence, when Mussolini arrived at the Palace, there were no partisan leaders to meet him and it became necessary for the Cardinal to kill time. "He entered the reception room," the Cardinal subsequently wrote, "with such a dejected look that the impression he gave me was that of a man nearly benumbed by an immense catastrophe."

Mussolini was received alone in the Cardinal's study while the remainder of the party were entertained in the anteroom by Father Bicchierai, the Cardinal's secretary, and other clerics. According to Cardinal Schuster's subsequent record of a conversation which lasted an hour and was remarkable only for its banality, he began by assuring Mussolini how much he "appreciated his personal sacrifice in thus initiating by capitulation a life of expiation in prison or in exile, in order to save the rest of Italy from final ruin." There was talk of the example of Napoleon, and Mussolini observed that his own empire of a hundred days was also about to expire; and he could only, like Bonaparte, accept his fate with resignation. There was also a discussion of past relations between fascism and the Church; and the Cardinal regretted that the Conciliation had not realized all the hopes of its protagonists, a failure which he ascribed to the conduct of certain Fascist dignitaries. Mussolini bore this rebuke with humble patience, and courteously referred to the services of the Catholic priests during his imprisonment at Ponza and Maddalena. There were desultory references to the reforms of Saint Charles Borromeo, to the Ambrosian rite, the Patriarchate of Moscow, and the Vatican. The clock ticked on as the two men waited.

"Seeing him somewhat depressed," the Cardinal's record continues, "I insisted that he accept at least a little comfort. Out of politeness he was persuaded to accept a glass of rosalio with a biscuit." This, the Cardinal informed him, was the manner in which St. Benedict had received King Totila at Montecassino; and he presented the Duce with a copy of his recently published life of the Saint. He hoped it would comfort him in the dark days to come and exhorted him to regard his Calvary as an expiation of his sins.

There was virtually no discussion of current affairs. Only at one point did Mussolini refer to his immediate plans: in the first stage, that is to say, on the following day, his army and militia would be dissolved; and then he would withdraw to the Valtelline with three thousand Blackshirts. The Cardinal inquired whether Mussolini intended to continue the war in the mountains, and he replied: "Only for a while and then I shall give myself up." When the Cardinal objected that the number of Blackshirts would be barely three hundred, Mussolini smilingly admitted it: "Perhaps there will be a few more, but not many more. I have no illusions."

It had been an exhausting business to keep the polite conversation flowing for an hour. The Cardinal records that Mussolini was not at all excited, but seemed rather to be a man moving listlessly to his destiny. At last the delegation of the National Committee of Liberation arrived: Cadorna, the commander of the partisan forces and son of the Italian commander-in-chief in the First World War, Marazza, and Riccardo Lombardi, representing the Left-wing Action Party. Meanwhile in the anteroom Bassi had learned to his amazement from the Cardinal's secretaries that the Germans had for two months been negotiating through the Curia the surrender of their army in Italy; and Cella told Graziani that General Wolff would be coming that day to the Palace to sign the armistice.

As this bombshell exploded in the Fascist ranks, the representatives of the National Liberation Committee were shown in. There were no greetings, and they, together with the Duce's party, were immediately introduced into the study where the meeting began. The Cardinal had offered to withdraw, but at Mussolini's request he agreed to stay, and presided over the two delegations, which were drawn up on either side of a table.

Mussolini on the Cardinal's signal opened the proceedings by asking Marazza what proposals he had to make. His reply was to the effect that the Committee expected the acceptance of unconditional surrender within two hours. The matter was urgent because orders were about to be given for a general partisan insurrection. The Fascist forces could concentrate in the Milan-Como-Lecco triangle, and would be guaranteed immunity as prisoners of war after laying down their arms, although subsequent proceedings might be taken against individuals.

Mussolini did not react visibly, but at the mention of an unconditional surrender, Graziani interrupted the conversation to reveal what he had been told in the anteroom about the imminent German surrender. Mussolini was astonished and indignant. Saying that he was the victim of a German betrayal, he broke off the meeting and declared that he would broadcast the facts to the people. In vain the Cardinal appealed for patience, and argued that the Germans had not yet signed anything. But Mussolini, suddenly deprived of his German prop, was completely disorientated and bewildered. "They have always treated us like slaves," he said indignantly, "and now they have betrayed us." He rose from the table and declared that his hands were now free. After undertaking to give the Liberation Committee an answer within an hour he hurriedly left the room, taking with him the Cardinal's *Life of St. Benedict.* In the car on the way back to the prefecture he angrily declared that the meeting was a plot designed to effect the capture of himself and of his government. After his experiences in July, 1943, he was not prepared to submit once more to arrest.

III

The Fascist chiefs, with the exception of those accompanying Mussolini, were gathered in the prefecture anxiously awaiting the issue of the meeting. They saw the Duce drive into the courtyard, jump out of the car, turn to his German escort commander and shout angrily: "Your General Wolff has betrayed us." He mounted the stairs rapidly and went into his office. His face was drawn, his German doctor Zachariae noted, and he wore the pallor of death. There were agitated discussions and recriminations. Mussolini accused Zerbino and Cella of having led him into a trap; a German officer, who came to announce that the escort was ready, was treated to a long denunciation of German faithlessness; and proposals and counterproposals for the next move were bandied about.

There was in fact little choice. It seemed hopeless to resume negotiations with the partisans; and in any event it would have been unrealistic to believe that in the prevailing atmosphere the Liberation Committee would have been in a position to implement an agreement for the orderly surrender of the Fascist forces. Two alternatives remained: a stand in the area around the prefecture, or a withdrawal to the Valtelline. The first offered little attraction, and Mussolini was genuinely reluctant to plunge Milan into a civil war. The second was the solution to which his mind had already become conditioned, and it had the added advantage of postponing the hour of reckoning.

Mussolini suddenly decided to order a departure for Como, the first stage on the road to the Valtelline. A column of passenger and armored cars with German escort was hurriedly organized. Meanwhile Mussolini made his hurried preparations for departure. Instructions were given that the troops should be freed from their oath of allegiance, the secret papers and a considerable sum of money were packed in a truck, and the last farewells were said in the courtyard. In the hubbub the Duce's followers debated among themselves what they should do, and as the minutes passed it became clear that the number of those prepared to accompany him was steadily diminishing. He seemed resigned to the defection of the fainthearted and made no effort to win them over.

Pisenti, the Minister of Justice, was left behind, nominally to represent the fallen Republic, and among those who stayed in the prefecture were Silvestri, Bassi, Pellegrini, the Minister of Finance, Moroni, Minister of Agriculture, and General Montagna. The small number who went with Mussolini included Graziani, Zerbino, Mezzasomma, Liverani, Tarchi, Barracu, Gatti, his son Vittorio, his nephew Vito, and the faithful Bombacci. In the wake of the convoy followed Clara Petacci with her brother Marcello and his family.

At 8 P.M. on April 25 the column pulled out of the courtyard of the prefecture and made for the highway leading to the lakes. A few minutes later the Cardinal's palace telephoned to obtain the Duce's reply to the Liberation Committee. Bassi replied that Mussolini had already left and that there would be no surrender or negotiation. During the night the remaining Fascist armed bands followed the Duce on the road to Como, and at 8 A.M. on April 26 the prefecture was quietly occupied by a detachment of Finance Guards on behalf of the partisans. The city was now completely in their hands.

The convoy arrived safely at the prefecture in Como shortly after 9 P.M. Mussolini was received by Buffarini, who had preceded him, and by the Fascist head of the province, who for some time had been in contact with the partisans. Once more Buffarini besought him to flee to Switzerland, and once more Mussolini firmly declined to leave Italian soil, saying that his plan was to stay in Como until he was joined by the armed bands due to leave Milan at dawn under Pavolini's command and those which had been diverted from Milan by radio. He may have been influenced by the circumstance that the Swiss chargé d'affaires had recently informed Mellini that the Swiss government would not give him hospitality.

There was a melancholy communal dinner at the prefecture, and it soon became apparent that even among the remaining leaders disintegration had set in. Mussolini was no longer in command of himself or of the situation. He was resolved not to be the cause of an effusion of blood, he intended no longer to call on the allegiance of his followers, and yet his instinct bade him refuse to surrender. It is not surprising that panic and defeatism should have spread through the ranks of the hunted men so suddenly bereft of his leadership. Many of them now favored some transaction with the partisans.

In the course of the evening the local chief of police reported that the situation was becoming dangerous, owing to the infiltration of partisans into the city. Although the federal secretary assured him that he could muster sufficient force to repel any attack, Mussolini decided to leave Como. He was anxious, as he had been in Milan, not to involve the city in warfare, and he was possessed of an elemental urge to evade capture by constant movement. He would go into the mountains, he declared. "Is it impossible that five hundred men should be found ready to follow me?"

Without waiting for Pavolini and his troops, Mussolini put in hand preparations for another immediate move. Where exactly he would go he did not know. But before leaving Como he wrote a last letter to his wife, whom he had been unable to reach on the telephone.

Dear Rachele, here I am at the last stage of my life, at the last page of my book. We two may never meet again, and that is why I am writing and sending you this letter. I ask your forgiveness for all the harm I have unwittingly done you. But you know that you are the only woman whom I have ever really loved. I swear it before God, I swear it before our Bruno in this supreme moment. You know that we must make for the Valtelline. Take the children with you and try to get to the Swiss frontier. There you can build up a new life. I do not think that they will refuse to let you in for I have always been helpful to them and you have had nothing to do with politics. Should they refuse, surrender to the Allies, who may be more generous than the Italians. Take care of Anna and Romano, especially Anna who needs it so badly. You know how I love them. Bruno in heaven will help you. My dearest love to you and the children.

Your Benito. Como. 27th April 1945, Year XIII of the Fascist Era.[6]

The letter was quickly delivered during the night at the neighboring Villa Mantero to the distraught Rachele, who was able after several attempts to reach Mussolini on the telephone. She urged him to flee to safety, but he could only repeat the advice given in his letter. So far as he was concerned, there was no longer any hope, and he was following his destiny. His voice was calm, but reflected a profound melancholy. To Rachele's protestations that there were Italians still ready to fight for him he replied that his followers, even his driver, had melted away and he was now quite alone. "I see that all is over."

IV

At about 3 A.M. on April 26 Mussolini left Como with Bombacci and the federal secretary, not without some delay caused by Lieutenant Birzer's insistence that the vehicles of his ecsort should be included in the convoy. He stopped at Menaggio, a few miles up the lake, where he was housed in the villa of the deputy federal secretary. There he was followed shortly afterwards by another column conveying Graziani and the remaining notables, who took up quarters in the local school. On their tail followed Clara and Marcello Petacci.

While Mussolini was incontinently fleeing from Como, Pavolini had been busy marshaling his slim forces in Milan. At dawn on April 26 his column of some two hundred vehicles, which included some artillery and armored cars, left Milan and reached Como safely after an uneventful journey. Here he learned that Mussolini had departed to Menaggio. He decided, foolishly as it turned out, to report to the Duce in Menaggio, leaving his troops in Como. He was driven there by the daughter of one of Mussolini's mistresses, the young Elena Curti, who had come in her own car to join him in his hour of need.

The Duce's leaderless and unplanned hegira now collapsed in utter chaos. In view of the attention they were attracting in Menaggio, Gatti organized the withdrawal of the ministers and officials to Cadenabbia, an operation which confirmed their impression that they were being invited to wander about the countryside without object or purpose. In a mood of utter hopelessness they debated their prospects, and Buffarini reverted to his favorite theme: an escape to Switzerland without waiting for Pavolini and his column. Graziani declared that it was his duty to return to his headquarters to share the fate of his troops; and he departed without further ado, accompanied by his two undersecretaries.

The now diminished party decided to return to Menaggio. On the way they met Pavolini, who having reported to Mussolini, was on his way back to Como to collect and bring up his troops. He also told them that Rachele had been refused admission to Switzerland and had returned to Como.

By the time Menaggio was reached a new plan had been hatched. Nerves were on edge and it had been represented that it would be safer to move to some deserted spot and there to await the arrival of Pavolini's little army. The whole party, still accompanied by Birzer and his escort, accordingly proceeded some two miles up the mountain road to Grandola, where they installed themselves in the

Hotel Miravalle, headquarters of the frontier militia. They were now only some ten miles from the Swiss border. There they waited with growing impatience for the appearance of Pavolini and his men. In Berlin Hitler, immured in his bunker, was waiting with equal impatience for relief by General Wenck's phantom army.

While they waited in the dreary little hotel, they listened to the radio giving the news of the latest Allied advances and of the proceedings of the Liberation Committee, which had taken over Milan and abrogated Mussolini's social legislation. There was also news of an ominous decree establishing popular courts of justice and war tribunals. Article 5 of the decree provided that "members of the Fascist Government and the leaders of fascism who are guilty of suppressing the constitutional guarantees, destroying popular liberties, creating the Fascist regime, compromising and betraying the fate of the country, and conducting it to the present catastrophe are to be punished with the penalty of death, and in less grave instances life imprisonment." Others specifically marked down for retributive justice were those in charge of Fascist squads guilty of violence, the leaders of the "insurrection" of October 28, 1922, and those guilty of crimes against the state since September 8, 1943.

This intelligence lowered the already shaken morale of the fugitives. It was cold with intermittent rain, and Mussolini walked in the dripping garden talking to Bombacci and Clara, who was showing signs of jealousy at the arrival of Angela Curti. The latter, however, soon disappeared on a bicycle, which she rode into Como with a view to expediting the arrival of Pavolini's column.

The hours passed without any word from Como. At about 4 P.M. Buffarini, Tarchi, and a former police chief of Bologna called Fabiani obtained Mussolini's permission to attempt a break into Switzerland at the neighboring frontier post close to Porlezza. They were, however, arrested on the way by propartisan Finance Guards. Fabiani, however, was able to escape and soon returned to Grandola with the news. Mussolini besought Birzer to take his escort to the rescue of the missing men, but the German refused on the grounds that he was under orders to stay with the Duce.*

* Both men were subsequently released by the Finance Guards. Buffarini was recaptured and after taking poison unsuccessfully was later shot in Milan. Tarchi escaped.

The incident aroused alarm in the Hotel Miravalle, since it demonstrated that hostile forces were on the doorstep, and spirits were still further depressed when Vezzalini (who had been one of the judges at the Verona trial) appeared with the news that he had been involved in an encounter with partisans while he had been traveling from Como to Menaggio with a small force in three armored cars. Two of his men had been killed and he himself had been wounded in the face.

It now seemed to the isolated and completely unnerved men that they were surrounded by their enemies, and they decided that it would be safer to return to the lakeside at Menaggio to await Pavolini's arrival. The column was reformed, and the diminished party drove in the rain to the militia barracks at Menaggio. A day had passed in which nothing had been done except to wander disconsolately in the country around Como. They were still as far as ever from their ostensible destination. Mussolini, now a prey to despair, could only make bitter remarks about his enemies and his friends.

In Como, however, events had moved fast. In Pavolini's absence at Menaggio the elements favoring surrender had gained the upper hand, and the Chief of the Province had decided to hand the city over to the partisans. When Pavolini returned at about midday on April 26 he found that his troops had been infected by the prevailing defeatism and were not prepared to continue the struggle. He was able after strenuous exertions to collect only a handful of men, and with these he drove northwards in the night of April 26/27.

At about 4 A.M. on April 27 Mussolini was awakened to be given the grim tidings: Pavolini had arrived in an armored car with Angela Curti and a few men, but without even the smallest detachment of troops. In despair an envoy was sent to Como to see whether any further force could be scraped up, but by the time he arrived the local Fascists had signed an instrument of surrender, and the partisans were in control of the city.

At the same time a German antiaircraft unit of some two hundred men, commanded by a Lieutenant Fallmeyer, had arrived in Menaggio from Como on its way to seek safety in the Tyrol. It was decided to take advantage of this opportunity to amalgamate Birzer's escort with the German antiaircraft unit, and under the protection of the combined force to move northwards. There was no longer much thought of a last stand in the mountains, for the Germans were intent on going home and there were no Italians to give battle. It was now only a question of evading capture, and it seemed that the German force was large enough to deal with any partisan formation which might be encountered.

V

The combined column moved out of Menaggio before dawn on April 27. With it traveled Elena Curti, Clara Petacci, and her brother Marcello. At about 7 A.M. they had reached Musso, where they were suddenly halted by a partisan roadblock. There was a brisk exchange of fire between the small partisan band and Pavolini's armored car, after which a white flag was hoisted and parleys began. It was about six in the morning. The local commander, Pier Luigi Bellini delle Stelle (Pedro), commanding the 52nd Garibaldi brigade, was summoned from his headquarters at Dongo a mile away to negotiate with the German officers. He explained that he was under instructions not to allow anyone to pass and the Germans retorted that they intended to carry out their orders to proceed to Merano. They added that they had no desire to enter into any conflict with the partisans. It seemed as if the parleys were deadlocked.

Both sides were, however, animated by the same purpose. Pedro's small, badly armed force was in no state to engage the Germans, whereas the Germans were only concerned to go home and had no stomach for a fight. The partisan tactics were to gain time and to rely on bluff. It was eventually agreed that the German commander, Lieutenant Fallmeyer, who had declared himself indifferent to the fate of the Italians attached to his convoy, should proceed with Pedro to partisan headquarters at Morbegno, some fifteen miles to the northeast to discuss an accommodation.

The convoy waited at the lakeside for nearly six hours. Eventually at about two o'clock Fallmeyer returned with the news that the partisans, who were determined to prevent the passage of any Italians, had made preparations to blow a bridge on the river Mera, nine miles to the north. They were, however, prepared to permit the Germans to proceed on condition that they allowed their vehicles to be inspected at Dongo to ensure that they contained no Italians. Fallmeyer pressed this solution on Birzer, who felt that he had no alternative but to comply. His little escort would have been insufficient to protect the Duce in an area now completely in rebel hands.

As a last expedient Birzer induced Mussolini to don a German greatcoat and helmet and to enter one of the German trucks. He hoped that in this disguise the Duce might escape attention at the control post in Dongo. Mussolini, like a man in a dream, climbed obediently into the truck, taking with him his precious pouch of secret papers. At the last moment Clara attempted to join him, but she was stopped by the Germans and compelled to return to her brother's car at the rear of the column.

At about three o'clock the Germans moved off, leaving Mussolini's followers in the hands of the partisans. Mussolini was now completely alone. Within a few minutes the column halted in the square at Dongo, where the agreed inspection was to take place. Lieutenant Fallmeyer accompanied the partisans in their search of each vehicle, and eventually the huddled figure in the German uniform was recognized as the Duce. There is little doubt that his presence in the convoy had been reported by the partisans at Musso. He was immediately hauled out of the truck by his exultant captors and taken through an angry, excited crowd to the Municipality. According to Urbano Lazzaro (Bill), second-in-command of the 52nd Garibaldi brigade, his face was waxen and his fixed, somewhat detached expression revealed an immense weariness, but not fear. He seemed to be bereft of will and spiritually dead. At last he was free from German tutelage. The German column, relieved of their incubus, gratefully pursued their march northwards.

Shortly afterwards Mussolini was joined in the municipal building by the remainder of his party, including Pavolini, who had been wounded in an attempt to escape by jumping into the lake. Marcello Petacci, who had attempted to pass himself off with a false diplomatic passport as a Spanish consul, had also been arrested with his family and Clara. He was detained in the local hotel for further investigation, while Clara, who had no papers and whose identity was still unsuspected, was consigned to the Municipality.

The capture of Mussolini, which was reported as soon as possible by telephone to Milan, was not an event with which the heterogeneous Committee of Liberation was equipped to deal. They were not a government, their members were scattered, and there was no machinery through which a quick decision could be reached in a matter of such importance. The immediate response was an instruction to treat the prisoner with every consideration and not to shoot, even if he should attempt to escape. It was evidently feared that the partisans might invoke the usual excuse for murdering a prisoner. But there was in Milan no clear idea as to what the next step should be. Only the Communists knew exactly what they wanted.

The Dongo partisans with fierce local pride seem to have been inspired by the desire to hold onto their important prize as long as possible, and in any event to surrender him to their superiors rather than to the Allies. Fearing that Mussolini might be snatched from them, they took him from the Municipality to the barracks of the Finance Guards at Germasino, in the mountains two miles from Dongo. There he was lodged in a cell, given supper, and, having regard to the instructions from Milan, invited to certify that he had been well treated. In a nervous hand he scribbled on a sheet of paper: "The 52nd Garibaldi Brigade captured me today Friday, April 27, on the square at Dongo. The treatment accorded to me during and after my capture has been correct." He seemed restless at times, his guards subsequently reported, but not afraid or in any way preoccupied with his fate.

He did, however, ask one favor of Pedro, the partisan commander: to say goodby on his behalf to Clara Petacci, who was under arrest in the Dongo Municipality, and to tell her not to think of him any more. This was the first intimation to the partisans that Clara was among the prisoners. Pedro duly carried out the commission and in a long interview with Clara, which he describes as affecting, eventually yielded to her entreaties to be allowed to rejoin her lover.

Meanwhile, later that night the partisans, fearing that Mussolini's presence at Germasino had become generally known, decided to move him again, this time to a villa at San Maurizio near Brunate, two miles northeast of Como on the other side of the lake. He was awakened from his sleep, and, in order to disguise him as a wounded partisan on the way to hospital, his head and face were so heavily bandaged as to render him unrecognizable. He submitted without a word to this treatment and was taken by car back to Dongo. It was raining heavily and very cold. On the square at Dongo Mussolini was allowed to alight to greet Clara Petacci. "Why have you decided to follow me?" Mussolini inquired, and she replied: "This is how I want it."

The party drove slowly in the direction of Como, Clara in a first car with a number of partisans and Mussolini in a second car, sitting behind with a young woman partisan, who played the part of a nurse. On the way they were constantly stopped by partisan detachments at their road blocks, who allowed them to pass without much difficulty. When, however, they reached Moltrasio, four miles from Como, they heard the sound of distant firing, and they were told by a local friend that the Allies had arrived that night in Como, where they were meeting some residual resistance on the part of Fascist forces. Fearing that, if they persisted in trying to reach Brunate, they might become involved in the fighting or fall into the hands of the Allies or the Fascists, they decided to turn back to Azzano, ten miles away, close to which lived a small farmer known to one of them as a man who had harbored partisans. The cars stopped at the lakeside on the far side of Azzano and in the still pouring rain the weary party climbed the steep, rocky path to the village of Bonzanigo. The short journey took a quarter of an hour, and Clara in her high heels, supported on each side by Mussolini and Pedro, was so exhausted that she was obliged to stop for rest. Eventually they knocked at the farmer's door. It was now three o'clock on the morning of April 28. They were at once admitted, given coffee to drink, and lodged as well as circumstances permitted in a double-bedded room on the second floor. There they slept the sleep of exhaustion, while at Milan their fate was being debated.

So many contradictory accounts have been given of the proceedings of the Liberation Committee that it is impossible to determine exactly what occurred. It is, however, certain that the Communist members of the Committee were resolved to execute out of hand Mussolini and the other members of the Fascist Republican government; and Togliatti subsequently claimed that he had given orders to this effect in his capacity of secretary of the Communist party and Vice-Premier of Italy.[7] The members of the committee who made themselves responsible for carrying out Togliatti's order were Luigi Longo and Walter Audisio, a former volunteer in the Spanish Civil War, who went under the names of Giovanbattista di Cesare Magnoli and Colonel Valerio. It seems that these two men persuaded their colleagues on the committee to entrust Colonel Valerio with the mission of bringing Mussolini back to Milan, without revealing that it was their intention that he should be brought back dead. In any event General Cadorna gave Valerio a pass, signed by the American liaison officer with the committee, requesting that he should be allowed to circulate freely in the execution of a mission entrusted to him by the National Liberation Committee.

Armed with this pass Valerio, accompanied by another trusted Communist, Aldo Lampredi, left Milan early on the morning of April 28 and drove to Como with an armed escort of partisans. At the prefecture he was received by the new prefect, to whom he represented that he was under instructions to convey Mussolini and the other Fascists captured at Dongo to Milan. According to one of Valerio's many subsequent accounts, the prefect displayed the petty jealousies of a bourgeois spirit, or in other words showed reluctance to allow Mussolini to be taken out of the hands of the local partisans. There was a long, acrimonious discussion, but Valerio's ruthless determination prevailed, and eventually he was allowed to pursue his way to Dongo.

There he arrived at about 2 P.M. only to find Pedro, the local partisan commander, equally uncooperative. Valerio was now in a frenzy. With every hour that passed the risk increased that the Allies would intervene or that some other circumstance would rob him of his prey. He brutally demanded that Pedro should forthwith hand over his prisoners; and when Pedro demurred on the ground that the 52nd Brigade, which had been responsible for their capture, should deliver them to the Liberation Committee, he retorted: "There is no question of that. I have come to shoot them." There was an altercation, but Valerio claimed that he was acting under direct instructions from the Committee and demanded a list of the Fascist prisoners at Dongo. When this was produced, he announced that Mussolini and Clara Petacci were to die. He then arbitrarily selected fifteen * from the list for execution, marking their names with a cross. Some of the men were in the Municipality, while four had been transferred during the previous night to the barracks at Germasino. It was agreed that while Pedro drove to Germasino to bring back the four men to Dongo, Valerio should proceed to Bonzanigo to fetch Mussolini and Clara. Pedro, while submitting to superior orders, was still hoping that the delay caused by this maneuver might yet frustrate Valerio's design. Accordingly, Valerio departed on his errand, having discarded Pedro, and taking with him two reliable members of the local partisan brigade.

Mussolini had awakened late and, after a simple meal provided by the farmer's wife, had spent the day waiting. At about 4 P.M. on April 28 Valerio broke into his room and announced that he had come to rescue him. Mussolini and Clara Petacci were hurried down the stairs and along a narrow lane to a waiting car. They drove for about a mile down a narrow mountain road in the direction of the lake. Suddenly the car stopped outside the Villa Belmonte, a substantial house standing behind a low stone wall. Mussolini and Clara were ordered out of the car, quickly placed against the wall on the left side of the gate, and riddled with machine-gun bullets at almost point-blank range.

Two men were left to guard the bodies while Valerio returned immediately to Dongo to complete his bloody work. The fifteen men selected for execution were hurriedly brought out on the square and lined up facing the lake. The protests of the mayor were angrily brushed aside. Only three minutes were allowed for the ministrations of a priest and the prisoners were shot down by a partisan squad. Immediately afterwards Marcello Petacci was also executed.

On the following morning, April 29, a commandeered moving van brought the bodies to a filling station in the Piazalle Loreto, the scene of the notorious execution of fifteen Italian hostages in the

* The fifteen were Barracu, Bombacci, Gatti, Liverani, Mezzasomma, Pavolini, Zerbino, Ruggero Romano, Minister of Public Works, Paolo Porta, head of the Fascist party in Lombardy, Alfredo Coppolo, Rector of the Bologna University, Ernesto Daquanno, Director of the Stefani agency, Mario Nudi, President of the Fascist Agricultural Association, Colonel Vito Casalinuovo, Mussolini's adjutant, Pietro Calistri, an air force pilot, and an obscure journalist Utimberger. The names of the last two are given in some works as Salustri and Hintermayer. But this is not borne out by the list of prisoners, of which a photostat is reproduced in Tamaro, III, 630.

preceding August. There, from a girder, were hung, head downwards, exposed to public execration, the corpses of Mussolini, Clara, Barracu, Pavolini, Mezzasomma, and Zerbino. To the pile of bodies lying beneath them was added the corpse of Starace, who had just been captured and summarily executed on the spot. Only four months had elapsed since Mussolini had been acclaimed in the streets of Milan. That evening the bodies were removed by order of the Allied authorities and Mussolini was given secret burial in the Musocco cemetery in Milan.*

Twelve years later it was considered safe to release the body to the family, and he was reburied in accordance with his own wish in his home cemetery of San Cassiano at Predappio where his son Bruno already lay. Clara also has her monument. On the spot where she died, on the road above Azzano, there stands at the gate of the villa a small marble cross bearing the inscription: Clara Petacci and the date of her death.

---

* The secret was not kept for long. In 1946 Domenico Leccesi, who later became a member of the Chamber of Deputies, with some other Neo-Fascists stole the Duce's corpse, which was traced some months later to the Franciscan monastery of the Angelicum at Pavia. It was secretly reburied in the Capuchin monastery at Cerro Maggiore, fifteen miles northwest of Milan. In August, 1957, it was handed over to Donna Rachele. He now lies under a tombstone bearing the emblem of the fasces.

Notes

CHAPTER ONE

1. P. Petit-Radel, *Voyage de l'Italie* (Paris, 1815), I, 256.
2. Giovanni Guareschi, *Don Camillo and the Prodigal Son* (London, 1952).
3. Benito Mussolini, *My Autobiography* (London, 1928), p. 18.
4. *Ibid.*, p. 19.
5. Gaudens Megaro, *Mussolini in the Making* (London, 1939), p. 22.
6. Cecil J. S. Sprigge, *The Development of Modern Italy* (London, 1943), p. 69.
7. B. Mussolini, *op. cit.*, p. 21.
8. Edvige Mussolini, *Mio fratello Benito* (Florence, 1957), p. 12.
9. B. Mussolini, *Il mio diario di guerra* (Milan, 1923), p. 127.
10. B. Mussolini, *My Autobiography,* p. 21.
11. Margherita Sarfatti, *The Life of Mussolini* (London, 1925), p. 59.
12. Emil Ludwig, *Talks with Mussolini* (London, 1933), p. 41.
13. B. Mussolini, *op. cit.*, p. 24.
14. Sarfatti, *op. cit.*, p. 65.
15. Ludwig, *op. cit.*, p. 196.
16. Giorgio Pini and Duilio Susmel, *Mussolini l'uomo e l'opera* (Florence, 1953), I, 42.
17. Ivon de Begnac, *Vita di Mussolini* (Milan, 1936), pp. 312–13.
18. Sante Bedeschi and Rino Alessi, *Anni giovanili di Mussolini* (Milan, 1939), p. 18.
19. *Ibid.*, p. 61.
20. *Ibid.*, p. 58.
21. De Begnac, *op. cit.*, p. 323.

CHAPTER TWO

1. Bedeschi and Alessi, *op. cit.*, letter VIII, p. 72.
2. *Ibid.*, letter X, p. 76.
3. *Ibid.*, letter XI, p. 76.
4. Sarfatti, *op. cit.*, pp. 80–81.
5. *Ibid.*, pp. 82–87.
6. *Ibid.*, p. 90.
7. Angelica Balabanoff, *My Life as a Rebel* (London, 1938), pp. 57–61.
8. Sarfatti, *op. cit.*, pp. 104–6.
9. *Ibid.*, pp. 113, 114, 118.
10. Armando Borghi, *Mussolini Red and Black* (London, 1935), p. 17.
11. B. Mussolini, *op. cit.*, pp. 27, 28.
12. Bedeschi and Alessi, *op. cit.*, letter XVII, p. 92.
13. Megaro, *op. cit.*, p. 71.
14. Bedeschi and Alessi, *op. cit.*, p. 26.
15. Beatrice Baskerville, *What Next, O Duce?* (London, 1937), p. 128.
16. Sarfatti, *op. cit.*, pp. 128–33.
17. B. Mussolini, *op. cit.*, p. 29.
18. Sarfatti, *op. cit.*, p. 136.
19. Paolo Monelli, *Mussolini, an Intimate Life* (London, 1953), p. 46.
20. Adolf Dresler, *Mussolini als Journalist* (Leipzig, 1938), pp. 8–11.

21. Pini and Susmel, *op. cit.*, I, 121.
22. Sarfatti, *op. cit.*, p. 152.
23. Dresler, *op. cit.*, pp. 14–15.
24. Pietro Nenni, *Ten Years of Tyranny in Italy* (London, 1932), pp. 20–21.
25. Borghi, *op. cit.*, p. 24.
26. *Ibid.*, p. 27.
27. *Ibid.*, p. 26.
28. Megaro, *op. cit.*, p. 211.
29. Rachele Mussolini, *My Life with Mussolini* (London, 1959), pp. 14–19; and Monelli, *Mussolini, op. cit.*, p. 22.
30. Balabanoff, *op. cit.*, p. 127.
31. Nenni, *op. cit.*, p. 21.
32. Pini and Susmel, I, 181, 182.
33. Carlo Silvestri, *Contro la vendetta* (Milan, 1948), p. 374.
34. Nenni, *op. cit.*, pp. 29, 30.
35. Cesare Rossi, *Mussolini com'era* (Rome, 1947), pp. 53, 54. Where not otherwise stated, references to Cesare Rossi relate to this book.
36. Pini and Susmel, *op. cit.*, I, 187.
37. Borghi, *op. cit.*, pp. 33, 34.
38. George Seldes, *Sawdust Caesar* (London, 1936), p. 21.
39. Sarfatti, *op. cit.*, p. 176.

CHAPTER THREE

1. Balabanoff, *Erinnerungen und Erlebnisse* (Berlin, 1927), p. 79.
2. Pini and Susmel, *op. cit.*, I, 199.
3. *Ibid.*, I, 202.
4. *Ibid.*, I, 201–4.
5. B. Mussolini, *op. cit.*, p. 33.
6. Pini and Susmel, *op. cit.*, I, 214.
7. *Ibid.*, I, 229.
8. Sarfatti, *op. cit.*, p. 193.
9. Pini and Susmel, *op. cit.*, I, 236, 237.
10. Sarfatti, *op. cit.*, p. 200.
11. Daniele Varé, *Laughing Diplomat* (London, 1938), pp. 213, 214.
12. Gaetano Salvemini, *Mussolini diplomatico* (Bari, 1952), p. 420.
13. Borghi, *op. cit.*, pp. 65, 66.
14. Alceste de Ambris, *Mussolini, la leggenda e l'uomo* (Marseilles, 1930).
15. Salvemini, *op. cit.*, pp. 425–27.
16. *Ibid.*, pp. 427–28.
17. B. Mussolini, *op. cit.*, p. 48.
18. Sarfatti, *op. cit.*, p. 203.
19. Salvemini, *op. cit.*, pp. 497–98.
20. Balabanoff, *Erinnerungen und Erlebnisse*, p. 144.
21. Seldes, *op. cit.*, p. 7.
22. *Ibid.*, p. 8.
23. B. Mussolini, *op. cit.*, p. 47.
24. Count Carlo Sforza, *Contemporary Italy* (London, 1946), p. 161.
25. C. Rossi, *Trentatre vicende mussoliniane* (Milan, 1958), pp. 391, 392.
26. B. Mussolini, *op. cit.*, pp. 52–53.
27. Monelli, *op. cit.*, p. 276.
28. B. Mussolini, *op. cit.*, p. 56.
29. Sarfatti, *op. cit.*, p. 232.

CHAPTER FOUR

1. Sarfatti, *op. cit.*, p. 238.
2. Pini and Susmel, *op. cit.*, I, 355.
3. Viscount Templewood, *Nine Troubled Years* (London, 1954), p. 154.
4. Pini and Susmel, *op. cit.*, I, 355.
5. B. Mussolini, *The Political and Social Doctrine of Fascism* (London, 1933). Translation of an article contributed in 1932 to the *Enciclopedia Italiana.*
6. Pini and Susmel, *op. cit.*, I, 377.
7. C. Rossi, *op. cit.*, p. 76.
8. Baron di San Severino, *Mussolini*

as *Revealed in His Political Speeches* (London, 1923), pp. 87–90.

9. Pini and Susmel, *op. cit.*, I, 391; and Mussolini, *The Political and Social Doctrine of Fascism, op. cit.*, p. 9.
10. San Severino, *op. cit.*, pp. 97, 98.
11. Pini and Susmel, *op. cit.*, II, 28.
12. J. N. Macdonald, *A Political Escapade; The Story of Fiume and D'Annunzio* (London, 1921), p. 47.
13. Sarfatti, *op. cit.*, p. 267.
14. Luigi Sturzo, *Italy and Fascismo* (London, 1926), pp. 121, 122.
15. C. Rossi, *op. cit.*, pp. 87, 88.
16. Pini and Susmel, *op. cit.*, II, 90–94.
17. Sarfatti, *op. cit.*, p. 281.
18. Borghi, *op. cit.*, p. 112; Seldes, *op. cit.*, p. 67.
19. Giovanni Giolitti, *Memoirs of My Life* (London, 1923), p. 445.
20. Spriggs, *op. cit.*, pp. 190–91. *See also* Federico Chabod, *A History of Italian Fascism* (London, 1963), p. 56.

CHAPTER FIVE

1. Benito Mussolini, *La rivoluzione fascista: scritti e discori di Benito Mussolini* (Milan, 1934), II, 165–88.
2. Seldes, *op. cit.*, p. 90.
3. Pini and Susmel, *op. cit.*, II, 132.
4. B. Mussolini, *My Autobiography*, p. 134.
5. *Ibid.*, p. 140.
6. *Ibid.*, p. 148.
7. Pini and Susmel, *op. cit.*, II, 154, 155.
8. Italo Balbo, *Diario 1922* (Milan, 1932).
9. The account of Balbo's operations is taken from his *Diario 1922*.
10. Nenni, *op. cit.*, pp. 9–14.
11. George Slocombe, *The Tumult and the Shouting* (London, 1936), pp. 148–53.
12. *Popolo d'Italia,* July 8, 1922.
13. Pini and Susmel, *op. cit.*, II, 162, 163.
14. *Ibid.*, 165.
15. B. Mussolini, *Scritti e discorsi, op. cit.*, II, 299-304.
16. Nenni, *op. cit.*, p. 119.
17. Arturo Rossi, *The Rise of Italian Fascism 1918–1922* (London, 1938), p. 231.
18. Pini and Susmel, *op. cit.*, II, 199.

CHAPTER SIX

1. B. Mussolini, *op. cit.*, II, 307–22.
2. C. Rossi, *Trentatre vicende mussoliniane* (Milan, 1938), p. 127.
3. *Ibid.*, p. 131.
4. B. Mussolini, *op. cit.*, II, 339–48.
5. Pini and Susmel, *op. cit.*, II, 231.
6. Balbo, *op. cit.*, pp. 195–98.
7. Sforza, *op. cit.*, pp. 255–56.
8. Intercepted telephone conversation. Efrem Ferraris, *La marcia su Roma veduta dal Viminale* (Rome, 1946), pp. 88–99.
9. *Ibid.*, pp. 143, 144.
10. A. Rossi, *op. cit.*, p. 296.
11. Pini and Susmel, *op. cit.*, II, 247.
12. B. Mussolini, *op. cit.*, II, 351–52.
13. Nino D'Aroma, *Vent'anni insieme* (Rome, 1957), pp. 138–39.
14. B. Mussolini, *My Autobiography*, p. 181.
15. Pini and Susmel, *op. cit.*, II, 258–59.

CHAPTER SEVEN

1. Related to the author by an informant who wishes to remain anonymous. Hereafter, such communications will be termed "Informant."
2. Aldo Castellani, *Microbes, Men and Monarchs* (London, 1960), p. 126.
3. Pini and Susmel, *op. cit.*, II, 149–50.
4. A. L. Rowse, *All Souls and Appeasement* (London, 1961), p. 25.
5. Ludwig, *op. cit.*, p. 70.
6. *Ibid.*, p. 123.
7. Arturo Carlo Jemolo, *Chiesa e stato in Italia negli ultimi cento anni* (Rome, 1948), p. 231.
8. Nenni, *op. cit.*, p. 36.
9. Ludwig, *op. cit.*, p. 122.
10. *Ibid.*, p. 158.
11. *Ibid.*, p. 65.
12. *Ibid.*, p. 65.
13. Richard Wichterich, *Benito Mussolini* (Stuttgart, 1952), p. 49.
14. Castellani, *op. cit.*, p. 134.
15. A. Rossi, *op. cit.*, p. 141.
16. Nenni, *op. cit.*, p. 38.
17. C. Rossi, *op. cit.*, p. 83.
18. *Ibid.*, pp. 164–65.
19. Ludwig, *op. cit.*, p. 155.
20. Informant.
21. Informant.
22. Count Galeazzo Ciano, *Diary, 1939–1943,* ed. Malcolm Muggeridge (London, 1947). Entry for September 18, 1939.
23. Enno von Rintelen, *Mussolini als Bundesgenosse* (Stuttgart, 1951), pp. 103, 104.
24. Varé, *op. cit.*, p. 210.
25. Speech to the Senate, March 11, 1926. *Scritti e discorsi, op. cit.*, V, 293.
26. Speech at Bologna, May 24, 1918. *Scritti e discorsi, op. cit.*, I, 319.
27. C. Rossi, *Trentatre vicende mussoliniane, op. cit.*, p. 377.
28. Ludwig, *op. cit.*, p. 155.
29. Ciano, *Diary,* Entry for March 15, 1939.
30. E. Mussolini, *op. cit.*, p. 147.
31. Dino Alfieri, *Dictators Face to Face* (London, 1954), p. 101.
32. Pini and Susmel, *op. cit.*, IV, 464.
33. Conversation with Goering. *Count Galiazzo Ciano's Diplomatic Papers,* ed. M. Muggeridge (London, 1948), p. 87.
34. Conversation with Ribbentrop. *Ibid.*, p. 145.
35. Castellani, *op. cit.*, pp. 126–31.
36. Pini and Susmel, *op. cit.*, II, 442.
37. C. Rossi, *op. cit.*, p. 186.
38. Margherita Sarfatti, *Dux* (Milan, 1926), p. 314.
39. Alfieri, *op. cit.*, p. 47. *See also* Filippo Anfuso, *Da Palazzo Venezia al Lagodi Garda* (Rome, 1957).
40. C. Rossi, *Trentatre vicende mussoliniane, op. cit.*, p. 390.
41. Ludwig, *op. cit.*, p. 216.
42. *Ibid.*, p. 70.
43. Pini and Susmel, *op. cit.*, II, 361.
44. Alma Mahler-Werfel, *Mein Leben* (Frankfurt, 1960), pp. 192, 286.
45. Kurt von Schuschnigg, *Ein Requiem in Rot-Weiss-Rot* (Zurich, 1946), p. 236.
46. C. Rossi, *op. cit.*, p. 209.
47. G. Ward Price, *I Know These Dictators* (London, 1937), p. 181.
48. Ludwig, *op. cit.*, p. 45.
49. *Ibid.*, p. 47.
50. E. Mussolini, *op. cit.*, p. 99.
51. Speech in Rome, June 22, 1925. *Scritti e discorsi, op. cit.*, V, 111.
52. *Gerarchia*, October 25, 1925.
53. Pini and Susmel, *op. cit.*, II, 335.
54. Sarfatti, *Dux, op. cit.*, p. 16.
55. E. Mussolini, *op. cit.*, p. 13.
56. B. Mussolini, *op. cit.*, II, 54.
57. Ludwig, *op. cit.*, p. 174.
58. B. Mussolini, *Fascismo, dottrine & institutione* (Milan, 1934), p. 30.
59. Balabanoff, *My Life as a Rebel, op. cit.*, p. 116.
60. Christopher Hibbert, *Benito Mussolini* (London, 1962), p. 54.
61. A. Rossi, *op. cit.*, p. 23.
62. R. Mussolini, *op. cit.*, p. 79.

63. Vittorio Mussolini, *Due donne nella Tempesta* (Rome, 1961), pp. 128, 129.
64. Franz von Papen, Memoirs (London, 1952), p. 279.
65. Adolf Hitler, *Adolf Hitler's Table Talk 1941–1944* (London, 1953), p. 10.
66. Hitler, *The Testament of Adolf Hitler* (London, 1961), p. 74.
67. Ludwig, *op. cit.*, p. 37.
68. A. Duff Cooper, *Old Men Forget* (London, 1953), p. 83.
69. Winston S. Churchill, *The Second World War* (London, 1949), II, 107.
70. *Ibid.*, II, 548.
71. Earl of Avon, *Facing the Dictators* (London, 1962), p. 133.
72. Informant.
73. Carlo Scorza, *Contemporary Italy* (London, 1946), p. 249.

CHAPTER EIGHT

1. Harold Nicolson, *Curzon: The Last Phase* (London, 1934), p. 290.
2. Related to the author by two members of the British delegation.
3. R. Mussolini, *op. cit.*, p. 50.
4. San Severino, *op. cit.*, p. 211.
5. *Ibid.*, p. 217.
6. *Ibid.*, p. 222.
7. *Ibid.*, p. 362.
8. C. Rossi, *Trentatre vicende mussoliniane, op. cit.*, p. 197.

CHAPTER NINE

1. Amerigo Dumini, *Diciasetti colpi* (Milan, 1951), p. 79.
2. *Ibid.*, p. 84.
3. The account of the judicial investigation is taken from Mauro del Guidice, *Cronistoria del processo Matteotti* (Palermo, 1954).
4. Informant.
5. The account of the trials is taken largely from Alessandro Schiavi, *La vita e l'opera di Giacomo Matteotti* (Rome, 1957).
6. Carlo Silvestri, *Contro la vendetta op. cit.*, pp. 280, 288.
7. G. A. Borgese, *Goliath: The March of Fascism* (New York, 1938), p. 262.
8. B. Mussolini, *op. cit.*, IV, 166.
9. *Ibid.*, IV, 176.
10. Enrico Caviglia, *Diario (1925–1945)* (Rome, 1952), pp. 3–4.
11. Carlo Silvestri, *Turati l'a detto: socialisti e democrazia cristianna* (Milan, 1948), pp. 39–40.
12. Caviglia, *op. cit.*, pp. 376–77.
13. Pini and Susmel, *op. cit.*, II, 382.
14. B. Mussolini, *op. cit.*, IV, 225.
15. Speech in the Chamber, May 26, 1927. B. Mussolini, *Scritti e discorsi, op. cit.*, VI, 62.
16. Pini and Susmel, *op. cit.*, II, 407, 408.
17. Caviglia, *op. cit.*, p. 337.
18. Informant.

CHAPTER TEN

1. Count Harry Kessler, Walther Rathenau (London, 1929), pp. 216, 217.
2. Slocombe, *op. cit.*, pp. 245, 246.
3. Salvemini, *op. cit.*, p. 97.
4. Letter to Sir William Tyrell of

October 18, 1925. Sir Charles Petri: *The Life and Letters of Sir Austen Chamberlain* (London, 1940), II, 287.

5. Luigi Salvatorelli and Giovanni Mira, *Storia d'Italia nel periodo fascista* (Turin, 1961), p. 411.

CHAPTER ELEVEN

1. Sforza, *op. cit.*, p. 278
2. Informant.
3. B. Mussolini, *Discorsi del 1929* (Milan, 1930), p. 77.
4. Informant.
5. Daniel A. Binchy, *Church and State in Fascist Italy* (London, 1941), p. 668.
6. Conversation with the author.
7. E. Mussolini, *op. cit.*, pp. 131–35.

CHAPTER TWELVE

1. Salvatorelli and Mira, *op. cit.*, p. 459.
2. Speech at the Capitol, December 31, 1925.
3. B. Mussolini, *Scritti e discorsi, op. cit.*, VII, 206.
4. Related by Grandi to Sir Ronald Graham. *See also* Salvemini, *op. cit.*, p. 317.
5. Vittorio Mussolini, *op. cit.*, pp. 130–37.
6. Informant.
7. E. Mussolini, *op. cit.*, p. 135.
8. Related by Count Grandi.
9. *Documents on German Foreign Policy*, Series C, II, 704–5. To be subsequently referred to as *G. F. P.*
10. *Ibid.*, II, 224–25.
11. A. Francois-Poncet, *Souvenirs d'une Ambassade à Berlin* (Paris, 1946), p. 183.
12. *G. F. P.*, pp. 10–13.
13. Elizabeth Wiskemann, *The Rome-Berlin Axis* (London, 1949), p. 36.
14. Alfred Rosenberg, *Das politische Tagebuch* (Tubingen, 1956), p. 28.
15. *Ibid.*, p. 28.
16. Paolo Monelli, *Mussolini piccolo borghese* (Milan, 1950), p. 202.
17. Prince Starhemberg, *Between Hitler and Mussolini* (London, 1942), p. 150.
18. Wiskemann, *op. cit.*, p. 36.
19. E. Mussolini, *op. cit.*, p. 147.
20. Speech to the Senate, May 20, 1925.
21. Starhemberg, *op. cit.*, p. 26.
22. *Ibid.*, p. 94.
23. *Ibid.*, p. 109.
24. *Ibid.*, pp. 168–71.
25. Salvatorelli and Mira, *op. cit.*, p. 767.
26. Ciano, *Diary* (*1937–1938*), Entry for December 24, 1934; Viscount Templewood, *Nine Troubled Years* (London, 1954), pp. 155–56; and Avon, *op. cit.*, p. 209.
27. R. Guariglia, *La Diplomatic Difficile: Memoires 1922–1926.* Translated from his *Ricordi* (Paris, 1955), p. 59.
28. *Ibid.*, p. 60.
29. Pompeio Aloisi, *Journal* (*25 Juillet 1932–14 Juin 1936*) (Paris, 1957). Entry for March 24, 1935.
30. Informant.
31. Emilio de Bono, *The Conquest of an Empire* (London, 1937), p. 57.
32. Lord Vansittart, *The Mist Procession* (London, 1958), p. 519.
33. *Ibid.*, p. 520.
34. Related to the author by Count Grandi.

CHAPTER THIRTEEN

1. De Bono, *op. cit.*, p. 54.
2. *Ibid.*, p. 13.
3. Wiskemann, *op. cit.*, p. 48.
4. Guariglia, *op. cit.*, p. 63.
5. E. Mussolini, *op. cit.*, p. 147.
6. Mario Toscano, "Eden at Rome on the Eve of the Italio-Ethiopian Conflict," *Nuova Antologia*, January, 1960.
7. Avon, *op. cit.*, p. 224.
8. De Bono, *op. cit.*, p. 161.
9. *Ibid.*, p. 161.
10. *British White Paper. Ethiopia No. 1* (Cmd. 5044), 1935, p. 13.
11. Guariglia, *op. cit.*, p. 67.
12. Wiskemann, *op. cit.*, pp. 51–52.
13. W. S. Churchill, *The Second World War,* I (London, 1948), p. 135.
14. *See* text of Grandi's memorandum reproduced in R. J. Minney (ed.), *Papers of Hore-Belisha* (London, 1960), pp. 101–2.
15. Salvatorelli and Mira, *op. cit.*, pp. 856–57.

CHAPTER FOURTEEN

1. Mario Donosti, *Mussolini e l'Europa* (Rome, 1945), p. 49; Salvatorelli and Mira, *op. cit.*, p. 894.
2. *G. F. P.*, III, 172.
3. *Ibid.*, IV, 37.
4. Pini and Susmel, *op. cit.*, III, 362.
5. *Journal Officiel, Chambre des Deputes,* December 5, 1936, p. 3370.
6. *G. F. P.*, III, 65.
7. Ciano, *Diary,* Entries for August 23, September 2, and September 3, 1937.
8. Ciano, *Diplomatic Papers,* pp. 8, 9, 20.
9. *Ibid.*, pp. 43–48.
10. Anfuso, *op. cit.*, pp. 27–28.
11. Ciano, *op. cit.*, pp. 56–60.
12. Anfuso, *op. cit.*, p. 29. When Lord Halifax visited Berchtesgaden in 1937 Hitler was again at pains to call his guest's attention to the distant prospect of Salzburg.
13. Informant.
14. Ciano, *op. cit.*, pp. 144–45.
15. Related to the author by the British military attaché.
16. *G. F. P.*, I, 1–2.
17. Ciano, *Diary,* Entry for January 31, 1938.
18. Paul Schmidt, *Statist auf der diplomatischer Buhne* (Bonn, 1949), p. 347.
19. Ciano, *Diplomatic Papers,* p. 90.
20. *Ibid.*, p. 146.
21. Schuschnigg, *Ein Requiem in Rot-Weiss-Rot, op. cit.*, pp. 42–43.
22. *G. F. P.*, I, 352.
23. Alan Bullock, *Hitler* (London, 1952), p. 394.
24. Ciano, *Diary,* Entry for March 12, 1938.
25. *Ibid.* Entries for April 23, 24, 1938.
26. *Ibid.* Entry for March 17, 1938.
27. Wiskemann, *op. cit.*, pp. 102–3.
28. Ciano, *op. cit.*, Entry for December 21, 1937.
29. Ciano, *Diplomatic Papers,* p. 162.
30. Ciano, *Diary,* Entry for November 16, 1938.
31. Pini and Susmel, *op. cit.*, III, 411-12.
32. Ciano, *op. cit.*, Entry for April 2, 1938.
33. Walter Schellenberg, *The Schellenberg Memoirs* (London, 1956), p. 53.
34. M. Magistrati, *L'Italia a Berlino* (Verona, 1956), pp. 163–64.

35. Hitler, *Hitler's Table Talk* (London, 1953), Entry for April 23, 1942.
36. D'Aroma, *op. cit.*, pp. 261-62.
37. Salvatorelli and Mira, *op. cit.*, p. 934.
38. Ciano, *op. cit.*, Entry for May 9, 1938.
39. *See* for example Ciano, *op. cit.*, Entry for March 13, 1938.
40. On this subject I am indebted to an excellent paper by D. C. Watt, "An Earlier Model for the Pact of Steel." *International Affairs,* XXXIII, No. 2. (1937).
41. Schmidt, *op. cit.*, p. 387.
42. Ciano, *op. cit.*, Entry for May 5, 1938.
43. Schmidt, *op. cit.*, p. 388.
44. Ciano, *op. cit.*, Entry for May 14, 1938.
45. *Il Pensiero Romagnolo.* "La filosofia della forza." A series of articles on Nietzsche published on November 29 and December 6 and 13, 1908.
46. Ciano, *op. cit.*, Entry for September 6, 1937.
47. A record of this interview is in Renzo de Felice, *Storia degli ebrei italiani sotto il fascismo* (Turin, 1961), pp. 149–51.
48. The facts are marshaled by Michaelis in "I rapporti italo-tedeschi e il problema degli ebrei in Italia (1922–38)," *Rivista di Studi Politici Internazionali,* April–June, 1961.
49. Text in De Felice, *op. cit.*, pp. 321–22.
50. Ciano, *op. cit.*, Entry for July 14, 1938.
51. Text in De Felice, *op. cit.*, pp. 611–12.
52. Text of Grand Council resolution in *ibid.*, pp. 347–50.
53. D'Aroma, *op. cit.*, p. 275.
54. Ciano, *op. cit.*, Entry for July 30, 1938.
55. *Ibid.*, August 22, 1938.
56. De Felice, *op. cit.*, p. 362.
57. *Ibid.*, p. 364.
58. Salvatorelli and Mira, *op. cit.*, p. 941.
59. Ciano, *op. cit.*, Entry for August 24, 1938.
60. *Ibid.*, August 29, 1938.
61. Salvatorelli and Mira, *op. cit.*, p. 942.
62. Ciano, *op. cit.*, Entry for July 10, 1938.
63. Magistrati, *op. cit.*, p. 200.
64. Ciano, *op. cit.*, Entry for June 17, 1938.
65. *Ibid.*, Entry for May 22, 1938.
66. *Ibid.*, May 26, 1938.
67. *Ibid.*, Entry for September 13, 1938.
68. Anfuso, *op. cit.*, pp. 68–69.
69. Ciano, *op. cit.*, Entry for September 25, 1938.
70. Ciano, *Diplomatic Papers, op. cit.*, p. 236.
71. Ciano, *Diary,* Entry for September 26, 1938.
72. *Ibid.*
73. William Shirer, *The Rise and Fall of the Third Reich* (London, 1961), p. 400.
74. Related by the Yugoslav military attaché to the British military attaché.
75. Ciano, *op. cit.*, Entry for September 29–30, 1938.
76. Anfuso, *op. cit.*, pp. 73–74.
77. Ciano, *op. cit.*, Entry for November 12, 1938.
78. *Ibid.*, Entry for December 16, 1938.
79. *Ibid.*, Entry for November 30, 1938.
80. Guariglia, *op. cit.*, pp. 94–95.
81. Ciano, *op. cit.*, Entry for October 29, 1938.
82. *Ibid.*, Entry for October 28, 1938.
83. Ciano, *Diplomatic Papers,* pp. 242–46.
84. Ciano, *Diary,* Entry for October 29, 1938.

CHAPTER FIFTEEN

1. Ciano, *op. cit.*, Entry for January 11, 1939.
2. *Ibid.*, Entry for March 10, 1939.
3. *Ibid.*, Entry for March 15, 1939.
4. Ulrich von Hassel, *Diaries 1938–1944* (London, 1948), p. 54.
5. Ciano, *op. cit.*, Entry for January 11, 1939.
6. Donosti, *op. cit.*, p. 152.
7. *Ibid.*
8. Ciano, *op. cit.*, Entry for March 21, 1939.
9. *Ibid.*, Entry for May 19, 1938.
10. *Ibid.*, Entry for October 27, 1938.
11. *Ibid.*, Entry for March 28, 1939.
12. Anfuso, *op. cit.*, p. 97.
13. Ciano, *op. cit.*, Entry for April 9, 1939.
14. *Ibid.*, Entry for April 16, 1939.
15. *Ibid.*, Entry for January 1, 1939.
16. *Ibid.*, Entry for April 16, 1939.
17. Rintelen, *op. cit.*, p. 61.
18. Pietro Badoglio, *l'Italie dans la Guerre Mondiale* (Paris, 1946), pp. 25–27.
19. Ciano, *Diplomatic Papers,* pp. 283–86.
20. Shirer, *op. cit.*, p. 468.
21. Ciano, *Diary,* Entry for May 13, 1939.
22. F. W. Deakin, *The Brutal Friendship* (London, 1962), pp. 1–2.
23. Ciano, *op. cit.*, Entry for May 25, 1939.
24. *Ibid.* Entries for April 29 and May 2, 1939.
25. Shirer, *op. cit.*, pp. 484–87.
26. Ciano, *op. cit.*, Entry for May 26, 1939.
27. Ciano, *Diplomatic Papers,* pp. 290–95.
28. Magistrati, *op. cit.,* p. 369.
29. Ciano, *Diary,* Entries for July 4, 22, and 28, 1939.
30. Information supplied by Count Magistrati to Miss E. Wiskemann, *op. cit.,* pp. 153–54. *See also* Magistrati, *op. cit.*, pp. 378–82.
31. Ciano, *op. cit.*, Entry for August 6, 1939.
32. For the account of these meetings I have relied principally on *Documents on German Policy,* Series D, VII; Ciano, *Diplomatic Papers;* Ciano, *Diary;* Schmidt, *Statist;* and Magistrati's *L'Italia a Berlino.*
33. Ciano, *Diplomatic Papers,* pp. 297–99.
34. Ciano, *Diary,* Entry for December 23, 1943.
35. *Ibid.*, Entry for August 11, 1939.
36. *G. F. P.*, VII, 56.
37. Ciano, *Diplomatic Papers,* pp. 299–304.
38. Ciano, *Diary,* Entries for August 13 and 14, 1939.
39. Donosti, *op. cit.*, p. 206.
40. Magistrati, *op. cit.*, pp. 418–19.
41. Ciano, *op. cit.*, Entry for August 20, 1939.
42. *Ibid.*, Entry for August 21, 1939.
43. Informant.
44. *G. F. P.*, VII, 560.
45. Ciano, *op. cit.*, Entry for August 23, 1939.
46. *Ibid.*, Entry for August 25, 1939.
47. *G. F. P.*, VII, 160.
48. *Ibid.*, VII, 240–43.
49. Hitler and B. Mussolini, *Lettere e documenti* (Milan, 1946), p. 7.
50. *G. F. P.*, pp. 291–93.
51. Hitler and B. Mussolini, *op. cit.*, pp. 10–11.
52. *Ibid.*, pp. 12–14.
53. Ciano, *op. cit.*, Entry for August 26, 1939.
54. Hitler and B. Mussolini, *op. cit.*, pp. 14–15.
55. *Ibid.*, pp. 15–16.
56. *G. F. P.*, VII, 346–47.
57. Hitler and B. Mussolini, *op. cit.*, pp. 16–17.
58. *Ibid.*, pp. 17–18.
59. Ciano, *op. cit.*, Entry for September 1, 1939.
60. Hitler and B. Mussolini, *op. cit.*, pp. 21–22.
61. *G. F. P.*, VII, 485–86.
62. *Ibid.*, VII, 509–10.
63. *Ibid.*, VII, 524–25.
64. *Ibid.*, VII, 538–39.

65. Ciano, *op. cit.*, Entry for September 4, 1939.
66. *Ibid.*, Entries for September 9, 10, 12, 1939.

CHAPTER SIXTEEN

1. Ciano, *op. cit.*, Entry for September 5, 1939.
2. Ciano, *Europe verso la catastrofe* (Rome, 1948), p. 462.
3. *G. F. P.*, VIII, 125.
4. Ciano, *Diary,* Entry for October 13, 1939.
5. Leonardo Simoni, *Berlino: ambasciata d'Italia 1939–1943* (Rome, 1946), p. 25.
6. Ciano, *op. cit.*, Entry for October 3, 1939.
7. *Ibid.*, Entry for November 9, 1939.
8. *Ibid.*, Entry for November 11, 1939.
9. *Ibid.*, Entry for November 20, 1939.
10. *Ibid.*, Entry for December 4, 1939.
11. *Ibid.*, Entry for November 27, 1939.
12. Ciano, *L'Italia de fronti al conflitto* (Milan, 1940).
13. Ciano, *Diary,* Entries for December 16, 17, 18, and 19.
14. Simoni, *op. cit.*, p. 45.
15. *G. F. P.*, VIII, 582.
16. *Ibid.*, VIII, 604–9.
17. Ciano, *op. cit.*, Entry for December 9, 1939.
18. *Ibid.*, Entries for September 24, October 6 and 9, and December 3, 1939.
19. Anfuso, *op. cit.*, p. 107.
20. *G. F. P.*, VIII, 184–91.
21. Ciano, *op. cit.*, Entry for October 1, 1939.
22. *G. F. P.*, VIII, 439–46.
23. Ciano, *op. cit.*, Entries for January 18, 19, and 23, 1940.
24. *Ibid.*, Entries for January 29 and February 7, 1940.
25. Sumner Welles, *The Time for Decision* (London, 1944), pp. 69–70.
26. Ciano, *op. cit.*, Entry for March 1, 1940.
27. *Ibid.*, Entry for March 7, 1940.
28. *Ibid.*, Entry for March 8, 1940.
29. *G. F. P.*, VIII, 871–80.
30. *Ibid.*, VIII, 882–93; and Ciano, *Europe verso la catastrofe,* pp. 512–27.
31. Schmidt, *op. cit.*, p. 477.
32. *G. F. P.*, VIII, 896–909.
33. Ciano, *Diary,* Entry for March 12, 1940.
34. Simoni, *op. cit.*, pp. 80–81.
35. Welles, *op. cit.*, p. 111.
36. Ciano, *op. cit.*, Entries for March 12, 13, 14, and 16, 1940.
37. *G. F. P.*, IX, 1–16.
38. Ciano, *op. cit.*, Entry for March 19, 1940.
39. Rintelen, *op. cit.*, pp. 81–82.
40. Deakin, *op. cit.*, p. 9.
41. Ciano, *op. cit.*, Entries for March 23, 27, 31, and April 2, 1940.
42. *Ibid.*, Entry for April 9, 1940.
43. *Ibid.*
44. *Ibid.*, Entries for April 11, 20, 28, and May 4, 1940.
45. Paul Reynaud, *In the Thick of the Fight* (London, 1955), pp. 402, 403.
46. Ciano, *op. cit.*, Entry for April 26, 1940.
47. Reynaud, *op. cit.*, p. 403.
48. Ciano, *op. cit.*, Entry for May 1, 1940.
49. Simoni, *op. cit.*, p. 101.
50. Llewellyn Wookward, *British Foreign Policy in the Second World War* (London, 1962), pp. 36, 37.
51. *G. F. P.*, IX, 271–72.
52. Ciano, *op. cit.*, Entries for May 2 and 3, 1940.
53. Anfuso, *op. cit.*, pp. 119–22; Ciano, *op. cit.*, Entry for May 10, 1940.
54. Ciano, *op. cit.*, Entries for May 10, 11, and 13, 1940.
55. *Ibid.*, Entry for May 16, 1940.

56. Churchill, *The Second World War*, II, 107–8.
57. Paul Reynaud, *La France a sauvé L'Europe* (Paris, 1947), II, 209.
58. *G. F. P.*, IX, 481–82.
59. *Ibid.*, IX, 484–86.
60. *Ibid.*, IX, 505.
61. Related by Count Grandi.

CHAPTER SEVENTEEN

1. Rintelen, *op. cit.*, p. 89.
2. Ciano, *op. cit.*, Entry for June 17, 1940.
3. Ciano, *Europa verso la catastrofe*, pp. 562–65.
4. Deakin, *op. cit.*, p. 11.
5. Ciano, *Diary*, Entries for July 18 and 19, 1940.
6. *Ibid.*, Entry for June 22, 1940.
7. *Ibid.*, Entries for July 2, 4, and 5, 1940.
8. Ciano, *Europa verso la catastrofe*, pp. 566–72.
9. *G. F. P.*, X, 209–11.
10. Churchill, *op. cit.*, II, 230.
11. Ciano, *Diary*, Entry for July 22, 1940.
12. Churchill, *op. cit.*, II, 230.
13. Ciano, *Europa verso la catastrofe*, pp. 574–76.
14. Ciano, *Diary*, Entries for August 6 and 8, 1940.
15. Simoni, *op. cit.*, p. 161.
16. Ciano, *op. cit.*, Entry for August 17, 1940.
17. Ciano, *Europa verso la catastrofe*, pp. 581–83.
18. Ciano, *Diary*, Entry for September 9, 1940.
19. *Ibid.*, Entry for September 17, 1940.
20. Ciano, *Europa verso la catastrofe*, pp. 586–91.
21. *Ibid.*, pp. 494–99.
22. Ciano, *Diary*, Entry for October 4, 1940.
23. Paul Schmidt, *Hitler's Interpreter* (London, 1950), pp. 194–95.
24. Ciano, *Europa verso la catastrofe*, p. 604.
25. Schmidt, *op. cit.*, p. 197.
26. Shirer, *op. cit.*, p. 801.
27. Ciano, *Diary*, Entry for October 12, 1940.
28. *Ibid.*, Entry for October 12, 1940.
29. Schmidt, *op. cit.*, p. 200.
30. Ciano, *Europa verso la catastrofe*, pp. 601–7.
31. Schmidt, *op. cit.*, p. 200.
32. Ciano, *op. cit.*, pp. 612–16.
33. Ciano, *Diary*, Entry for November 20, 1940.
34. Hitler and B. Mussolini, *op. cit.*, pp. 71–77.
35. Ciano, *op. cit.*, Entry for November 22, 1940.
36. *G. F. P.*, XI, 671–72.
37. Ciano, *op. cit.*, Entry for December 4, 1940.
38. *Ibid.*, Entry for December 6, 1940.
39. Alfieri, *op. cit.*, pp. 82–84.
40. *Simoni*, *op. cit.*, p. 187.
41. Alfieri, *op. cit.*, pp. 87–88.
42. Ciano, *op. cit.*, Entry for December 10, 1940.
43. Simoni, *op. cit.*, p. 190.
44. *Ibid.*
45. *G. F. P.*, XI, 990–94.
46. Ivone Kirkpatrick, *The Inner Circle* (London, 1959), p. 195.
47. Ciano, *op. cit.*, Entry for October 13, 1941.

CHAPTER EIGHTEEN

1. Donosti, *op. cit.*, pp. 245–48; Wiskemann, *op. cit.*, pp. 247–48; and Simoni, *op. cit.*, pp. 196–200.
2. Ciano, *op. cit.*, Entry for January 3, 1941.
3. Alfieri, *op. cit.*, p. 93.

4. Ciano, *Europa verso la catastrofe,* pp. 628–29; Rintelen, *op. cit.,* pp. 124–26; Alfieri, *op. cit.,* pp. 91–98; and Ciano, *Diary,* Entry for January 18, 1941. *G. F. P., op. cit.,* XI, 1127–33.
5. Department of State, *The Spanish Government and the Axis* (Washington, 1946), pp. 28–33.
6. Anfuso, *op. cit.,* p. 153.
7. Ciano, *Europa verso la catastrofe,* pp. 631–43.
8. Ramon Serrano Suñer, *Entre les Pyrenees et Gibraltar* (Geneva, 1947), pp. 227–29.
9. Anfuso, *op. cit.,* p. 155.
10. Ciano, *op. cit.,* pp. 646–47, footnote.
11. Ciano, *Diary,* Entry for January 18, 1941.
12. *Ibid.,* Entry for January 24, 1941.
13. *Ibid.,* Entry for January 25, 1941.
14. For contemporary German criticism of Mussolini's judgement on this issue, *see G. F. P.,* XI, 1225–27.
15. Ciano, *op. cit.,* Entry for June 10, 1941.
16. *Ibid.,* Entry for May 13, 1941.
17. Ciano, *Europa verso la catastrofe,* pp. 660–61.
18. Ciano, *Diary,* Entry for June 6, 1941.
19. Hitler and B. Mussolini, *op. cit.,* pp. 104–8.
20. Ciano, *op. cit.,* Entry for June 30, 1941.
21. Deakin, *op. cit.,* pp. 15–16.
22. Simoni, *op. cit.,* p. 248.
23. Ciano, *op. cit.,* Entry for June 26, 1941.
24. Anfuso, *op. cit.,* p. 205.
25. Ciano, *Europa verso la catastrofe,* p. 671.
26. Alfieri, *op. cit.,* p. 157.
27. Anfuso, *op. cit.,* pp. 237–40.
28. Rintelen, *op. cit.,* p. 149.
29. Ciano, *op. cit.,* p. 685.
30. Ciano, *Diary,* Entries for September 24, 25, and 26, 1941.
31. Ciano, *Europa verso la catastrofe,* pp. 679–86; and Ciano, *Diary,* Entry for October 25, 1941.
32. Ciano, *Diary,* Entry for November 24, 1941.
33. Ciano, *Europa verso la catastrofe,* p. 693.
34. *Ibid.,* pp. 694–97.
35. Ciano, *Diary,* Entry for December 25, 1941.
36. *Ibid.*
37. *Ibid.,* Entry for December 19, 1941.
38. Hitler and B. Mussolini, *op. cit.,* Letter of December 29, 1941, pp. 116–18.
39. Ciano, *op. cit.,* Entry for December 22, 1941.
40. *Ibid.,* Entries for December 27, 1941, and January 2, 1942; and Mussolini's statement to the Council of Ministers: "The war will last long—three to four years." (Deakin, *op. cit.,* p. 16.)

CHAPTER NINETEEN

1. Ciano, *op. cit.,* Entry for January 6, 1942.
2. *Ibid.,* Entry for February 22, 1942.
3. *Ibid.,* Entry for April 2, 1942.
4. *Ibid.,* Entries for February 8 and 20, 1942.
5. Suñer, *op. cit.,* p. 273.
6. Felix Kersten, *The Kersten Memoirs, 1940–1945* (London, 1956), p. 158.
7. Deakin, *op. cit.,* p. 35.
8. Ciano, *op. cit.,* Entries for February 2 and 4, 1942.
9. Ciano, *Diplomatic Papers,* pp. 481–84; and Hitler and B. Mussolini, *op. cit.,* pp. 118–22.
10. Ciano, *Diary,* Entry for April 29, 1942.
11. Deakin, *op. cit.,* p. 19.
12. B. Mussolini, *Memoirs: 1942–1943* (London, 1949), p. 219.
13. Ciano, *Diary,* Entries for July 2 and 3, 1942.

14. G. Bottai, *Vent'anni e un giorno* (Milan, 1949), pp. 227, 228.
15. Ciano, *op. cit.*, Entry for July 24, 1942.
16. B. Mussolini, *Memoirs,* p. 219.
17. Ciano, *op. cit.*, Entry for September 27, 1942.
18. Bottai, *op. cit.*, p. 231.
19. Ciano, *op. cit.*, Entry for November 6, 1942.
20. B. Mussolini, *Memoirs,* p. 3.
21. Schmidt, *Statise auf der Diplomatischen Buhne*, p. 564.
22. Ciano, *op. cit.*, Entry for November 12, 1942.
23. *Rommel Papers, op. cit.*, p. 369.
24. Deakin, *op. cit.*, pp. 84, 85.
25. Bottai, *op. cit.*, p. 239.
26. Ciano, *op. cit.*, Entries for December 18 and 19, 1942.
27. Deakin, *op. cit.*, pp. 122, 123.
28. Pini and Susmel, *op. cit.*, IV, 205.
29. Caviglia, *op. cit.*, pp. 383–85.
30. Ciano, *op. cit.*, Entry for January 15, 1943.
31. Deakin, *op. cit.*, pp. 148–49.
32. Bottai, *op. cit.*, p. 253.
33. Deakin, *op. cit.*, p. 151.
34. *Ibid.*, p. 198.
35. *Ibid.*, p. 207.
36. *Ibid.*, pp. 203–5.
37. *Ibid.*, pp. 216, 217, 249.
38. *Ibid.*, p. 217.
39. Simoni, *op. cit.*, Entry for April 11, 1943.
40. Schmidt, *op. cit.*, p. 551.
41. *Ibid.*, Entry for May 6, 1943.
42. Deakin, *op. cit.*, pp. 279–80.
43. *Ibid.*, pp. 281, 282.
44. Anfuso, *op. cit.*, p. 279.
45. Deakin, *op. cit.*, p. 323.
46. *Ibid.*, pp. 283–84.
47. *Ibid.*, p. 286.
48. *Ibid.*, pp. 353–55; and Wiskemann, *op. cit.*, p. 298.
49. Deakin, *op. cit.*, p. 356.
50. R. Mussolini, *op. cit.*, p. 120.
51. Rintelen, *op. cit.*, p. 196.
52. Deakin, *op. cit.*, pp. 337–40.
53. *Ibid.*, p. 341.
54. Rintelen, *op. cit.*, p. 206.
55. Deakin, *op. cit.*, p. 373.
56. *Ibid.*, p. 374.
57. *Ibid.*, p. 373.
58. *Ibid.*, p. 375.
59. *Ibid.*, pp. 376, 377.
60. Tamaro, *Due ami di storia, 1943–45* (Rome, 1950), I, 186–87.
61. Bottai, *op. cit.*, pp. 281 ff.
62. Deakin, *op. cit.*, p. 392.
63. B. Mussolini, *Memoirs,* p. 49.
64. Deakin, *op. cit.*, p. 382.
65. Alfieri, *op. cit.*, p. 236.
66. *Ibid.*, pp. 237–38.
67. Rintelen, *op. cit.*, p. 212.
68. Alfieri, *op. cit.*, pp. 240, 241.
69. Schmidt, *op. cit.*, p. 567.
70. Alfieri, *op. cit.*, p. 245.
71. Deakin, *op. cit.*, p. 407.
72. Alfieri, *op. cit.*, p. 246.
73. Deakin, *op. cit.*, p. 408.
74. B. Mussolini, *op. cit.*, p. 221.
75. Deakin, *op. cit.*, p. 408.
76. Rintelen, *op. cit.*, p. 214.
77. Deakin, *op. cit.*, p. 409.
78. *Ibid.*, p. 409.
79. Rintelen, *op. cit.*, p. 215.
80. Deakin, *op. cit.*, p. 410.
81. Alfieri, *op. cit.*, p. 248.
82. Deakin, *op. cit.*, pp. 410, 411.

CHAPTER TWENTY

1. Rintelen, *op. cit.*, p. 215.
2. Deakin, *op. cit.*, p. 420.
3. *Ibid.*, pp. 421–423.
4. J. Goebbels, *Diaries* (London, 1948), Entry for July 25, 1943.
5. Anfuso, *op. cit.*, p. 282.
6. Deakin, *op. cit.*, pp. 423, 424.
7. B. Mussolini, *op. cit.*, p. 52.
8. Deakin, *op. cit.*, p. 428.
9. Interview with Grandi in *Milano Sera,* January 16, 1946.
10. B. Mussolini, *op. cit.*, p. 53.
11. Deakin, *op. cit.*, p. 426.
12. *Ibid.*, p. 430.
13. Interviews with Grandi in *Corriere della Sera,* February 9, 1955, and *Milano Sera,* January 16, 1946.

14. B. Mussolini, *op. cit.*, p. 53.
15. Bottai, *op. cit.*, pp. 290, 291.
16. Albert Kesselring, *Soldat bis zum letzten Tag* (Bonn, 1953), p. 229.
17. B. Mussolini, *op. cit.*, p. 54.
18. Deakin, *op. cit.*, pp. 435–37.
19. *Ibid.*, p. 431.
20. B. Mussolini, *op. cit.*, p. 55.
21. Grandi, interview in *Milano Sera*, January 16, 1946.
22. Bottai, *op. cit.*, p. 302.
23. B. Mussolini, *op. cit.*, pp. 55–61.
24. *Ibid.*, p. 61.
25. Grandi, interview in *Milano Sera*, January 17, 1946.
26. Deakin, *op. cit.*, p. 443.
27. Deakin, *op. cit.*, p. 450.
28. B. Mussolini, *op. cit.*, p. 63.
29. Alfieri, *op. cit.*, p. 340.
30. Bottai, *op. cit.*, pp. 316, 317.
31. Grandi, interview in *Milano Sera*, January 17, 1946.
32. The texts of the three motions, Grandi's, Scorza's, and Farinacci's, are printed in Deakin, *op. cit.*, pp. 455, 456.
33. B. Mussolini, *op. cit.*, p. 64.
34. Pini and Susmel, *op. cit.*, IV, 253, 254.
35. *Ibid.*, IV, 254.
36. Conversation with Admiral Maugeri. B. Mussolini, *op. cit.*, p. 222.
37. R. Mussolini, *op. cit.*, pp. 126, 127.
38. Deakin, *op. cit.*, p. 467.
39. B. Mussolini, *op. cit.*, p. 78.
40. Deakin, *op. cit.*, p. 459.
41. B. Mussolini, *op. cit.*, p. 79.
42. *Ibid.*
43. R. Mussolini, *op. cit.*, p. 130.
44. Deakin, *op. cit.*, p. 460.
45. A record of this conversation is printed in Tamaro, *op. cit.*, I, 72.
46. Deakin, p. 465.
47. *Ibid.*
48. R. Mussolini, *op. cit.*, p. 130.
49. B. Mussolini, *op. cit.*, p. 80.
50. Deakin, *op. cit.*, p. 469.
51. B. Mussolini, *op. cit.*, p. 81.
52. Deakin, *op. cit.*, p. 470.
53. *Ibid.*
54. B. Mussolini, *op. cit.*, p. 82.
55. Deakin, *op. cit.*, p. 538. The account written by the doctor is printed in Tamaro, *op. cit.*, I, 72.
56. B. Mussolini, *op. cit.*, p. 83.

CHAPTER TWENTY-ONE

1. Deakin, *op. cit.*, p. 474.
2. The texts are printed in Tamaro, *op. cit.*, I, 46, 47.
3. Deakin, *op. cit.*, p. 473.
4. B. Mussolini, *op. cit.*, pp. 83–85.
5. *Ibid.*, pp. 217, 218, note.
6. Maugeri's account in *ibid.*, pp. 218, 219.
7. Maugeri's account in B. Mussolini, *op. cit.*, pp. 220, 221.
8. B. Mussolini, *op. cit.*, p. 88.
9. E. Mussolini, *op. cit.*, p. 202.
10. B. Mussolini, *op. cit.*, pp. 228, 229.
11. E. Mussolini, *op. cit.*, pp. 198, 202. There is a photostat of these two letters.
12. Deakin, *op. cit.*, pp. 541, 542.
13. Maugeri's account in B. Mussolini, *op. cit.*, p. 233.
14. B. Mussolini, *op. cit.*, p. 131.
15. Maugeri's account in *ibid.*, pp. 231–43.
16. B. Mussolini, *op. cit.*, pp. 92, 93.
17. Her account is in *ibid.*, pp. 244–53.
18. B. Mussolini, *op. cit.*, p. 251.
19. R. Mussolini, *op. cit.*, p. 139.
20. Goebbels, *op. cit.*, Entry for September 15, 1943.
21. Deakin, *op. cit.*, pp. 554, 555.
22. Goebbels, *op. cit.*, Entry for September 22, 1943.
23. Anfuso, *op. cit.*, p. 326.
24. *Ibid.*, p. 328.
25. This information was subsequently given to the prefect Giocchino Nicoletti, who published an account of his conversation with Mussolini in the *Cor-*

riere D'Informazione, February 14/15, 1948.

26. Goebbels, *op. cit.,* Entry for September 17, 1943.
27. The texts are printed in Tamaro, *op. cit.,* I, 586, 587.
28. Goebbels, *op. cit.,* Entry for September 23, 1943.
29. Anfuso, *op. cit.,* p. 318.
30. Rudolf Rahn, *Ruheloses Leben* (Dusseldorf, 1949), p. 235.
31. Anfuso, *op. cit.,* p. 323.
32. Deakin, *op. cit.,* p. 563. *See also* Anfuso, *op. cit.,* p. 335.
33. Pini and Susmel, *op. cit.,* IV, 334, 335.
34. Text in Tamaro, *op. cit.,* I, 590–93.
35. R. Mussolini, *op. cit.,* p. 145.
36. Tamaro, *op. cit.,* I, 590–93.
37. Goebbels, *op. cit.,* Entry for September 19, 1943.
38. Deakin, *op. cit.,* p. 567.
39. Professor Edmondo Cione, quoted in Mino Caudana and Arturo Assante, "Dal regno del sud al vento del nord," *Il Tempo,* February 25, 1961.
40. Deakin, *op. cit.,* p. 568.

CHAPTER TWENTY-TWO

1. Deakin, *op. cit.,* p. 571.
2. Text in Tamaro, *op. cit.,* II, 47–49.
3. Deakin, *op. cit.,* p. 576. A longer, but substantially the same, version of this letter is printed in Tamaro, *op. cit.,* II, 205–8.
4. Deakin, *op. cit.,* p. 606.
5. Goebbels, *op. cit.,* Entry for September 23, 1943.
6. Pini and Susmel, *op. cit.,* IV, 342.
7. *Ibid.,* IV, 336.
8. *Ibid.,* IV, 349.
9. Deakin, *op. cit.,* p. 607.
10. Pini and Susmel, *op. cit.,* IV, 345.
11. Deakin, *op. cit.,* p. 617.
12. Deakin, *op. cit.,* pp. 618–20.
13. Goebbels, *op. cit.,* Entry for November 18, 1943.
14. Deakin, *op. cit.,* p. 624.
15. *Ibid.,* p. 627.
16. Text in Tamaro, *op. cit.,* II, 249–53.
17. Deakin, *op. cit.,* p. 628.
18. Tamaro, *op. cit.,* II, 221.
19. Carlo Silvestri, *Contro la vendetta, op. cit.,* p. 111.
20. Deakin, *op. cit.,* p. 631.
21. *Ibid.,* p. 632.
22. Tamaro, *op. cit.,* II, 214, 215.
23. *Ibid.,* II, 215, 216.
24. Pini and Susmel, *op. cit.,* IV, 355.
25. Tamaro, *op. cit.,* II, 350.
26. Anfuso, *op. cit.,* p. 410.
27. Deakin, *op. cit.,* pp. 633, 634.
28. *Ibid.,* p. 636.
29. Tamora, *op. cit.,* II, 350.
30. Deakin, *op. cit.,* p. 635.
31. Pini and Susmel, *op. cit.,* IV, 383.
32. Deakin, *op. cit.,* p. 637.
33. Text in Tamaro, *op. cit.,* II, 363, 364.
34. This account is based on the statement made by General Harster to Duilio Susmel (*Vita sbagliata di Galeazzo Ciano* (Rome, 1963), pp. 328–37).
35. Deakin, *op. cit.,* p. 638.
36. Tamaro, *op. cit.,* II, 353.
37. Text in Deakin, *op. cit.,* pp. 650–53.
38. *Ibid.,* p. 639.
39. Pini and Susmel, *op. cit.,* IV, 387.
40. Tamaro, *op. cit.,* II, 354; Pini and Susmel, *op. cit.,* IV, 387.
41. Text in Tamaro, *Ibid.,* II, 364–69.
42. Texts in Deakin, *op. cit.,* pp. 642, 643.
43. *Ibid.,* p. 643.
44. *Ibid.,* p. 641.
45. Text in *ibid.,* pp. 644, 645.
46. Record of Mussolini's conversation with Mazzolini on January 12. Text in Tamaro, *op. cit.,* II, 369–71.
47. Pini and Susmel, *op. cit.,* IV, 388.
48. Tamaro, *op. cit.,* II, 369–71.

49. Deakin, *op. cit.*, p. 646.
50. Text in *Ibid.*, pp. 647, 648.
51. Tamaro, *op. cit.*, II, 371.
52. Otto Skorzeny, *Secret Missions* (London, 1957), p. 108.
53. Pini and Susmel, *op. cit.*, IV, 413.
54. *Ibid.*, IV, 427.
55. *Ibid.*, IV, 407.
56. *Ibid.*, IV, 427.

CHAPTER TWENTY-THREE

1. Deakin, *op. cit.*, p. 664.
2. Tamaro, *op. cit.*, II, 425.
3. Text in *Ibid.*, II, 419.
4. *Ibid.*, II, 442–44.
5. Deakin, *op. cit.*, pp. 668–70.
6. *Ibid.*, pp. 672, 673.
7. *Ibid.*, p. 673.
8. *Ibid.*, p. 677.
9. *Ibid.*, p. 681.
10. *Ibid.*, p. 682.
11. Anfuso, *op. cit.*, p. 435. A record of the meeting is printed in Tamaro, *op. cit.*, III, 58–67.
12. The account of the Klessheim conference is taken from Deakin, *op. cit.*, pp. 678–89.
13. Pini and Susmel, *op. cit.*, IV, 417.
14. Tamaro, *op. cit.*, III, 30.
15. Pini and Susmel, *op. cit.*, IV, 417.
16. Deakin, *op. cit.*, p. 693.
17. Charles Delzell, *Mussolini's Enemies: The Italian Anti-Fascist Resistance* (Princeton, 1961), p. 401.
18. Deakin, *op. cit.*, pp. 696, 697.
19. *Ibid.*, pp. 697–700.
20. John Wheeler-Bennett, *The Nemesis of Power* (London, 1953), p. 644.
21. Schmidt, *op. cit.*, p. 582.
22. Quoted in *Corriere D'Informazione,* March 9/10, 1946.
23. Wheeler-Bennett, *op. cit.*, pp. 645, 646.
24. Deakin, *op. cit.*, pp. 709–13.
25. Tamaro, *op. cit.*, III, 270.
26. Deakin, *op. cit.*, p. 728.
27. *Ibid.*, pp. 735, 736.
28. Pini and Susmel, *op. cit.*, IV, 454.
29. *Ibid.*, IV, 455.
30. *Ibid.*, IV, 473.
31. Caudana and Assenti, *op. cit.*, *Il Tempo,* March 31, 1961.
32. Pini and Susmel, *op. cit.*, IV, 475, 476.
33. Text in Deakin, *op. cit.*, pp. 776-78.
34. Anfuso, *op. cit.*, p. 2.
35. Informant.
36. An account of these last conversations is in Pini and Susmel, *op. cit.*, IV, 481, 498, 499; and E. Mussolini, *op. cit.*, pp. 225–27.

CHAPTER TWENTY-FOUR

1. Text in Pini and Susmel, *op. cit.*, IV, 506–8.
2. Deakin, *op. cit.*, p. 797.
3. *Ibid.*, p. 801.
4. Tamaro, *op. cit.*, III, 514.
5. Pini and Susmel, *op. cit.*, IV, 486.
6. R. Mussolini, *op. cit.*, p. 176. The date on the letter is incorrect. It was written on the night of April 25.
7. *Corriere della Sera,* March 9, 1947.

Biographical and Explanatory Notes

ALFIERI, Dino. B. 1886. Minister of Press and Propaganda 1936–39; Ambassador to the Holy See 1939–40; Ambassador to Germany 1940–43. He was vain, trivial, and inefficient, but he was not so stupid as to support Germany's enslavement of Italy. He voted against Mussolini in the Grand Council and was condemned to death in his absence at Verona. He died after the war.

AMBROSIO, General Vittorio. B. 1879. Chief of Army Staff 1942–43; in 1943 replaced Cavallero as Chief of General Staff of Armed Forces. Was a moving spirit in the effort of the army to get rid of Mussolini. For a short time he was a member of Badoglio's Military Provisional Cabinet. Subsequently was appointed by Badoglio to be Inspector-General of Italian Army.

AOSTA, Amedeo, Duke of. B. 1898, d. 1942. Son of a cousin of King Victor Emmanuel III, who always regarded him with a certain jealousy and suspicion. He was Viceroy of Abyssinia 1937–41; surrendered to the British at Amba Alagi on the May 19, 1941, and died the following year in captivity.

BADOGLIO, Pietro, Marshal of Italy, Duke of Addis Ababa. B. 1871. Chief of Army Staff 1919–21; Ambassador to Brazil 1924–25; Chief of General Staff of Armed Forces from 1925; Governor of Libya 1928–33; assumed Command of Italian forces in Abyssinia in 1935; Viceroy of Abyssinia 1936, when he became Duke of Addis Ababa and received the Collar of the Annunziata. Later that year he resumed his post of Chief of the General Staff. He resigned in 1940 because of the fiasco of the Greek War. Remained unemployed until the King appointed him Prime Minister after the fall of Mussolini. In 1944 he resigned after the liberation of Rome, and he died not long afterwards.

BALBO, Air-Marshal Italo. B. 1896, d. 1940. One of the picturesque and combative figures of the Fascist movement in its early days. Member of the Quadrumvirate of the March on Rome. Minister for Air 1929–33. He was always an object of jealousy and suspicion on the part of Mussolini, who gladly banished him to be Governor-General in Libya 1933–40. There he still further ill-disposed the Duce by openly criticizing the alliance with Germany. In June, 1940, he was killed when his aircraft was accidently shot down over Tobruk by the Italians.

BIANCHI, Michele. B. 1882, d. 1930. In the early days was one of Mussolini's closest personal associates. Member of the Quadrumvirate of the March on Rome, when he used his influence to oppose the efforts of De Vecchi and Grandi to compromise. He was the first Secretary of the Fascist Party. Undersecretary of the Interior 1928–29; Minister of Public Works 1929–30. His premature death removed a man who had as much influence with the Duce as anyone outside the family circle.

BONOMI, Ivanoe. B. 1873. Reformist Socialist. Prime Minister 1921–22. Received the Collar of the Annunziata. After 1922 retired into private life. In 1944 elected President of the Rome Committee of National Liberation. After the fall of Rome succeeded Badoglio as Prime Minister 1944–45. Died soon after the war.

BOTTAI, Giusseppe. B. 1895. Early Fascist. Under-Secretary in Ministry of Corporations 1926–29; Minister of Corporations 1929–35; Governor of Rome 1935–36; Minister of Education 1936–43. An articulate critic of Mussolini during the war. Sentenced to death in his absence at Verona. Went into hiding, but returned to Italy in 1948 and died not long afterwards. His memoirs are a valuable source.

CAVALLERO, Count Ugo. Marshal of Italy. B. 1880, d. 1943. Commander-in-Chief in East Africa 1937. Replaced Badoglio as Chief of General Staff 1940–43. Considered excessively subservient to the Germans. In 1943 he committed suicide, almost certainly because he knew that he could no longer conceal his involvement in the military plot against Mussolini.

CIANO, Countess Edda. B. 1910. Daughter of Mussolini. Married Ciano 1930. Fled to Switzerland with Ciano's diaries in 1944. Expelled from Switzerland in 1945, interned in Lipari, and subsequently sentenced to two further years' internment. Amnestied in 1946. Now lives in Italy.

CIANO, Count Galeazzo. B. 1903, d. 1944. Son of Count Constanzo Ciano, one of Mussolini's earliest followers. Entered Diplomatic Service 1925. Married Edda Mussolini 1930. Minister for Press and Propaganda 1935–36; Minister of Foreign Affairs 1936–43; Ambassador to Holy

See 1943. Received Collar of the Annunziata. Voted against Mussolini. Escaped to Germany. Was returned to Italy, arrested, and tried at Verona. Executed on January 11, 1944.

CORPORATIONS, THE CORPORATIVE STATE. The idea of a state and legislature based on guilds and professional associations was adopted by Mussolini, but it was not an original Italian conception, having been advocated many years previously by Walther Rathenau among others. It was never fully applied in Italy, although the Legislature became Corporative rather than elected.

The Corporative theory seems to have some appeal in the Soviet Union. After the war whenever German unity was discussed, the Soviet delegates invariably insisted that in any future legislature of a united Germany representation must be found for what they described as the "mass organizations."

DE BONO, Emilio, Marshal of Italy. B. 1866, d. 1944. A professional soldier who supported Fascism in its early days. Member of the Quadrumvirate of the March on Rome. Senator 1923. Chief of Police 1922–23, but resigned after Matteotti's murder. Minister of Colonies 1929–35; Commander-in-Chief in Abyssinia at outbreak of war, but soon dismissed and replaced by Badoglio. Received Collar of the Annunziata. Condemned to death at Verona and executed on January 11, 1944.

DE VECCHI, Cesare Maria. B. 1884. Member of the Quadrumvirate of March on Rome. Royalist in sentiment, he was out of sympathy with the revolutionary aspirations of the early Fascists. As a politician and administrator he was a failure. Senator 1925; Ambassador to the Holy See 1929–35; Minister of Education 1935–36; Governor of the Dodecanese 1936–40. Sentenced to death in his absence at Verona. Escaped, and died after the war in Italy.

ELENA, Queen of Italy. B. 1873. Princess Petrovic Niegos of Montenegro. Married Victor Emmanuel III in 1896. In appearance a rugged daughter of the mountains, she was a woman of character who exercised a strong influence on her husband. After his abdication in 1946 she left Italy with him.

FACTA, Luigi. B. 1861, d. 1930. Prime Minister from February to October, 1922. It was his weakness and incapacity which opened the door to Mussolini. After the advent of Fascism to power Mussolini magnanimously made him a Senator, a post which he held until his death.

FARINACCI, Roberto. B. 1892, d. 1945. An early and extremist member of the Fascist Party. Mussolini, who disliked and despised him, appointed him Secretary of the Fascist Party 1925–26 and used him to destroy the power of the party bosses. In 1926 he defended Matteotti's murderers. He was violently anti-Semite, anti-Vatican, and pro-German to a point which often annoyed the Duce. After the fall of Mussolini the German Ambassador flew him to Germany, where he became a leader of the extremist Fascist Republicans. Mussolini refused to employ him under the Salò Republic. Nevertheless in April, 1945, partisans arrested him in Northern Italy and executed him after summary trial.

FASCISM, THE FASCIST PARTY. It is commonly thought that the Fascists derived their name from the bundles of rods carried by the Roman lictors. In fact it had for some time been the custom in Sicily anl elsewhere to apply the term *fasci* to groups. Consequently it was no innovation when during the First World War Mussolini founded his *Fasci di Combattimento* in Milan. For some time the Fascists were a movement rather than a political party, and most of the early Fascists, who despised politics, opposed any change. But Mussolini, who saw that he had no political future unless backed by a party, was able in 1922 to carry his followers with him in founding the Fascist Party. It was only after he had seized power and it became the thing to revive the glories of the Roman Empire, that the connection between the *fasci* and the lictors was established and that the lictor's bundle became the official emblem of the Party.

GIOLITTI, Giovanni. B. 1842, d. 1928. The Grand Old Man of Italian politics. Became Prime Minister for the first time in 1892. Thereafter he was for thirty years in and out of successive Liberal administrations, many of which he led. He was Prime Minister for the last time in 1920–21. When Mussolini came to power in 1922 Giolitti was at first disposed to give him qualified support. But after the murder of Matteotti he passed over to the opposition. His last speech in Parliament in March, 1928, was an attack on Mussolini's law creating a Corporative Legislature. Four months later he died.

GIURIATI, Giovanni. B. 1876. Lawyer. With D'Annunzio at Fiume. Secretary of Fascist Party 1930–31. Collar of the Annunziata 1932. Senator 1934. He was a member of the extremist wing of the party. After the war was imprisoned in Italy, but was subsequently released. He now lives in Rome.

GRANDI, Dino. B. 1895. One of the earliest Fascists, who played a prominent part in the civil disorders which wracked the North of Italy in 1921 and 1922. He opposed the so-called truce with the Socialists. Nevertheless in October, 1922, he favored a political compromise, an attitude which again threw him into conflict with Mussolini. Subsequently his ability earned him a succession of high posts under the Fascist Government: Undersecretary of the Interior 1924–25 and of Foreign Affairs 1926–29; Minister of Foreign Affairs 1929–32; Ambassador in London 1932–39; President of Chamber 1940–43; Minister of Justice 1940–43. Collar of the Annunziata 1943. Leader of the political revolt against Mussolini. Sentenced to death in his absence at Verona. Fled to Lisbon. After many years of exile in Portugal and Brazil returned to Italy. Now lives at Modena.

GRAZIANI, Rodolfo, Marshal of Italy. B. 1882. Viceroy of Abyssinia 1936–37; Governor of Libya 1940–41; dismissed after his defeat by Wavell and remained unemployed. In 1943 he was with difficulty persuaded to accept the post of Minister of War in the Salò Government. Escaping capture by the partisans, he surrendered to the Allies on April 29, 1945. He was imprisoned by the Italians but was subsequently released. He died shortly afterwards.

MUTI, Ettore. B. 1902, d. 1943. Appointed Secretary of the Fascist Party 1939–40, largely at Ciano's instance. But he proved a dismal failure. After Mussolini's fall he was arrested and shot by the Badoglio police, allegedly while attempting to escape. He was subsequently elevated by the Republican Government to the status of a national martyr.

NENNI, Pietro. B. 1891. Republican extremist. Imprisoned in 1911 with Mussolini. An interventionist in the First World War, he became a Socialist in 1921. Went into exile in 1926. Was arrested in France in 1943 by the Gestapo, was sent to Italy and imprisoned at Ponza. Since the Liberation he has led the Italian Socialist Party.

ORLANDO, Vittorio Emanuele. B. 1860. One of the leading Liberal politicians who appeared in successive administrations in the pre-Fascist era. Became Prime Minister in 1917 after the Caporetto disaster and led the Italian Delegation at Versailles. As a protest against fascism resigned his seat in the Chamber in 1925, but he supported the Abyssinian venture. After the Liberation of Rome became President of the Chamber. He died five years later.

PALAZZO CHIGI. An old Roman palace begun in 1562 and centrally situated at the corner of the Corso and the Piazza Colonna. Mussolini soon transferred his Foreign Office from the Consulta Palace—its traditional seat—to the Chigi. Thereafter the Italian Foreign Office was termed the Palazzo Chigi, just as the Foreign Offices in Paris, Berlin, and Vienna had been known by their locations: the Quai D'Orsay, the Wilhelmstrasse, and the Ballplatz.

The Italian Foreign Office has now moved to commodious, modern, stone and marble premises on the northern fringe of Rome. Yet most of those who have worked in both buildings seem to hanker after the mixture of dusty shabbiness and grandeur in the Chigi.

PALAZZO DI VENEZIA. Begun about 1455 by Pope Paul II. In 1560 it was given by Pius IV to the Republic of Venice, with which it came in 1797 into the possession of Austria. From then it was the residence of the Austrian Ambassador to the Vatican. It ceased to be Austrian property after the First World War, and shortly after his accession to power Mussolini transferred the Prime Minister's office to the Palazzo Venezia. It was here that meetings of the Grand Council and Cabinet were held. Thus the Palazzo Venezia came to be spoken of as the seat of government in much the same way as the term "White House" is used in Washington.

QUADRUMVIR. For tactical reasons Mussolini decided to entrust the direction of the March on Rome to four *Quadrumviri:* Balbo, Bianchi, De Bono, and De Vecchi. They signed the proclamation and thus achieved a publicity and prestige which would otherwise not have been theirs. Nevertheless none of them received high office in Mussolini's first government and none of them, with the possible exception of Balbo, gained any particular distinction in Italian public life.

THE QUIRINAL. One of the Hills of Rome, which gave its name to the former Papal Palace built there in 1574 by Gregory XIII and added to by subsequent Popes. In 1870 the Quirinal Palace became the town residence of the Kings of Italy, and since then the term "the Quirinal" was used to describe the Italian monarchy and civil government in Rome as against the Vatican. Thus the two diplomatic corps were said to be accredited respectively to the Quirinal and to the Vatican or Holy See.

ROSSI, Cesare. B. 1887. One of Mussolini's early intimates. As head of the Fascist Press Bureau, he became involved in Matteotti's murder. He was arrested and in retaliation published a memorandum implicating Mussolini. He subsequently escaped to France, where he conducted anti-Fascist propaganda. In 1928 he was lured over the frontier into Italy and sentenced to 30 years by the Special Tribunal. The liberation of Italy did not bring him freedom, for in 1945 he was sentenced to four years and two months for Fascist crimes by an Italian Court. He was released in 1947 after being acquitted, for lack of evidence, of the murder of Matteotti. He is now living in Rome.

SCORZA, Carlo. B. 1897. A prominent member of the early Fascist gangs. Appointed Secretary of the Party in April, 1943, with the special task of dealing with defeatism. Played an equivocal role before and during the meeting of the Grand Council, and after Mussolini's fall. He was subsequently tried and acquitted by a neo-Fascist Court. Arrested in 1945 by the Italian authorities, he escaped. In 1949 he was amnestied and he returned to Italy.

SQUADRISTI. In the early militant days the Fascists were organized in detachments or squads termed *squadre*. The members of these detachments were *squadristi*. Later the term was applied to men who had been early militants in much the same way as early Nazis were called "*Alte Kämpfer*" (Old Fighters).

STARACE, Achille. B. 1889, d. 1945. He held the post of Secretary of the Party from 1931–39, a period longer than any other incumbent. A somewhat primitive character, he was less interested in party policy than in uniforms, decorations, and the organization of mass rallies. After 1939, when his dismissal was universally acclaimed, he remained loyal to Mussolini, though he did not receive office in the Salò Government. He was massacred by partisans in Milan on the day following Mussolini's death.

TOGLIATTI, Palmiro. B. 1893. One of the founders of Italian Communism. Member of the Comintern in Moscow. Returned to Italy in 1944. Minister without Portfolio in Badoglio government March–June, 1944; Vice-Premier in Bonomi Government 1944–45; Minister of Justice 1945–47. Claimed responsibility for killing of Mussolini. Still leads Italian Communist Party.

UMBERTO, Prince of Piedmont. B. 1904. In May, 1946, after the abdication of King Victor Emmanuel he became King Umberto II of Italy. A month later a national plebiscite decided by a narrow majority in favor of a Republic, and he left Italy. He now lives in Portugal.

VICTOR EMMANUEL III, King of Italy. B. 1869, d. 1947. Ascended the throne in 1900. A man of limited intellectual capacity, but possessed of a certain native shrewdness. Became increasingly ineffective as he grew older. In 1944 he named the Crown Prince, Lieutenant of the Realm and transferred to him the powers of the Crown. In 1945 he abdicated and sailed for Egypt. He died the following year.

Bibliography

There is an enormous collection of works on every aspect of fascism. They cover the theory and practice of fascism; specific events in the pre-Fascist and Fascist eras such as the Fiume affair, the March on Rome, the murder of Matteotti, the treaties with the Holy See, the Abyssinian War, the Spanish Civil War; the Italian campaigns in the Great War, the fall of Mussolini and his rescue, the Verona trial, the proceedings of the Salò Republic, and Mussolini's end. There are also books on Fascist foreign policy, on Italian relations with Germany, on Mussolini's life at various periods, and an array of memoirs by civilian and military actors on the Italian stage. Few of these works claim to be impartial, since they are written for the most part by avowed supporters or opponents of the system.

In addition there has been since the war a flood of contributions to Italian dailies and periodicals, designed to meet the apparently insatiable demand for information about Mussolini. It would have been difficult to trace all these, and I have not attempted to do so, for most of them are unreliable and of fugitive interest. I have, however, used some of them by reference to the work of other writers; and I have only listed those significant items which seem to me to have been hitherto overlooked or which have appeared too recently to figure in previous works.

The third and most important source is constituted by the Italian, British, and German documents which have been published. These are supplemented by the invaluable German and Italian "collections," of which substantial extracts are published for the first time in Deakin's *The Brutal Friendship*. An interesting point about the documents is that the records of the various transactions, whether they be Anglo-Italian or Italo-German, are in substantial agreement. This is attributable to the fact that they were for the most part written not by the principals, but by officials trained to make accurate reports. There are of course differences of emphasis, since representatives of one country may attach greater importance to a particular aspect of a problem than the other party to the negotiation. Nevertheless there is a striking degree of uniformity. A case in point is Anthony Eden's conversations with Mussolini on Abyssinia, where the British and Italian records are in harmony.

Ribbentrop constituted an unhappy exception. It was his practice to tinker with Schmidt's accurate records in order to present himself in a more favorable light. I had occasion in Marburg in 1945 to examine the originals of the records of all Ribbentrop's conversations with foreign politicians. In a large number of cases there were deletions or marginal embellishments which were patently dishonest.

The only book which purports to cover in detail the whole of Mussolini's life is *Mussolini l'uomo e l'opera* by Giorgio Pini and Duilio Susmel. It is written somewhat in the form of a war diary and catalogues in chronological order Mussolini's movements, speeches, interviews, and conversations. It is not impartial, and it is inaccurate in places. Nevertheless, with its notes and extensive bibliography it is useful, particularly for Mussolini's early days and for the end, when Pini was at Mussolini's side as Undersecretary in the Ministry of the Interior.

Another general work is *Storia d'Italia nel periodo fascista* by Salvatore and Mira, an excellent account of the political evolution of Italy under Mussolini. It is fully documented, impartial, and accurate. Tamaro's six volumes, with their wealth of illustrations, are particularly valuable for the reproduction of a large number of documents.

For Mussolini's early days I have had to rely largely on the dubious *My Autobiography,* Margherita Sarfatti's *Life of Mussolini,* Angelica Balabanoff's two books, Marcel Bezancon's *Mussolini in der Schweiz,* Ivon di Begnac's *Vita di Mussolini,* and *Anni giovanili di Mussolini* by Sante Bedeschi and Rino Alessi. This last book contains some interesting letters. Some of Mussolini's contemporaries have also published reminiscences in the press.

Balbo's *Diario 1922,* though necessarily suspect, gives a good picture of Fascist excesses in northern Italy. For the March on

Rome a useful supplement to Salvatorelli and Mira is *La marcia su Roma veduta dal Viminale* by Efrem Ferraris.

The murder of Matteotti and the subsequent trials are competently dealt with in Schiari's *La Vita e l'opera di Giacomo Matteotti* and Mauro del Giudice's *Cronistoria del processo Matteotti.* Neither Dumini nor Rosso is reliable.

On the Conciliation and relations with the Vatican the standard work is Binchy's *Church and State in Fascist Italy.* The detailed negotiations are related in much detail from the Vatican side in Francisco Pacelli's diary and from the Quirinal side in Biggini's book, based on Mussolini's personal files. I am indebted for the loan of this rare work to Mr. F. W. Deakin. Biggini, it will be remembered, subsequently became a member of the Salò government. Arturo Jemolo's book *Chiesa e stato in Italia negli ultimi cento anni* is a useful general historical work.

Sir Ronald Graham was ambassador in Rome from 1921–1934, and I have drawn on information which he gave me while I was serving under him.

For the period 1937–1943 I have made much use of Ciano's *Diary.* It is the product of a man as vain and mercurial as Mussolini himself. It is full of contradictions and represents Mussolini at times as better and at times as worse than he was. It was almost certainly touched up, and it cannot be accepted as accurate in every particular. But it is of value as reflecting Mussolini's changing moods and describing the impact on him of events. There is no reason to question the picture which Ciano presents.

On the birth of the Axis the leading authority is Mario Toscano. I am also indebted to D. C. Watt for his contributions. On the general question of Italo-German relations Elizabeth Wiskemann's book is invaluable. It was written at a time when much of the material now available had not been opened, but nothing has since appeared to invalidate her conclusions. Alan Bullock and, to a lesser degree, William Shirer have of course dealt authoritatively with the problem of Germany's relations with Italy, as seen from Berlin. The German and Italian documents form the basic record of the transactions between the two countries.

The maltreatment of the Jews has been the subject of a detailed study in Renzo de Felice's *Storia degli ebrei italiani sotto il fascismo.* Other useful contributions are Carpi's "Il problema ebraico nella politica italiana," Cohen's "Mussolini and the Jews," and Michaelis' "Il problema degli ebrei in Italia."

For the period 1943–1945 I have relied very largely on Deakin's *The Brutal Friendship.* It is difficult to do justice to this work, which does not seem to have been properly appreciated, presumably because reviewers were unable to read it carefully in the time allotted. With scholarly thoroughness and critical humor the author unfolds and interprets a massive array of documents. His conclusions are unassailable. I am also indebted to C. F. Delzell for his *Mussolini's Enemies: The Italian Anti-Fascist Resistance.*

Of the vast number of memoirs I found the following most useful: Alfieri, Anfuso, Bottai, Caviglia, Magistrati, Rahn, Rintelen, Cesare Rossi, Schmidt, Silvestri, Simoni, and Starhemberg. But, as the notes show, I have drawn on many other works.

Of my informants some wish to remain anonymous. In order not to discriminate I have described them all in the notes as "informant." The only informants whom I have identified are Cardinal Pizzardo, the last survivor of the Conciliation, who kindly gave me his views on the impact of that transaction; and Count Grandi, who took much trouble on my account both in correspondence and in conversation.

For an historical assessment of the whole period a useful work is Chabod's *History of Italian Fascism,* published in 1963. I read it after this book had been written, but it did not cause me to modify my conclusions.

Ackermann, Werner, *Matteotti besiegt Mussolini.* Karlsruhe, 1947.
Alfieri, Dino, *Dictators Face to Face.* London, 1954.
Aloisi, Pompeio, Journal (25 Juillet 1932–14 Juin 1936). Paris, 1957.
Ambris, Alceste de, *Mussolini, la leggenda e l'uomo.* Marseilles, 1930.
Amendola, Giovanni, *La nuova democrazia.* Naples, 1951.
Anfuso, Filippo, *Da Palazzo Venezia al Lago di Garda.* Rome, 1957.
Aron, Robert, *The Vichy Régime 1940–1944.* London, 1958.
Ashton, E. B. [E. Basch], *The Fascist: His State and His Mind.* London, 1957.
Avon, Earl of, *Facing the Dictators.* London, 1962.
Badoglio, Pietro, *L'Italie dans la Guerre Mondiale.* Paris, 1946.

———, *Rivelazioni su Fiume*. Rome, 1946.

Balabanoff, Angelica, *Erinnerungen und Erlebnisse*. Berlin, 1927.

———, *My Life as a Rebel*. London, 1938.

Balbo, Italo, *Diario 1922*. Milan, 1922.

Barnes, J. S., *The Universal Aspects of Fascism*. London, 1928.

Baskerville, Beatrice, *What Next, O Duce?* London, 1937.

Bedeschi, Sante and Rino Alessi, *Anni giovanili di Mussolini*. Milan, 1939.

Begnac, Ivon de, *Palazzo Venezia*. Rome, 1959.

———, *Vita di Mussolini*. Milan, 1936.

Belline Delle Stelle, Pier Luigi and Urbano Lazzaro, "La fino di Mussolini." *Epoca*, December 4, 11, 18, 25, 1960.

Bezançon, Marcel, *Mussolini in der Schweiz*, Zurich, n.d.

Biggini, Carlo Alberto, *Storia inedita della Conciliazione*. Milan, 1942.

Binchy, Daniel A., *Church and State in Fascist Italy*. London, 1941.

Bonnet, George, *Défense de la Paix*. Two vols. Geneva, 1946.

Bono, Emilio de, *The Conquest of an Empire*. London, 1937.

Bonomi, Ivanoe, *Dal socialismo al fascismo*. Rome, 1924.

Borgese, G. A., *Goliath: The March of Fascism*. New York, 1938.

Borghi, Armando, *Mussolini Red and Black*. London, 1935.

Bottai, G., *Vent'anni e un giorno*. Milan, 1949.

Braunthal, Julius, *The Tragedy of Austria*. London, 1948.

Brinon, F. de, *Mémoires*. Paris, 1949.

Bullock, Alan, *Hitler*. London, 1952.

Cancogni, Manlio, *Storia del squadrismo*. Milan, 1959.

Carofiglio, Mario Fusti, *Vita di Mussolini e storia del fascismo*. Turin, 1950.

Carpi, D., "Il problema ebraico nella politica Italiana," *Rivista di Studi Politici Internazionali*. January–March, 1961.

Castellani, Aldo, *Microbes, Men and Monarchs*. London, 1960.

Caudana, Mino and Arturo Assante, *Dal regno del sud al vento del nord*. 209 instalments, *Il Tempo*, January 15–September 17, 1961.

Cavallero, Ugo, *Commando supremo: Diario 1940–43 del capo di stato maggiore generalo*. Bologna, 1948.

Caviglia, Enrico, *Diario 1925–1945*. Rome, 1952.

Celovski, Boris, *Das münchener Abkommen von 1938*. Stuttgart, 1958.

Chabod, Federico, *A History of Italian Fascism*. London, 1963.

Chiurco, G. A., *Storia delle rivoluzione fascista*. Five volumes. Florence, 1929.

Churchill, Winston S., *The Second World War*. Six vols. London, 1948–1953.

Ciano, Count Galeazzo, *Diary 1937–1938*. London, 1952.

———, *Diary 1939–1943*. London, 1947.

———, *Diplomatic Papers,* edited by Malcolm Muggeridge. London, 1948.
———, *Europa verso la catastrofe.* (The Italian version of the above.) Rome, 1948.
———, *L'Italia di fronto al conflitto.* Rome, 1940.
Cione, E., *Storia della Republica Sociale Italiana.* Rome, 1950.
Cohen, Israel, "Mussolini and the Jews." *Contemporary Review,* December, 1938.
Cooper, A. Duff, *Old Men Forget.* London, 1953.
Currey, Muriel, *Italian Foreign Policy 1918–1932.* London, 1932.
Danese, Orlando, *Mussolini.* Mantua, 1922.
D'Aroma, Nino, *Vent'anni insieme.* Rome, 1957.
Deakin, F. W., *The Brutal Friendship.* London, 1962.
Delcroix, Carlo, *Un uomo e un popolo.* Florence, 1928.
Del Giudice, Mauro, *Cronistoria del processo Matteotti.* Palermo, 1954.
Delzell, Charles, *Mussolini's Enemies: The Italian Anti-Fascist Resistance.* Princeton, 1961.
Department of State, *The Spanish Government and the Axis.* Washington, 1946.
Dinale, Ottavio, *Quarant'anni di colloqui con lui.* Milan, 1953.
Documenti Diplomatici Italiani, Rome, 1952 *et seq.*
Documents on British Foreign Policy, London, 1948 *et seq.*
Documents on German Foreign Policy. London, 1946 *et seq.*
Dolfin, G., *Con Mussolini nella tragedia.* Milan, 1950.
Dollmann, E., *Roma nazista.* Milan, 1951.
Dombroski, Roman, *Mussolini, Twilight and Fall.* London, 1956.
Donosti, Mario, *Mussolini e l'Europa.* Rome, 1945.
Dresler, Adolf, *Mussolini als Journalist.* Leipzig, 1938.
Dulles, Allen, *Germany's Underground.* New York, 1947.
Dumeni, Amerigo, *Diciasette colpi.* Milan, 1951.
Esch, P. A. M. van der, *Prelude to War: The International Repercussions of the Spanish Civil War.* The Hague, 1951.
Falivena, Aldo, "25 Luglio. Storia di un giorno." *Epoca.* July 30, August 6, 1961.
Feiling, Keith, *The Life of Neville Chamberlain.* London, 1946.
Felice, Renzo de, *Storia degli ebrei italiani sotto il fascismo.* Turin, 1961.
Fermi, Laura, *Mussolini.* Chicago, 1961.
Ferraris, Efrem, *La marcia su Roma veduta dal Viminale.* Rome, 1946.
Finer, Herman, *Mussolini's Italy.* London, 1935.
Fiori, Vittorio de, *Mussolini, the Man of Destiny.* London, 1928.
Foot, Michael ["Cassius"], *The Trial of Mussolini.* London, 1943.
Forbes, Rosita, *These Men I Knew.* London, 1946.
François-Poncet, André, *Au Palais Farnése.* Paris, 1961.

———, *Souvenirs d'une Ambassade à Berlin*. Paris, 1947.

Fusco, Gian Carlo, "Quelle che Mussolini tenne nascosto al Duce." *Il Giorno,* October 29; November 1, 3, 8, 10, 15, 17, 22, 24; December 1, 1961.

Garratt, Geoffrey T., *Mussolini's Roman Empire*. New York, 1938.

Gentile, G., *Origini e dottrina del fascismo*. Rome, 1929.

Georges-Roux, *Mussolini*. Paris, 1960.

Germino, D. L., *The Italian Fascist Party in Power*. Minneapolis, 1959.

Giolitti, Giovanni, *Memoirs of My Life*. London, 1923.

Gisevius, H. B., *To the Bitter End*. London, 1948.

Goebbels, J., *Diaries*. London, 1948.

Graziani, R., *Io ho difeso la patria*. Milan, 1948.

Guareschi, Giovanni, *Don Camillo and the Prodigal Son*. London, 1952.

Guariglia, R., *La Diplomatie Difficile*. (French version of his *Ricordi 1922–1946*). Paris, 1955.

Halifax, Earl of, *Fulness of Days*. London, 1957.

Hassell, Ulrich von, *Diaries 1938–1944*. London, 1948.

Henderson, Nevile, *Failure of a Mission*. London, 1940.

Hinsley, F., *Hitler's Strategy*. Cambridge, 1951.

Hitler, Adolf, *Table Talk 1941–1944*. London, 1953.

———, *The Testament of Adolf Hitler*. London, 1961.

Hitler, Adolf and Benito Mussolini, *Lettere e documenti*. Milan, 1946.

Hollis, Christopher, *Italy in Africa*. London, 1941.

International Military Tribunal, *Trial of the Major War Criminals*. Forty-two volumes. Nuremberg, 1947–1949.

Istoricheskiy Arkhiv, Volume V. Moscow, 1962.

Jemolo, Arturo Carlo, *Chiesa e stato in Italia negli ultimi cento anni*. Rome, 1948.

Kemechy, L., *Il Duce*. London, 1930.

Kersten, Felix, *The Kersten Memoirs 1940–1945*. London, 1956.

Kesselring, Albert, *Soldat bis zum letzten Tag*. Bonn, 1953.

Kessler, Count Harry, *Walther Rathenau*. London, 1929.

Kirkpatrick, Ivone, *The Inner Circle*. London, 1959.

Kordt, Erich, *Nicht ans den Akten*. Stuttgart, 1950.

———, *Wahn und Wirklichkeit*. Stuttgart, 1948.

Laffan, R. G. D., *The Crisis over Czechoslovakia*. Survey of International Affairs 1938. Vol. 11. London, 1951.

Leto, G., *OVRA*. Bologna, 1961.

Longhitano, Rino, *La Politica religiosa di Mussolini*. Rome, 1937.

Ludwig, Emil, *Talks with Mussolini*. London, 1933.

Lussu, Emilio, *Enter Mussolini*. London, 1936.

Macartney, Maxwell H. H., *One Man Alone*. London, 1944.

Macartney, Maxwell H. H. and Paul Cremona, *Italy's Foreign and Colonial Policy 1914–1937*. London, 1938.

Macdonald, J. N., *A Political Escapade: The Story of Fiume and D'Annunzio*. London, 1921.

Mack Smith, D., *Italy: A Modern History*. Ann Arbor, 1959.

MacOysan, H. A., "Interview with Grandi." *Milan Sera*. January 12, 14, 15, 1946.

Magistrati, Massimo, *L'Italia a Berlino. (1937–1939)*. Verona, 1956.

Mahler-Werfel, Alma, *Mein Leben*. Frankfurt, 1960.

Martelli, George, *Italy against the World*. London, 1937.

Massock, Richard, *Italy from Within*. London, 1943.

Megaro, Gaudens, *Mussolini in the Making*. London, 1938.

Michaelis, M., "Il problema degli ebrei in Italia (1922–1938)." *Rivista di Studi Politici Internazionali*. April–June, 1961.

Ministère des Affaires Etrangères, *Le Livre Jaune Français*. Paris, 1939.

Minney, R. J., *The Private Papers of Hore-Belisha*. London, 1960.

Monelli, Paolo, *Mussolini, an Intimate Life*. London, 1953.

———, *Roma, 1943*. Rome, 1946.

Munro, Ian S., *Through Fascism to World Power*. London, 1933.

Mussolini, Benito, *Discorsi dal banco di deputato*. Milan, 1929.

———, *Discorsi del 1929*. Milan, 1930.

———, *Dizichario mussoliniano,* Edited by Bruno Biancini, Milan, 1940.

———, *Fascism, Doctrine and Institutions,* 1934.

———, *Il mio diario di guerra*. Milan, 1923.

———, *Memoirs: 1942–1943*. London, 1949.

———, *My Autobiography*. London, 1928.

———, *Opera mia*. Edited by Edoardo and Duilio Susmel. Thirty-two volumes. Florence, 1951–61.

———, *The Political and Social Doctrine of Fascism*. London, 1933.

———, *Scritti e discorsi*. Milan, 1934.

———, *Testamento politico*. (Interview with G. C. Cabella.) Rome, 1948.

Mussolini, Edvige, *Mio fratello Benito*. Florence, 1957.

Mussolini, Rachele, *My Life with Mussolini*. London, 1959.

Mussolini, Vittorio, *Due donne nella tempesta*. Rome, 1961.

———, *Vita con mio padre*. Milan, 1957.

Namier, L., *Diplomatic Prelude: 1938–1939*. London, 1948.

———, *Europe in Decay*. London, 1950.

———, *In the Nazi Era*. London, 1952.

Nenni, Pietro, *Ten Years of Tyranny in Italy*. London, 1932.

Newman, E. W. Polson, *Italy's Conquest of Abyssinia*. London, 1937.

Nicoletti, Gioacchino, "Ultimo colloquio a Gargnano." *Corriere d'Informazione* 13–14, 14–15, February, 1948.

Nicolson, Harold, *Curzon: The Last Phase*. London, 1934.

Pacelli, Francesco, *Diario della conciliazone*. Vatican City, 1959.

Papen, Franz von, *Memoirs*. London, 1932.

Petit-Radel, P., *Voyage de L'Italie*. Paris, 1815.
Petrie, Charles, *The Life and Letters of Sir Austen Chamberlain*. London, 1940.
———, *Mussolini*. London, 1931.
Pini, Giorgio, *The Official Life of Mussolini*. London, 1939.
Pini, Giorgio and Duilio Susmel, *Mussolini l'uomo e l'opera*. Four volumes. Florence, 1953.
Prezzolini, Giusseppe, *Fascism*. London, 1926.
Price, G. Ward, *I Know These Dictators*. London, 1937.
Pagliese, E., *Io difendo l'esercito*. Naples, n.d. (postwar).
Ragionieri, Ernesto, *Socialdemocrazia tedesca e socialisti italiani 1875–1895*. Milan, 1961.
Rahn, Rudolf, *Ruheloses Leben*. Düsseldorf, 1949.
Re, Emilio, *Storia di un archivio: le carte di Mussolini*. Milan, 1946.
Reynaud, Paul, *La France a sauvé l'Europe*. Two volumes. Paris, 1949.
———, *In the Thick of the Fight*. London, 1955.
Ribbentrop, J. von, *The Ribbentrop Memoirs*. London, 1954.
Rintelen, Enno von, *Mussolini als Bundesgenosse*. Stuttgart, 1951.
Roatta, Mario, *Otto millioni di baionette*. Milan, 1946.
Rommel, E., *The Rommel Papers*. Edited by B. H. Liddell Hart. London, 1953.
Rosenberg, Alfred, *Das politische Tagebuch: 1934/35 und 1939/40*. Göttingen, 1956.
Rossato, Arturo, *Mussolini: colloquio intimo*. Milan, 1922.
Rossi, Arturo [Angelo Tasca], *The Rise of Italian Fascism 1918–1922*. London, 1938.
Rossi, Cesare, *Mussolini com'era*. Rome, 1947.
———, *Trentatre vicende mussoliniane*. Milan, 1938.
Rowse, A. L., *All Souls and Appeasement*. London, 1961.
Royal Institute of International Affairs, *Information Department Papers No. 16. Abyssinia and Italy*. London, 1935.
Salvatorelli, Luigi and Giovanni Mira, *Storia d'Italia nel periodo fascista*. Turin, 1961.
Salvemini, Gaetano, *Mussolini diplomatico*. Bari, 1952.
San Severino, B. Quaranta di, *Mussolini as Revealed in His Political Speeches*. London, 1923.
Saporiti, Piero, *Empty Balcony*. London, 1947.
Sarfatti, Margherita, *The Life of Mussolini*. London, 1925.
———, *Dux* (an Italian version of the above). Milan, 1926.
Schellenberg, Walter, *The Schellenberg Memoirs*. London, 1956.
Schiavi, Alessandro, *La Vita e l'opera di Giacomo Matteotti*. Rome, 1957.
Schmidt, Paul, *Hitler's Interpreter* (a shortened English version of the below). London, 1950.
———, *Statist auf der diplomatischen Buhne*. Bonn, 1950.

Schneider, Herbert. W. *Making the Fascist State*. New York, 1928.
———, *The Fascist Government of Italy*. New York, 1936.
Schuschnigg, Kurt von, *Ein Requiem in Rot-Weiss-Rot*. Zurich, 1946.
———, *Farewell Austria*. London, 1938.
Seldes, George, *Sawdust Caesar*. London, 1936.
Sforza, Carlo, *Contemporary Italy*. London, 1946.
Sheridan, Claire, *To the Four Winds*. London, 1957.
Shirer, William L., *Berlin Diary*. London, 1942.
———, *The Rise and Fall of the Third Reich*. London, 1962.
Silone, Iganzio, *The School for Dictators*. London, 1939.
Silvestri, Carlo, *Contro la vendetta*. Milan, 1948.
———, *Turati l'ha detto*. Milan, 1948.
Simon, Viscount, *Retrospect*. London, 1952.
Simoni, Leonardo, *Berlino: imbasciata d'Italia 1939–1943*. Rome, 1946.
Skorzeny, Otto, *Geheimkommando*. Stuttgart, 1930.
———, *Secret Missions* (an abridged translation of the above). London, 1957.
Slocombe, George, *The Tumult and the Shouting*. London, 1936.
Sprigge, Cecil J. S., *The Development of Modern Italy*. London, 1943.
Starhemberg, Prince Ernst, *Between Hitler and Mussolini*. London, 1942.
Stationery Office, *Ethiopia No. 1* (Cmd. 5044). London, 1935.
Steer, G. L., *Caesar in Abyssinia*. London, 1936.
Sturzo, L., *Popolarismo e fascismo*. Turin, 1924.
———, *Italy and Fascismo*. London, 1926.
Suñer, Ramon Serrano, *Entre les Pyrenées et Gibraltar*. Geneva, 1947.
Susmel, Duilio, "Margherita Sarfatti." *Il Tempo*. November 18, 1961.
———, "Mussolini e Vittorio Emanuele, amici e nemici." *Oggi*, October 5, 12, 19, 22, 29, and November 5, 1962.
———, *Vita sbagliata di Galeazzo Ciano*. Rome, 1963.
Tamaro, Attilio, *Due anni di storia 1943–1945*. Three volumes. Rome, 1950.
———, *Venti anni di storia 1922–1943*. Three volumes. Rome, 1953.
Taylor, A. J. P., *The Origins of the Second World War*. London, 1961.
Teeling, William, *The Pope in Politics: The Life and Work of Pope Pius XI*. London, 1937.
Templewood, Viscount, *Nine Troubled Years*. London, 1954.
Thomas, H., *The Spanish Civil War*. London, 1961.
Thompson, Geoffrey, *Front Line Diplomat*. London, 1959.
Toscano, Mario, "Eden at Rome on the Eve of the Italo-Ethiopian Conflict." *Nueva Antologia*. January, 1960.
———, *Le origine diplomatiche del patto di acciaio*. Florence, 1956.
Toynbee, Arnold, "Abyssinia and Italy." *Survey of International Affairs 1935*. Vol. II. London, 1936.
Vansittart, Lord, *The Mist Procession*. London, 1958.

Varé, Daniele, *Laughing Diplomat*. London, 1938.

Watt, D. C., "An Earlier Model for the Pact of Steel." *Royal Institute of International Affairs,* 1957.

———, "The Rome-Berlin Axis 1936–1940. Myth and Reality." *Review of Politics*. October, 1960.

Weizsäcker, Ernst von, *Erinnerungen*. Munich, 1950.

Welles, Sumner, *A Time for Decision*. London, 1944.

Wheeler-Bennett, John, *Munich, Prologue to Tragedy*. London, 1948.

———, *The Nemesis of Power*. London, 1953.

Wichterich, Richard, *Benito Mussolini*. Stuttgart, 1952.

Willis, Fred C., *Männer um Mussolini*. Munich, 1932.

Wiskemann, Elizabeth, *The Rome-Berlin Axis*. London, 1959.

Woodward, Llewellyn, *British Foreign Policy in the Second World War*. London, 1962.

Zangrandi, Ruggero, *Il Lungo viaggio attraverso il fascismo*. Milan, 1962.

Zara, Philippe de, *Mussolini contre Hitler*. Paris, 1938.

Acknowledgment

I should like to express my indebtedness to those who helped me to write this book. They include: former colleagues and many people in Britain, Italy, France, and Germany who took much trouble to answer questions and supply information; the London Library and the Wiener Library, who gave indispensable help and showed much forbearance; Sir Ashley Clarke, formerly British Ambassador in Rome; Miss Vinceguerra of the Information Department of the British Embassy in Rome and her father Professor Vinceguerra, the Italian historian; Count Grandi who gave me much of his time; the warden of St. Anthony's College, Oxford, who lent me a number of books from his collection and from whose admirable work *The Brutal Friendship* I have culled much valuable material, which he has generously allowed me to reproduce; my publisher who has given me more help than I had a right to expect; and my secretary, Miss Fitzgerald. Finally I should like to thank my wife who has read the manuscript in its various stages and has made many helpful suggestions, which I have adopted. She has shown particular patience when, as often happened, fierce pride of authorship caused me incontinently to reject her advice.

Index

THE AUTHOR AND HIS BOOK

SIR IVONE KIRKPATRICK *was born at Wellington, India, in 1897 and was educated at Downside. In World War I he was wounded at Gallipoli and won the Belgian Croix de Guerre. Afterwards he entered the British Diplomatic Service, serving first at Rio de Janeiro and later in the British Foreign Office. From 1930 to 1938 he was a member of the British Embassy in Rome, the Legation to the Holy See, and the British Embassy in Berlin. During World War II Kirkpatrick became Director of the Foreign Division of the Ministry of Information and then adviser on foreign policy and Controller of European Services for the British Broadcasting Company. Later he was named Deputy Commissioner of the British Control Commission for Germany and Political Adviser to SHAEF under General Eisenhower. After World War II, Kirkpatrick was the British High Commissioner for Germany, completing his Foreign Service career as Permanent Under-Secretary of State of the Foreign Office. Upon his retirement in 1957, he became Chairman of the British Independent Television Authority and is now Joint President of the Channel Tunnel Study Group and Chairman of the British National Bank. He has contributed articles to* The New York Times, *and* The Times *and* The Daily Telegraph *of London. His book* The Inner Circle *was published in 1959.*

MUSSOLINI: A STUDY IN POWER *(Hawthorn, 1964) was designed by Stefan Salter. It was set in type by the Pyramid Composition Company and printed and bound by Montauk Book Manufacturing Company, both of New York City. The body type is Caledonia, invented in 1938 by William Addison Dwiggins, a New Englander who based his design on Scotch typefaces; his typeface was accordingly named "Caledonia," the ancient name for Scotland.*

A HAWTHORN BOOK

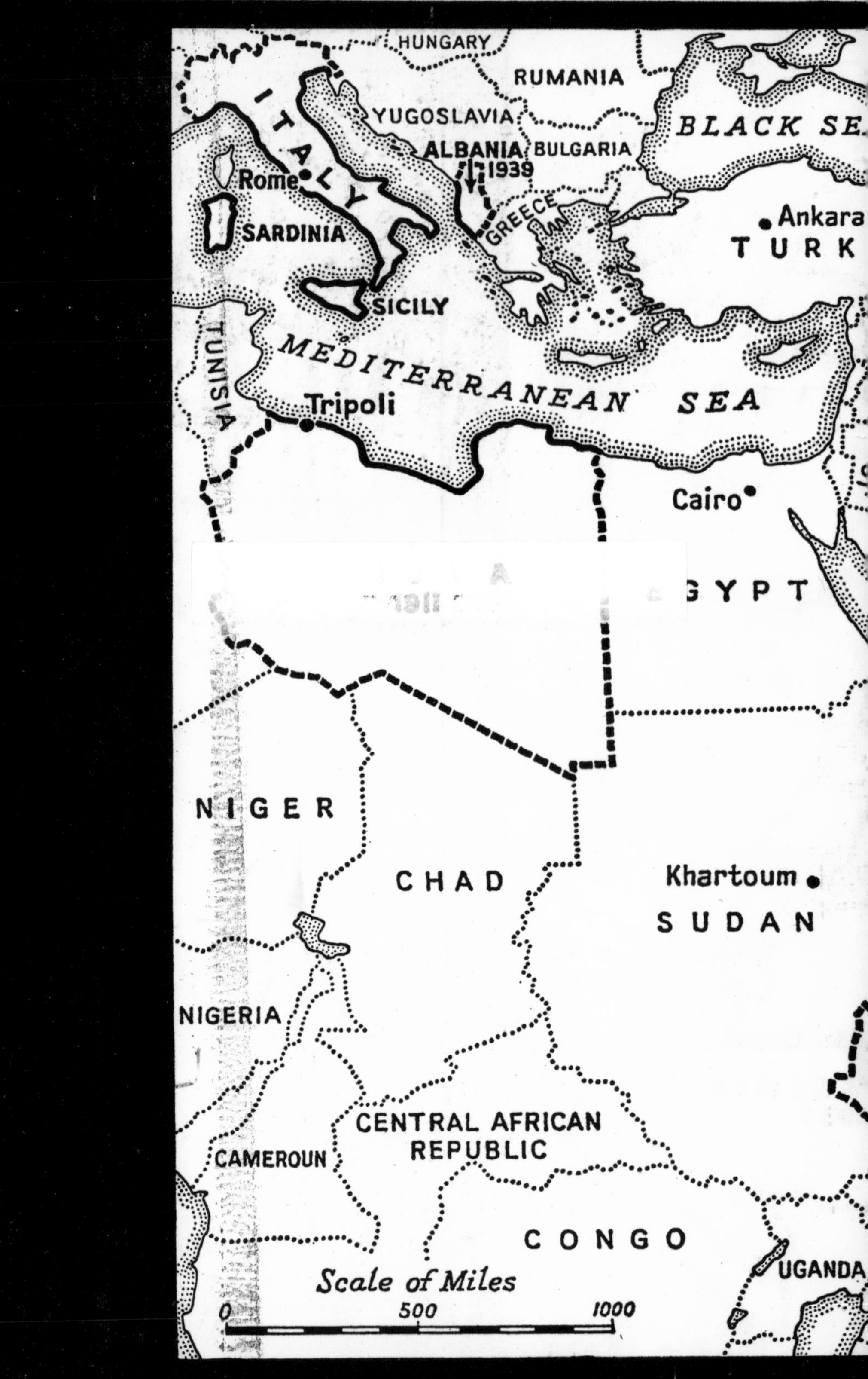
HUNGARY
RUMANIA
YUGOSLAVIA
ITALY
BLACK SE
ALBANIA
BULGARIA
1939
Rome
Ankara
SARDINIA
GREECE
TURK
SICILY
TUNISIA
MEDITERRANEAN SEA
Tripoli
Cairo
GYPT
NIGER
CHAD
Khartoum
SUDAN
NIGERIA
CENTRAL AFRICAN
REPUBLIC
CAMEROUN
CONGO
UGANDA
Scale of Miles
0
500
1000